HUMAN RIGHTS IN PHILOSOPHY AND PRACTICE

Human Rights in Philosophy and Practice

Edited by

BURTON M. LEISER
Distinguished Professor of Philosophy
Adjunct Professor of Law
Pace University

TOM D. CAMPBELL
Professor of Law
The Australian National University

Routledge
Taylor & Francis Group
LONDON AND NEW YORK

First published 2001 by Dartmouth Publishing Company and Ashgate Publishing

Reissued 2018 by Routledge
2 Park Square, Milton Park, Abingdon, Oxon OX14 4RN
711 Third Avenue, New York, NY 10017, USA

Routledge is an imprint of the Taylor & Francis Group, an informa business

A Library of Congress record exists under LC control number: 2001022329

ISBN 13: 978-1-138-72169-2 (hbk)
ISBN 13: 978-1-138-72168-5 (pbk)
ISBN 13: 978-1-315-19422-6 (ebk)

Contents

List of Contributors

Akanmidu, R.A., *University of Ilorin, Nigeria*
Arango, Rodolfo, *Universität Kiel, Germany*
Bauböck, Rainer, *Institut für Hörere Studien, Germany*
Benditt, Theodore M., *University of Alabama, USA*
Brennan, Samantha, *University of Western Ontario, Canada*
Campbell, Tom, *The Australian National University, Australia*
Choi, Chongko, *Seoul University, South Korea*
Cooper, James M., *California Western School of Law, USA*
Dahbour, Omar, *Hunter College of the City University of New York, USA*
Gill, Emily R., *Bradley University, USA*
Gupta, Nidhi, *Jaipur, India*
Halmai, Gabor, *Lórand Eötvös University School of Law, Hungary*
Humbach, John A., *Pace University, USA*
Jain, Meenakshi, *Jaipur, India*
Miller, Seumas, *Charles Sturt University, Australia*
Nunan, Richard, *College of Charleston, USA*
Papadopoulos, Thrassyvoulos, *Kiel, Germany*
Sampford, Charles, *Australian National University, Australia*
Seel, Gerhard, *Universität Bern Institut für Philosophy*
Sterba, James P., *University of Notre Dame, USA*
Stoilov, Yanaki B., *Sofia University, Bulgaria*
Swan, Peter D., *Carleton University, Canada*
Tan, Kok-Chor, *Queens University, Canada*
Tideman, Nicolaus, *Virginia Polytechnical and State University, USA*
Usami, Makoto, *Chukyo University, Japan*
Vallentyne, Peter, *Virginia Commonwealth University, USA*
Wolcher, Louis E., *Washington School of Law, USA*
Xanthaki, Alexandra, *University of Keele, UK*

Series Preface

The objective of the Dartmouth Series in Applied Legal Philosophy is to publish work which adopts a theoretical approach to the study of particular areas or aspects of law or deals with general theories of law in a way which focuses on issues of practical moral and political concern in specific legal contexts.

In recent years there has been an encouraging tendency for legal philosophers to utilize detailed knowledge of the substance and practicalities of law and a noteworthy development in the theoretical sophistication of much legal research. The series seeks to encourage these trends and to make available studies in law which are both genuinely philosophical in approach and at the same time based on appropriate legal knowledge and directed towards issues in the criticism and reform of actual laws and legal systems.

The series will include studies of all the main areas of law, presented in a manner which relates to the concerns of specialist legal academics and practitioners. Each book makes an original contribution to an area of legal study while being comprehensible to those engaged in a wide variety of disciplines. Their legal content is principally Anglo-American, but a wide-ranging comparative approach is encouraged and authors are drawn from a variety of jurisdictions.

Tom D. Campbell
Series Editor
The Faculty of Law
The Australian National University

Preface

In the early summer of 1999, some five hundred philosophers, lawyers, judges, and other scholars from every part of the world convened at Pace University in New York City for the Nineteenth World Congress on the Philosophy of Law and Social Philosophy. It was an especially apt opportunity for scholars and practitioners to meet members of their professions who represented vastly differing legal, political, and social cultures and traditions.

The diversity did not end, however, with geography, politics, and legal traditions. It extended to the participants' philosophical and legal interests and specializations as well. Thus, plenary and concurrent sessions were devoted to such highly theoretical topics as the nature of law and legal reasoning to pressing ethical and political issues such as law and the environment, the rights of women, artificial intelligence and computer ethics, and the impact of scientific discovery and technological advances upon the law. Indeed, participants were treated to a most unusual lecture and performance entitled "Philosophy and Law in Opera" by Maestro Joseph Colaneri of the Metropolitan Opera. Thus, participants had an exceptional opportunity to communicate with one another and to exchange views on a variety of levels.

The sponsoring organization, the International Society for the Philosophy of Law and Social Philosophy (known by its German initials, IVR), has traditionally published the papers that are presented at its world congresses. Naturally, those presented at the Nineteenth World Congress are being published as well under the official imprints of the IVR. In a departure from tradition, the editors of this volume have selected a number of outstanding papers in a particular area of the philosophy of law for publication in a form that is likely to be more readily accessible to a wide audience.

In order to preserve the atmosphere and diversity of the World Congress, the papers selected for this volume on human rights represent men and women from many parts of the world—from North America, Australia, western and eastern Europe, Africa, Japan, India,

South Korea. They also offer a broad picture of contemporary thinking in many areas of legal and ethical concern, including the grounds for the universality of human rights; the rights of women, minorities, cultural groups, and indigenous peoples; the scope and limits of international protection of human rights; the relation between the rights of individuals and the rights of people collectively to protect the environment and other aspects of our common patrimony; the problem of ex post facto laws being applied to violators of human rights and the jurisdiction of later regimes to try and punish such violators; and the right of self-determination as opposed to the interests of existing nation states.

In view of the fact that the papers in this volume have come to us from scholars whose linguistic traditions vary so greatly, we have decided to respect their several stylistic traditions. Thus, we have made no effort to impose an artificial uniformity upon our contributors in such matters as spelling (e.g., "honor" as opposed to "honour"), the use of single as opposed to double inverted commas in various contexts, the form of citations and footnotes, and the like. Even within a single tradition, such stylistic matters may differ widely among, say, sociologists, philosophers, and lawyers. To assume that any one of them is more "correct" than the others strikes as being singularly inappropriate in a volume that is dedicated to celebrating the very diversity that its authors represent.

We cannot let this opportunity pass without expressing our deep appreciation to all of those who worked so hard to make the Nineteenth World Congress on Philosophy of Law and Social Philosophy a success. It is impossible here to name them all, but we extend our special thanks to the many participants from all over the world who contributed papers and participated in the discussions at the Congress; the philosophers at Pace University; and the many members of the university's faculty, staff and administration without whose hard work the Congress would have been impossible; Dr. Richard Podgorski, former provost, and Dr. Marilyn Jaffe-Ruiz, provost of the university, whose support was absolutely vital; Dr. Enrico Pattaro, president of the IVR; and the executive committee of the IVR for their invaluable support, guidance, and assistance.

Finally, I wish to thank my co-editor, Professor Tom Campbell, for the splendid job he has done in making this a volume of truly outstanding scholarly papers; my student aide, Ms. Amy Manna; and my research assistant, Ms. Oxsana Stupachenko, who have devoted countless hours to helping us organize, edit, and format this work.

Burton M. Leiser
Pace University
Briarcliff Manor, New York

Part I
The Philosophy of Rights

1. Libertarianism, Motivation and Rights*

SAMANTHA BRENNAN

Introduction

Broadly speaking, there are two different paths to libertarianism. First, one might believe in "too little" morality, and hold that we must construct rules for human co-operation out of the bare materials of self-interest and rational agreement. Second, one might believe in "too much" morality, and hold that there are aspects of morality so strong as to severely limit the powers of government. On the first path we find contractarians, such as David Gauthier and Jan Narveson. On the second we find rights theorists, such as Robert Nozick. But membership in the second camp need not be limited to Lockean-style rights theorists. This paper takes up the concern that certain moral considerations, more Kantian than Lockean, lead to libertarian conclusions.

In this chapter I present and examine two arguments for political libertarianism.[1] The arguments are Kantian in flavor,[2] focusing on the moral significance of ones motive for action, and on the moral significance of autonomy. Both arguments begin by granting that there are very strong obligations to aid those in need, but go on to deny - for different reasons - the further claim that we ought to enforce those obligations. According to the first argument, forcing others to do what morality requires of them cannot succeed, since what morality requires of them is doing what is right for the right motives. In forcing others to fulfill their obligations we rob their actions of moral worth. According to the second argument, even if we could force others to do what morality requires of them, we are morally forbidden from doing so. Individuals have rights, which protect their moral autonomy.

The version of libertarianism that results from these two arguments is a kind of libertarianism that I find it useful to refer to as "political libertarianism." I think it is important to distinguish a libertarianism, which says we may not *enforce* from moral obligations to aid from the stronger libertarian view that moral obligations to aid do not *exist*. I call this second, stronger view "moral libertarianism."[3]

Having presented and examined the two arguments in the first two sections of this chapter, in the third section I present Robert Goodin's response to the Kantian-libertarian argument and show why his response is inadequate to deal with the challenge.

Before I begin an examination of the two arguments - the argument from the moral significance of motive and the argument from the moral significance of moral autonomy - I want to say a little more about them. The first argument is consequentialist in nature, where what is to be promoted is moral worth. This argument criticizes attempts to force others to do what is required of them at the level of the good, as opposed to the right. According to this argument, forcing others to do their duty will fail because of the essential role motive plays in creating moral value. The second argument is non-consequentialist. This argument criticizes attempts to force others to do what is required of them at the level of right action. According to this argument, even if we could force others to do what is required of them, we are morally forbidden from doing so because in doing so we infringe their rights. It is a useful strategy in ethics to separate out, as much as one can, questions about the good and the right. We try first to see which states of affairs are good, and then we ask whether a state of affair's being good is sufficient reason to bring that state about. For this reason I will examine the argument from the moral significance of motive first.

The Argument from the Moral Significance of Motive

On a roughly Kantian account of morality's demands what we are required to do is to perform the right action for the right reason. According to this argument, force would rob the action of its moral worth by substituting prudence for duty as the motive for right action.[4] Welfarist policies, according to this line of argument, remove moral worth from the act of helping the needy through the payment of taxes by fining or jailing persons who fail to pay their taxes.[5]

Now once one agrees that one's duty consists in not just performing right action but also performing it for the right reason, it seems that there is an element of paradox in forcing someone to do her duty. Strictly speaking, all that we can force others to do are the acts that are required as *part* of their duties; we cannot get them to fulfill their duties *completely* (since we cannot get them to do it for the right reason). Although I recognize this to be true, for the purposes of this paper, I will speak about forcing people to do their duties. This is to be understood as shorthand for "forcing them to do the actions that are required as part of their duties."

I was first struck by the strength of the Kantian argument when considering the moral preferability of two possible worlds.[6] Call them Kant's World, or KW for short, and the Welfarist World, or WW for short. In both worlds there are haves and have-nots.[7] In KW, the haves act out of a direct concern for their moral duty and give a great deal of their wealth to the have-nots. In WW, the have-nots receive just as much from the haves but the giving is coerced. Haves who refuse to give their wealth will be punished by the state. If the amount of giving is equal between the worlds - setting aside here the question of just how much giving is required of the haves, and assuming that they are both giving as much as is required whatever that amount may be - I have the intuition that KW is a morally preferable world. After all, in both worlds all of the right acts are performed, but KW has something extra, namely acts which have moral worth. And if, as good Kantians, we value moral worth above all else, then KW is in all ways superior to WW. According to Kantian morality, the good acts in WW count for nothing if they were not done out of concern for moral duty.[8]

Is KW morally superior to WW? Some people will argue that it is not. In what follows I consider three responses to the claim that KW is morally superior.

First, it might be objected that in KW all that is present is *mere* charity while in WW the requirements of justice are being met. Surely a world that contains justice is superior to one that does not. If this is right, then it is a mistake to claim that the worlds are equivalent but for the presence of moral worth. But this objection is based on a misunderstanding of what is meant by "charity" and "justice." There are two things one might mean by the distinction between charity and justice. It may be that we use "charity" with reference to private acts of aid, while reserving the term "justice" for public, or state-organized, aid. But if this is what is meant, then there is no distinction in kind between the aid given in KW and the aid given in WW, only a difference in how the giving is co-ordinated.[9] It is difficult to see how this distinction could carry the moral weight required by the objection. However, it may be that we use "charity" to refer to acts of aid, which are optional, and "justice" to refer to acts of aid, which are required. It is because the giving in KW is optional that it falls under the category of mere charity, and not justice. However, if this is what is meant by the distinction between charity and justice, then all the acts of aid, in both KW and WW, will turn out to be acts of justice. From the point of view of morality, the act of giving to the have-nots is required in both worlds. It is only when we conflate the requirements, or demands, of morality with the requirements of the law that this error arises. Morality can require us to perform acts about which the law is silent. Such acts are not optional, morally speaking, and so the acts of giving in KW are not mere acts of charity. Neither way of interpreting the distinction between charity and justice counts against the moral superiority of KW.

Second, one might object that in a real Welfarist World much of the giving is not coerced. In a democracy, at least, a majority of the citizens will have explicitly endorsed the government's plans for taxation and spending (assuming that these plans were a publicized part of the electoral platform). And so, given that a majority has consented to taxation, one might go on to argue that the acts of the majority retain their moral worth.[10] There are many responses one could make to this argument. I will give just two. While it may be true that some of those who vote for the welfarist party do so out of a concern for their moral duty to those in need, not all of the majority will be so motivated. Some of the majority will be the needy who, it can be argued, vote for the welfarist government out of self-interest, rather than a sense of duty. Also, it seems to me that this objection poses too strong a connection between voting and endorsement of a plan for taxation and welfare. Consider that if one opposes welfare funded through taxation and one is given a choice between voting for three parties - a party, X, with a mildly redistributive platform, a party, Y, with a moderately redistributive platform, and a party, Z, with a strongly redistributive platform. In this case it should be clear that a vote for X, while the rational choice for a person opposed to welfare funded through taxation (since X minimizes a bad thing), does not constitute endorsement of the redistributive elements of X's electoral platform.

Third, one might object that the moral superiority of KW over WW depends on the claim that the acts of giving in WW were coerced and hence not performed with the right motive. In WW, so the original argument went, threat of punishment made prudence, and not attention to moral duty, the reason for acting. However, one might object that we cannot assume from the presence of laws backed by threat of punishment what peoples' actual motives were in giving aid. After all, our actions can be over determined. It is consistent with there being a legal requirement for the haves to aid, that the haves aid out of respect for their moral duty. Recognition of the moral requirement can exist alongside recognition of the legal requirement. Indeed, this is likely the case for many people in our society today. To determine if the acts of aid on the part of the haves have moral worth, we can apply a counterfactual test. Would the haves have provided aid were the legal requirement absent? If the answer is "yes" in all cases, then it is possible that KW and WW are equal with regards to the amount of moral worth present in the worlds. All we are left with then is an epistemological problem in the case of WW - how to tell which motive is doing the work in moving the haves to action? - which does not exist in the case of KW. But there is no longer a case for claiming that KW is necessarily morally superior to WW.

Where do we go from here? It seems we are forced to grant that if all of the haves in WW have concern for their moral duty as a sufficient motive for giving aid, then the two worlds are morally equal. So granted. It is *possible* that KW and WW are equal in terms of moral worth. But how likely is it that all of the haves in WW have concern for moral duty as a sufficient motive for action? Not very. And as long as at least one of the haves gives from prudential motives, then KW is morally superior. So the comparison between KW and WW is not as straightforward as it first seemed. The superiority of KW is based on a contingent fact, albeit one, which seems very likely to be true, namely that not everyone in WW is sufficiently motivated by moral duty.

If we make the rather weak assumption that some of the haves in WW are not sufficiently motivated by moral duty, then it looks as if KW is morally superior to WW, even if the comparison is between more moral worth and less, rather than between more moral worth and none.

Having responded to the two objections, we can conclude that KW is superior to WW, though its superiority is not as great as we might have thought. Given the (possibly weak) superiority of KW, we can now ask what conclusions follow about the morality of enforced aid in this world. It seems to me that *if,* in the real world, the choice were between KW and WW, we ought to opt for KW on the grounds that we can be certain that KW contains more moral worth. This follows since the giving of aid in KW will be contrary to self-interest, while in WW government sanctions work to make giving aid in one's self-interest. One might also worry about the longer term, detrimental effects of enforced aid on one's motive to assist others.[11]

But is the choice now really between WW and KW? Let me introduce for consideration another possible world, SW (which can either stand for Selfish World or Suffering World). As in KW, in SW there is no enforced aid. But unlike KW, in SW few of the haves act on the obligation to provide aid. Some of the haves fail to recognize that they have such an obligation. Others recognize the obligation but choose to place little weight on moral reasons in their deliberations. Since a few of the haves do act on their moral duty, there are some acts with moral worth, but there are also a great many needy people. How does the introduction of SW change things? What is the *real* alternative to WW?

Whether KW or SW is the real alternative to WW will depend upon certain facts about the motivation for giving in WW. There are two distinct possibilities.

First, consider what WW would have to be like if it were possible to transform WW into KW. If we could remove force from co-ordinated acts of giving and retain the same level of aid to the needy, then it must be the case, given our assumptions about the high level of charitable giving in KW, that a great amount of giving in WW is done from a sense of moral duty. If we could move from WW to KW, then it would have to be the case that the same amount of moral worth is present in both worlds. Assuming that KW is a real alternative to WW, the worlds are morally equal. However, there are two additional considerations in favor of KW. The first is greater epistemological certainty about peoples' motivations for giving. The second is lack of worry about the potentially undermining effects of enforced aid. While Kantian considerations of moral worth lead to the conclusion that if WW could be transformed into KW, then the two worlds are morally equal, these two additional considerations tip the scale in favor of KW.

Second, consider what WW would have to be like if it were only possible to transform WW into SW. If the removal of force from co-ordinated acts of giving leads to drastically lowered levels of charitable giving, then it must be the case, given our assumptions about the low level of charitable giving in SW, that a great amount of giving in WW is done from fear of punishment, not out of a sense of moral duty. And so, if the choice is between WW and SW, that is, if SW were what our world would be like without enforced aid, then we can assume that not much moral worth is present in either world. Again, from the point of view of concern for moral worth, the two worlds are roughly equal. However, one additional consideration, which spoke in favor of KW above, also speaks in favor of SW, namely we can be certain about the amount of moral worth that is there in SW. And so this additional consideration tips the scale in favor of SW.

But for me, while I am convinced of the moral superiority of KW over WW, I am not convinced that SW is better than WW. Why not? I find that I am not prepared to sacrifice great amounts of human welfare for the sake of moral worth.[12] What this shows me is that while Kantian considerations about the moral importance of motive matter, they are not the only factor which affects my moral intuitions about cases; human happiness matters as well. Given equal amounts of human happiness in

KW and WW, I think that the addition of moral worth in KW makes a difference and so breaks a tie. But given a choice between worlds which greatly differ in amounts of human happiness - where WW contains much more happiness than SW - I do not think that the differences in amount of moral worth weigh heavily enough to favor SW.

So far this is all no more than a mere reporting of my intuitions and an attempt at locating their source. But I take it these intuitions are common enough that it is worth wondering whether we might develop a more moderate Kantianism, a mixed deontology that takes account of human happiness, in addition to moral worth. Thoroughgoing Kantians, however, ought to prefer both KW and SW to WW, and ought not to endorse enforced aid.

The Argument from the Moral Importance of Moral Autonomy

Considerations of moral worth aside, many people believe that there are moral rights, which prevent us from forcing others to do their moral duty. We can incorporate into our moral theory any factor, which we think has moral importance in one of two places. We can recognize the value as one to be promoted as part of a consequentialist ethic. Or we can give the value a different sort of recognition by incorporating constraints, which protect it. It is this second way of incorporating autonomy into a moral theory which I think is the more usual route to go and with which I will concern myself here. On this view, even if Smith had a moral duty to aid Green, a third party, Isaac, would not be permitted to force Smith to help.

Why wouldn't Smith volunteer? We can imagine two possibilities. First, Smith does not believe that he has a duty to aid. Second, Smith recognizes the duty but fails to be sufficiently motivated. Perhaps he has other motivations, which speak against the act in question. Either way Smith has rights, which protect him from Isaac forcing him to do his duty.

Let's consider two responses to the rights-based argument against forcing Smith to do his moral duty. A first response one might make to this argument is to deny that rights of this sort, rights that protect one's failure to do one's duty, exist. Such rights would be rights to do wrong and we might want to deny that there can be such rights at all. Perhaps one thinks there is something paradoxical about moral protections for wrongdoing. I do not think that attempts to deny the existence of rights to do wrong are likely to succeed. I find myself persuaded by Waldron's examples in his paper "A Right to Do Wrong."[13] Consider just the first example Waldron gives: "Someone uses all the money that he has fairly won in a lottery to buy racehorses and champagne and refuses to donate any of it to a desperately deserving charity." Further examples of Waldron's are even more persuasive; they are ones in which the person failing to live up to their duty does so from a strong moral conviction. In these cases the moral agent disagrees about what actions duty demands. What makes me think of rights to do wrong as protecting moral autonomy is that they allow others to decide for themselves what is required, and to decide what weight those requirements ought to have in their personal decision-making.

A second response to this argument allows that there are rights, which protect our failing to do what duty demands, but denies that such rights are absolute. On one plausible view about rights all, or at least most, rights have thresholds. For example, one might believe that a right can be justifiably infringed when enough is at stake for those who will benefit from the right's infringement. Various accounts have been offered for thresholds for rights. These accounts vary in the details but agree that a certain total amount of good must be at stake for those who will benefit from that right's infringement, and that this amount must be significantly greater than the amount the right bearer would be harmed, were the right infringed.[14] Consider the following example: Suppose that Amelia has a right to her money. If rights have thresholds, then there may be circumstances in which we can justifiably take A's money, even though in doing so we infringe her rights. (In such a case we may speak of Amelia's rights as having been justifiably infringed, or overridden.) Suppose that one such circumstance is that a group of people will go hungry without access to Amelia's money. We have the power to help by taking Amelia's money but not enough money to help on our own. In this case then, the benefits to the group justify the infringement of Amelia's right. And so, according to this moderate threshold theory of rights, rights can be overridden when by doing so we bring about a great amount of good.

A third response builds on the second. One might believe that rights have thresholds, but that these thresholds are even lower when the right bearer has a duty to perform the act in question. The above discussion of Amelia took place without reference to Amelia's duties. If the good that can be brought about by infringing Amelia's right is so great as to justify that infringement, it seems that the good must also be great enough to generate a duty on Amelia's part. Surely Amelia ought to volunteer her money to the hungry group. If we grant that Amelia has a right to her money, and we grant that she has a duty to aid those in need, then we can go on to ask whether the right and its threshold are affected by her duty. To put the question more generally: Are the strength of individual rights affected by individual moral duties?

What one might expect is that the presence of a duty weakens the right in question, making its threshold lower than when no such duty exists. To test our intuitions for such a weakening effect, we need a pair of contrast cases, one in which a duty exists and the other in which it does not. This presents a challenge. Under what circumstances will the amount of good that can be attained by infringing a right be enough to justify doing so, but not enough to also generate a duty on the part of the right bearer? It looks as if all cases of justified infringements might be cases in which a duty is also present, because the same circumstances, which justify the infringement, will also generate a duty to aid.

One place we might look for such an example concerns imperfect duties. Imperfect duties are those duties, which need not be discharged at all times and in all manners. Moral agents retain discretion as to when and how the duties are fulfilled. Duties to charity are commonly thought to be imperfect, for example. This being the case we can contrast Bart, who has provided aid to the full extent needed (say, the last nine times he has been presented with the opportunity to aid), with Amelia, who given the same opportunities to aid as Bart has always refused to provide assistance. Suppose that now some set of circumstances exists which would justify infringing Bart's right. Suppose further that given his past actions we can all agree that Bart has no perfect duty to aid. Similarly, suppose such a set of circumstances exists for Amelia. But in Amelia's case, given her past actions, we do hold that she has a perfect duty to aid on this occasion. Is it easier to justify infringing Amelia's right than Bart's?[15] It seems to me that it is. And one plausible explanation of the reason it is easier to justify infringing Amelia's right is that the threshold of her right is lower, given the presence of a perfect duty to aid.[16]

Another way we might generate a pair of contrast cases concerns special, rather than general, duties. Suppose that Amelia has contracted to donate a set amount each month to a charity, while Bart has not. In this set of cases there may be enough at stake to justify infringing either right, Amelia has a duty while Bart does not. Again, we can ask whether less need be at stake to justify infringing Amelia's right? Has her duty weakened her right? My sense of the matter is that Amelia's right is weakened by the existence of her duty.

This suggests that the relationship between rights and duties is more complex than has previously been thought. On the standard utilitarian picture, duties to promote the good arise whenever we can, by our actions, bring about a net increase in the overall good. But many people believe that morality cannot be so demanding. My colleague, Jones, may appreciate my morning mug of cappuccino more than I will, but it seems a stretch to claim from this that I have a duty to give him my cappuccino. A moderate view about duties is that they kick in when we can, by our actions, bring about a *significant* increase in the overall good.[17] Consider if I have the option of giving my cappuccino, not to Jones, but rather to a hungry, homeless person, Mary, who spends part of each day sitting outside the building where I work. It seems to me that it is reasonable to think that I have a duty to help Mary, but not Jones, because one action leads to a significant increase in the overall good and the other a rather small increase. According to this moderate view about duties, duties to aid kick in at some point above the point of net increase in the overall good. On this view, then there will be a gap between what maximizes the good and what one ought to do - a first-person option. However, where rights protect our actions, there is second gap, between what duty demands and what others may force us to do, a third-party option. The amount of increase in the overall good required for you to be able to justifiably take my cappuccino away and redistribute it against my will, will be greater than either a net increase (the utilitarian standard) or simply a significant increase (the moderate view about duties). And finally, whether duties exist or not, there is a point at which our rights give out and can be overridden, where the duties of others to abide by our rights gives way.

On the account I have here just briefly sketched, there are rights to do wrong - to fail to do one's duty - but such rights are not absolute. They have thresholds, which are sensitive to the existence of duties. The theory may not be Kant's but I find it an attractive picture of morality.

Robert Goodin's Response: Collective Responsibility

The final response to the Kantian arguments I would like to consider comes from Robert Goodin's recent book *Utilitarianism as a Public Philosophy.*[18] Goodin takes on both of the Kantian arguments for political libertarianism discussed in this paper, though he does not break them apart quite the way I do. His first response, found in Chapter 2, is that in cases where collective responsibility is involved (where your doing your duty depends on my doing my duty) you do have a right to force me to fulfill my obligation. His second response, in Chapter 3, is to argue against the moral significance of motive. For the purposes of this paper, I will concentrate on the first of these two lines of argument. Why the first? It is more original. It is no surprise that Goodin, a utilitarian, will deny that motives matter.

Goodin's Chapter 2 argument, which he applies specifically to two cases - welfare and national defense - consists in two moves. First, he argues that some of our individual moral duties are actually collective duties. Second, he argues that force or coercion is morally permissible in the case of collective duties. Writes Goodin: "Whereas compelling people to do their individual moral duties might be impermissible, it is perfectly permissible to compel people to play their necessary parts in discharging collective responsibilities."[19]

What is a collective duty? On Goodin's account a collective duty is one that we cannot meet individually. The duty's being met depends upon co-ordination between individuals. Is welfare a collective duty, on Goodin's account? It becomes one when it is transformed from an imperfect duty to aid to a perfect duty to do one's part in an organized scheme to aid others. But I am not sure that Goodin's argument is quite right. If I get his sense of collective duties, your doing your bit is necessary for me doing my bit. And so for example, if you own the boat and I own the oars, and a third person is drowning, we have a collective duty to rescue. Neither can do it on their own. In this case, the rescue is an all or nothing business. But welfare does not work quite this way. My helping others does not depend on your doing so. There are matters of degree and while it is true that a volunteer welfare scheme would have less to give than a mandatory one, it is not the case that without the participation of all, I am prevented from fulfilling my duty to aid.

However, suppose that there were collective duties of the sort Goodin is discussing. One might wonder whether force is morally permissible even in the case of collective duties. What am I allowed to do in order to fulfill my duties? Remember, collective duties are those in which I cannot discharge my share of the duty without the co-operation of others. Return to the boat scenario. May I steal the boat, thus infringing your property right, in order to discharge my share of the collective duty to rescue? It seems to me that I can, but that the right explanation for this lies not in the terrain of collective responsibility, but in the rather more straightforward terrain of thresholds for rights. In cases where the good to be gained is quite small, my sense is that I cannot force your participation should you fail to live up to your moral duty.

And so, Goodin's response is not a satisfactory response to the Kantian arguments for libertarianism. To my mind, he fails to show that welfare is a collective duty (in his sense of this term) and he fails to show that force is a permissible response to individuals failing to discharge their share of collective duties.

In conclusion, all is not lost for Kantians who do not want to be libertarians. The argument from motive is a much weaker argument that one might have initially thought. The argument from rights can be dealt with by moving to a more moderate account of rights, one that allows that all rights have thresholds.

Notes

* Thanks to Tracy Isaacs, Thomas Hurka, Jan Narveson and Mariam Thalos for helpful comments on earlier drafts on this chapter.

1 The scope of this paper is limited in the following ways. In my discussion of libertarianism I focus on welfare as one deviation from the libertarian state. I recognize that the modern state contains other elements which would not be justified, were libertarianism true, and I believe the argument given in the case of welfare could be extended to cover these other elements. Also, in this paper I don't ask the broader question of whether any state is justified. Some philosophers have thought that Kantian considerations of autonomy addressed here lead to the conclusion that no state has moral authority. See Robert Paul Wolff's *In Defense of Anarchism*, Harper Colophon Books, 1970.

2 In this paper I do not claim that Kant himself would support the arguments I'm putting forward for examination. Yet, the premises of the arguments are certainly ones, which have been attributed to Kant, and the intuitions they appeal to are in a broad sense "Kantian." And so, for the purposes of this paper, I call the argument "Kantian."

3 We can also make distinctions between varieties of moral libertarianism. On some libertarian views, it is a good thing to aid those in need even if we are not obligated to do so. On this view, all charity is supererogatory. On other libertarian views, we are not obligated to aid those in need and further, doing so is a bad thing. And according to a still stricter libertarian view, aiding those in need is morally forbidden.

4 This assumes that Kantians should care about moral worth. For an alternative view, see "Should Kantians Care about Moral Worth?" Walter Schaller, *Dialogue*, Vol. XXXII, No. 1, Winter 193, pp. 25-40.

5 I set aside here the issue of whether welfarist policies always accomplish the task of getting one to perform the right action for the wrong reason. In the usual case, one pays taxes out of a fear of punishment - thus the act is an act of the agent, though coerced. But should one refuse to pay, then the funds will be taken - in cash or in kind - and in this case, it is less plausible to claim that the act of paying taxes is an act of the agent's. If a thug demands my wallet while threatening to hit me if I do not and I hand over the wallet, we can claim that the giving up of the wallet was an act of mine. If I refuse to hand over the wallet and the thug takes it from me by force, then it is incorrect to attribute an action to me. Likewise, if the government took payment for taxes owed by force, the relevant action belongs to the state, not the individual.

6 Thanks to Michael Milde for discussing the comparison with me during a meeting of the Ethics Reading Group at Western.

7 I am leaving out of consideration a more optimistic third world where there are no people in need. Versions of this optimistic world have been endorsed by socialists and libertarians alike. Some socialists agree with Marx's claim that a true socialist state would be beyond scarcity and so material need would disappear. Likewise, some libertarians believe that because the market would flourish in the absence of

state controls we would all, including the poor, be better off without the state. I do not find either version of this optimistic third world persuasive.

8 This version of the argument appeals to Kantian intuitions but it has something in common with certain arguments in feminist ethics. Some feminist moral theorists believe it is better to act out a direct sense of caring for others than to have justice dictate one's actions. And so we could compare Welfarist World to Caring World in much the same fashion as we compared WW to KW.

9 We can imagine a state-organized but voluntary welfare scheme where one gave by opting to donate a certain percentage of one's pay.

10 Thanks to Andrew Brook for presenting me with this line of objection.

11 It is an interesting topic for empirical research just how much enforced giving affects one's motivation to aid. For example, people often mention that the average American gives far more to charity than the average Canadian as evidence for the claim that enforced giving reduces the motivation for altruistic giving. But this claim misses two points. First, as I have noted, it may be that in paying their taxes gladly Canadians are just as motivated by moral duty as are Americans. They simply prefer co-ordinated action. Second, it fails to take into account the presence in the U.S. of tax incentives, which make donating money or goods to charity in one's self-interest.

12 If both human welfare and moral motives matter, this raises the question of the relative importance of these two values. Is there any amount of human welfare we would be prepared to sacrifice for an increase in actions stemming from the morally correct motive? For an exploration of these issues as they relate to virtue and human welfare, see Thomas Hurka, "How Great a Good is Virtue?" *The Journal of Philosophy*, Volume 95, Number 4, 1988, pp. 181-203.

13 Jeremy Waldron, "A Right to Do Wrong," *Ethics*, 92, October 1981, pp. 21-39.

14 For two such accounts, see Judith Thomson's presentation of the High Threshold Thesis in *The Realm of Rights* (Harvard University Press, 1990), and my "Thresholds for Rights," *Southern Journal of Philosophy*, Volume 33, Number 2, 1995, pp. 143-168.

15 I will not ask whose right we ought to infringe, given a choice between infringing Bart's or Amelia's. This is because, given their past behavior, there may be egalitarian reasons for calling on Amelia over Bart.

16 Of course this is not the only explanation of why the threshold of Amelia's right is lower than the threshold of Bart's right. It may be that less is at stake for Amelia than is at stake for Bart. Perhaps Bart is nearly bankrupt from past giving, while Amelia is well-off. If the threshold of a right is a function of harm to the right bearer were the right infringed, then less being at stake for Amelia will result in a right with a lower threshold. For a defense of the claim that harm is a factor on which the strength of rights is based, see my "How is the Strength of a Right Determined?: Assessing the Harm View," *American Philosophical Quarterly*, Volume 32, Number 4, 1995, pp. 383-394.

17 Of course, just when duties kick in is a difficult question. The view I've sketched here as the moderate view about duties is frequently endorsed but rarely given in detail. My quick presentation of the issue is not meant to suggest that these questions about detail are easily answered. The utilitarian view, while not so accommodating of our intuitions, does possess the virtues of clarity and simplicity.

18 Robert Goodin, *Utilitarianism as a Public Philosophy*, Cambridge University Press, 1995.

19 P. 41, *Ibid.*

2. Human Rights, Truth, MacIntyre, and Putnam's Pragmatism

THRASSYVOULOS PAPADOPOULOS

This paper is about Alasdair MacIntyre's criticism of human rights and its connection with his theory of truth and rationality. In the beginning there is an account of Alasdair MacIntyre's conception of human rights and a brief description of the place this conception occupies in his philosophy. A criticism of a crucial point in this philosophy will lead to a very different way of viewing human rights. This is inspired by Hilary Putnam's efforts to renew pragmatism.

MacIntyre and Witches

In one of his most famous aphorisms MacIntyre has no mercy on human rights: "there are no such rights and belief in them is one with belief in witches and unicorns" (MI 1985:69). The reason for this, he continues, is that every attempt to give good reasons for believing that there are such rights has failed, just as the case is with believing that there are witches and unicorns.

A rather less bluntly put, but equally radical thesis of MacIntyre concerning human rights runs as follows:

> "...both the conception of rights characteristically invoked by those engaged in this conflict over rights, and the rhetorical procedures used to advance claims to rights embodying this conception, are such that to invoke them or employ them is already to have entangled oneself in error. The dominant contemporary idiom and rhetoric of rights cannot serve genuinely rational purposes, and we ought not to conduct our moral and political arguments in terms derived from that idiom and rhetoric." (MI 1991A:96)

To call these positions radical at such an early point in the argument is not a mark of prejudice; it is rather a recognition of the importance of the consequences they could have if they were vindicated, as well as of the fact that they are quite strange to the majority of western moral and political philosophers, let alone lawyers ...

Which considerations lead MacIntyre to these claims?

He thinks that a characteristic feature of western social and cultural orders is their inability to solve conflict over important moral problems rationally. Debates concerning such problems degenerate to confrontations of assumptions, because, according to MacIntyre, the adherents of rival positions appeal to incommensurable standards. They use, he continues, conceptions of the moral good which initially were developed and could be rationally defended only in certain theoretical and social contexts. But today these conceptions are deprived of their contexts with the result that they have become expressions of mere (i.e. emotional) preference. MacIntyre claims that moral discourse in our culture has indeed taken the form ascribed to any moral discourse by some positivist thinkers (notably Stevenson and Ayer). He borrows the term "emotivist" from those thinkers, in order to describe our present moral condition.

The most important reason for this moral disaster is, according to MacIntyre, the failure of what he calls "the enlightenment project". To put it in a nutshell, he believes that the philosophers of the enlightenment set out to substitute what they regarded as discredited, traditional and superstitious moral forms with a kind of secularized morals that can claim the allegiance of every rational person. As different thinkers as Hume, Bentham, Diderot and Kant - among others - had tried to formulate moral principles, which any sufficiently reflective rational person must necessarily comply with. MacIntyre holds that these efforts have failed.

This failure has led to persistent confusions in Western culture. One of them, according to MacIntyre, is that the enlightenment has bequeathed to its cultural heirs a set of rival moral beliefs each one of which is presented by its adherents as if it were the only rational way to ground moral comportment. MacIntyre tells us that it doesn't surprise him that what he considers to be the failure of those efforts (of rationally solving moral problems) in post-enlightenment western cultures has led some thinkers to the assumption that reason is helpless in this realm. (He has the emotivists and Kierkegaard in mind.)

Another consequence of the failure of the enlightenment project is, according to MacIntyre, that what he sees as the ongoing, unsettled and insoluble conflict among rival moral standpoints has led to the introduction of a set of moral concepts in western cultures, debate over which appears to be rationally justified, but, in his view, really isn't. The result of this, he says, is that these allegedly rationally grounded concepts can be put to the service of the pursuit of a set of rival and incompatible goals. Just because they conceal the purposes they serve, MacIntyre calls these concepts useful fictions. The most important of them are the concepts of human rights and of utility. This is how MacIntyre comes to think of human rights as if they had the rational status of witches and unicorns.

Once we've noticed that, we can proceed with MacIntyre's claim that even the invocation or employment of rights by the sponsors of rival rights theories is necessarily misleading.

He believes so, because

> "Rational debate over the application of moral, indeed, more generally, of evaluative concepts, requires that there be some standard, independent of the desires, preferences, and wills of the contending parties, to which appeal can be made in trying to show why the reasons supporting one point of view are superior to those supporting another. In the absence of such a standard, there is nothing to distinguish genuinely rational moral or evaluative disagreements from any other clash of conflicting desires, preferences, and wills." (MI, 1991A:97)

At this point MacIntyre's argumentation no longer aims at mere, however severe, cultural criticism, but takes a more strictly philosophical turn. His claim is a) that rationality is context-bound, and b) that it demands that appeals be made to standards external to what one wants or feels. Not a few philosophers would find a) and b) to be incompatible with each other. They would say something like "you can't pair contextuality with objectivity of standards". I'll examine the validity of this claim later. For the sake of the argument it is important that it becomes clear if and how MacIntyre succeeds in making this claim plausible.

To achieve this we now have to turn to MacIntyre's theory of rationality.

MacIntyre and Rationality

Macintyre puts forward a conception of moral particularity which he considers to be alien to liberal individualism. In his opinion the social features of human existence are not contingent; on the contrary, he thinks they are constitutive of personal, moral, and intellectual life. I see this as a partial recognition of some moral autonomy, because this conception seems to be compatible with something like responsible individuality. MacIntyre (MI, 1985:221) believes that what he accepts as a fact, namely that

> "the self has to find its moral identity in and through its membership in communities... does not entail that the self has to accept the moral

> limitations of the particularity of those forms of community. Without those moral particularities to begin from there would never be anywhere to begin; but it is in moving forward from such particularity that the search for the good, for the universal, consists."

This is undoubtedly a good argument for the importance of cultural context, but the question still remains: what kind of rationality is it, in terms of which one is to identify the theoretical and practical limitations in one's particular tradition, in terms of which one is to move forward toward the universal, or in terms of which one can choose which tradition-based community is the most adequate?

The answer to that question is the central issue of many chapters of "Whose Justice? Which Rationality?". One of the most important assumptions of this book is to be found at the start (MI, 1988:4). MacIntyre says that modern authors who are influenced by the Enlightenment way of thinking ignore "the inescapably historically and socially context-bound character which any substantive set of principles of rationality, whether theoretical or practical is bound to have".

Nevertheless, he agrees with Aristotle that the basic laws of logic hold in every tradition. Despite that, "observance of the laws of logic is only a necessary and not a sufficient condition for rationality, whether theoretical or practical" (MI, 1988:4). Which then are the sufficient conditions for rationality?

According to MacIntyre (MI, 1988:7), we must recover the following conception of rationality:

> "...conception of rational enquiry as embodied in a tradition, a conception according to which the standards of rational justification themselves emerge from and are part of a history in which they are vindicated by the way in which they transcend the limitations of and provide remedies for the defects of their predecessors within the history of that same tradition."

Although standards of rationality are, according to MacIntyre, relative to a tradition, there are certain possibilities to consider certain standards as better in that they transcend the limitations and remedy the defects of their predecessors. What exactly does this mean? Is it a mark of superior rationality? There seems to be a possibility of bridging gaps between rival traditions, even of comparing them to a degree. The reason to suppose that is MacIntyre's following thesis (MI, 1988:9-10):

> "an acknowledgement of the diversity of traditions of enquiry, each with its own specific modes of rational justification, does not entail that the

differences between rival and incompatible traditions cannot be rationally resolved."

How is this possible?

MacIntyre (MI, 1988:351) claims that "there is no set of independent standards of rational justification by appeal to which the issues between contending traditions can be decided."

What he wants to say is that what rival traditions share (lists of virtues, conceptions of the self, metaphysical cosmologies, and even logical intelligibility) is so different that it doesn't seem to be sufficient to solve the conflict between such traditions. On the other hand, wasn't it MacIntyre who claimed that such conflicts can be solved rationally? Although some traditions are presumably rival, they share something that enables them to solve their disagreements rationally, because MacIntyre insists that relativism and perspectivism are *not* the consequences of his conception of rationality. The answer is: in order to discover what these traditions share, one should look at the actual practices of enquiry of inquirers. This kind of historical account (of the Aristotelian, Augustinian, Scottish Enlightenment and liberal traditions) is exactly what MacIntyre has given in WJ. Such a study, he claims, can

> "provide an account of the rationality presupposed by and implicit in the practice of those enquiry-bearing traditions with whose history I have been concerned..." (MI, 1988:354)

MacIntyre calls this kind of enquiry tradition-constitutive and believes that its characteristic rationality includes some well-defined stages through which it increasingly achieves intellectual maturity. He distinguishes three such stages (MI, 1988:355) "a first in which the relevant beliefs, texts, and authorities have not yet been put into question; a second in which inadequacies of various types have been identified, but not yet remedied; and a third in which response to those inadequacies has resulted in a set of reformulations, reevaluations and new formulations and evaluations, designed to remedy inadequacies and overcome limitations."

One important inadequacy is, according to MacIntyre, "incoherences in the established system of beliefs"; another one is "a lack of resources for offering or for justifying answers to new questions" (MI, 1988:355). Conversely, achieving consistency and comprehensiveness seem to be general marks of rationality, things to be achieved by all inquirers in any tradition.

In MacIntyre's scheme it is clear that, although enquiry and evaluation are always relative to a tradition, to a particular set of beliefs, so that rational progress is always formulated in the particular terms a tradition currently employs, it still seems that historical study of traditions of rational enquiry can show certain common criteria which mark success or failure at rational enquiry.

> "The identification of incoherence within established belief will always provide a reason for enquiring further, but is not in itself a conclusive reason for rejecting established belief until something more adequate because less incoherent has been discovered." (MI, 1988:359)

MacIntyre calls radical cognitive impasses in traditions of enquiry "epistemological crises". Although these are supposed to be particular to every tradition of enquiry, he presents again general standards for solutions to any epistemological crisis. A solution must be more "systematic and coherent" than its predecessor, it must "provide an explanation" for past difficulties, and it must stand in "some fundamental continuity" with the past beliefs (MI, 1988:362).

Now the interesting case is when a tradition in an epistemological crisis encounters a hitherto alien tradition. This tradition may be able to recognize, after learning the language of the alien tradition, that

> "it is possible to construct from the concepts and theories peculiar to it what they were unable to provide from their own conceptual resources, a cogent and illuminating explanation - cogent and illuminating, that is, by their own standards - of why their own intellectual tradition has been unable to solve its problems or restore its coherence." (MI, 1988:364)

But the real problem, in MacIntyre's opinion, is that a sense of substantive continuity is not had in this solution to the crisis. "Derived as it is from a genuinely alien tradition, the new explanation does not stand in any sort of substantive continuity with the preceding history of the tradition in crisis" (MI, 1988:365). So, MacIntyre continues, to accept the new tradition's solution requires "an acknowledgement... that the alien tradition is superior in rationality" (MI, 1988:365).

This argument is not very clear. MacIntyre says that in such cases there is no substantive continuity between the old and the new, but how exactly can we tell a substantive continuity from a too abstract or general one? He has claimed that although traditions share standards, these are not *sufficient* to rationally solve disagreements. This generates the question of whether he wants a *total* solution (and of how would this look like) or whether a partial would do.

MacIntyre's answer would be that only a total solution would be acceptable, because without such a solution we could not achieve commensurability of standards of the rival traditions. This need for commensurability stems from his view that - though there may be observable procedural and substantial points of resemblance between two conflicting traditions of enquiry - each such system has its own standards of measure and interpretation, explanation, and justification internal to itself. In this view, this means that

> "there are indeed no shared standards and measures, external to both systems and neutral between them, to which appeal might bc madc to adjudicate between their rival claims. The two systems of thought and practice are incommensurable..." (MI, 1991B:109)

MacIntyre stresses that this kind of incommensurability has a historical character, i.e. it occurs over a certain period of time, which, in turn, means that two traditions of enquiry can be incommensurable at one stage of their development and yet become commensurable at another. The question rises again: how can this happen?

First of all, says MacIntyre (MI, 1991B:110), it can be the case that the members of each of the two or more contending parties will agree (by providing sufficient grounds for their assertions) that what they are referring to is indeed the same subject matter. Nevertheless, he goes on, the standards which determine how the true / false distinction is to be applied are at this stage still different and mutually exclusivc.

But the sharing of a certain subject-matter (MacIntyre uses the terms "descriptive characterization" and "associated reference") by two or more incommensurable and rival conceptual schemes is, according to MacIntyre, not enough for them to reach commensurability.

> "It is at a second level of characterization that predicates are applied in accordance with standards internal to and peculiar to each of the rival standpoints and such that each set of standards excludes the possibility of application for key predicates of its rivals. And this use of predicates will give expression to distinctive modes of observation, of seeing as and of imagining, as well as of reasoning." (MI, 1991B:110)

This can serve as a description of the phenomenon of untranslatability, which, in MacIntyre's view, may, but need not, be associated with and arise from incommensurability. Nevertheless, he claims that to achieve translatability is an initial step toward transforming the relationship between two or more originally incommensurable standpoints. How can this initial step be made?

Of course, MacIntyre says, untranslatability of one "language-in-use" into another does not entail that all mutual understanding is precluded.

But such an understanding can be achieved only by inquirers who inhabit both conceptual schemes, both traditions. Such people can be only those adherents of each standpoint who manage to learn the language of the rival stand-point so good that it becomes for them a "second first language".

MacIntyre holds that only these persons will be able to understand what it is in the rival tradition that they reject, but that they will still have to reject it anyway. This is because of the standards of their own framework by which the alternative will inevitably be judged false. The question that MacIntyre asks at this point is how this transformation of the incomprehensible to the inescapably rejected does constitute an advance in the conversation.

His answer is that we can speak of such an advance if, and only if, at least one of the contending parties enriches its conceptual arsenal by grasping the concept of incommensurability and, as a result of it, recognizes two things: "that its own rejection of the rival alternative up to this point was indeed inevitable and that, were the adherents of that rival alternative in like manner to understand their opposing point of view, the same inescapable act of rejection would have to ensue" (MI, 1991B:112).

MacIntyre and Truth

The acquisition of the concept of incommensurability by the adherents of one of the rival traditions of enquiry is in MacIntyre's view very important, because, from an Aristotelian point of view, it implies the conclusion that *no rational encounter*, "no dialectical appeal to mutually acknowledged principles of any kind" had taken place or "could so far have taken place". We have now reached a very crucial point in MacIntyre's argument. He holds that it is only through rational encounter with a rival theory that one can test its claims to *truth*.

His conception of truth is also presented in a very clear way, since he identifies truth with adaequatio intellectus ad rem (MI, 1991B:112) which is a rather traditional formulation of the correspondence theory. He adds that in no way should truth be confused with warranted assertibility, because

> "Warranted assertibility is always from the point of view of and in accordance with the standards of some one out of the rival incommensurable points of view. But what makes the concept of truth distinctive is precisely that it holds or does not hold independently of point of view. To claim truth for some expression of the relationship of a mind to

> its objects or for that relationship itself is to claim that this is how things are, no matter how they seem from points of view." (MI, 1991B:113)

Of course, MacIntyre continues, one can only make a claim to truth from within one particular point of view, one conceptual scheme, one tradition of enquiry, but this claim is not about how things appear according to the standards of that tradition; it's a claim about how things are, "a claim in terms of fundamental ontology" and that's why, he says, such a claim characteristically involves a claim that no consideration made from any other point of view can "overthrow or subvert" that claim.

From this conception of truth it follows, according to MacIntyre, a) that problems concerning the warranted assertibility of rival incommensurable views can be solved sufficiently (by the standards of rational warrant of each view the rival view would fail) and b) that progress in rational enquiry leads toward agreement within any tradition of rational thought and action but need not lead toward agreement or convergence of views between adherents of rival and incommensurable traditions.

How, then, can it become possible that two or more rival and incommensurable standpoints achieve commensurability? After all, MacIntyre, unlike relativists and perspectivists, repeatedly stresses that a genuine rational encounter between such standpoints can take place.

Incommensurability Revisited

He begins his argument by stating that traditions of enquiry as a rule have long and complex histories of internal development in the course of which they have been confronted with and have more or less successfully overcome problems and difficulties. If now, according to MacIntyre, two or more rival and incommensurable traditions have reached the stage described above (beyond partial incomprehension and misrepresentation of the other by enriching their linguistic and conceptual resources), they may see that an accurate representation of the other involves regarding it as a historically developing body of theory and practice with its own internal standards of success and failure in respect of its particular problems and difficulties.

Such a construction of histories is crucial, says MacIntyre, because it may lead the adherents of the one standpoint to the recognition that theirs is rationally inferior to some other rival and incompatible standpoint. He believes that for this recognition to take place two conditions must both be fulfilled:

> "the first is that its own history, as narrated in the light of its own standards, the standards internal to it, should lead in the end to radical and, so far as it is possible to judge, irremediable failure..." (MI,1991B:117)

MacIntyre adds that it is not necessary that the adherents of such a tradition of enquiry recognize that failure; it is enough, he says, that they would have recognized it had they viewed matters in accordance with their own internal standards. The second condition is:

> "that the adherents of this alternative rival tradition be able to provide the resources to explain why their own tradition failed by its own standards of achievement and, more precisely, why it succeeded and why it failed at just the points and in just the ways in which by those same standards it did succeed and fail." (MI, 191B:118)

Those resources must not, in MacIntyre's view, be available within the tradition whose failure is being explained.

He claims that when both of these conditions are satisfied, it is rational for the adherents of the tradition of enquiry which failed to transfer their allegiance to the tradition which explained why.

We should not forget at this point that, according to MacIntyre, these conditions are only satisfied if each of the competing standpoints is judged by its own internal standards and not by shared standards allegedly sufficient for rational evaluation, let alone neutral and independent standards. This means that the conditions can be satisfied only when the two rival and incompatible traditions of enquiry are incommensurable.

MacIntyre's conclusion is that incommensurability does not preclude (at least not always) rational encounter and debate and that when the development of two rival and incommensurable bodies of theory and practice reaches a point at which it is possible to pose the question, "in a detailed and substantive way", of whether the two conditions above are satisfied (or seem likely to be in the near future), then these two systems have become commensurable. For this reason, he holds, the way towards the recognition of the importance of making rational encounter between two incommensurable bodies of theory and practice possible requires, as a necessary first step, that the adherents of each standpoint provide for themselves a history of the other, written from that other's point of view and employing the other's standards of rational success or failure.

Such a way of writing the history of a tradition of enquiry shows, in MacIntyre's opinion, a more general aspect, as well: how conversation between rival traditions of enquiry, rooted in very different cultures, has to proceed, if it is to be fruitful. He considers two features of all such conversations to be crucial: the admission of fallibilism and the inescapability of contextualism.

> "We can only learn what intellectual and moral resources our own standpoint... possesses, as well as what intellectual and moral resources its rivals may possess, when we have understood our own point of view in a way that takes with full seriousness the possibility that we may in the end, as rational beings, have to abandon that point of view. This admission of fallibilism need not entail any present lack of certitude, but it is a condition of worthwhile conversation with equally certain antagonists." (MI, 1991B:121)

> "...in comparing two fundamental standpoints at odds with each other... we have no neutral, independent standpoint from which to do so. We... cannot find any legitimate standing ground outside the context of the points of view." (MI, 1991B:121)

What we can do instead, MacIntyre says, is to compare comparisons: our comparison of our standpoint to theirs with their comparison of their standpoint to ours.

We have seen so far how it is possible in MacIntyre's philosophy that contextualism and a kind of absolutism (although he never uses this word, I think it's an adequate concept for describing his theory of truth) can fit together. Rationality, he holds, a) is context-bound, and b) requires an acknowledgement of victory/defeat in respect of truth which is independent of point of view. Moreover, MacIntyre holds that a "strictly realist conception of truth" as the one described above is a presupposition of the possibility of a rational dialogue between traditions of enquiry (MI, 1996:682), because it is exactly this shared presupposition of the contending enquirers in respect of truth that can generate rational progress.

Truth, Rights, and Politics

The consequences of MacIntyre's conception of truth for his conception of human rights are now clear: since, according to his theory, without the assumption of and the commitment to a strong realist correspondence theory of truth there can be no rational progress toward solutions of conflicts between rival traditions of enquiry or genuine rational debate between such traditions, it follows that in a debate over the concept of human rights their adherents cannot rationally ground their claims, because theirs is at best a commitment to warranted assertibility and not to truth and it is only a vindication of their claims to truth that could prove their standpoint to be rationally superior. Just because proponents of human rights theories cannot rationally justify their claims, says MacIntyre, they have substituted for the traditional notion of rational justification "of one among competing rival bodies of theory some notion of pragmatic context-bound justification, according to which justification is relative to the contingent purposes and agreements of those who engage in activities of justification in the course of their conversation with each other" (MI, 1991B:115).

It is obvious that a critical assessment of MacIntyre's ideas on human rights has to involve criticism of his conception of truth. But, first of all, I turn to his provocative assertion that belief in human rights is one with belief in witches and unicorns.

It is not right that the reason we don't believe in witches and unicorns is the failure of the attempts to show *that* there are witches and unicorns. The reason why we don't believe in them is that we're better off with theories and practices that exclude their existence than with the ones that do not. In the case of human rights this means that MacIntyre has to show why we should stop believing in them or, rather, what politics and which institutions are better.

Now MacIntyre has definitely rejected the notion that his sweeping philosophical summary of Western thought suggests that he is proposing we should *return* to a traditional, i.e. pre-modern, society governed and informed by a perfect, conflict-free moral order. What he has said, is that, although there has never been such a society, even the loss of the *ideal* of such an order in the course of the transition to modernity "in exchange for the impoverished moral orders of modernity raises the sharpest of questions" (MI, 1991A:102). On the other hand, he has written very little on the politics of the society (or the societies) favoured by his theory (e.g. MI, 1990:216-236, 1991A:106-110), anyway too little to be able to convince anyone that life in the kind of community he envisages would be so much better than life in the "impoverished moral orders of modernity" with their "useful fiction" of human rights. Even if human rights were fictions and even if Western modernity were morally impoverished, how would MacIntyre's alternatives look? MacIntyre has yet a lot of theoretical (as well as practical) work to do in this respect (and this is something he is well aware of).

There are some thinkers who have described the politics that MacIntyre's views tend to favour as appalling. One of these thinkers is Hilary Putnam (P, 1992:185). Putnam thinks that the politics that views such as MacIntyre's can justify is a politics of an immunization of institutionalized oppression from criticism, because they involve, whether deliberately or not, an abandonment of the idea

> "that it would be good for the victims of oppression to know of alternative ways of life, alternative conceptions of their situation, and to be free to try for themselves which conception is better" (P, 1992:185 - 6)

The Theory of Inquiry

In other words, Putnam holds that these politics "block the path of inquiry", because they silence the voices of criticism, which is crucial to inquiry. (Inquiry is seen by Putnam and the classical pragmatists in its wide sense, i.e. human dealings with problematical situations.) Putnam, like the classic American pragmatists Peirce and Dewey, views inquiry as a *cooperative* activity (P, 1995:70), as a "cooperative human interaction with an environment'. He stresses the importance of both interaction ("the active intervention, the active manipulation of the environment") and cooperation with other human beings.

Intervention, he tells us, is connected with pragmatist fallibilism, which is stronger than the mere granting of the possibility of a well-confirmed-in-the-here-and-now theory being disconfirmed in the future. Pragmatic fallibilism teaches us that some ideas won't be falsified, unless we go out and actively seek falsifying experiences. Putnam believes that only those ideas have proved their worth which are repeatedly put under strain. This conception of falsification stems from the pragmatist model of inquiry which is one of a *group* of inquirers - not of a single scientist in his study or lab, like the positivist model - who try to produce ideas and test their value.

It is very important to note that, according to the pragmatists, this awareness of human fallibility should by no way, and indeed cannot, produce universal scepticism. One of the most vital insights of pragmatism is that one can, and indeed should, be both fallibilistic and anti-skepticist. As Putnam (P, 1995:68) puts it:

> "The fact that we have sometimes been mistaken in even very fundamental belief cannot, by itself make me doubt any specific belief."

But, all the same, this point doesn't give us a reason for trusting any particular belief either. What kind of method would enable us to find out which of our beliefs are really justified?

The pragmatist answer to this question would, first of all, rule out the possibility of the requested method being an algorithm, which solves all of our epistemological problems. Such a thing is held to be just a philosopher's fantasy, a metaphysical apriorism (P, 1995:63-64 and 1994:245-264). Nevertheless, Putnam says, the lack of such an algorithm and of a metaphysical guarantee that any of our beliefs or methods will never need revision, "does not mean that we don't know *anything* about inquiry" (P, 1995:69). Our experience has taught us a lot about how inquiry should be conducted - and that some of this applies to all kinds of inquiry, and not to some particular subject-matters. What we have learned - be it in science or in ethics - can provide us with maxims (Putnam uses this concept in its Kantian meaning), not algorithms, and maxims themselves require contextual interpretation.

It is at this point that we can see the importance that pragmatists attribute to criticism, for it is criticism generated by cooperation that prevents any interpretation or application of maxims from being in practice merely subjective (as would be the case, according to the pragmatists, when an isolated inquirer is at work). As William James has written (quoted in P, 1995:72) even the notion of "truth" makes no sense in such a "moral solitude" for "truth presupposes a standard external to the thinker" (cf. P, 1994:172).

Putnam adds that it is of great importance that cooperation must be of a certain kind in order to be effective. For instance, he says, it must respect the principles of discourse ethics (P, 1995:72; on differences between discourse ethics and pragmatism see also P, 1987:53-56 and 1994:232-233), autonomy, and symmetric reciprocity, which are absolutely indispensable for the scientific enterprise, because the latter requires "the unimpeded flow of information and the freedom to offer and to criticize hypotheses" (P, 1992:198). Of course, pragmatists are not blind to the role power plays in the history of science, but they have a normative notion of science. They don't only consider the above requirements to be important to good science - that could also apply to the case that scientific theories and hypotheses were, in the end, to be tested by the application of an algorithm - but,

> "the very *interpretation* of the *non*-algorithmic standards by which scientific hypotheses are judged depends on cooperation and discussion structured by the same norms. Both for its full development and for its full application to human problems, science requires the *democratization of inquiry*.' (P, 1995:73)

According to the pragmatists, this is especially true of the application of science, which is also a test of the hypotheses applied and should be under democratic control. Moreover, the pragmatists never accepted the dichotomy pure science/applied science (cf. P, 1994:198-220). They consider these activities to be interdependent and interpenetrating.

The same goes for instrumental values and terminal values, if we follow pragmatism. This means that, although the above justification of the democratization of inquiry is, in part, instrumental (science helps us attain knowledge and other goods and goals), it is also terminal, in the sense that a) even goal-oriented activity is also guided by norms of rationality which have become terminal values for those who act (P, 1994:160-169) and b) knowledge is very often a terminal value for most of us.

We have seen that, according to the pragmatist normative conception of what is to be scientifically rational, it is not just a sociological-descriptive fact that the norms under which we choose, generate and evaluate theories are part of the nature of scientific inquiry. "These norms describe the way we *ought* to function when the aim is knowledge" (P, 1995:74).

Nevertheless, this is not to be taken as a mere empirical correlation: inquiry, which follows these norms does not produce knowledge as fire produces warmth. On the other hand, it could be the case that inquiry, which does not follow these norms does produce knowledge and justification. As Putnam says "concepts of knowledge are essentially contested concepts; they are always open to reform" (P, 1994:174) and they cannot be "analytically" defined once and for all. Instead, he adds, the applicability of our present conceptions is being constantly tested and the norms which partly constitute that conceptions represent values which may now be terminal but they are not immune to criticism. This situation is, of course, difficult to deal with, but, according to Putnam, John Dewey wanted us to see it as typical.

Against the possible accusation that pragmatism tries to derive ethics from science (or from a theory of inquiry) Putnam defends his theses by saying that he is well aware of the fact that, notwithstanding a certain overlap between scientific values and ethical values, these values remain different. Nevertheless, Putnam agrees with Dewey that there is a close connection between inquiry and ethics. They give two reasons for that assumption.

First, all cooperative activity involves a moment of inquiry, otherwise it would be very difficult to see if the activity is carried on successfully ("going smoothly") or not. That is why Putnam believes that "what is essential to the rational - or, to use the word that Dewey preferred, the *intelligent* – conduct of inquiry is thus, to some extent, essential to the *intelligent conduct of all cooperative activity*." (P, 1994:174)

This is how the extension of democratization to more and more institutions and relationships in the modern world is to be explained.

The second reason is that ethics itself requires inquiry. It is a fact that we all act as ethical fallibilists: we have all criticized and often abandoned many inherited values (this is not to say that all of us have criticized the same values) and "the more we do that the more we come to see ethical disputes as disputes that are to be settled by intelligent argument and inquiry, and not by appeals to authority or to a *prioiri* principles" (P 1994:175). Putnam knows that this doesn't *prove* that there are objective norms or principles or even situation-specific values. However, James and Dewey claim, *if* there are such norms (they speak of "ethical facts") to be discovered,

> "*then* we ought to apply to ethical inquiry just the rules we have learned to apply to inquiry in general. *For what applies to inquiry in general applies to ethical inquiry in particular*." (P, 1994:175)

It follows that, if the above considerations are right, then an ethical community (according to Putnam, a community which wants to know what is right and good) should organise itself democratically, because democratic standards and ideals are "the prerequisites for the application of intelligence to inquiry" (P, 1994:175).

Of course the pragmatists recognize the possibility of a tyrant giving his scientists, say physicists, a certain freedom of discussion in some areas, a kind of freedom that is forbidden in the society. But John Dewey argued (and this is an empirical presupposition) that societies that organise themselves undemocratically and hierarchically limit the rationality of those at both ends of the hierarchy. The intellectual growth of the oppressed is limited, and the rulers are forced to construct rationalizations to justify their position (cf. P, 1992:180-200).

Even the physicists of the example would, according to Dewey, become so removed from the society and from common interests "as to become a class with private interests and private knowledge, which in social matters is not knowledge at all" (cf. P, 1994:217). Dewey firmly believed that inequality in distribution of power inevitably produces a one-sided growth, and, therefore, cognitive distortion in the privileged.

Criteria

At this point, however, a question could arise: even if ethical inquiry is democratically organized, even if the participants cooperate respecting the norms of discourse ethics etc. under what *criteria* should they judge success or failure of the inquiry?

The pragmatist response to this question has three parts:

First, nobody starts from the position of doubting everything. In any actual discussion the participants share a lot of factual and value assumptions that are not disputed in that actual discussion. It is also often the case that it is exactly by appeal to those values (the ones that are not disputed in that discussion) and not to any universal criteria that a disagreement is seen as resolved. We are never in the position, imagined by the positivists, of having a large stock of factual beliefs and no value judgements, and having to decide whether our first judgement is warranted, i.e. of having to infer our very first "ought" from a whole lot of "ises".

Putnam adds, that it can happen that the accepted criteria can "conflict with themselves." In that case rational reconstruction is called for, provided it is seen as just one among other ways of resolving problems, and not as the way to the discovery of universal principles applicable to all situations. We could add, at this point, that it would be perfectly compatible with Putnam's views to state that, in the case of such a conflict, *trade-offs* must be made, and there is no formal rule or method for making such trade-offs. As Quine (from whom I borrowed this term) has said, the decisions we make are, "where rational, pragmatic" (cf. Quine, 1961).

Second, the pragmatists hold that one can often tell that a problem is resolved without applying any set of criteria (cf. P, 1994:198-220) and that we have all made this experience in our lives. It can be, for instance, that the solution we found to a problem would not have been judged as good by any "criteria" we regarded as binding at the beginning of our search for a solution. Or it can be that *after* having solved an individual or a collective problem we may not know if it was an ethical problem or some other kind of problem. These situations occur every day and nothing is bad or wrong in such solutions. What this can help us see, is that we neither have nor require one single criterion for judging warranted assertability in ethics any more than we do in any other area. As Dewey believed, the authority of philosophy is not the authority of a field invested with knowledge of such a criterion or set of criteria.

> "As philosophy has no private store of knowledge or methods for attaining truth, so it has no private access to good. As it accepts knowledge of facts and principles from those competent in science and inquiry, it accepts the

> goods that are diffused in human experience. It has no Mosaic or Pauline authority of revelation entrusted to it. But it has the authority of intelligence, of criticism of these common and natural goods." (Dewey, cf. Putnam, 1992:188)

This brings us to the third part of the pragmatist answer to the "By what criteria" question. If pragmatists do not believe that inquiry requires criteria, in the sense of algorithms or decision procedures, either in the sciences or in daily life, they do believe that there are some things that we have *learned* about the nature of inquiry from the conduct of inquiry. It is, for instance, distinctive about Dewey that he never ceased stressing the importance of and applying the idea that what holds good for inquiry in general holds for value inquiry in particular (cf. Putnam, 1994:198-245 and 1992:180-200). Things that hold good for inquiry in general are, for instance, the principle of fallibilism (in the strong sense mentioned above), the principle of experimentalism (try out different solutions to problematical situations and, if this is not possible, examine carefully what solutions other people have found and reflect on the consequences) and the bundle of principles which fall under the title "democratization of inquiry" (cf. P, 1995A).

At this point it is important to stress that the pragmatists don't hold that the belief in the possibility of ethical objectivity goes together with the belief that there are no undecidable cases (contrary to Dworkin) or no problems which cannot be solved (at least not in the study, i.e. some of them can only be solved by engaging in politics).

What they do hold is

> "that once we give up the metaphysical claim that *there cannot be* such a thing as ethical objectivity, and once we observe that objectivity in other areas is strongly connected with values, we can begin to see not just that ethical objectivity might be possible, but, more important, that investigating ethical problems requires just the values that have come to be linked with the open society." (P, 1994: 176)

Fundamental democratic institutions like freedom of thought and speech are, among other human rights, such values. Like all values they are not immune to criticism (nor can they be grounded *a priori*), but they are constitutive of the next best way of conducting inquiry (in this case the inquiry of living together in a society) that we have learned in practice.

It should be clear by now that Putnam's defense of moral objectivity has got nothing to do with either moral apriorism or authoritarianism. This is crucial, because MacIntyre's example has shown us that not every defense of moral objectivity is good and that in trying to refute moral skepticism we can easily end up providing a rationale for deeply anti-democratic politics or at least for the maintenance of the status-quo.

But MacIntyre wouldn't have great problems with granting that Putnam's sort of moral objectivity can establish the possibility of there being warranted assertibility in ethics. However, he would say, such an account of objectivity cannot support any claim to *truth* (for the reasons mentioned above). So Putnam still has to show the relation of warranted assertibility to truth.

Realisms and Truth

Putnam's defence of moral objectivity is intertwined with his views on realism (the question of how mind and language hook on to the world) and truth. According to the present version of these views (note that Hilary Putnam has changed his opinion on these matters twice in the last twenty-five years; cf. P, 1994B), truth cannot be defined, but there is a lot of philosophically important things to say about how we employ the notion of truth and how it relates to other semantical and epistemological notions. These are very complicated and very fascinating matters, but before we get lost in them let us see how MacIntyre's conception of truth could be criticized from Putnam's present point of view.

Clearly the correspondence between mind and its objects, the correspondence between words and things "as they are" which is the core of MacIntyre's theory of truth has got nothing to do with a correspondence within language, i.e. it is not a verbal correspondence (against which nothing is to be said). Instead, it is a substantive property that lies outside of language and explains the fact that we accept statements as true or not true (a verbal correspondence could not play this role). This conception of truth assumes a fixed set of objects (this is, among other things, what "strict realism" amounts to), which are mind-independent and are "out there" and a fixed relation between statements in any language and these mind-independent objects.

Against MacIntyre's conception of correspondence Putnam would hold that

a) there are many possible uses of the notion of an "object" (not just one) and reality cannot fix the use of this word;
b) the world cannot "single out" a unique correspondence between objects and words or determine a unique correspondence between words and "items in the universe of discours" (cf. P, 1990:173).

If this criticism is justified - and I believe it is - there are important consequences for the whole theory of Alasdair MacIntyre. Above all his explanation of the possibility of a rational dialogue between different traditions of inquiry and the rational solution of conflicts between them, his opinions on the nature of value judgements, his account of the relationship of theory to praxis, and, of course, his criticism of human rights as being a concept which cannot be rationally defended, because commitment to it is just a commitment to warranted assertibility and not to truth - his truth - are bound to fail.

So far, so good, but nothing has been yet said about the relation of warranted assertibility to truth. After all, Putnam claims that we have learned some things from inquiry and the application of the standards that experience has taught us are necessary to the "intelligent" conduct of inquiry in science as well as in ethics can enable us to distinguish (however fallibly) better from worse solutions to problematical situations. For a pragmatist, this suffices to establish the "existence" of warranted assertibility in this area.

However, this establishment of warranted assertibility should not be confused for a definition of truth as warranted assertibility under "ideal" (i.e. good enough) epistemic conditions (Putnam's previous conception of truth). That would be just another kind of conception of truth as a "substantive property" (remember that the correspondence in MacIntyre's theory is a substantive property, too.)

Putnam holds that he doesn't any more see that we are forced to choose between the alternatives: truth as a substantive property (whatever this might be) or truth as one among many versions of "deflationism" or "disquotationalism", which is, roughly, the theory that "p" is true = p.

He thinks that disquotationalism in the version that was defended in the late philosophy of Wittgenstein has an insight, but that many present-day deflationists severely pervert that insight. The insight in Wittgenstein's disquotationalism is

> "that to call a claim true is not to assert anything *above and beyond* the claim itself; in particular, it is not to claim that all 'representation' has a 'substantial property'." (P, 1995A:74)

To avoid skepticism, we don't need the metaphysical realist picture of a "funny metaphysical something" that stands back and guarantees our claims or explains the very possibility of thinking (as opposed merely to giving expression to one's subjectivity). A corollary of this is that MacIntyre's account of the debates over human rights (and other notions) as being hopelessly emotive is wrong. Wittgenstein and Putnam reject the idea that being able to make ordinary claims to truth about the external world (e.g. "there is a chair in this room") and denying that truth is reducible to making statements with a funny sort of "substantial property" are incompatible.

The problem with deflationism, according to Putnam, is that it very often goes together with reductionism, i.e. the theory that thoughts, judgements and beliefs are reducible to "marks and noises" or to so-called "representations" in the brain, which our community has taught us to associate with conditions for being conclusively verified. This conception of truth as verification is called verificationism and it is also a very central feature of antirealism, too, and Putnam strongly rejects antirealism.

It would be an enormous digression to go into the realism-antirealism debate, and since I am mainly concerned with refuting central theses of MacIntyre, who is no antirealist at all, but rather a metaphysical realist, I confine myself to stressing that antirealism is the label for a bunch of theories all of which claim that there is no world independent of our representations (perception, thoughts, beliefs, judgements, desires etc.) of it and that we can see how intelligent people can come to support such an unbelievable claim if we consider a) that their main concern is to avoid what Putnam calls metaphysical realism and/or postulating magical powers of the mind in its hooking up to the world and b) that they see no other option to do that than making such claims. I repeat that I am well aware of the fact that I am doing injustice to antirealism with such a brief and rough description, but I already digress and we have to go on.

Now, Putnam rejects verificationism on the grounds that truth is not *always* something that can be verified, i.e. the limits of truth are not always the limits of warranted assertibility. There can be statements that may be true, but there are no conditions under which we can verify that they are true and the very notion of "conditions" for verifying them may make no sense. An example is the statement "there do not happen to be intelligent extraterrestrials". Although it may be impossible to verify that this is the case (even under "ideal" conditions), we all understand what it means that it may be true.

Another thing that's wrong with deflationism, as long as it goes together with verificationism - which it almost always does - is that, by identifying understanding with verification abilities, it cannot properly accommodate the truism that certain claims about the world are not merely assertible or verifiable, but true.

Putnam believes that the right alternative to thinking of truth as a substantive property like the metaphysical realists do, is not deflationism or verificationism (let alone antirealism) but common-sense ordinary realism, namely the claim that empirical statements already make claims about the world - many different sorts of claims about the world - whether or not they contain the words "is true" (P, 1994B:501).

On the other hand, Putnam believes that it would be a mistake to reject what is right in verificationism, namely that

> "a great deal of scientific talk does depend for its full intelligibility on the provision of the kind of thick explanatory detail that is impossible if one has no familiarity with the use of scientific instruments." (P, 1994B:502)

This brings us to the point that, even if the limits of truth are not always the limits of warranted assertibility, it would be a big mistake to suppose that truth can always transcend warranted assertibility under good enough conditions. The reason is that

> "the ability to refer to things is not something that is guaranteed by the very nature of mind... reference to things requires information-carrying interaction with those things, and that is enough to rule out the possibility that truth is in all cases radically independent of what we can verify." (P. 1995:17)

We have seen that Putnam rejects the metaphysical realist conception of truth as a substantive property (the fantasy that the form of all knowledge claims is fixed once and for all in advance together with the myth that there is just one way in which a knowledge claim can be responsible to reality - by corresponding to it) and the verificationist account of truth on the grounds that truth is sometimes recognition-transcendent, because what goes on to the world is sometimes beyond our powers to recognize (let alone to verify) even if we can conceive it. We do know that he has not an antirealist account of truth either.

What we haven't yet answered is the imaginary question: "but is then the disquotationalism he supports synonymous with that Tarski's?" The answer is no. Tarski held that it is a theorem of logic that each sentence is either true or false and this theorem is called bivalence.

Now, Putnam does not believe that this is right. To put it in a nutshell, he holds that a sentence may fail to have a truth-value, for instance because of the vagueness of its terms (e.g. "the number of trees in Canada is even") or even because it is possible that not only may there be cases in which there is no determinate truth-value (or, say, right answer), but that it may be indeterminate which those cases are (second order vagueness). "True" is not a mere device for disquotation. To put it as Wittgenstein would,

> "Our understanding of what truth comes to, in any particular case (and it can come to very different things), is given by our understanding of the proposition, and that is dependent of our mastery of the 'language game', by which Wittgenstein means here 'the whole, consisting of language and the actions into which it is woven'." (P, 1994B:513)

Even if I presented a very incomplete picture of the problem of truth and some of the connected matters, I hope that I have succeeded in making it clear that our learning from practice and experience enables us to formulate claims to warranted assertibility in every field, including ethics and that making such claims and being engaged in the practice of criticizing them does amount to a commitment to truth. Institutionalized values such as human rights are social conditions of that practice and therein lies maybe not their foundation (Begründung), but their justification.

References

Alasdair MacIntyre

1985: *After Virtue*. London: Duckworth.

1988: *Whose Justice? Which Rationality?* London: Duckworth.

1990: *Three Rival Versions of Moral Enquiry*. London: Duckworth.

1991A: *Community, Law, and the Idiom and Rhetoric of Rights*, in: 26(2) Listenings 96-110 (1991).

1991B: 'Incommensurability, Truth, and the Conversation between Confucians and Aristotelians about the Virtues', in: Deutsch, Eliot (ed.), *Culture and Modernity*. Honolulu: University of Hawaii Press, 1991.

1994: 'A Partial Response to My Critics', in: Horton, John and Mendus, Susan (eds.), *After MacIntyre*. Oxford: Polity, 1994.

1996: 'Interview', in: Deutsch, Z. Philos, *Berlin 44* (1996), 671-683.

Hilary Putnam

1987: *The Many Faces of Realism*. LaSalle, Ill.: Open Court.

1990: *Realism with a Human Face*. Cambridge, Mass. and London: Harvard UP.

1992: *Renewing Philosophy. Cambridge*, Mass. and London: Harvard UP.

1994: *Words and Life*. Cambridge, Mass. and London: Harvard UP.

1994B: 'Sense, Nonsense, and the Senses: An Inquiry into the Powers of the Human Mind' in: 91 *The Journal of Philosophy* 445-517 (1994).

1995: *Pragmatism. An Open Question*. Oxford: Blackwell.

1995A: 'Are Moral and Legal Values Made or Discovered? and Replies', in: 1 *Legal Theory* 5-19 and 69-80 (1995).

Willard Van Orman Quine

1961: 'Two Dogmas of Empiricism', in: *From a Logical Point of View*. Cambridge, Mass.: Harvard UP.

3. Towards a Natural Justice of Rights Relationships

JOHN A. HUMBACH*

For a social species such as ourselves, having a psychological repertoire replete with emotions sparked by human interchange, it is relationships not rights that people really live for. What we really want from others is not our abstract rights but right relationships. Rights are at best a means to right relationships, a way of providing background conditions in which right relationships can be established and developed. Ultimately, however, no depersonalized system of rights and rules can mediate, except in a crude and clumsy way, the intricacies of interactions among persons. As the fundamental legal concepts for a global society, rights alone produce only a poor simulation of actual right relationships, and a moral focus on rights alone supports and fortifies tendencies toward anonymization and de-personalization that come at the expense of human individuality. In short, a relationship of rights is to a right relationship what a paint-by-numbers picture is to a genuine work of art, a set of boxes that can never be the match of something whose ineffable beauty can only be produced from the heart.

I.

Most people today associate "justice" primarily with rights. However, as developmental psychologists have observed, children growing up not only come to recognize the justice of rights, but they also learn to organize their moral thinking in other ways as well.[1] There is not merely the justice of rights but also another and distinctive kind of justice, the justice of right relationships. The two are very different.

The justice of rights is a justice of entitlements. It is a conception of justice in which personal entitlements are the fundamental moral objects in view and their enforcement is crucial. By contrast, the justice of right relationships treats human *relationships*, not rights, as the fundamental moral objects, with no crucial role for entitlements at all. While the justice of rights is grounded in rules about entitlements, the justice of right relationships arises out of the human attachments and connections that people form in the course of daily life. At its core, the justice of right relationships is the intrinsic good that inures to persons who live in interaction with others whose fundamental moral concern is to maintain the quality and mutual worth of their relationships, instead of insisting on their rights.

In the legalistic outlook of our times, rights-consciousness abounds in thinking about justice, and many people, especially lawyers, see a pre-eminent role for rights and norms as almost synonymous with justice itself. Unlike the relational justice, the justice of rights can be implemented only by a conscious recollection, analysis and application of rules and other norms.[2] As a result, rights and norms play a disproportionately large role in our intellectual understanding of justice and they seem practically indispensable if there is to be any justice at all. By contrast, the justice of right relationships does not rest on a conscious application of rules and norms and, as a consequence, we tend to overlook the importance that relational justice has in our day-to-day lives. However, both the regulatory justice of rights and the relational justice of right relationships offer bases for resolving conflicts and achieving social justice. Indeed, it will be maintained here, the justice of right relationships provides the better basis by far.

II.

Rights are lines in the sand, legal boundaries that must not be crossed, with punishments for transgressors. If people all stay on their own sides of the lines, the "justice of rights" is achieved. It neither allows less nor demands any more, and the actual effects of acts on others are not a required concern, at least not for individuals. Those effects were all dealt with, in an abstract sort of way, when the lines of the law were laid down. Thus, you can do as you please, chips falling where they may, as long as you are "within your rights." More formally, then, a relationship of rights is a bounded interaction of morally independent individuals. If everyone stays in their rule-defined bounds, then the relation is deemed to be "just."

Right relationships cannot be as precisely defined as rights because they are intrinsically indefinite. Their indefiniteness is indeed their virtue, as it allows them to provide individualized justice that is tailored to particularized human beings and connections instead of the rigid, pre-canned justice of rights. Though not definite, however, right relationships can still be described, and their description is generally this: Right relationships are human relations in which each (or all) seek, without abandoning themselves, to be attentive and responsive to the needs and emotions of one another, quite apart from considerations of entitlement. There are also several important "negative" markers of right relationships, namely that they must be free of systematic oppression, exploitation or manipulation. That is, a relationship is not "right" if participants seek to overbear in power (oppress), to overreach in resources (exploit), or to mislead for selfish advantage (manipulate). These negative markers cannot, of course, be taken as precise categories - else they would reduce to mere "rights," a rigid one-size-fits-all. Instead, consonant with providing individualized justice for particular persons and attachments, what counts as, say, "oppression" will necessarily vary with the particularized needs and capabilities of the human beings in question. For example, the appropriate proportions of power in a given parent-child relationship are obviously not likely to be the same as those among most spouses. In consequence, the "test" of whether a relationship is right, or not, cannot be the simple analytical application of affirmative and negative markers. The rightness of a relationship can be measured, ultimately, only by whether it is felt to be right by those concerned. It is not that feelings are always per se reliable (in particular, there must be alertness for the distorting effects of manipulation). However, in this as in all matters ultimately of the heart, the proof is in the tasting, not the analysis.

The justice that is enjoyed in a right relationship is reciprocal, but that does not necessarily mean reciprocal entitlements. A tit-for-tat reciprocity of entitlement is characteristic of the justice of rights but not the justice of right relationships. Rather, the reciprocity of right relationships needs go no further than the mutual and effective commitments of both (all) members to one another. It is the reciprocity that exists when the members of a relationship all value the relationship for the values they get from it. Different members may value a relationship in very different ways and for very different reasons. The specific values that each receives may be entirely incommensurable with those received by the other(s), so that the measured tit-for-tat that is expected in relationships of rights may often, in fact, be literally impossible to compute - but it is characteristic of right relationships that "nobody is counting." In right relationships it is not tit-for-tat but the members' mutual and effective commitments to one another and to maintaining the values of their connection that is the basis of justice.

This should not be read to imply that rights and rules are not also sometimes important. For one thing, a robust background of legal rights can help promote the relational justice of right relationships by stabilizing social contexts so that acquaintanceships and, hence, relationships can be formed. Also, the regulatory justice of rights is useful as a last resort, for cases in which relationships have broken down to the point that serious oppression, exploitation or manipulation will occur unless entitlements are enforced.

Nevertheless, the regulatory justice of rights is a very poor proxy for the justice of right relationships, and systems of rules creating lines in the sand (rights) are in no way a substitute for genuinely right relationships. A relationship of rights is to a right relationship what a painting-by-numbers is a genuine work of art, at best a crude and awkward substitute for the real thing.

To view right relationships as the fundamental moral objects in human interactions is strongly reminiscent of the feminine "ethic of care," identified and described by Carol Gilligan.[3] In her important and ground-breaking work, Gilligan has shattered the prevailing notion that rights-based thinking is the sole legitimate approach to questions of moral concern. By uncovering an actual, living alternative way to view moral problems, the relation-oriented "ethic of care," Gilligan has provided an influential corrective to the legalistic, rights-obsessed moral myopia of the late 20th century. However, Gilligan describes her ethic of care as a moral perspective that is *distinguished from* justice rather than as a *kind* of justice.[4] She appears to have concluded, moreover, that the "care" perspective emerges from the particular experience of growing up female, making it more likely to be the moral orientation of females than of males.[5] These qualifications are debatable.[6]

In any case, the ideal of right relationships as fundamental moral objects, and as a kind of justice superior to a rigid justice of rights, goes back at least 23 centuries. For example, at the end of a lengthy disquisition on justice, Aristotle wrote of an alternative that he called *epieikes*, the "better" kind of justice that results when a person "does not insist upon his rights to the damage of his neighbors, but is content to take less than his due, although he has the law on his side."[7] Although *epieikes* is not the same as legal (rule-based) justice, Aristotle insisted nevertheless that it was "a kind of justice."[8] Aristotle saw *epieikes* as "a rectification of legal justice," a rectification that is necessary because, in prescribing legal rules, it is "plainly impossible to pronounce with complete accuracy upon such a subject-matter as human action."[9] "For where the thing to be measured is indefinite the rule must be indefinite..."[10] Apparently too, Aristotle saw this "better" kind of justice as entailing the affirmative concerns and care that are characteristic of the best human relationships, writing: "If people are *philios* [in loving relation, such as parent and child, lovers or friends], there is no need for [ordinary rule-based] justice between them... Indeed it seems that justice, in its *supreme* form, assumes the character of *philia* [amity/love]."[11] In sum, it appears that Aristotle saw two kinds of justice: the justice of rights, *i.e.,* legal justice, and the "better" justice, the *epieikes,* of right relationships.

Right relationships may seem to be, compared with hard and robust rights, a rather pale and undependable basis for preserving a quality that is as significant and weighty as "justice." In fact, however, people always have relied and still rely, most of the time, on right relationships rather than enforced entitlements to bring justice to their lives. In their families, in their workplaces, among neighbors, between landlords and tenants, in shopping - and the list goes on - almost never do people have recourse to actual legal rights. Even when we do make claims of right in the course of controversy, it is almost always purely a rhetorical (and often erroneous) reference. True, rights and their defining rules lie in the background of most human interchanges and, in cases of litigation, these background rights and rules are brought forward to demarcate the entitlements at hand. For the most part, however, in most people's day-to-day lives, rights are not a major factor in either what people give or what they get in their interactions with others. Although ideas of rights, vaguely understood, may provide a suggestive plane of reference for right relationships, rights certainly do not define right relationships, nor do they define the level of general satisfaction that people have with respect to the justness of their lives.

To add perspective, it should be recalled how recent an innovation the artifice of rights really is. For millions of years, our early human ancestors and their earlier hominid predecessors had no such thing as rights. That does not mean there was no such thing as "justice," or that individuals had no sense of the just and unjust. On the contrary, the ethological evidence is that our pre-rights ancestors probably had a fairly distinct sense of what we would call justice. It is merely that this justice was not channeled into rights but was realized directly in the interactions that occurred within right relationships. It was the relationships themselves that were the *fons et origo* of justice. Even today, higher primates seem to sense something like "justice" when it comes to exchanges of food or grooming and to retribution for affronts and violations of the expected behavior patterns. Children within a family or, more generally, people sharing a common household or even workplace, similarly evolve common expectations in the course of interactions with one another, amounting to a shared understanding of what counts as just treatment and what does not. Such shared understandings arise quite naturally as people interact within the give-and-take milieu of their social lives. Enforced with help of and, in turn, reinforcing the likewise natural bonds of affection, attraction or amity that help hold the relationship together, these common expectations provide a very stable grounding for justice within the relationship. They are, however, a far cry from the sorts of defined, condition-dependant entitlements that we normally refer to as rights. Again, they are to rights what the forms and shapes on a beautiful painting are to a paint-by-numbers imitation of it.[12]

III.

The more recent history of humankind can be seen as the history of a passage from the justice of right relationships towards a regulatory justice of rights and norms. As people came to live in large societies of thousands and even millions, instead of in the small social bands of pre-agriculture, individuals found themselves in multiple overlapping relationships with countless others, most of whom they did not even know. This change did not in itself prevent the building of right relationships: A right (or wrong) relationship can be anything from a one-shot encounter to long-term living together. But new challenges did emerge as people in relationships became more and more remote and anonymous to one another. After all, even though people are still willing to risk their lives for their countrymen, most people feel far less bonded to mere compatriots than to members of their own families, and they do not personally know or have relations of trust with most of them at all. As it has become ever more common for people to find themselves in anonymous interactions of standardized types, the creation of standardized "rights" has acquired obvious utility.

The Romans faced this need on a large (imperial) scale comparatively early on, and they developed in the Roman law a very refined system of rights, and they gave these rights, at least in theory, a high moral priority over other considerations. *Fiat justitia, ruat coelum*, exclaimed the Roman motto: "Let right be done though heavens may fall." Clearly the Romans had absorbed the concept of applying rights and rules while "letting the chips fall where they may." Nevertheless, the traditional and natural justice of people in commitment with right relationships as their fundamental moral objects still has much vitality. As stated earlier, most people for most of the time have relied and still rely on right relationships rather than rights as the primary basis of social justice. The relational justice of right relationships still has not been supplanted by the regulatory justice of rights.

One reason people tend to keep rights in the background is because rights are, in actual fact, not very practical for day-to-day use, but work well only as weapons to bring out on those occasions when legal battles erupt to supersede ("resolve") the ordinary conflicts of life. One of the practical problems with rights is that, in order for them to be faithfully utilized, they have to be recalled, analyzed and interpreted for each of the plethora of cases to which their prescription runs. Another practical problem is that, as observed by Aristotle, legal rules must of necessity be written to provide for the general case, the most usual kind of case. Because of the infinite nuance of life, however, rules (and, hence, the rights they prescribe) often do not work well to meet the particularized, context-specific moral challenges that later arise.

Indeed, one might say, except when applied to de-personalized "persons" engaged in standardized exchanges, the clumsy stiffness of abstract rules and rights almost *always* miss the moral mark. If individual human beings and their personal interactions were stamped out like standardized rivets and rights, then right relationships could always emerge from carefully structured rights. However, unlike the rights defined by rules, we and our relationships are not uniform entities like rivets in a row, and the problem of unjust application becomes ever more acute in relationships that are closer and more intricate, to the point where bullheaded insistence on rights can actually be detrimental to relationships and interests of the persons in it. Rights can be the enemy of right relationships.

The great bastion of right-oriented thinking is, of course, the law. In the legal orthodoxy of today, rights and rules are the only explicitly recognized embodiments of justice, with the fostering of right relationships being considered more and more a by-product, at best, of the legal system's operations. Moreover, the law's policy priorities evince, in anything, an ever growing faith in rights as the sole path to social justice. Better to stand on your rights and regard your relationships as replaceable than to foster relationships at the expense of personal rights.

This is not a trend that can continue indefinitely. While respect for individuals' rights is supposed to be the very foundation of good human relations, the justice of rights has the unfortunate side effect of supporting and fortifying tendencies toward anonymization and de-personalization that come at the expense of the very human individuality rights are supposed to assure. Because, however, the justice of rights is a profoundly inept substitute for the justice of right relationships, a reaction will come and, in that reaction, the law's current obsession with rights and norms will be radically de-emphasized in favor of the more ancient, individualized and "natural" justice of right relationships.

IV.

Nowhere is the modern regime of rights more clear, and the legal lines in the sand more painfully enforced with inflictions, than in the area of criminal justice. Every interaction between a criminal offender and his or her victim is not merely a violation of rights but also, at least prima facie, a profoundly wrong relationship. However, the moral orientation of "right relationships" as the basis of social justice produces some very different conclusions from those that would follow from a purely rights-based approach to the problem of criminality.

We in the United States have a generally benevolent form of government, and live in a society where life, liberty and the pursuit of happiness are supposedly "inalienable" rights and where official brutality, if not entirely absent, is at least considered to be a deplorable exception. Yet, millions of people every year encounter government as an unsympathetic force for evil in their lives. These are the people who find themselves, their loved ones or others with whom they identify not merely excluded from social communion but deliberately subjected to systematic suffering inflicted by and in the name of government. We call this infliction punishment and, in general, regard it as justified despite our larger ideals about the wrongness of treating people badly. A variety of reasons or rationales are given for the infliction of punishment - deterrence, incapacitation (restraint), rehabilitation and retribution. Essentially, however, the thinking about what to do about the problem of criminality revolves around two basic kinds of goals:

- to give offenders what we feel they *"deserve"*
- to *minimize* crime and victims

These two basic kinds of goals (which may or may not, as an empirical matter, actually be compatible *at the margin*) correspond, in turn to two different views as to the proper role of law in dealing with social harms. The first is to view the proper role of law as *rectification*, a backward looking view that seeks to restore the balance of justice or entitlements that the offender has put asunder. It is, at its core, a matter of rights. The second is to view the proper role of law as the *modification of human behavior*, a forward looking view that seeks to prevent or minimize social harms in the future. It is, at its core, a matter of establishing and preserving relationships and habits of relationship in which all are attentive and responsive to the effects of their conduct on others, and do not seek to oppress, exploit or manipulate.

The classic strategy of rectification is simple restitution, taking back the ill-gotten gain and returning it to the person who has been unjustly deprived. In the crime of theft, for example, the stolen item is taken from the thief and returned to the owner. By the simple enforcement of personal entitlement, justice is restored. However, many kinds of crime do not admit of any straightforward restitutionary rectification. Assaults, homicides and other destructive acts cannot be literally "taken back." They can only be met by further destructive acts, this time with the offender (and those who care about him) as the victims, but this does not actually "put things back." The criminal is said to have a "debt" that must be "paid," to have "blame," which makes him "deserve" to be harmed, but these ideas are merely fictive constructs, and they no more correspond to anything measurable in physical reality than the idea that the offender is a Tauris or Sagittarius. From a physical standpoint (which is to say, as a scientific matter) these non-material "qualities" are fundamentally illusions - very powerful illusions, like the illusion that the world is flat or that the sun rises in the east, but they are illusions nonetheless. Nor are they harmless illusions, not if they lead our society to spend billions of dollars in deliberate efforts to inflict human suffering. To administer punishment to those who do harm may be useful as a way to appease frustrations: "It looks like slavery not to requite evil."[13] But that still does not prove that the suffering is "deserved," merely that it is useful.

The goal of minimizing crime and victims presents considerations that are very different from those of rectification. Rather than looking back, and trying to undo what was done, it tries to look forward and prevent bad things from happening the first place. In general this means taking steps to neutralize the threat of persons who, for whatever reason, pose an unreasonable risk of harm to others. While such threat of unreasonable risk may be evinced in many non-criminal ways, for purposes of the present discussion I will focus on those who have already committed crimes and been caught, so the question is: What to do with them? Here, too, punishment is an option - indeed, it is the favorite option of orthodox rights-oriented thought.

The infliction of punishment as *deterrence* is not founded on the notion that the offender "owes" anything per se (or else we are still talking retribution). Rather it is founded on the instrumental notion that the infliction will "deter" (*lit.* scare away) people from similar harmful behavior in the future. The deterrence effort may be aimed at the offender himself - a sort of tough-love mode or rehabilitation - or it may be aimed at making an "example" of the offender, so others will be dissuaded from crime.

There can be no question that, at least within limits, deterrence strategies can be efficacious: Aggression is an effective way to modify the behavior of others. By creating instrumental "rights" as tools of deterrence, the law supplies a formal structure with which to mount campaigns of aggression against those whose conduct we do not like. However, the evidence does not necessarily bear out the seemingly boundless faith that people sometimes seem to have in the deterrent effects of punishment. Deterrence has limits. Inflicting human suffering will usually affect the behavior of those targeted, but the change may not always be in the direction that is desired. It may, for example, breed resentments that only makes things worse. Already, America has a higher rate of imprisonment (which is to say, a lower rate of freedom) than any other country in the world. As prison populations swell, our current morality of reprisal may be reaching the limits of its ability to make a better world.

Deterrence theory is, essentially, an economic theory of crime: It holds that if you want to reduce crime you need merely raise its "price." It is rooted in the idea that people tend to act "rationally," that they *calculate* the expected gains and costs of acts in choosing what to do. The justice of rights similarly assumes that people are calculative in making their decisions. Indeed, the calculative assumption is perhaps even stronger in rights-justice than in economics, since the latter treats the assumption of rationality as being descriptive only of the average of behavior. By contrast, the justice of rights demands more than that rights be observed "on average," insisting instead on the ideal that every person's rights be upheld in every situation. This means in turn that efforts to realize the justice of rights requires a degree of calculative ratiocination in every situation, identifying the pertinent rights of all concerned and figuring out what observing those rights entails.

Like modern economic theory, the theory of deterrence and the idea of justice as rights are vulnerable to defects in their root assumption, namely, that people act rationally. This is much-sifted ground, and here is not the place to review the usefulness of the economist's assumption of rationality. A couple of points bear noting, however. First, there is the still-unanswered question of whether and how people can *ever* act rationally. For example, David Hume argued that, strictly speaking, rationality can never motivate human actions unless it is coupled with desire - and these desires, these limbic emotions that translate rational thought into acts, almost surely add their own deflections on the way.[14] Indeed, the whole drama of human life depends, in great degree, on the regularity with which the passions overcome reason. Then there is the problem that, as a logical matter, it would be rather spooky if the results of reason alone ever *could* directly determine the specifics of people's actions. The immediate product of mental reasoning is merely an idea in the mind, specifically, the logical conclusion that the reasoning entailed. Without repealing a couple of laws of physics, it is hard to see how a mere non-material idea, rational or otherwise, could ever in itself change or deflect the course material events, whether those events be the motions of human muscles or the synaptic discharges in the neurons that direct those motions.

Even assuming, however, that we can make the mind-to-body leap from rational mentation to action, there is another reason why rationality can be only a limited factor in determining what people do: Even the most dispassionately logical mental process is always limited by the short list of factors and considerations that actually come to mind. Nobody can think about things that do not occur to them, and nobody has the ability to rationally canvas the entirety of his or her memory banks to find and appropriately weight all the things they "know" that might rationally bear on a given choice. Indeed, the particular factors and considerations on which our thinking actually operates are always brought to awareness, complete with presumptive weights, by the operation of mental processes that lie beneath the surface - entirely beyond our ken. Even though these subsurface mental processes crucially constrain our choices, by selecting and provisionally weighting the operative options, there is no way whatever to assure that these processes are rational, uninfected by emotions, or otherwise unflawed. This is a very serious limitation on the power of ratiocination. People are able to be quite rational in reflecting on the matters they are aware of, but they have nothing like complete rational control over which things pop into their minds and enter into such reflections. As a result, even if the final stages of reaching a decision are carried out in a completely rational way (whatever that may mean), every decision is nevertheless conditioned, controlled and profoundly limited by mental operations that are completely outside the reach of rational control.

In short, we can be reflective, but we can never hope to exert rational control over the selection of things that we reflect about, the factors and considerations that we take into account. This fact is of the utmost importance to any consideration of deterrence as a justification for deliberately inflicting punishment. For to the extent that punishments do not in fact modify behavior for the better they are merely gratuitous and inhumane inflictions that serve only to increase the total amount of suffering in the world.

There is, in fact, substantial evidence that rational analysis and the punitive "prices" put on crimes do not play their intended role in the choice processes of many perpetrators. Among other things, much of criminality occurs because the certain people are so constituted or disposed (due to experience, intelligence and other factors) that they systematically underweight the longer term consequences of their acts while substantially overweighting the expected short term gratifications.[15] That is to say, their emotions (weightings) at any given time cause them to reach systematically false conclusions about what their future emotions (weightings) will be, and when that future time arrives they come to rue the consequences of their previous impulses. As seen by people who discount the future in a more "normal" way, these perpetrators do not appear to be acting rationally at all, not even from the perpetrators' own selfish point of view. Their calculations about others' rights, when such occur at all, seem to be immensely distorted.

In summary, while deterrence works in many individual cases, it is quite another thing to extrapolate to the conclusion that deterrence also works as a global strategy. The ideal of deterrence wildly underrates what Carol Gilligan has called "the awesome power of the irrational" in determining human behavioral choices.[16] If our goal is to modify human behavior for the better, it may turn out that devising a general theory of the irrational is much more helpful than continuing our dogged pursuit of the logically limited rationality-based models of rights and of deterrence economics.

V.
Rights, Right Relationships and the Irrational

For people imbued with the post-Renaissance dogmas of rationalism, the idea is vexatious that there are situations in which the rational answer is the wrong one: A familiar example may help elucidate how easily this can occur. Consider the principle of "the greatest good for the greatest number." Like every such general moral principle, this one leads to mostly "good" choices as well as some obviously bad ones. One of the bad ones that the principle implies is that it would be right to cut the vital organs out of a healthy person in order to use them for transplants to save the lives of ten others. It "feels" wrong, and such dissonances between our common moral sense and the logical implications of moral principles are a favorite diversion for students of elementary ethics. What typically happens when people work through thought experiments that evoke such dissonances is that they carefully engage themselves in a rational thought process and then they reject the conclusion on the basis of mere *feeling*. The powerful feeling that the logical conclusion is repellent is taken to be a more dependable guide to justice and moral rectitude than the outcome of logic. This is not merely a matter of choosing non-rationally. It is to make a choice that is counter to reason; it is *ir*rational. We allow our hearts to overrule our minds.

Almost everyone has no trouble understanding the metaphor of letting one's heart overrule one's mind, but what does it really mean? How can it be a good thing? Actually, what is happening is perhaps not nearly as mysterious as the "heart" metaphor suggests.

Psychologists note that knowledge can be divided into two very different categories - declarative and procedural. Declarative knowledge is like a recipe that can be recited and consciously followed, step by step, to produce a result. Procedural knowledge, by contrast, consists of that which we know but cannot say - how to ride a bicycle, being a classic example, but there are vastly more, encompassing indeed most of what we know how to do. Most children beyond a few years of age can speak their native language with almost perfect grammatical regularity (according to their local dialect), reliably finding and applying words, usages and inflections that the ever shifting contexts require. Yet, until they receive formal training none has much if any ability to "recite" the rules they are implicitly following. Even an adult who can recite all of the grammatical rules of her native language does not use this declarative knowledge in actually forming speech. Indeed, a person would be tongue-tied if she were forced to think declaratively of all applicable grammatical rules while constructing sentences (and, in trying to use foreign languages, learners do sometimes become tongue-tied for precisely because of this).

So it is, too, with building and maintaining relationships (like linguistic communication, a continuous social interchange). It is no more possible to produce a right relationship by following a declarative knowledge of the rules of right and wrong than it is to communicate linguistically by consciously applying a declarative knowledge of the rules of its grammar - or to ride a bicycle by consciously applying the "rules" for maintaining balance, propulsion, direction, and so on.[17]

The distinction between declarative and procedural knowledge corresponds to a crucial difference in the mode of realization of the regulatory justice of rights as compared with the relational justice of right relationships. The justice of rights emerges from conscious use of a declarative knowledge of rights and rules, while relational justice is produced by an implicit application of the procedural knowledge people have of how to treat each other in a wide and subtly nuanced variety of contexts. A person may often find it hard to cite a rule or "principle" explaining why she did exactly what she did in furtherance of a relationship, for there often are no rules or principles, as such: "The heart has reasons that the reason does not know."[18]

To illustrate this point in terms of a very attenuated (and, hence, simple) relationship, consider this example: In a large parking lot, a red convertible sits unattended with its top down and a valuable camera on the seat, in plain view. Three people walk past and see the camera, one at a time. In each case, nobody else is around. Each reacts differently:

- Mr. Able sees the camera but it does not even occur to him to steal it.
- Mr. Baker has a thought to steal the camera but, on reflection, decides not to (for whatever reason).
- Mr. Charles has the thought to steal the camera, and he does so.

The salient moral difference among these three might be summarized as follows:

- Mr. Able is in *right relationship* with (anonymous) others, whose interest in possessions he implicitly respects. His operative knowledge of justice is procedural (like the operative knowledge of the rules of language).

- Mr. Baker, by contrast, uses *rules about rights*, such as "stealing is wrong" or, the more selfish "it is wrong to risk to my liberty," but his ratiocination, his reflections, produce only an imitation of a genuine right relationship. His operative knowledge of justice is, in this case, only declarative.
- Mr. Charles is neither in right relationship nor does he act in accordance with rights, at least not *others'* rights. He does not even imitate a right relationship.

Obviously, using rules about rights, as Baker did, is better than nothing at all in making behavioral choices. It is, however, inferior to right relationships, where connections and attachments to others, rather than respective entitlements, are the *fundamental moral objects* to be realized. That is, it is better when persons are acting vis-à-vis one another allow themselves to be guided by what, in their interaction, occurs to them as they strive to make attentiveness and responsiveness to the effects of their acts on others (right relationships) their fundamental moral objects. For such persons, the right choices come not from rational calculations about rights but rather from their procedural moral knowledge or, metaphorically, "from the heart" - their approach being similar to that of an artist approaching a canvas or a virtuoso approaching a sonata, with perhaps a few rules in the background but with a certainty that no application of rules will ever produce a beautiful or splendid result.

But, one might object, what assurance can there possibly be that the behavioral choices that "occur" from the heart (*i.e.*, out of procedural moral knowledge) will be respectful of the others' rights? Such a question assumes, of course, that rights and not right relationships are the fundamental moral objects and the ultimate criteria of justice. The answer is that there is no assurance. Whether the behavioral results of procedural moral knowledge will be in accord with the others' rights depends on, as much as anything, how those rights are defined. If the results "violate" the other's rights, it may be that the legal prescription of the rights is morally flawed, not the behavioral choice. (For instance, a few years back when rape laws still gave husbands a legal right to non-consensual copulation with their wives, behavior consonant with a right relationship would have denied husbands that particular "right"). Of course, a person trying to do what seems best to promote right relationship might misjudge and err, just as a rights-oriented person may misconceive or misapply rights. However, at a guess, the average person's procedural knowledge of right relationships is probably a better guide to good relations with others than his declarative knowledge of rights. Persons who try to build or maintain right relationships by means of calculative, rights-based thought probably either end up either rejecting many of the rights-specified conclusions or (as perhaps too often happens) they stand on their rights, insist on them, and damage or destroy the relationship.

Again, this is not to say that rights-defined entitlements cannot exist in right relationships, but the norms that create such right relationships are, in their complex application to the vast diversities of human life, virtually impossible to state, let alone to apply in a recipe-like way. The world of the justice of right relationships is one for which, to paraphrase the prophet Jeremiah, the law is written on people's hearts,[19] where the most important knowledge of justice is not declarative but procedural.

In summary, even if rights are indispensable as a last resort, it is a perversion of moral purpose to turn things around, as modern society has, and apply them as a first resort. In our concern to continue the moral progress of humankind, we may therefore have come about as far as we can with the assumptions of rationality and the rights-oriented approach that the prevailing economics-type assumption of "rationality" suggests. We may need to search for a general theory of the irrational to get to the next moral stage of humanity's moral advance, the stage where the norms of how we treat each other are "written on people's hearts." The concept of right relationships will have a central role in any such general theory.

VI.
Moving from a Justice of Rights to a Justice of Right Relationships

If the justice of right relationships is not produced by calculations about personal entitlements, the question arises: What can be done to promote its production and wider realization? In particular, what is the role of law?

It would be, of course, entirely antithetical to the character of relational justice to suppose it possible to make a set of legal rules that define right relationships and then expect that people's following those rules would ipso facto cause the justice to result. A government can simply legislate rights into being, as happens every day, but right relationships cannot be legislated.

Because right relationships are largely the product of procedural knowledge about how to treat others, the justice of right relationships requires that people have and apply that knowledge. The question is not, however, so much a matter of providing the knowledge as it is of removing the barriers to its application. Even those who act most viciously are generally also able, when it suits their purpose, to seem conscientious and caring toward others. Indeed, it seems a fair hypothesis that the "right relationship" reaction - the disposition to be attentive and responsive to the others' needs and emotions -

does not have to be and, perhaps, cannot be taught any more than you can (or need to) teach a person how to feel hunger. However, just as people can be taught to repress their hunger drives, so likewise a normal acculturation in a modern social environment does much to inculcate barriers to acting in right relationship.

A significant part of the challenge is, therefore, educational - to neutralize the barriers to acting in right relationship by, for example, acculturating young people with social attitudes of tolerance and flexibility in the face of others' inevitable flaws, and teaching that "getting even" or insisting on rights irrespective of the effects on others is not an admirable sign of spunk or machismo but an immature surrender to reprehensible appetites. Rips and tears in the fabric of relationships should be taught as occasions for mending, not as occasions to dissolve what still remains.

Of course, there may be relationships that have become damaged beyond mending and, for them, the only resort is to the safety net of rights in order to protect the human dignity of the participants. However, a too-strong consciousness of those rights will lead to their being invoked too soon, either as a bludgeon to pound somebody or as an escape hatch for premature exit. When that happens, rights end up being part of the problem rather than part of the solution.

The question of whether to prefer rights or the relationship when troubled times arrive is, of course, very much a matter of the moral perspective of the persons facing the moral choice. As Carol Gilligan has noted, the relationship-oriented "try to change the rules in order to preserve relationships" while the rights-oriented "in abiding by these rules, depict relationships as easily replaced."[20] This difference reflects a difference in acculturation. However, relationships often are not so easily replaced as people may conceive, especially the ones that are most important to our lives. They take too long to establish and build. Yet, there are people, especially in the field of law and enforcement, who make whole careers out of pressing for the dissolution troubled relationships and urging those in them to exit. To honor these endeavors is, however, to send the wrong message. The law need not cooperate. Instead, the law can mute its own extreme rights-consciousness in the way it defines its central task of "dispute resolution" and make the fostering of relationships, rather then abstract rights, its primary end in view.

The justice of rights and relational justice differ enormously in their approach to the conflicts and clashes of human social life. In particular, to pursue relational justice is to seek to actually *resolve* disputes rather than just *subliminalize* them, pushing them beneath the surface. The idea that the enforcement of rights actually resolves conflicts is, in most cases, nothing but illusion. The actual "resolution" of disputes means mending tears in the fabric of relationships and, if possible, fostering the establishment of right relationships in the place of manifestly wrong ones. This can only happen, however, when all of those concerned come away feeling they have reached an accord that is respectful of the equal dignity and the legitimate claims and needs of everyone concerned. It is only then that a right relationship can begin to form and build.

All the law usually does today is to designate "winners" and "losers" based on rights and duties. Conflicts are deemed resolved when some of the disputants see themselves up against such overwhelming government power that they lose heart and give up the fight. The force of the law drives the discord to a hidden place where it festers or slowly atrophies. The losers may be quieted, but the conflict has not gone away. It is merely out of sight, subliminalized. However, a right relationship can never be founded on an exercise of sheer force. Picking winners does little or nothing to reconcile the losers to their fate. Therefore, in its winner/loser mode of functioning, the law does little or nothing to bring people back together and repair the rents in the social fabric. It merely tends to bolster the disputants' detachment and alienation from each other. By forcing losers to capitulate, it leaves the dissension intact.

The mistaken view that overwhelming force can truly resolve disputes occurs because people let their sense of legal rights replace their natural human sense of caring about others. It occurs when justice discourse is dominated by rights, rules and rule-defined personas such as "offenders," "victims," "tortfeasors," "contract-breachers," and the like. Lawyers especially can talk and write at tremendous lengths, prattling on about rights, rules and abstract persons without once making mention of the effects they might have on the quality of actual lives. The law is not, however, about abstract quantities but about real people, who never quite fit its pre-cast molds.

When disputes actually come to law, the justice of right relationships means (among other things) elevating mediation and reconciliation over litigation and "victory" as the strongly preferred ways of dealing with the parties. Today it is taken for granted that every person is absolutely entitled to pursue litigation in order to enforce rights and has little obligation to engage in non-litigative processes that could truly resolve rather than merely subliminalize conflicts. One measure that would elevate mediation and reconciliation efforts over litigation and "victory" is to require them as a mandatory prerequisite to litigation, with any sign of foot-dragging, subversion, or absence of good faith in the mediation process to count as a distinct negative in any litigation that ensues. The law should take care not to reward people who insist on their rights while disdainful of care, connection and responsiveness. It should recall Aristotle's counsel that the better kind of justice occurs when people do not insist on their rights to the injury of others. For those who still insist on victorious vindication, who insist on seeing their enemies gnash with their teeth and melt away, that victory should be simply denied.

In the case of criminal justice, the justice of right relationships requires that the primary effort should be to reestablish the harmdoer in a network of relationships that will return him to a law-abiding life. People who live in tightly bonded association with others within a web of responsive relationships are the most unlikely of all to commit antisocial acts. In the framework of right relationships the deliberate infliction of human suffering on the metaphysical ground that harmdoers "deserve" to suffer is an oppression that would simply never occur. There may be uses of deterrence, where this is the most humane alternative in light of the interests of all concerned, but there is never a place in the justice of right relationships for inflicting serious or permanent suffering purely for suffering's sake - no matter how satisfying it may feel to the inflictor.

How would an approach of relational justice reestablish the offender in a web of right relationships? People learn from experience. They evolve in their behaviors to adapt to the conditions in which they find themselves, whether those conditions be the dog-eat-dog environments of present-day prisons and jails or the tightly bonded attachments of right relationships among the law-abiding. If you want to create a population of individuals who are well adapted to life in a given kind of social setting, you create that kind of social setting (with its mores) and put the population in it. People who pose unreasonable risks need to be carefully supervised and subjected to restraint, but that does not mean prison must be brutish and nasty. The ugly gang-dominated social existence in today's prisons teaches relationships, but it does not teach right relationships.

In bringing about any move from our justice of rights to a justice of right relationships, lawyers are key. It is the lawyer's habits of thought that support the citizen's obsession with "rights," and in a culture of right relationships the lawyer's habits of thought must correspondingly support a robust concern with relationships - with mediation, reconciliation and genuine resolution of disputes. As the United States Chief Justice Warren Burger has said: "In their highest role, lawyers should be the healers of conflicts and, as such, should help the diverse parts of a complex, pluralistic social order function with a minimum of friction. Lawsuits ought to be the last resort - like war."[21] The Chief Justice then quoted Abraham Lincoln, whose counsel to lawyers was: "Discourage litigation. Persuade your neighbors to compromise whenever you can. Point out to them how the nominal winner is often a real loser - in fees, expenses, and waste of time. As a peace-maker the lawyer has a superior opportunity of being a good man."[22]

Too many people act like the only really "right" relationship is the relationship of victor and vanquished. This is not necessary, but it is the salient moral contingency of our times. It can be changed, but until it is changed, our human race will forever fall morally short.

Appendix
A Summary Comparison of Rights vs. Right Relationships

Rights: entitlements as fundamental moral objects
RRs: human connections and attachments as fundamental moral objects

Rights: *depersonalized* bases for action
RRs: *context-specific* bases for action

Rights: are about expressible norms
RRs: are about responsiveness to maintain relationship

Rights: calculative (within the domain of economics)
RRs: non-calculative (outside the domain of economics)

Rights: implemented by use of declarative knowledge
RRs: produced by use of procedural knowledge

Rights: the subordinate values (= means)
RRs: the paramount values (= ends)

Rights: tit-for-tat reciprocity
RRs: reciprocity in overall relationship, specific values offered based on immediate specificity of respective needs (where the thing measured is indefinite, the rule must be indefinite)

Rights: legalistic - "let chips fall where they may"
RRs: "equitable" - responsive character of moral responsibilities

Rights: devices to transfer choice, to impose will
RRs: social structures to harmonize choices, to reconcile wills

Rights: "Mine is mine" (resources, choices, other scarce values)
RRs: "We're in this together" (resources, choices, other scarce values)

Rights: rigid, and often in conflict
RRs: adaptive, resolvers of conflict (*cf.* II Cor. 3:6)

Rights: stress detachment, "contractism," obsession with self
RRs: stress attachment, connection, responsiveness to others

Rights: our rule-oriented mode
RRs: the way we usually live our lives

Rights: male
RRs: female
(supported by some empirical data, but debatable)

Rights: adjudication, with winners, losers
RRs: mediation and reconciliation, with mutual adaptation

Rights: subliminalize conflicts and disputes
RRs: resolves conflicts and disputes
(when a party thinks he can win, rights are enemy of right relationships)

Rights: "paint-by-numbers" relationships
RRs: genuine works of art

Notes

* J.D. *summa cum laude*, Ohio State University (1966). Professor of Law, Pace University School of Law, White Plains, New York.

1 See, e.g., Mapping The Moral Domain (Carol Gilligan, et al. eds., 1988); Justice and Care: Essential Readings in Feminist Ethics 93 (Virginia Held, ed., 1995). See generally Carol Gilligan, In a Different Voice: Psychological Theory and Women's Development (1982).

2 See infra part V.

3 Carol Gilligan, 'In a Different Voice: Psychological Theory and Women's Development' (1982).

4 See, e.g., Carol Gilligan and Jane Attanucci, 'Two Moral Orientations', 73, in *Mapping the Moral Domain* (Carol Gilligan, et al. eds., 1988).

5 Carol Gilligan, 'Moral Orientation and Moral Development', *Justice and Care: Essential Readings in Feminist Ethics,* 31-46 (Virginia Held, ed., 1995); Carol Gilligan and Grant Williams, 'The Origins of Morality in Early Childhood Relationships', in *Mapping the Moral Domain,* 111-37 (Carol Gilligan, et al. eds., 1988).

6 Gilligan's empirical conclusions as to gender differences in moral perspectives have been criticized on the basis of further studies. See *Justice and Care: Essential Readings in Feminist Ethics* 63 and 182 (Virginia Held, ed., 1995).

7 Aristotle, *Nicomachean Ethics*, Bk. V, ch. XV (J.E.C. Welldon, trans., 1987).

8 Id.

9 Id.

10 Id.

11 Id. at Bk. VIII, ch. I (italics denote emphasis added, and original Greek substituted in translation). The translator used the words "friends" and "friendship" but acknowledged in a footnote that these terms were not adequate to convey the meanings of the original Greek. Id. note 1. Aristotle's description of philia in its many aspects justifies, in my view, the conclusion that he is referring to a much broader concept than that encompassed by the English word "friendship," and had in mind a relational concept that was essentially congruent with paradigmatic right relationships.

12 Rights may not merely seem a maladroit basis for good human relationships but, compared with right relationships, rights may also be far less conducive to economic efficiency, as well. Empirical research by Ernst Fehr and Simon Gächter shows that assurances of material incentives in principal-agent relationships (rights) "cause a strong crowding out of voluntary cooperation," Ernst Fehr and Simon Gächter, Do Incentive Contracts Crowd Out Voluntary Cooperation, Institute for Empirical Research in Economics, Working Paper Series, Working Paper No. 34 (2000), available at <http://papers.ssrn.com/paper.taf?ABSTRACT_ID=229047>, "making agents less willing to cooperate voluntarily." id. at 26. "[T]he crowding out is sufficiently strong so that incentive contracts are on average less efficient than contracts without incentives." Id. at 26.

13 Aristotle, op.cit supra note 7, at Bk. V, ch. VIII.

14 See David Hume, *A Treatise of Human Nature* Bk. II, Pt. III, Sec. III (L.A. Selby-Bigge ed., 2d ed. 1978 [1789]).

15 See Richard J. Herrnstein and James Q. Wilson, *Crime and Human Nature* 49-56 (1985).

16 *Mapping the Moral Domain,* xvi (Carol Gilligan, et al. eds., 1988).

17 For a discussion illuminating a possible gender-contingent reason why some people have superior procedural knowledge of the strategies of right relationship, see D. Kay Johnston, Adolescents' Solutions to Dilemmas in Fables - Two Problem Solving Strategies, in Carol Gilligan, et al., *Mapping the Moral Domain*, 49, 66-67 (1988) (drawing on the work of L.S. Vygotsky and N. Chodowrow).

18 Blaise Pascal, *Pensées* 106 (Maxi-Poche Classiques Français 1995).

19 Jeremiah 31:33.

20 Carol Gilligan, 'In a Different Voice: Psychological Theory and Women's Development', 44 (1982), quoted in Claudia Card, *Gender and Moral Luck*, reprinted in *Justice and Care: Essential Readings in Feminist Ethics,* 93 (Virginia Held, ed., 1995).

21 Remarks of Warren E. Burger, Chief Justice of the United States at the Dedication of Notre Dame London Law Centre: The Role of the Lawyer Today, 59, *Notre Dame L. Rev.* 1, 2-3 (1983).

22 Id., quoting Abraham Lincoln, 'Notes for Law Lecture', in II *Complete Works of Abraham Lincoln,* 142 (J. Nicolay and J. Hay, ed., 1894).

4. Collective Moral Responsibility

SEUMAS MILLER*

In this paper I will offer an account of the notion of collective (moral) responsibility. In essence, I will argue that collective responsibilities are joint responsibilities of individual persons. My account is individualist in that I do not ascribe collective responsibility to groups or other collective entities as such. On the other hand, I am able to eschew extreme forms of individualism by virtue of my use of the notion of a jointly held responsibility. A joint responsibility is a responsibility that a single individual could not possess on his own. Moreover, in the case of joint responsibilities there is interdependence of possession; each relevant individual has a responsibility, but only on the condition that the other individuals have that responsibility.

I also use this account of collective responsibility as joint responsibility to try to deal with a number of puzzles that have arisen in relation to collective responsibility. Before turning to collective responsibility we need first to get clearer on the general notion of responsibility.

Moral Responsibility

There are number of different senses of responsibility. Sometimes to say that someone is responsible for an action is to say that the person had a reason or reasons to perform some action, then formed an intention to perform that action (or not to perform it), and finally acted (or refrained to act) on that intention, and did so on the basis of their reason(s). Moreover, it is assumed that in the course of all this the agent brought about or caused the action, at least in the sense that the mental state or states that constituted his reason for performing the action was causally efficacious (in the right way), and in addition, that his resulting intention was causally efficacious (in the right way).[1]

This above described sense of being responsible for an action is different from other well-known cognate senses of responsibility. The latter include what might be termed "bare responsibility". An agent has bare responsibility for an action if and only if (i) he intentionally performs (or refrains from performing) the action and; (ii) the intention causes the action (or omission). The latter also include the notion of a responsible agent - as distinct from someone being responsible for an action. An agent is a responsible agent if he or she is not insane, is not under the influence of drugs, and so on. Finally, there is being responsible for an action in the sense of freely performing the action. This notion of a freely performed action is notoriously difficult to pin down. According to one popular line of thought a freely performed action is an action such that the agent could have done otherwise. But this line of thought has been heavily criticised, and the analysis of the notion of a freely performed action remains an essentially contested one.[2]

I will dub the first of these above senses of being responsible for an action "natural responsibility". It is the first sense of being responsible that I need for my purposes in this paper.

In the interests of brevity and simplicity, the discussion in this and the following section will assume that the points made in respect of action can be made - suitably adjusted - in relation to intentional omissions. This is a controversial assumption, and, strictly speaking, not quite correct. But in my view it is near enough to the truth. Specifically, an agent can intentionally not do something that he has a moral obligation to do, and thereby be held morally responsible for his intentional omission. Consider someone who intentionally does not throw a life jacket to his drowning father in order to secure his inheritance. In the last section of this paper I look at some problems that arise in relation to collective responsibility for omissions.

What I have called, "natural responsibility" is not the only sense of the term, "responsibility".[3] On other occasions what is meant by the term, "being responsible for an action", is that the person in question occupies a certain institutional role, and that the occupant of that role is the person who has the institutionally determined duty to decide what is to be done (or not done) in relation to certain matters. For example, the mechanic has the responsibility to fix the brakes on my car when it goes in for a service, irrespective of whether or not he does so, or even contemplates doing so.

A third sense of "being responsible" for an action, is a species of our second sense. If the matters in respect of which the occupant of an institutional role has an institutionally determined duty to decide what is to be done (or not done), include ordering other agents to perform or not perform certain actions, then the occupant of the role is responsible for those actions performed (or not performed) by those other agents. We say of such a person that he is responsible for the actions of other persons in virtue of being in charge of them or of being the person in authority over them.

The fourth sense of responsibility is in fact the sense that we are principally concerned to elucidate, namely, moral responsibility. Roughly speaking, an agent is held to be morally responsible for an action (or intentional omission) if the agent was responsible for that action (omission) in one of our first three senses of responsible, and that action (omission) is morally significant.

The ways in which an action (omission) can be morally significant are too many and varied to be detailed here. They include instances of infringing or conforming to a moral principle or right, causing great good or evil and being motivated by a moral emotion. I will say more about the scope of this notion of a morally significant action later. Suffice it to say here that this notion is relatively narrow, and needs to be contrasted with wider moral and ethical notions, such as the ones expressed in phrases like, "it was a good or bad thing to do" or "it ought or ought not to be done". Indeed I hold the view that most of the actions of most people are without moral significance, in this sense of moral significance. So I do not accept certain versions of utilitarianism which are committed to the view that all or most of our actions (omissions) are morally significant because they contribute causally to the sum of pain/pleasure or happiness/unhappiness or desire satisfaction/dissatisfaction of someone or other at some stage or other.

At any rate I can now make the following preliminary claim concerning moral responsibility.

(1) If an agent is responsible for an action (omission) in the first, second or third senses of being responsible, and the action (omission) is morally significant, then - other things being equal - the agent is morally responsible for that action (omission), and can reasonably attract moral praise or blame and (possibly) punishment or reward for performing the action (omission).

Here the "other things being equal" clause is intended to be cashed in terms of exculpatory conditions, such as that he was not coerced, he could not reasonably have foreseen the consequences of his action, and so on.

Further this definition is a definition of a central species of individual (as opposed to collective) moral responsibility. There might be other species of individual moral responsibility, including weaker notions. For example, one might be less morally responsible for an unpremeditated act of wrongdoing, or for an outcome that was a foreseen consequence of one's action, but not intended. Further, there are various gradations of "action" in respect of which one has moral responsibility. Consider a person who fires a bullet at his business competitor with the intention of killing him. Coincidentally the person suffers a terminal heart attack a split second before the bullet arrives.[4] Given the notion of natural responsibility, on which the above definition of moral responsibility in part relies, the shooter is not morally responsible for the death of the person. This is so notwithstanding the fact that the shooter would have killed his competitor if the competitor had not suffered a heart attack. On the other hand, it is consistent with the above definition to hold that the shooter is morally responsible and blameworthy for a closely related action, namely attempted murder. It is also consistent to hold that the shooter is morally responsible for shooting his competitor. It is even consistent to hold that the shooter is almost as bad, as he would be if the competitor had not suffered a heart attack. To those who hold that he is just as bad, I would reply that what one actually does counts for more (even if sometimes not much more) than what one would have done, but for luck.

If a person is responsible for some action in the second or third senses of being responsible, then typically that person is institutionally accountable for it. To say that someone is institutionally accountable in this sense, is to say that he or she is required to be called to account for, and to justify, the action in question to some institutional body or person. Sometimes institutional accountability brings with it institutional, including legal, liability, and an adverse judgment on the part of those to whom one is accountable can result in the infliction of punishment.

If a person is morally responsible for some action then they can be held accountable, and hence liable in a number of ways. Personal accountability is accountability to oneself, and typically involves the provision of justifications to oneself for actions one is morally responsible for. Failure to provide adequate justifications may result in feelings of guilt. Personal accountability is, as they say, accountability to one's own conscience.

As members of a community or society we are also accountable to others in a number of ways for actions for which we are morally responsible. If these actions are criminal actions we are legally accountable for them. Such actions are subject to legal scrutiny and judgment. Moreover, sanction, including punishment by imprisonment can flow from an adverse legal judgment.

But we are also held informally accountable by other people for actions for which we are morally responsible. Our friends and the other members of the community to which we belong will often subject our actions to moral scrutiny for the purposes of determining moral responsibility and moral culpability. Moreover, adverse judgment is typically followed by expressed attitudes and actions, which signal moral disapproval, contempt and so on. Such judgment making and expressed disapproval constitutes a process of holding individuals accountable. And while this process is informal and may carry no legal sanctions, it is one that can powerfully influence our behaviour, often by generating feelings of shame.

Having distinguished four senses of responsibility, including moral responsibility, and distinguished each of these from accountability and liability, let me now turn directly to collective responsibility.[5]

Collective Moral Responsibility

As is the case with individual responsibility, we can distinguish four senses of collective responsibility. There are doubtless a number of different varieties of collective responsibility. However, in my view the core notion of collective responsibility, or at least one quite central notion of collective responsibility, arises in the context of joint actions, as opposed to individual actions.

I have offered a detailed account of joint actions elsewhere, but let me offer this brief account of joint action.[6] Roughly speaking, two or more individuals perform a joint action if each of them intentionally performs an individual action, but does so with the true belief that in so doing they will jointly realise an end which each of them has. Having an end in this sense is a mental state in the head of one or more individuals, but it is neither a desire nor an intention. However, it is an end that is not realised by one individual acting alone. So we have called such ends, collective ends. For example, you and I lifting a table is a joint action, since you lift one side and I the other, each of us lifts his side truly believing the other will lift his, and each of us has as an end that the table be lifted.

Agents who perform a joint action (or refrain from performing a joint action) are responsible for that action (omission) in the first sense of collective responsibility. Accordingly, to say that they are collectively responsible for the action (omission) is just to say that they performed the joint action (refrained from performing it). That is, they each had a collective end, each intentionally performed their contributory action (omission), and each did so because each believed the other would perform his contributory action (omission), and that therefore the collective end would be realised.

Again, if the occupants of an institutional role (or roles) have an institutionally determined duty to perform some joint action (or refrain from performing it) then those individuals are collectively responsible for its performance (omission), in our second sense of collective responsibility. Here a joint duty is a composite duty consisting of the duty each of us has with respect to the realisation of some collective end, and the duty each of us has to perform a certain specified action in order to realise that end. More precisely, I have the duty to realise a collective end by means of doing some action, believing you to have performed some other action for that self-same end. The point about joint duties is that they are not discharged by one person acting alone.

There is a third sense of collective responsibility corresponding to the third sense of individual responsibility, but it is not a species of joint responsibility. You will recall that the third sense of individual responsibility concerned those in authority. Here we need to distinguish two kinds of case. If the matters in respect of which the occupant of an institutional role has an institutionally determined duty to decide what is to be done (or not done) include ordering other agents to perform or not perform certain actions, and the actions in question are joint actions, then the occupant of the role is individually responsible for those joint actions performed (or not performed) by those other agents. This is our first kind of case, and it should be set aside, since it does not involve collective responsibility in our target sense.

In the second kind of case it is of no consequence whether the actions performed by those under the direction of the person in authority were joint actions or not. Rather the issue concerns the actions of the ones in authority. In what sense are they collective? Suppose the cabinet of country A (consisting of the prime minister and senior politicians) collectively decides to exercise their institutionally determined right to order their army to attack country B during peacetime. The army does what it was ordered to do. Moreover, the cabinet is collectively responsible for starting the war in some sense of collective responsibility.

There are a couple of things to keep in mind here. First, the notion of responsibility in question here is institutional, not moral, responsibility. Therefore nothing we are about to say commits us to ascribing moral responsibility to institutions or organisations or collectives as such. Second, we need to distinguish the notion of joint responsibility from other possible notions of collective responsibility.

The cabinet is not jointly responsible for the attack. The reason that it is not jointly responsible, is that the directive to the army is not a joint order. Rather it is single order issued by a single institutional authority, namely, the cabinet. Accordingly, these kinds of case of (so-called) collective responsibility are not cases of joint responsibility. Rather they are special cases of individual responsibility, except that the individual in question is not a natural person, but an institutional body. In fact they are cases of what I have termed elsewhere, joint institutional mechanisms.[7]

There might be cases of joint institutional responsibility, but they are relatively few. This is because for the purposes of avoiding confusion, lines of authority need to be clear, and a given order needs to be issued by a single authority.

What of the fourth sense of collective responsibility, collective moral responsibility? Collective moral responsibility is a species of joint responsibility. Accordingly, each agent is individually morally responsible, but conditionally on the others being individually morally responsible. This account of collective moral responsibility arises naturally out of the account of joint actions. It also parallels that given of individual moral responsibility. So a set of agents are collectively moral responsible for a joint action (or omission) if the agents are collectively responsible for that joint action (omission) in one of our first two senses of collective responsibility, and that joint action (omission) is morally significant.

In addition, I suggest that if a collective entity is responsible for an "action" in our third sense of collectively responsible then the members of that collective are collectively - which is to say, jointly - morally responsible for that "action". Thus in the war example, the individual members of the cabinet are collectively - which is to say, jointly - morally responsible for starting the war in virtue of jointly deciding that the cabinet issue an order to attack to the army.

Thus we can make our second preliminary claim about moral responsibility.

(2) If agents are collectively responsible for a joint action (omission) in the first or second senses of collective responsibility, or if agents are the members of a collective which is responsible for an "action" ("omission") in our third sense of collective responsibility, and if the joint action (omission) or the "action" ("omission") is morally significant then - other things being equal - the agents are collectively morally responsible for that joint action (omission), or for that "action" ("omission") and can reasonably attract moral praise or blame, and (possibly) punishment or reward for performing the action (omission) or "action" ("omission").

There are a number of points that should be made concerning collective - as opposed to individual - moral responsibility. First, unlike individual moral responsibilities, collective moral responsibilities are often generated by collective moral rights.[8] For example, perhaps the East Timorese have a collective moral right not to be invaded and subjugated by the Indonesians. If so, perhaps there is a collective moral responsibility on the part of other nations or the UN to intervene and prevent this (collective) rights violation. The reason that collective rights tend to generate collective responsibilities - as opposed to individual responsibilities - is that collective rights violations call for collective action; individual action tends not to be sufficient.

Second, there is the so-called problem of many hands. In the context of a social group or an organisation there are many actions, outcomes and spheres of activity to which many different persons in fact contribute. Because of the cooperative nature of activity in social groups and organisations it is often unclear who is actually responsible for some untoward outcome, and the extent of their contribution to that outcome. An example that comes to mind in the recent history of policing is the investigation of Police Superintendent Harry Blackburn. After a lengthy police investigation, Blackburn was falsely accused of being a sex offender. However, in the course of the investigation hypotheses were accepted without adequate testing, evidence eliminating Blackburn as a suspect was discredited, witnesses were extensively prompted, and so on.[9] The point of interest here is that these errors, acts of negligence and so on, were not committed by one person, but by quite a large group of individuals, each of whom was supposedly being guided by their own judgment. So the question arises as to how moral responsibility is, as it were, to be parceled out. And of course there are the corresponding questions as to how accountability and liability are to be ascribed to these different individuals.

Clearly in some situations one or more agents has a greater degree of responsibility than another by virtue of, say, being a leader. However, this does not settle the issue as to whether all the equally participating agents could be fully responsible, or whether responsibility should be shared around. Zimmerman has argued for the former position.[10] I find his main argument unconvincing. Specifically, he argues that there is no relevant difference between instances of individual responsibility and cases of collective responsibility because in each case the action of any individual is only a necessary condition for the outcome. Even in a case of individual responsibility the individual relies on the presence of other necessary conditions. So his action is not sufficient. However, this overlooks the fact that in the kinds of collective action that he discusses there is interdependence of action. It is not simply that the action of the other person is a necessary condition for my action, it is also the case that my action is a necessary condition for the action of the other agent. But this is not so in the standard case of individual action. Here the background necessary conditions will typically obtain whatever I do. This difference is a relevant difference, since in collective action the action of each agent is not only necessary for the outcome, it is also necessary for the action of the other agent. So perhaps the other agent is not fully responsible. (On the other hand, the other agent's action is also necessary for the action of the first agent.) I say more about interdependence, and also the related and relevant phenomenon of collective ends, below. However, I do not have the space here to address the issue of sharing moral responsibility. Suffice it to say that I am a pluralist. I believe that there will be cases of collective responsibility in which each agent is fully responsible for the outcome, and cases where he or she is only partially responsible.

I have argued elsewhere that, unlike individual human beings, macro-entities, including organisations, do not have moral agency, and therefore do not have moral responsibility.[11] Macro-entities are not agents, and therefore not moral agents. From the fact that they are not agents of the sort that can be ascribed intentions and beliefs it follows that they cannot be moral agents, and cannot therefore be held morally responsible or accountable.

In the following sections I will look at four puzzles that arise in relation to collective moral responsibility; two problems in relation to collective responsibility for actions, and two problems in relation to collective responsibility for omissions. In the light of my views on collective moral agency, I will only be discussing the moral responsibility of individual human persons.

Collective Responsibility for Actions: Two Puzzles

The notion of collective responsibility apparently gives rise to a number of puzzles. In this section I will explore two of these.

Overdetermination

The first puzzle arises in collective action situations in which the outcome of the collective action is overdetermined by the actions of the agents involved.[12] Suppose, for example, that each of eleven men inflicts a single stab wound on a twelfth man, John, intending to kill him. Assume the stabbings are simultaneous. John dies from his wounds, however seven stab wounds would have been sufficient to kill him. That is, seven stab wounds are individually necessary and jointly sufficient to kill John. Therefore, no single stab wound (of the eleven) is either necessary or sufficient for John's death. So not one of the eleven men performed an action, which was either necessary or sufficient for John's death. But if a person has not performed an action, which was either necessary or sufficient for a person's death, surely that person cannot be held responsible for the person's death. So none of the eleven men is responsible for John's death. But if none of the eleven is responsible then no one is responsible. For the cause of John's death was the stab wounds, and these were performed by the eleven men.

It might be said that nevertheless the eleven men were collectively responsible for John's death. But even this appears to be false, since only the actions of seven were necessary for John's death. So at best we are entitled to conclude that (an unspecifiable) seven of the eleven men were collectively responsible for John's death, but no individual was responsible. This conclusion is very unpalatable indeed. For one thing, it sets up an unbridgeable gap between collective responsibility and individual responsibility; a collective can be responsible for an outcome, even though none of its members are. For another, it licenses the commission of immoral acts, so long as they are collective actions involving overdetermination; individual perpetrators are not responsible for heinous crimes, so long as they commit those crimes collectively and their actions overdetermine the outcome.

Moreover, the same kind of argument can be used to deprive those who collectively produce goods, of the benefits of their efforts. Suppose instead of inflicting stab wounds on John, the eleven men had each scored twenty runs in a one innings World Cup cricket game, and this score of 220 turned out to be too difficult for the opposition to achieve. In reply, the opposition team could only manage a score of 139. So 140 of the 220 scored by the eleven was sufficient for victory in the game. Since each of the eleven men only scored 20 runs, none of the innings was either necessary or sufficient for the victorious batting total of 140. Accordingly, not one of the eleven was responsible, and so no one was responsible. But in that case the eleven should not individually receive their payments for scoring a higher total than their opponents and thereby winning the game.

We first need an analysis of the kind of collective actions at issue. We have one at hand; the above described account of joint actions. So we can conceive of such cases of collective action as actions directed to a collective end; in our first example, the collective end is the death of John, in our second, the production of a victorious batting total. Each of the eleven has the collective end as an end. Moreover, each of the eleven performs the act of stabbing (or the hitting of 20 runs) as a means to the collective end he has.

So far so good, but now comes the crucial point. The actions of the eleven agents are interdependent. That is, each performs his contributory action, if he believes the others will perform theirs, and each does so, only if he believes this. Why are the actions interdependent? They are interdependent because each rightly believes he cannot realise the collective end by acting on his own, but equally rightly believes that the outcome will be achieved if all act together.

This interdependence has to be sharply distinguished from the necessity and sufficiency (for the realisation of the collective end) of the actions considered in themselves. Certainly, if the action of one (or two or three or four) of the eleven had not been performed and the actions of the other ten (or nine or eight or seven) were performed, the outcome would still have been achieved. However, the point to be made is that - given the interdependence mentioned above - if it is believed by ten of the agents that the eleventh agent has not or will not perform his contributory action, then the other agents will not perform theirs. If we assume that the agents are positioned to know what the other agents have or will do, then interdependence ensures that each agent's action is in fact necessary for the outcome. For if the eleventh agent does not or will not perform his contributory action then the other ten will believe that he has not or will not perform it, and they will not perform their contributory actions.

In short, given interdependence of action (and knowledge of one another's intentions and actions) each of the contributory actions is necessary for the outcome, and so each agent can be held responsible for the outcome. Consider the stabbing example. The individual act of stabbing by one agent is necessary if the other agents are to stab. Therefore, the eleven acts of stabbing are individually necessary (and jointly sufficient) for the death of John. So each of the agents is responsible, and each can be punished. Now consider the cricket example. Assume that no one will bat if the others are not prepared to bat. If so, the eleven batting innings are individually necessary and jointly sufficient for the victorious batting total.

In response to this the following counterexample might be put forward. Assume that each of the eleven knows that the actions of seven of their number will be sufficient to ensure the realisation of the end. Therefore, the structure of the interdependence is as follows. Each stabs if and only if six of the others stab. Here there are three salient possibilities. One possibility is that each knows which seven of the eleven are the ones who will do the stabbing. In that case each of the seven stabs if and only if the other six stabs, but the remaining four do not stab, and no-one believed that they would stab. Moreover, none of the four have as a collective end - or any other sort of end - that John be stabbed to death. Accordingly, while each of the four might desire the death of John, and foresee it, the four are not responsible, either individually or collectively, for the death of John.

A second possibility is that none of the eleven knows what the others have done until it is too late. (It is a case of stabbing in the dark.) So while each knows that only seven stabs are necessary, all eleven stab, since everyone knows that no-one will know (until it is too late) whether and how many of the others have stabbed. If this is the situation, then the interdependence has been misdescribed. It is not the case that each stabs if and only if six others stab. Rather, each stabs if and only if all ten of the others stab. So each is responsible in virtue of performing an action, which was in the circumstances necessary for the outcome.

A third possibility is that while each knows that only seven stabs are necessary, and each stabs in full view of the others, nevertheless each agrees to stab. Not only are the stabs of the last four agents not necessary for John's death, they are known to be unnecessary at the time they are performed. Here the point to be made is that all agents agreed to stab and did so only on condition all the others did. So the actions of the last four agents were in fact necessary for the actions of the first seven. The interdependence of action has the form each x's if and only if the others x, in virtue of the agreement the agents made with one another. Accordingly, the eleven agents are individually and collectively responsible for John's death.

There is a further set of closely related apparent counterexamples to our analysis. Suppose that the actions of the eleven men consist of two, not one, joint action. Suppose each of five of the men stabs on condition the other four do. And suppose that each of the remaining six men stabs on condition the other five do. Suppose, further, that five stabs are sufficient to kill John. Accordingly, one joint action is sufficient to kill John. Accordingly, no agent's action is either, directly or indirectly, necessary or sufficient, for John's death. So no agent is responsible for his death.

This reply does not work as it stands. For each of the joint actions is a sufficient condition for the death of John, and each of the agents performed an action which was a necessary part of that sufficient condition. Therefore each agent is morally responsible for the death of John. But let us complicate matters. Assume that there are not two, but three, joint actions, two of which are jointly sufficient for the outcome, but no one of the joint actions is sufficient on its own.

In that event those who perform one of the three joint actions do so on the assumption that one or the other or both of the other joint actions will be performed. So there is interdependence of action. Moreover, the three joint actions have a single collective end viz. whatever collective end each of them had initially. Accordingly, each of the three joint actions is an indirectly necessary part of a sufficient condition for the outcome. So again the putative counter-example has been accommodated.

Unfortunately, this is not the end of the matter, for there is yet another related problematic example. Assume that there are only three agents who stab John but that two stabs are sufficient to kill John. Assume that Freddy's stab is not necessary because the other two agents are jointly going to kill John, and they do not need or want Freddy to be involved. Freddy is adamant that he will contribute, and so stabs John at the same time as the others, notwithstanding the fact that his action is unnecessary. (His action is neither directly or indirectly necessary.) Here there are two possibilities, Freddy 1 and Freddy 2. Freddy 1 would not have stabbed John if his act of stabbing had been necessary to kill John. Freddy 1 does not have John's death as an end. Rather he simply wants to make a superfluous contribution. Not having John's death as an end, and not having performed an action that was either necessary or sufficient, leaves Freddy 1 with *significantly* diminished moral responsibility. Freddy 2 is more troublesome.

Freddy 2 would have stabbed John if one of the others had failed to do so, and at the time when he stabbed John he hoped that his action would turn out to be necessary. We can conclude that Freddy 2 has John's death as an end, notwithstanding the fact that his contributory action was neither, directly or indirectly, necessary or sufficient. Freddy 2 appears to have *slightly* diminished moral responsibility.

Layered Structures of Joint Action

Let us now consider a more complex kind of case. Consider an army fighting a battle. Assume that it is a just war. (Or assume that it is a very unjust war; even a genocidal war.) In what sense are the individual soldiers morally responsible for victory? No action of any soldier was either necessary of sufficient for victory. Moreover, the army itself is divided into separate groups e.g. the infantry, the tank division, and so on. Accordingly, while, say, one infantryman might be engaged in joint activity with the fellow members of his squad, he is not thus engaged with other parts of the army. Indeed, he may not even know who these people are, or what precisely any one of them is doing at a given time. Clearly the above-described analysis of basic joint actions is going to be inadequate, at least as it stands. Moreover, the account of collective responsibility, which was generated, on the back of that notion of a basic joint action is likewise going to be inadequate.

At this point the notion of, what I have termed elsewhere, a layered structure of joint actions needs to be introduced. Suppose a number of "actions" are severally necessary and jointly sufficient to achieve some collective end. Call these "actions" level two actions. Suppose, in addition, that each of these level two "actions", is itself - at least in part - a joint action whose component actions are severally necessary and jointly sufficient for the performance of the level two "action" in question. Call these component actions, level one actions. So the collective end of the level one actions is the performance of the level two "action". One illustration of the notion of a layered structure of joint actions is in fact an army fighting a battle. The members of the mortar squad jointly operate the mortar in the first phase. The set of tanks jointly move forward firing in the second phase. Finally, the set of foot soldiers jointly position themselves to hold the ground vacated by the retreating enemy force. The actions of each of the individual foot soldiers, mortar squad members and individual members of the tank team are level one actions. However, the infantry and the cavalry (the tanks) and the mortar squad jointly act to defeat the enemy. Each of these "actions" is a level two action.

Now suppose that such a layered structure of joint actions involves our above-described property of indirect responsibility. Suppose that each of the level one actions is only necessary for the realisation of the collective end it contributes to, at some critical threshold of level one actions. In short, each of the individual actions is a necessary component of a sufficient condition for the realisation of the collective end; but the actions overdetermine the outcome - there is more than one sufficient condition. Accordingly, none of the level one actions is either necessary or sufficient for the outcome it contributes to. However, the actions of one member of the mortar squad are a necessary part of a condition, which is sufficient for mortar to be fired. Finally, suppose that each of the level two actions is itself only necessary for the realisation of the collective end it contributes to, at some critical threshold of level two actions. Accordingly, none of the level two actions is either necessary or sufficient for the outcome it contributes to However, (say) the combined infantry and cavalry level two actions are a sufficient condition for securing victory.

I suggest that many collective action scenarios can be conceived as layered structures of joint actions involving indirect responsibility. This indirect responsibility is typically not for the most part the indirect responsibility generated when the participation of each is a necessary condition for the participation of the others. Rather the indirect responsibility in question is that generated when a given agent's action is a necessary part of a condition which is sufficient for the realisation of an outcome, though it is not the only sufficient condition.

Collective Responsibility for Omissions: Two Puzzles

Thus far we have been considering problems that arise in relation to collective moral responsibility for actions. Let us now consider two puzzles that arise in relation to collective moral responsibility for omissions.

Kitty Genovese

The first problem can be illustrated by the following redescription of an infamous incident that took place in New York in 1964.

> "On the night of March 13-14, 1964 thirty-eight New Yorkers were awakened in the early hours of the morning by the frenzied cries for help of a young woman, Kitty Genovese, the victim of a savage physical assault perpetrated by a man who had accosted her while she was on her way home. Over a period of about forty minutes, the assailant made several separate attacks on her, while she struggled, battered and bleeding, to reach the sanctuary of her apartment. Her screams of anguish and her calls for help were heard by at least thirty-eight neighbours, who, in the privacy and anonymity of their own homes, witnessed her struggle, yet offered no assistance in any form, whether through direct intervention or through the simple expedient of telephoning the police. A neighbour finally summoned the police, after first calling a friend to seek advice as to what to do. A patrol car arrived on the scene within two minutes but this prompt assistance was too late to save the young woman, who died on the way to hospital. It is clear that Kitty Genovese was a victim not only of her assailant's viciousness, but also of her neighbours' inaction."[13]

The first question that arises in relation to this scenario is the question as to who is to be the one to intervene by calling the police. Most, if not all, of the neighbours are capable of telephoning the police, but no one did until it was too late. There is clearly a moral obligation, but it does not attach to some one person without attaching to any other person; nor does it seem to attach to everyone simultaneously, since it is only one phone call that is needed. Perhaps the obligation is disjunctive in form; either you or I or him or her or...has a moral obligation to ring the police.

So if someone rings the police, then the others have not failed to discharge their individual moral obligations. On the other hand, if no-one rings the police then each has failed to discharge their individual moral responsibility.[14] In short, we have interdependence of individual moral responsibility to intervene; though not joint moral responsibility to intervene.

Let us now consider a variation on the Kitty Genovese episode. Assume that in this second scenario the neighbours do not have access to phones, and so would themselves have to physically intervene. Let us assume that one (or even two or three neighbours) acting on their own are likely to be unsuccessful, and indeed would put at risk their own physical well-being. What is needed is collective action by, say, a dozen or so. Certainly, the sight of all thirty-eight neighbours coming toward the attacker resolutely and in a threatening manner, would have been sufficient to ward him off, and thereby save Kitty's life.

On the second version of the scenario, if each neighbour fails to intervene the overall result is the same as in the first version; the death of Kitty. However, in the second version (seemingly) no neighbour is responsible for Kitty's death. This is because the intervention of a single neighbour would be neither necessary nor sufficient to protect her life.

Now let us attend more closely at the second version. To save Kitty's life requires collective action, but it does not require the participation of all the neighbours, rather some critical threshold of, say, ten, is required.

Accordingly, each neighbour can act in such a way as to constitute a necessary component of a sufficient condition for saving Kitty's life. The sufficient condition comprises the actions of ten neighbours. If so, we can invoke our argument from the last section, and conclude that there is an indirect responsibility on the part of each of the ten to so act, and this indirect responsibility exists in virtue of the joint moral responsibility of all ten to act.

The existence of this joint moral responsibility is consistent with the existence of disjunctive moral responsibility of the following sort. If ten neighbours act, and thereby save Kitty's life, it is not morally obligatory for the remaining twenty-eight to do anything. On the other hand, if no-one acts then all are morally responsible for her death.

The Kitty Genovese episode illustrates the general moral imperative not to allow the basic rights of others to be violated.[15] This moral imperative generates obligations to cooperate and/or put in place cooperative schemes, including institutional mechanisms. To see this consider the following different version of the Kitty Genovese scenario.

Suppose the would-be murderer of Kitty was threatening all of the neighbours' lives, and not just Kitty's. Assume that if each acts on his own, no-one will protect him/herself from the murderer. Now assume that the neighbours could thwart the murderer if they cooperated with one another by, for example, coming to one another's assistance should he attack any one of them. No single murderer would dare attack thirty eight people simultaneously. So it is in the rational self-interest of each of the neighbours to act collectively to prevent individual harm to each of them. Notice also that this cooperative arrangement enables each neighbour to protect all his or her neighbours, including Kitty. And surely a neighbour is under a moral obligation to comply with an arrangement that protects the lives of others as well as him/herself, and with no overall cost to himself. (Whatever the costs attendant upon complying with this arrangement they are surely outweighed by the benefit of preserving one's life.) Naturally, each of the neighbours might be tempted to free-ride. After all, ten to twelve is sufficient to thwart the murderer. However, the point is that each is under a moral obligation to contribute. It is the established, and explicitly agreed to, cooperative scheme, and its purposes, that determines moral obligations; not the small contribution to the success of the scheme by each of the parties to it.

Now let us return to the earlier version of the scenario, and assume that it is only Kitty's life that is in question – the neighbours' lives are not threatened. Surely each neighbour should have as a collective end the prevention of Kitty's death by means of the sort of cooperative arrangement mentioned above. Under such a scheme, each neighbour would intervene conditionally on the others intervening, in virtue of the commitment on the part of each to the collective end of preserving the life. So the act of intervention on the part of each, is a necessary condition for the act of intervention on the part of the others. Accordingly, the intervention of each is a necessary condition for the prevention of Kitty's death, and so each is responsible for avoiding that outcome.

What is the moral principle in question here? Presumably it is the moral principle already invoked, namely, that one should act jointly with others to prevent the violations of basic rights. However, there is a difference in this version of the scenario in that each of the neighbours is now acting in a manner, which involves an overall cost to him/herself.

Doubtless this is true. However, two points can be made in response to this. First, the cost is minimal. Second, the cost is surely outweighed by the moral obligation to prevent the violation of basic rights.

Frank Jackson's Puzzle

A second puzzle is one described by Frank Jackson.[16] Assume that there are a thousand bandits who each steal a thousand beans from a thousand villagers. On the first scenario each bandit steals a thousand beans from a single given villager. (Following Jackson, call this the vertical version.) Since the villager has no beans he dies, and the individual bandit who stole all his beans is responsible for his death. Further, the overall consequence of each bandit stealing a thousand beans is the death of all one thousand villagers.

On the second scenario each bandit steals one bean from each villager. (Following Jackson, call this the horizontal version.) The overall result is the same as in the first scenario, namely, the death of 1000 villagers. (For their part, the bandits do not need the beans; the beans are pure profit.) However, seemingly no bandit is responsible for the death of any single villager. For the action of any one bandit in respect of one villager cannot make a difference to whether that villager lives or dies; one bean is neither here nor there in the diet of a villager.

Let us get a little clearer on the notion of making a difference. There appear to be four ways in which one could be said to make a difference in relation to harming others.

First, my action (or refraining) is necessary and sufficient to ensure that there is no harm done. I, and I alone, can ensure that there is no harm done. This is the case with each of the bandits in the first scenario, but not with any of the bandits in the second scenario.

Second, my action (or refraining) is sufficient, but not necessary, to ensure that there is no harm done. Acting (or refraining) alone, I can ensure that there is no harm done, though I am not unique in this respect, since others can also ensure that there is no harm done. (It also follows that I cannot ensure that harm is done, though my action (or refraining) is necessary to ensure that harm is done.) This is not the case with any of the bandits in either of the scenarios.

Third, my action (or refraining) is necessary, but not sufficient, to ensure that there is no harm done. I cannot ensure that there is no harm done, but if I do not act (or refrain) then harm will be done. This is not the case with any of the bandits in either of the scenarios.

Now let us attend more closely to the scenarios. There are two different ways of taking these scenarios. On the first way there is collective action. That is, the bandits cooperate with one another to steal all the villagers' beans. The collective end is to steal all the beans in order to starve the villagers to death. (Or perhaps they steal 1000x1000 beans in order to sell them in bulk for export, but do so in the full knowledge that the result would be the death of the villagers.)

Here there is interdependence of action; each steals 1000 beans if and only if the others steal 1000 beans. So each bandit performs a contributory "action" (theft of 1000 beans) which is necessary if the others are to likewise perform their contributory actions. Further, the combination of the actions of all the bandits is sufficient for this outcome.

Notice that the action of any one bandit - given the actions of all the other bandits - is not necessary to achieve the outcome. And of course, the action of any one bandit is not sufficient. Accordingly, in terms of our taxonomy of three ways in which someone could make a difference, seemingly no bandit can make a difference. But matters are more complex than this.

There is interdependence of action. So each bandit's action is necessary, if the other bandits are to perform their actions. To this extent each bandit's action is necessary for the realisation of the collective end of starving the villagers to death. It remains the case that each bandit's action is not necessary for this outcome, given the other bandits perform their actions. But the point is that the other bandits will not perform their contributory actions, if the bandit in question does not perform his.

The upshot of this is that we have in effect introduced a fourth way in which an agent can make a difference to an outcome. He can perform an action the performance of which is necessary for the actions of other agents; the combination of only most of these actions being sufficient for some outcome. In keeping with the discussion in earlier sections, let us say that in such cases the agent's action is indirectly necessary for the outcome.

Accordingly, we are entitled to conclude that each of the 1000 bandits are responsible for the death of the villagers in virtue of the fact that in each case their action made a difference to this evil outcome.

A crucial point to be made here is that on this rendering of the example, it does not matter whether the bandits achieved the outcome according to the horizontal or the vertical version of the scenario. Either way the actions of each bandit were (directly or indirectly) a necessary condition for the evil outcome; for the death, that is, of all the villagers.

It might be argued that this first rendering of the example is unrealistic, or at any rate that there is an alternative way of describing matters, and that on this alternative description of the first rendering the problem posed by Jackson remains.

Specifically, it is highly unlikely - the argument runs - that the interdependence involved in a case of collective action involving 1000 agents is complete. That is, it is highly unlikely that each bandit performs his contributory action only if all the others perform theirs. Surely it is more plausible that there is a relatively indeterminate threshold of compliance, which is necessary for each to perform his contributory. That is, each bandit performs his contributory action only if a majority (or perhaps most) of the others perform their contributory actions.

The existence of examples with such a threshold structure of interdependence is uncontroversial. Here we need to distinguish two sorts of examples involving thresholds. The first sort are clearly not counterexamples. For in these cases interdependence is still complete, albeit indirect. Consider the following six person example. Suppose A will go to the football only if B and C go; B will go only if C and D go; C will go only if D and E go; D will go only if E and A go; E will go only if A and B go. Given this structure, no one will go unless all the others go.

However, there is a second sort of example. Consider a situation involving 100 people and the indeterminate threshold, "most". Each will go to the football only if most of the other 99 go. Here there are two possibilities; first, that no-one much cares who in particular goes, so long as most do, or; second, that each prefers that the most be comprised of certain individuals. In the latter case, the situation in which there is a specific minority that all the rest prefer not to go is ruled out. Let us consider the first possibility.

Here the action of each individual is necessary at a certain indeterminate threshold if the others are to perform their contributory actions. However, the point is that each is going to perform his contributory action if most of the others do - no-one is seeking to free ride. So everyone performs his contributory action. Moreover, since there is no specifiable (albeit indeterminate) most upon which the actions of everyone depended, the situation is essentially equivalent to the example of the six people. That is, interdependence is complete, albeit indirect via (various different) sets of most of the agents.

On the second rendering of the example, there is no collective action. Rather each bandit steals 1000 beans independently of what the other bandits do; albeit with knowledge of what the other bandits are doing, and of the consequences of their actions.

In scenario one each bandit is individually responsible for the death of one villager. This is not so in scenario two.

Does it follow from this that - as Jackson claims - no-one is responsible for the deaths of the villagers in scenario two? I do not think so.

Scenario one illustrates the obvious moral imperative to avoid seriously harming someone. Since each bandit knows that if he steals 1000 beans from a given villager then the villager will die. So there is a clear moral imperative for the bandit not to steal the 1000 beans.

But scenario two also illustrates this general moral imperative not to cause serious harm to others. After all, the combined actions of the bandits leave 1000 villagers dead. But there is a difference between the moral imperatives illustrated in the two scenarios.

In scenario one the actions of one bandit will cause the death of the villager. Accordingly, the relevant version of the general moral imperative to avoid harming others is: You should avoid performing an individual action, which will seriously harm another person.

Scenario two is somewhat different. Consider first the obligations of the villagers. Assume that if each acts on his own no-one will prevent the bandits from stealing their beans. Now assume that the villagers could thwart the bandits if they cooperated with one another by, for example, storing all their beans in one place and guarding it together. No single bandit would dare attack 1000 villagers. So it is in the rational self-interest of each of the villagers to act collectively to prevent individual harm to each of them. Notice also that this cooperative arrangement enables the villagers to protect all the beans, and hence the lives of their fellow villagers. And surely a villager is under a moral obligation to comply with an arrangement that protects the lives of others, and with no overall cost to himself. (Whatever the costs attendant upon guard duty they are surely outweighed by the benefit of preserving one's life.) Naturally, each of the villagers might be tempted to free-ride. After all, 999 villagers is sufficient to dissuade theft by any one bandit. However, the point is that each is under a moral obligation to contribute on grounds of fairness, and also agreement. It is the established, and explicitly agreed to, cooperative scheme, and its purposes, that determines moral obligations; not the infinitesimal causal contribution to the success of the scheme by each of the parties to it.

Now consider the moral obligations of the bandits, and do so on the assumption that each bandit is concerned about the avoidable death of a villager. While each bandit ought to be, and indeed is, concerned about the plight of the villagers, the problem is that seemingly the actions of any one bandit in stealing one bean from each villager will not make any difference. To be sure. However, the question that needs to be asked is whether there is a feasible and salient cooperative scheme, which, if established, would redress the plight of the villagers.

Clearly there is such a scheme. Each bandit could refrain from stealing beans conditionally on the others refraining from stealing beans! (Or at least each bandit could content himself with stealing, say, 500 beans, conditionally on the others so doing.) After all, each bandit is concerned about the deaths of the villagers, and the bandits are mutually aware how the deaths are caused, and how the deaths could be avoided.

In other words, each bandit should have as a collective end the prevention of the deaths of the villagers by means of each stealing (say) less than 500 beans. Under such a scheme, each bandit would refrain from stealing on condition the others so refrained, in virtue of the commitment on the part of each to the collective end of preserving the lives of the villagers. So the act of refraining from theft on the part of each, is a necessary condition for the act of refraining on the part of the others. Accordingly, the action of each is a necessary condition for the avoidance of the evil outcome, and so each is responsible for avoiding that outcome.

What is the moral principle in question here? Presumably it is the moral principle already invoked in relation to the villagers, namely, you should act collectively with others to prevent serious harm to people. However, there is a difference in that the bandit is now acting against his self-interest.

Doubtless this is true. However, two points can be made in response to this. First, the bandit does not need the beans he forgoes, while the scheme to which he contributes preserves the lives of the villagers; in this case the avoidance of serious harm outweighs his self-interest. Second, the "act" of stealing 1000 beans is a moral wrong.

Notes

* Seumas Miller is Professor of Social Philosophy, Director of the Centre for Professional and Applied Ethics, and Head of the School of Humanities and Social Sciences, at Charles Sturt University, Australia.

1 See Donald Davidson 'Freedom to Act' in (ed.) Ted Honderich *Essays on Freedom of Action* (London: Routledge and Kegan Paul, 1973) and John R. Searle *Intentionality* (Cambridge University Press, 1983) Chapter 3.

2 See (ed.) John Martin Fischer *Moral Responsibility* (London: Cornell University Press, 1986) p.14f. For attempts to analyse free action, and related notions of autonomy, by recourse to higher order attitudes see Harry G. Frankfurt 'Three Concepts of Free Action' in (ed.) Fischer op.cit. and Gerald Dworkin *The Theory and Practice of Autonomy* (Cambridge University Press, 1988). For accounts of one's responsibility for one's character see (ed.) Ferdinand Schoeman *Responsibility, Character and the Emotions* (Cambridge University Press, 1987).

3 The discussion of responsibility in this and the following section is a version of points made in my 'Individualism, Collective Responsibility and Corporate Crime', *Business and Professional Ethics Journal* vol.16 no.4 1997.

4 This is a version of an example provided by Dean Cocking.

5 On the notions of joint and collective responsibility see: D.E. Cooper *Collective Responsibility Philosophy* vol.43 1968; R.S. Downie *Collective Responsibility*

Philosophy vol. 44 1969; Joel Feinberg *Doing and Deserving* (Princeton University Press, 1970) chapt.9; Virginia Held 'Moral Responsibility and Collective Action' in (ed.) Peter A. French *Individual and Collective Responsibility* (Schenkman Publishing Company, 1972); Dennis F. Thompson *Political Ethics and Public Office* (Harvard University Press, 1987) chapt.2; Michael J. Zimmerman *Essay on Moral Responsibility* (Rowman and Littlefield, 1988) and 'Sharing Responsibility' *American Philosophical Quarterly* vol.22 no.2 1985; Larry May (ed.) *Collective Responsibility* (Rowman and Littlefield, 1991); Steven Sverdlik 'Collective Responsibility' ch*Philosophical Studies* vol.51 1987.

6 Seumas Miller 'Joint Action' *Philosophical Papers* vol. xxi no.3 1992. See also Seumas Miller 'Intentions, Ends and Joint Actions' *Philosophical Papers* vol.xxiv no.1 1995, Margaret Gilbert *On Social Facts* (London: Routledge, 1989), Michael Bratman 'Shared Cooperative Activity' *Philosophical Review* vol.101 no.2 1992 and Raimo Tuomela *The Importance of Us* (Stanford: Stanford University Press, 1995)

7 Ibid. See also 'Individualism, Collective Responsibility and Corporate Crime' op.cit.

8 See Seumas Miller 'Collective Rights', *Public Affairs Quarterly* (in press) and 'Collective Responsibility, Armed Intervention and the Rwandan Genocide', *International Journal of Applied Philosophy*, vol.12 no. 2 1998.

9 Seumas Miller, J. Blackler and A. Alexandra, *Police Ethics* (Sydney: Allen and Unwin, 1997) p.133.

10 Michael J. Zimmerman 'Sharing Responsibility', *American Philosophical Quarterly* vol.22 no.2 1985.

11 See Miller Individualism, Collective Responsibility and Corporate Crime op.cit. See also Peter A. French, *Collective and Corporate Responsibility* (New York: Columbia University Press, 1984).

12 There are less developed discussions of the first three of my four puzzles in my 'Collective Responsibility, Armed Intervention and the Rwandan Genocide' op. cit.

13 Leon Shaskolsky Sehleff *The Bystander; Behaviour, Law, Ethics.* (Lexington, Mass.: Lexington Books, 1978) pp. 1-2.

14 I accept positive rights, such as the right to security and subsistence. Such rights give rise to individual and collective responsibility. For the case in favour of positive rights, and how rights generate responsibilities, see Henry Shue *Basic Rights* (Princeton: Princeton University Press, 1996).

15 Ibid.

16 Frank Jackson 'Group Morality' in (ed.) P. Pettit, R. Sylvan and J. Norman *Metaphysics and Morality: Essays in Honour of J J C Smart* (Oxford: Blackwell, 1987).

5. Are Human Rights Universal?

YANAKI B. STOILOV

Introduction

Are human rights universal indeed? Such a question does appear, at first sight, to be bizarre. This is due to the widespread conception, underlying a number of international instruments as well, that human rights are universal by nature. The World Conference on Human Rights, held in Vienna in 1993 asserted that "all human rights are universal, indivisible, interdependent and interrelated." Quite a few researchers also deem the universality of human rights to be all but an axiom. Such assertion derives probably from the concept that the universality of human rights is an intrinsic trait of theirs, a prerequisite for their existence. Thus, the conclusion about the legal existence of human rights is drawn from the unsubstantiated assumption about their universal nature. Whereas in terms of politics and ideology the employment of such approach is hardly surprising, from a scientific point of view it is inadmissible. Inadmissible indeed, because it involves no distinction between the perception of human rights as a moral imperative and as a legal category; between the rights of man and the rights of the citizen; between the rights as a subject of legislative policies and as an element of the positive legal order.

In truth, the unverified assertion of universality of human rights conceals their actually limited scope. The recognition of such limitedness and probing the reasons therefore is of benefit to the human-rights cause. A critical scrutiny into the problem of human rights would truly conduce to establishing the instances of replacing the humanitarian for the political aspect of the human-rights issue. Such approach would contribute also to finding the appropriate ways and means for a general augmentation of human rights as well as for their protection.

Human rights should not be proclaimed to be something that is absolute as is often the case with the absolute sovereignty of the national state. The analogy in this instance is really convenient: just as state power is limited, inter alia, by a number of legal claims to it, so are human rights restricted by a number of factors, inclusive of their existence as rights of the citizen.

The traditional liberal concept of human rights often eludes a number of essential queries: who is vested with the right to lay down the catalogue of "universal rights"; what is the criterion of universality of rights – their legal recognition or their enjoyment by all individuals alike; is the idea of universal human rights compatible with the relativism of their observance in respect of the human beings from various nations and civilizations; and, finally, who shall be entitled, at an international level, to render legitimate decisions whether human rights have been violated, and who then shall be empowered to legitimately sanction and redress such violations.

I. From the concept of human rights – to universal rights

The concept of universal human rights derives from the natural-law theory. This mainly philosophical doctrine impacted the legal acts of the American and French revolutions of the late 18th century. The Declaration of Independence (1776) and The Declaration of the Rights of Man and of the Citizen (1789) proclaimed the universal validity of human rights. Nowadays, the Universal Declaration of Human Rights (1948) proclaims in its very first article that "All human beings are born free and equal in dignity and rights."

Despite such accomplishments, human rights have not yet attained their alleged universality. What is at issue here are not so much the human-rights violations whose complete avoidance seems really impossible, but rather the large-scale deviations from the principle of human rights' universality. This cheerless inference should not prevent us from drawing yet another conclusion – the history of human rights is the history of their augmentation. Such augmentation has been following several lines – the swell in the variety of claimed rights, the growing numbers of those entitled and the expanding territorial spread of human rights.

1. The swelling catalogue of human rights

Human rights are based on the concept of property in its philosophical sense. John Locke defined the complex notion of property to include life, liberty and estate. This is the basis where the first generation of fundamental civil and political rights derive from. The better part of such rights are a negative expression of individual freedom (England's Habeas Corpus Act of 1679). Their role is to safeguard the inviolability of every individual against the arbitrary interference with his privacy and life. The first-generation rights ensure autonomy and security of the person in the area of personal and property relations, as well as the opportunity to exert influence on government.

Belonging to the second generation of human rights are the economic, social, and cultural rights. These rights derive from the late 19th century and have increasingly pervaded first labour and employment, and then social-security relations. Social, economic and cultural rights augmented with the development of public education networks, health care systems, etc. Such rights require the intervention of the state for the purpose of providing favourable conditions for social realization of the human personality and in assuring access to certain goods and welfare. The most notable development of social and economic rights was witnessed during the ascendancy of the welfare state in the third quarter of the 20th century.

The third generation of solidarity rights, largely discussed during the last quarter of the 20th century, extended still further the range of human rights. The institution of a new group of claimed rights is a clear indication that the set of generally accepted human rights is not an unchanging or unchangeable list. There are continuous discussions about whether new rights should be included, such as the third-generation rights to development, to a clean environment, and to peace, as well as the rights of minorities.[1] The emergence of this new generation of heterogeneous rights relates to the ongoing changes in an individual's environment, i.e. his technological, natural and informational surroundings. This has given rise to the need to protect the individual as a consumer, as well as to protect his privacy, etc.

Consequently, paralleling the expanding scope of legal regulation is an expansion of the human-rights system. Thus, the growing acceptance of the principle of human rights has concurred with the expansion of the catalogue of basic rights. It keeps growing yet larger as well as more and more diversified. The evolution of human rights, incongruous as it may be, has lead to their augmentation as well as to their penetration into all domains of social life.

2. The growth of individuals entitled to the variety of human rights

Parallel to the ever growing variety of rights is the expanding circle of those who are entitled to possess such rights. It is the extension of human rights to every person on Earth that largely determines their general or universal character. Human rights are regarded as universal in the world of states as we know it: all individuals have such rights.[2] Normally, the recognition of new rights leads – sooner or later – to an increase in the number of those who claim them.

Rights, even though conceived as rejection of the Mediaeval conceptions of privilege, were at least in the beginning established and enjoyed as privileges. The example of the English Magna Carta of 1215 is remarkable. By such solemn grant of liberties and rights the aristocracy provided for itself autonomy in its relations to the King as well as opportunities to partake in the political decision-making.

Long after most of the rights were proclaimed universal they were in truth enjoyed by a small group of the public alone. Over a prolonged period of time the pretension that "all men like us are equal", and the various equal-rights amendments to the U.S. Constitution showed the evolution in meaning through "all men and women like us are equal" into the modern egalitarian "all people are equal".[3] The history of the establishment and augmentation of a number of rights, such as the suffrage for instance, is an illustration that for many a year after the grant of a right it used to be in fact a privilege enjoyed by some of the citizens alone. Thus, historically rights were at the time of their adoption merely a "form" of politically universal rights; they were not really rights of all citizens, i.e. of all persons within the body politic. As evidence here we can cite the permanent exclusion, from the right to vote, of women and slaves in the U.S. at that time and for almost a century (or a century and a half) afterwards.[4] Thus, it was no earlier than during this last century that even in such countries where the right to vote was first recognized it has become really universal with regard to all adults not legally disqualified in their particular states.

The establishment of the constitutional principles of non-discrimination and equality of all citizens before the law has given a most crucial impetus to the growth of population entitled to the various human rights. Thus, a number of such rights were gradually claimed and shared by larger and yet larger groups of people, until eventually they have been granted, in principle, to every citizen and some have even grown to be almost universal.

3. The expanding spread of human rights

The answer to the queries concerning the universality of human rights is certainly dependent on their spatial distribution as well. The human-rights "geography" is indicative of whether and to what extent they are recognized, respected, observed and realized in the various countries and regions worldwide.

For the better part of their existence, human rights, notwithstanding their proclaimed universality, have been recognized on the national plane alone. There is ample evidence that even within one and the same country such rights were not initially extended to all cases and to all the various levels of governance. The rights of the Bill of Rights in the U.S., while nominally universal, were actually rights of all persons (excepting slaves, of course) only under federal law. Thus, they were not governing legal rights, in all important cases, of literally all persons.[5] Both the personal and the geographical abridgment of the basic rights was formally abolished in the U.S.A. only after the Civil War, and in truth – even much later.

It cannot be disputed that for the time being the safest way to promote and expand the legitimate scope of human rights is the respect for and observance of the same or similar, in terms of content, rights within the various national legal systems. Such process has been certainly enhanced by the adoption and ratification of the international human rights instruments.

In the years following World War II the three-piece International Bill of Rights was adopted and established to include a comprehensive catalogue of all important traditional rights. Thus, for the first time in history the issue of universality of human rights was brought up and addressed from the aspect of international law. With the increase in the number of states that have adopted and ratified the international human rights acts, the world has witnessed at least a nominal expansion of the legitimate territorial scope of human rights. Another notable development of such process has been the adoption of a number of regional human-rights instruments.

The transformation of the human-rights idea into truly universal human rights is a very long process that has no ending. Like the pursuit of any glorious aspiration, the accomplishment of human-rights universality is on the one hand a noble ideal for many a person, while on the other hand has been the subject of manifold political speculations.

The transition from the human-rights idea to the establishment of universal rights is the logical result of the overall economic, political, cultural and legal advancement. And such result can hardly be achieved solely by logical deductions, and certainly not by legal instruments alone, either. What it really takes is much political and social struggle. Rights, including the "natural rights" of the liberal tradition, are the historic result of age-old struggles.[6] The history of human rights, incongruous as it may be, is the history of their legal recognition and advancement. In consequence of the processes discussed herein, as well as through a number of legislative, jurisdictional and other acts, the basic rights of the citizen, of the person have started to be conceived as human rights. The increase in the human rights diversity, the growing circles of the people that enjoy them, and the expanding territorial range of their distribution is in itself an evolution of the basic rights. Thus, they in practice have approached the idea of universal human rights and constitute its more or less successful realization.

The evolution of rights is closely related to the development of national states and the liberation of a number of nations from colonial domination, to the establishment of civil equality, the rule of law and the welfare state. The changes in the social conditions have their impact on the content of claimed rights. Hence, notwithstanding the human rights advancement, each age brings forth yet new problems and puts human rights through the mill. Consequently, there is a need to explicate the current challenges and obstacles confronting human rights.

II. Challenges and obstacles to the universality of human rights

The obstacles posed to human rights today are the most formidable ever challenges to their large-scale distribution and assurance. Such obstacles are the expression of some fundamental contradictions:

First, there is the contradiction between the human, humanistic aspect of the rights, and their body politic existence as the rights of the citizen;

Second, there is the contradiction between the formal equality of people with regard to their basic rights, and the considerable social and economic inequalities between them;

Third, there is the contradiction between the universalization of rights via the spread of Christian culture and the particularism and relativism of the rights related to the different traditions of the various nations and civilizations.

1. Citizenship and human rights

The establishment of human rights is customarily concurrent with the foundation of the national state and of the institute of citizenship.

It is the bitter truth that in manifold places worldwide the setout of the national state and the establishment of citizenship went hand in hand with violence and with intolerance against minority groups. In many states the human-rights idea coexisted for what seems ages not only with unequal treatment of the people representing different racial, ethnic, faith or other groups, but with their persecution as well. Even the recognition of the universal citizenship failed to preclude, did not preclude through most of the 20th century, has not precluded up to now the ethnic cleansing and victimization. Very often actively involved in brutal acts are state authorities as well, particularly in the course of armed conflicts.

Yet, citizenship is conducive to a nation's consolidation. It is also instrumental in the universalization of the rights within the personality and territorial jurisdiction of a given state.

Active civil rights, taken generically, are simply political rights universal within a given society. They are beneficial ways of acting, or ways of being treated, that are specifically recognized and affirmed in law for each and all citizens there (or, ideally) for all individual persons there and are actively promoted.[7] At the same time, however, citizenship draws a dividing line with respect to persons' legal status, and in particular, in regard to their rights. Human rights understood as universal, moral (and legally) supreme rights, often conflict with the norm recognizing the legal sovereignty of states within a system of states.[8] In this context, citizenship is an impediment to the complete universalization of rights. Hence, human rights are only universal inasmuch as all the different states establish and protect principally the same rights. This is either the result of the existence of comparable social, economic and political conditions as well as congruous cultural traditions, or is attained by concluding international agreements imposing on the states the obligation and responsibility to recognize and observe specific rights. In addition, states assume obligations, including at the international level, not only to their citizens' rights, but in certain areas and to some extent with respect to other persons as well.

The operation of the universal international-law instruments in the area of human rights conduces to their harmonization, even though the rights remain essential elements of different legal orders. The establishment of common standards in the human-rights domain is not in a position to rule out their being disregarded by certain states, nor their limited enjoyment in consequence of the restrictive role of citizenship. Moreover, citizenship is the last personal privilege, the last remaining factor of discrimination, the last pre-modern remnant in the difference of status – in contrast to the proclaimed equality and universality of human rights.[9] Citizenship is like a screen and certainly not all the rights can pass through it. This applies particularly to such typically political right as the franchise, which for the time being does not exist outside of the vinculum between the citizen and the state (or the respective political commonwealth where such state belongs). However, if each and every citizen did really possess the right of voting and could enjoy it freely in their states, this would provide sufficient grounds to assert that suffrage has become universal without being extraterritorial.

The parallel recognition of certain rights by the individual states does not in itself surmount the juridical nationalism in the field of rights. Even nowadays the legal intensity of the relation between a subject and the worldwide legal order is still much lower than the intensity of the connection between a citizen and the domestic law.[10] Therefore, the projection of the internationally recognized inventory of human rights upon the national legal systems is just prerequisite but not sufficient for their realization. Pronouncing rights to be universal does not at all make up for the lack of symmetry between their recognition in principle and the obligations of the institutions tasked with their satisfaction. There are a number of rights whose exercise involves some limitations and rather complex rules and procedures concerning foreigners. Such inconsistency affects rights and freedoms deemed to be intrinsic to the human nature, i.e. rights of man regardless of his citizenship. To cite an example, many is the state where the right to freedom of movement is formally recognized, while applicable at the same time are visa restrictions allowing the competent authorities to use discretion in granting or denying foreigners free access to their territory. Such category of restrictions are even stricter in the area of social rights.

This practice – acclaimed by some and disapproved by others – is a reality deriving from each state's responsibility to maintain public order within its borders, and to regulate the distribution of wealth among the members of the public. This status quo will hardly undergo a radical change as long as the responsibility to ensure certain living standards as well as the respect for human rights remains prevailingly the care of the individual states.

The contradiction between the humanistic aspect of claimed rights and their presence under state control could be abated by taking citizenship outside the boundaries of a single state. We should endeavor to preserve the republican heritage, if we ever really may, by transcending the confines of the national state.[11] The formation and development of national, regional communities could serve to bridge the concept of universal rights on the global plane with the rights of the citizen at the national level.

The European experience provides evidence in favour of such opportunity. The European Convention for the Protection of Human Rights and Fundamental Freedoms provides for a procedure whereunder persons whose rights have been violated by a particular state shall refer their cases directly to and seek protection from the European Court of Human Rights. Thus, an international judicial institution operates as the superior instance in relation to the national jurisdiction.

The growing integration within the European Union has also been conducive to the expanding scope of human rights and the growing instances of their enjoyment. In the present political situation in Western European countries there are not very strong reasons for not giving all civil and social rights to all men and women – whatever their actual citizenship might be, who are resident in that particular country. Even political rights could be conceded to non-citizens if these are de facto members of the political community, for instance, if they have grown up or have been working in it.[12] Thus, the state institutions of the European Union countries assume the responsibility to assure the individual rights of all people belonging to the community.

One possible solution to the antinomy between the universality of rights and the citizenship might be the enactment of an European Constitution with a higher degree of validity compared to all other sources, whether national or of the European Union.[13] The adoption of such instrument would be truly instrumental in overcoming the current variances in the treatment of human rights within the different legal systems. The greatest difference, however, as regards the universalization of rights would make a social, economic, and political integration, along with the attendant increase in the social capacity of the communities partaking in such integration. Such steps could lead to some discernible positive results in the human-rights domain only if combined with efforts aimed at eliminating extreme inequality and destitution.

2. Formal equality and social inequality with regard to human rights

The gradual elimination of privileges and of restrictions based on qualification and other requirements, has been expanding the circle of those entitled to basic rights. This has to a large extent contributed to displacing the inequality with regard to human rights laid down in the law itself. The principle of equality before the law lays the stress upon its equal application. However, this principle in itself is not in a position to abate the inequality in the distribution of rights, let alone to surmount the polarization within the society.

The contradiction between the formal equality of people with regard to their basic rights, and the considerable social and economic inequalities between them derives from the open market environment, from the bitter competition within which such rights are exercised. At the same time, the distribution of rights should not just reflect the economic and social inequality, but ought to compensate and abate it as well. Otherwise it could lead to greater political instability and exacerbated inequality between the haves and have-nots of the world. By some measures, the ratio of income inequality between the world's richest 20 percent and the poorest 20 percent roughly doubled from 1960 to 1990.[14] The income inequality results in inequality with regard to the distribution of rights. Consequently, the growing economic and social inequality, manifested as inequality of income, sets up a barrier to the attainment of universality of rights.

What universality of human rights, and particularly of social, economic and cultural rights, can we speak of when hundreds of millions of people are in practice denied access to a number of such rights, meaning that they are deprived from the attendant goods as well. Exacerbated inequality most normally coexists with growing destitution.[15] Poverty is in its essence a factor of discrimination whose extremes deprive manifold people from basic rights.

The inequality of rights is manifested globally, i.e. between the people from the so called developed world, on the one hand, and those from the periphery, on the other, as well as nationally, i.e. between the people within many countries. The greatest danger to the development of human rights and democracy is the growing economic gap between citizens within countries.[16] A rise in inequality is evidenced even in most of the best developed states. The other America is made up of: 40 million people with no health insurance, 45 million below the poverty threshold and 52 million illiterate. Some 50 million of those living in the European Union member-states are poor and 18 million are homeless. The earnings of just 225 moneyed tycoons (exceeding a billion U.S. dollars) is equivalent to the annual income of nearly 47 percent of the world's population, that is of the world's poorest (some 2.5 plus billion people).[17] The growth in inequality leads to polarization of the people depending on the rights they enjoy. Such polarization, despite the solemn declarations of universality of rights and the gestures of concern about their assurance, has left hundreds of millions of people across the globe in possession of rights that hardly cover their destitute existence.

Ironically, inequality is growing at a time when the triumph of democracy and open market was supposed to usher in a new age of freedom and opportunity. At the same time while rich nations get richer, the poor population continues to grow.[18] Hence the relative expansion of poverty goes hand in hand with the absolute increase in the numbers of the people subsisting either at or below the living wage. In such proportions inequality loses its healthy effect and instead of stimulating individual and social development starts causing desocialization and confrontation. A situation like this cannot but erode the legal systems, inclusive of the human rights setup.

The reasons for the situation as described derive, in general, from the disparities of today's global economy. While the latter has contributed to a vast increase in the potential capacity of the economic system to produce necessary goods and services, expanded levels of productivity have not translated into a corresponding reduction in levels of global poverty. The expansion of output in this system takes place by "minimizing employment" and compressing workers' wages. This process in turn backlashes on the levels of consumer demand for necessary goods and services: unlimited capacity to produce, limited capacity to consume.[19] Such developments are manifested even worse in certain Eastern European countries and seem to provide a lucid explanation for their social troubles of today. When assessing the impact of earnings, employment and social services, the post-Cold War economic collapse in parts of eastern Europe appears to be deeper and more destructive than that of the Great Depression.[20] With the downsizing of the economic potential there are less and less assurances of the respect for and observance of the economic and social rights. Ongoing is a rapid polarization between the people with regard to the distribution of such rights. The lack of congruity with the notable advancement of political rights puts the entire system of the rights and democratic progress to a severe test, indeed.

The rights that people really possess, are those by which it is easiest to judge whether human rights are universal. The entirety of the rights an individual enjoys, his social and his economic rights in particular, reflect his living standard and well-being. This cluster known as the right to a standard of living includes pursuant to Article 25 of the Universal Declaration of Human Rights "food, clothing, housing and medical care and necessary social services, ..." The wish to underline the meaning of this aggregate of rights and to ensure their exercise by each and every person has found its theoretical expression, too. The recent thought being devoted by some human-rights scholars to the concept of a "right to live" – going beyond the notion of a "right to life" – is interesting conceptual development.[21] Such elaboration of the human-rights conception requires over and above the guarantees for each individual's right to life, assurances for his existence plus the provision of appropriate conditions and sufficient means for adequate living and development of person.

Nowadays poverty and social inequality discredit the pronounced universality of human rights. Without curbing those phenomena, the concept of universal rights will not have an earthly chance indeed of ushering in the genuine rights for everyone. Here, however, we are faced with a controversy on a point of principle. The self-contradiction of liberal ideology is total. If all humans have equal rights, and all peoples have equal rights, we cannot maintain the kind of inegalitarian system that the capitalist world economy has always been and always will be.[22] Capitalism brought about the conception of the universal human rights and paved the way to the establishment and the development of human rights as one of the pillars of the contemporary legal system. But because of its nature, capitalism is incapable of ensuring true universality of human rights. What is at issue here is not the achievement of some sameness of all specific rights possessed by the different people. This is neither feasible, nor will be helpful to the advancement of society. What we do need, however, are changes that will ensure that each person and the humans of all peoples are entitled to enjoy the basic rights to the end that their dignified existence and their right to exert influence on the management of public affairs be safely guaranteed.

3. Universalism and particularism of human rights

The very concept of universality of human rights involves the understanding that they are equally possessed by every man, regardless of his national, ethnic, religious, cultural and other traits. In support of such perception are the basic international human-rights instruments which relate the rights primarily to the person's human nature and only then to its individual particular expressions.

The history of human rights provides evidence that they emerged in the western Christian civilization. It was from there and mainly through such culture that they have spread to other cultures and civilizations as well. At the same time, in a number of non-western cultures, notably the Hindi society, the Islamic and the Arab worlds, and African traditions, individuals are not accorded rights as in the west: in the Confucian or Vedic traditions, duties are considered more important than rights, while in Africa it is the community that protects and nurtures the individual.[23] The cultural and ideological diversities and the divergent views on such issues as the nature of relationship between the individual and society, and between rights and duties exert the strongest influence on the assessment of the role of human rights. The wide range of such assessments determine the relativism of the human-rights conceptions and the particularism of the legal systems with their intrinsic rights.

In this perspective there is a need to work out a definition of the status of rights which may find its place half-way between moderate ethnocentrism and cautious universalism. It cannot be expected that citizenship rights, including the fundamental rights of liberal tradition, will be accepted as "natural" rights with a universal valence and neutrality towards cultures.[24] Otherwise, equally detrimental to human rights could be both cultural hegemonism and cultural separatism. In the first case, a nation may claim, from a position of its culture or civilization, to forcibly impose "world order" based on is view of "human rights". In the second case there is the claim of exceptionality allowing a nation or a civilization to disregard all universal standards of the human rights.

As a set-off to such extremes, the difficult but helpful approach to human-rights development and distribution involves the quest for the point of contact, the common ground of the various legal systems in the human-rights domain and a display of tolerance for the cultural diversity. It is of extreme importance for the evolution of the human rights that official institutions should in truth establish and respect at least a core of standard human rights which everyone can exercise, without even any need to renounce an individual's right (provided it has been freely exercised and positively not in violation of anybody else's rights) to swing towards cultures that do not take the human-rights conception.

The globalization of today's world contributes to its universalization. A part of such universalization is the formation of a more or less shared comprehension of the human rights. Thus all the human cultures must have a minimum core of prima facie values. First, prima facie value propositions, belonging to this core, are objectively valid in the sense that their validity (or their truth) does not depend on an individual's preference and cultural background, either. But such prima facie propositions do not logically imply a moral judgment in any particular case. On the other hand, the final evaluations are necessarily relative to a certain culture. When speaking about universal values, people see the first side of the problem. When speaking about relativism, they see the second one.[25] The achievement of at least minimum core understanding of the value and significance of human rights is a prerequisite for their universal nature. At the same time, without tolerance for the cultural, religious, etc. peculiarities in the content of rights and in the mechanisms of their realization, even what is believed to be a common core might easily be lost.

The adoption of the concept of human rights and their legal institution conduce to changing the conditions with a view to rendering them more favourable for the establishment of human rights. At the same time, without the existence of a favourable social, economic and cultural environment to generate the need for human rights and to promote their advancement, there is a strong possibility that they will be rejected or at least regarded with suspicion.

The balance between the universal and the particular in the content of rights according to their social and economic purpose and cultural background, although with some difficulty, could be struck by a variety of measures, including legislation. Thus, for instance, if the right to reproduction of the human individual is interpreted in principle to be a universal right, it could be treated either more broadly or more narrowly according to the different attendant conditions and depending on whether there is a population explosion or a decline in population. To insist on reproductive rights by ignoring this possibility on the grounds that these rights must be adequate, since the worries are real and we have reasons to attach importance to the happiness and misery of people now and in the future.[26]

Placing restrictions on the realization of some human rights when such restrictions are not discriminatory and are prompted by the actual conditions in a particular society, is not in contradiction with the principle of universality of rights. Such contradiction would be apparent only where certain human rights have been ignored completely.

The competition between the universalization of the human rights and the cultural distinctions of the individual societies at the end of the 20th and the beginning of the 21st century is demonstrated more and more distinctly. Globalization generates a world-wide society where people and nations are losing some of their hitherto identity. In the post-Cold War era they seem to me disposed to seek shelter and development within the various civilizations. People define themselves in terms of ancestry, religion, language, history, values, customs, and institutions. They identify with cultural groups: tribes, ethnic groups, religious communities, nations, and, at the broadest level, civilizations. People use politics not just to advance their interests but also to define their identity.[27] A logical consequence from this is the ever growing cultural relativism of rights, which, without repudiating the concept of human rights, necessitate their conformity with the aforesaid, broadly speaking, civilization distinctions.

Some writers even believe that in the post-Cold War world, the most important distinctions among peoples are not ideological, political, or economic – they are cultural.[28] The common cultural identity is anticipated to exert strong influence on the manner of perceiving human rights. However, such identity will hardly be sufficient to establish a uniform disposition towards human rights even within one and the same civilization in case the variances between the social classes, between the rich and the poor, and between the other distinct economic groups continue to expand.

Laying the stress on the cultural and civilization distinctions is helpful when it serves to blend together the universal validity of basic rights and the particular conditions for their enjoyment. It may become dangerous, though, when such particularities are used to substantiate exceptionality which abrogates the validity of human rights itself.

III. Is global protection of human rights a possibility indeed?

The pretension that human rights are universal ought to include also their protection not only on the national plane, i.e. by the state, but internationally as well, i.e. by the various international institutions. Moreover, there is the need to discuss the opportunities of expanding and enhancing such protection in all cases when any state disregards or violates the rights of its citizens or of other persons under its jurisdiction. It is in the solving of this problem that the contradiction between human rights and the sovereignty of the state stands out most noticeably.

There is no easy solution to the issue of competition between the principles of universality of human rights and the supremacy of state. Even with the radical solution, where preference is given to the supremacy of human rights to the power of state, a pair of queries need be posed: who has the right to verify the human-rights violations, and who shall have the power to penalize the violating states?

An attempt at establishing a specialized mechanism of protecting human rights on the global plane was made with the International Covenant on Civil and Political Rights and the Optional Protocol thereto. These instruments empower the Human Rights Committee at the request of state parties or of persons to probe into reported violations of internationally recognized rights by a particular state. The strength of these two acts is their weakness all the same – they provide for exchange of information, amicable solutions and conciliation procedures. After all, the outcome of the considerations of the issue by the Committee is the adoption of a statement communicated to the concerned parties.

The International Court of Human Rights in Hague, established under the UN Charter, has the power to hear cases involving human rights, if they constitute a violation of international convention (Art. 38, subpara 1, item "a" of the Statutes of the International Court). Allowed to bring cases to the Court are only states (Art. 34, subpara 1). Hence, claims against states that violated human rights cannot be entered by persons, nor by international organizations.

The institution recently of international tribunals for certain crimes and even of a common international penal court has not sufficed to find solutions to the many issues related to the protection of human rights and mainly to the prevention of large-scale violation.

In the post-World War II period the UN Security Council in a number of cases played deterring and balancing role with regard to the world power to the end of maintaining international peace and security. The Security Council's military capacity, however, never developed because of the formation of the large military and political alliances shortly after the establishment of the United Nations.

In the post-Cold War era, in the absence of stability and balance between the world powers the world has witnessed a growing number of armed local and regional conflicts provoked by large-scale human-rights violations and causing in turn still graver humanitarian consequences.

The latest glaring example is the Kosovo crisis and the war in Yugoslavia. The strikes against Yugoslavia, which started in defense of human rights, led to the commitment and provoked much more flagrant human-rights violations than the ones they had to redress. The NATO operations against Yugoslavia, despite the pronounced humanitarian motives for their initiation, cannot change the aggressive nature of this act. At the same time, the inability to employ the existing institutional mechanisms to prevent mass human-rights violation and to protect the victims provokes actions eroding the international legal order.

The actual joining of the roles of world court of justice and a punitive detachment by one organization or a state without even legal grounds derived from the international law cannot be of service to human rights. The establishment of "new world order" by force and disregarding peace poses a threat to the surroundings – humanitarian, environmental, economic, social that is needful in order to have human rights exist and be realized.

The United Nations Organization is facing the dilemma to adapt to the changed conditions and play an active role in ensuring peace and stability, and hence human rights, or prove to be unnecessary. It is necessary to set up a working mechanism that will allow the carrying out of monitoring and inspections any time there are large-scale reports about human-rights violations by the authorities of a particular state. In accordance with the findings made, binding instructions may be issued to the failing state authorities. If the employment of such measures has failed to produce results and the violations have not been redressed, it might be then resorted to sanctions, inclusive of the use of force. This must, however, be authorized, by mandate of the UN Security Council or in another fashion if it will be established by way of international law. The application of such measures requires at least minimum separation of international powers, i.e. separation of the institutions tasked with the performance of monitoring, inspections, control and forcible enforcement of the decisions for international human-rights protection.

At the threshold of the 21st century the finding of the best solutions to the human-rights issues depends on the character of the state. The state has the potential to set the appropriate conditions for the protection of human rights only if it displays ethnic, religious, etc. tolerance, if the national identity is not enforced by coercion and violence against any of the ethnic and other minority groups, if the boundaries of the states are not changed, but grow more and more open instead. It remains for us to see whether at this new turning point in history the humanity and the politics will manage to not repeat the ill-fated experience of this elapsing century, full of conflicts and wars, that lead to grave and large-scale human-rights violations.

Notes

1 Andreas Follesdal, 'Justifying Human Rights: The Challenge of Cross-cultural Toleration,' in *Challenges to Law at the End of the 20th Century*, 4 vol., p. 39, IVR World Congress, Bologna, 16-21 June 1995.

2 Ibid., p. 37.

3 Charles V. Edward, 'The Future of Rights and Democracy in a Multi-cultural Society,' in *Challenges to Law at the End of the 20th Century*, 4 vol., p. 14.

4 Rex Martin and Stephen M. Griffin, 'Constitutional Rights and Democracy in the U.S.A.: The Issue of Judicial Review,' in *Challenges to Law at the End of the 20th Century*, 2 vol., p. 162, 17 IVR World Congress, Bologna, 16-21 June 1995.

5 Ibid.

6 Luca Baccelli, 'Citizenship and Membership,' in *Challenges to Law at the End of the 20th Century*, 4 vol., p. 58.

7 Rex Martin and Stephen M. Griffin, op. cit., p. 166.

8 Andreas Follesdal, op. cit., p. 37. I have not touched herein upon the issue of the conflict of interest between the individual and the state, as well on the complex link between 'majority rule' and human rights within one and the same nationally organized community and state. On these issues see Andreas Follesdal, op. cit., p. 38 and 40, and Rex Martin and Stephen M. Griffin, op. cit.

9 Luigi Ferayoli, 'Beyond Sovereignty and Citizenship. For a World Constitutionalism,' *Contemporary Law*, University of Sofia, 'St. Climent Ohridski', Faculty of Law, Sofia, 1995/No 6, p. 74.

10 Daniel Valchev, 'The Human Rights and the Modern State,' *Contemporary Law*, Sofia, 1997/No 6, p. 119.

11 Jurgen Habermas, 'The European National State – Achievements and Limits. On the Past and Future of the Sovereignty and the Citizenship,' *Bulgarian Law Review*, Sofia, 1996/No 1, p. 117.

12 Massimo La Torre, 'Citizenship and Beyond. Remarks on Political Membership and Legal Subjectivity,' in *Challenges to Law at the End of the 20th Century*, 4 vol., p. 87.

13 Luigi Ferayoli, op. cit., p. 76.

14 Stuart Eizenstat, 'Learning to Steer the Forces of Globalization,' The International Herald Tribune, 22 January 1999, p. 6.

15 For data on the almost immeasurable growth of poverty see UNDP, *Poverty in Transition*, New York (1998).

16 The New Yalta: Commemorating the 50th Anniversary of the Declaration of Human Rights in the RBEC Region, New York 1998, p. 15.

17 Ignacio Ramonet, 'Nouveau siècle', *Le Monde diplomatique*, Janvier 1999, p. 1.

18 Nancy Birdsall, 'Life is Unfair: Inequality in the World,' *Foreign Policy*, Summer 1998, pp. 77, 79.

19 Michael Chossudovsky, 'Global Poverty in the Late 20th Century,' *Journal of International Affairs*, 1998, 52, 1, pp. 304, 306.

20 Ibid., p. 295.

21 Shashi Tharoor, 'The Universality of Human Rights and Their Relevance to Developing Countries,' a paper presented at the *International Conference on Human Rights* at the International Academy for Development of Freedom, Sintra, Portugal, 14-16 November 1988, p. 20.

22 Immanuel Wallerstein, 'After Liberalism,' New York, 1995, p. 161.

23 Shashi Tharoor, op. cit., p. 7.

24 Luca Baccelli, op. cit., p. 62.

25 Aulus Aarnio and Alexander Peczenik, 'On Values Universal or Relative?,' in *Challenges to Law at the End of the 20th Century*, 2 vol., p. 6.

26 See Amartya Sen, 'Legal Rights and Moral Rights: Old Questions and New Problems,' in *Challenges to Law at the End of the 20th Century*, 2 vol., p. 210 et seq.

27 Samuel P. Huntington, *The Clash of Civilizations and the Remaking of World Order*, New York, 1996, p. 21.

28 Ibid., p. 28.

Part II
Constitutional Rights

6. The Role of the Constitutional Courts in the Development of Legal Systems

GABOR HALMAI

I. The Hungarian Approach of Judicial Review

One of the goals of the transformation beginning in 1989 in Hungary was to create a constitutional regime, for which it was indispensable to institutionalize some means for the protection of constitutionality.

The Organization of the Constitutional Court

According to the "republican" amendment of the constitution of October 23 1989[1] and the Act on the Constitutional Court framed simultaneously[2] the first Constitutional Court in Hungarian legal history started to function on January 1, 1990. The court was set up prior to the democratic parliamentary elections to ensure the constitutionality of legislation in the time of transition and its establishment was urged primarily by the governing party, since it had greater opportunity to name judges to the court before the elections than after them. In compliance with the agreement concluded at the roundtable talks, the successor party of the Hungarian Socialist Workers' Party could name two judges out of the first five to the court. A further two judges were nominated by the Opposition Roundtable, while the fifth one was an independent judge accepted by all parties concerned. It has been much debated whether the newly formed body can be considered legitimate, having been constituted by a parliament of dubious legitimacy. So when the Act on the Constitutional Court finally came into force in November 1989, it consisted of only five members, and the nomination of another five judges was left to the parliament elected in the spring of 1990. The remaining five vacancies were to be filled by the parliament in power in the fifth year of the Constitutional Court's activity following a second general election. In late 1994, i.e., prior to the election in question, the total number of the constitutional judges was determined to be eleven.[3] The reduction took place because the experiences of the previous five years showed that a body of fifteen members would not be able to function well, and it would not be wise to set up two senates, as the failure of the German system showed.

A nominating committee consisting of one member of each parliamentary faction puts forth a recommendation as to the nomination of the members of the Constitutional Court. The fact that the committee is composed of an equal number of representatives delegated by the individual parties eliminates the dominance of the stronger parties in the nomination of the judges, which is a guarantee for the political neutrality of the Constitutional Court. Another guarantee is that from among the nominees of outstanding theoretical knowledge and at least twenty years of professional practice, the judges are elected by a two-thirds majority vote of all members of parliament, considering the opinion of the constitutional committee of the parliament. The appointments are for nine years and can be renewed once.

To guarantee the independence of the Constitutional Court, the law defines cases of incompatibility. Accordingly, the judges of the court shall not be members of parliament, members of local administrative bodies, trade union leaders and members of any political party, and shall not pursue any gainful occupation except for scientific, educational, literary, and artistic activity. The independence of the judges is guaranteed also by the fact that they enjoy the same immunity as the members of parliament, immunity that can be withdrawn only by a decision of the plenary session of the Constitutional Court.

The Constitutional Court judges appoint from among themselves the president and the vice-president of the court for a term of three years, whose activity in co-ordination and representation naturally does not affect the independence of the judges.

The Constitutional Court makes its final and universally binding decisions by a majority of votes. The more significant cases require the plenary session, while governmental regulations and regulations of lower levels require only chambers of three judges.

The Jurisdiction of the Court

The Constitutional Court of Hungary has an exceptionally wide jurisdiction even in international comparison since in the beginning it had to control the activity also of the former, not quite legitimate, parliament. Since at the time of the formulation of the separate act on the Constitutional Court, i.e., in the summer of 1989, the forces of the opposition were not yet sure of the outcome of the democratic elections, they meant to build in guarantees also against the next Parliament and Government alike. It was, therefore, not by chance that the Constitutional Court was given too many functions to control both the legislative and the executive power in the new system of government, created by extensive amendments to the constitution. Its position was further strengthened by the lack of some important institutions for the protection of law. Namely, there were no administrative courts to guarantee the legal functioning of administration, and the ombudsmans mentioned in the constitution had not been elected, either. Should another type of parliament, e.g., a bicameral one, have been elected, balancing the power of legislation would have required a different approach also on the part of the Constitutional Court.

Until 1998 the Hungarian Constitutional Court reviewed the constitutionality of a bill, when a motion to this effect is submitted by the parliament, its permanent committees, or a group of at least fifty MPs. Once the unconstitutionality of a bill or part of it had been established, the parliament or the individuals or organs submitting the motion had to see to its being corrected. However, the Constitutional Court voluntarily renounced this right in 1991, saying that it would mean interference with the legislative process. The decision was brought in connection with the motion of fifty-two MPs of the opposition against the first compensation act not yet passed by parliament.[4] In 1998 the Hungarian Parliament wanted to cancel the possibility of preventive norm control. The bill was challenged before the Constitutional Court, which ruled that it is not unconstitutional to abolish this institutions. The preventive control of acts passed but not yet promulgated can still be initiated by the president of the republic. Once declared unconstitutional, the president cannot promulgate the act before its being made constitutional by parliament. This is what happened, for example, in the case of the compensation act.

The other method is regressive abstract norm control. The need to systematically review the constitutionality of the surviving elements of the old legal system existing parallel with the renewed constitution has made this the main function of the Hungarian Constitutional Court. Regressive norm control can be initiated by anyone, even if they are not affected by the regulation in question. So the unique method of the Hungarian Constitutional Court has made the citizens participants in the process of the transformation of the old legal system. Such "popular actions" have led to several decisions by the Constitutional Court influencing decisively the organs of the state and, still more, the regulation of fundamental human rights. It was in the wake of such civic motions that the administrative courts were set up in Hungary and the death penalty abolished, the general use of the PIN number declared as unconstitutional, and the criticism of public officials allowed.

In such a motion the petitioner can suggest the full or partial nullification of the legal regulation or statute challenged. By such an *actio popularis*, any citizen of the country can challenge any legal regulation and even administrative regulations such as, for example, ministerial decrees. Regressive norm control can be initiated also by ordinary court judges. A judge can suspend the case and initiate proceedings before the Constitutional Court in any case pending before him, if he considers the legal provision to be applied in the case unconstitutional.

The decision of annulment generally applies only prospectively. One of the exceptions is when it is more favourable for a convict in a case to establish unconstitutionality retroactively, i.e., counting from the counting to power of the given regulation. In that case. the Constitutional Court is bound to prescribe the revision of the criminal procedure.

This "self-triggering" mechanism of the Hungarian Constitutional Court quite unknown in other countries, manifests itself also in cases when the legislative organ has created an unconstitutional situation not by sanctioning an unconstitutional regulation but by neglecting to carry out its legislative duties. Such a procedure can be initiated by the Court ex officio and also by any citizen of the country. Once the omission has been established, the legislative body has to comply with the request of the Constitutional Court to fulfil its duty. Such an omission happened, for example in the case of the Media Act.[5] It reveals the limitations of the authority of the Constitutional Court that several Parliamentary terms have passed and the Media Act was only passed in 1996.

Those whose rights have been violated by the application of an unconstitutional legal provision may turn to the Constitutional Court with a constitutional complaint for the violation of their constitutional rights, after having unsuccessfully tried all other means of gaining legal remedy. This is the only case when the power of the Hungarian Constitutional Court is not as wide as that of other European Constitutional Courts, in that it cannot deal with direct individual complaints against an administrative or judicial decision not challenging the constitutionality of the norms on the basis of which the decision has been brought. Due to these limitations, the number of the complaints presented to the Hungarian Constitutional Court in the past nine years does not amount even to 1% of the total number of potential claims. The Hungarian constitutional judges tried to breathe life into the lifeless institution of complaint more than once in the past few years, and their first decision serving as a precedent annulled a judgement in a concrete case.[6]

The Constitutional Court decides individual cases on the basis of its interpretation of the various provisions of the constitution, but it is authorized, on the claims of specified bodies, to interpret constitutional provisions also in an abstract manner, without reference to particular cases, which is also a very strange phenomenon in international comparison. Such abstract decisions have been made in connection with the constitutional powers of the president of the republic.[7]

II. The Jurisprudence of the Court in the First Nine Year Term

The first nine year cycle of the Hungarian Constitutional Court's proceedings have come to an end. I am certain that these nine years will enter into not only Hungarian political and public law history as the era of the Sólyom Court, but—and what is at least as important to a genuine constitutional judge/court—into legal text books as well.[8] In the final days of the "era" a seemingly inconsequential decision was born,[9] which appropriately enough remained completely without reverberations in the political life as well as in the confines of (Constitutional) legal circles. The matter seems all the more frivolous since the Court closed its proceedings without bringing forth a decision on the motions with respect to the debate between the Prosecutor's Office and the Parliamentary Commissioners on civil rights about the scope of their jurisdiction. Three among the eleven Constitutional judges at the time disagreed with halting the proceedings. Their dissenting opinion was articulated by the same László Sólyom who since its inception and for the ensuing nine years was not only the administrative director of the Court but also its outstanding and determining Justice, and who originally presented the case before the Court.

Intimating the significance of his dissenting opinion is the fact that László Sólyom, who two months after the decision was handed down, stepped down from his position as President and Justice, in an interview about the future of the Constitutional Court proceedings assessed the decision as a turning point.[10] In response to the journalist's inquiry, in which she asked about the Constitutional Court's earlier decision being reviewed possibly by the new Court, the departing President called attention to two dangers. He saw the first in that the activism of the Court would be moderated; the second, in that with respect to the scope of competences, a limited interpretation in adherence to the letter of the law would become dominant in the Court. In addition, Sólyom expressed a further concern in the interview: based on certain signs during the past few years, he thought that the 1992 decision on the right of free speech [deleting "blasphemy" as bearing on the case in the public's incitement to riot—G.H.] would not receive a majority opinion today. He based this conclusion on the fact that he had prepared over a year ago the proposed judgment on the constitutionality of punishment by law for using symbols of tyranny, which however, he did not present before the Court because he assessed that the "unusually liberal viewpoint" of the proposal would not receive the vote of the majority.

In other words, László Sólyom, expressed or implied, presented three issues about the new composition of the Bench: with respect to the interpretation of the Constitution it would be less activist; it would represent a more conservative interpretation in its attitude; and as for the scope of jurisprudence it would adhere more closely to the letter of the law than its founding fathers did. The subject of this study are these three premises and through it the first nine years of the Hungarian Constitutional Court's proceedings.

Liberal versus conservative decisions and judges

Let us begin perhaps with the question most difficult to answer. Is it demonstrable that the fundamental legal decisions of the Sólyom era were characterized more by a liberal perspective than can be expected from the new Court. One of the starting points for arriving at an answer is to try to group the existing and new Justices according to liberal and conservative attitudes. Except that this task is not easy even in the case of those Justices who have nine years of constitutional decision making behind them; never mind those who are new to this Bench and their earlier work is not discernible from this perspective because say, as a corporate attorney, or perhaps an intern judge, or even as a university professor and author of professional publications they were not forced to take a position as to their liberal or conservative views.

In addition, we must also consider the problem that any liberal or conservative majority ruling by a court may not necessarily reflect directly the views of the judges so ruling. In evaluating the Sólyom Court's nine years for example, a writer in one of the weekly newspapers stated that among the initial members of the Constitutional Court it is quite possible that not a single one was liberal in the political interpretation of the word; nevertheless, it was this public legal institution that accomplished the most toward the consolidation of Hungarian liberal democracy.[11] The author explains this entire fact by that the Justices, in the interest of an objective and values they deemed more important, were able to rise above the conceptual boundaries of their own world views. Let us disregard for the moment that the writer uses liberalism at times in the context of politics and at others, in terms of world view; whereas in the case of a constitutional judge the term has relevance only as an ideology that determines a legal position. Even in this last regard, I feel that Sólyom was in fact a liberal Justice,[12] and as I have already mentioned, the weight of his understanding was far more significant than that of anyone else. Moreover, his influence exceeded the inevitable result stemming from his status as President in the role of *primus inter pares*. Sólyom's liberal views could be imprinted on cardinal decisions he either prepared or merely influenced because he was the one most receptive to the theoretical implications of the decisions; the others often followed opinions held in high esteem, which brought domestic or foreign professional recognition.[13] Beyond Sólyom's overriding influence, the liberal viewpoints of the decisions were of course determined by the substantially more liberal than today socio-political environment at the beginning phase of the change in regime.[14]

If we take an overview of the major decisions of the first nine years, beginning with the abolishment of the death penalty, through the fundamentals for the freedom of information, to the freedom of speech in the broad context, they are in fact permeated by a consistently consequential liberal viewpoint. Perhaps the only decisions to fall out of line are the freedom of religion and abortion. I think Sólyom's liberal views came into conflict with considerations of his conscience. I offer the same explanation for the decision by Sólyom which reflects a conservative position, namely, his decree that the state's limit on minors' participating in organizations established to protect the interest of homosexuals is constitutional.[15]

Among the Constitutional Court's interpretations of the ruling on the freedom of expression, it defends its decision to eliminate from the penal code the position on incitement to hatred on grounds that it is unconstitutional in this form of inciting the public to riot, in that the right to freedom of expression protects that right without consideration of the value or truthful content of that opinion, because this alone corresponds to the ideological neutrality of the Constitution.[16] In knowing this understanding it is not difficult to guess what Sólyom's proposal may have contained on the constitutionality of the penal code's position on criminality in the use of symbols of tyranny. At best, it is difficult to imagine what may have been of an "unusually liberal viewpoint" in it. Much more at issue may be why Sólyom just prior to the end of his mandate could no longer prevail upon the somewhat changed composition of the Court to accept his opinion, unchanged in comparison to his earlier position. It is my opinion however, that the Justices who took their seats by the end of 1998 were no more conservative than those who stepped down since; as I have stated previously, the latter cannot be called liberal either.

Of course, not to cast doubt on the liberalism of Sólyom's position with respect to his aborted proposal, but for the sake of completion it must be noted that toward the end of his mandate it seemed as if a certain uncertainty could be detected in his views on freedom of opinion. The first tangible evidence of this was the dissenting opinion he wrote with Tamás Lábady on the constitutionality of the last censorship regulation of the press law. Under the interpretation of the passage stemming form 1986, on the initiative from the Prosecutor, the Court—among other things in the case of news which infringes on public morals and/or the individual rights of others—prohibited public dissemination of the publications of the press, while the Prosecutor suspended the news until the Court's legal decision was final. The five Constitutional Justices representing the majority decision decreed censorship in violation of the Constitution only in the instance of news violating individual rights where the Prosecutor introduced the motion without the consent of the injured party. László Sólyom in the jointly registered dissenting opinion extended the sphere of cases of unconstitutionality to the Prosecutor's power to suspend newspaper distribution by citing violation of public morality; but they did not object, in the name of protecting morality, to the Court's power to ban press materials which did not violate the rights of individuals nor resulted in criminal acts. Of course, Sólyom and Lábady's opinion is "more liberal" than that of the other Justices representing the majority, and especially more so than the view of those two Constitutional Justices who in another dissenting opinion ruled the entirety of the legislation constitutional.[17] The question is merely whether one can consider an opinion liberal which opinion legitimizes censorship regulations at the end of the Twentieth Century.[18] It is a separate novelty of this 5:4 decision that Sólyom became part of the minority with those Justices (and not for the first time toward the end of his mandate) with whom he so often constituted the majority in former years. Among them Tamás Lábady, to this day on the same platform as he, can be called his most faithful ally. As we shall see, Justices Lábady and Tersztyánszky followed the President in the minority decision in the case of the *Ombudsman vs. the Prosecution*, while Justice Zlinszky by that time having already stepped down from the Court.

The suspicion of uncertainty however, can arise with respect to those issues of freedom of speech that Sólyom did not have time to complete within his official tenure. In addition to the already mentioned penal code passage on the use of symbols of despotism, the motions that have been waiting for years for a decision also fall into this category, motions which state as unconstitutional the new regulation in the penal code on the violation of the use of national symbols and the modified position of public incitement to riot. In connection with the foregoing, Sólyom's words are quite chatty in the *Fundamentum* interview, as if they seemed to reflect a confutation of the arguments of a political liberalism: "With respect to national symbols, two motions were submitted to us, which educate us about American flag-burning, and about the fact that vulgar and damaged individuals compensate for their inadequacies with national symbols, and this 'national cohesive consciousness' in the sociological soil for nationalism and fanaticism." A few lines later, this impatience is further revealed in legal argument: "Here at home, the simplistic logic is put forward that after adopting the decision in the New York v. Sullivan case we should adopt the ruling on flag-burning as well..."[19] Whereas, it would require separate proof that the defense of freedom of opinion without consideration of truthful content or value—which was already mentioned in ruling 30/1992.(V 26.) AB—and in its wake subsequent and other decisions as well, emphasized the nation's demand for guaranteed ideological neutrality; why would it also not apply to so-called symbolic speech, like flag-burning and violation of other national symbols.

In the text on public incitement to riot, truncated by the Constitutional Court, the element in the new position was repeatedly replaced by the Legislature, the prohibition of unpurposeful "other actions that can be used to engender hatred," also barely corresponds to the test established as a result of the 1992 decision. Sólyom also makes this unequivocally clear in the interview, in which he also makes a promise to ensure a decision prior to his stepping down: "The Legislature didn't even pay attention in the incitement to hatred decision that two other tests also played a part: the unique character of the assailed goods as well as the threshold of danger."[20] As we have stated, the ruling did not come to pass, moreover–in contrast to the prohibition against symbols of despotism—nor did Sólyom comment in this regard about the completion of the motion to present. The text of the interview, however, betrays in this case as well the possible causes for delay in the decision when it refers to the International Commission of Jurists—which holds a consultative status in UNESCO and the Council of Europe—questioning the incitement ruling and requesting the Hungarian government to clarify the relationship between the Constitution and the agreement against discrimination.[21] Except that for as long as the Hungarian Parliament does not modify the content of the basic ruling, the Constitutional Court is exclusively bound by it in its reaching a judgment.[22]

"Activist human rights fundamentalists" vs. "Parliamentary legal allies"

As Ronald Dworkin established in connection with the American Supreme Court's decision on abortion, the moral interpretation of the Constitution may be represented by both liberal and conservative Justices;[23] in like manner, the activism represented on issues of fundamental law in the case of the Hungarian Constitutional Justices is not simply a matter of liberal or conservative viewpoint either.

In Hungarian jurisprudence literature Béla Pokol was the first to attempt relatively early, and for this reason an aborted evaluation and categorization of the proceedings into "activist human rights fundamentalists" and "Parliamentary legal ally" on the part of the Constitlutional Court and certain Justices during the first two years.[24] The essence of Pokol's fundamental law activism-criticism is that the Constitutional Court's practice of abolishing law cannot be based on such "super abstract" fundamental legal formulas as rule of law, human dignity or equal protection.

Thawing out the "general rights of individuals"

The "great turn" toward activism according to Pokol took place at the proclamation of the 8/1990.(IV.23.) AB ruling. This decision judged unconstitutional the pre-transition regulation of the Labor Code, which empowers labor unions to represent workers—even if they happen to be non-union members, perhaps even against their expressed will—without their separate power of attorney. The basis for the abolishment was the rule of human dignity in the Constitution, which the Constitutional Justices (on the recommendation of Sólyom presenting Justice of the case) in their justification of the decision considered an expression of "the general rights of individuals." This right, which does not appear in the Constitution, is according to Sólyom's view "thawed out" from the right to human dignity, a "birthright;" namely, it is such a subsidiary fundamental right that the Constitutional Court as well as all the courts in every instance can cite it in defense of individual autonomy if none of the specifically named fundamental laws apply to the case in question." Pokol considers this quoted reference the "credo of activism," whereby in his view even the constitutionally binding minimum on which to base the Constitutional Court's decisions disappeared and merely the bare sense of justice remained as their basis.

Pokol of course, correctly prognosticated that the thawed out avalanche will gather momentum in the course of years to come. The

Justices determined in ruling 57/1991.(XI.8.) AB that "the right to self-identity and self-determination is part of the 'general rights of individuals.'" Further, this right includes everyone's most personal right to discover their blood origin. The following year, decision 22/1992.(IV.10) AB decreed unconstitutional the requirement that enlisted officers request permission from their superiors to marry, on the basis that the right to marry, as part of the right to self-determination, is such a fundamental right so as to stand under Constitutional guardianship. One can also include here the treatment as birthright under the right of human dignity. Ruling 14/1995. (III.13.) on the right of gay couples to live life in partnership, in which the Court—based on Sólyom's presentation—unanimously decreed that there can be no cardinal rule Constitutional differentiation between persons living together in emotional and material partnership on the basis of gender, because individuals have to be judged based on the principle of equal dignity. In this case, the Court cited the Constitution's prohibition on discrimination and did not frame new legislation, but as Sólyom later commented, it could have done so.[25]

Ruling 9/1990.(IV.25.) on the constitutionality of positive discrimination, according to Pokol carried the activist line further in that through the application of Ronald Dworkin's formula on the requirements of "treatment as persons of equal dignity" it dissolved the contradiction between Paragraph 1, Section 70/A of the Constitution that formally declared equality under the law, and Paragraph 3, which implies equality in content and requires the development of equal opportunity as a constitutional objective. Sólyom acknowledges "the Dworkin effect" in the *Fundamentum* interview; moreover, he once and for all professes his faith in the Dworkin principle as the basis of activism and the moral interpretation of the Constitution: "The first rulings with reference to positive discrimination seemingly follow [Dworkin's] argumentation verbatim, according to which in the final analysis we must reach a solution that in terms of usefulness to society creates equality, while as a tool, it is equipped with inequality at the same time. This is the philosophy of affirmative action. Dworkin provided reinforcement on behalf of precisely this issue of the system of morality; namely, how autonomous is the Court when it reaches a borderline case. In his view, within an unbiased neutral reading of the Constitution, numerous possibilities for interpretation exist, but the moment a person arrives at a border line in a 'hard case,' it is here that the judge's moral perspective and reading play a part."[26]

The Right to Life: the Death Penalty and Abortion

Ruling 23/1990(X.31) AB abolishing the death penalty, according to Pokol characterizes the duality of concurring opinions at the peak of activism on the one hand; and on the other, the first articulation of dissenting opinions by the "Parliamentary legal allies" position which dismissed these. Based on Pokol's evaluation, among the concurring opinions Sólyom's demonstrates the unmistakable signs of activism in two references; namely, in that the President of the Court recognizes on the one hand the Constitutional Court's relationship to Parliament; and on the other, to the Constitution. In the former regard, Pokol considers the following statement key to the Sólyom position: "Parliament, according to its pleasure can uphold, abolish or reinstate the death penalty—for as long as the Constitutional Court gives no final word as to the penalty's constitutionality." Pokol interprets this text as Sólyom obviating the possibility of subsequent reinstatement of the death penalty thereby, even by way of constitutional amendment, empowering the Constitutional Court as a result with the right to declare a Constitutional Amendment unconstitutional. (In essence, Pokol also attributed the same activist intention to extend power to the concurring opinion that Constitutional Justices Lábady and Tersztvánszky registered jointly.) Of course, it is possible to interpret both Sólyom's and Lábady et al.'s text in such a manner; at the same time, subsequent actions would rather support the interpretation that the Justices thought that: after the decision by the Constitutional Court, Parliament's ability to act as Legislator, and not as constitutional law-maker, ceased to exist with respect to reinstating the death penalty. This is what the 1994 decision seems to confirm, in which the Court having determined its lack of jurisdiction rejected the motion that initiated a review of one of the statues within the Constitution.[27] Sólyom's words confirm the same thing in his *Fundamentum* interview, even if in its articulation it awakens certain doubts about his own opinion: "The majority of the Constitutional Court finds no need to examine the constitutionality of Constitutional Amendments, although theoretically it could be justified."[28]

The second disclosure associated with the Sólyom-type activism, which has since become quite renowned because of the concurring opinion attached to the decision on the death penalty, is the concept of the "invisible Constitution:" "The Constitutional Court must continue its work in articulating the underlying theoretical concepts in its interpretation of the Constitution and the laws inherent within it, such that it creates a coherent system by its judgments, which serves...as an 'invisible Constitution' above the Constitution, from the secure criterion of constitutionality, and for this reason it is expected not to come into conflict with the new Constitution about to be established, nor with future Constitutions." Although it is true that in subsequent opinions Sólyom did not repeat the expression that visibly irritated politicians, nevertheless, he never gave up its contents, which his words also confirm in a 1997 interview: "Our Constitutional Court proceedings in the interest of coherency—especially in the 'hard cases'—modulate on the boundary of drafting a Constitution, I never denied this."[29] He reiterated this again in a separate interview in 1998, shortly before stepping down, in which he discussed the misconception by many of the concept of an "invisible Constitution;" and later, when the reporter confronted him with the question as to whether he would retract the metaphor, he replied: "No. What I have written, I have written. In those days, the Constitution was amended monthly, as daily politics happened to desire. It was precisely for this reason that I wanted to point out that the Constitution is of a higher order; it is not merely the strict order of technical regulations, but of principles. We had to discern these principles by our decisions, clarify, elucidate and apply them, because no one can determine them from mere one-line paragraphs and simple sentences. Of course, it is possible to pass Constitutional Court decisions by retreating behind the letter of the law—there are examples for such in Europe and Asia as well."[30]

In the course of the decision on the death penalty, in terms of the first open difference of opinion based on an activist understanding of and as the clear articulation of fundamental law, which won at least a silent majority, Pokol addresses the once and for all "Parliamentary legal ally," Péter Schmidt's dissenting opinion, according to which "Although interpretation of the Constitution belongs under the sphere of jurisdiction of the Constitutional Court, dissolution of contradictory constitutional regulations is the right and obligation of Parliament, [which is] vested with the power to enact constitutional legislation. The Constitutional Court cannot usurp this right."

Among those Justices who wrote concurring opinions to the considerably laconic argumentation in the shared decision in favor of abolishing the death penalty, Pokol only considers Tamás Lábady and Ödön Tersztyánszky's aforementioned joint opinion as similarly activist to Sólyom's; he does not comment on János Zsilinszky, and evaluates András Szabó as someone who "relates to the Parliamentary legal alliance with more of an indifference, in the same way that no explicitly activist dissertations can be discovered from him either."

In several 1991 decisions however, Pokol believes to have discovered further dissent vis-à-vis Sólyom activism on the part of certain

Justices. He evaluates Géza Kilényi's dissenting opinion as such, attached to the already mentioned decision 57/1991.(XI.8) AB for example, in which he argued as follows: "As of the present time, among the Constitutional Courts functioning in the world today, the Constitutional Court of the Hungarian Republic has the broadest spectrum mandate and concomitant stockhouse of tools in the area of constitutional enforcement. However, even this unusually broad legal mandate is not without limits, which does not mean that the Constitutional Court can do whatever it considers necessary in the interest of the Constitution... No matter how worthy a motive behind it, any attempt to wish to ameliorate a violation of the law at any price—in a given case even by ignoring the boundaries of its jurisdiction—is unacceptable." With this Kilényi, with whose dissenting opinion Péter Schmidt, the "Parliamentary legal ally," also joined, argued against the unacceptability of the theory of "extant law" incorporated into the majority decision, stating that the Constitutional Court has no jurisdiction to review the constitutionality of the practice of applying the law; moreover, it cannot "prosecute" the Legislature by abolishing the statute that under correct interpretation does not otherwise violate the Constitution because of the unconstitutional interpretation of the application of the law by organizations. According to Kilényi, the Constitutional Court's jurisdiction only extends to explaining in the justification for its decision, which is that interpretation in a given legal regulation that when taken under consideration is not regarded in opposition to the Constitution. Subsequently, the Constitutional Court unabashedly applied this "constitutionally conferment interpretation," which was gentle on the legal system in force, a solution taken from German Constitutional Court practice, which redeemed placing the legally regulated statute outside the jurisdiction of what may also be interpreted in opposition to the Constitution. Except that Pokol was mistaken in that Kilényi et al.'s counter-argument did not refer to the activism exhibited in the moral interpretation of the Constitution but—as the explicit allusion in the text indicates—he took exception to the all too broad spectrum of interpretation, in his view, of the Constitutional Court's jurisdiction. It is a different matter that it is Kelényi who is mistaken in that his preferred interpretation of constitutional conformity does not indicate a "disregard of the limitations of jurisdiction." He disagrees about this error from Sólyom who on the principle that the part is contained within the whole, does not consider the constitutional conformity interpretation of legal regulations as exceeding the province of jurisdiction: "If we have once [been given] the right to determine that the legal regulation under attack is against the Constitution, we then have the right to prevent its unconstitutional application."[31] In fact, in this case the Constitutional Court—instead of abolishing the legally regulated provision it judged to be unconstitutional and charging the Legislature to create a new standard—it interpreted the regulation and not the Constitution, for which it has no mandate under any jurisdiction whatsoever; moreover, such an interpretation that is binding for all is unequivocally a positive creation of law.

The other "distancing" Pokol believes to have caught is in János Zlinszky's concurring opinion attached to Ruling 64/1991.(XII.17.) AB, that is, to the first decision on abortion, in the following train of thought: "If the position of the initiators of the motion is that in our society today recognition under the law of the full nature of a fetus' individual rights is justified, they find agreement with legal enactment and can do so with an affirmative decision on the constitutional level. This position cannot be 'sneaked in' on the basis of interpreting the Constitution's text." It is quite true that "sneaking into" the Constitution, as referred to by Zilinszky, that a fetus is a legal entity would have far exceeded the boundaries indicated by Sólyom as regards Constitutional wording, except that until that time the Constitutional Court never took the risk. This position was only represented by Tamás Lábady, initially as a parallel justification to the first, 1991, decision on abortion and subsequently as a dissenting opinion to the second, in 1998. In his view it can be deduced from the Constitution that a fetus must be considered human from the moment of conception, namely, a legal entity; for this reason, it is exclusively in cases of danger to the mother's life that termination of pregnancy can be regarded as Constitutional.

János Zlinszky's opinion referred to by Pokol represents therefore, not a distancing from activism, merely from its extremist expression, as had been rejected by all the other Justices as well. There remained plenty of activism in Zlinszky's opinion as well as in all the others, especially in defending the interests of the legally non-human fetus. The most important expression of this is the institution of the state's responsibility to protect life, which does not appear in the Constitution, and which Sólyom deduced from the right to life and considered necessary to apply in the case where the Legislature/Constitution-maker does not regulate a fetus' existence as a legal entity—in the way that this in fact took place in the crafting of the 1992 law on the protection of fetal life. Except that the idiosyncrasy of this conservative activism is that it treats it as equal to women's right to self determination; furthermore, in specific cases it considers a certain responsibility of state foremost, which is missing from the Constitution, and which in the legal sense has no subject.[32]

Government organizational issues: competences of the President of the Republic and independence of the courts

1. The dilemma of activism-pacifism did not divide the Court exclusively in matters of fundamental law only, but at times on issues of government organization. Such were the decisions handed down in 1991-1992, which dealt with the interpretation of the President of the Republic's legal sphere of influence under the Constitution. The motions for a constitutional interpretation—in the interest of the Constitutional Court deciding on the political debate that had emerged between the Prime Minister and the Head of State—were submitted in part by the Prime Minister himself, and partly by the majority of the ruling Party's ministerial and Parliamentary committees. Forced into decisions that had a political effect in nature, the majority of Constitutional Justices—under the leadership of Sólyom, who as a civil lawyer delivered the opinion of the Court on this issue of public law—accepted the task of circumscribing the head-of-state jurisdictions when the constitutional text offered nothing to grasp whatsoever. The main subject of the confrontation among the Justices was the politically most sensitive question in the media war then in progress, that of the interpretation of the President's legal sphere of appointment. Sólyom et al. determined that the Head of State can only reject the appointment, that is, its necessary acceptance, in the instance of a lack of a legal regulation governing it; and if in the course of investigating the person proposed for nomination, he has substantial cause to conclude that implementing it would seriously disturb the country's democratic process.[33] Géza Kilényi, Péter Schmidt and Imre Vörös in their dissenting opinions however, judged that the Constitutional Court in its interpretation of the regulations on the legal sphere to name appointments exceeded its jurisdiction; that the decision surpassed the interpretation of the Constitution's applicable regulations and that it already belonged in the realm of Constitutional legislation.

The same conceptual division was repeated in reply to the Prime Minister's question as to whether the President's exercise of the right to appoint was subject to a deadline. Sólyom et al. responded to the issue, obviously motivated by a concrete matter, by introducing the Constitutional demand of a "reasonable deadline," whereas Kilényi et al. preserved their earlier dissenting opinions.[34] The Head of State's reluctance to execute the specific appointments resulted in further Prime Ministerial motions, to which the majority responded again with an abstract but extremely applicable constitutional interpretation of the case at hand, while the other three answered with the obligatory dissenting opinions.[35]

2. The other important government organizational decision of the Constitutional Court addressed the position of the courts in the system of separation of powers. At the same time, this was the first decision, 38/1993. (VI.11.) AB, in which the Constitutional Justices instead of abolishing a legal regulation that had been applied unconstitutionally, articulated constitutional injunctions in the provisional sections of the ruling that bound everyone equally. Fundamentally, behind the scenes of the motions stood the ongoing disputed practice of the then Minister of Justice's appointment of county court presidents. Namely, the Minister interpreted the judicial organizational law in the course of the appointments such that in effect even in the case of a single vote at the full judiciary meeting the nominee's support came into effect. In fact, the inappropriateness of the legal interpretation was just as obvious as in an earlier instance (Ruling 57/1991.(XI.8.) AB) by the Supreme Court, when the Constitutional Justices referring to the unconstitutional "extant law" abolished the objectionable regulations. In contrast to this practice, they upheld in this case the unconstitutionally applied rule and determined its interpretation such that it conformed to the Constitution. The Court first took position on the issue of whether it was constitutional at all to order the right to nominate to other branches of power. After an affirmative answer to this question, they determined the boundaries that resulted from the separation of nominations by an "external" organization from the branches of power. Accordingly, in nominating judges and judicial leaders it is constitutional to demand that it neutralize the politically-based effect of nominations from another branch of power; or the Judicial Branch of power's material effect on the public good or else, on the balance outside the Judicial Branch of power. The effect of the Judicial Branch of power on the public good must exhibit, embodied in the judges' positions, judicial independence and neutrality of the Judicial Branch; and that their position exercise material influence on the nomination. All of which is to say, understandably, that in contrast to the interpretation by the Minister, the support of the majority of the judicial court is necessary.

In the concurring opinion attached to the ruling, Péter Schmidt agreed with the merits of the decision, according to which the judicial organizational law is not unconstitutional. In his opinion however, its constitutionality is based on the fact that the Constitution, beyond declaring judicial independence, does not determine the constitutional bases for the relationship between the Executive and Judicial powers. Consequently, it does not follow from the Constitution that in order to balance the external nominating sphere of influence within judicial organizations it is necessary to operate judicial bodies; nor, of course, that it could not be so. Péter

Schmidt, faithful to his earlier position on the consistently strict interpretation of the jurisdiction of the Constitutional Court, also emphasized that it is not the task of the Constitutional Court to transform the principles of the Constitution into concrete legal regulations, as it is also not to adjudicate the basic law in cases where it lacks the guarantees for the requirements contained therein.

According to Antal Ádám's dissenting opinion, the possibility of infringing on judicial independence is inherent in the Minister of Justice's right to appoint, as expressed in the law. Imre Vörös in his dissenting opinion likewise deems unconstitutional, stemming from the requirements of separating the branches of power, the executive branch's involvement in judicial proceedings, which is not balanced by the deficient regulations of judiciary self-government organizations. Vörös at the same time—again adhering consistently to his notion of passivism in jurisdiction—also deemed the Constitutional Court proceeding troublesome in that it attempts to determine the constitutionally supportable content from among several interpretations of the law, as if it were protecting the law in effect and trying to avoid abolishment based on opposition to the Constitution. In the case of fundamental laws he considers the possibility of multiple interpretations itself to be an infringement of legal security. According to Vörös' understanding, as expressed elsewhere, the Constitutional Court has no jurisdiction to interpret the law or other legal regulations, the jurisdiction guaranteed for the interpretation of the Constitution does not extend to the whole of the legal system.

Social rights

The development of the Justices' activism with respect to social rights was interesting under the Sólyom era. László Sólyom himself in 1990 already made his own passivist position clear in his concurring opinion to Ruling 31/1990.(XII.18.) AB: "The Constitution does not determine any measure or cognizance of welfare support; the determination and implementation of all such is the responsibility and obligation of the Legislature and government." The polarization of the judicial positions was first palpable in Ruling 24/1991.(V.18.) AB, in which the majority (Sólyom, Lábady, Ádám, Herczegh, Schmidt and Tersztyánszky) rejected at the time reviewing the merits of the numerous motions on socialized medicine and the pension system, up until their codification, then in progress, was completed. In contrast, according to the dissenting opinions of four Constitutional Justices (Kilényi, Szabó, Zilinszky and Vörös) the motions could have been adjudicated. Underlying the two positions however, conceptual differences lay hidden, which became apparent from the dissenting opinions that addressed the issue's merits. Based on this, pensioners have the right to social security under what is surmised in Paragraph 70/E of the Constitution, and this cannot be revoked by the state.

The second "collision" came to pass in relation to Ruling 26/1993. (IV.29) on the stability of the value of pension funds. The four minority Constitutional Justices of four years ago were forced again to write a dissenting opinion. This time however, the majority explained its interpretation as to the merits of their position as well, in the presentation of Tamás Lábady. Accordingly, it is not a violation of the right to social security if the agreed upon increase in pensions and other benefits does not reach the measure of inflation. The majority decision also pointed out that there is no correlation between the right to social security governed under Paragraph 70/E of the Constitution, that is, the right to benefits, and the right of ownership guaranteed under Paragraph 13. According to the position of the six Constitutional Justices, based on the so-called welfare rights, the basis of social welfare benefits for pensioners and other rightful constitutional beneficiaries is not the right of ownership, but the right expressed in the Constitution to allocation of provisions.

A series of adjudicated decisions on certain elements in the government's economic stabilization package in 1995, brought a change in the majority ruled Constitutional Court's interpretation of social rights. In this decision, and even prior, in Ruling 43/1995. (VI.30) AB, the Court on the basis of its interpretation of welfare benefits as an acquired right, abolished numerous regulations of law. The Constitutional Court determined that legal security, as the most essential conceptual element of constitutional statehood and the conceptual basis for the protection of acquired rights, is of special significance from the perspective of stabilizing welfare systems. In this way, in the case of long-term support under the child welfare system, the Legislature has the right to change the entire legal regulation of support. However, the Constitutional requirement related to legal security for those affected in changing to a new system is the guarantee of sufficient preparation time to adapt to the changed regulations and for organizing the family's household finances based on the new conditions. It was necessary for the Constitutional Court in its justification of the decision to change its 1993 acknowledged interpretation on pension benefits, and now take a position such that in all cases of social security services where the element of security plays a part, the constitutionality of a decrease in services or their abolition is to be judged according to the criteria of preservation of property.

The development of the interpretation in connection with social rights demonstrated in practice therefore that as a departure from the usual characteristics, Sólyom et al., who represented a "passivists" position in the beginning but who in terms of the other fundamental law happened to be activist (at least Sólyom, Lábady and Tersztyánszky), joined Kilényi et al. in their untrue-to-form activism, and this is how the "Bokros package" decision passed with such surprising unanimity—which according to accounts additionally irritated the government leadership.

Referendum issues

The 1997 unanimously voted decisions of the Constitutional Court on matters of plebiscite demonstrate an interesting permutation of activism and passivism. In this regard the members of the Court represented partly an activist and partly passivist interpretation. The retreat into the background of the original division was probably facilitated by the fact that the fundamentally political nature of the debates among the Parliamentary parties used the Constitutional Court as an arbitrating judge, which at times reluctantly and at others, sensing the political flavor of its role, took position on the side of either one or another (predominantly one) political player.[36]

The series of 1997 Constitutional Court decisions in connection with the plebiscite was launched by the opposition parties' petition-signing initiative on land issues and the Government's wish to prevent this through a determination of its relationship to initiating plebiscites in a relatively "activist" Ruling 52/1997(X.14.)AB. In this the Court articulated the unequivocally correct concept according to which priority is granted to a plebiscite that must be called based of obligation, in contrast to one that can be called on discretion. At the same time, it raises misgivings that the Constitutional Court judged the abstract interpretation of the Constitution to "give direction to the matters in progress," and with this indirectly declared Parliament's posting the plebiscite initiated by the Government as unconstitutional. The intention of the Constitutional Justices to influence the specific matter is clearly shown by the unmistakable threat in the Ruling according to which "procedural infringement of the Constitution in the course of creating legislation—including that of a law based on an unconstitutionally called plebiscite—may draw the abolition of the law in its wake, even in the absence of constitutional enmity in the law's content."

The activism in the constitutional interpretation by the Constitutional Justices is especially evident if we compare it with the concept which the Court followed in its first year, in Ruling 31/1990.(XII.18) AB. Referred to as an expression of self-restraint in connection with an abstract constitutional interpretation, this Ruling however, already leads into the realm of jurisdictional activism. Ruling 16/1991.(IV.20) AB belongs to this circle as well, which Béla Pokol also assessed as the restraint of "political activism." In this Ruling—on presentation by chief activist Sólyom—the Court voluntarily declined the opportunity to exercise a preliminary examination of draft laws, which may be initiated by at least fifty Parliamentary representatives in cases where the final text before the final vote on a legislative proposal has not yet been formulated.

Naturally, behind the politically activist and passivist concepts that emerged in the decisions already discussed—at least in the initial periods—political division was doubtlessly palpable among the Justices as well. The most pliable demonstrations of this were the 1991-1992 constitutional interpretations in connection with the jurisdiction of the President of the Republic. Interestingly, this division did not appear in the decisions which the political players initiated also with the intent of forçing the Constitutional Court into a decision they can directly apply politically. Such was the case in 1995 with the Bokros package, as well as the 1997 motion in connection with the plebiscite. The only explanation for the reason these decisions were unanimous was the solidarity among the Justices that emerged in the course of the years, despite the obviously continued presence of differences in political concepts. (Beyond common interest, this was probably reinforced by the insecure status the political realm evoked as a result of not filling the vacant judicial seats, as well as additional negligences.) At the same time, disappearance of the political division did not represent either in the interpretation of the "Constitution nor in connection with expansion of the spheres of jurisdiction the unification of positions. One of the differences between the two kinds of activism is that while the first is proudly embraced by activist human rights fundamentalists, everyone tries to deny the latter. This is illustrated by Sólyom's *ars poetica*, articulated in his 1998 BUKSZ interview: "I am an activist by conviction, if we do not mean by activism that one trespasses his jurisdiction. Activism means that the Court upholds its decision even in borderline cases."[37]

Jurisdictional activism versus strict interpretation of competencies

Before we take a position in the question of whether Sólyom's Court was characteristic of extending beyond jurisdiction, it is worth analyzing the experience of the nine years from the perspective of interpretation of the more important decisions on competences as they are incorporated in the constitutional law and their jurisdictional-modification by the Court. We should like to state at the beginning that the jurisdictional activists are not differentiated from the passivists by the fact that the former interpret every jurisdiction broadly and the latter strictly, by and large. The self-restraint exercised with respect to certain jurisdictions, even in the case of the same Justice, does not preclude activism in relation to other legal rights. This was the case in the preliminary constitutional examination, from which the otherwise activist held Justices tried to absolve themselves.

Preliminary norm control and the process of legislation

As I have previously stated, the first Ruling 16/1991.(IV.20.) AB in connection with this that contained self-restraint, was presented by László Sólyom himself before the Court, and it was supported unanimously.[38] In the decision, which was brought as a result of the motion submitted by 52 opposition party Parliamentary representatives in opposition to the first draft of the compensation law which had not yet been voted upon, the Constitutional Justices denied the exercise of jurisdiction on the justification that as a result the Court would interfere in the process of legislation which had not yet been concluded. In the context of the justification, this interference remains a threat for as long as the final version of the legal proposition had not taken form; and this is from the moment of the completion of the vote on modification of the motion and before calling the final vote. In those times, it was in fact a matter of a moment because according to the House Rules one act was directly followed by another. The Constitutional Court's determination of cause therefore, in essence meant that it also became physically impossible to submit the preliminary motion for constitutional examination that satisfied the Court's requirements. The argument is entirely acceptable; it is a different question that as a result, the Constitutional Court denied exercise of its jurisdiction as embodied in a law currently in force; therefore, it was not simply a strict interpretation of jurisdiction, but rather, its *contra legem* interpretation.

Afterwards, in 1998, as if acknowledging the Court's exercise of self-restraint, Parliament amended the law on the Constitutional Court and abolished the possibility of preliminary constitutional review of legal proposals.[39] As a result, the institution of preliminary examination for constitutional compliance of recognized but not-yet-proclaimed laws, Parliamentary Rules and international agreements became restricted to review initiated by the President of the Republic and the Government.

The abstract interpretation of the Constitution as "advisory opinion"

As I have already mentioned, the initial understanding of the Constitutional Court with respect to the abstract interpretation of the Constitution was determined by the self-restrictive character of Ruling 31/1990.(XII.18) AB. At the time the Constitutional Justices unanimously rejected the motion by the Finance Minister in office, in which he asked for an "advisory opinion" on the constitutionality of various governmental ideas about raising the interest on long-term housing loans that were earlier transferred at a preferred rate. According to the Constitutional Court's justification, if they were to interpret the jurisdiction of their constitutional interpretation in the abstract sense, it could easily lead to a situation where the respective legislative bodies could ask for a "constitutional interpretation" before the creation of not only legislation, but also governmental moreover, ministerial decrees. This however, argued the Justices, would lead to the Constitutional Court's assuming legislative, moreover executive responsibility and—in direct opposition to the principles on government organizations embodied in the Constitution—would eventuate in a certain "Constitutional Court government."

At the same time in 1997, by way of the constitutional interpretation on the plebiscite, as discussed earlier, the Constitutional Court assumed the odium of Constitutional Court governance after all—again unanimously—because although through otherwise correct contextual decisions of legal standing, they had expanded their own jurisdiction to a seemingly almost unrecognizably broad base. In response to the questions raised by the ombudsman, within the framework of the abstract interpretation of the Constitution, they did in fact examine the specific decision of Parliament with respect to its call for a plebiscite, for which they did not otherwise have authority based on the regulations to date. On the other hand, with a view toward the future, they established this jurisdiction; moreover, they deleted a section from one of the regulations of the law in force on plebiscite, altering thereby the content of the legal regulation. The law on plebiscite made review by the Constitutional Court on the Parliamentary decision to reject the call for a plebiscite possible only if the rejection were "based on confirmation without a result." The Legislature's intent was completely evident: Parliament did not wish to give jurisdiction to the Constitutional Justices in cases where Parliament's negative decision is justified by a motion's unconstitutional or illegal status. How did the Constitutional Court "solve" the situation in this case? They deleted the words "based on confirmation without a result" from the text, making examination of their own jurisdiction unlimited in every instance of a rejection thereby.

What other than assuming the task of the Legislature can this be called, which the Justices in 1990 were still reluctant to undertake. If the Constitutional Justices, instead of placing outside legal force the law they reviewed and decreed unconstitutional and entrusting the Legislature with framing the new constitutional text, wrote the text themselves—even if it was by erasing parts of a sentence—they would have been no longer exercising negative but positive legislation, which is not in the power of any Constitutional Court in the world, nor can it be.

The constitutional complaint, as genuine legal remedy

The Hungarian Constitutional Court, charged with the most extensive authorization in the world on the issue of examining the jurisdiction of abstract constitutional compliance—in contrast to the German, Swiss, Spanish and Austrian partners—was not authorized from the beginning to review the constitutionality of concrete judicial and government administrative decisions, at least not without having to examine the constitutionality of the standard that served as a basis for the specific decision as well. This deficiency of the direct complaint in the Hungarian regulation, meant that the Constitutional Court complaint procedure codified in 1989 did not fulfill its actual function as a legal remedy. (Since this hybrid complaint-solution was no other than a motion for examination of abstract constitutional compliance in a specific matter, which had no effect on the solution to the given case whatsoever; the ratio of complaint did not exceed one percent of all submissions to the Constitutional Court.) Members of the Constitutional Court who professed an extended interpretation of jurisdiction already attempted to breathe life into the seemingly dead institution of constitutional law complaint in Ruling 57/1991. (XI.8) AB.

The Court, in a majority decision delivered by Tamás Lábady, determined in the case of a judicial procedure that was already legally in force and decisively defended paternity, that it conclusively forever divested a child from her/his right to personally intercede in her/his own behalf in clarifying the origin of her/his bloodlines; and that this resulted in infringement of the child's general individual rights. For this reason, the Constitutional Court determined the inapplicability of the regulation in violation of the Constitution in the matter under complaint and—in the parts of the legal regulation that were unconstitutional—once and for all eliminated the judicial judgments under attack; moreover, it ordered birth certificate data changed as a result of judgments that caused infringement of the law, to be reinstated to their original status. According to the justification, it was the only way the function of legal remedy to the constitutional law complaint could be made effective in a specific case; and as a result the right of minors for self-determination and self-identity guaranteed under the Constitution was also correctly positioned, that is, it provided opportunity that once they reached the age of adulthood, based on their own decision, they could personally initiate clarification of their family status and origin of their blood line. The justification attempts to also explain on what basis the Constitutional Court took the liberty to eliminate any kind of judicial judgment in the absence of any jurisdictional regulation with respect to this matter. The judicial argumentation interprets the absence of legal authority in that while the law on the Constitutional Court does not regulate its manner of legal procedure, in certain cases the manner of legal remedy for infringement of the law must be determined by the Constitutional Court itself. The ruling was met by stringent criticism both from the President of the Supreme Court, as well as representatives from the juridical community, stating that the Constitutional Court slipped onto the not to be permitted territory of legal enforcement, infringing thereby the jurisdiction of the Supreme Court to pass judgment and legal remedy.[40]

Dissenting opinions from the Constitutional Justices appeared not in connection with the judicial judgment but with the elimination of the legally regulated statutes that served as its basis. The majority opinion judged the statutes under attack in violation of the Constitution on the basis that judicial practice—adhering to the interpretation of the law by the Supreme Court—applied these with consistently unconstitutional attribution. According to the justification, the Constitutional Court has interpretive jurisdiction only with respect to the Constitution's provisions, and has no independent power to interpret law. (It is worth remembering this argument because a few years later, the same Justices' authentication of the interpretation of Constitutional conformity of laws created this selfsame non-existent jurisdiction.) For this reason, the Constitutional Court had to examine the constitutional complaint of text from the perspective of understanding and content under which understanding legal procedure applied it; that is, it had to compare the "extant law" with the content of the Constitution's provisions. It was the theory of "existant law" that Géza Kilényi in his dissenting opinion and Péter Schmidt in alliance with him found unacceptable. According to their position, the Constitutional Court has no jurisdiction to examine the constitutionality of the application of law in practice; furthermore, it cannot "punish" the

Legislature because of unconstitutional interpretation of the law on the part of organizations applying the law by deleting a statute that under correct interpretation does not otherwise violate the Constitution. Beyond extending the realm of jurisdiction, it also causes legal uncertainty if they consider the content of the legal regulation not according to the text as it appears in *Magyar Közlöny [Hungarian Official Gazette]* but as that which it "attributes to the permanent and unified application of the law in practice." According to the assumption of the two Constitutional Justices, the Constitutional Court would instead have the right to explain in the justification to its ruling which is that interpretation of a given measure in a legal regulation which when taken at its root does not allow them to consider the regulation unconstitutional. As we can see, it is here that the basis for the subsequent practice of the interpretation of constitutional conformity first appeared.

In connection with the conflict that emerged as a result of Ruling 57/1991.(XI.8.) AB between the Constitutional Court and the Supreme Court on the interpretation of the extension of the constitutional legality of complaint-jurisdiction, a solution offered itself in the possibility of a compromise which emerged in the course of the process of preliminary preparations for a new Constitution in 1995. Under the interpretation of the proposal formulated by the two courts and presented to the preliminary drafters of the Constitution, in matters of fundamental law the final decisions would continue to be brought by regular courts; at the same time, in the case of infringement of rights guaranteed under the Constitution, it would be possible to request the Constitutional Court to take a theoretical position, which would subsequently bind the decision of the regular court in consideration of the matter at the time of passing judgment. Although with this solution the Constitutional Court would not have been authorized to be the actual final adjudicator of complaint on constitutional legality, nevertheless, with its assessment of constitutionality the case would have the ability to exercise binding influence on the fate of a specific issue.[41] With interruption of the process of drafting a preliminary Constitution however, enactment of this proposal also failed. The two courts, even in the absence of codification, attempted a solution from among the existing legal requirements. In the case of the legally binding denial of registration by the court of a gay rights association called "The Rainbow Partnership for Gay Rights," the Supreme Court in the course of examining the petition turned to the Constitutional Court with a motion for constitutional interpretation. The Supreme Court in the end decided the case using the contents of the Constitutional Court's ruling.[42]

In the absence of a legislative solution, in the course of a complaint in a specific court case brought before the Constitutional Court in 1998, the Court again had to address the constitutional problem in connection with application of the legal requirements in successful constitutional complaint. Ruling 23/1998 (VI.9.) AB, again delivered by Tamás Lábady—referring in several instances to the 1991 decision—repeatedly emphasized that according to Paragraph 57 (5.) of the Constitution, constitutional complaint has the quality of an actual legal remedy and for this reason its effectiveness must bear legal consequences. These legal consequences must extend to the examination of the merits of a legally closed case, since this is the only means the principle element of the legal remedy can succeed; namely, medicament of the legal infringement. Although the unanimous decision determined that specifically regulating the constitutional complaint in terms of a legal remedy does not follow under duress from the Constitution's Paragraph 57.(5); however, if the Legislature opened up this opportunity, it is its constitutional responsibility to create such procedural regulations through the application of which the infringement of law in fact becomes remediable. If it should fail to do so, it is infracture of its right to legal remedy. From another perspective, failure to act also incurs infringement of the principles of legal security because while the ruling passed by the Constitutional Court in the complaint case is binding on the court holding the proceedings of the case, the procedural regulations through application of which the court would gain argument for the decision by the Constitutional Court are missing. Based on the foregoing, the Constitutional Court determined that Parliament committed an unconstitutional omission in proceedings other than that of criminal, by not regulating the procedural consequences of and not excluding application of the legal regulation determined unconstitutional in specific cases by the Constitutional Court.

The novelty of the 1998 ruling compared to that of 1991, is that the Constitutional Justices through this means—at least provisionally—refrained from abolishing the judicial judgment comprising the subject of the complaint. They were satisfied with setting a deadline for the Legislature to create the procedural regulations; they suspended to an even later time any proceedings directed to abolishing the court ruling, providing an opportunity thereby for the court itself to bring a decision based on appropriate procedural regulations compliant with the ruling of the Constitutional Court.[43] It must be noted, however, that the Constitutional Justices merely reclaimed as much of the activism they exhibited in the 1991 ruling, so as to not delete immediately the court judgment, but gave a chance to the Legislature, and as a result to the court, to come to a decision.

However, in the event of delay by the Legislature, deletion of the court decision by the Constitutional Court, like the sword of Damocles, continues to be suspended in the ruling, without the Court's feeling as a result the need to explain on the basis of what legal authority it would do such.

"Jurisdiction-alteration" on the part of the Constitutional Court

In this chapter there was discussion among the Court's various members on the extended or strict interpretation of the legally guaranteed jurisdiction of the Constitutional Court. As we have seen, the extended interpretation also frequently burst open the framework of the given jurisdiction, and in fact resulted in the institutionalization of a new sphere of authority. This is what László Sólyom named somewhat euphemistically "jurisdiction-alteration" enacted on the part of the Court.[44] Sólyom himself classifies application of the Italian institutional-ancestry of "extant law" to this position. He views transplantation of the exercise of "interpretation in conformity with the Constitution (Verfassungskonforme Auslegung)" imported from Germany, as its reverse; that is, on the practice that in order to interpret the legal regulations to be examined from the demands deduced from the Constitution, they determine an abstract "province of constitutional interpretation," embracing as a result all the unregulated power of the interpretation of legal regulations that are subject to everyone. A similar kind of extension of jurisdiction activism is evidenced by the Constitutional Court deleting the regulations that were to have come into force in the aforementioned Bokros-package in connection with social rights, where it attempted to compensate for the absence of its so-called "temporary action" institution, also existing in Germany; namely, suspension of the implementation of the constitutional compliance examination until a decision on the ruling.[45]

However, another new jurisdiction emerged in the wake of the two 1997 rulings discussed earlier, one of which (Ruling 4/1997.(I.22.)AB) extended the Constitutional Court's authorizations for retroactive constitutional examination of international agreements; the other, by deleting a section of the jurisdictional regulation, created the Court's supervisory competence of legal authority to reject in every instance the call for plebiscite (Ruling 52/1997.(X.14) AB).

An American author in a book on the Supreme Court that serves as a model for the United States and in many respects for the Hungarian Constitutional Court as well, attempted to group the eras of the Supreme Court based on the role of the Chief Justices.[46] He grouped the sixteen presidencies during the two hundred years into three categories. One is represented by the "super" Chief Justice, in the manner of Earl Warren who directed the Court; the second is associated with a weak-handed Chief Justice, as for example, Warren Burger, who was directed by the Court; finally the third, under the rule of William Rehnquist, still effective as of today, allows for several determinant individuals to direct the Court (for example, William Brennan). It can be of no doubt that the Hungarian Constitutional Court's Sólyom Era, can be compared to the Warren Court, in which the President of the Court strived to lead the defense of the Hungarian Constitution in a liberal activist direction, both with respect to the Constitution, as well as in the interpretation of jurisdiction.

III. What Next: Legislator vs. Court

In my opinion, the Hungarian Constitutional Court can be freed from all political implications only if it is moved nearer the ordinary courts instead of legislation in the system of the separation of powers.

Another alternative to the Constitutional Court's decision making in the sphere of fundamental human rights is that these cases should be tried by the ordinary courts as stipulated by §70/K of the constitution.

In contrast, the Hungarian ordinary courts have not exercised judicial review even though they are authorised to do so. In my opinion, it would, therefore, be the best solution to invest the Constitutional Court with jurisdiction as regards the real constitutional complaint. In those cases, the decisions would not be limited to cases where the regulations forming the basis of the challenged administrative or judicial decisions are deemed unconstitutional, and the activity of the Constitutional Court would come closer to the activity of the regular courts.

It is not only the need to strengthen jurisdiction in the field of fundamental human rights that would justify such a change but also the fact that to my mind, a Constitutional Court based primarily on abstract review will not stand the test in the long run. At the time of reviewing an old legal system existing in parallel with the new constitution, it was justified to set up a system like that and even complement it with the institution of popular action. However, once the old legal system is reconciled with the new Constitutional regulations and principles, the Hungarian system can also change over to a norm based on cases and controversies.

In the course of the preparation of the new constitution, a process, which started in 1995, and not yet finished, the possibility of a compromise arose, according to which cases concerning the fundamental rights would belong to the jurisdiction of the regular courts in the future as well. But in connection with rights guaranteed by the constitution, a theoretical decision could be requested from the Constitutional Court that would be binding for the ordinary court before which the case is pending. In this case, the Constitutional Court would not have the power to decide constitutional complaints in itself but would be able to influence the outcome of the particular cases in this respect.

Notes

1 Act XXXI of 1989 on the amendment of the Constitution.
2 Act XXXII of 1989 on the Constitutional Court.
3 Act LXXIV of 1994 on the amendment of the Constitution. By that time, however, the body consisted of only nine members, one of its former members having been elected judge of the International Court in The Hague. His post was not filled by the Parliament until 1996.
4 Decision no. 16/1991.
5 Decision no. 37/1992.
6 Decision no. 57/1991.
7 Decision no. 48/1991, and no. 36/1992.
8 The author of these lines is grateful to Fate for the opportunity to have served during the first six and a half years of what may be called in the most honorable sense of the word, revolutionary, as the immediate colleague of László Sólyom.
9 Decision 42/1998. (X.2.)AB.
10 Cf. "Farewell to Donáti Street. One on One with László Sólyom, departing President of the Constitutional Court" *Magyar Hírlap [Hungarian Newspaper daily]*. 1998 November 28.
11 cp. Balázs Weyer: Mértékmentés. Azt első magyar Alkotmánybíróság 1989-1998. (A Rescue of Measure: the first Hungarian Constitutional Court, 1989-1998.) *MaNcs*, 1998 November 26.
12 I am of this opinion despite the fact that Sólyom in an interview he gave explicitly refuted that the justices and with this himself and five others be categorized as liberal-conservative pairing.
13 Cf. A "nehéz eseteknél" a bíró erkölcsi felfogása jut szerephez. Sólyom Lászlóval, az Alkotmánybíróság elnökével Tóthe Gábor Attila beszélget. (In difficult cases" a judge's moral concepts comes into play. Attila Tóth Gábor in a conversation with the President of the Constitutional Court. (Henceforth, *Fundamentum* interview.) *Fundamentum*, 1997/1. Page 33.

14 It is interesting that in the theoretical sense, Sólyom's only true opponent in the beginning was Imre Vörös, who also held a similarly liberal view. Beyond politically inspired differences of opinion (cf. references to the Constitutional Court in the media debate between the President of the Republic and the Prime Minister), perhaps the effect of "two men on a horse" also played a part in that their conflicts intensified for no apparent reason, as a result of which Vörös, tiring of the secondary role, hardly called notice to himself with any significant opinion during the second phase of the cycle. It is in this way that issues that came up for discussion subsequently could remain free of liberal criticism. Some of these matters in which Sólyom's liberalism was not apparent—in 1996, the prohibition of minors to participate in gay rights organizations; in 1997, the Church's role in public education; in 1998 the decision on second abortions—became more obvious as time went on.

15 Perhaps the only small sign of this is the change in understanding among members of the political arena on the issue of the death penalty. Nine years after the Constitutional Court abolished the death penalty, the current Prime Minister of the FIDESZ government, at that time professing to be liberal, said about the death penalty that it "stands on traditional values," and considers the issue "worthy of serious debate and requiring serious debate." Interview with Prime Minister Viktor Orbán, Kossuth Rádio, 1998 December 23.

16 In defending his decision in the question of abortion, Sólyom's religious belief, according to which it would be an act significant on par only with the abolishment of slavery if he were to acknowledge the human status of a fetus. In the interview conducted with hom, Attila Tóth Gábor in response to his statement in this regard, acoording to which any reader of the decision would feel that the Constitutional Court would have preferred to prohibit abortion, Sólyom replied honestly: "A Constitutional Judge does not decree based on what he would prefer most to do." *Fundamentum* interview, page 38.

17 Decision 21/1996. (V.17.) AB. Cf. Gábor Halmai—Kim Lane Scheppele, "Constitutional Protection for Homosexuality in Hungary," *East European Human Rights Review*, 1997/1.

18 Decision 30/1992. (V.26) AB. Cf. For a detailed analysis, Gábor Halmai "Criminal Law as Means Against Racist Speech?," *Journal of Constitutional Law in Eastern and Central Europe 1997/1.*

19 Cf. the dissenting opinion of Ödön Tersztyánszky and János Zlinszky to decision 20/1997 (III.19.)

20 Cf. a detailed criticism of the decision by Gábor Halmai in Freedom of Expression in Hungary, *Journal of Constitutional Law in Eastern and Central Europe*, 1998. In criticism of the liberality of the decision it is also a matter for evaluation that the legislature—for whom the Constitutional Court subsequent to its elimination of the entire passage because of the sections it considered unconstitutional, gave over half a year as of October 31, 1997 to amend the regulation—missed the deadline, allowing the entire paragraph on censorship to default.

21 *Fundamentum* interview, page 42.

22 Ibid.

23 Ibid. Page 43.

24 For a more detailed account of the Constitutional Court's changes of procedure and its possible causes with respect to freedom of speech, cf. Gábor Halmai, A sajtószabadság határainak módosulásai. (Modifications in the Boundaries of Freedom of the Press); Mária Vásárhelyi- Gábor Halmai (editors), And 'A nyilvánosság rendszerváltása' (*The Public's Change of Regime),* Új Mandátum Könyvkiadó [New Mandate Book Publisher}, Budapest, 1998, pages 95-112.

25 Dworkin first described his view on this in *The New York Review of Books,* August 13, 1992 in his article, "The Center Holds!" Later, he expressed his concept on the moral interpretation of the Constitution in his book, *Freedom's Law,* which appeared in 1996.

26 Cf. Constitutional Judicial Practice. Béla Pokol: A magyar parlamentarizmus (*Hungarian Parliamentarism),* Cserépfalvi, Budapest, 1994. Chapter Five.

27 He stated in the *Fundamentum* interview that they could have designated as a separate right in the ruling [had they so desired], that a couple has the right to be recognized as such independent of their gender. Page 37.

28 Ibid. Page 32.

29 Rule 23/1994. (IV.29.) AB. Antecedent to the issue was that the Constitutional Court in its decision 3/1990. (III.4.) AB declared unconstitutional that regulation of the law on the right to vote, according to which a citizen who was out of the country on the day of election would have been impeded in voting. Prior to the first democratically held elections Parliament did not wish to amend the law, for this reason it preferred to insert into the Constitution the limitation declared as unconstitutional by the Constitutional Justices. Prior to the 1994 elections, some Hungarian diplomats serving abroad attacked this constitutional passage at the Constitutional Court; the Court however, determining that it was outside its jurisdiction despite the fact that for as long as the regulation appeared only in the law and not in the Constitution, it declared its contents unconstitutional.

30 *Fundamentum* interview, page 34. Despite the phrasing's double meaning, they did not attach a concurring nor a dissenting opinion to the ruling referenced above.

31 Ibid. Page 37.

32 Csilla Mihalicz: Interjú Sólyom Lászlóval, az Alkotmánybíróság volt elnökével. (Interview with László Sólyom, former President of the Constitutional Court), BUKSZ Winter, 1998, page 438.

33 Ibid. Page 442.

34 Read his criticism in more detail: Gábor Halmai, Mérsékelt, de egyértelmű szigorítás Az Alkotmánybíróság ellentmondásos abortusz-döntéséről. (Measured, But Unequivocal Restriction. On the Constitutional Court's Controversial Decision on Abortion), *Népszabadság* [daily newspaper], 1998 November 28.

35 Decision cp. 48/1991. (IX.26.) AB.

36 Rule 8/1992. (I.30) AB.

37 Rule 36/1992.(VI.10.) AB. Unfortunately, the President of the Constitutional Court, subsequent to the President of the Republic's continued reluctance to take steps in the particular matter based on the Court's abstract instructions, stepped out of character in one or two statements made to the press and left no doubt as to which half's conduct in his opinion was constitutionally unacceptable.

38 For a detailed criticism of the 1997 plebiscite decisions, see Gábor Halmai, Népszavazás és alkotmánybíráskodás. (Plebiscite and Constitutional Court Judicial Proceedings), *Beszélő,* 1998, March.

39 BUKSZ interview, page 437.

40 János Zlinszky, author of the single concurring opinion, was not of dissimilar position on the question of jurisdiction but partly as regards compensation [coupon system for nationalized private property].

41 Law I. 1998.

42 The President of the Supreme Court in a statement of protest cited Paragraph 70/K of the Constitution, according to which lawsuits in connection with violations of fundamental rights belong in the domain of regular courts. *HVG*, 1998 May 1.

43 The presenting Constitutional Justice, in his study that appeared in the same volume of the periodical, repeats the argument expounded in the justification on the ruling, according to which a solution for a actual legal remedy in the specific case was offered exclusively through the elimination of the judicial judgment. Tamás Lábady, "Constitutional Judicial Proceedings Seeking its Place," *Világosság [Lucidity]*, 1993/1, page 39.

The author of these lines similarly criticized the decision in several articles, as having been brought *contra legem* as a result of the extended interpretation of the jurisdiction of the Constitutional Court. cp. Gábor Halmai, Az alkotmányjogi panasz—jelen és jövendő? (The Constitutional Complaint—Present and Future?), *Bírák Lapja*, 1994./3-4, page 46.

At the same time I do not share the concept hidden behind the criticisms whereby based on the principle of division of power and the factor of the interpretation of the Constitutional Court's independent power it is to be avoided that the Body charged with preserving and protecting the Constitution become part of the Judicial Power. On the contrary, I think that the position of the Constitutional Court in the system of separation of powers ought to be moved by means of constitutional and legal correction of its jurisdiction toward the direction of the courts, rather than its proximity at present to the Legislature. See first, Gábor Halmai, Tiszta Amerika? Alkotmánybíráskodás és Alkotmánybíróság (Pure America? Constitutional Judicial Proceedings and the Constitutional Court), *Világosság [Lucidity]*, 1993/7; and later, Merre tovább Alkotmánybíróság? (Which Way Forward Constitutional Court?), *Beszélő [Narrator]*, 1996/4, page 80.

44 For an explanation of the agreement, see Gábor Halmai-Péter Paczolay, Az Alkotmánybíróság. (The Constitutional Court) In, Alkotmányos elvek és esetek. (Constitutional Principles and Cases), COLPI, 1996, page 40.

The fundamental justification for denial of the court registration was the fact that the founding regulations of the association did not exclude membership of those under 18 years of age. The motion, based on Article 67, Paragraph 1 of the Constitution, in connection with an interpretation of the state's tasks with respect to the physical, mental and moral development of children, asked for an answer to the question whether the right to association for those under 18 years of age, guaranteed under Article 63 Paragraph 1, could be restricted in a legal manner. For criticism of the Constitutional Court's ruling containing an affirmative reply, see the work referenced in Footnote 9.

45 Parliament did not fulfill its legislative responsibility as of the deadline, 1998 December 31, determined by the Constitutional Court, nor as of the writing of these lines (1999, April), in the consequence of which the court of course was unable to come to further decision.Cf. Ruling 43/1995. (VI.30.) AB and Ruling 44/1995 (VI.30.) AB.

46 Bernard Schwartz, *Decision: How the Supreme Court Decides Cases*. Oxford University Press, New York, 1996.

7. On Constitutional Social Rights*

RODOLFO ARANGO

Constitutional social rights have been obscured by the ideological discussion concerning liberal and economic, social and cultural human rights.[1] At a philosophical level, this question has been discussed mainly in relation to the difference between negative and positive rights[2] or to their correlative duties not to interfere and to provide services.[3] Some economists, sociologists and state theorists have taken the social rights question to concern the role of the state in the distribution of goods and services in a market economy[4] or the character of the state and its functions[5] in a global world.[6] In constitutional law, the matter of social rights has been discussed in relation to constitutional interpretation. E.g., it was maintained that such rights can be derived from the principle of equality.[7] All these perspectives are undoubtedly important, but insufficient. Now, it is time to analyse the concept of constitutional social rights from the perspective of legal theory.

The concept "constitutional social rights" refers to rights to the social minimum providing for basic needs.[8] Basic needs are represented by such basic goods as are necessary to lead a life with dignity and self-respect. Examples for these basic goods are food, clothes, shelter, minimal medical aid, minimal education, work and social security.

Constitutional social rights usually are not contained in written western constitutions.[9] Still, several constitutional courts[10] and constitutional and legal theorists[11] have recognised such a "*Recht auf Existenzminimum*" in the interpretation of the constitutional texts. We are therefore justified in asking whether there are any constitutional social rights in modern constitutional democracies despite the fact that these rights are not expressly written down in the constitution.

The central thesis of this paper is that the question whether there are any constitutional social rights in modern democratic constitutions could not be answered until now, because we lacked a developed concept of rights.[12] Such a concept of rights will be presented now.

1. A Developed Concept of Rights

A developed concept of rights[13] is composed of two parts. First, it is a three-level concept – as Alexy has pointed out with his distinction between rights as normative positions, reasons for rights and enforcement of rights.[14] Second, it states the criteria for its adequate use; that is, it offers a standard which permits the recognition of the violation of rights in every case. A developed concept of rights must be described as follows:

> "A right is a normative position based on valid and sufficient claims, whose unjustified non-recognition imminently harms the right-bearer".

Now, I describe the two parts of a developed concept of rights. Later I will show the relevance of such a concept to understand the concept of constitutional social rights.

a. The First Part of the Concept of Rights

According to the proposed concept, the concept of rights in its first part consists of three elements: 1) a normative position, 2) valid claims for this normative position, and 3) the sufficiency of the valid claims on which this normative position is based.

1) *Normative position* The identification of rights with normative positions within a normative system emphasises three aspects of rights: The "position" in which an individual is situated means that she or he (or it by animal rights) is in a concrete relation to others;[15] but this is not a simple factual position. It is a normative or deontic position within a normative system that bonds a second part – duty-bearer – commanding him to do or to abstain to do something. Considered as a normative position, a right is the outcome of an imputation of a deontic status to valid claims. Such a concept of rights resolves the problem of the ontological status of rights, i.e. the problem whether they exist as empirical facts or as metaphysical entities. It assumes that we – human beings – ourselves confer rights, not God or the Nature. The question is not *what* rights are, but *how* normative positions are to be grounded. This is done by the fulfilment of the validity criteria of claims.

2) *Valid claims* Normative positions are based on claims, that is, on reasons raised searching for recognition. Claims are different from

emotions, interests or needs.[16] Although emotions, interests and needs are the factual basis of claims, they are not sufficient conditions for grounding a normative position. Therefore, valid arguments are needed additionally. The insufficient differentiation between the anthropological or axiological levels on the one hand and the linguistic level on the other hand causes multiple errors in the foundation of rights. Emotions, interests or needs are turned into normative positions via the recognition of valid claims. This change of levels can only be warranted of constitutive rules[17] which make claims about emotions, interests, or needs valid claims. But, when is a claim valid? An example illustrates the point. A new-born baby cries when it has hunger or pain. These cries are the expression of emotions that we interpret as claims for protection. But why are these cries not the exercise of a right? To be so, they have to fit constitutive rules that turn the brute fact of the cry into an institutional fact (i.e. the exercise of a right). Claims – like reasons – need to be valid to be recognised as rights. They have to fit rules of validity to become normative facts.

As regards validity, we have to distinguish between moral and legal validity. Law and morality have different constitutive rules. Each one conduces to a different kind of rights. Much speculation is raised in philosophical and legal theory intending to clarify the relation between moral and legal validity.[18] What is clear, is that neither moral and legal rights nor moral and legal validity should be confused, if we hope to conserve the critical force of morality over law.[19] So, the cries of the baby can be seen as facts that, because of constitutive rules – like "parents must take care of their children" – turn out to be institutional facts. Constitutive rules give validity to the claim that is the base of a moral right of the baby[20] to receive the protection of the parents. Generally, civil statutes of western countries also recognise these claims by positive norms about legal rights, giving their representatives or the state itself the legal possibility to intervene in the defence of children. But moral and legal constitutive rules are not co-extensive. Claims can be transformed – through constitutive rules of moral speech – into moral rights, but remain extra-legal institutional facts. This is interesting in the case of human rights. Having moral character and being stated in international declarations and covenants, human rights press and urge their recognition as fundamental constitutional rights.[21]

3) *Valid and sufficient claims* We cannot exclude conflicts between valid claims of different individuals. Valid claims for normative positions ground prima facie rights, i.e. rights which are not definitive. When different valid claims conflict, there must be a rational resolution of the

conflict. Only valid claims that can be objectively recognised as sufficiently grounded can be seen as definitive rights and be enforceable by the judiciary. Thus, the principle of proportionality[22] (*Verhältnismäßigkeit-sprinzip*) becomes the heart of the constitutional balancing of conflicting valid claims for prima facie rights The sufficiency of a valid claim to justify a definitive right, can only be determined by balancing reasons for and against it in the concrete case. This is the very meaning of the deontological character of rights: it can only be delimited by balancing normative valid reasons and not pragmatic ones.[23]

This first part of the proposed concept is not enough for a complete description of the language of rights, specially positive rights. Positive rights raise different problems, the overcoming of which requires the complementation of the concept of rights. As Hart exhorted some time ago, a theory of rights is to be developed, which gives fully account of the use of the language of rights by constitutional lawyers.[24] The second part of the proposed concept of rights aims at partially fulfilling Harts' exhortation. It consists of criteria to evaluate the lawfulness of the consequences, which an unjustified non-recognition of valid and sufficiently grounded claims would have for an individual. This second part recovers the important criterion of the "direct individual detriment",[25] which was proposed by Bentham for the recognition of rights.

b. The Second Part of the Concept of Rights

The second part of the concept of rights consists of a two-parts criterion, which permits to recognise the violation of a right. The second part of the concept of rights immunises it against indetermination, and therefore against non-recognition of their violation. First I shall explain why the second part is necessary. After that I shall explain its functioning.

Is the second part of the concept of rights really necessary? The first part – right as normative position based on valid and sufficient claims – is insufficient because it does not take into account the peculiarity of positive rights and works with a very primitive conception of causality.[26]

Negative rights have duties of forbearance as correlatives, i.e. duties to abstain from doing something. This characteristic of negative rights has conduced some authors to affirm that they are absolute or universal, because they count for everybody in all circumstances. This structure of negative rights seems to facilitate the recognition of its violation. The violation of a right is seen as caused by a concrete act that presupposes the infringement of the duty to forbear. The occurrence of this act can be easily recognised and its illegality established. The practice of constitutional law shows, however, that conflicts between prima facie rights have to be taken into account. This requires one to accept that rights are not absolute but relative, and that the enforcement of rights is a more complex process of balancing than it was taken to be before.

Positive rights have duties to do (to serve, to provide) something as their correlatives. This raises the problem of knowing *how* a positive duty is to be fulfilled and *who* is obliged to fulfil it.[27] The indetermination of content and duty-bearer communicates to the recognition of the violation of positive rights. These difficulties lead some authors to the conclusion that positive rights are not really claim-rights[28] before they have been determined by the legislator. The violation of rights through action can be recognised more easily than the violation through omission. The omission of duties to do something can have different and multiple causes. Because of the indeterminateness of the bearer of the duty and the content of the right, it is not easy to establish the cause of a violation. A direct, simple causality between act and violation does not work in the establishment of an omission to fulfil a positive duty. Here we are confronted with the dilemma either to deny that the recognition of a violation of positive rights is reasonably possible, or to construct a hypothetical condition which makes this recognition possible. Because all rights are to be taken seriously, the construction of such a reasonable criterion must be attempted. How does the second part of a developed concept of rights function? The recognition of a violation of a positive right depends on the construction of objective conditions (criteria) which eliminate the indetermination of the content of the right (or its correlative duties) and of the duty-bearer. These conditions consist of 1) an imminent individual harm and 2) an unjustified non-recognition of a valid and sufficient claim.

1) *Imminent individual harm* The imminence of an individual harm is the key to solving the problem of the indetermination of the right's content. When a child is drowning in a pool it is clear which is the content of the duty of the adult that stays beside the swimming pool observing the situation. What is required to fulfil the right corresponds to that which has to be done to avoid its violation. In an urgent situation it is normally obvious what has to be done. Only in tragic cases, when acting implies to take the risk of an imminent harm, it could be said that an omission is not sufficient condition of a harmful consequence.

A developed concept of rights has a conceptual, necessary relation with the responsibility theory.[29] It shows that not only acts but also omissions are to be taken as sufficient causes of harm.[30]

When the mother does not nourish the baby and nobody notices it, the baby can die. But when the child gets no education, an ill person has no medical aid or an adult has no work, the imminence of the harm can be questioned. It could be said that this is a problem of personal responsibility or a problem of individual preferences that can not be objectively solved, because preferences are relative and incommensurable.[31] The central key to knowing when an omission is a sufficient condition of an individual harm, is the *urgency*[32] of the situation. To determine it we have to imagine what could happen if the basic need is not satisfied despite of imminence of the individual harm.

The problem of the determination of the right's content (and of the correlative duties) can be solved by abandoning an abstract theory of "basic goods" or of the ideal priority of liberty-rights.[33] These theories are always relative. It's important to notice that the urgency of a situation in which basic needs are not secured is an objective state of affairs.[34] It can be demonstrated with counterfactual arguments, which show what can happen when an individual basic need is not fulfilled immediately, that is, when a valid and sufficient claim is not recognised.[35]

The "urgency situation-thesis" solves the problem of the indetermination of the right's content. But is it able to solve the problem of indetermination of the duty-bearer, as well?

2) *Unjustified non-recognition of a valid and sufficient claim* The non-recognition of a valid and sufficient claim can be justified or unjustified. It may be justified, if a different person than the defendant is primarily obliged to fulfil the correlative duty. But the non-recognition of the right by the subsidiary obligated (e.g. the state) is unjustified, if the primarily obliged person fails to fulfil his duty, thus impeding the realisation of the positive right, and if this failure threatens imminently to harm the right-bearer.[36]

H. Shue has convincingly argued that multiple duties and multiple duty-bearers can correlate to a single right.[37] In the case of the moral right to life, it is clear that there is not only a correlative duty not to kill, but also the positive moral duty to assist persons whose life is endangered. This evidence complicates the recognition of the violation of the right by omission of the duty. The plurality of duty-bearers questions the existence of the right and makes difficult the recognition of its violation.

Modern law departs from a premise: the autonomy of the individual. This principle implies two other ones: the principle of

> personal responsibility and the principle of subsidiarity. According to the first, the individual is responsible for her destiny. According to the second principle, an individual has to be assisted when he is not able to take his own fate in his hands. The family, the national community or the human community are possible subsidiary duty-bearers in cases where the weight of the burdens is too great for an individual or a narrow group of persons (supererogatory duties).
> The problems raised by the existence of multiple duty-bearers – and multiple possible right's violators – can also be resolved by looking at the urgency of the situation. The urgency of the situation activates the principle of subsidiarity. If another primary duty-bearer – the family according to law or the state according to the national constitution – is not able to fulfil his positive duties, the recognition of the right cannot be simply denied. This raises the question whether non-recognition is justified or not.
>
> A non-recognition of a valid and sufficient claim is justified if one of the duty-bearers is not primarily obliged to fulfil it. This is the case, for example, if not the state, but the parents are primarily obliged to provide for the education of their children; also it is the case, when not the world community, but the national community according to the human rights declarations and covenants is obligated to provide for constitutional social rights. But if the primary duty-bearers are factually unable to fulfil their duties, the refusal to recognise and enforce a valid and sufficient claim can be unjustified. The continuance of this omission by the subsidiary obliged person is a sufficient condition to declare the violation of the right.

The conjunction of these two conditions, the imminence of the individual harm and the unjustified non-recognition of a valid and sufficient claim, resolves the problem of indetermination of the right. It may be seen as a consequentialist criterion of the violation of a right. They complement the first part of a developed concept of rights.

The consequentialist criterion, which the second part of the concept of right consists of, refers to the urgency of a situation and the necessity to act immediately to avoid an avoidable harm. This is an objective fact that, in accordance with the underlying constitutive rules of the constitutional order (e.g. principles of equality and of personal security), becomes an institutional legal fact (constitutional fundamental right). The objective quality that activates the potential duty of the state to act is determined by the urgency of the circumstances.

An example may help to clarify this urgency case. If the claims raised by the baby are no longer attended to by the parents or surrounding persons, it will certainly suffer harm. This is also the case with very old or disabled persons, as E. Tugendhat[38] has convincingly pointed out. Should they be left alone in circumstances where they cannot factually react against the threats of life or the infringement of the legal duties by their relatives or national community? For a Kantian[39] or Habermasian[40] perspective, these duties are moral burdens (supererogatory duties), not legal duties, unless the democratically elected legislator expressly incorporate them into a statute. Habermas – like Kant – dismisses the recourse to the social state because he fears the negative effects of state paternalism for individual autonomy. But in doing so, he sacrifices the baby and the old or ill persons who are temporally or definitively unable to take part in politics. More problematic in Habermas is that he also neglects the active role of constitutional law (specially through the judiciary) in the larger realisation of factual equality.

2. Relevance of a Developed Concept of Rights for the Concept of Constitutional Social Rights

The complementation of the first part of the concept of rights is unnecessary at the level of civil law or in societies without modern democratic constitutions. But, with the acceptance of the private ownership of the means of production, the existence of a modern constitutional democracy[41] and the economic interdependence in a global world,[42] an underdeveloped concept of rights is no more acceptable. The arguments given until now to reject an underdeveloped concept of rights have a moral character. But when the principle of equal treatment is introduced into the constitution, these arguments gain constitutional relevance.[43]

So we can formulate and justify a new concept of constitutional social rights, based on a developed concept of rights as is presented in this paper. This new concept is immunised against the objection that such rights are indeterminate. It also shows that valid and sufficient claims to a social minimum providing for basic needs can be objectively recognised, not from the Rawlsian theory of justice[44] *a priori* "basic goods", but from the perspective of a moderate rule-consequentialism.[45] This new concept of constitutional social rights says:

> "A person has a constitutional right to a social minimum providing for basic needs, when – despite the urgency of the situation – the state omits to act, harming him or her without constitutional justification".

This is an abstract concept of constitutional social rights which illustrates the logical structure[46] of all constitutional social rights, e.g. of the right to food, the right to health, the right to education, the right to shelter, the right to work and the right to social security.

Notes

* I would like to thank Dr. Carsten Heidemann for the correction of the English version of this paper. Of course, all remaining mistakes are mine.

1 D.D. Raphael (ed.), Political Philosophy and the Rights of Man, London 1967; F.A. Hayek, Law, Legislation and Liberty, Vol. 2 The Mirage of Social Justice, London/Henley 1976, p. 103; R. Nozick, Anarchy, State, and Utopia, Oxford 1974, preface ix.; P. Koller, The Scope of Human Rights, Rechtstheorie, Bh. 17 (1993), p.253 ff.

2 J. Feinberg, Social Philosophy, Englewood Cliffs, N.J. 1973, p. 59 ff.; Ch. Fried, Right and Wrong, Cambridge, Mass./London 1978, p. 110 ff.; G. Pincione, On The Relative Stringency of Negative and Positive Moral Duties, ARSP Bh. 68 (1998), p. 40 ff.

3 J. Feinberg, The Moral and Legal Responsibility of the Bad Samaritan, ARSP Bh. 23 (1985), p. 216 ff.; E. Garzón Valdés, Allgemeine positive Pflichten und ihre Begründung, in: Argentinische Rechtstheorie und Rechtsphilosophie heute, E. Bulygin und E. Garzón Valdés (ed.), Berlin, 1987, p. 167 ff.; H. Shue, Mediating Duties, Ethics 98 (1988), p. 688. J. Raz, The Morality of Freedom, Oxford 1986, p. 170 ff.; O. O'Neill, Towards Justice and Virtue, Cambridge 1996, p. 128 ff.

4 H. Ehmke, Wirtschaft und Verfassung, Karlsruhe 1961, p. 20, 43 ff. C. R. Sunstein, Free Markets and Social Justice, Oxford 1997, p. 3

5 E. Forsthoff (ed.), Rechtsstaatlichkeit und Sozialstaatlichkeit, Darmstadt 1968, p. 186 ff.; T. Campbell, The Left and Rights, London 1983, p. 193 ff.; P. Kolowski/A. Føllesdal (eds), Restructuring the Welfare State, Berlin/Heidelberg 1997.

6 O. O'Neill, Transnational Justice, in: D. Held (ed.), Political Theory Today, Oxford, 1991, p. 276-304; P. Koller, Der Geltungsbereich der Menschenrechte, in: S. Gosepath/G. Lohmann (eds.), Philosophie der Menschenrechte, Frankfurt a.M. 1998, p. 112 ff.

7 Against this thesis are R. Dworkin, Freedom's Law, Cambridge Mass. 1996, p. 36 and C.S. Sunstein, The Partial Constitution, Cambridge, Mass./London 1993, pp. 148-149. For the thesis are F.I. Michelman, On Protecting The Poor Through The Fourteenth Amendment, Harvard Law Review 83 (1969), p. 7 ff. and L. Tribe, American Constitutional Law (1978), p. 1079 ff.

8 In German constitutional law, this concept corresponds to the concept of '*Recht auf Existenzminimum*'. See R. Alexy, John Rawls, Theorie der Grundfreiheiten, in: Philosophische Gesellschaft Bad Homburg/Wilfried Hinsch (eds.), *Zum politischen Liberalismus*, Frankfurt a.M. 1997, p. 281.

9 L. M. Diez-Picazo/M.-C. Ponthoreau, The Constitutional Protection of Social Rights: Some Comparative Remarks, European University Institute, Florence 1991, p. 9, 10, 13, 17, 25.

10 In Germany: BVerfGE 40, 121 (133,134), BVerfGE 82, 60 I (85). In Switzerland: Schweizerisches Bundesgericht (Bger) Lausanne, II. Öffentliche Abteilung, 29. September 1995, EuGH 1996, p. 208. In Colombia: ST- 531 de 1992.

11 H.L.A. Hart, 'Bentham On Legal Rights', in: Oxford Essays in Jurisprudence, A.W.B. Simpson (ed.), Oxford 1973, p. 194-195 (see specially fn.90); F.I. Michelman, Welfare Rights in a Constitutional Democracy, Washington University Law Quarterly 3 (1979), p. 680; R. Alexy, Theorie der Grundrechte, 2nd Ed., Frankfurt a. M. 1994, p. 454 ff.; C.S. Nino, 'On Social Rights', in: A. Aarnio/ S.L. Paulson/O. Weinberger/G.H. v. Wright/D. Wyduckel (eds.), *Rechtsnorm und Rechtswirklichkeit*, Berlin 1993, p. 295; J. Rawls, Political Liberalism, New York 1993, pp. 228-230.

12 This insufficiency in the analysis of the language of rights was pointed out by H.L.A. Hart (fn. 11), p. 201. It is also surprising that theories of law of philosophers like Rawls or Habermas make use of an underdeveloped concept of rights. This handicap affects the system of rights that they propose to regulate social life under a legitimate positive law.

13 'A developed concept of rights' is one which reproduces entirely the language of rights – including not only negative, but also positive rights – and states the criteria for determining its violation.

14 R. Alexy (fn. 11), p. 164; R. Alexy, 'Individual Rights and Collective Goods', in: C.S. Nino, Rights, Aldershot et al. 1992, p.163.

15 'Rights are relationships, not things', I. M. Young, Justice and the Politics of Difference, Princenton 1990, S. 25; 'It [A right, R.A.] is a relationship and a social practice, and in both those essential aspects it is an expression of connectedness', F.I. Michelman, Justification and the Justifiability of Law in a Contradictory World, Nomos, Vol. XVIII, 1987, S. 91.

16 J. Habermas, Richtigkeit und Wahrheit DZPhil 46 (1998), S. 183.

17 J. Searle, The Construction of Social Reality, London 1995, pp. 43 ff., 48.

18 See for example J. Habermas, Between Facts and Norms, Cambridge 1996, p. 82-83; J. Habermas, The Inclusion of the Other, Cambridge, Mass. 1998, S. 191-192.

19 H.L.A. Hart, 'Positivism and the Separation of Law and Morals', in: H.L.A. Hart, Essays in Jurisprudence and Philosophy, Oxford 1983, p. 77.

20 N. MacCormick, 'Children's Rights: A Test for Theories of Right', in: C.S.Nino (fn. 14), p. 305.

21 R. Alexy, 'Die Institutionalisierung der Menschenrechte im demokratischen Verfassungsstaat', in: S. Gosepath/G. Lohmann (fn. 6), p. 254 ff.

22 R. Alexy (fn. 11), p. 100.

23 S. Freeman, 'Utilitarianism, Deontology, and the Priority of Right', *Philosophy and Public Affairs* 23 (1994), pp. 313, 348-349.

24 H.L.A. Hart (fn. 11), p. 201.

25 'If the statement that a law intends to benefit an individual and so confers a right upon him is interpreted as meaning no more than that its breach constitutes a direct individual detriment, then we have a criterion for determining when laws confer individual rights which avoids difficult inquiries into "actual" legislative intent', H.L.A. Hart (fn. 11), p. 188.

26 See Rodolfo Arango, Der Begriff der sozialen Grundrechte (chapter 3) (Ph.D. Dissertation, Kiel 1999).

27 E. Garzón Valdés (fn. 3), p. 168; H. Shue (fn.3), p. 688-689.

28 J. Feinberg, Rights, Justice, and the Bounds of Liberty, Princeton, N.J. 1980, p. 140 f.; E.-W. Böckenförde, 'Die sozialen Grundrechte im Verfassungsgefüge', in: E.-W. Böckenförde, Staat, Verfassung, Demokratie, 2nd Ed., Frankfurt a.M. 1992, p. 154.

29 The relation between the theory of risks and social rights is explored by K.-H. Ladeur in 'Social Risks, Welfare Rights and the Paradigm of Proceduralisation', European University Institute, Florence (Working Paper Law No. 95/2), San Domenico 1994; W. Lübbe, Verantwortung in komplexen kulturellen Prozessen, Freiburg/München 1998.

30 H.L.A. Hart/T. Honoré, *Causation in The Law*, 2nd Ed., Oxford, 1985, p. 33 ff.; C.S. Nino, *The Ethics of Human Rights*, Oxford 1991, p. 206.

31 K.J. Arrow, *Social Choice and Individual Values*, 2nd Ed., New Haven/London 1963, p. 9.

32 'Urgency is a two-faced notion. In moral arguments appeals to relative urgency seem to be appeals to a consensus about how much people care about certain benefits, protections, etc. The structure of such arguments is first to claim that everyone admits in his own case that, as, being protected against certain consequence is more important then enjoying some other benefit', T.M. Scanlon, 'Preference and Urgency', *The Journal of Philosophy* 19 (1975), p. 667.

33 J. Rawls, *A Theory of Justice*, Oxford/London/New York 1971, § 11, § 15, §16; J. Rawls (fn. 11), S. 178, 187.

34 'The claims of needs suggest a sense of urgency. [...] We can postpone listening to a piece of music or going to a party, but we can't postpone the consumption of water when thirsty, or food when hungry, or medical attention when ill', P. Dasgrupta, *An Inquiry into Well-Being and Destitution*, Oxford 1993, p. 39-40.

35 T.M. Scanlon explains the importance of empirical and counter-factual arguments by the recognition of rights: '[T]he view that there is a moral right of a certain sort is generally backed by something like the following: (i) An empirical claim about how individuals would behave or how institutions would work in the absence of this particular assignment of rights (claim-rights, liberties, etc). (ii) A claim that the result would be unacceptable. This claim will be based on valuation of consequences [...], taking into account also considerations of fairness and equality. (iii) A further empirical claim about how the envisaged assignment of rights will produce a different outcome', id., 'Rights, Goals, and Fairness', in: J. Waldron (ed.), *Theories of Rights*, 6th Ed., Oxford 1995, S. 146.

36 At the level of private law, the injured person can be compensated for the violation of her right. But, at the level of constitutional law, it is unreasonable to wait until the right is violated to be able to claim for its protection.

37 H. Shue, *Basic Rights*, Princeton, N.J. 1980, p. 60.

38 E. Tugendhat, *Vorlesungen über Ethik*, 3rd ed., Frankfurt a.M. 1995, p. 358.

39 A. Wildt, *Zum Verhältnis von Recht und Moral bei Kant*, ARSP 83 (1997), S. 159.

40 J. Habermas, *The Inclusion of the Other*, Cambridge, Mass. 1998, S. 191-192.

41 R. Dreier, 'Konstitutionalismus und Legalismus', in: *Rechtsstaat und Menschenwürde*, A.Kaufmann/E.-J. Mestmäcker/H.F. Zacher (eds.), Frankfurt a.M. 1988, S. 87; R. Alexy, *Grundrechte im demokratischen Verfassungsstaat* (manuscript 1993), S. 1; R. Dahl, *On Democracy*, New Haven/London 1998, S. 178, 180 ff.

42 H. Shue (fn. 3), p. 694; E. Tugendhat, *Die Kontroverse um die Menschenrechte*, in: S. Gosepath/G. Lohmann (fn. 6), p. 60.

43 '(O)nce it is allowed that there are some – any – constitutional rights beyond those literally spelled out in the constitutional text or rigorously deducible from it, then

importance just has to become a crucial constitutional variable. This is true partly because interests and claims often conflict or, in other words, rights entail costs, and the significant must take precedence over the petty. It is true also because some rights presuppose others, and some rights, even if not all, presuppose one's having passed beyond the struggle for existence and for the marks of minimum social respect', F. I. Michelman, (fn. 11), pp. 679-680.

44 For Rawls in *A Theory of Justice*, the distribution of wealth and income – which is presupposed in the recognition of constitutional social rights – is a matter of the second principle of justice [id., p. 61]. The matters regulated by the second principle of justice (including the social minimum) are matters under the competence of the legislator (id., p. 276). They do not form part of the constitutional text. 1993 Rawls modifies his position. In *Political Liberalism* he writes: '[...] a social minimum providing for the basic needs of all citizens is also an [constitutional] essential' (J. Rawls, *Political Liberalism*, New York 1993, p. 228-229). With the acceptance of a "social minimum for basic needs", Rawls embraces Frank I. Michelman's thesis that "constitutional social rights" are to be part of democratic constitutions (id., p. 236). Although Rawls does not make clear whether "a social minimum specified by basic needs" has to be taken as a constitutional fundamental right (see the critique of R. Alexy (fn. 8), p. 303). This irresolution in the characterisation of the constitutional essentials may be explained by the fact that Rawls does not offer a developed theory of rights. H.L.A. Hart correctly maintained that Rawls offers a controversial and incomplete theory of rights, id., 'Utilitarianism and Natural Rights' in: H.L.A. Hart (fn. 19), p. 194.

45 T.M. Scanlon (fn. 32); id., (fn. 35); A. Sen, 'Rights and Capabilities', in: *Morality and Objectivity*, T. Honderich (ed.), London et al. 1985, p. 130 ff.; A. Sen, Welfare Economics and Two Approaches to Rights', in: J. Casas/ F. Schneider (eds.), *Current Issues in Public Choice*, Cheltenham/Brookfield 1996, p. 23.

46 This logical structure is: $U \wedge P \rightarrow RisD$ (1), i.e. when an urgent situation (U) and legal and factual possibilities to act (P) are given, then the individual (i) has a right (R) against the state (s) to do (D) what's necessary to avoid the unconstitutional consequence. At the level of the theory of principles, the logical structure of the concept of constitutional social rights may be expressed as follows: (P1...Pm *P* Pn ... Px) $U \rightarrow RisD$ (2), i.e., when the principles P1 to Pm have priority over the principles Pn to Px at the urgent situation U, then the individual (i) has a right (R) against the state (s) to do (D) what's necessary to avoid the unconstitutional consequence. I thank Prof. Dr. Robert Alexy for the hint.

8. Modest Judicial Restraint

THEODORE M. BENDITT

Introduction

It is perhaps surprising that after more than 200 years there is substantial disagreement in the United States about the nature of its government and the role of its Constitution. One of the profound differences concerns the relationship between self-government and the liberties protected by the Constitution. According to one side, self-government is central. What the founders established, and what our government should be, is a system in which disputed issues are decided by popular decision-making processes, in particular, majority vote among elected representatives. There are limitations, expressed in the Constitution, on what the majority can do, but these are, and should be seen as, minimal and occasional. What this means to those on this side of the argument is that the language of the Constitution imposes, and should be seen as imposing, only minimal constraints. Strategies for reading the Constitution should therefore be adopted which are in accord with both the design and the proper nature of American government; such strategies will, of course, rule out expansive readings of the Constitution.

I will call the foregoing the "self-government-first" camp and contrast it with the "liberty-first" approach. This side believes that what is central, both in the design of our government and in what it should be, is the acknowledgement and protection of individual liberties. The primary purpose of government, in this view, is to protect people's liberties, and all agencies of government should be maximally bent toward this end.

In some ways there is no real debate between self-government-first and liberty-first—the American political system embraces both self-government and liberty, and everyone would agree that all genuine constitutional rights should be respected in the fashioning of laws and that within that framework popular decision-making processes are free to do whatever seems appropriate. What gives life to the debate is disagreement about the rights protected by the Constitution. Self-government-first argues either that a fair reading of the Constitution yields minimal limitations on legislative competence, or, more strongly, that the importance of self-government should *lead* us to read the abstract language of the

Constitution as containing only minimal limitations on legislative competence. Liberty-first argues, to the contrary, that a fair reading of the Constitution yields a more robust set of rights.

The difference between self-government-first and liberty-first about the extent of the limitations on popular decision-making naturally spills over to their views about the role of the courts. Every member of government, legislator as well as judge, has a duty to uphold the Constitution, which embraces the responsibility to ascertain what the Constitution requires. In the American political system, however, ultimate authority to determine what the Constitution embraces is assigned (except for the rare constitutional amendment) to the courts. Self-government-first and liberty-first, accordingly, have different ideas about how judges should determine what is embraced in the Constitution. That is, they have ideas not only about the substantive content of the Constitution, but about the techniques to be used in reading or interpreting the document.

There is another difference, of some importance, between self-government-first and liberty-first in resolving the foregoing issues, namely, the extent to which our ideas on these subjects are to be guided by the words of the Constitution itself, and the extent to which extra-constitutional considerations apply. This comprehends, on the one hand, such things as the specific intentions and expectations of the founders, and, on the other, ideas about the overall nature and character of American government.

Judicial Review and Constitutional Interpretation

All constitutional actors, including legislators, are obligated to the Constitution and thus must interpret it. Which agency, then, should have the authority to make final decisions about what the Constitution is to be taken to say or mean? Though history has assigned this prerogative to the courts, doubts have continually been raised about the legitimacy of this assignment on the ground that judicial review is undemocratic. The argument is that the essence, the very point, of democracy is that decisions are to be made by the majority (though sometimes a plurality) of citizens or their elected representatives. Disputed questions are to be submitted to the popular decision-making process, and the majority rules. To assign such issues to the courts, it is argued, is to ignore "the people," or the majority, and to substitute as decision-makers men and women who, though serious and able, are often not elected, if elected usually serve for very long terms, and are not even supposed to be responsive to public opinion. This is claimed to be counter to democracy, which is taken to be, at its heart, rule by the people as determined by majority voting.

This conception of democracy plays an important role in many views about how the Constitution is to be read. On the one hand, it is true that majoritarianism is clearly limited by provisions in the Bill of Rights. But partisans of self-government demand that these provisions be read in such a way as to minimize the limitations. Two different strategies have been employed toward this end. One is to embrace a theory of meaning that has the desired result (sometimes the desired outcome is at least part of the reason for embracing the particular theory of meaning, other times perhaps not). A different tack is simply to approach the issue directly—not via a theory of meaning, but by taking a view of the proper roles of legislatures and courts.

The former approach, including reading the Constitution in terms of plain meaning, original intent, or some versions of original understanding, has been much discussed in the literature and, though still maintained by numerous scholars and a large portion of the public, has, in my judgment, been properly exploded by Professor Dworkin and others; it will not be discussed here. The other approach, variously called judicial restraint or judicial deference, holds that courts should deliberately defer to the popular decision-making branch of government except in limited, and perhaps even exceptional, circumstances. This view, held by Judge Learned Hand, Justice Robert Jackson, and others, will be discussed later on.

Professor Dworkin

Professor Dworkin's views are fairly well known by now,[1] so a limited presentation of them should be adequate here. Dworkin's aim is to convince us that the Constitution is to be read in a certain way, that when the Constitution is read in this way we see that it protects a rather broad array of rights, that self-government-first rests on a mistaken idea of democracy, and that once this is seen the purported difficulties with judicial review disappear.

Central to Dworkin's approach is what he calls the moral reading of the Constitution, which is a multi-stage procedure. First, we note that some provisions of the Constitution (such as the equal protection and due process clauses) state or contain abstract moral principles.[2] Next, we refine our understanding of the principles by seeing how the Constitutional provisions have been applied in the past. Then, for each principle, we ascertain its "true ground" and determine what novel cases it extends to. Finally, we unify the entire document into a set of consistent and coherent moral principles (this is the notion of law as integrity), adjusting our understanding of each so that they will fit together. For example, the goal of the Due Process Clause is to protect basic liberty, which includes protecting individual privacy. An application of that principle to procreation yields a principle of procreative autonomy, which says that "A state may not curtail liberty, in order to protect an intrinsic value... when the decisions it forbids are matters of personal commitment on essentially religious issues... (FL, 101-2)." This general principle is formulated by looking for a morally justifiable idea that can be seen as underlying existing decisions we are inclined to accept; it is then extended, via the principle of integrity, to other cases that fall under it. Dworkin maintains that the moral reading is not a proposal he is offering, but is in fact, though largely unacknowledged, the approach that has long been taken to constitutional interpretation.[3]

Even though the moral reading requires exercises in moral judgment, there are, Professor Dworkin holds (and I agree) right answers to moral/constitutional questions. The argument (or at least an argument) for there being right answers is that each of us who puts forward an answer thinks it better than the alternatives, which amounts to thinking it right; no one can think his position better than another and at the same time think an alternative equally good. This is so even though one might acknowledge that his or her own answer might not be correct, and might refrain, on grounds of humility or lack of confidence, from declaring it to be "the right answer." Nor is the notion defeated by the fact that, for some purposes, such as constructing public institutions, one may step outside the framework of her or his own beliefs and adopt, for that purpose, a point of view that recognizes that competing answers exist (one of which *might* be correct).[4]

The moral reading of the Constitution, together with there being right answers to constitutional issues, leads to a position quite contrary to the self-government-first approach, for it yields a wide array of constitutional limits on popular decision-making. From this perspective, therefore, to favor a greater role for popular decision-making is to recommend *ignoring* certain rights fairly embraced by the language of the Constitution. One thing that this makes clear, according to Dworkin, is that judicial review is not the issue. The moral reading of the Constitution is incumbent on *all* officials, legislators as well as judges.

> The moral reading... is not a theory about who must ask these questions, or about whose answer must be taken as authoritative... What shall we say about the remaining questions, the institutional questions the moral reading

> does not reach? I see no alternative but to use a result-driven rather than a procedure-driven standard for deciding them. The best institutional structure is the one best calculated to produce the best answers to the essentially moral questions of what the democratic conditions actually are... (FL, 34).

There are, Dworkin believes, extra-constitutional reasons for assigning this task to the courts, and in any event our history has so assigned it.

But what of the argument from democracy—the worry that assigning final authority to make these determinations to the courts is antimajoritarian and thus antidemocratic? Dworkin believes that this concern rests on an incorrect view of what democracy is; it is not, he holds, to be equated simply with popular decision-making, but rather with popular decision-making that meets certain conditions. Majority rule, he argues, has no moral standing in itself. To be sure, it is a way of getting things decided, but its *value* consists in a majority decision being a genuine expression of what the community thinks, and it cannot do this unless all are included, and on equal terms. This, then, is what constitutional limitations on popular decision-making are all about—the rights that must be recognized if we are all to be moral members of the community (FL, 21-6). In the case of abortion, for example, Dworkin believes that to force on a woman the community's opinion about the intrinsic value of human life is to fail to treat her with equal concern and respect (FL, 98-9); to do this is to fail to regard her as a full member in the moral community and thereby fails to fulfill the conditions that make democratic decisions justifiable and obligatory. Democracy is popular decision-making subject to certain conditions (which Dworkin calls the democratic conditions), and if those conditions are not met, "there can be no objection, *in the name of democracy*, to other procedures that protect and respect them better" (FL, 17; emphasis added).

Identifying Constitutional Rights

While many constitutional issues involve the application of an acknowledged right to new circumstances, or at least to a new statute, on occasion the principle a court relies on has never been previously acknowledged, at least explicitly and officially. Critics see this as creating new rights; defenders see it as identifying rights that are in fact "in" the Constitution. Even granting, however, that such rights are in the Constitution, the fact is that they have never before been acknowledged, explicitly and officially (though it will sometimes be claimed, perhaps reasonably, that there are past cases, now seen as precedents, that have implicitly been decided on the basis of such principles).

What are the bases for recognizing constitutional rights that have not previously been overtly acknowledged. Even though this should not be regarded as the creation of new rights, we need some idea about when it is appropriate to recognize previously unrecognized constitutional rights. One possibility is to say that we don't need any special bases—all rights that are in the Constitution are rights we are entitled to, and we are entitled to them as soon as we are satisfied that they are in the Constitution.

Consider the recognition of the right to privacy and its extension to abortion:

> In the important 1965 case of *Griswold v. Connecticut*... the Court decided that a state may not prohibit the sale of contraceptives to married persons, and in later cases it extended the ruling to unmarried persons as well... Justice Blackmun [in *Roe v. Wade*] cannot be charged with erring in treating *Griswold* as a precedent he was obliged to respect. But once one accepts that case as good law, then it follows that women do have a constitutional right to privacy that in principle includes the decision not only whether to beget children but whether to bear them. *Griswold* and the other privacy decisions can be justified only on the presumption that decisions affecting marriage and childbirth are so intimate and personal that people must in principle be allowed to make these decisions for themselves, consulting their own preferences and convictions, rather than having society impose its collective decision on them. (LD, 106)

Professor Dworkin says "it follows" from *Griswold*'s holding that the right of privacy applies to contraception that it also applies to abortion. In what way does it follow? If it can at all be said to follow, it does so as a matter of moral judgment, by seeing the ideas underlying the right of privacy as also embracing abortion. But it is possible, as a logical matter, to see the point of the right of privacy differently, or to see something about abortion that takes it out of the class of cases in which individual privacy is important, or to believe that privacy is not the dominant value in the abortion situation. Even if the determination that the right of privacy extends to abortion is morally correct, it still requires an independent exercise of moral judgment—no less than the initial determination that there is constitutional right of privacy required moral judgment.

Justice Blackmun had a decision to make: either the right to privacy embraces abortions or it does not; one answer is right and the other is not. He had an opinion on the matter, but so did others, and the right answer does not certify itself. The institutional response (what the Supreme Court would hold, as opposed to what Justice Blackmun believed) was going to be decided by a vote in which the majority on the court would prevail. Should Justice Blackmun (and the other justices) have consulted only his own moral sense (including the way in which, as he saw it, certain moral principles undergird existing law)? This is, I believe, what Professor Dworkin recommends. The claim of those advocating judicial restraint, on the other hand, is that judges need to consult more than their own moral evaluations, however careful and well informed they are. This is, of course, an issue of continuing concern, going beyond the abortion decisions, for the moral reading of the Constitution makes it extraordinarily likely that there are still other rights buried in the abstract language of the great clauses of the document.

Presumption of Constitutionality

As pointed out above, some constitutional issues involve recognizing rights that have not previously been recognized. All constitutional issues, however, involve deciding whether a right, whether newly or previously recognized, applies in the case at hand. In dealing with such issues our courts have steadfastly taken the position that legislation is presumed to be constitutional. The presumption is explained in the following excerpt from *Parham v. Hughes*, a 1979 Supreme Court decision dealing with a challenge to a Georgia law:

> State laws are generally entitled to a presumption of validity against attack under the Equal Protection Clause. . . Legislatures have wide discretion in passing laws that have the inevitable effect of treating some people differently from others, and legislative classifications are valid unless they bear no rational relationship to a permissible state objective. . . Not all legislation, however, is entitled to the same presumption of validity. The presumption is not present when a State has enacted legislation whose purpose or effect is to create classes based upon racial criteria, since racial classifications, in a constitutional sense, are inherently "suspect." . . And the presumption of statutory validity may also be undermined when a State has enacted legislation creating classes based upon certain other immutable human attributes. . . In the absence of invidious discrimination, however, a court is not free under the aegis of the Equal Protection Clause to substitute its judgment for the will of the people of a State as expressed in the laws passed by their popularly elected legislatures. "The Constitution presumes that, absent some reason to infer antipathy, even improvident decisions will eventually be rectified by the democratic process and that judicial intervention is generally unwarranted no matter how unwisely we may think a political branch has acted." . . . The threshold question, therefore, is

> whether the Georgia statute is invidiously discriminatory. If it is not, it is entitled to a presumption of validity and will be upheld "unless the varying treatment of different groups of persons is so unrelated to the achievement of any combination of legitimate purposes that we can only conclude that the legislature's actions were irrational."[5]

Of course, the same applies to the acts of the federal legislature. The Court in *Parham* was presented two classifications alleged to be problematic. One, a distinction between legitimate and illegitimate children, was acknowledged to be "suspect," but the Court observed that the basis for regarding it as suspect was not present in the statute being challenged. The other, a distinction based on gender, was held to be a legitimate distinction in the case being considered. Having decided that no fundamental rights were at issue in the case, the Court went on to say that the statute was entitled to a presumption of constitutionality, meaning that it was to be held valid unless irrational.

The rationality test is, Professor Dworkin observes, "a very weak restriction" (LD, 104)—though it should be noted that its being weak is just another way of saying that there is a presumption that legislation is constitutional. But why is it weak? Why, given a court's concern to protect people's rights, does it presume, at least when it is satisfied that no fundamental rights are at risk, that a statute is constitutional, rather than undertake its own examination? It is not, after all, as if there are *no* rights involved. Why should courts leave some rights to the mercies of legislatures, even though they might, based on their own moral readings, see matters differently? Putting the matter more strongly, when a court refuses to examine a statute on the basis of a presumption of constitutionality, it is, or at least may be, refusing to recognize a right that one of the parties has *so that the legislature will have the final word on the matter.* The only alternative to this would be for the court to decide *all* such cases, on the basis of its own moral reading—that is, to apply the principles it finds in the Constitution *all the way down.*

If we agree that courts do not and should not apply constitutional principles all the way down (this will be discussed further on), the question is where the line should be drawn between the sorts of cases in which a court should substitute its judgments for a legislature's, and those in which it should not. In answering this, however, it is important to be aware of another dimension of the matter, for we must notice that in determining what *our* rights are, the courts are at the same time determining the bounds of *their own* power, as well as that of the legislatures. When the courts find that a right not heretofore regarded as fundamental is indeed fundamental, or that a fundamental right is at risk in a type of situation not previously thought to put it at risk, they at the same time discover that the extent of their power is greater than it had been thought to be. Thus, in establishing, or in re-examining, the line between cases in which there are fundamental rights needing protection and cases in which there are not, it is very important to observe that below the cut-off, *wherever it is*, lies the prerogative of the popular decision-making bodies—the area in which the presumption of constitutionality applies. Accordingly, any decision as to the applicability of our fundamental rights is at the same time a decision as to the division of authority and power between courts and legislatures.

The notion that the courts are more likely to get right answers about fundamental rights is not an adequate response to the issue of which agency should decide questions about rights (i.e., about where to draw the line), for, if the courts are more likely to get right answers, this will be true no less for the application than for the identification of fundamental rights, so long as moral principles are in play. To answer the question, courts must take a view as to the proper role of courts vis-à-vis legislatures; they must take a view about the allocation of power in our legal/political system.

In drawing this line, courts can take one of two approaches. First, they can make decisions solely on the basis of considerations internal to the relevant clauses of the Constitution, perhaps by giving them a moral reading. Second, they can include in their thinking institutional considerations regarding the role of popular decision-making bodies in our governmental structure; that is, they can, in deciding what is fundamental within our institutional structure, entertain some combination (weighing) of moral considerations and political (institutional/structural) considerations. Professor Dworkin, as I read him, argues for the first approach. Those favoring some notion of judicial restraint, I believe, can be taken to favor something like the second approach. They believe that independent of the considerations that are involved in the moral reading, there are structural considerations that have weight in their own right and that need to be brought to bear (somehow) in deciding what the courts will hold our fundamental rights to be, and which must be weighed against judges' substantive views about rights. This in implicit in Justice Rehnquist's 1984 statement of the presumption of constitutionality: "the presumption of constitutionality which attaches to every Act of Congress is not merely a factor to be considered in evaluating success on the merits, but an equity to be considered in favor of applicants in balancing hardships."[6]

Presumption of Constitutionality: The Role of Compromise

Part of the rationale for the presumption of constitutionality is to be found in the political importance of compromise, including compromise of principle. Consider the case of *Fullilove v. Klutznick*, decided in 1980. In 1977 Congress passed the Public Works Employment Act which included a Minority Business Enterprise provision which said that at least 10% of federal funds granted for public works projects must be used to procure services or supplies from businesses owned by minorities. Congress passed the law after extensive hearings showing, to its satisfaction, that traditional procurement practices in the building trades perpetuated the effects of past discrimination. The Supreme Court held that this was a legitimate legislative goal and that the MBE provision was a legitimate means to achieving the objective. It seemed important to Chief Justice Burger, who wrote the opinion for the Court, that "Congress have necessary latitude to try new techniques" even though they "may press the outer limits of congressional authority." Chief Justice Burger's opinion makes it clear that the Court is giving Congress a lot of leeway to deal with its problem: "Petitioners have mounted a facial challenge to a program developed by the politically responsive branches of Government. For its part, the Congress must proceed only with programs narrowly tailored to achieve its objectives, subject to continuing evaluation and reassessment; administration of the programs must be vigilant and flexible; and, when such a program comes under judicial review, courts must be satisfied that the legislative objectives and projected administration give reasonable assurance that the program will function within constitutional limitations." In support of this judicial attitude the opinion quotes from Justice Robert Jackson:

> The Supreme Court can maintain itself and succeed in its tasks only if the counsels of self-restraint urged most earnestly by members of the Court itself are humbly and faithfully heeded. After the forces of conservatism and liberalism, of radicalism and reaction, of emotion and of self-interest are all caught up in the legislative process and averaged and come to rest in some compromise measure such as the Missouri Compromise, the N.R.A., the A.A.A., a minimum wage law, or some other legislative policy, a decision striking it down closes an area of compromise in which conflicts have actually, if only temporarily, been composed. Each such decision takes away from our democratic federalism another of its defenses against domestic order and violence. The vice of judicial supremacy, as exerted for ninety years in the field of policy, has been its progressive closing of the avenues to peaceful and democratic conciliation of our social and economic conflicts.[7]

It is clear that the approach in *Fullilove* is responsive to the Court's view of both the political need for legislative compromise and its appreciation of the role and prerogatives of Congress is dealing with the country's problems. The Court did not attempt to make its own finding about the present effects of past discrimination; it accepted that Congress had in good faith made such a finding (in later cases the Court refused to accept the bare claim, in the absence of an appropriate factfinding procedure, of the need to remediate the continuing effects of past discrimination). And it accepted the legislative determination, at least on a provisional and experimental basis, that racial and ethnic distinctions were a reasonable way to address the problems. It is perhaps easy to read the outcome of *Fullilove* simply as a liberal decision (though notice the votes cast by various justices) on preferential treatment. I am more inclined, though, to take it at its word—as a decision that confronts not only the substance of the Equal Protection Clause but the relative responsibilities of courts and Congress in our constitutional structure. One does not have to agree that the Court got it right to agree that the structural issue has something (indeed, much) to do with the outcome.[8]

What are Principles?

If there is a case for a presumption of constitutionality in cases involving the application of recognized constitutional rights to new circumstances or new statutes, what about the more visible and often notorious cases in which courts recognize rights that have not previously been recognized, cases in which the role of principle is most in evidence?

What are principles? Sometimes we speak of "general principles," such as that one should keep promises, not harm others, be considerate, and help others. In a similar vein are some of the principles that Professor Dworkin discussed in his earlier writings—that no one should profit from his own wrongdoing. that manufacturers of potentially dangerous items have special obligations of care, and others. These "general" principles identify considerations that are always relevant but not always decisive. They are considerations that argue for or against some course of action or outcome. They are weighed against one another, and their weights are variable, depending on the circumstances—in a given situation one principle might carry more weight than another, and in a different the reverse may be true, though there will be something else we can point to that explains the difference. Principles thus work in groups.

This is not the notion of principle that Dworkin advances in later writings, where it is found instead in the ideas of "acting on principle," "having principles," "being principled," having convictions, and standing for something. Principles as employed in these contexts are matters of pressing moral importance, not merely considerations having some degree of weight that are balanced against others. Weighing and balancing are still in the picture, but these considerations are very weighty and can't easily be overridden, and some might be so important that nothing can be taken to override them.

There are what I will call subjective and objective aspects of the foregoing notion of principle. If we suppose that there are objective truths in morality, then principles have whatever weight they (objectively) have and we can be correct or incorrect in our assessment of this. On the other hand, a person can *treat* a moral consideration as a principle—i.e., treat it as very important, perhaps so important that nothing will be taken to override it. A person who does this may be correct or incorrect in so regarding a moral consideration; if incorrect, she or he will be treating as a principle something that is not.

There is also a situation-relative use of the idea of principle. Something might not be of substantial moral importance in itself, but might become important in a given set of circumstances, and a person who insists on it, especially when it might be safer not to do so, is often said to be acting on principle or standing for some principle. For example, a person who takes an unpopular stand on an issue (say, in a faculty meeting or some other public/political setting) might be said to be standing on principle, even if what is at stake is not at the level of urgency of life and death, liberty, and basic human dignity.

Professor Dworkin's philosophy of law employs the objective (but non-situation-relative) notion of principle. He finds the idea that there are moral principles of this sort embedded in the Constitution very exciting, saying that their scope is "breathtaking" (FL, 73) and that "the American ideal of government not only under law but under principle as well is the most important contribution our history have given to political theory" (FL, 6). It is important to observe that the principles Dworkin calls upon have to do with individual rights: "Arguments of principle attempt to justify a political decision that benefits some person or group by showing that the person or group has a right to the benefit" (TRS, 294). (Actually, it is unclear whether Dworkin thinks that all principles involve rights, or only a subclass of principles that might be called fundamental; it is likewise unclear whether the claim that arguments of principle involve rights is intended to be stipulative.) Moral principles of this sort hardly seem to admit of compromise. Is there, though, a place for compromise? And if so, is there a place for a presumption of constitutionality when courts consider challenges to laws reflecting such compromises?

Compromises of Principles

Many legislative results can only be seen as contests among different interests, where principle is hard to find. Professor Dworkin expresses doubt about the role of principle in the legislative arena, saying that "when political controversies are decided by legislatures or other elected officials, the decision is likely to be guided by what most people want" (FL, 344), rather than on the basis of principle. But there are many publicly discussed issues, such as public support for private education, abortion, preferential treatment, and the death penalty, in which matters of principle seem quite prominent. It is hard to see the abortion issue as being decided by what people *want* as opposed to what they *think right*; it is hard to see what individual interests would be promoted by one outcome or another. It is easy, though, to see the push and shove of controversy as reflecting people's principles, and to regard the public and the legislative debates as involving only, or at least primarily, principles. Nevertheless, legislative results on such matters might involve compromise, each side getting something that *its* principles favor. If this is the case, then, I suggest, there is an argument for a presumption of constitutionality.

Suppose, for argument's sake, that the members of a court are inclined to accept, on principle, the idea that anti-abortion statutes are constitutional (contrary to what Professor Dworkin believes the Constitution requires), and that their own basis for thinking them right makes no exception for rape and incest. Suppose a statute that comes to them makes exceptions for rape and incest and that in the legislature there were thorough arguments of principle on all sides of the issue, both as to whether abortion should be legal at all and whether it should be legal in cases involving rape or incest. Suppose, finally, that a bill comes forward that compromises some of the issues,[9] and it passes. What is the proper course for judges who themselves are inclined to believe that the exceptions are inconsistent, in principle, with the principles they find persuasive against abortion? (It is irrelevant that there might be principles that justify both the general anti-abortion statute and the exceptions; the point is that the judges considering the case don't believe there are such principles.) Professor Dworkin, as I understand him, believes the responsibility of judges is to act on what they themselves think are the controlling moral/constitutional principles, regardless of what any in the legislature think. But why, given the history of popular deliberations on the issue, should the judges not at least think about whether the legislative compromise ought to be respected, even if they disagree with it? That does not preclude them, if they think it important enough, from rejecting the compromise.

In *Law's Empire* Professor Dworkin argues against compromise, specifically, a form of compromise that yields what he calls "checkerboard" laws. A difference of opinion about the justice of strict liability laws might be accommodated by a law imposing strict liability on the manufacturers of automobiles but not washing machines. Such a compromise, even though each side might favor it as yielding more justice (or less injustice) than one of the alternatives (though less than another), is nevertheless unacceptable because it "treat[s] people differently when no principle can justify the distinction" (LE, 180). The injustice in this is that "it affirms for some people a principle it denies to others" (LE, 183); such an inconsistency of principle constitutes a lack of integrity. This defect does not exist, though, where a distinction reflects a prioritization of principles. "Would you not think a statute prohibiting abortion except in the case of rape distinctly better than a statute prohibiting abortion except to women born in one specified decade in each century? . . . You see the first of these statutes as a solution that gives effect to two recognizable principles of justice, ordered in a certain way, even though you reject one of the principles" (LE, 183). Statutes reflecting prioritization of principle do not suffer from the defect of incoherence of principle.

So Professor Dworkin is not opposed, on grounds of principle, to suitable compromises, namely, those reflecting a prioritization of principles. It would seem, then, that he is not opposed, on grounds of principle, to certain legislative compromises. The issue, then, is how judges who do not agree with the prioritization should respond to such a legislative compromise. I suggest that, in cases of this sort, it would be appropriate for courts to give some weight to the very fact that the law being challenged reflects a compromise of principles that has been reached by a legislature. In a suggestive remark (in a footnote) Professor Dworkin entertains the thought that checkerboard solutions "can be justified, if at all, only on the grounds of a fair allocation of political power between different moral parties" (LE, 435). Though Professor Dworkin does not commit himself in this remark to the idea that checkerboard solutions might actually be justifiable, the notion of the allocation of political power as a possible basis for justification is worth paying attention to. I propose borrowing the suggestion that, not checkerboard laws, but compromises of principle reached by appropriate moral parties (legislatures) have a claim on other moral parties (courts) that have to deal with them in some way. Specifically, I think it appropriate that courts presume the constitutionality of such laws, understanding that their own role demands that they overturn them if they are not merely different from what the judges might have decided on their own, but are beyond acceptability.

These thoughts can be extended, finally, to cases in which, rather than a prioritization of controversial principles, there is instead a debate over principles and the resulting statute reflects only one of the competing principles. Consider the case of *Pierce v. Society of Sisters,*[10] concerning a 1922 Oregon law requiring all children to attend public schools, in which the Supreme Court held that one of our essential liberties, protected by the Due Process Clause of the 14th Amendment, is the right to control the education of our children. The issue presented in the case is certainly one of principle; whatever interests are involved are clearly not as powerful as the principles that motivate people on this question, and even if they are, they are likely to be strongest on the part of those favoring private education. (Of course, there are the interests of the private schools themselves, which stand to lose students and very likely go out of business; it is of no little interest that the case was brought by such a school, which was allowed to make its case on the basis of the (purported) rights of the students who attended the school.) Surely those who voted for the law (there was a referendum) were aware that many people held the view that they have the right to control the education of their own children. And surely those favoring private education were aware that many people held views such as that society would be better if education were the same for all, or that private education promotes class divisions, or unacceptable inequality, or whatever. And surely there was a debate, probably robust (since there was a referendum), on the issue. In light of this, what is the proper course for judges? Should they, as Professor Dworkin maintains, act on what they themselves think are the controlling moral/constitutional principles, regardless of what the majority who voted for the law think? But, once again, why, given the history of popular deliberations about the issue, should the judges not at least think about whether the majority view about the principles ought to be respected, even if the judges disagree with it? Once again, that does not preclude them, if they think it important enough, from deciding against the majority. Respecting a presumption of constitutionality is not a counsel of complete deference to the legislative branch. What is does is raise the bar; it tells judges that it is only in especially egregious cases that they ought to substitute their own idea of the determinative principles for those adopted by other constitutionally recognized agencies.

Reasons for a Presumption of Constitutionality

The Value of Compromise

Justice Jackson, referred to earlier, speaks of democracy as a process of "composing oppositions." "The measure of success of a democratic system," he observes, "is found in the degree to which its elections really reflect rising discontent before it becomes unmanageable, by which government responds to it with timely redress. . . . It must be remembered that our democratic system can succeed in composing oppositions only if the effort is made while the separation is not extreme."[11] Indeed, Jackson maintains, historically the Supreme Court does not have a very good record when it comes to overruling the "popular branches," in the sense that "In no major conflict with the representative branches on any question of social or economic policy has time vindicated the Court."[12] Many would dispute this remark with respect to a number of the Supreme Court's decisions since Jackson wrote, but that does not upset the point that courts do well to advert to the composing of oppositions that are frequently presented in contested legislation, and to regard it as a factor to be considered in deciding on the constitutionality of a law.

Against these cautions Professor Dworkin offers the benefits of robust public arguments of principle. In reply to Judge Learned Hand's (no doubt extreme) idea of judicial restraint, which rests on the good of public participation in the important decisions that its legislatures make, Professor Dworkin maintains that much better debate is associated with court decisions, which are decisions of principle, rather than legislative decisions, in which issues of principle are clouded by single-issue pressure groups and political intimidation of legislators. Important court decisions are typically followed (note: not preceded, but followed, after, as some would see it, the damage is done) by robust debate, which may lead to such decisions being "elaborated, expanded, contracted, or even reversed, by future decisions." (FL, 345).

But it is doubtful that the robust debate of principles is such a good thing that it supports Dworkin's view not only of the Constitution but also of the role of the courts. Confronting principles notoriously raises the stakes in a matter of controversy; it has the tendency to harden positions and make people intractable. In their book *The Abuse of Casuistry* Stephen

Toulmin and Albert Jonsen report on their participation in a national conference on biomedical research. The eleven commissioners had substantially different backgrounds, yet they were readily able to come to agreement on many specific proposals. "Serious differences of opinion began to appear only when individual commissioners went beyond the stage of formulating practical proposals and explained their individual *reasons* for participating in the collective recommendations."

> Members of the commission were largely in agreement about their specific practical recommendations; they agreed what it was they agreed about; but the only thing they could not agree on was *why* they agreed about it. So long as the debate stayed on the level of particular judgments, the eleven commissioners saw things in much the same way. The moment it soared to the level of "principles," they went their separate ways. Instead of securely established universal principles, in which they had unqualified confidence, giving them intellectual grounding for particular judgments about specific kinds of cases, it was the other way around.[13]

In a related vein Robert Paul Wolff oncc remarked that

> It is much easier to accept a compromise between competing interests . . . than between opposed principles which purport to be objectively valid. The genius of American politics is its ability to treat even matters of principle as though they are conflicts of interest. (It has been remarked that the genius of French politics is its ability to treat even conflicts of interest as matters of principle.)[14]

Professor Dworkin, by contrast, applauds confrontation of principle in spite of its problematics and notes with approval that the French and American orientations have been reversed:

> . . . in spite of all the violence . . . the public discussion of [abortion] in America has involved many more people, and has been more successful in identifying the complex variety of moral and ethical issues involved, than in other countries where a political compromise was engineered. In France, for example, this was done more in the interest of avoiding intense public discussion than of reflecting it. . . (FL, 345)

Allocation of Power

There is nothing in the history of the establishment of our governmental structure, or in the public understanding of that structure, either in the past or at present, suggesting that our legislatures—and by extension the public—do not have a legitimate role to play where fundamental principles are concerned. Professor Dworkin concedes this in saying that the moral reading applies to legislatures as well as courts and that the question of which entity establishes authoritatively the meaning of the Constitution is determined by considerations extrinsic to it. Accordingly, to regard legislative determinations of principle, and a fortiori the public debate that frequently accompanies them, as not entitled to any special weight is to fail to treat the legislature as a co-equal branch of government. Our courts regularly express the view that they and the legislature are co-equal branches of government, which they take to mean that legislative determinations are to be respected and not overturned lightly. Even if this pronouncement sometimes appears to be honored only in the breach, it expresses a widely understood view of the allocation of power and responsibility between courts and legislature.

As noted earlier, Professor Dworkin's conception of principle is not completely clear—specifically, it is not clear whether all moral principles involve rights. If they do not, and if some considerations of public welfare (broadly understood) rise to such a level of importance that we might want to say they underwrite moral principles, then it is particularly important to pay attention to legislative determinations of principle, because legislatures are the institutions specifically charged with protecting and promoting welfare. Consider the dictum that the right of free speech does not entitle one to shout fire in a crowded theater. Is public safety merely a goal (as if we could choose not to protect it)? Or do we recognize as a principle that public safety is to be protected? The latter clearly puts legislatures in the business of dealing with issues of principle and thereby obligates courts to give weight to legislative determinations of principle.

The presumption of constitutionality is not a counsel of slavish adherence or of legislative supremacy. Courts have the power and the obligation to overrule where, in their opinion, a legislature's resolution of issues of principle is intolerable. No opinion is expressed here as to what "intolerable" should mean, or, in fact, whether that is a suitable term. The point is that the existence of a legislative determination of principle not only does, but should publicly be recognized to, raise the bar to some degree—a degree to be determined by courts giving due respect to the presumption of constitutionality.

The Appropriateness of Humility

Earlier it was observed that it is a mistake to assume that review by the judiciary is the equivalent of protection of individual rights, for judges are simply people who may or may not be more able than legislators, governors, and presidents, and after the judges consider an issue they make their decisions by a simple vote. They are, on the whole, more likely to get the right results, because they have more experience considering matters of principle, have their eyes on a larger picture (that is, other legal decisions and principles as applied in other cases), and are more removed from the pressures of political decision-making. On the other hand, in many cases in which principles play a prominent role judicial determination is preceded by debate among a large number of people, many of whom are intelligent, serious, and legally informed. These considerations, when they actually occur, should lead anyone to give some credit to the outcome of such deliberations and to be quite sure of his or her ground before insisting on a different outcome.

Integrity and Community

Professor Dworkin holds that the proper conception of democracy has to do with the conditions under which we can be said to govern ourselves, to be self-legislating, and thereby come under a moral obligation to comply with laws. This occurs when we are constituted as a single community under a coherent set of laws and principles that reflect our implicit ideals, for only in such circumstances do we undertake a commitment to each person to treat him or her the same as others, which we do by applying the same principles to everyone: ". . . a general commitment to integrity expresses a concern by each for all that is sufficiently special, pervasive, and egalitarian to ground communal obligations according to standards for communal obligation we elsewhere accept" (LE, 216).

Critics have observed that, in Dworkin's philosophy, the integrity that is achieved (or perhaps only sought) is not necessarily a *shared* set of principles. In response to Dworkin's "Law's empire . . . is an interpretive, self-reflective attitude. . . . It is a protestant attitude that makes each citizen responsible for imagining what his society's public commitments to principle are" (LE, 413). Dennis Patterson responds that "Ultimately the act of putting the practice "in the best light" is something individuals (including judges) do. Interpretation is not intersubjective for Dworkin, but deeply personal."[15] In a similar vein Jeremy Waldron observes that "The integrity of a substantive theory of social policy or social practice is the integrity of a single mind: but we are faced with many minds and many theories on almost every issue."[16] The point is that community has much to do with the principles people consciously accept; someone's idea of the web of principles we are morally committed to by those we consciously accept may be a possible basis for community, but as yet does not underwrite an actual one.

It is indeed important, as Professor Dworkin intimates, that we can look each other, even strangers, in the face and acknowledge that we owe them certain things as a matter of justice or fairness or procedural due process and that we are committed to treating all in precisely the same way. It may be that our mutual commitment to this can provide an explanation of our obligations to obey the law. But treating everyone the same in this sense can occur only if integrity is in fact achieved and everyone sees it as having been achieved. For if it is not achieved, then people are being treated differently, and in any event if people do not believe it is achieved, then they will not accept that they are part of a community that gives rise to political obligations. Without widespread acceptance of principles it is difficult to speak of a community of principle.

Notes

1 Four of Professor Dworkin's books are cited in the text; page references appear with the following abbreviations: FL is *Freedom's Law* (Harvard University Press, 1996), LD is *Life's Dominion* (Alfred A. Knopf, Inc., 1993), LE is *Law's Empire* (Harvard University Press, 1986), and TRS is *Taking Rights Seriously* (Harvard University Press, 1978).

2 "According to the moral reading, these clauses must be understood in the way their language most naturally suggests; they refer to abstract moral principles and incorporate these by reference. . . ." FL, 7. For a different view, see Antonin Scalia, A *Matter of Interpretation*, pp. 3-47; Dworkin comments at pp. 115-27.

3 "There is . . . a striking mismatch between the role the moral reading actually plays in American constitutional life and its reputation" (FL, 3).

4 It is important, though, to recognize that it is a mistake to see the issue of judicial review as posing a choice between the right answer and a legislature's (possibly wrong) answer to a moral/constitutional issue. If this were the choice, one would always prefer the former, but that would not be an argument for judicial review, for review by the judiciary is not the equivalent of getting the right answer. The real choice is between a legislature's answer and a court's answer, and even if we think a court is more likely to get it right, perhaps because it is more likely to pay attention to principles, it is still the case that each individual judge comes to her or his own opinion and that the outcome rests ultimately on a vote. Courts are majoritarian institutions. See Jeremy Waldron, 'Freeman's Defense of Judicial Review', *Law and Philosophy*, 13: 27-41 (1994).

5 441 U.S. 347, 99 S.Ct. 1742, 1745-46 (1979).

6 Walters v. National Association of Radiation Survivors, 466 U.S. 1323, 105 S.Ct. 11, 12 (1984).

7 448 U.S. 448, 100 S.CT. 2758, 2781 (1980), quoting from Robert H. Jackson, *The Struggle for Judicial Supremacy* (New York: Vintage Books, 1941), p.321.

8 In Wygant v. Jackson Board of Education, 476 U.S. 267 (1986) and in City of Richmond v. J. A. Croson Co., 488 U.S. 469 (1989) the Supreme Court held that Fullilove did not apply on the grounds that an unsupported legislative claim that a statute designed to favor minorities is remedial, is inadequate under the Equal Protection Clause, and that general societal discrimination, without some sort of showing of past discrimination in the area for which a 'remedial' statute is passed, is likewise inadequate. Furthermore, unlike the state-based statutes in those cases, Fullilove involved an act of Congress under a special grant of power under section 5 of the 14th Amendment. The Court in Croson says (pp. 500-1): "The factfinding process of legislative bodies is generally entitled to a presumption of regularity and deferential review by the judiciary. . . But when a legislative body chooses to employ a suspect classification, it cannot rest upon a generalized assertion as to the classification's relevance to its goals. . . A governmental actor cannot render race a legitimate proxy for a particular condition merely by declaring that the condition exists. . . The history of racial classifications in this country suggests that blind judicial deference to legislative or executive pronouncements of necessity has no place in equal protection analysis." See also Adarand Constructors, Inc. v. Pena, 515 U.S. 200 (1995).

9 " . . . it would be a mistake to suppose that persons who compromise with one another . . . necessarily compromise their moral integrity. To see why, it is important to distinguish: (1) what one judges ought to be done about a matter that happens to be in dispute, leaving aside any consideration of the fact that there is a dispute; (2) what one judges ought to be done, all things considered. When an issue is in dispute there is more to be considered than the issue itself—for example, . . . the intrinsic good of participating in a process in which each side must hear the other side out and try to see matters from the other's point of view, the extent to which the matter does admit reasonable differences of opinion, the significance of a settlement in which each party feels assured of the other's respect for its own seriousness and sincerity in the matter. Taking all of this into account, a person of goodwill might well decide that compromise is the wisest course." Arthur Kuflick, 'Morality and Compromise', in *Compromise in Ethics, Law, and Politics* (ed. By J. Roland Pennock and John W. Chapman (New York, NYU Press, 1979).

10 268 U.S. 510 (1925).

11 Supra n.6, p.316.

12 Ibid., p.x.

13 Albert R. Jonsen and Stephen Toulmin, *The Abuse of Casuistry* (Berkeley and Los Angeles: University of California Press, 1988), p.18.

14 Robert Paul Wolff, 'Beyond Tolerance', in Robert Paul Wolff, Barrington Moore, Jr., and Herbert Marcuse (eds.), *A Critique of Pure Tolerance* (Boston: Beacon Press, 1965), p.21.

15 Dennis Patterson, *Law and Truth* (New York: Oxford University Press, 1996), p.83, n.75.

16 Waldron, op. cit., p. 34.

9. Democratising Human Rights

TOM CAMPBELL*

The institutionalisation of human rights, a process which is necessary for their adequate implementation, involves the concretisation and positivisation of human rights. This, in turn, brings into renewed focus persistent disagreements over the correct content, form and valence of human rights. The nature and extent of these controversies make it unreasonable to lodge the power to articulate the specifics of human rights in legal form which lack moral authority and democratic accountability. There is no available epistemology of human rights that warrants confidence in the role of courts as the effective authors of human rights. Further, judicial review of legislative action on the basis of human rights is internally inconsistent in so far as it negates self-determination and potentially damaging to the moral authority of human rights discourse itself by reducing it to the status of just another branch of law. This essay examines ways of rendering the institutionalisation of human rights more democratic and looks at this issue in the context of recent developments in the constitutional law of Australia and the United Kingdom.

Human Rights

The concept of human rights captures moral insight into the equal worth and importance of all human beings and the political commitment to give this moral insight institutionalised existence through adopting a system of rights and duties which can be used to assert, protect and enhance basic human interests. Hence the importance of articulating the specific content of human rights and providing mechanisms to monitor and enforce these specific contents, processes which are unattainable without appropriate legal and political institutions. A legislative commitment for human rights does not exclude more generalised roles for human rights discourse in political rhetoric, civic education and the moral consciousness of civil society. However, these more diffuse roles themselves involve an orientation towards the achievement of the more specific and focussed roles of generating positive laws and procedures which protect the fundamental interests that we choose to identify as human rights. This institutionalisation of human rights is fundamental to the realisation of the aspirations which are signalled by the more generalised and rhetorical human rights discourse. The contemporary *telos* of human rights must be specific articulation and application of hitherto unacceptably abstract formulations.

Enormous progress has been made over the past fifty years towards the general acceptance of the idea of human rights and the political and legal frameworks for their enunciation and enforcement. This has involved what is sometimes called the concretisation of rights, that is their specific formulations in a manner applicable to particular circumstances, and the positivisation of human rights, namely the recognition by identifiable political and legal acts as authoritative sources of human rights law.[1] Such concretisation and positivisation is necessary if we are to identify what is and what is not a violation of human rights in a particular polity, or regional or global group of polities, and hope to install some mechanisms for reducing abuses of rights and obtaining redress. Moves towards the concretisation and positivisation of human rights involve what is in effect a massive legislative enterprise embedded in a substantial jurisprudence of case law. There has also been a rather more limited development of institutional mechanisms for policing the articulated rights, mechanisms which lead to further concretisation of previously more abstractly formulated rights.

The twin enterprises of official articulation and specific application have reawakened certain dormant problems about human rights which threaten to undermine their moral standing and political effectiveness. These problems have been long commented on by philosophers, while being in practice avoided by practitioners. They relate to the inherent controversiality of concrete formulations of human rights.

The controversies surrounding the articulation of human rights are varied and deep. They relate to the nature, the identity, the material content, the form and the valence (or power) of human rights and their associated correlative duties. Agreement can be readily achieved and palpably felt when we affirm the right to life or the right to freedom of expression or the right to a fair trial, but when it comes to expressing these rights at a level of specificity which enables us to systematically identify violations of, for instance, the right to life, or determine the scope of freedom of expression or decide whether a fair trial requires, for example, free legal aid, then that consensus diminishes and may evaporate altogether.

While some of this disagreement can be put down to perceived cultural backwardness or the distorted perspectives of selfish interests, a great deal of human rights controversy is genuine moral difference rather than a manifestation of special pleading and self-interest alone. It is clear that these differences run deep into cultural roots and individual identity and are not confined to the peripheries of a basically agreed core. Moreover, such disagreement is expanding for at least three reasons: (1) the increasing respect being given to differing cultural traditions and personal perspectives, which makes it more difficult to brush aside unfamiliar norms, (2) the developing demands for more compliance with human rights which involves giving more and more attention to the fine detail of human rights articulation and protection, and (3) the ever more apparent indefensibility of failing to give equal status and importance to economic and welfare interests alongside the traditionally more prized civil and political rights.

The phenomenon of profound and widespread disagreement about specific human rights need not lead us to despair of the intelligibility or the utility of human rights discourse. It must, however, heighten concern about the modes of institutionalising human rights in a period of positivisation and pluralism. In particular, we need to look more carefully at what might be the appropriate democratic input into the articulation of the rights that we require governments to follow and courts to administer. Thus, the long-standing debate about the democratic nature of judicial review of legislation for the protection of human rights must be intensified in the face of a growing acceptance of the judicialisation of human rights articulation.

The current tendency is to look to courts not simply for the application of human rights but more and more for the active creativity required to determine their justiciable content. A constitutionalised mechanism, which may have worked well in some jurisdictions at some periods of their history, is being generalised into a required part of any globally acceptable system of government. Given the growing scope and range of human rights which has already reached the point where there is scarcely a political issue that does not have a substantial human rights dimension, the juridification of the specification of human rights increasingly undermines the role of electorally based politics and thereby diminishes one of the few institutions of modern society that embody respect for the individual. Human rights-based judicial review of electorally legitimated laws poses a long-term threat not only to self-government but to human rights themselves.

Disagreement

It is easy to illustrate and explain the correlation between specificity and disagreement. We may note the relative ease with which the international community adopts lists of vaguely worded human rights in contrast with the unending disputes over how these highly generalised statements are to be "interpreted", that is, given useable content. In this area, more than any other, "interpretation" is a euphemism for disguised invention.

Disagreement arises first at the point of the most general notions which underlie the concept of human rights: equality and dignity.[2] These are uncontroversial enough starting points but in themselves are quite incapable of generating agreement as to specific rights. This is well illustrated by recent attempts to use the notion of human dignity to condemn any form of cloning involving human genetic material.[3] Such assertions seem self-evident to some and bemuse others. Clearly, what counts as an affront to dignity is paradigmatically a cultural and personal variable.

Further disagreements arise at the point of identifying those abstract rights which are to be accorded the status of human rights. Historically, the greatest disagreement has been as to the comparative status of civil and political rights on the one hand and social and economic rights on the other. The current stalemate on this issue at the international level, which is more or less mirrored in some domestic constitutions, is that both are equally important, but the former are mandatory while the latter remain merely aspirational.[4] This is an unstable compromise which fails to take on board the expensive nature of many civil and political rights and the eminently realisable content of many social and economic rights.[5] To this controversy must now be added the complications arising from more recent demands for community-based rights, such as group self-determination, which have been introduced both to supplement and curb the more traditional list of civil and political rights.[6] Clearly, any major human interest capable of protection and furtherance by government action or inaction is now a candidate for human rights status. The idea that there is a limited and clearly defined list of human rights is no longer defensible.

If we could agree on the rights to be included in a list of fundamental rights, we would then disagree as to the content and scope of each right which we have so identified. Such disputes bring to the fore basic divergences of emphasis between those who see basic human interests as coalescing around human happiness and well-being (the welfare, utility or humanitarian dimensions) and those who see them as having more to do with the overlapping but distinct notion of the human capacity for choice and self-determination (the liberty, deontological or autonomy dimensions). Priority often goes to the latter over the former, perhaps because of the perceived ease of concretisation and implementation, particularly when rights in general are regarded as freedoms involving only negative correlative duties which require only inaction. Yet, many people experience a fundamental unease about such prioritising, sensing that it is rooted in an ideological preference for liberties which are compatible with extensive economic inequality over the relief of those sufferings which are most acutely felt by the masses of those impoverished people whose lives lack the material prerequisites of any conception of a dignified existence. This conflict between negative liberty and the preconditions of happiness is the stuff of many but by no means all human rights disagreements.

If we were to agree on the content and scope of the identified rights, we would still disagree as to the form these rights should take. Disputes abound about such matters as the nature of the correlative obligations (the duty of the state not to interfere as against the duty of the state to promote the fundamental interests in question), and about who has these correlative duties (states, corporations, or everyone). We diverge on whether these rights give the right holders options to control the conduct of others, or simply provide some protection for the identified interests without giving the individual the power to demand or waive their rights.[7] Disagreement here is about the role of the state and the autonomy of economic systems, and is therefore immense and unending.

If we were to agree on the form as well as the content of the identified rights, we would still disagree about the valence or power of each right when it comes into conflict with other rights, about whose identification, content form and valence we may also disagree. We would also disagree about its valence when it has to be weighed against other legitimate social and political values which may not themselves count as rights, as is required by most recently adopted human rights systems.[8]

In summary, disagreements about human rights relate to the bases of our moral consciousness of human rights, identification of the fundamental rights all human beings have equally, the nature of the obligations which correlate with these rights, and what it means to say that someone has a right in any case. These controversies deepen with our uncertainty as to whether the idea of the human individual is at base either that of an utterly distinct and self-sufficient entity or that of a being situated in and partly constituted by significant social relationships and groupings. They include the most basic political controversies on the role of states, for human rights were invented to express the view that states have certain justifying functions and certain limits to what they can do if they are to retain their legitimacy. They involve our view of the relationship between political and economic institutions. We are not dealing here simply with a few exceptional (although no doubt very important) issues such as abortion, capital punishment and defamation, but with the entire panoply of human rights discourse.

How are we to understand and react to this pervasive human rights disagreement? What follows, constitutionally and politically, from the fact that to posit human rights in a pluralistic polity or a culturally diverse globe is to let loose a culture of controversy? Many human rights activists and organisations ignore human rights disagreement as an academic matter which does not affect their efforts to reduce the gross violations of human rights that mark our world today as ever before. This is an understandable pragmatism for those who know torture or genocide when they see them and want to do something about them. Yet this laudable desire to get on with the humanitarian job needs to be supplemented by some careful analysis of human rights controversies; otherwise, the moral force of the appeal to human rights will be weakened by disagreements which will not go away and which eat at the foundations of our working moral certainties. If we seek to have more than ad hoc political reactions to human rights violations and wish to promote a human rights consciousness deep in the framework of our societies, attention must be given to the public procedures for dealing with human rights divergences.

Certainly legal philosophers must confront the issue of human rights disagreement. It must be accepted that we cannot explain this disagreement away in terms of enlightened versus unenlightened views, or in the contrast between moral and immoral cultures. We must also accept that religious faiths, which are usually not amenable to "rational" criticism, are bound to play a part in human rights disagreement and that we cannot discount the significance of religion in the lives of a substantial majority of the human race. And we must take full note of the fact that while the philosophical argument about whether there are objective moral "truths" is unsettled and probably not amenable to settlement,[9] it is demonstrably the case that no epistemology of morals has provided a technique whereby it is feasible to reach rational agreement as to what these moral truths might be.

This is well documented in the glorious retreat of John Rawls in first proposing and defending a method for reaching justified agreement on fundamental rights through the methodology of the original position, the veil of ignorance and the device of reflective equilibrium,[10] and then withdrawing into an acceptance of this as simply a device for promoting political consensus within a certain type of liberal society.[11] It is not to denigrate this enterprise to say that Rawls does not provide a practical technique for resolving moral disagreement in a manner which gains consensus or invites epistemological confidence. The same applies to the sources from which Rawls's position is drawn, whether it be Kantian universalisability and respect for persons, Adam Smith's impartial spectator or Aquinas's natural reason. Such theories may give us some reason to believe that there is moral truth, and may well provide well grounded methods for making progress in moral knowledge, but they serve more to identify genuinely moral disagreement than to resolve it.

It is not difficult to see why this is the case. Such formal criteria as impartiality are essentially sieves which are useful for seeking to exclude certain unacceptable attitudes, such as those which clearly do not take the interests of all equally into account, but retain a mammoth diversity of view as to what, for instance, those interests are and what importance is to be attached to them. Essentially, such methods involve a commitment to the equal worth of all human beings but leave it an open question as to what constitutes that worth. They are therefore powerless to resolve value disagreements, although they may give us some guidance as to how some moral errors of a discriminatory sort may be reduced.

Similar comments may be made about Ronald Dworkin's heroic efforts to prove a reasoned basis for distinguishing the right and the good, as in the contrast between issues of principle and matters of policy.[12] Dworkin's approach has the advantage of being rooted in the interpretation of the jurisprudence of particular jurisdictions. This enables him to call in aid the idea of coherence and "fit" as a formal way of determining the principles which may be drawn from that jurisprudence,[13] but he now readily acknowledges that the choices involved in determining the substantive outcome of the interpretive process are the moral judgments of the individuals who seek to determine what they regard as the most acceptable of the alternative coherent readings that may be discerned in a particular set of legal materials.[14] At worst this returns us to the state of anarchy from which legal systems are meant to deliver us, at best it gives unwarranted authority to the moral views of a tiny minority of individuals.

Since the moral authority of any body of law has to be argued either from an independent moral assessment of the content or the process whereby that content has come about and the moral judgments involved in coming to the "best" view of a legal tradition also have to be established independently of that tradition, in so far as the Dworkinian method has relevance to our human rights disagreement, we must fall back on his moral theory which is often insightful and illuminating, but clearly no more of an epistemological engine for the effective resolution of moral disputes than its rivals.

Perhaps the most promising moral methods on offer in contemporary philosophy are those discourse theories which emphasise the role of actual rather than hypothetical dialogue in the process of reaching agreements which have claims to being based on truth or derived from some form of epistemological legitimacy.[15] The view that acceptable moral deliberation must include the free and informed and equal participation of all those who are affected by a particular decision is profoundly attractive for a number of reasons. It captures a social situation which pressures participants to take an impartial and inclusive view. It encourages the provision of all available evidence or information which is relevant to the matter in hand. It is tolerant with respect to the criteria of relevance that are involved. It holds the promise of limiting the extent of any coercion that might result from the decision in question.[16]

However, the attractions of the theory have as much to do with the prospect of generating consent and hence minimising political compulsion, or the opportunity they present for bargaining under "fair" conditions, as they have to do with the epistemological benefits of equal participant dialogue. This promise is a major plus for a pragmatic political philosophy, but not a triumph for moral epistemology. Compulsion may be minimised at the price of inaction which is costly in terms of the well-being of those involved and the bargains struck might be less than fair unless we have unrealisable equalities of prior holdings and future opportunities. What remains with respect to moral epistemology, however, seems to take us no further than the promises of impartiality which we have already acknowledged to be at best helpful and certainly insufficient in the quest of justified claims to moral truth. In fact the retreat to a procedural approach to moral dialogue can be read as an abandonment of the philosophical search for substantive justified moral agreement in favour of a pragmatic method of attaining a workable political consensus.

It is, therefore, part of the context of any discussion of human rights disagreement that we do not have an available moral epistemology which can deliver rational agreement on human rights, however "impartial" those who seek to implement that epistemology may be. This must make us cautious about underplaying the extent and significance of human rights disagreement when we turn to the difficult problem of how to constitutionalise human rights in the circumstance of controversy.

Constitutionalising Human Rights

How should we go about settling disagreements over the fundamental rights and duties which we want to see enforced above all other considerations in our society? What are the constitutional implications of the controversiality of human rights?

First, we need to be clear about objectives. If we only seek to identify a core list of rights about which there is relatively little disagreement even at the point of concretization, then we may adopt what I call the "torture model" of human rights, accepting as human rights only those rights whose content is clear and whose violation is unquestionably inhumane. We can then concentrate on reducing their incidence.[17] Such an approach may have some validity in connection with international enforcement of human rights at this stage but it is quite inadequate as a domestic and regional tactic, for, as we have seen, it leaves so much out of the reckoning and produces at best a very minimal catalogue of human rights.

What we require, it must be remembered, is justified agreement at a level of specificity at which human rights are applied to particular sets of events, not simply agreement on some general formulation. We must seek a concrete, not a generalised agreement. At that level, even torture is not totally uncontroversial with respect to scope and valence. There is no prospect of identifying a core of human rights of sufficient specificity to be taken out of the normal political process and given to some neutral umpire to administer and enforce.

This all means that it is very difficult to conceive of establishing a justiciable Bill of Rights within a constitution that is adequate to contemporary expectations as to the application of human rights to specific situations of everyday life. There may be advantages to listing human rights in a constitution if it is designed only to set out fundamental aspirations to guide the public life of that polity, thus setting goals for its citizens and their governments. But there is no prospect of having in a constitution a Bill of Rights that is capable of being applied through standard methods of statutory interpretation. The question then becomes, how is the necessary specificity to be obtained?

The standard answer is that concretisation is to be sought through the progressive jurisprudence of courts charged with the task of applying that Bill of Rights, either through a common law methodology of case-by-case development in accordance with canons of precedence and analogy, or allowing more open discretion to judges to apply the moral principles involved as they see fit on the particular occasion. If there is no such jurisprudence to hand, it may be acquired by adopting the global case law arising from constitutional and international courts all over the world. These approaches provide only process answers to the problem of institutionalising human rights in situations of disagreement. Inevitably it gives rise to a multiplicity of inconsistent human rights jurisprudence that is a mine for illustrations of the controversial nature of human rights content and valence.

Given that the point of human rights is mainly to curb and direct the actions of governments, it is understandable that authority to enforce such rights is separated from government itself. The problem is, however, that in the case of abstract human rights, application requires extensive and creative specification. Given the indeterminate variables surrounding human rights discourse, the task of enforcement against democratic government means taking on a legislative role, thereby undermining the democratic values it is intended to defend. Avoiding the perceived tyranny of the majority or their representatives brings with it another tyranny, the rule of the unaccountable elites who are given the task of making crucial value judgments on behalf of the majority of citizens. We have seen that we cannot evade this by saying that the choice and definition of rights does not involve controversial value judgments. Nor can we claim that there is a moral methodology which, if adequately informed by relevant information, is best handled by a small group of individuals trained in these techniques and capable of grasping the relevant information. All this is more than evident as we study the right-based constitutional law of various jurisdictions. There is the evident controversiality of specific decisions. There are marked disagreements between courts in different jurisdictions and in the same jurisdictions at different times. There is greater awareness that the mode of reasoning involved is moral not legal, consequentialist as well as deontological and often incurably ad hoc and unprincipled.

If, nonetheless, we want to insist that judiciaries are in a better position to have a stab at these difficult matters than either the populace in general or their elected representatives, then we are effectively abandoning the legitimacy of electoral democracy. Leaving human rights positivisation to judiciaries may be tolerable if the matters involved are limited, clearly distinctive and uncontroversial; but they are none of these things. There is in principle and increasingly in practice no matter that lies beyond their scope. Few issues do not have a human rights dimension and few human rights issues in concrete application are not eminently contestable.

We have seen that it is not feasible to retreat to a core of uncontroversial rights. Indeed, it has become apparent that, unless the scope of human rights is broadened, they will become more and more associated with a controversial ideology which will not be able to survive global economic downturns. The scope of human rights has already become so wide and so intrusive that it must be brought under the democratic control of those affected by the wholly laudable and necessary positivisation of the traditional aspirational affirmations of the equal dignity, significance and worth of all human beings. As social and economic rights are given their inevitable place in the pantheon of enforceable rights, juridical power to effectively determine the content of human rights will become all-encompassing.

Indeed, we are already approaching the paradoxical position that judicial review of legislation, itself a form of legislation, which is introduced to protect fundamental rights negates some of these very rights, particularly the rights of self-determination and political equality. Jeremy Waldron has lucidly presented this paradox with respect to self-determination, where the principle of self-determination is used to take away the right of citizens to share in the making of decisions that have a profound impact on their well-being.[18]

Judicial review of legislation threatens human rights in other ways. Without going so far as to endorse discourse ethics as a rationale which requires involving in decision-making all those affected by decisions which are binding on them, we should note the need to involve the population as a whole in the process of positivising human rights so that they come to own these rights, identify with them and retain a commitment to them. Once controversial human rights decisions are made by electorally unaccountable courts, those affected by these decisions come to reject them as the imposition of the values of others on what is rightfully their concern. The problem with trusting in constitutional courts is what to do when electorates perceive that judicial review of legislative power together with the impact of global economics have all but pre-empted anything they might want to decide for themselves. At that point there may be an alienation from human rights which derives from the fact that the system denies in practice equal concern and respect in the name of these very values. Human rights law will then become just another system of law whose authority is detached from the moral insights that gave it birth, with the added defect that it is constitutionally virtually unchallengeable.

The Australian Tangle

Nothing I have said is intended to suggest that the solution to the eternal problem of who guards the guardians is an easy one. Nor do I suggest that there have not been significant advances made through constitutionalising human rights. If nothing else, it certainly puts human rights on the political agenda. I do, however, argue that we need to have regard to how we may further democratise human rights with respect to the articulation of their content, form and valence.

At this point it may be as well to particularise, for the situations in different jurisdictions are sufficiently disparate to warrant divergent approaches to our problem. For instance, it is almost unthinkable in the United States to suggest the abolition of the Supreme Court's power of judicial review; consequently, normative US constitutional law has to operate within the framework of competing suggestions as to how the Supreme Court ought to exercise its powers.[19] Despite the pressures of constitutional globalisation, most other jurisdictions have more choice in the matter and even in the United States it is feasible to consider increasing the role of non-judicial organs of government in the articulation and furtherance of fundamental rights.

Two jurisdictions which have some flexibility in this regard are Australia and the United Kingdom. Until recently, both polities could have been said to be distinctive amongst western democracies in having no modern Bill of Rights, although Australia has, of course, since its inception in

1901, a written constitution which includes some rights that may be viewed as human rights and the UK has a long political history of affirming political rights against government. An interesting divergence now is that the UK has moved towards incorporating the European Convention on Human Rights (ECHR), while Australia has backed away from the tentative steps taken by its High Court towards protecting something like human rights through the backdoor mechanism of reading such rights into a constitution whose founders explicitly rejected the Bill of Rights approach.

The Australian system has, from time to time, thrown up proposals to adopt a Bill of Rights on the US model but, in part because of the unusual difficulty in achieving changes to the constitution, not even modest proposals to that effect have succeeded. Proposals for a statutory Bill of Rights have also failed.[20] There is, of course, substantial protection of the substance of human rights through the common law and statutes, including very specific human rights legislation in the field of anti-discrimination law with respect to race and gender both at state and federal level.[21] More recently a few rights which at least resemble some of the widely accepted human rights have been found to be implied within the Constitution.[22]

The lack of more formal recognition of human rights in the Australian Constitution is regretted by many influential Australians including many members of the senior judiciary who regard human rights as inadequately protected within the Australian system.[23] This has produced an unusual level of judicial activism in relation to two such areas of perceived human rights deficit. One of these is the situation of the indigenous peoples of Australia, and another has to do with freedom of speech, particularly with respect to defamation law.

The history of dispossession and oppression of aboriginal peoples following the European settlement is an unhappy and by contemporary standards an outrageous one, for which, it is argued, there have been insufficient remedial responses or even acknowledgment. The complex matters involved have been addressed by statute, in land rights legislation reserving extensive territories for aboriginal peoples, and in constitutional changes to achieve formal equality for Australia's indigenous people which was explicitly limited in the Constitution,[24] but no satisfactory solution to the cumulative affects of this disastrous history, acceptable to the aboriginal peoples, has emerged.

The audacious and unexpected common law decision in the case of *Mabo*, native title, was introduced to Australia for the first time.[25] Given the disparate and uncoordinated judgments of the several justices, so familiar in common law jurisdictions, it is not easy to summarise the grounds for the decision, but it is probably not misleading to say that they included overriding previous legal authorities, using Canadian, American and New

Zealand precedents, on the basis of a new reading of the facts of Australian history – namely that the land was not, after all, "terra nullius" or effectively uninhabited at the time of European settlement. To this was added a moral affirmation that the way in which land was acquired during that settlement was shameful by today's standards,[26] making it unacceptable to take the view that, just because the sovereignty of the Australian state is based on settlement rather than conquest, this means that there can be no room for the recognition of native title based on prior presence and occupation. Staying within the factual and legal realities of the constitution under which the High Court obtains its authority, it was decided that those peoples who could demonstrate a continuing connection with the land could acquire native title which allowed them to use that land for traditional activities in ways which are compatible with the user rights of those having other forms of tenure over that land. A subsequent case, *Wik*, determined that such rights are not necessarily extinguished by the granting of pastoral leases.[27]

Relating this story to my critical scheme is by no means easy. It can be read as an example of judges acting in a progressive way to protect oppressed minorities when Parliaments fail to do so, thus demonstrating the desirability of court-based initiatives in solving human rights problems. However, this could be read either as demonstrating the capacity of the common law to deliver human rights solutions without using a Bill of Rights, or as bolstering the case for giving more scope to such interventions through the instrument of a Bill of Rights, which might have brought the matter to resolution much sooner or avoided the mistaken rulings in the first place. In this context, it should be noted that the recognition of native title in *Mabo* and *Wik* is in effect a very limited one, being confined to traditional usage and giving rise to no claims for compensation as a result of the original expropriations involved.

On the other hand, the problems of achieving social change through courts deciding these matters on a case by case basis, especially when drawing on moral principles which invite moral reassessment of social practices and institutions are well illustrated by the *Mabo* decision which produced uncertainty and confusion in the area of property law without the prospect of significant tangible improvements for aboriginal peoples. It is hard not to think of such ad hoc developments as being inevitably exceptional, generally inefficient and perhaps unnecessarily disruptive and even counterproductive.

As a common law decision, *Mabo* is, of course, subject to legislative review and refinement. And this is what has happened, first in the Native Title Act 1993 (Cth) which broadly accepted the *Mabo* decision and put in place procedures for dealing with claims to native title, and the Native Title

Amendment Act 1998 (Cth) which places a more restrictive interpretation on native title and seeks to secure the certainty of pastoral leases which had been put in doubt by a further decision of the High Court in the *Wik* case. By any account some legislation was necessary because of all the practical questions left unanswered by the *Mabo* decision. However, the particular enactments are highly controversial, particularly the way in which the Amendment Act favours pastoral leases over native title rights. Aspects of this act can be seen as discriminatory in that they are systematically unfavourable to a form of title which disproportionately, indeed entirely, affects one racial group. Hence, the prospect of challenges to the Native Title Amendment Act under Australia's racial discrimination legislation, and the strong critique, abruptly repudiated by the Australian government, made by the UN Human Rights Committee.

Without entering a contentious debate about the desirability of the outcome, we can view the recent legal and political history of native title in Australia as an example of courts, on the initiative of parties, putting a human rights issue on the political agenda, but in a way which allows the elected legislature to address the issues more systematically and with more political legitimacy. It is interesting and important to note that the Australian government's response to *Mabo* and *Wik* and crucial points in the cases themselves were directly affected by the Racial Discrimination Act 1975, a standard anti-discrimination statute which makes it unlawful to legislate in a way which disadvantages one racial or ethnic group by, for instance, abolishing native title without paying compensation. To that extent, the *Mabo* scenario can be taken to demonstrate the effective role of statutory human rights law and makes this appear a fruitful way of promoting human rights which does not require entrenchment.

What, then, of the other Australian development - implied constitutional rights - as a path to rectifying injustice, as perceived from the highest court? A series of decisions, stemming from *Australian Capital Television* and *Nationwide News*,[28] determined that Australia has a constitutional right to freedom of political communication. Moreover, this right has been used to require that the common law of defamation must not violate the constitutional right to freedom of communication.[29] As a result Australia now has a version of *New York Times v Sullivan*,[30] with a reversal of the burden of proof as to malice on the part of the defendant and the addition of the requirement that the publication of the material in question was "reasonable in the circumstances". On the other hand, and somewhat paradoxically, the original *Australian Capital Television* decision struck down a law which was designed to reduce the power of finance in electoral campaigns, thus ruling unconstitutional, on the grounds that it was incompatible with representative government, a system of political broadcasting not unlike that in place in the United Kingdom, which was designed to enhance freedom of speech by reducing the impact of finance in political campaigning.

While the High Court has recently confirmed its position as to the freedom of political communication, it is at pains to reiterate that this is not an individual right to freedom of speech but a requirement for making representative government work. Moreover, no clear methodology has emerged for developing this right or discovering other implied constitutional rights with a human rights flavour. Indeed, after a barrage of public criticism, the current justices are suspicious of deducing rights from broad concepts such as representative government, especially if these are taken to carry theories of government with them, and have no clear way of deciding the scope and valence of such rights, despite some use of European ideas of "proportionality" as well as more traditional Australian concepts of "balancing".

As a result, some commentators are urging further developments in the methodology of the common law and statutory interpretation, encouraging the tendency to make liberal use of overseas precedents and international treaties in the "interpretation" of the law. Interestingly, this raises the prospect of constitutionalising the common law since a High Court endorsement of a common law decision may now include a strong presupposition that it is compatible with the Constitution, including the rights implied therefrom. In some cases this will make it more difficult for the Parliament to alter a common law decision reached with cognisance of implied constitutional rights.

All this could be said to amount to a tangle if not an outright mess. The situation is the outcome of the High Court's desire to keep government within the bounds of what are perceived as at least quasi-human rights. It has produced very few tangible gains in terms of a progressive (if controversial) view on the substance of human rights. The benefits accruing to aboriginal people of the *Mabo* and *Wik* decisions are as yet minimal. The ensuing political controversies have poisoned some ethnic relationships and in part prompted the emergence of unexpectedly right-wing political parties and policies. On the other hand *Mabo* and *Wik* may be seen as better than nothing and a psychological boost to the original inhabitants of the land. Defamation law does not seem to have markedly altered in practice and halting steps to improve freedom of communication with respect to access have been thwarted. Moreover, something of the onus for protecting human rights is perceived to have passed from the Parliaments to the courts but the courts do not seem to have the wherewithal to make a consistent and significant ongoing impact. Australia may, therefore, be said to have the worst of both worlds, with the High Court unable to fulfill its promise and the Parliament cagey about venturing into human rights legislation.

The United Kingdom Compromise[31]

In contrast to the Australian constitution which is so unchangeable that Australia entered the new millennium with a Head of State who resides in another country, the tradition of parliamentary sovereignty has recently revealed just how malleable the British constitution can be. The Human Rights Act 1998 may turn out to be a minor or a major change in the constitution of the United Kingdom but either way it has to be viewed as part of a global trend towards the legal institutionalisation of the idea of human rights. This can only be welcomed if it places the identification and protection of fundamental human interests nearer the centre of the public agenda, but the entrenchment of court-based determinations of the content and form to be given to the concept of basic rights is a potentially dangerous development to the extent that it leads to the juridification of politics and the distancing of the prioritisation and concretisation of human rights from the domain of representative politics. Human rights will be the weaker if they are seen as the impositions of controversial interpretations of basic rights without the scope of democratic accountability.

The alternatives facing the United Kingdom with respect to the European Convention on Human Rights (ECHR) are quite restricted in the context of its membership in the European Union. Some constitutional changes are clearly required to remove the anomalies arising from British courts being unable to take significant cognisance of the ECHR even although its citizens may challenge their decisions at the European Commission of Human Rights and the European Court of Human Rights. The Human Rights Act appears to be at the modest end of the range of alternatives, but it may be no more than a staging post to a fully-fledged domestic Bill of Rights, in which case there will be a difficult debate on which specific rights and what mode of entrenchment is to be adopted. In fact, the emergence of a so-called home grown Bill of Rights seems an increasingly unlikely outcome as the problems of drawing up such a Bill become more apparent. If a stop-gap Human Rights Act turns out to be a more permanent feature of the British constitution, the ECHR may continue to have relatively slight impact on British courts, but its import will depend largely on the way that British judiciaries respond to the opportunities which it creates for more activist judicial roles. There is a possibility that the Bill could encourage judicial creativity not only in statutory interpretation but also in the development of the common law in line with European Human Rights jurisprudence.

It may not be easy to restrict the impact of the Act to minor questions of interpretation. Interpretation is itself a slippery term which is now used much more widely than simply in relation to making a selection between different readings of ambiguous statements and is often equated with highly flexible forms of legal reasoning.[32] Interpretation may involve creative concretisations of vague statements in order to give justiciable meaning to those statements, a process which goes far beyond resolving ambiguities.[33] With respect to more specific statements of rights, "interpretation" is taken to include how we read legal texts to determine whether or not there is an ambiguity which needs to be addressed as well as the process of resolving that ambiguity. The attempt to distance the ECHR from making or unmaking UK law and confining its use to the clarification of obscurities comes up against the thesis that obscurity is not something which comes on the face of a statement but emerges from the pre-existing state of mind of those who seek to give meaning to a form of words.

Although these points may be overstated in that they ignore the existence of relatively stable understandings of verbal patterns within particular cultures, there is no doubt that the existence of the ECHR does impact on how domestic laws are read in the first place. The Convention affects what seems clear and what does not as well as which clarifications are to be preferred. And so, while it is possible to sustain a fair working distinction between understanding and interpretation in a legal culture where there is sufficient precision and continuity of discourse, this process is undermined by the introduction of unspecific principles as a guide to the so-called interpretation of pre-identified ambiguities and obscurities.

Further, it is not clear what will be made of the requirement of Section 6 that public authorities must conform to the ECHR. This may be read (or "interpreted") as permitting or even requiring courts, which are explicitly identified in the Act as public authorities, to develop the common law so that it is increasingly in harmony with the Convention. This may not be the intention of the Act's sponsors, but, in a fluid constitutional situation involving the changing role of courts, it is possible that judiciaries will modify their working assumptions as to how statutes, including the Human Rights Act, are to be interpreted. Certainly, there are available theories of interpretation, particularly in the human rights sphere, which place few limitations on judges' power to understand the enactments of the legislature in accordance with generalised norms which permit cognisance of purposes other than those in the mind of the legislators.

Putting these two points together, if British judiciaries choose to develop the common law along the lines of the precedents established in the European Court of Human Rights and the decisions of the Commission (which they are not obliged to do), and if they systematically 'interpret' any Parliamentary modifications of the common law in such a way as to make them compatible with the ECHR, there is little that can be demonstrated to be legally wrong in their conduct. A situation could emerge in which there is increased impetus to develop the common law without the sense of illegitimacy that at present accompanies significant changes unapproved by Parliament. This will decrease the legal and political capacity of the Parliament to exercise its theoretical sovereignty by passing legislation which can decisively override common law developments.

It is argued that this will not happen, on the grounds that current decisions of the European Court are not threatening in this way, and that there is no will on the part of the British judiciaries to take on such wider powers. This may well be so in the short term, but relatively small constitutional changes have to be seen against the wider process of change, and we cannot easily extrapolate from current decisions and attitudes to what will be the case in ten, twenty or fifty years' time. This might not matter if the constitutional changes were readily reversible as is the case under the traditional doctrine of the sovereignty of parliament. However, what may emerge is a process of de facto entrenchment whereby reversibility is effectively disallowed or made more difficult politically. As the European Union develops, the sovereignty of Parliament is no longer a fixed point of British constitutional law. It therefore becomes imperative to look at possible long term consequences under different legal cultures, different judiciaries and different political situations, noting that some of these differences will themselves be the result of promoting a juridification of political issues by giving an ever increasing law-making role to judges. It would appear that the Act gives encouragement to liberal methods of interpretation which have the potential to undermine the traditional ethics of adjudication that require a basic commitment to respecting the intention of the legislature as expressed in the enacted text.

Working through these potential implications of the Human Rights Act may require a new model of the separation of powers which provides bounds within which judiciaries and legislatures can work cooperatively so that human rights are more at the centre of a political debate in which citizens can participate more fully. This model requires elements of tension and partnership between the legislative, executive and judicial branches of government. An enhanced role for Parliamentary committees is one emerging feature of such a model. The Declaration of Incompatibility outlined in Section 4 of the Act, which permits the courts to declare a statute incompatible with the ECHR, but not to invalidate it on that account, could prove to be an ingredient which helps to shape the political agenda and attract Parliamentary and media attention in a way which improves the quality of political discourse and encourages a human rights focus for constitutional partnership. In such ways the Human Rights Act could be an enduringly beneficial constitutional development which contributes to a relatively stable and sensible model of the relative roles of judges, parliamentarians and populace in the identification and development of specific concrete rights.

Conclusion

Much of the case for an entrenched Bills of Rights together with judicial review of legislation is based on a critique of the available alternative: human rights legislation. This negative mode of argument ignores the facts that there is no simple and logical solution to the majoritarian problem and there are even stronger arguments to be made against transferring large and unchallengeable power to small, unelected and unrepresentative bodies.

The debate about the democratic or undemocratic nature of judicial review of legislation is bedeviled by repeated *ignoratio elenchi*, non-sequitur and much democratic pessimism. Thus, it is frequently argued that, since democratic procedures can be used to diminish democracy itself, therefore non-democratic safeguards must be in place to protect democracy from itself. Certainly, the vulnerability of democracy is not in doubt, but this does not establish that democratic procedures, even imperfect ones, are not the best protection against the demise of democracy that is available. Again, it is frequently argued that, since democratic systems must utilise majoritarian procedures, minorities must be protected by non-democratic institutions. This neglects the possibility that majorities may sometimes decide what is in the best interests of everyone and not only themselves. If this is dismissed on the grounds that human beings are irretrievably selfish, this immediately undermines the claim that there can be some other institution, run by people who are not selfish, which is better fitted to protected minorities.

There is a formally insoluble problem of how to render accountable those whom we entrust with constitutionally ultimate power. This problem can be mitigated by dividing that power - the checks and balances approach. But unless this is a recipe for gridlock, as when each separated power has a veto on state action, there must be some *primus inter pares*, some body or person with the power to break through and make an enforceable decision. The question therefore remains, where should such power lie.

It is in this context that there is evidently a crisis in the evolution of democracy brought on by the political successes of the human rights movement and with it the respectability, indeed the felt necessity, of constitutional arrangements which incorporate rights-centred judicial review of legislation. As this mode of politics becomes more dominant, and there is a steady increase in the jurisprudence which gives concrete content to abstract rights, there are clear threats not only to those political human rights which are part of the idea of democracy itself, but also to the perceived moral legitimacy of human rights themselves.

Notes

* Professor of Law, The Australian National University.

1 See Tom Campbell et al, (eds.), *Human Rights: From Rhetoric to Reality* (London: Blackwells, 1986).

2 Note the opening words of the Preamble to the Universal Declaration of Human Rights: "Whereas recognition of the inherent dignity and of the equal and inalienable rights of all members of the human family is the foundation of freedom, justice and peace in the world".

3 Thus, Deryck Beyleveld and Roger Brownsword, 'Human Dignity, Human Rights and Human Genomes' *61 Modern Law Review* (1999),

4 Vienna Declaration of Program of Action, 14 *Human Rights Law Journal* (1993), 352.

5 Thus, C. Fabre, 'Constitutionalising Social Rights' 6 *Journal of Political Philosophy*, 1998, 263.

6 See H.J. Steiner and P. Alston, *International Human Rights in Context* (Oxford: Oxford University Press, 1996), chapter 14.

7 These themes are all explored in Tom Campbell, *The Left and Rights: A Conceptual Analysis of the Idea of Socialist Rights* (London: Routledge and Kegan Paul, 1983).

8 A typical example is Article 16.2 of the American Convention on Human Rights.

9 For an account of this debate, see J.L. Mackie, *Ethics: Inventing Right and Wrong*, (Harmondsworth: Penguin Books, 1977).

10 J. Rawls, *A Theory of Justice (*Oxford: Oxford University Press, 1972).

11 J. Rawls, *Political Liberalism*, (New York: Columbia University Press, 1993).

12 R. Dworkin, *Taking Rights Seriously* (London: Duckworth, 1977).

13 R. Dworkin, *Law's Empire* (London: Fontana, 1986).

14 R. Dworkin, *Freedom's Law: The Moral Reading of the American Constitution* (Cambridge: Harvard University Press, 1996).

15 Jurgen Habermas, *The Theory of Communicative Action*, (Boston: Beacon Press, 1984-87), and *Between Facts and Norms* (Cambridge: Polity Press, 1996).

16 For a balanced discussion of the epistemological benefits of deliberative democracy, see C. Nino *The Constitution of Deliberative Democracy* (New Haven, Yale University Press, 1993).

17 Of course, what counts as "torture" is itself contentious at its fairly generous margins: see C.A. MacKinnon, 'On Torture: A Feminist Perspective on Human Rights' in K.A. Mahoney and P.Mahoney (eds.) *Human Rights in the Twenty-First Century: A Global Challenge* (Dordrecht: Martinus Nijhoff, 1992), 21.

18 Jeremy Waldron, 'A Rights-based Critique of Constitutional Rights', 13 *Oxford Journal of Legal Studies*, 1993, 18-51.

19 Yet, see Mark Tushnet, *Taking the Constitution Away from the Courts* (Princeton: Princeton University Press, 1999).

20 Bills introducing a statutory Bill of Rights made some progress in 1973, 1983 and 1985.

21 Commonwealth legislation includes the Racial Discrimination Act 1975, the Sex Discrimination Act 1984 and the Disability Discrimination Act 1992.

22 Most particularly *Australian Capital Television Pty Ltd v The Commonwealth* (1992) 177 CLR 108 (concerning freedom of political communication).

23 For a recent contribution to the debate, see George Williams, *A Bill of Rights for Australia* (Sydney: UNSW Press, 2000).

24 The unamended section 51 (xxvi) enabled the Parliament to make laws with respect to "The people of any race, other than the aboriginal race in any State, for whom it is deemed necessary to make special laws". The qualification with respect to "the aboriginal race" was removed by the 1967 referendum.

25 *Mabo (No.2) v Queensland* (1992) 175 CLR 1.

26 Two of the justices wrote of "the conflagration of oppression and conflict which was, over the following century, to spread across the continent to dispossess, degrade and devastate the Aboriginal peoples and leave a national legacy of unutterable shame".

27 *Wik Peoples v Queensland* (1996) 187 CLR 1.

28 *Nationwide News Pty Ltd v Wills* (1992) 177 CLR 1.

29 *Theophanous v Herald & Weekly Times Ltd* (1994) 182 CLR 104; *Lange v Australian Broadcasting Corporation* (1997) 189 CLR 520.

30 376 US 254 (1964).

31 This part of the essay reproduces some material from T. Campbell, 'Human Rights: a Culture of Controversy', 26 *Journal of Law and Society*, 1999, 6-26.

32 See A. Marmor (ed.) *Interpretation and Legal Theory* (Oxford: Oxford University Press, 1992) and B. Bix (ed.), *Law, Language and Legal Determinacy* (Oxford: Clarendon Press, 1993).

33 This and related problems are examined in an important article that casts doubt on the utility and clarity of the model on which much of the Human Rights Act is based: A.S. Butler, 'The Bill of Rights Debate: Why the New Zealand Bill of Rights Act 1990 is a Bad Model for Britain', 17 *Oxford Journal of Legal Studies*, 1997, 323-45.

10. Judicial Protection of Human Rights in India

MEENAKSHI JAIN

Introduction

In 1966, the General Assembly of the United Nations adopted two Covenants viz., (i) the Covenant on Civil and Political Rights, and (ii) the Covenant on Economic, Social and Cultural Rights envisaging the implementation system of the protection of human rights. India became a party to these two Covenants in 1979 by making the Instrument of Accession. Various measures have been taken to implement them. This paper will discuss protection of human rights by the Supreme Court of India. Most of them have been laid down in Part III of the Indian Constitution as fundamental rights with the aim of guaranteeing the protection of these rights against illegal invasion by the state.[1] The implementation of these rights by the Supreme Court may be studied, for the sake of convenience, under the four categories:

1. Fundamental rights specified by the Covenant and adopted by the Indian Constitution;
2. Other rights provided in the Covenant but not specifically laid down in Part III of the Constitution;
3. Rights recognised in the Covenant neither guaranteed in Part III of the Constitution nor regarded as fundamental in the beginning by the Supreme Court;
4. Rights provided in the Covenant but not agreed to by the Government of India, however enforced by the Supreme Court.

Fundamental Rights Specified in the Constitution

The Indian Constitution under the caption of "fundamental rights" has specifically recognised many rights which have been provided in the Covenant. Articles 20 (3), 21, 22, 23 and 25 of the Indian Constitution specifically deal with those rights. Equality before law, prohibition of discrimination on the grounds of religion, race, caste or sex and equality of opportunity in the matter of public employment have been guaranteed under articles 14, 15 and 16 (i) of the Constitution. They are similar to articles 14 (1) and 25 (c) of Covenant on Civil and Political Rights. The right to liberty of movement, freedom to choose one's residence, the right of peaceful assembly, and the right to freedom of association with others enshrined in articles 19 (1) and (2), 21, 22 (1), 12 (1) of the Covenant on Civil and Political Rights have been guaranteed to the citizens in different clauses of article 19 (1) of the Indian Constitution. Clause 1 to 3 of article 20 i.e., (i) prohibition of *expost facto* operation of criminal law; (ii) conferring of immunity against double jeopardy and (iii) protection against self-incrimination are equivalent to articles 15 (i), 14 (7), and 14 (3) (g) of the Covenant on Civil and Political Rights. The right to life and security of person laid down in article 6 (1) and 9 (1) of the Covenant has been specified in article 21 of the Constitution. Article 22 of the Indian Constitution proceeds to enact protection against arrest and detention in certain cases corresponding to the provisions of article 9 (2) (3) and (4) of the Covenant. Further, prohibition of forced or compulsory labour provided in article 8 (3) of the Covenant has been laid down under 23 of the Constitution. The right to religion and worship enshrined in article 25 of the Constitution corresponds to article 18 (1) of the Covenant.

Other Rights Provided in the Covenant but not Laid Down Specifically in Part III of the Constitution

There are a number of other rights, which have been provided in the Covenant on Civil and Political Rights but have not been specifically laid down in Part III of the Constitution. The earlier view of the Supreme Court was that no such right is applicable in India unless legislation has been enacted to give effect to it because under article 253 of the Constitution, Parliament alone has the power to make laws for the implementation of any treaty, agreement or covenant.[2] Later on it changed its view and held that rights which are not specifically mentioned in the Constitution may be regarded as fundamental rights if they are an integral part of a named fundamental right or partake of the same basic nature and character as specific fundamental rights. However, the Supreme Court of India enlarging the meaning and scope of the fundamental rights gave a broad and liberal interpretation to life and personal liberty of a man. For example, the Covenant lays down that every human being has the inherent right to life and security and no one shall be arbitrarily deprived of his life. Though the right has been embodied in article 21 of the Indian Constitution but the

Supreme Court in the beginning imparted a very narrow interpretation to the term "right to life and personal liberty", which was certainly not in the consonance with the true spirit of the covenant. However, in 1978 in *Menka Gandhi* v. *Union of India,*[3] the Supreme Court through a remarkable decision gave a new dimension to article 21 and introduced procedural due process into Indian Constitutional law through creative interpretation inspired by judicial activism.

This new interpretation to article 21 brought about significant reform in the administration of criminal justice for under-trial prisoners who unduly languish in jails for a long time in India. The percentage of these under-trial prisoners has always been high.[4] They are of two categories viz., (1) those who were denied bail by the courts on account of their involvement in serious offences; and (2) those who could not furnish bail for one reason or the other. In the State of Bihar that condition was so bad that many of these under-trial prisoners had been in jails for years before their trial had been commenced. A woman advocate brought public interest litigation in the court, which after examining the matter thoroughly gave various directions in a series of decisions, known as the *Hussainara Khatoon*[5] decisions. In the majority of these cases, it was found that a large number of under-trial prisoners afflicted by extreme poverty, ignorance and illiteracy could not seek relief from the courts on account of a lack of awareness, assertiveness or availability of machinery. Moreover, the major impediment in the way of providing access to justice to the deprived and vulnerable sections of the community was the traditional rule of *locus standi*. This rule which was evolved in the context of a private right-duty pattern required that if legal injury was caused or a legal wrong was done to any person, he alone could bring an action in a court of law for judicial redress and no one else could do so on his behalf. This restricted rule of *locus standi* closed the doors of justice to large masses of people in India. The Supreme Court, with a view to providing easy access to justice to the underprivileged segments of society, expanded the scope of the doctrine of *locus standi*. It provided that where legal injury is caused or legal wrong is done to persons or class of persons who by reason of poverty or disability or a socially or economically disadvantaged position, cannot approach a court of law for justice, any member of the public or social action group acting *bona fide* can bring an action seeking judicial redress for the legal injury caused or legal wrong done to such person or class of persons. This can be done even by addressing a letter to the Court. Thus, there came into being public interest litigation in the Supreme Court and High Courts in India and new jurisdiction was evolved by the Supreme Court, namely, epistolatory jurisdiction. Much of the development of human rights jurisprudence in India, particularly in favour of the weaker sections of Indian society, has taken place as a result of public interest litigation.

The Supreme Court in the *Hussainara Khatoon* case[6] found that there were quite a few women prisoners who were in jails without even being accused of any offence, merely because they happened to be victims of an offence or they were required for the purpose of giving evidence and therefore it directed their release immediately.

The Supreme Court also found that there were a number of under-trial prisoners who had been in jails for periods longer than the maximum term for which they could have been sentenced, if convicted, and yet their trials had not commenced. It reprimanded the administration as well as the judiciary in the State of Bihar for this shocking state of affairs which betrayed a complete lack of concern for human values and directed that these under-trial prisoners should be "released forthwith, as their further detention would be unlawful and in violation of their fundamental rights under article 21".[7]

Free Legal Aid

Article 14 (3) (d) of the Covenant provides the right to legal assistance to a person against whom a criminal charge has been levied and in cases where the interest of justice so required, and without payment by him in such case if he does not have sufficient means to pay for it. In the Indian Constitution, unfortunately, there is no such enumerated, constitutional right. Article 22 (1) does provide that no person who is arrested shall be denied the right to consult and to be defended by a legal practitioner of his choice, but the Supreme Court in *Janaardhan Reddy* v. *State of Hyderabad,*[8] held that this provision does not carry with it the right to free legal aid. In 1976, by the 42nd Amendment of the Indian Constitution, article 39A was introduced so as to provide legal aid to economically depressed classes.

This article merely contains a directive to the state. This directive is not an obligation enforcement in a court of law and does not confer a fundamental right on the accused to secure free legal assistance. The state, no doubt, took steps by legislation to achieve the goal of cherished human values of personal liberty at the state's cost only in hard cases. Section 303 of the Code of Criminal Procedure, 1973 provides:

> Any person accused of an offence before a criminal court, or against whom proceedings are instituted under this code, may be defended by a pleader of his choice.

Section 304 of the above Code provides, *inter alia*, that the sessions judge will provide a pleader at sessions trial to an accused at the state's expense, if the accused is not represented by a pleader or he has no sufficient means to engage a lawyer. The Advocates (Amendment) Act, 1973, also authorises the Bar Council of India and the State Bar Council to provide legal aid to the poor and in achieving the goal of cherished human values of personal liberty at the state's cost in certain hard cases.

Notwithstanding the provisions for legal services in the above mentioned enactments, the courts took a longer period to appreciate the spirit of provisions. A bare reading of these provisions conveys that the accused have been given the right to consult and be defended by a lawyer. The judicial attitude, however, softened gradually and in *Bashira* v. *State of U.P.*[9] the Supreme Court construed Rule 37 of the U.P. High Court Rules as a mandatory one. The rule *inter alia* authorised the sessions court at its discretion to provide legal assistance to an accused person. Judicial activism since then has continued with added vigour. The Supreme Court was distressed to see that the sessions judge did not take seriously the need to appoint a state counsel for undefended accused in "grave" cases.

The Supreme Court further filled the constitutional gap through creative judicial interpretation of article 21 following the *Maneka Gandhi* case. in *M.H. Hoskot* v. *State of Maharashtra*[10] and also in the *Hussainara Khatoon* case,[11] it held that a procedure which does not make legal services available to an accused person who is too poor to afford a lawyer and who would, therefore, have to go through the trial without legal assistance cannot possibly be regarded as reasonable, fair and just. The right to free legal assistance is an essential element of reasonable, fair and just procedure for a person accused of an offence and it must be held implicit in the guarantee of article 21.[12] The Supreme Court thus directed that on the next remand dates when the under-trial prisoners were produced before the magistrate, the state government should provide a lawyer at its own cost for the purpose of making an application for bail and opposing remand. In *Khatri* v. *State of Bihar*,[13] the Supreme Court further held that the state cannot avoid its constitutional obligation to provide legal services to a poor accused person by pleading financial or administrative inability.

Right to Bail

Article 9 (3) of the Covenant says "It shall not be the general rule that person awaiting trial shall be detained in custody, but release may be subject to guarantee to appear for trial, at another stage of judicial proceedings, and should occasion arise, for execution of the judgment. In the *Hussainara Khatoon* case[14] it was also considered as to when and under what circumstances bail should be granted and what the nature of such bail should be. One of the major reasons for denying justice to the poor by keeping them for years in pre-trial detention is the highly unsatisfactory bail system in India. It suffers from the erroneous assumption that risk of monetary loss is the only deterrent against fleeing from justice. The Code of Criminal Procedure, even after its reenactment in 1973, continues to adopt the same antiquated approach as the earlier code enacted towards the end of the last century and when an accused person is to be released on his personal bond, it insists that the bond should contain a monetary obligation requiring the accused to pay a sum of money in case he fails to appear at the trial. Moreover, as if this were not a sufficient deterrent to the poor, the courts insist that the accused should produce sureties who will stand bail for him and these sureties must again establish their solvency to be able to pay up the amount of the bail in case the accused fails to appear to answer the charge. This system of bail operates very harshly against the poor and it is only the non-poor who are able to take advantage of it by getting themselves released on bail. The Supreme Court in this case was of the view that the risk of monetary loss is not the only deterrent against fleeing from justice, but there are other factors, which act as equal deterrents against fleeing. If the court is satisfied, after taking into account, on the basis of information placed before it, that the accused has his roots in the community and is not likely to abscond, it can safely release the accused on his personal bond. The Supreme Court, therefore, laid down certain conditions for granting bail to the accused.[15] The court further pointed out that even where an accused person is released on a personal bond it is necessary to caution the court that the amount of the bond which it fixes should not be based merely on the nature of the charge, but the bond should depend upon the individual financial circumstances of the accused and the probability of his absconding. The Supreme Court, thus, by its judicial activism, helped to advance the right in article 9 (3) of the Covenant.

Right to Be Tried without Undue Delay

Article 14 (3) of the Covenant declares that everyone against whom a criminal charge has been levied shall be tried without undue delay. The Constitution does not expressly provide that a person has a right to be tried without undue delay. In the *Hussainara Khatoon* case,[16] the Supreme Court held that though speedy trial is not specifically enumerated as a fundamental right, it is implicit in the broad sweep and content of article

21, which deals with the right to life and liberty. Justice Bhagwati in this case observed:

> No procedure, which does not ensure a reasonably quick trial can be regarded as "reasonable, fair or just" and it would fall foul of article 21 There can, therefore, be no doubt that speedy trial, and by speedy trial we mean reasonably expeditious trial, is an integral and essential part of the fundamental right to life and liberty ensured in article 21.[17]

The Supreme Court again in *Kadra Pehadiya* v. *State of Bihar*,[18] where four persons were confined to Pakud Jail for about eight years without trial, took the matter aggressively. It observed that it is a crying shame upon the adjudicatory system, which keeps men in jail for years without a trial.

Right of Prisoners to Be Treated with Humanity

Article 10 (1) of the Covenant provides that all persons deprived of their liberty shall be treated with humanity and with respect for the inherent dignity of the human person. There is no such provision in the Indian Constitution which safeguards against the discretionary and brutal treatment given to prisoners. In *Charles Shobharj* v. *Supdt, Central Jail, Tihar, New Delhi*,[19] where the petitioner complained of the barbaric and inhuman treatment inflicted on him and that intentional discrimination was made against him, the Supreme Court held that the right to life is more than mere animal existence or vegetable substance. Even in prison a person is required to be treated with dignity and one enjoys all the rights specified in article 19 and 21. It restricted such treatment and regarded it as violation of the right to life guaranteed under article 21. It further ordered the removal of bar-fetters on the petitioner. The Supreme Court again in *Francis Coralie Mullin* v. *Union Territory of Delhi*,[20] held that the right to life protected under article 21 is not confined merely broad matrix the right to the use of every faculty or limb through which life is enjoyed as also the right to live with basic human dignity. The Supreme Court thus elevated immunity against torture or cruel, inhuman or degrading treatment or punishment to the status of a fundamental right under article 21, thought it is not specifically enumerated and a fundamental right in the Constitution and incorporated under article 7 of the Covenant.

In *Sheela Barse* v. *State of Maharashtra*,[21] the treatment of women in police lock-ups came up for discussion. It is a well known fact that conditions in police lock-ups are far from satisfactory. In the case it was complained that there was custodial violence to women prisoners while they were confined in the police lock-ups in Bombay. In a report submitted by Dr. Desai, the Supreme Court gave detailed directions with a view to improving the conditions in the lock-ups and providing adequate protection to the arrested persons and particularly to women confined in the police lock-ups.

The Supreme Court also condemned the use of handcuffs in chaining prisoners in *Prem Shankar Shukla* v. *Delhi Administration.*[22] It held in the case that no prisoner shall be handcuffed or fettered routinely or merely for the convenience of the custodian or escort. The compulsion of security must be so pressing that no alternative will work except handcuffs. There must be material sufficiently stringent to satisfy a reasonable mind that there is clear and present danger of escape of the prisoner who is being transported by breaking out of police control and further that by adding to the escort or other strategy, he cannot be kept under control. The judicial officer before whom the prisoner is produced must also interrogate the prisoner to find out whether he has been subjected to handcuffs and, if he has been, the escorting officer must be asked to explain his action. The court in the case also struck as arbitrary and irrational, the classification of prisoners for the purpose of handcuffs into "better class" and "ordinary class" and laid down that the same criterion must apply in all cases whether a prisoner should be handcuffed or not.

In the *Sunil Batra* case,[23] the Supreme Court also expressed itself emphatically against solitary confinement of a prisoner whether under sentence of death or otherwise. The court was of the view that solitary confinement has a degrading and dehumanising effect on the prisoner.

Right not to Be Imprisoned for Inability to Fulfill a Contractual Obligation

Article 11 of the Covenant on Civil and Political Rights provides that no one shall be imprisoned merely on the ground of inability to fulfill a contractual obligation. However, in Part III, this right has not been specifically provided. The Supreme Court in *Jolly George Verghese* v. *Bank of Cochin,*[24] held that to cast a person in a prison because of his poverty and consequent inability to meet his contractual liability is a violation of article 21 of the Constitution. He also held that freedom from imprisonment for non-payment of debt is covered under article 21 of the Constitution.

Right to Shelter

The Supreme Court has guaranteed right to shelter in *Chameli Singh* v. *State of U.P.*[25] It held that the right to shelter is a fundamental right under

Article 21 of the Constitution. Right to live guaranteed in any civilised society implies the right to food, water, decent environment, education, medical care and shelter. These are basic human rights known to any civilised society. All civil, political, social and cultural rights cannot be exercised without them. Shelter for a human being is a home where he has opportunities to grow physically, mentally, intellectually and spiritually.

Right against Delayed Execution

The Supreme Court has held that delay in execution of death sentence exceeding 2 years would be sufficient ground to invoke the protection of Article 21, i.e. right to life and personal liberty.[26]

Prevention of Sexual Harassment of Working Women

Women who generally work in the offices have to face problems against sexual harassments by their bosses and colleagues. The Supreme Court held in *Smt. Vishakha* v. *State of Rajasthan*,[27] that it is the duty of the employer or other responsible persons in work places or other institutions whether public or private, to prevent sexual harassment of working women. Express prohibition of sexual harassment which includes physical contact and advances, a demand or request for sexual favours, sexually coloured remarks, verbal or non-verbal conduct of sexual nature should be noticed, published and circulated in appropriate ways. Appropriate work conditions should be provided in respect of work leisure, health and hygiene to ensure that there is no hostile environment towards women at work place.

Professional Obligation of Doctors

In *Parmananda Katara* v. *Union of India*,[28] the Supreme Court held that it is the professional obligation of all doctors, whether in government or private to extend medical aid to the injured immediately to preserve life without waiting legal formalities to be complied with by the police under the Code of Criminal Procedure.

Similarly in *Paschim Bang Khet Mazdoor Samiti* v. *State of West Bengal*,[29] the Supreme Court held that the denial of medical aid by government hospital to a person suffering from serious head injuries and brain hemorrhage, because of non-availability of beds, amounted to violation of right to life under article 21 of the Constitution.

Right to Livelihood

In *D.K. Yadav* v. *J.M.A. Industries,*[30] the Supreme Court held that the right to life includes the right to livelihood and therefore termination of the service of a worker without providing him reasonable opportunity of hearing is unjust, arbitrary and illegal.

Right to Health and Medical Assistance

In *Vincent Parikur langara* v. *Union of India,*[31] the General Secretary of Public Interest Law Service Society, Cochin, asked the Supreme Court for directions to the government in public interest to ban import, manufacture, sale and distribution of such drugs, which were recommended by the Drugs Consultative Committee and also asked for cancellation of all licenses authorising import, manufacture, sale and distribution in respect of such drugs. The Supreme Court held that the right to maintenance and improvement of public health is included in the right to live with human dignity enshrined in article 21.

In *Consumer Education and Research Centre* v. *Union of India,*[32] the petitioner filed a petition for the protection of the health of the workers engaged in mines and asbestos industries with adequate mechanism for diagnosis and control of the silent killer disease "asbestosis". The Supreme Court held that the right to health and medical care is a fundamental right under article 21 of the Constitution, which makes the life of workmen meaningful and purposeful with dignity of person. Right to livelihood includes better standard of life, hygienic conditions in work place and leisure.

State of Punjab v. *Mohinder Singh Chawla,*[33] the Supreme Court held that it is now settled that the right to health is integral to the right to life. If the government servant has suffered an ailment, which requires treatment at a specialised approved hospital and on reference the government servant had undergone such treatment, then it is the duty of the state to bear the expenditure incurred by the government servants.

Equal Pay for Equal Work

State of Haryana v. *Rajpal Sharma,*[34] teachers in privately managed, aided school in Haryana are entitled to same salary and inflation allowance as is paid to teachers in Government school because the teachers at both places have to perform similar duties and bear similar responsibilities.

Right to Education

In *Mohini Jain* v. *State of Karnataka*,[35] the Supreme Court held that the right to education is fundamental right under article 21 of the Constitution, which cannot be denied to a citizen by charging higher fee known as capitation fee. The Supreme Court was of the view that the right to life under article 21 and the dignity of an individual cannot be assured unless it is accompanied by the right to education.

Non-citizens Entitled to Right to Life

Right to life and personal liberty guaranteed under article 21 is not limited to citizens only but also to non-citizens. They are equally entitled to right to life. In *National Human Rights Commission* v. *State of Arunachal Pradesh*,[36] a public interest litigation was filed by the Commission regarding 65,000 chakamas who migrated from Bangladesh and settled in the State of Arunachal Pradesh, but the All Arunachal Pradesh Student Union had threatened to forcibly expel them from the state. The Supreme Court held that it is the Constitutional duty of the state to protect the life and liberty of every person whether citizen or non-citizen.

Rights Recognized in the Covenant neither Guaranteed in the Fundamental Rights nor Recognised as Fundamental in the Beginning by the Supreme Court

There are certain rights which although recognised in the Covenant are neither guaranteed in Part III of the Constitution nor have they been regarded by the Supreme Court as fundamental. For example, the right to privacy has been stipulated in the Covenant on Civil and Political Rights under article 17 (1) which says that no one shall be subjected to arbitrary or unlawful interference with his privacy, family, home or correspondence, nor to unlawful attacks on his honour and reputation. But this right is not guaranteed in the Indian Constitution. In *Kharak Singh* v. *State of U.P.*[37] it was held by the Supreme Court that the "domiciliary visits" were an infringement of the right to privacy and violative of the citizen's fundamental right to personal liberty guaranteed under article 21 of the Constitution. In the *State of Maharashtra* v. *Madhukar Narayan*,[38] a police inspector visited the house of one Banubai in uniform and demanded to have sexual intercourse with her. On refusing he tried to molest her. The Supreme Court held that the right to privacy is available even to a woman of easy virtue and no one can invade her privacy as and when he likes. In *People's Union for Civil Liberties* v. *Union of India* and another,[39] the Supreme Court held that right to hold a telephone conversation in the privacy of one's house or office without interference can certainly be claimed as right to privacy.

Rights Provided in the Covenant but not Accepted by India in the Instrument of Accession

India while acceding to the Covenant on Civil and Political Rights had made certain reservations. They have been laid down in the Instrument Accession by way of the Declaration of 1979. It specifies the conditions of its willingness to become a party to the Covenant. They, thus, restrict the application of the Covenant on it. The effect of the declaration is that the Covenant will be binding on India subject to the provisions stipulated therein. The Supreme Court, however, in order to give relief to the people enforced the provisions of the Covenant.

Article 9 (3) of the Covenant provides that any person "who has been the victim of unlawful arrest or detention shall have an enforceable right to compensation". While acceding to the Covenant, the Government of India declared:

> (ii) With reference to Article 9 of the International Covenant on Civil and Political Rights, the Government of India takes the position that the provisions of the Article shall be so applied as to be in consonance with the provisions of clauses (3) to (7) of Article 22 of the Constitution of India. Further, under the Indian Legal System, there is no enforceable right to compensation for persons claiming to be victims of unlawful arrest or detention against the State.[40]

The Supreme Court in a few cases through its judicial activism took the lead in bringing the provisions of the Covenant under the purview of fundamental rights. The Supreme Court ordered for the first time in 1983 in *Rudul Sen* v. *State of Bombay*,[41] the payment of compensation of Rs. 30,000 (equivalent to 2308 U.S. dollars) to the person unlawfully detained by the Government for 14 years. In the case, the petitioner was acquitted by a sessions court on 3 June 1968. Consequently, the court holding the detention illegal ordered the State of Bihar to pay to the petitioner as an interim measure. The Court further made it clear that the petitioner was not precluded "from bringing a suit to recover appropriate damages from the state and its erring officials".[42] In *Bhim Singh* v. *State of Jammu & Kashmir* a Member of Jammu and Kashmir Legislative Assembly was detained by the police on the eve of the Assembly session. From the facts of the case the Supreme Court came to the conclusion that "Shri Bhim Singh was not produced either before the magistrate on 11th or before the sub-judge on 13th, though he was arrested in the early hours of 10th of September, 1985".[43] According to article 22 (2) of the Indian Constitution, persons arrested or detained "shall be produced before the nearest Magistrate within twenty-four hours". On the given facts the court found that the conduct of the police officers "was a gross violation of Shri Bhim Singh's constitutional rights under article 21 and 22 (2)".[44] Though his unlawful detention could be attributable to "Minions, in the lower rungs of the ladder", the court did not have the "slightest doubt that the responsibility lies elsewhere and with the higher echelons of the government of Jammu and Kashmir.[45] Since the constitution rights of Bhim Singh were violated with impunity", he must be "suitably and adequately compensated".[46] The court, thus, directed the state of Jammu and Kashmir to pay Rs. 50,000 (equivalent to 3854 U.S. dollars) to the petitioner.

Conclusion

In this paper only a few very important cases concerning basic human rights have been discussed. it will, however, be seen from these cases that a number of rights which are not specifically provided in the Constitution in Part III as "fundamental rights" have been regarded as fundamental and are available to individuals though the process of creative interpretation. The indifferent attitude of the government and consciousness amongst the judges of the Supreme Court as to India's commitment and its obligation undertaken through the ratification of the Covenant have changed the trend of the decisions of the court. They did not wait for the new enactment to come. They instead interpreted the fundamental rights, which are specifically mentioned in the Constitution by name in such a way that the rights enshrined in the Covenant which do not find a place in the Constitution may be available to the citizens. In fact this entire human rights jurisprudence has been the result of a most startling and remarkable development of the law following upon the landmark decisions in the *Maneka Gandhi* case. This new jurisprudence, which has been evolved by the judiciary is the result of case-to-case development of which an attempt has been made to give a synoptic view so that the various dimensions and facts of this new jurisprudence may be appreciated. It has been a most fascinating development and it should be a matter of pride and satisfaction to the people of India. The Supreme Court has played a very important and significant role in this regard. It has expanded the reach and ambit of the fundamental rights rather than attenuate its meaning and content. It has interpreted the Constitution in such a liberal way that the rights provided in the Covenant have been made available to the people in India. Article 21 together with article 19 of the Indian Constitution cover practically all aspects of personal freedom. They embrace both procedural and substantive rights and include all varieties of rights to exercise personal freedoms, which could fall under a broad concept of human rights. The Supreme Court, as and when cases have gone before it, has always given the widest possible interpretation of fundamental rights so as to take sympathetic and human consideration.

In India many rights provided in the Covenant on Civil and Political Rights are available to a person either by virtue of their being in Part III of the Constitution, or because of the bold and liberal interpretation given by the Supreme Court by enlarging the meaning and scope of the specific fundamental rights, but in practice things are quite different. These rights are not available to the masses especially to the poor, ignorant and illiterate people. They are deprived of these rights because of the lack of enthusiasm and consciousness towards their rights. Lack of effective implementation of the laws by the authorities, the rough attitude of the police, administrators, judges and policy-makers are also responsible for the violation of human rights to a great extent.

Notes

1 See Beg J. in A.D.M. Jubalpur v. S. Shukla, A.I.R. 1976 S.C. 1207 at 1293.
2 See Birma v. State of Rajashan; A.I.R. 1951 Raj. 127; Nanka v. State of Rajasthan A:I.R. 1951 Raj., 153; Maganbhai Ishwarbhai Patel v. Union of India A.I.R. 1969 S.C. 793, J.G. Verghese v. Bank of Cochin A.I.R. 1980 S.C. 470.
3 Maneka Gandhi v. Union of India A.I.R. 1978 S.C. 597 at 640-641.
4 In 1981 out of 1,410,767 total prisoners on 30 June 1981, there were 87,144 under trial prisoners i.e., 6.15 percent of the total.
5 Hussainara Khatoon v. State of Bihar (i) A.I.R. 1979 S.C. 1360; (ii) 1979 S.C. 1369; (iii) 1979 S.C. 1377, (iv) A.I.R. 1979 S.C. 1819.
6 A.I.R. 1979 S.C. 1369.
7 Id. at 1369.
8 A.I.R. 1952 S.C. 227.
9 A.I.R. 1969 S.C. 1313.
10 A.I.R. 1978 S.C. 1548.
11 A.I.R. 1979 S.C. 1369.
12 Id. at 1376.
13 A.I.R. 1981 S.C. 928.
14 A.I.R. 1979 S.C. 1360.
15 Id. at 1364.
16 1979 S.C. 1365.

17 Ibid.
18 A.I.R. 1981 S.C. 939.
19 A.I.R. 1978 S.C. 1514.
20 A.I.R. 1981 S.C. 746., See also D.K.Basu v. State of West Bengal A.I.R. 1997 S.C. 610.
21 A.I.R. 1983 S.C. 378.
22 A.I.R. 1980 S.C. 1535., See also citizen for Democracy v. State of Assam (1995) 3 SCC 743.
23 Sunil Batra v. Delhi Administration A.I.R. 1978 S.C. 1675.
24 A.I.R. 1980 S.C. 470.
25 (1996) 2 SCC 549.
26 T.V.Vatheeswaran v. State of Tamil Nadu A.I.R. 1981 S.C. 625.
27 A.I.R. 1997 S.C. 3011.
28 A.I.R. 1989 S.C. 2039.
29 (1996) 4 SCC 37.
30 (1993) 3 SCC 258.
31 (1987) 2 SCC 165.
32 (1995) 3 SCC 42.
33 (1997) 2 SCC 83.
34 A.I.R. 1997 S.C. 449.
35 (1992) 3 SCC 666.
36 (1996) 1 SCC 742.
37 A.I.R. 1963 S.C. 1295.
38 A.I.R. 1991 S.C. 207.
39 (1997) 1 SCC 307.
40 Emphasis added.
41 A.I.R. 1982 S.C. 1986, See also P.A.Narayan v. Union of India (1998) 3 SCC 67.
42 Id. at 1089.
43 A.I.R. 1986 S.C. 494.
44 Id. at 499.
45 Ibid.
46 Ibid.

Part III
Minority Rights

11. How to Justify the Rights of Political Minorities

GERHARD SEEL

The issue I want to discuss is normally referred to in the literature as 'the right to national self-determination'.[1] It is understood by this that the holders of such a right are 'peoples' or 'nations'.[2] In this paper I shall avoid this terminology because it is a matter of dispute as to which group qualifies as a people or a nation. Instead, I shall follow a subjective approach to that question, speaking not of peoples or nations but of political minorities.

In my terminology, a political minority is a group of citizens of a given state who strive for the establishment of an autonomous or independent state on a determined part of the given state's territory. The rights I shall try to justify are as follows:

1. The right of each member of the group to form an association or political party with the aim of promoting peacefully their political aspirations.
2. The right of that association or party to a democratic vote in the determined part of the given state in order to find out whether a qualified majority of the population living in that region (60%) accepts the creation of the new state.
3. The right to the transformation of the given state into a federal state, and the establishment of a new state that will become a part of the federal state, on condition that said vote has reached the requested majority.

I consider these rights not as positive rights granted by the positive law or constitution of a given state, but rather as non-positive or moral rights which oblige the legislators of any given state to grant these rights in the positive law or constitution of that state, i.e. to transform them into positive rights.[3]

I am, of course, not the first to give such a justification, and further there is a certain agreement in the relevant literature that such rights should be generally recognised.[4] Why, then, is it worth addressing the issue again?

This seems to be necessary for the following reasons:

1. Non-positive or moral rights do not exist in the way those things or facts exist. Things and facts, at least for a realist, exist independently of any theory, which states or proves their existence. Therefore they can be discovered by a theory. Rights, on the other hand, cannot be discovered by a theory, as already existing entities. They exist only insofar as a theory successfully justifies our acknowledgement of them: there are no rights without justification. So the slightest weakness of the justifying theory will affect the rights themselves.
2. Any theory that tries to justify non-positive rights has to take moral skeptics seriously, who simply deny the existence of any non-positive or moral rights whatsoever, and present arguments in favour of their position, which are not easily refuted.
3. A close look at the relevant literature shows that almost nobody takes skepticism seriously, and that most of the arguments in favour of political minority rights either rest on strong silent assumptions or show some logical deficiency.

Therefore a new critical examination of the issue is necessary. I shall attempt this by asking the following questions:

1. Who is the holder of the rights in question?
2. What is the source of (the reason for) these rights?
3. What is the exact content of these rights?

These questions are logically connected in such a way that the answer given to one of them affects the answer to be given to the others. Moreover, the second question appears to be the fundamental one. According to the answers given to it we can distinguish three main types of theory that attempt to justify political minority rights: these are the value theory, the interest theory and the contractualist theory. I shall take each of these theories in turn, and criticise it from a skeptical point of view.

I

The value theory of rights[5] is actually the most currently popular way to justify non-positive (moral) rights. Its main thesis is that the ultimate source of any moral right is the intrinsic value of the bearer of that right. For instance, in environmental ethics we often find the argument that because a sane environment has an intrinsic value it has the right to protection and safeguard. Similarly, in the present debate, advocates of political minority rights often argue that because the culture of each people has an intrinsic value, and the preservation of that culture presupposes self-government, each people has a right to self-government. As the sources of these rights are intrinsic values, the bearers of the rights are the entities that have those values. Hence, it is claimed, the bearers of the right to self-government are not the individual members of the political minorities, but rather the groups themselves.

Let us analyse the logical structure of this type of argument. It starts from the following principle:

P1 Any entity that has intrinsic value has the right to existence and preservation against everybody able to promote that aim.

P2 As a second premise the argument employs a statement affirming that social entities (groups) of a certain type (i.e., having a certain set of properties) have intrinsic value.

From these two premises one can deduce that entities of the specified type do have the right to exist and to be preserved.

P3 In order to deduce from this conclusion that the specified type of social entity has also a right to self-government, the argument employs an auxiliary premise stating that the preservation of that entity presupposes self-government.

It is easy to attack each of the three main premises of the argument.

P1 presupposes that value judgements can be true or false in an explainable way. Now, this is more than doubtful. To be sure, in recent years the thesis that there are objective values has gained supporters. Nevertheless, I consider the usual criticism of that thesis to be sound and convincing. For instance, J.L. Mackie has argued that entities of the required kind would be very strange, and that there is neither a consensus about values nor a scientific method, which could bring such a consensus about.[6]

But even if we accepted the objective value thesis, we would not be obliged to accept P1. For it is far from obvious that 'having intrinsic value' implies 'having a right to exist'. According to my conception 'A has a right to exist' does not simply mean 'A world in which A exists is a better world than a world in which A does not exist'. It rather means that some identifiable subject of action (an individual or a collective agent) is under an obligation to promote or preserve the existence of A by acting accordingly, and that correspondingly A (or his authorised representative) has a claim against him. In order to deduce the latter from the former, you either need a valid bridge-principle or you must show that for logical or semantical reasons the former implies the latter. I do not see how one could convincingly argue for either of these.

P2 consists of a set of concrete value-judgements. Consequently, we usually find in theories of the first type a catalogue of properties that a social entity must have in order to qualify for the moral right in question.

Supporters of the present theory believe that these properties or a combination of them confer intrinsic value on a social unity. The trouble is that there is no agreement at all on these crucial properties. Margalit and Raz (1995, 82-85) for instance, propose the following six properties:

1. Common character and common culture;
2. Transmission of that culture from one generation to the next;
3. Membership by mutual recognition;
4. Importance of the group-membership for the self-identification of the individual member;
5. Independence of the membership from any achievement;
6. Largeness of the group that excludes familiarity with all members.

Others add a common language and a common history as qualifying features. However, when it comes to justifying their claims, the proponents have little or nothing to say. Furthermore, one might argue on the basis of a different set of criteria that the given state has intrinsic value and therefore has a right to be protected against separation from one of its parts. In fact, the enumeration of qualifying properties seems to be a rather arbitrary procedure.

There is only one kind of argument that seems to avoid this arbitrariness. Communitarian authors often argue that the intrinsic value of cultural groups is grounded in the fact that individuals need membership in cultural groups for their self-esteem and self-identification.[7] I shall not discuss to what degree this is exactly right. However, it seems to me that even if it were, it would only be a reason why individuals wish the preservation of the group they belong to, rather than a reason which justifies its intrinsic value or its objective right to exist, unless, of course, this wish in itself is sufficient to ground such a value or such a right.

Finally, P3 states an instrumental relation between the preservation of a group and the fact that it enjoys self-government.[8] History indeed shows that sometimes self-government has contributed to, or even proved necessary for, the preservation of a culture, but in other cases there has been no connection between the political status of a group and the flourishing of its culture. But this point aside, there prevails a deeper misunderstanding in the above kind of argument. The classical political philosophy from Hobbes to Kant did not understand self-government as a means to the preservation of a people or a culture. It was either conceived of as a means to the preservation of individuals (Hobbes) or as a means to the preservation of the freedom and rights of the individual (Rousseau and Kant). To be sure, communitarian philosophers want to overturn this classical conception. But in order to achieve this, they must show what is wrong with it. Prima facie at least, the classical conception seems more convincing than the communitarian alternative.

Let us now turn to the second type of theory, the interest theory of rights.[9] As its label indicates, this theory holds that interest is the primary source of moral rights.[10] In a way, this position is more plausible than the value theory. Normally, people claim to have a right to something only if they are interested in that thing. However, we may doubt that having an interest in something is sufficient or even necessary to having a right to it. At least in the domain of positive rights there are many things we are interested in without having a right to them; and, vice versa, there are things we have a right to although we have no interest in them. For instance, I have the right to be a candidate in the next election, but I am not at all interested in such a candidature. I cannot see that this should be different in the domain of moral rights.

Another weak point in the present theory is the enlargement of the set of entities having interests. According to it, in order to have an interest in something, it is not at all necessary to be conscious of that interest or to be able to manifest it. It is sufficient to have a kind of teleological mode of existence. Consequently, the supporters of this type of theory attribute interests to plants, biotopes, biological species and, concerning our question, to cultures and groups. A skeptic would, of course, question this teleological view of the world. He might with good reason deny a teleological character to entities that do not consciously pursue goals. It is especially doubtful that cultures or groups have interests unless they have given themselves an internal organisation enabling them to articulate interests unequivocally.

But even if we accepted this, my first critical objection would be sufficient to reject this theory. Its supporters could, of course, try to improve it by speaking of legitimate interest instead of plain interest. Legitimate interests are interests, which deserve respect and protection. But in this case, they would have to show which interests are legitimate, and on what grounds. So the burden of proof rests with them.

Finally, I doubt that entities that do not have the capacity for deciding and willing could possibly be bearers of rights.[11] As we shall see later, in order to be a possible bearer of rights it is even required that a being be able to understand what a rule is, what an obligation is and what it means to follow a rule and to fulfil an obligation. This is the case for groups whose internal organization enables them to form an unequivocal group will. Ethnic groups, however, do not necessarily have such an internal organisation.

Concerning the legitimisation of interests the third type of theory (the contractualist theory), is in a much better position. In fact, contractualist theories offer a plausible basis for the distinction between legitimate and non-legitimate interests. According to T.M. Scanlon's[12] version of contractualism, the following criterion of right and wrong holds:

An act is wrong if its performance under the circumstances would be disallowed by any system of rules for the general regulation of behaviour, which no one could reasonably reject as a basis for informed, unforced general agreement. Consequently, an interest is legitimate if and only if its protection would be granted by any system of rules, which no one could reasonably reject as a basis for informed, unforced general agreement. So, if and only if no one could reasonably reject a rule, which protects the existence of a minority group, this group has a moral right to exist.[13]

This conception raises many skeptical questions. The most important of these asks how we should understand the condition of reasonable rejectability. Which are the reasons that allow someone to reject a general agreement concerning a general rule of behaviour? Scanlon's answer to that question is that in order to have such a reason it is not sufficient that the rule in question hurts my interests - it must also hurt me harder than it hurts the opposite interests of others.[14] This of course requires comparability of interests, as Scanlon rightly acknowledges.

Now, as I argued before, it is doubtful that entities that can neither feel nor express interests are potential interest-bearers. Therefore, the notion of group-interests itself seems to be thus far unjustified. Furthermore, even if there were authentic group interests, it still would be unsettled, how a general law could hurt them harder than, say, the opposite interests of individuals. Let us envisage a case where the interests of a group are opposed to the interests of individuals. For instance, the existence of a group could be in danger because too great a number of members want to leave the group. In this case, the interest of those individuals in leaving the group is opposite to the interest of the group to hold onto its members. In such a case we need to compare group interests with the interests of individuals in order to know who would be more disadvantaged, the group (if the law allows individuals to leave) or the individuals (the law forbids leaving). Without knowing this nobody could ever tell who has a reason to reject a law which favours the interests of the opposite party. But in order to make this comparison one ought to be able to put oneself in the shoes of the group, and judge how badly it would feel if its interests were not protected. This seems completely impossible. Therefore, the comparability of group interests and interests of individuals is highly questionable. This is my first reason for not following this version of contractualism in my justification of political minority rights.

But there is another, more fundamental reason. Scanlon's contractualism rests on the assumption that people have a motivation 'to justify one's actions to others on grounds they could not reasonably reject'.[15] Though he does not claim that this motivation is universal or natural he still believes that it 'is quite strong in most people' (p.117). However, this is too weak a starting-point on which to ground a general theory of moral rights. What a contractualist theory needs is an argument showing that everybody should be so motivated. Only on this basis will the theory provide us with the kind of justification of political rights we are after. That is why I cannot accept the third type of justification either, even though it comes very close to my own way of founding moral rights. In the next section, I explain what my way consists of.

II

Let us make a fresh start. In the first section, I used skeptical arguments against he three most prominent types of justification given in the debate about political minority rights. Now I must keep my promise to take skepticism seriously in my own justification of these rights. I must show that my theory withstands skeptical attacks. In order to do this, I shall envisage a skeptic who does not accept non-positive (moral) rights at all. The only kind of rights he admits are positive rights, and he argues that positive law is the only conceivable form of law.

Let us first clarify the difference between positive and non-positive law.

Def.1 A juridical norm is a positive norm if and only if its validity stems from an act of legislation by a legislative organ of a state which has the power and the intention to punish transgressions of that norm.

Def.2 A juridical norm is a non-positive or moral norm if and only if its validity is independent of any positive legislation and relies essentially on a theoretical justification.

Note that these definitions allow a norm to be both positive and moral.

Now, the skeptic will argue that there is no norm that fulfils the definition of a non-positive norm because there is no possible justification of the validity of a norm that does not finally rely on an act of legislation.

The only way to overcome this kind of skepticism involves showing that the type of validity, which the skeptic does recognise, i.e. positive validity, presupposes the validity of at least one non-positive norm. I have showed this in detail in a forthcoming article;[16] for now a brief sketch of my argument must suffice.

In order to justify the validity of positive norms, we need so-called bridge principles. These are conditionals or biconditionals that have a practical proposition and a theoretical proposition as arguments. They say, in other words, that something should be the case if and only if something else is the case. An instance of such a bridge principle could be the following:

A positive norm x is valid in the state y if and only if x has successfully passed a procedure of legislation according to the rules of the constitution of y.

An other good example would be Hans Kelsen's 'Grundnorm', which says that a legal norm is valid if and only if it has been put in force in accordance with the rules of the constitution of a state and if it shows efficiency over a sufficiently long period of time, i.e. if it is implemented by most of the citizens during a long period.[17]

Now, it is evident that bridge principles have no justifying force unless they are valid themselves. Radical positivists or conventionalists try to show that this validity in turn can only have positive grounds. This means that it is itself grounded in a bridge principle of the above type. But it can easily be shown that this leads either to an infinite regress or to a vicious circle, neither of which is acceptable. The right conclusion to draw from this is that positive norms presuppose for their validity at least one valid non-positive norm. This is the reason why Hans Kelsen characterises his 'Groundnorm' as 'nicht gesetzt, sondern vorausgesetzt'.[18]

So, either one renounces the claim that positive law is valid, or one must admit the general thesis that there is at least one non-positive norm binding any being who either gives or lives under positive law. Of course, the sceptic can still opt for the first possibility. But if so, he is no longer morally entitled to blame or punish any transgressor of positive laws. If we want to avoid this consequence, we must look for a practical proposition that does the job of a bridge principle in justifying positive law and has to be accepted by everyone as valid.

Before attempting this, we should reflect briefly on which method to follow. Of course, we could choose just the first principle that seems to do the job, for instance Kelsen's Grundnorm. However, we would then again expose ourselves to skeptical objections. These can only be avoided, or at least minimised, if we look for a principle that has the following properties:

1. It should be as weak as possible. This will make it less vulnerable to criticism, and more acceptable for most people.
2. It should be as fundamental as possible. This means that in the ideal case its validity will depend on no other principle, and the validity of any other practical principle will depend directly or indirectly upon it.
3. It should be a practical proposition and not just a theoretical one.

I have explained elsewhere how to find and justify such a principle.[19] Here I can only give an outline of my main argument. It relies on my conception of rationality and practical validity. I define rationality as the capacity of a being to make decisions by applying decision criteria and especially by using general decision criteria, i.e. rules. Further, I take rational beings to be free to apply a given criterion or not. They exercise this freedom by deciding whether they will apply the criterion in a given decision situation. Analogously with the difference between object language and metalanguage, I call this kind of decision 'metadecision'. Now, the question is whether in the metadecision I can also apply a criterion and what this criterion could be. The answer is that there is indeed a possible criterion for the metadecision and that this consists of a practical proposition saying that the given criterion should be applied in the first-order decision. I use this idea in defining the concept of practical validity:

A practical proposition or a norm is valid if and only if it should be applied by any subject that is in a decision situation that falls under it.

Practical validity in this sense differs radically from theoretical validity, i.e. truth, in respect of its validity conditions. The validity of a practical proposition does not ultimately depend on the way reality is, but rather on its logical relation to other valid practical propositions and on the capacity of rational beings to put practical propositions into force, i.e. their nomothetical power.

In fact, rational beings are capable and entitled to put into force practical propositions or norms by binding themselves, either on their own or with others. Where does this strange power to put oneself under an obligation stem from and how is it justified? I hold that this power is grounded in the following principle that I consider being the most fundamental practical principle:

> *Rational beings are morally obliged to make their decisions not blindly but in a rational way, i.e. to use criteria in their decision making.*

This obligation cannot be justified by, or deduced from, any other practical principle; rather, any justification of other principles depends on it. So my defence of it must proceed via a transcendental argument: Somebody who denies the validity of the above principle must admit that the use of decision-criteria and the following of rules is completely up to each decision maker and that nobody is ever under an obligation to use a particular criterion or to follow a particular rule. This means that no practical principle could possibly have practical validity. On the other hand, the above principle is extremely weak. It demands merely that each rational being put into force decision-criteria, which she will use in her decision-making; and it authorises each rational being to do so. It does not prescribe any content for those criteria leaving it up to everyone which criteria they want to follow.

Although the normative principle just reached is very weak, I can use it in the construction of a theory that allows us to justify non-positive juridical norms. All I need in order to do this is to enlarge its scope: A person who, according to the principle of rationality, sets up a system of decision criteria or norms for himself, simultaneously acquires the capacity to live in accordance with himself, i.e. to avoid the mutual opposition and adversity of his decisions and of his willing. The norm of practical rationality can therefore also be understood as the commandment to live coherently, as the Stoics had already said.

Now, as soon as several people communicate and interact in their decisions, we must consider a possible enlargement of the scope of this principle: reason demands not only that a person be coherent with herself but also that persons be coherent with each other in their decisions. We should not, of course, commit the fallacy of supposing that this enlargement follows analytically from my practical principle.[20] In order to avoid such a fallacy, we must look carefully for a different justification of the enlargement I propose.

Let us attempt an analogy with another enlargement of the scope of a fundamental principle, one, which is usually accepted in the domain of theoretical behaviour. We normally consider as valid a practical principle that obliges everybody to make his beliefs coherent. By enlarging the scope of this principle, we obtain a norm that obliges those who are engaged in a common theoretical endeavour to seek a system of common coherent beliefs by way of argument and theoretical proof or rebuttal. This enlargement, though not obtained analytically, is unproblematic, because a group of researchers cannot obtain a satisfying theory without reaching a system of common coherent beliefs. Prima facie, one could believe that the enlargement of the scope of my practical principle is acceptable for the very same reasons.

However the analogy I established is not sufficient to yield that conclusion. A comparison of the realm of practical validity with the realm of scientific truth can make this clear. In the latter, according to the correspondence theory of truth, a proposition's truth or falsehood depends primarily on its relation to reality, with agreement between the scientists playing only a secondary, methodological role. However, in the realm of morality, as has been argued, the validity of a norm or the rightness of an action is defined not in terms of correspondence to a reality that is independent of human action, but rather in terms of an obligation to decide and to act in a definite way. This obligation has its very source in a property which all rational beings share, namely rationality. Therefore, the idea of agreement here not only guarantees the reaching of validity, but is constitutive of it. To justify this fundamental role, the analogy with theoretical agreement is clearly insufficient. We must analyse further the relations between practical validity, rationality and intersubjectivity.

The first point here is that rationality could not possibly be a privilege of one or a few human beings. If one has it, then all must have it. Now, if owing to her rationality, one human being is under a moral obligation, then all human beings will be as well. That means that concerning the principle of rational decision all human beings are under the same obligation; all understand the same obligation and recognise, as far as they view other human beings as rational, that all are under the same obligation. Therefore, everybody is a possible judge of everybody else, as far as the fulfillment of the fundamental duty is concerned.[21] Indeed, if there is, pace the skeptics, a difference between making the morally right and the morally wrong decision for an individual subject, then every rational being is a possible judge concerning this difference. No one can therefore avoid asking for moral approval from everybody else, nor can he consider himself morally justified as long as someone has good reasons to disapprove of his decisions and actions.

Secondly, if someone, in order to avoid moral disapproval by others, refuses to recognise them as rational beings, this refusal is not justified as long as he has no reason to believe that they are not rational beings. To deal with the possibility of the non-recognition of others as rational beings I need therefore a second practical principle that obliges any rational being to recognise other rational beings as such. This principle was first formulated by the German philosopher Fichte.

Thirdly, if someone has no good reason to disagree with the decisions and actions of other rational beings, he is obliged to give them his agreement. The burden of proof lays therefore with the one who disagrees with another.

The three points taken together show that as soon as there is a plurality of rational beings communicating with each other, the idea of practical validity goes together with the idea of intersubjective agreement. This is just what I meant when I formulated the principle of the coherence of the decisions of a group of communicating and mutually interfering persons. This gives us at the same time a better reason to adopt contractualism then the one Scanlon advances.

However, the content of this obligation is moral, not juridical. But we can easily reach a practical norm that has a juridical content by asking how best to comply with that obligation. A first way to do that consists in deciding and acting in such a manner that nobody is harmed or disadvantaged by one's decisions and actions. This is what Christian morality asks according to the famous verse: And unto him that smiteth thee on the one cheek offer also the other (Luke, 6:29). This way to obtain the agreement of others is neither the only one, nor the best. Nobody can reasonably refuse to agree with the decisions and actions of another if those decisions and actions comply with norms, which they have enacted together. So those who wish to avoid Christian morality and have no other way to gain the agreement of others are morally obliged to create, together with all others, an institution (the State) which makes it possible to live under commonly agreed positive law. This clearly is a norm of juridical content and accordingly the first norm of the law of reason.

From this norm we can deduce a first group of human rights: the so-called rights of political participation. These rights are all founded in the following principle: Every rational being has the right, against any other rational being with whom she communicates, to the common creation of a state, and to be accepted as a full member of that state. This principle will serve as a starting-point when I now come to the justification of the rights of political minorities.

III

According to a contractualist foundation of law, as developed in the preceding section, communicating persons have both non-positive rights and non-positive obligations against each other. These rights and obligations concern the creation of a state and the putting in force and administering of positive law. So the creation of positive law is itself a moral obligation, as contractualist justifications of the state have always argued. But in their legislation persons are not perfectly free. Rather, the limits and contents of positive law are regulated by further non-positive rules. The first and most general of these is the following:

A rule of behaviour qualifies as a possible positive law if and only if no one could reasonably reject it as a basis for informed, unforced general agreement.

In order to apply this principle, we need to know what is meant by a 'reason to reject a rule'. As we have seen, this cannot simply be a subjective interest or a subjective will of a person. It should rather be defined as a legitimate interest or will. But under what conditions is an interest or a will legitimate?

The following answer seems initially plausible: An interest or will of a person is legitimate as long and as far as its realisation is compatible with the realization of the corresponding interests and wills of anybody else.

However, it is not clear how I can apply this criterion, because interests and wills of persons are not only very often opposed to one other but also very different in kind and intensity. So, how can we know that the realisation of our interests is compatible with the realisation of the interests of everybody else? This can be answered by switching from the concrete and very diverse interests of each person to the metainterest that all persons have in common, i.e. the interest in the opportunity to pursue one's own interests as freely and as efficiently as possible. Traditionally, philosophers have called this opportunity 'freedom'. Thus, Kant declared: 'Freedom (independence from the constraining intention of someone else), as far as it can exist together with each others freedom according to a general law, is the only original right every human being is entitled to due to his humanity' (Metaphysics of Morals, AA VI, 237).

Following Kant, I define:

An interest or will of a person is legitimate if and only if its realisation is compatible with an equal freedom of anybody else.

Now, a man can restrict the freedom of another man in two ways: he can hinder him directly or he can make the other's actions impossible by withholding the necessary means. Positive law must regulate both kinds of restriction in order to assure everybody an equal freedom in pursuing his own interests.

However, this must be done according to the principle of legal minimalism:

The restriction of the freedom of everybody by law should never go beyond the level necessary to protect everybody's equal freedom.[22]

This level is determined by the exterior conditions of life, and can be more or less elevated. In the ideal case where nobody can interfere with the actions of others, no restriction of the freedom of anybody would be allowed. Law in this case would have to allow each to do whatever he liked. But normally, people interfere positively or negatively in their actions, and this makes it necessary to restrict their freedom accordingly.

Let us now examine whether on this basis I can justify the non-positive right of a political minority to self-government. Prima facie, an affirmative answer seems obvious. If people interfering in their actions are morally obliged to regulate these by positive law, then the members of groups living in the neighbourhood must have the moral right to form a state. But given that a political minority is a group living in an already existing state, the groups covered by this right are not political minorities. The question therefore is whether the existence of positive law in a state nullifies the right of groups living in that state to create a different state on its territory. Two arguments speak in favour of this: 1. By creating a state, the individuals have already honoured their moral obligation to live under commonly agreed laws. There is no further obligation to do this a second time. As the right to create a state is dependent on this obligation, it will be nullified as soon as there is no longer any obligation. 2. The obligation to create a state implies the obligation to observe the laws of that state. If, therefore, the positive laws of a state do not authorize secession or another kind of self-government on the territory of that state, then the members of a group living in that state cannot have a moral right to self-government. Both arguments constrain us to have a closer look at the obligations and rights implied in the right to create a state, in order to find a basis for the justification of political minority rights.

1. Let us first consider the contingent historic fact that the world contains more than one state. This fact is again connected with an other contingent historic fact, namely that in the building of states men applied the principle of territorial division rather than that of ethnic or cultural division. In this way we are confronted with a plurality of states which are separated from one another by territorial borders, and which all lay claim to sovereignty. It was one of Kant's greatest insights that states, which interfere with each other's actions, are to be treated by the philosophy of rights in the same way as individuals are. They have the obligation to regulate their interactions by commonly agreed positive laws and, in order to put such laws in force, to form a state of states. This means that the claim to sovereignty of each state is invalid. Sovereignty must be the privilege of the all-embracing state of states and, in the case of the particular states, be replaced by special legislative competencies. For the same reason, the building of states of states must be followed up until we reach as the highest possible legislating body, a world state. The latter therefore is the only genuinely sovereign state.

What reason really demands us to realise, according to this conception, is not just a state, but a federal state. This principle of federalism is only implemented with the creation of a federal world state that guarantees every member state its rights against other member states and its competence in the inner legislation.

Now, if this reasoning beginning from the obligations and rights of individuals, and leading to obligations and rights of ever more embracing states, ends in its bottom-to-top movement with the justification of a federal world-state, one might ask whether the reverse movement starting from the world state and going down to the individuals must not yield the same result. Let us suppose for the sake of argument that the only legislating body is a non-federal world state. Is such a state entitled to forbid by positive law any creation of particular federal states on its territory? If it were, we would get a non-symmetric situation with the bottom-to-top reasoning yielding a different result than the top-to-bottom reasoning. However, this would be very strange. Therefore, I doubt that a world state could reasonably have such a power. In order to prove this point, I need a deeper analysis of the content of the agreement reached in the creation of a state.

2. I said at the outset that the purpose of a state is the putting into force of positive rules of behaviour that make it possible for everybody to agree with what anybody else does. A rule of behaviour, I further argued, qualifies for positive legislation if and only if nobody has a reason to reject it. A good reason to reject a law would be the fact that it restricts one's freedom more than is necessary, or more than it restricts the freedom of others. Though this rule is formal and general it may make it very difficult to reach an actual agreement between the members of a state. Indeed, the more numerous are the members of a state, and the more their interests and values differ, the more difficult will it be to reach an agreement between them regarding a common rule of behaviour. It is very likely in this case that someone has a reason to reject a rule, or at least believes that he has. Therefore, it seems reasonable to limit the common positive legislation to those who share a minimum stock of values and beliefs, and to agree with the others that, given the difference in values and beliefs, every group has the right to regulate their own affairs. This leads us to the apparently paradoxical obligation to agree to disagree.

There is a further consideration that leads to the same conclusion. I said before that one has a reason to disagree with some one else if and only if his intentions and actions risk interfering with one's own intentions and actions. Therefore, the need for a common legislation concerns first of all those people who actually interfere in each other's actions. Consequently the density of regulation should be proportionate to the density of interaction. Now, it is more likely that closer neighbours interfere with each other than do people who live at a greater distance. The age of globalisation has only modified this triviality, and has not invalidated it.

This brings us to the following conclusion. Close neighbours more greatly need the regulation of their interactions by positive law than do people who live at a greater distance from each other. People who share common values and beliefs agree more easily on such regulation. The sharing of common values and beliefs happens, in turn, more often within groups living territorially close together, though the contrary is by no means excluded. One should therefore first try to form states on the basis of the latter, and leave it to international law and federal states to regulate the interactions that reach beyond that.

Let us now come back to the two arguments against political minorities given above. The second argument is of course not convincing. For I am looking for non-positive rights and not for positive law. If the latter could make the former inefficient, the endeavour to argue for non-positive rights would be entirely pointless. So if the positive law of a state does not recognise the rights of political minorities, and those rights are justified on the level of non-positive law, then the members of this state and especially its political decision-makers are morally obliged to introduce those rights in positive law. This is what I mean by 'non-positive right', as introduced at the outset.

It is more difficult to rebut the first argument. Does the existence of positive law nullify the right to create a different state and a different system of positive law? To answer this question we must recall the criterion of a just positive law, which was established in the preceding section. According to that criterion, a positive law is not just if somebody who is under it could reasonably reject it because it restricts her freedom in an unnecessary or unequal manner. This criterion can of course be used by the members of a political minority as well. If and only if they can show that the positive laws of the state they live in restrict their freedom in an excessive or unequal way, and the majority refuses to change those laws, do the members of the minority have a non-positive right to self-government. For this is here the only way to let both groups, the majority and the minority, have their own way of regulating their internal interactions by law, and to re-establish the agreement between the groups on a higher level. This shows that the existence of positive law can in no way nullify non-positive rights.

The latter, though, are not unconditional rights. They depend on the general principle of all legislation, namely the principle of justified rejection. This is a formal condition, which has the advantage of avoiding the panoply of material conditions advanced in the literature. I no longer need to discuss criteria like common language, common history, ethnic identity and so on. Nevertheless, these material criteria can have a role in the application of my formal criterion. If, for instance, by the law of a state the members of a minority are not allowed to speak their language, this clearly is a violation of the principle of just legislation and gives the members of the minority the right to self-rule.

As a general principle, we can formulate the following conditions on the right to self-government of a political minority:

The members of a political minority have the non-positive right to self-government if and only if they have good reasons not to agree with the existing laws and the majority refuses to change them. Good reasons to reject existing laws are, as we have seen, the facts that they unnecessarily and unequally restrict the freedom of members of the minority. In order to show this, it is sufficient to prove that self-government of the minority would avoid these restrictions without in turn imposing unnecessary and unequal restrictions on the majority - for if it restricts them unnecessarily it is Pareto-sub-optimal, and if it restricts them unequally it is unjust.

Having uncovered the source of non-positive rights, and justified on this basis the rights of political minorities to self-government, I should finally be more precise concerning the bearers and the content of these rights. I have argued that groups can only be bearers of rights if they have an internal structure that enables them to form an unequivocal group will. This is the case for a state or an association, but not necessarily for an ethnic or linguistic or religious group. Therefore, the primary bearers of the right to self-government must be the individual members of those groups and not the groups themselves. It is the rights of the individuals, which are possibly violated by a system of positive law. Therefore, if this violation justifies self-government, this right must belong to the individuals too. The question, however, is how these rights must be articulated in order to make the creation of a new state, and of a collective bearer of rights, possible. The first right which individual members of a political minority must have is the right to form an association or a political party. This right is independent of the question whether or not their claim to self-government is finally justified. But in order to make this claim, and to argue for it in the political arena, they must be given the right to form an association or a party. Once an association or a party has been constituted, it is a potential bearer of rights as well, unless its internal structure does not yield the building of a common will.

However, the rights of the political association of a minority do not nullify the rights of its individual members. To be sure, the political party of the minority must have the right to fight peacefully for self-government. But the right it fights for lies with the individuals and not with the party. Therefore, the first step to implement that right must be a general scrutiny of the political will of the population living on the territory of the presumed future state, to make sure that in forming that state no new injustice is made. Only if it is the clear will of a qualified majority of the inhabitants of the territory can steps be taken to build a new state on it.

The right to self-government is not identical with a right to secession. It normally should go together with the transformation of the former state into a federal state. This ensures that the interactions between the two groups of the population of the former state continue to be regulated by a commonly agreed law. The only case in which a secession is justified is the one in which the majority refuses all co-operation with the minority in a common federal state. However, even in this case it is necessary that both states become members of an embracing system of law.

Finally, as soon as the new state is formed, it is a bearer of rights. The most fundamental of these rights is the right to recognition by the other states as having equal rights.

As a general rule we might say: A political minority living on a sufficiently large territory of a given state, and having a sufficiently large majority, has the right to the creation of a separate state on that territory if and only if a) the positive laws of the given state restrict unnecessarily or unequally the freedom of its members and b) the terms of the separation guarantee the equal freedom of the former majority.

Notes

1 In today's international law, we find protections of three collective interests of peoples: a) physical existence, b) self-determination and c) natural resources. My discussion concerns only the second. But it is clear that one can protect the second only if one protects the first as well. I conceive these interests as the interests of the individual members of the group in question.

2 The Charter of the United Nations affirms the 'Principle of Self-determination'. The two human rights Covenants say: 'All peoples have the right of self-determination'. The term 'nation' is also used in the political context, but it is left open whether the two terms have the same meaning or not.

3 Cp. the definitions given below.

4 Margalit and Raz (1995, 79) emphasise this agreement, they still find that there is dispute 'concerning the precise definition of the right, its content, its bearers, and the proper means for its implementation'. I shall try to answer these questions too.

5 Cp.

6 Cp. J.L. Mackie, *Ethics, Inventing Right and Wrong*, Penguin Books 1977, p.36-39.

7 Cp. Margalit and Raz (1995, 86-87).

8 Cp. Margalit and Raz (1995, 88).

9 See Leslie Green, 'Two Views of Collective Rights', in: *Canadian Journal of Law and Jurisprudence*, Vol. IV, No.2, 1991.

10 Joseph Raz seems to hold this thesis, cp. his definition of a right according to which 'X has a right if and only if X can have rights and, other things being equal, an aspect of X's well-being (his interest) is a sufficient reason for holding some other person(s) to be under a duty'. I do not accept this definition because I think that an interest is never a sufficient reason for another's duty.

11 Concerning this point, I agree with L.W. Sumner, *The Moral Foundations of Rights*, Oxford 1987, 209.

12 Cp. T.M. Scanlon, 'Contractualism and Utilitarianism', in: *Utilitarianism and Beyond*, ed. A. Sen and B. Williams, Cambridge University Press 1982, p.110.

13 T.M. Scanlon is not concerned with political minority rights in his paper. The conclusion I mention is not a conclusion Scanlon draws, but a conclusion that logically follows from his general theory of contractualism.

14 Cp. Opus citatum p.113.

15 Cp. Opus.citatum, p.116.

16 G. Seel, Wie weit kann man den praktischen Naturalismus treiben.

17 Cp.Hans Kelsen, Reine Rechtslehre.

18 (Trans. 'not enacted, but presupposed'.)

19 Cp. G. Seel, Ist der praktische Begruendungsregress abschliessbar?

20 Utilitarians did not always pay enough attention to the danger of committing an analogous fallacy when they obtained the principle of act utilitarianism by enlarging the scope of the subjective principle of egoistic interest maximisation. Indeed from the duty that each has maximally to satisfy his own preferences it does not follow that everybody has a duty maximally to satisfy the preferences of all.

21 The so called 'realm of aims' - formula of Kant's Categorical Imperative stands clearly in this relation.

22 Cp. H. Obelel, 'Praxisgeltung und Rechtsgeltung', in: *Lehrstuecke der praktischen Philosophie und der Aesthetik*, ed. K. Baerthlein und G. Wolandt, Basel 1977, p. 106.

12. Cultural Citizenship: Minority Rights and Political Community

RAINER BAUBÖCK

Cultural Citizenship

When T.H. Marshall (1965) analyzed the evolution of citizenship in England he identified three components, which he called civil, political and social citizenship and associated with the institutions of the judicial system, parliamentary democracy and the welfare state. Did he forget about cultural citizenship? Is there a need for supplementing the traditional conception of liberal citizenship with cultural minority rights? A growing number of liberal intellectuals seem to say no. After two decades where multiculturalism was very much the *Zeitgeist*, a certain fatigue and impatience has set in. In the US, affirmative action and bilingual education programs have been rolled back in the voting booth and in the courts. Prominent intellectuals have accused multiculturalism of "disuniting America" (Schlesinger 1992), of fostering a "culture of complaint" (Hughes 1993) and "culture wars", which have wracked the American society and have distracted the liberal left from its egalitarian goals (Gitlin 1995). Some rehabilitate the melting pot for a "next American nation" (Lind 1995) while others advocate a "postethnic America" in which cultural affiliations are no longer based on descent, but on revocable consent (Hollinger 1995). We find similar critiques of multiculturalism in Canada (Bissoondath 1994, Gwyn 1995), where the concept was first introduced as a public policy in 1971, in Australia and Western Europe.

These books illustrate a shift from the liberal discourse of rights towards a new emphasis on integration. It is part of my argument that this juxtaposition is misleading. The language of rights, and even conflicts about rights, are part of what integrates liberal democracies. It is both morally wrong and politically naïve to think that appealing to a shared civic identity is sufficient to integrate marginalized groups whose grievances have been brushed aside. Iris Young's (1990) proposal that citizenship has to be group-differentiated in response to discrimination and oppression is still convincing in this regard. What critics fear is that cultural minority rights instrumentalize public policies for maintaining contested cultural traditions and practices while at the same time immunizing internally oppressive communities from interference. It is not at all difficult to gather anecdotal evidence, which lends credence to these accusations. But the case against multiculturalism rests upon a whole series of gross generalizations, which are certainly facilitated by the ambiguities of the concept itself.

There is an underlying theme, which justifies retaining the concept. Paraphrasing John Rawls we may identify this as the fact of cultural pluralism, i.e. the persistence and salience of internal distinctions within contemporary societies, which are marked by religion, language, ethnic origin, racial category or different ways of life. Accepting this fact is an important starting point for normative analysis. It excludes approaches that believe that these differences can be eventually overcome by assimilation or can be neutralized by separating groups. However, this starting point is merely the acknowledgement of a problem and does not necessarily point towards the way, how to resolve it. Recognizing it as a problem is necessary to get beyond the naïvité of celebratory multiculturalism, which dominated much of the early manifestations before the 1990s and which rested on the belief that affirming the value of diversity is already a solution to identity conflicts. Once we shed this idea there is no single normative principle of multiculturalism that could tell us how to respond to claims for cultural rights. What we have to do to make sense of these claims is disaggregate them and consider then how established principles of liberal democracy and equal citizenship could apply to them or may have to be amended in response to a plausible challenge. I propose to disaggregate along three axes: first, by distinguishing various cultural practices and the types of claims they tend to create; second, by looking at categories of minorities that are differently positioned in their relation to the political community; and, third, by considering how general principles may have to be modified by considering the particular context in which they have to be applied. The cultural practices which I will discuss are those associated with religion and language, the categories of minorities are immigrant and non-immigrant ethnic and national groups and the relevant contexts are particular projects or historical traditions of nation-building which shape the political institutions and public discourses of multicultural societies. There are, of course, many more relevant practices, categories and contexts to be considered, but the picture which emerges from these few ones is already sufficiently complex to destroy any idea of multiculturalism as a single phenomenon or principle which is either to be defended or to be overcome.

I will defend the view that the liberal principle of neutrality is insufficient for determining the limits of religious toleration and is inapplicable to claims for language recognition. Religious pluralism goes beyond neutrality in acknowledging first, that in some countries religious communities form a constituent group of the political community; second that nonliberal religious ways of life may have a particular value for their members and for the wider society; and, third, that it may sometimes be better to overcome inequalities by extending existing privileges of religious communitics to minorities rather than by abolishing them. Linguistic diversity presents a different set of problems because liberal states cannot avoid establishing one or a small number of languages and have a duty to provide a shared public culture. Whether we regard minorities as disadvantaged and entitled to compensatory recognition of their languages depends on our conception of the social functions of language. I argue that languages are not merely a means of communication but carry a specific identity value and serve as markers for political boundaries. The latter of these three functions distinguishes between the claims of immigrant and national minorities. In the final section of the paper I consider whether making this distinction is morally and politically justified.

How should we then answer the initial question about a cultural component of citizenship? Two contrasting responses will not do: a first one that asserts that there is no need to go beyond the Marshallian framework because all reasonable cultural claims can be satisfied within it; and a second one that adds a distinct national-cultural dimension to democratic citizenship. The Marshallian approach is blind towards the cultural nonneutrality of liberal states; the liberal nationalist one acknowledges and justifies it but fails to fully grasp its implications for minority citizenship.

Let me consider first the proposition that one can exhaustively classify all cultural rights as civil, political or social ones and that whatever normative principles apply to the distribution of these rights should also be applied to settle cultural claims. If this were the case there would be no need to add a separate cultural dimension to Marshall's right-based conception of citizenship. In this view, the rights of cultural minorities are primarily covered by the civil element of citizenship. The free exercise of religion or the free use of a minority language in private communication is guaranteed through the liberties of free speech, association and assembly. These rights are, however, strictly "culture-blind". In liberal democracies they are regarded as universal human rights that do not depend on any particular classification of the beneficiaries as members of a cultural community or even as nationals of a state.[1] The political element of citizenship circumscribes the cultural privileges of national majorities. It applies to legislative decisions that give official status to a certain language, that subsidize theatres and museums through tax money or celebrate historical and religious events by declaring them public holidays. These decisions are collective ones: every citizen has an equal right to participate or to be represented in them, but they bind also those who oppose them. In a liberal democracy the scope of legitimate majority rule is, however, constrained by constitutional safeguards for individual liberties. Finally, the social rights of citizenship specify the fundamental duty of the state in the area of cultural policies. Every child has the right to public education that teaches it a national language and introduces it in a broader sense to a national culture and history. This secondary cultural socialization is meant to provide all with equal opportunities in societies marked by inequalities of class and gender.

Such a Marshallian framework for cultural rights does not merely identify the basic liberties and entitlements, but reflects also the differentiation of categories of beneficiaries in contemporary democracies: the negative cultural liberties are strictly universal, public education is an entitlement for all residents and their children, whereas political participation rights are a citizen privilege and generate legitimate benefits for majorities. Legal provisions for cultural minorities that transcend this framework may then be regarded as a result of pragmatic accommodation rather than as grounded in moral rights. Yet this does not capture at all the nature of minority claims, which use the language of civil, political and social rights to challenge this initial distribution of rights and benefits as unfair and press for special exemptions, for symbolic recognition and material support.

The liberal-nationalist approach wants to make an explicit element of citizenship that Marshall had tacitly assumed: that integrating a class-ridden society through equal citizenship presupposes a prior sense of national community with specific cultural attributes. In this perspective, the willingness to share the burdens and benefits of political cooperation results from a prior national identity that makes citizens see themselves as part of a transgenerational community. In contrast with earlier ethno-racial views of the origins of nations, contemporary liberal nationalists[2] acknowledge the insights of "constructivist" accounts of nationhood.[3] These emphasize the role of the modern state and economy in bringing about the common culture, which is then retrospectively associated with the historic origins of the nation. The evolution of citizenship is thus closely connected to the promotion of national public cultures and identities. From this perspective it makes sense to add to Marshall's triad a distinctive fourth component that consists of the collective identity and the rights, but even more so the obligations and the daily practices that tie individuals to particular national communities. The history of national conflicts has also shaped the internal structure of contemporary polities. Nearly all nation-states have their own ethnic or indigenous minorities who have never been fully incorporated into a mainstream national identity. A small number of contemporary states are multinational federations, which formally break down their citizenship into constituent national components. And in some cases their national identity links minorities to a foreign state whom they regard as their national homeland and to whom they turn as an external protector of their rights. Illiberal nationalist ideologies make internal and external citizenship rights a prerogative of members of the dominant national community and demand that minorities either assimilate or be excluded. In contrast, liberal nationalist approaches defend universal, inclusive and pluralistic conceptions of citizenship. They affirm everybody's right to a national identity and allow for a differentiation of citizenship along these lines.

The problem with many of these latter theories is that they associate cultural identities too closely with national ones. National communities share an aspiration to, or an achieved status of, self-government. In order to be, or to become, self-governing, a community must be organized territorially[4] and must develop a standardized cultural repertoire. Internally, this repertoire consists of a written language serving as a general medium of communication and of symbols evoking a common origin and *destiny*; externally it provides markers for the boundaries that identify the group vis-à-vis others. These two features of territoriality and cultural standardization make national-cultural identities building blocks for constructing the basic units of political community. National identities are embedded in a public culture shared throughout a political community. Other cultural identities are more like dividing lines within civil society – they undermine the very image of a homogeneous political community that is supported by national-cultural identities. Culture in this broader sense encompasses all the various practices and symbols through which people collectively organize their lives and try to make sense of the world (Geertz 1973; Parekh forthcoming). Communal identities built around shared practices and beliefs subdivide national communities and cut across them in many different ways. It is therefore misleading to think of national cultures as "societal" (Kymlicka 1995) or "encompassing" (Margalit and Raz 1990) in the sense that they contain within themselves all these other practices and beliefs as internal components or options (Waldron 1992, 1996; Buchanan 1999; Carens forthcoming, chap. 3).[5] Liberal nationalists generally understand the encompassing quality of a national culture as that of a thin roof that leaves a lot of space for cultural diversity underneath in civil society. But this division of spheres still ignores that for some deeply held beliefs and cherished practices a dominant national culture, a free market economy and a liberal democracy are hostile environments. Religious identities are often more encompassing than national ones by stretching over many different countries and linguistic identities frequently cut across national borders by linking a group to an external homeland. National identities are therefore not generally superordinate, neither in terms of range nor in terms of weight. Religious, linguistic and ethnic identities are constrained by national identities, rather than contained within them. These constraints are sources of serious political and legal conflicts. Postulating a shared national identity, as a precondition of a liberal conception of citizenship is unhelpful for understanding such claims and will further downgrade them.

Cultural citizenship is indeed a missing element in Marshall's account and more generally in liberal political theory. A political theory of multiculturalism should not be construed as apart from, or opposed to, liberal democratic citizenship but ought to be grounded in the same considerations about what kind of rights and institutional arrangements are necessary in order to make individuals full and equal members of a well-integrated political community. But taking culture into account is not an easy task. The specific disadvantages that make some culturally defined minorities unequal citizens are not covered in Marshall's class-based account of citizenship. Nor is it sufficient to add a national dimension to the three he has identified. Finally, there appear to be neither a single unifying normative principle nor distinct political institutions of cultural citizenship. Civil, political and social citizenship respond to the normative ideas of liberty, democracy and social justice and are upheld by the separate institutions of the judicial system, parliaments and welfare services. Neutrality, toleration and recognition have been suggested as different approaches to cultural diversity, but, as I will try to show, none of these is an overarching norm that we could apply to all cultural identity claims. There is also no single political institution that specializes in reproducing and maintaining cultural citizenship. The education system is certainly a primary candidate for this role, but the public culture of a society is shaped by a much wider range of institutions including all three branches of government as well as the mass media. My hope is that we may learn more about cultural citizenship by examining how liberal democracies have differentiated rights and obligations in response to types of cultural practices, categories of minorities and polity-building projects. In this paper I shall, however, not give a historical or comparative account in the

Marshallian tradition, but shall focus instead on normative principles that have been suggested as guidelines for coping with cultural diversity.

Religious Diversity and the Limits of Neutrality

Liberalism has historically developed as an answer to the challenge of religious diversity. Its starting point was religious toleration, which has gradually been transformed into the stronger doctrines of religious neutrality and separation between church and state. Nowadays, liberal theorists tend to think of toleration as an implication of neutrality, or of neutrality as the liberal mode of toleration. It is this view that I want to challenge. I will first suggest that toleration is supported by power-based, rights-based and value-based reasons. Only the second among these coincides with the liberal ideal of neutrality. We may have to move beyond neutrality if all three reasons remain relevant for democratic citizenship in multireligious societies. I will consider whether the three reasons might nevertheless converge towards an ideal of neutrality. This is a possibility, but it depends on rather exceptional circumstances that cannot be conceptually presupposed. While liberals may thus maintain the ideal of religious neutrality, they have to face a real world where not all groups are willing to accept their reasons and where existing democratic states are imperfectly neutral.

Michael Walzer has, first, distinguished toleration as an institutionalized arrangement between groups from tolerance as an attitude of persons towards other persons' identities or practices (Walzer 1997: xi). Second, toleration is a negative form of recognition. It does not imply approval or support and need not even imply respect (ibid.: 11). What is recognized is a conflict and what is respected is the need for peaceful coexistence (ibid.: 5). Toleration occurs within and between cultural communities. Internally it defines the limits of acceptable deviant or dissident behaviour below a threshold of sanctions, ranging from verbal disapproval to physical punishment, shunning within the group or expulsion from membership. In contrast, intergroup toleration concerns behaviour that is internally approved within the "tolerated" community but would be sanctioned inside the "tolerating" one. Cultural toleration by the state combines both forms. It is internal insofar as the members of cultural communities are subjects or citizens.[6] At the same time, it is external toleration because it involves a separation of a public political realm from the internal life of cultural communities. Practices that would be unacceptable within public political institutions or even within civil society are accepted as long as they occur within an internal domain of the community in question. Thus a liberal state that otherwise enforces gender-neutral job descriptions, will tolerate that the Catholic Church discriminates against women in the appointment of priests.

The civil liberties listed in the human rights catalogues and in liberal democratic constitutions establish a generalized regime of toleration that can defuse many of the conflicts that have torn apart other societies. In a way this reduces the need for toleration. The state does not protect my neighbour's religion, which I may find offensive, but protects us both from each other by giving us an equal liberty to practice our beliefs. This still leaves a fair amount of more contested instances of toleration in the strong sense, where groups are singled out for special exemptions from generally enforced rules. In several countries, Jehovah's Witnesses are exempted from military service, Sikhs are exempted from motorcycle helmet laws and Jews and Muslims are permitted ritual slaughtering of animals which would otherwise be prohibited under animal welfare legislation.[7]

Public toleration has to be supported by public reasons. There are three such reasons, each of which characterizes a different kind of toleration. Citizens may support the toleration of practices, to which they otherwise strongly object, if they are too weak to interfere with them, if they enjoy a common set of rights that protect these practices, or if their negative judgment is balanced by some other positive value that they see in these practices. Toleration can thus be power-based, rights-based or value-based. The first type is what John Rawls (1993) calls a *modus vivendi*. It results from a lack of power to expel another community or to coerce it into conformity. A truce may emerge from a balance of power between opponents of roughly equal strength or may be imposed by a stronger force above them. Where the balance is kept for a long time, it will generate its own benefits and expectations of further peaceful coexistence. The second reason for toleration emerges from sharing a set of rights that protect controversial practices. As a bearer of rights to practice my religion I can relate to those who follow a different light as members of a broader community of law that guarantees our freedom to be different. The widest such community is grounded in universal human rights. Democracy provides a more robust reason for rights-based toleration by addressing persons affiliated to different cultural communities as both individual rights-bearers and as collectively governing themselves. Finally, a third reason for toleration involves balancing competing values. I may be an agnostic or atheist, who regards religious beliefs as profoundly irrational, but I may still see much value in the social commitments and the moral inspiration that other people derive from their faith.

The dominant public reason for toleration in a liberal democracy is of course rights-based and it covers a broad area of freedom for religion, language and different ways of life. Classical liberal theorists like John Locke and John Stuart Mill were mainly concerned with grounding toleration in negative duties of government forbearance. Locke thought it "necessary to distinguish exactly the business of civil government from that of religion, and to settle the just bound that lie between the one and the other" (Locke 1956b: 128) and claimed that "the business of laws is not to provide for the truths of opinions, but for the safety and security of the commonwealth" (ibid.: 153). Mill widened the sphere of toleration dramatically by declaring the prevention of harm to others to be "the only purpose for which power can be rightfully exercised over any member of a civilized community" (Mill 1972: 78), ruling thus out of court government interference with practices that are harmful only to those voluntarily engaged in them but not to outsiders. Both the separation of state and religion and Mill's harm principle may, however, fail to provide clear standards in conflicts about cultural minority rights: Do Sunday closing laws violate separation? Are blasphemy or hate speech laws covered by the prevention of harm to others? Rather than merely relying on principles for limited government, liberal democracies have spelled out more specific catalogues of fundamental individual rights. These rights are interpreted and protected by independent courts and turn non-interference into a corresponding state duty derived from these rights.

But rights should not be regarded as the only reason and the ultimate threshold for toleration. Power-based reasons and value-based reasons have some independent weight and may expand a liberal regime of toleration beyond what can be justified on the basis of equal rights alone. In a political community where some illiberal cultures are regarded as constituent communities, there will be strong power-based reasons for accommodating them and tolerating exemptions from general obligations of citizenship. Even if one does not see any value in their particular ways of life, the need for obtaining their political cooperation may still justify concessions. Where such toleration only reflects a balance of power that does not allow liberal forces to prevail it will be regarded as merely temporary. However, toleration may also be justified in a different manner that is more consistent with a commitment towards equal citizenship. Liberal democracies may have to tolerate illiberal practices if they want to transform a deeply divided society into a liberal democracy without oppressing any of its constituent parts. Coercive imposition of the full range of liberal rights and obligations on illiberal communities may fatally undermine this democratic project. The limits of toleration will then in part be determined by a political process of negotiating the terms of common citizenship between communities, each of which has a stake in the polity and a threat potential that others cannot ignore. Arrangements like in Israel, where religious courts adjudicate personal law concerning marriage and divorce,[8] or in India, where secular courts use religious law for their decisions in these matters, are obviously not fully liberal but may be justified by these concerns.[9]

The other reason for extending toleration beyond what is implied in liberal citizenship is quite different. Liberal democracies are frequently willing to tolerate illiberal practices among minorities who have no constituent status in the polity and little strategic power. This case requires balancing the value of membership in such a community against that of full citizenship. The decision of the US Supreme Court in Wisconsin v. Yoder[10] to grant the Old Order Amish an exemption from the general state requirement of school education until the age of 16 demonstrates a balancing of this kind.[11] Jeff Spinner (1994: 105-8) has suggested an argument for granting special toleration to a group like the Amish that is exactly opposite to the power-based rationale. It is because they voluntarily renounce many of the benefits of citizenship such as social security or voting rights that one should reduce the burdens that citizenship obligations put on their way of life. However, liberal citizenship does not generally allow for such an opting out of the citizenship compact while staying within the jurisdiction. Once this were made a rule that applies to individuals independently of their cultural or religious affiliation[12] this would clearly undermine the equality of status and rights that characterize liberal citizenship. In enforcing the laws throughout a territory and ascribing citizenship at birth a liberal state forms a political community that is not a voluntary association. Citizens may opt out of that community by emigration, but not by exempting themselves from benefits and burdens shared by all other residents. The kind of toleration displayed towards the Amish is not based on a principle of free choice between full or partial citizenship. It is hard to justify unless one assumes that the Amish way of life has considerable value for those who choose it and that they would be unfairly disadvantaged if the full scale of citizenship obligations were imposed on them.[13] While a liberal state may not positively endorse a specific religious way of life, it can recognize the disadvantage that results from a lack of neutrality of liberal citizenship towards different ways of life. As in the case of integrating powerful illiberal minorities, such recognition can count as public reason that aims at making the democratic polity more inclusive.

With a few significant exceptions liberal political theorists defend a rights-based account of toleration. Two theorists who outline alternative approaches are Chandran Kukathas and Bhikhu Parekh. Kukathas starts from a *modus vivendi* between cultural communities. He does not presuppose the existence of a common political authority (a "we" which tolerates "them") but sees "the public realm as an area of convergence of different moral practices" (Kukathas 1997: 84). Parekh argues for a value-based perspective. In his view, a liberal society ought to embrace "the plurality of values that results from cultural diversity and it has a duty to engage in a dialogue with the minority about its disputed practices" (Parekh 1996: 262). But such a society defends also its own "operative public values" and may legitimately ban practices that violate these values" (Parekh 1995: 216). In contrast with rights-based accounts, both power-based and value-based ones regard the limits of toleration as highly variable in different contexts.[14] A difficulty with both views is that they do not seem to provide us with either a procedure or a goal that could generate a stable consensus among groups who will share a common political authority. I suggest then that the best starting point for delimiting the proper scope of toleration, and more generally of cultural minority rights, is this need for common citizenship. Liberal democratic citizenship is not merely a set of universally valid rights and duties, but also a project of building a political community in a particular society at a particular historic moment. Keeping this focus in mind should help to develop a context-sensitive account of minority rights that avoids the twin dangers of relativism and context-blind universalism. We will then take the more universalistic rights-based reasons for toleration as a starting point and go beyond them by considering power-based reasons that emerge from the composite nature of a particular polity and value-based reasons that apply to specific groups and their distinct ways of life.

The contemporary debate about multiculturalism is less concerned with the composite nature of many political communities than with the value of cultural community and diversity in society. A reason for this is that multiculturalism is not primarily a demand for toleration, but for positive recognition (Taylor 1992, Honneth 1992). In the debate about liberal responses to this request, recognition is contrasted with neutrality. The standard argument against public policies of cultural recognition is that this would transform cultural difference into unequal citizenship. Treating citizens with equal respect and concern requires a neutral or even culture-blind approach in public policies. Pluralists respond to this by challenging the basic assumption that a liberal state is, or can be, neutral towards cultural distinctions in civil society. The common denominator that allows to add all the disparate demands of multiculturalism into a general argument for minority rights is the idea that the public culture of the wider society is not a neutral context for the flourishing of different cultural practices and identities, but systematically privileges some and disadvantages others. This complaint includes a value claim and a policy demand. The policy demand is that political institutions ought to respond by transforming the public culture or by compensating the disadvantaged groups, but this makes sense only insofar as the practices and identities that are said to be disadvantaged are valuable and deserve some public protection or promotion. Adding the "fact of non-neutrality" of the liberal state to the "fact of pluralism" (Rawls 1993) in civil society appears to provide thus a general justification for recognition demands. Even policies aiming at restoring neutrality will have to identify and recognize the cultural groups that had hitherto been disadvantaged. However, this argument is not sufficiently fine-grained. Before we accept it we will first have to examine in which way specific practices and identities may be disadvantaged and how liberal states can honour cultural value claims without undermining the equal status of their citizens.

Let me consider two liberal responses to cultural value claims. A standard reply builds on the basic value of autonomy. In Joseph Raz's definition "the ideal of personal autonomy holds the free choice of goals and relations as an essential ingredient of individual well-being" (Raz 1986: 369). Liberals may then assert that harm for nonconsenting others is the proper threshold for toleration while uncoerced individual choice is what makes a practice or identity valuable. But this would grossly misinterpret most cultural value claims. First, the element of choice is generally absent in gender, racial, ethnic and also some religious identities that are acquired at birth and are socially constructed as immutable attributes of personal identity. Second, even for those practices that can be seen as autonomously chosen, the value is never derived from choice alone, but the choice is regarded as valuable because the practice is. If choice itself conferred value to a practice or identity then starting to smoke cigarettes would have to be seen as valuable as long as one does not expose others to hazards of passive smoking. Liberal theorists have therefore been careful to describe autonomy as involving morally important choices between different conceptions of the good life. Having a choice only between bad or trivial options does not make a person autonomous (Raz 1986: 374-7). Furthermore, authors like Rawls and Kymlicka have shifted the emphasis from an activist conception of autonomous choice as individual self-creation to the less demanding requirement that our conceptions of the good and our ends in life, even if they have been inherited or have been strongly shaped by our social environment, should be experienced as our own rather than as imposed from the outside and should remain open to revision or rejection. But this raises two further questions: First, if a person is only autonomous when she has a choice concerning important and valuable options for her life, then the value of these options cannot depend entirely on her freedom to choose. Although the value of a moral conception of the good or of an affiliation to a community may increase if these can be chosen, their characterization as good rather than as bad or trivial must be prior to choice. If this is so, then they are presumable still good if they are not chosen but unquestionably accepted as given. Second, although persons may be able to revise or reject any socially constructed identity with which they grow up, including gender or "racial" ones, the vast majority will accept these as describing the kinds of persons they are and will interpret their meaning for their lives without questioning the basic identity itself. Cultural pluralists like Bhikhu Parekh extend these arguments to religious or ethnic communities, many of which strongly believe that membership cannot be chosen or abandoned at will. Making personal autonomy a criterion for assessing the worth of such membership is then inconsistent and blocks a genuine understanding of cultural value claims.

Will Kymlicka (1995: 82-93) has developed an alternative liberal theory that seems to escape this critique by reversing the causal relation between autonomous choice and cultural value. He suggests that membership in, or access to, a societal culture is valuable not because it is chosen, but because it enables individuals to choose by providing them with a wide range of meaningful options for their lives. Without a secure cultural background, individuals would not be able to know the value of these options. However, this is a tough standard for assessing claims of cultural minorities who often cannot, or do not want to, provide their members with a wide range of options.[15] If a culture has to be societal in order to enable individuals to become autonomous, three different kinds of cultural minorities will fail to qualify. First, there are groups whose cultural claims are not sufficiently comprehensive to provide a full range of options for their members. A minority of immigrant descent may, for example, wish to preserve their language of origin as a second spoken language among their group of origin while accepting that their members' opportunities will primarily depend on their participation in the wider public culture. Second, membership in some groups is a liability rather than an asset because of pervasive discrimination in the wider society. In reaction to persistent social segregation, racialized minorities like African Americans have developed urban counter-cultures, which provide their members with a quite limited set of opportunities and choices but still articulate a desire for self-respect and external recognition of cultural value. Third, many indigenous and religious groups explicitly reject the liberal conception of autonomy and emphasize instead inherent obligations of their members to the community or to divine authority. The more comprehensively a religious community shapes the lives of its members, the less likely it is to cherish or promote personal autonomy in the liberal sense. When religion pervasively regulates everyday life as in orthodox Judaism and Islam, or when it constitutes a whole way of life, as it does for the Amish, this may satisfy to the fullest extent one of Kymlicka's criteria for the value of culture: that it allows us to lead our lives from the inside and provides us with an interpretation of our options which makes them meaningful to us. But such religious creeds necessarily deny the other element of liberal autonomy, which is the freedom to critically examine and radically revise one's chosen ends (Kymlicka 1995: 80-2).

Kymlicka's autonomy-value of cultural membership is too narrowly geared towards liberal national cultures that are institutionally complete; share a language of public life, a bounded territory, and a general commitment to liberal democracy. We will have to go beyond this if we acknowledge that cultural practices and identities of the other three kinds can also be valuable (rather than being merely tolerable). We may, for example, question that cultures serving as a background for individual autonomy have to form mutually exclusive constituencies, each of which is institutionally complete and coextensive with a political community. It seems natural to assume that access to a wider range of cultural diversity and mélange will offer more resources for individual autonomy (Waldron 1995, 1996). Although individuals do not actually choose most of their cultural affiliations, they may still be able to merge divergent cultural influences to which they are exposed into cultural patterns, which make sense for their lives. Yet this move still does not account for the value of those cultures, which are internally coherent and externally exclusive but do not endorse liberal autonomy.

Similar difficulties for liberal theory emerge from taking seriously the policy demands implicit in cultural minority claims. *Prima facie* the claim that the liberal state cannot be culturally neutral seems to apply only to language but not to religion. If religious neutrality is both desirable and achievable then multicultural claims based on religious difference seem to carry little weight. Let me therefore consider what I see as the best defense of liberal neutrality. If the argument fails this will further strengthen the case for a pluralist perspective.

Liberals generally affirm that in a society where citizens affirm many different creeds, the state has to remain neutral. It must neither establish a particular religion by turning it into an official attribute of the state, nor interfere with its citizens' choices by subsidizing or suppressing any particular religious or nonreligious perspective in society. Stated in this way, neutrality appears to be a meta-norm, which entails the more specific requirements of secular political power and toleration of religious minorities. Secularism and toleration are independent of each other and go well together only when both are derived from liberal neutrality. The Jacobin regime during the French revolution and communist states in the 20th century were secular but notoriously intolerant towards religion.[16] In contrast, liberal neutrality is incompatible with establishing atheism or even agnosticism as an official ideology. Liberal secularism is thus of a particular kind: first, it is not antireligious, but nonreligious and, second, its mandate is merely to create a secular state, but not to spread secularism throughout society. Similarly, religious toleration is no particular hallmark of the liberal tradition and is compatible with religious establishment. The 17th century doctrine of *cuius regio, eius religio*, which ended the long period of religious wars in Europe, buttressed an international regime of toleration (Walzer 1997: 19-22) between sovereign states, each of which had its official religion. The Ottoman Empire is an often-quoted example for domestic religious toleration. Indeed, it can be said to have been much more tolerant than contemporary liberal states because the millet system granted Christian and Jewish communities extensive powers of self-government. Liberalism greatly reduces these powers by treating religious communities as voluntary associations. It stands for a quite specific form of toleration. Whereas previous regimes had divided political powers along religious lines, liberal toleration emerges from a separation between state and civil society.

The rights-based argument for toleration, which emphasizes the limits of legitimate political coercion, can be straightforwardly applied to support religious neutrality. As an institutionalized monopoly of violence the state is inevitably coercive. However, such coercion is only legitimate if it can be rationally endorsed by all subjected to a political authority from a perspective where they regard each other as free and equal citizens. While citizens may agree that many of their preferences and interests will be legitimately overruled by majority decisions, their liberty to form their own religious beliefs and moral convictions is part of what makes them free and equal citizens and must not be exposed to collective decisions within the political community. But liberal states must not only refrain from coercing their citizens into accepting religious doctrines or from invoking any such doctrines in their legislation, they must also protect the freedom of religious exercise. It is a misconstruel of the liberal view to see religion as a strictly private matter in the sense that it may be practiced within the confines of one's home. Religious beliefs are private only in the sense that they cannot expect support from government institutions. But religion is of course an eminently social phenomenon: It is practiced in association with others who share the same beliefs but also in the public square where people may profess their faith and try to convince others. Treating religious communities as voluntary associations and opening the public square for free religious speech allows the state to retain a neutral stance that is not biased against religious activities. It provides these communities with the necessary social space and legal protection for free exercise, while making their numerical strength and material assets entirely dependent on the support they can muster among citizens.

A second argument for neutrality is related to power-based reasons for toleration and emphasizes political stability. It starts from the "fact of pluralism". The diversity of irreconcilable religious and moral views is an intrinsic feature of a liberal society. There is no hope that all citizens will ever agree on the most fundamental questions of how to live a good life. It is precisely because these views do often have strong political implications that liberal states must not privilege any particular doctrine of this sort. The most dangerous implication of profound religious convictions is that their followers generally prefer quite rationally to live among other people who share their faith. In a strictly monoreligious society everybody sees her faith recognized by others and nobody's beliefs are exposed to prejudice, ridicule or contempt.[17] However, the desire to create such a society by instrumentalizing state power for propagating the true creed produces an endless chain of violence. Liberal states cannot suppress this wish by establishing a secular civic religion. But they must carve out of society a political sphere where religious affiliation does not count and where all are treated as equal citizens and full members of the same political community. Initially, a religiously neutral state may be no more than a grudgingly accepted *modus vivendi* between warring factions none of which is strong enough to crush the other one. However, where it persists over time, a consensus can emerge that supports this arrangement from the perspectives of citizens who are affiliated to the various religious communities. This hope should not be grounded in the expectation that in a liberal society all religious doctrines will eventually converge towards some form of moderate Protestant theology that endorses state neutrality because of its belief in the freedom of individual conscience.[18] Political stability in a multireligious society can only come about if citizens attribute some independent value to their rights as members of the political community. A neutral liberal state protects not only agnostics and minority religions from the pressure exercised by a dominant majority, but it equally protects the liberty of members of this majority by stripping their religious authorities of any coercive political power.

A third reason for neutrality recognizes the value of sincere religious commitments. The argument is that the association with political power corrupts religious faith and makes it shallower. In all great world religions there have been internal resistance movements against the worldly temptations of political power. The impact of secular liberal ideas on religious faith has probably been strongest in the established churches of Britain and the Scandinavian states. In Israel there are voices among orthodox Jews deploring present arrangements that give religious authorities substantial power in matters of family law and public education (Leibowitz 1992).[19] Some religious communities view any kind of involvement in politics as improper and as an aberration from the single-minded pursuit of the right path towards salvation. Others have fewer problems with using political power as an instrument for their goals, but they may be aware that the secularization of political power in western democracies has gone so far that orthodox faith can today better survive in relative isolation from the world of politics. Where such arguments gain ground, neutrality will not only be endorsed by those religious views that harmonize well with a fairly liberal conception of individual autonomy, but may even be supported by those most opposed to the liberal philosophy.

Taken together, these three arguments present a fairly strong case for the legitimacy and stability of religious neutrality. Yet there is a problem with how well they go together and how well they fit the parallel arguments for toleration, which I stated in the previous section. Consider first, an obvious tension between the arguments for neutrality. Only the first is a classic liberal one, whereas the second one is akin to civic republicanism, which attributes great value to membership in the political community, and the third one is genuinely pluralistic, emphasizing the integrity of beliefs and practices. For a libertarian theory that focuses exclusively on limited government or for a comprehensive liberalism that makes autonomy the central value there is no need to compromise with these other perspectives. The second and third argument for neutrality are mainly concerned with the stability of political institutions in a multireligious society. If we think that limited government is the solution to conflicts that deeply divide societies along religious lines, then appealing to a sense of common citizenship would be the wrong thing to do, as it must raise citizens' aspirations to stronger political and social rights. Similarly, if we believe that most orthodox religions hamper their members' development into autonomous persons who critically examine and question their fundamental beliefs and goals, then we can hardly appeal to the interest of nonliberal religious communities in preserving their integrity by staying aloof from political power.

The Rawlsian project of political liberalism, however, which is concerned with reconciling liberal justice and stability in diverse societies, could embrace such an overlapping consensus of quite different perspectives on a political norm of religious neutrality as an ideal result. For this more ecumenical liberalism another problematic inconsistency arises between the reasons for toleration and for neutrality. Only the rights-based reasons converge towards the same arrangements, whereas the power-based and value-based ones pull into different directions. The support of the latter for neutrality is clearly more conditional and depends on a number of fortunate circumstances, such as an already well-established liberal democracy with a strong citizenship identity, or the preponderance of non-politicized forms of religious orthodoxy. Where such conditions are present to a lesser degree, these two arguments will endorse a more extensive regime of religious toleration that deviates to some extent from the norm of a religiously neutral state. Although neutrality may indeed be supported from various religious and political perspectives there is no necessary convergence towards this norm even in liberal societies. It seems therefore that our previous conclusion that religious toleration has a broader scope than neutrality remains valid in many real world cases.

Examining western democracies where the most favourable conditions for religious neutrality are present we find that they, too, are rarely faithful to this ideal. All of them guarantee the free exercise of religion, but fail in different degrees to be perfectly neutral towards religious identities in their societies. The most obvious illustration is the choice of Sunday (or Saturday in the case of Israel) as a weekly day of rest, but other examples abound. In the US, which has the strictest regime of separation of church and state among these states, the pledge to the flag recited every morning by children in public schools proclaims allegiance to "one nation under God" and the federal and state governments support churches financially through tax exemptions and subsidies for charitable activities. In France where *laïcité* is an official doctrine, the most important Catholic holidays are public holidays and Catholic private schools are largely financed by the state under the pretext that they receive this money only for teaching the general national curriculum. In Britain and in Scandinavian countries there are established Anglican or Protestant churches and in many Central and Southern European states the Catholic

Church enjoys special privileges based on bilateral treaties with the Vatican state.

Some of these deviations from neutrality are more severe than others. Seats for Anglican Bishops in the British House of Lords are more problematic than seats for representatives of religious bodies in a local government board providing services to homeless people. And some provisions would be rather costly to abolish. Imagine that all government offices had to make sure that they remain open on Sundays so as not to discriminate against Jews and Muslims (Walzer 1998). Perfect neutrality is difficult to achieve with regard to all the activities of public administration that necessarily interact with civil society and its many religious organizations. While no liberal state can grant political power to religious authorities or can enforce religious doctrines through its laws, there is a grey area where symbolic recognition and material support result from the fact that legislators represent the interests of religious constituencies and that civil servants have to cooperate with religious organizations in order to implement some government policies. Instead of setting a rigid interpretation of neutrality as a benchmark by which all present states must fail, one could introduce the weaker test how religious and nonreligious minorities fare under given arrangements. Yet this plausible move has important consequences, which may lead us further away from perfect neutrality.

Faced with deeply entrenched imperfections of neutrality, liberals may choose among two options: They can either advocate redesigning government so that it better approaches a neutral standard, or they can spread the unevenly distributed benefits more evenly among those groups that are disadvantaged by the present arrangements. Let me call these the strategies of neutralization and of pluralization. My conjecture is that once the basic requirements of free exercise and separation of religious authority and political power have been secured, there is no general principle that tells us which of these two paths should be preferred.[20] The question is then what to do about the other aspects in which liberal states fail to be neutral. A case in point is the debate on blasphemy laws in the UK triggered by the Rushdie affair (Parekh 1990, Poulter 1998: 101-4). The exclusive protection of Christian beliefs against insult by others is not justifiable on liberal grounds. Abolishing all blasphemy laws in the name of free speech enhances prima facie liberal neutrality. But one could also make a non-religious argument that in certain contexts blasphemy can be a form of collective defamation and insult or even incitement to hatred and violence toward an ethnic group and that it should in such cases not be protected as free speech. The question is then whether it is better to adopt a strategy of pluralization and extend the protection previously granted to one group to all others that can make similar claims. Another example is denominational religious instruction in public schools in a number of European states. The historical origins of this arrangement are privileges for dominant Christian churches. The neutral solution is to ban all religious instruction from the public school curriculum and to replace this subject with a course in ethics or history of world religions. But some countries have gone the other way by providing registered minority religions with the same opportunities already enjoyed by dominant Christian denominations.[21] Is there something to be said for the latter policy? First, religious freedom is not endangered as long as participation in these courses is optional. And, second, offering religious instruction for minorities in state schools may serve some public policy concerns better than a strict separation of church and state in education. It can help winning the trust of parents and creating a more mixed and better-integrated student body by slowing the drift towards private schools. It may also undercut the demand for sometimes abusive forms of religious instruction outside the control of school authorities (e.g. in fundamentalist Koran schools) and can create a framework of cooperation between religious leaders and public authorities that is conducive to the social integration of minorities.

Imperfect neutrality that privileges a dominant religion is problematic because it violates a basic principle of equal citizenship. Strategies of neutralization and pluralization are both fit to improve such a situation of unjustifiable inequality, but they move into opposite directions. Furthermore, each of the two strategies implies specific costs that may in certain cases outweigh benefits. Policy reform involves therefore often genuine dilemmas. The major objection against neutralization is that it generally misrepresents the demands of those minorities who feel most strongly discriminated under the existing arrangement. Muslims in Britain certainly did not want blasphemy laws to be abolished – they even do not want the Anglican Church to be disestablished (Modood 1998) – and Muslims in Austria and Germany would not see their situation improved if religious instruction were banned from public schools. Policy demands of cultural minorities are not merely about equal treatment but are coupled with value claims. Neutralization is then not implausibly interpreted as devaluation. Moreover, religious minorities can point out that neutralization will often be a much less effective way to redress the balance. After having been formally disestablished a dominant religion that has shaped the public culture of a society over many hundred years will find it much easier to retain its influence with policy-makers and public administrations than will a socially marginalized religious minority.

The strategy of pluralization, on the other hand, has its own disadvantages. It can quickly lead to a proliferation of demands for exemptions that undermine general legal norms, for material support that becomes a drain on public resources and for symbolic recognition that is ultimately self-defeating if granted equally to all groups.[22] If the underlying norm that justifies pluralization from a liberal democratic perspective is equal citizenship, then there seems to be no way of stopping short of fulfilling all similarly grounded requests. Will liberal democracies then have to allow every sufficiently large religious sect as well as atheists, socialists, feminists, environmentalists and others to teach their worldviews in public schools parallel to religious instruction provided by registered denominations?[23] After a full cycle of pluralization policies of this sort the outcome could then be a new fairly neutral equilibrium, where, however, the social sphere controlled by religious and other cultural collectivities has been greatly expanded at the expense of public institutions and common citizenship. Multiculturalism might then become a Trojan horse whose apparently progressive agenda merely serves to further dismantle core institutions of the democratic welfare state such as public education.

Yet these fears about stumbling down a slippery slope of multicultural recognition seem to me exaggerated in most cases. First, claims are generally group-specific: there is little indication that ethnic or political-ideological groups demand the same kind of recognition as religious groups. Distinctions between different kinds of cultural and political groups that reflect their particular interests in certain activities are not necessarily discriminatory. A liberal state can support non-governmental organizations in various ways if the services they provide are beneficial for a public policy goal. If religious organizations enjoy special privileges in school education, political parties running for elections can instead be guaranteed access to public media, feminists ought to be supported when they set up shelters for battered women and environmental groups should be consulted in decisions about the location of hazardous waste dumps. Second, claims for recognition and support may be easier to limit than those for special exemptions. When a liberal state grants such exemptions it unilaterally renounces the enforcement of a generally valid law. This may be justified by showing that the tolerated practice is essential for maintaining a distinct and valuable way of life and does not violate basic requirements of liberal citizenship.[24] In contrast, recognition and subsidies create a reciprocal relation between the state and the group. Political authorities can thus attach strings to their support; they can limit it to those practices of religious organizations that serve a public policy purpose (such as the provision of general education or welfare services) and they may regulate these activities to prevent abuse. This involvement can even warrant making distinctions between different kinds of religious communities, judging not the value of their beliefs, but the public value of their activities. Some religious sects can then be legitimately excluded from support if their practices are exclusively focused towards proselytizing and provide no services that are valuable from a public policy perspective.[25] Third, the goal to preserve common public institutions for all citizens need not be undermined by a pluralization strategy but can instead serve to orient it. As I have argued above, it may for example lead to a preference for providing religious education in public schools over subsidizing private religious schools.[26]

This is a plea for soft neutrality, which advocates broader toleration and a more equitable distribution of public support and recognition, not for abandoning neutrality altogether. At the level of universal principles, all liberal states ought to guarantee the free exercise of religion and they must not use their coercive power for promoting a religion or invest religious authorities with such coercive power. But each country has its own historical experience with religious diversity and a constitutional tradition of interpreting the general requirement of separation between the state and religion. These particular arrangements will be continuously challenged and tested in politics and in the courts.[27] The path of reform will rarely be dictated by a universal principle of neutrality and more often by evaluating how the existing institutions and policies affect minorities in a given context.

Linguistic Diversity and Unequal Recognition[28]

Can we model the rights of linguistic minorities after the principles of religious toleration and neutrality? The analogy certainly supports a right to use a minority language not merely in domestic, but also in public contexts. Members of a linguistic minority must be free to associate and promote their language, for example by establishing their own press and audiovisual media or by conducting their business in their own language.[29] If religious toleration implies a right to private religious schools the same must be true for linguistic groups. It is still slightly inappropriate to call this a principle of linguistic toleration. Cultural nationalists who value linguistic homogeneity may grudgingly tolerate a minority language. But from a liberal perspective there is no recognition of conflict involved here. There are illiberal religious practices and beliefs that may have to be tolerated in a liberal society, but there are no illiberal languages. A liberal state should thus be neutral rather than tolerant towards the diversity of languages spoken by its citizens in their daily lives. Freedom of speech does not only protect the content of speech but also the choice of language.

Article 27 of the 1966 International Covenant on Civil and Political Rights covers these rights for both religious and linguistic of minorities: "In those States in which ethnic, religious or linguistic minorities exist, persons belonging to such minorities shall not be denied the right, in community with the other members of their group, to enjoy their own culture, to profess and practice their own religion, or to use their own language." One difficulty with this is, of course, to determine which groups qualify as minorities. Some states have simply denied, against all evidence, the existence of native linguistic minorities in their territories and many more would disagree that immigrant groups could fall under this heading.[30] Still, the rights implied in this article are primarily negative liberties that impose on governments only duties of non-interference rather than of recognition or assistance. Denying any such rights to immigrant groups would therefore entail explicit discrimination that singles them out by way of special prohibitions and this is clearly unjustifiable in a liberal democracy.[31]

The analogy between religious and linguistic freedom is, however, quite limited. I have argued that liberal states guarantee the free exercise of religion and embrace a norm of neutrality, which they achieve only imperfectly. Yet how could they ever endorse an ideal of neutrality with regard to the languages of public life?[32] In pre-modern states the legitimation of political authority was generally justified in religious terms. A demand for religious neutrality would then have seemed either absurd or radically subversive. In modernity, much the same seems to be true for the intimate linkage between, on the one hand, political legitimation and, on the other hand, policies of linguistic homogenization. Gellner's theory of nationalism (1983), which links the need for general communication in a standardized form to the industrial division of labour, is obviously relevant here. The theory has been often criticized as functionalist, i.e. as explaining a contingent social development by a postulated systemic need for a certain outcome. This lack of explanatory power can be overcome if we add the powerful agency of the modern state as a second reason to the structural requirements of the economy. For the rapidly expanding state bureaucracy a standardized language became not only a requirement for internal communication, but also an instrument of social control over the general population. Finally, representative democracy adds a third and normative reason to these two. Democratic elections and political decisions presuppose that citizens understand the issues on a nation-wide political agenda and are able to form their opinion in a public discourse on candidates and programs. None of these three reasons requires a completely monolingual citizenry. But all three demand that each language of public life must exist in a standardized form and must be taught at schools and studied at universities. The number of such official languages will necessarily be limited.[33] A modern liberal democracy can be *pluralistic* by giving official status to several language groups and by assisting smaller and dispersed ones, but it cannot possibly be *neutral*. Even if it does not formally adopt an official state language, it will nevertheless de facto establish it through its own public institutions.[34] Modern languages are not merely means of communication and markers of regional or ethnic identities in civil society, but also instruments for the political organization of society. They are public goods whose production and reproduction demands large-scale investment of public resources. A strictly neutral state that left this task to markets or to the forces of self-organization in civil society would not be a democracy, as we understand it today. It would resemble a minimal state (Nozick 1974) reduced to a territorial monopoly of violence.[35]

What normative conclusions we draw from this fact will depend on how we assess the value of a particular language for individuals and groups. I will consider three approaches that highlight different values: language as a means of communication, as an aspect of personal identity and as a political boundary marker. These views should be seen as complementing each other. Taken together they enable us to distinguish universal from particular language rights.

One possible answer to the fact of linguistic establishment suggests that there is nothing wrong with this. Ought implies can. If states cannot be neutral, they do not have to treat all languages equally. They must only respect negative liberties of linguistic minorities but need not provide them with public recognition or resources for protecting and promoting their own languages. Let me call this the liberal assimilationist argument. Its first claim is that religion and language are not merely different in their historical importance for political legitimation, but also in their moral status. For liberals religious toleration and the separation of church and state are ultimately grounded in respect for the moral integrity of individuals. Imposing a faith through the use of political power violates the moral autonomy of individuals to form and revise their own conceptions of the good. It is this liberal norm, which does not seem to apply to linguistic diversity. People pray in various languages, but they do not believe in a language. Languages enable us to communicate about facts, emotions and ideas, including various religious or moral beliefs. In contrast with the holy languages of religious scripts or oral traditions among ethno-religious groups, modern national languages, which are taught in public education seem to be entirely free of religious signification and can be used to express utterly different worldviews. By imposing a certain language of instruction in public education the state does not seem to violate the moral autonomy of parents or their children who have been raised in a different language.

A second difference between language and religion reinforces this argument. The number of languages in which individuals can be simultaneously competent is limited by their cognitive capacities, while the number of religions they can simultaneously profess is limited by the doctrinal content of these religions. Human beings are just as capable of combining various religions into a syncretic system of beliefs as they are of speaking more than one language. But all monotheistic world religions condemn the worshipping of other Gods. Some among them severely sanction apostasy and conversion to another religion. In contrast, learning a second or third language does not lead to a loss of identity or of status in one's original language community. A requirement to assimilate into a common national language need then not imply that all citizens become monolingual by completely abandoning the use of any other than the national idiom.

Minority languages may still become extinct over the course of a few generations when their languages do not enjoy official status and are not taught in public schools. However, if the only linguistic right that states ought to protect is the liberty to use a language in communicating with other members of the same language group, then such assimilation can be seen as entirely voluntary. One could even claim that teaching a minority language in compulsory education is discriminatory for these minorities. Like affirmative action it singles them out for special treatment, which may in itself reinforce majority prejudice and social segregation, but unlike affirmative action it offers them something that is of no advantage for their social status and mobility in the wider society.

All the arguments listed so far rely on what Joseph Carens (1994:172) has called a thin theory of language. Such a theory regards language merely as a medium for communicating messages between human beings. The communicative value of competence in a certain language increases with the number of people with whom it allows me to exchange messages, with the amount of stored information it gives me access to and with the complexity of messages that can be expressed in this language. The more widely used a language and the richer its vocabulary the higher is its communicative value. From this perspective we could simply rank all languages assigning higher value to written languages over those that exist only as oral vernaculars and giving the highest value to the major world languages. This model is still too simplistic. The communicative value of a language for an individual depends also on how likely she is to establish contact with other speakers of this language and how important that contact is for her goals. A monolingual speaker of English who moves to rural France will still find that her native language has little value there. This communicative barrier will be more important if she is looking for employment there than if she is just visiting as a tourist. However, because competence in a language is itself a powerful factor shaping the pattern of future contacts, we cannot establish first the pattern of contacts an individual is likely to make during her lifetime and then assess the communicative value that learning a certain language might have for her. This self-reinforcing mechanism of language distribution accelerates with the spread of communication technology and with the rate and distance of geographical mobility. The overall effect is an ever-increasing communicative value of globally dominant languages over the merely regional or local ones.

If the task of public education were simply to provide future citizens with skills that give them the widest possible opportunities, then languages should be primarily chosen by their communicative value. From this perspective, making the teaching of isolated minority languages like Welsh or Basque obligatory throughout a region should not be considered a right but rather a disadvantage as it deprives children of opportunities to learn other languages with a higher communicative value. Similarly, it would be wrong to divert scarce resources to programs that offer children of immigrants a choice to learn their parents' native languages in school. This theory would support linguistic assimilation into the larger language pools as beneficial for the members of minorities.

There are a number of objections against this line of argument. First, we can doubt the idea that languages are morally neutral media. While modern languages are not strictly tied to religious worldviews, they are still markers of cultural and political forms of membership, which may have to be respected in their own right. The theory of language underlying the assimilationist argument is therefore too thin (Carens 1994: 172). It ignores the significant differences between primary acquisition of a "mother tongue" in the family and secondary linguistic socialization. A thick theory emphasizes the identity value of language, which has an individual and a collective dimension. For individuals, the language they have grown up with retains a special emotional and cognitive significance. It determines not only their opportunities, but shapes also a cultural habitus and their way of interpreting the world. The acquisition of a mother tongue makes an individual a member of a language community whose own collective identity depends on maintaining alive the use of the language among its members. At this collective level, language maintenance allows to achieve a continuity of high cultural and folk traditions across generations. The idea that people somehow "belong" to their original language group is reinforced by the observation that after adolescence most people can no longer learn to speak a foreign language without accent. In this perspective, our first language is not so different after all from a religion that we have grown up with. Both can be eventually abandoned, but they will always remain a part of what has shaped our selves.

Thick theories provide a normative justification for a politics of language recognition. While learning a second or third language increases an individual's opportunities, being deprived of an environment where she can use her first one and can relate to the cultural traditions of her original language community may lead to a loss of self-esteem, that is, of an individual's relation to herself as a recognized member of a social group in whose achievements she can take pride.[36] For majority children the transition from oral capacities in their mother tongue to learning a standard form of the national language is relatively smooth. For minority children it may be an experience of devaluation of, and estrangement from, their family background. The loss of a mother tongue due to compulsory school education will also hurt adult immigrants who find it more difficult to communicate with their children or grandchildren or depend on them for communication with the authorities of the host country. If speaking a minority language carries also a social stigma and diminishes social and economic opportunities as well as self-respect, then one should remove the stigma rather than press people into abandoning their language. Protecting minority languages may thus be a matter of justice and not merely of utility.

Although these are reasonable arguments, I would not fully subscribe to the thick theory. The main reason is that it does not allow to distinguish between immigrant and other minorities. However, it is simply an empirical fact that most immigrant groups in western democracies assimilate over the course of several generations into the language of their host country without being recognizably hampered in their psychological development or their social opportunities. The process of transition may be difficult and in some respects painful, but this is not sufficient for giving primacy to the mother tongues of immigrant minorities over the task of learning a national language. What the argument does support is some supplementary teaching of "heritage languages" as well as bilingual education programs that smooth the transition and use the implicit grammatical knowledge acquired by first linguistic socialization for learning the national language as a second one. This should be considered as a relevant interest and a prudent policy in immigration societies, but not necessarily as a matter of justice and fundamental rights.

In order to make a stronger case for linguistic conservation policies the thick theory would have to be applied at the collective rather than the individual level. One might say that even if individual members of minorities have an interest in assimilating, they have this interest only because the given social context deprives them of opportunities for retaining their native language. Their community as a whole may then have a collective interest in redrawing the balance through language maintenance programs that reduce the assimilation pressure. This is a perfectly liberal argument, but it stops short of condemning assimilation as such and does not warrant state intervention in order to preserve a language that has already been abandoned by its native speakers. Other arguments about the collective identity value of endangered minority languages are more difficult to accept. Some invoke a collective obligation towards one's culture of origin. Granting that such obligations can be strongly felt by the members of a cultural community it is still illegitimate for the state to enforce them against those who do not see themselves bound by them. Internal enforcement within the community will often be a special interest of professional élites such as teachers, journalists, artists and political leaders. In the absence of democratic accountability within minority communities there is a real danger that language maintenance programs may not represent a truly collective interests of these groups. Another argument defends linguistic diversity as a collective interest of the wider society or even of humankind. A greater diversity of languages may enrich the public culture of a society or can help to establish better communication with neighboring countries in the region. And the extinction of small language groups reduces the cultural wealth of the human experience and is in that sense certainly a loss for humankind. However, such reasons do not always support language maintenance policies in a particular context. On the one hand, small and isolated linguistic minorities will not improve their countries' communication with neighbouring societies. On the other hand, the assimilation of linguistic diasporas of immigrant or transborder minorities whose language is firmly established in a national homeland does not contribute to global language extinction. From a normative perspective, there is a more important objection against these kinds of arguments: Policies of linguistic conservation should be rejected if they are merely based on the "external preferences" of those who are not minority members themselves.[37] The external value of linguistic diversity[38] should only be counted where it coincides with a collective interest of the groups concerned in maintaining their language.

There is another reason for rejecting liberal assimilationism, and this is that languages do not merely transport cultural knowledge but also mark collective identities of a political kind. Let me call this the political theory of language. If the thin and thick theories emphasize the *pragmatic* and *expressive* aspects of communication, the political theory stresses the *strategic* use of languages for staking claims to collective self-government. National and ethnic identity is in most cases connected to membership in a language group. Quite often, the demand for recognizing a minority language by teaching it in public schools is derived from a broader demand for recognition of a minority as a distinct political community and building-block of a larger federated polity. In officially multilingual countries like Switzerland, Belgium, Spain, the UK or Canada several language groups claim political powers that enable them to establish their idiom as the dominant one in their provinces' schools and public life. What kind of justification is there for this demand? Most members of the smaller language groups in these countries are bilingual and understand the majority language. Wouldn't it serve their integration into the wider polity if they had to use the majority language in courts and in communication with political authorities? Neither are all of these languages immediately threatened by extinction.[39] For these groups political self-government is not primarily a means to protect their languages or to facilitate communication, but the other way round – they want to preserve the regional language border in order to maintain their claims to self-government within a federation. If a national linguistic minority became a minority in its own province through intermarriage, immigration of other groups,[40] or emigration of its own members, this would undermine its rights of autonomy and special representation at the federal level. In liberal democratic federations provinces have no powers to directly control these forms of mobility. But they may preserve their status by making their language dominant in public life. As long as they respect the rights of linguistic and other minorities living in their territory there is no fundamental liberal objection against granting them the same powers that dominant national majorities enjoy in unitary states and officially monolingual federations.

Language rights of this kind are derivative of self-government, which has an intrinsic value for a liberal democratic perspective. There is no good reason why the right to self-government should be confined to presently independent states. In order to be self-governing a political community must extend across several generations, live in a bounded territory and share a public culture. The desire for self-government among national minorities can be met within multinational federations or by adopting special arrangements for autonomy. In composite polities of this sort citizenship is not only functionally differentiated, but also territorially. Citizens are simultaneously members of a constituent unit and of the larger federation.

Democratic self-government implies legitimate powers to establish languages as those of public life. The choice of these languages is tied to particular nation-building projects and is not dictated by either the thin or the thick theory of language. States support languages not merely for the convenience of communication – they do not have to make English a national language even where it is the most widely spoken second language and the de facto lingua franca. And the choices of Hebrew as the official language of Israel or of Irish as the second official one in Eire demonstrate that state languages need not even be widely spoken as first languages among the original population. The justification of such linguistic establishment cannot be assessed by the criteria of communicative value or personal identity value. What we need to examine is the legitimacy of the claim to self-government and the underlying nation-building project.

What this argument does, is limit the strongest language rights to those groups, which can also claim some kind of territorial self-government. This is not say that they all have to establish their particular languages. First, self-governing minorities have a right, but certainly not a duty to do this. Some national minorities are not identified by a particular language but by a religious or political tradition. If the primary task were to preserve the diversity of languages then Scottish nationalists should presumably attempt to establish their version of Gaelic. Yet, in contrast with Wales, Scotland's history and legal institutions are so clearly distinct from England's that the near extinction of the Gaelic language has not dissolved the perception of national difference. Second, indigenous groups who enjoy some territorial autonomy may have both the right and the desire but will often be unable to fully establish their languages simply because there are too many different languages and most groups are too small to be supported by a fully developed educational system.[41]

Although strong language rights are generally derived from territorial self-government, this does not mean that non-self-governing minorities cannot enjoy some of these rights, too. In Canada, both Anglophones in Québec and Francophone communities in some of the other provinces can send their children to public schools where their own language is the medium of instruction. This arrangement expresses the idea that Canada is not merely a federation of provinces, one among which is a distinct nation, but is also a bilingual federation that guarantees its language groups certain not strictly territorial rights. Still, this nonterritorial bilingualism could hardly have been sustained over time without the strong territorial self-government enjoyed by Québec as a Francophone province.

Another objection to be considered is that for immigrant minorities, too, their languages of origin may have some political value. At least among the first and second generations a native language provides a marker for a distinct community with particular interests. Media, schools and businesses that use these languages may serve as rallying points for mobilizing around these interests. However, using a minority language for purposes of identification and mobilization in this way still aims at "renegotiating the terms of integration" into the wider society (Kymlicka 1998a, chap. 3) rather than at political autonomy.

The three theories of language that I have discussed are not strictly incompatible. However, if we see them as complementary we cannot put all the burden of justification for language rights on one theory only. The thin theory applies to all individual human beings and grounds a general principle of linguistic toleration, i.e. a basic right to the free use of minority idioms in private life and in civil society. Additionally, it creates a moral obligation to teach immigrants and their children the language of their countries of residence in order to facilitate their integration as future citizens. Finally, considering the different communicative value of languages suggests that governments should increase opportunities for all citizens by teaching them foreign languages. As failing to do so would not violate anyone's liberties or claims to equal respect, this last point is, however, a matter of good policy rather than a moral obligation. The thick theory of language applies again to all individuals, but it identifies them as members of distinct groups and it is not equally strong for all these groups. For nearly everybody her or his mother tongue has a special importance. But for dispersed and immigrant minorities, competence in the language of the surrounding society will be even more important for their future opportunities. A liberal interpretation of the thick theory must therefore allow for voluntary assimilation. Governments may have to improve the conditions under which this shift takes place and this should include a promotion of transitional bilingualism among the first and second generation. However, that is not sufficient to establish a more general obligation to maintain linguistic diversity. Finally, the political theory of language applies only to some groups and not to others. Not all linguistic minorities have the capacity or desire to exercise territorial self-government and not all can reasonably claim to be constituent historical parts of the larger political community. If immigrant groups raised such demands, or if their demands were misinterpreted in this way, this would merely serve as a pretext for reinforcing their unequal status and segregation.

This account is skeptical towards the assertion of a fundamental linguistic human right "to learn the mother tongue, including at least basic education through the medium of the mother tongue" (Phillipson et al. 1995: 2), especially if this is interpreted as a right "to have it developed in formal schooling through being taught through the medium of it" and is seen to be "inherent in everyone, even those who leave their community of origin and migrate or flee to another country or community" (ibid.: 12). However, denying this does not imply that immigrants can only claim a right to use their original languages in domestic life and in their own associations, media and private educational institutions. The dichotomy between, on the one hand, human rights to the free use of a language and, on the other hand, group rights of self-governing national minorities to establish their language as the dominant one in public life does not exhaust the full range of rights. We should think of these as the end points of a continuum. Bilingual education in public schools falls in between the two poles and there are good reasons for promoting it for immigrant minorities.

The rights of religious minorities do not generally depend on whether they are immigrants or have been part of the population for many generations.[42] The strategy of pluralization, which I have briefly discussed in the previous section, creates positive entitlements based on considerations of equity. Historic privileges such as religious instruction in public schools or the funding of private education may then be extended to other religious minorities. Such provisions will of course depend on numbers and geographical concentration and immigrant minorities may often be disadvantaged in these respects. However, this is a matter of practicality and limited resources and not of justification for the existence of a right. Minority language rights are limited by similar considerations, but they are additionally differentiated according to the particular type of minority involved. There are justified demands for recognition beyond the basic layer of civil rights to the free use of languages. Immigrant groups exposed to pressures of linguistic assimilation can expect that their native languages receive some public support in order to facilitate their integration into the wider society while permitting them also to retain social ties to their countries and cultures of origins. But the right to establish a language as an official one belongs to the constituent groups of the polity and this limits the danger of proliferating demands.

Immigrants and National Minorities

Making this distinction between different kinds of minorities appears at first glance morally arbitrary. Why should one group enjoy the strong power of self-government, which permits them to establish their national culture while immigrants are denied this privilege? Is this not a differentiation of cultural citizenship that denies equal respect by relying on dubious criteria of descent and national origin? If we accept Kymlicka's basic claim that secure belonging to a cultural community is a primary social good and a precondition for individual autonomy, then it would seem that migrants are even more disadvantaged than national minorities. In Liberalism, Community, and Culture Kymlicka argued that minorities have to invest more resources to maintain their cultural structure than national majorities for whom it is provided as a public good (Kymlicka 1989: chap. 9). Yet immigrants face even more obstacles to maintain or recreate their culture of origin than do territorially concentrated national and aboriginal minorities and might therefore deserve more protection (Tempelman 1999: 28). The hierarchy of minority rights assigned to immigrant and national minorities respectively is plainly rejected by Parekh (1997: 62; Parekh forthcoming) while other authors want to see it more as a continuum rather than a dichotomy (Carens 1997: 43-5; Young 1997). In this section I will consider six reasons that could support the salience of the distinction. I present them in an ascending order of plausibility.

Kymlicka's main argument is that all individuals have an equal right to cultural protection but can waive this right by leaving the country where their culture is established as a public one.[43] This move appears somewhat inconsistent within his theory that denies the relevance of choice between different cultural affiliations and emphasizes instead the inclusive nature of national cultures into which we are born. It is also not obvious that individuals ought to be free to waive their rights to primary goods.[44] Apart from these problems at the level of theory the argument has also counter-intuitive implications. One obvious objection, of which Kymlicka is aware,[45] is that refugees and those who immigrate with their parents at an early age or are born in the host country have not voluntarily left the country where their culture is fully protected and ought therefore to enjoy the same cultural rights of self-government as national minorities. Finally, as Bhikhu Parekh has pointed out, "just as immigrants come voluntarily, the receiving country admits them voluntarily" (Parekh 1997: 62). Immigrants are under a moral obligation to waive some of their cultural rights only if the receiving society is under no duty to grant them these rights. We need thus a prior reason why immigrants cannot claim the same rights as national minorities.

It is somewhat more plausible to see immigrants as waiving some cultural rights after settlement in the receiving society. This second argument would assume that both groups do have the same kinds of rights, but immigrants choose, for whatever reason, not to claim full cultural autonomy. The difference is then merely one of empirical patterns of voluntary integration, but has no moral foundation. In the first argument, the morally unconstrained choice is whether to immigrate, but this choice entails a moral obligation to renounce certain cultural rights. According to the second reason the receiving society is obliged to offer immigrants all cultural rights available but immigrants are free to choose which ones among those they want to activate. This would, of course, imply that a group of immigrants that wishes to segregate from the surrounding society and to establish its own separate public culture ought to be free to do so.

A third argument builds on needs and interests. In Joseph Raz's theory, the moral force of rights is not derived from choices but from interests. X has a right if "an aspect of X's well being (his interests) is a sufficient reason for holding some other person(s) to be under a duty" (Raz 1986: 166). We might then say that, in contrast with national minorities, immigrants generally do not have a fundamental interest in recreating their culture of origin as a public culture in the receiving society, or if they have such an interest that it is not sufficiently strong to create a duty for the state to establish their culture. Three objections could be raised against an argument along these lines. First, its validity depends on how we determine the immigrants' interests. If we consider their actual choices as revealing their true interests we are back to the previous argument. If we think (as Raz does) that persons may be wrong about their interests, there is a danger of paternalism. Who are we to tell immigrants that a certain kind of cultural integration is in their best interests? Second, interests may be shaped by a morally unfair bargaining position. Immigrants will have a strong interest in learning the language of the host country if this is the price they have to pay for equal opportunities. The question is then whether the initial situation of diminished opportunities for native speakers of immigrant languages is not itself unfair.[46] Third, if we think that it is not inherently unfair to tie equal opportunities to such cultural integration we will have to ask why national minorities should not also be seen as having an overriding interest in integration into the dominant national culture. I believe that it is generally true that immigrant and national minorities have different interests. However, we still have to show why they are different and why immigrants are not unfairly prevented from developing the same cultural interests as national minorities.

The fourth argument is about the feasibility of allocating the same rights to both types of minorities. It is once again compatible with the view that immigrant and national minorities may have the same moral claims to cultural protection. While the second argument regards the translation of these claims into positive rights as emerging from individual and collective choices of the rights-bearers, we now have to consider whether such a spontaneous distribution of rights is constrained by scarce resources. As Cass Sunstein and Stephen Holmes (1999) have recently reminded us, rights are not cost-free. This is true for all rights, but there is an important difference between negative liberties, which require general enforcement mechanisms against illegitimate interference, and positive entitlements that allocate public funds directly to specific persons or groups in order to enable them to enjoy the right. The difference is not primarily one of costs (a libertarian state with few provisions for public education and welfare may have to spend a lot more on police and prisons) but concerns the demands of equality. Where scarce resources are needed to provide specific groups with "enabling rights" cost-efficiency and trade-offs with other public policy goals have to be considered. Immigrants may then often be disadvantaged merely because they reside territorially dispersed throughout the country. The liberties of free religious exercise and free use of a language are not constrained in this way. Although immigrants may not be deprived of opportunities to practice their religion or speak their language of origin when they live isolated from their ethnic community, this affects in no way their right to do so. Yet assigning teachers and school hours for minority language education means diverting scarce money and time from other important public purposes and needs to be justified in terms of the relation between costs and beneficiaries. Even more obviously, territory cannot be infinitely subdivided in order to satisfy the interests of all language groups to have their language established as a public one. At the end of this process all would have the same rights but there would not be any public space left within which any language can be hegemonic. This argument is perfectly reasonable, but it is merely contingently related to the distinction between immigrants and native minorities. On the one hand, certain immigrant minorities live in sufficiently dense urban and regional concentrations. Should South Florida be made an autonomous territory so that the Cuban community can fully establish its language and culture there? And there are, on the other hand, historical native minorities, such as Eastern European Jews and Roma before the Holocaust, who cannot muster regional majorities because they are either territorially dispersed or not sedentary. Should they be treated as immigrants?

What the pragmatic feasibility argument omits is the historic dimension of minority rights. The fifth argument, which is also suggested by Kymlicka, answers to this objection. It puts a positive weight into the scale pan of national minority claims that tips the balance in their favor. National minorities have been previously self-governing and were either voluntarily or coercively incorporated into the larger state (Kymlicka 1995: 10-13). If incorporation is voluntary it leads to a multinational federation in which each constituent part secures for itself the necessary rights to preserve its own culture. If it is coercive, as in the case of all aboriginal groups, the minority has a right to have its powers of self-government restored or, if that is no longer possible, to at least some compensatory protection for its culture. In contrast, a receiving country has no special historical obligations towards immigrants who have come voluntarily or as refugees.[47] It may, however, have some obligations of this kind towards the descendants of slaves whose forebears were also coercively "incorporated" or towards immigrants from (former) colonies. Immigrants' cultural rights would then not only be constrained by conditions of feasibility, but also by the absence of special obligations. Yet it is somehow awkward to derive strong cultural minority rights exclusively from special historical obligations. First, we have to explain why agreements concluded long time ago under quite different circumstances should be still honored today and why injustices committed long time ago should still give rise to claims for restitution. Second, if we go back far enough in history, the distinction between native and immigrant minorities becomes increasingly blurred. In the end we are all descendants of immigrants and at some point in time nearly all groups have been coercively incorporated into another state territory. Third, even if we could establish a clear lineage and the ongoing moral relevance of historical agreements and injustices, there would still remain a nagging doubt why prior occupancy of a territory by a group should give it exclusive rights to self-government in a world where Locke's proviso for legitimate first acquisitions that "there is enough and as good left in common for others" (Locke 1956a: 15) can no longer be satisfied. Why should newcomers have weaker cultural rights than members of territorially self-governing groups?

The sixth argument takes a step back by asking the prior question why immigrants should not form self-governing minorities in the first place. If certain cultural rights are derived from claims to self-government then the justification for differential treatment must focus on the legitimate conditions for exercising self-government. In liberal democracies territorial self-government has four characteristic features: it is territorially inclusive, historically continuous, provides a shared public culture, and is federally disaggregated in multinational societies. Let me briefly explain each of these features and how they apply to immigrants and national minorities.

First, in a liberal democratic perspective, self-government rights cannot be the exclusive prerogative of culturally defined communities. If government is exercised territorially by issuing laws that are binding for all residents, then it is prima facie the whole resident population of the territory that enjoys the right to govern itself by choosing its rulers or institutions of government. At this level, the argument cannot distinguish between natives and newcomers. Its practical implication is that after a reasonably short period resident immigrants must be treated as citizens or be given the right to become citizens through naturalization. In a second sense, self-government is a historical project. All polities are imagined as transgenerational communities. They build upon a common past and are oriented towards a common future. In this sense, newcomers must accept that the political institutions, which are already in place when they enter, have been formed by the particular historical experiences of previous generations and can be changed only incrementally to reflect their own specific interests. Immigrants cannot change the past of their new society, but the society can and ought to change the narratives of its own past to include the histories of immigrants and it ought to give immigrants a voice in determining the future of the polity (Bauböck 1998). Third, territorial self-government implies a right as well as a duty to provide a common public culture that serves as a medium and background for public education, political deliberation and economic and social mobility. Such a public culture is necessarily associated with a particular majority tradition, but it must be accessible and open for change to reflect the experiences of all groups in the self-governing polity, including recent immigrants. In a fourth sense, self-government is a collective right of distinct political communities that need not coincide with the whole population and with the territorial borders of an independent state. Most present borders are the result of war and oppression directed against rival claims to territory. There is no good reason for considering the claims of victorious nations as more legitimate than those of vanquished national minorities. Yet it is also impossible to grant every group that aspires to territorial self-government its own independent state. The obvious solution for this dilemma is devolution of political power that grants territorial autonomy to historic communities with a constant desire and capacity to be self-governing. In some cases this leads to a special status for minorities within a polity that embraces a mononational conception of *itself*. The status of Puerto Rico or of Indian tribes in the US is an example for such arrangements (Kymlicka 1998b: 77), which in a way resemble the religious exemptions discussed above. Other states are organized as multinational federations so that the polity itself is regarded as a composite of constituent national communities.[48] In such federations national minorities enjoy a collective right of self-government within their territory and an individual right to participate as equal citizens in the self-government of their national entity and of the larger state. Once immigrants are admitted as citizens they have the same rights of participation, but they have no collective right to establish their own self-governing territories where their culture dominates the public sphere.

The reason for this is the territorial nature of self-government. If we lived in a world where political communities were organized merely on a membership basis with no reference to territorial residence, immigrants would have exactly the same cultural rights as all other groups. Such a deterritorialized system of political communities ought to be unattractive for liberals regardless of whether membership is inscriptive or freely chosen. Its effect would be that people who meet in streets, neighborhoods or at work no longer share a citizenship which commits them towards a common public good. In order to maintain their political power, political groups would have to constantly police the boundaries of their membership and enforce uniformity inside. The territorial bases of political power allow for inclusive citizenship shared between groups with different identities and interests. Non-territorial forms of voluntary association and minority rights can flourish only against the background of a territorially defined domain for the rule of law and democratic representation.

Given the territorial structure of self-government immigrants who import their self-government rights into a "receiving society" are simply invaders. This is what colonial settlers did in the Americas, in South Africa, Australia and New Zealand. For just that reason Immanuel Kant restricted a right of free movement as the core of a future cosmopolitan citizenship to a right to visit other countries rather than to settle there (Kant 1984). I can imagine a future world in which free movement between states includes a right to settle and becomes thus like an internal migration within liberal states, but none where immigrant groups could claim a separate territory in order to become self-governing. This still allows for a number of exceptional cases. Although they are under no obligation to do so receiving states may cede parts of their territory to an immigrant group, they may invite a group to form a territorially cohesive community within the state or they may grant such a group a strong form of non-territorial cultural autonomy that allows it to remain separate from the wider society. Groups of immigrant descent may also acquire self-government rights when they have in fact become national minorities by occupying over a long time a separate territory and maintaining a distinct culture. The history of colonialism is marked by many different population movements ranging from European settlers to Asian indentured laborers and African slaves. In a number of colonies immigrants brought there as indentured workers were segregated from both white colonialists and the indigenous population and have retained their distinct cultural identities and urban concentrations.[49] However, in postcolonial contexts these groups have more often fought to gain equal citizenship and protection for their economic activities than demanded to be treated as a self-governing national minority. A transformation of immigrant groups into national minorities is even less likely to occur if the society is liberal democratic. These societies offer immigrants their citizenship rather than a piece of their territory.[50] And inclusion into citizenship stimulates economic and social mobility and undermines the kind of persistent territorial and cultural segregation that could eventually produce a consolidated national minority.[51]

Conclusions

My conclusion is therefore that in liberal societies immigration does not give rise to self-government rights and to those cultural minority rights that are a derivative of self-government. This argument generalizes the "political theory" of language that I have outlined in the previous section. I think that it is compatible with three of the other reasons for distinguishing the claims of immigrant and national minorities – namely the interest, feasibility and historic claims arguments. Moreover, I believe that the self-government argument helps to answer some of the puzzling questions that these others have left open. It provides a prior reason why immigrants' and national minorities' interests and historical claims are different and it effectively resolves the problem of the feasibility argument to clearly distinguish between the two categories.

A focus on self-government prepares the ground for a more contextual normative analysis of multicultural claims. This is the third axis of disaggregation I have suggested in the beginning of this paper. Territorial self-government in liberal states gives, on the one hand, a dominant regional or state-wide majority a legitimate power to shape the public culture of the society but commits, on the other hand, this majority also to respond to internal cultural diversity by transforming its own culture and accommodating minorities. Some projects of nation-building deny such commitments and lead to illiberal forms of establishing a dominant culture. It should be possible to develop a normative critique of national self-government on these grounds.[52] We can easily compile a list of national policies that *prima facie* violate the constraints on self-government that I have advocated: the way in which Israel defines itself as a Jewish state and discriminates against its Arab citizens, the restrictions for immigrants' access to English schools in Québec, the preferential treatment of ethnic German immigrants over Turkish ones in Germany, the French refusal to recognize any ethnic minorities, the denial of bilingual schools and topographical inscriptions for Austria's regional linguistic minorities and many more policies of this kind. However, it would be futile to assess any of these without attention to historical context. It is a contradiction in terms to think that universal principles apply to self-governing communities everywhere in the same way and completely determine the range of permissible policies and acceptable arrangements. If this were true, such communities could no longer govern themselves but would instead have to be governed by some global authority that enforces uniform principles of liberalism all over the world.

The normative distinction between immigrant and national minority claims, for which a theory of liberal self-government provides the best argument, should not be misinterpreted as a strict dichotomy. Many groups fall somewhere in between these two and their claims are accordingly of a mixed kind. There are old linguistic minorities such as Danes and Sorbs in Germany or Slovenes and Croats in Austria who do not aspire to self-government because they cannot muster a majority in any subdivision of the territory; there are dispersed groups of self-governing national or aboriginal minorities such as Francophone Canadians outside Québec or off-reservation members of Indian tribes; there are ethno-religious sects like the Amish or Hutterites who do not want self-government but demand wide-ranging exemptions to preserve their ways of life; there are ethnic communities such as Mexican Americans in the South-West of the US who were originally coercively incorporated but whose distinctiveness today is primarily maintained through ongoing immigration. All these groups and their claims fall somewhere on a continuum. But in order to describe this continuum it is necessary to identify its endpoints. This is how the distinction between immigrant and national minorities should be interpreted.

Finally, not all cultural rights can be located on this continuum. It serves to assess those claims that are derived from the fact of non-neutrality of the public national culture. But it does not answer to complaints about imperfect neutrality towards the diversity of religious practices and moral views. I have argued that an attempt to promote equal citizenship will sometimes justify toleration and recognition beyond liberal neutrality. This opens another dimension for cultural group rights that is largely independent of the differentiation of linguistic and self-government claims. The best liberal theorists of our time often focus too exclusively on either the one or the other. Rawls' political liberalism is too heavily bent towards problems associated with religious diversity and operates with a model of a closed and mononational society. By contrast, Kymlicka's defense of comprehensive liberalism seems to me unconvincing as a response to persistent conflicts that result from the coexistence of liberal and nonliberal communities within democratic states.

There is not yet a fully satisfying answer to the question how societies that are deeply divided along religious, linguistic, racial, ethnic and national lines can remain integrated as democratic polities. But there are certainly many different answers that seem to have worked at different times in different places. Political theory should be willing to learn from these experiences. Where minority rights succeed in integrating historically oppressed and alienated groups into a common citizenship, but deviate from liberal norms of neutrality or equal treatment, it may be the norms that need to be corrected rather than the institutions.

Notes

1 Western democracies that still restrict such liberties for foreign residents are in this respect illiberal.

2 Among others: Raz and Margalit (1990), Tamir (1993), Miller (1995), Philpott (1995), MacCormick (1996), Moore (1997).

3 Among the most influential constructivist or modernist theories of nationalism are those of Gellner (1983), Anderson (1983), Hobsbawn (1990) and Smith (1987).

4 National communities in exile or diaspora still define themselves territorially by referring to a historic homeland where they want to become self-governing.

5 In times of crisis and mobilization a national culture may crowd out or invade other cultural practices and acquire a simultaneously political, religious and racial character. Such a truly encompassing national identity undermines liberal citizenship and is of course not what liberal nationalists have in mind.

6 I do not discuss here the toleration of cultural practices across state borders. The international state system is in this respect a maximally tolerant arrangement, which limits legitimate foreign intervention to very few exceptional circumstances (Walzer 1997:19-22).

7 For a discussion of these and other examples see Poulter (1998), Levy (1997), Parekh (1996).

8 Gavison (1999), Shachar (1998).

9 Liberals in these societies will still defend the women, men and children whose individual rights as citizens are sometimes sacrificed in such decisions. If the need for developing a common citizenship is what justifies this form of toleration in the first place, any particular outcome that violates this idea can be challenged under the same principle. Neutralist liberals will call on the state to abolish these forms of partial autonomy, while pluralist liberals will generally press for internal reform, which respects the special status of the group but expects it to equally respect the integrative norms of the political community.

10 Wisconsin v. Yoder, 406 U.S. 205 (1972).

11 See the controversy between Richard Arneson and Ian Shapiro (1996), who criticize the Court's decision because they see the task of school education as promoting critical thinking among future citizens, and Shelley Burtt (1996) who defends the decision because she sees the Amish parents fulfilling their duty to provide their children with the resources necessary to choose and live a good life.

12 Spinner thinks that freedom of religious exercise is not essential for justifying Yoder and suggests that the same reasoning should apply to secular communities (Spinner, 1994: 107).

13 This reason need not necessarily lead to legal protection for illiberal practices. In many cases toleration will merely consist in a lack of legal enforcement.

14 In an earlier essay Kukathas defended the view "that there is at least one right which is of crucial importance: the right of the individual to leave a community or association by the terms of which he or she no longer wishes to live" (Kukathas 1992: 117).

15 See critiques of this aspect of Kymlicka's theory by Tomasi (1995), Parekh (1997), Weinstock (1998), Tempelman (1999).

16 One could of course claim that Robespierre's cult of Reason or Marxism-Leninism were really attempts to establish civic religions, which, however, failed quite miserably.

17 The fact of religious diversity is certainly one that theological doctrines must be able to account for. One argument may be that God has dispersed His chosen people among the infidels in order to test the strength of its faith. Another one might be linked to proselytism and tell those who know the truth to go and convert others. Such beliefs will, however, obviously not generate *respect* for diversity. A more tolerant creed may think that God has chosen not to fully reveal Himself to any human being so that all religions can only partially approach a truth that ultimately cannot be known. But even this latter view need not support a social preference for living in a multireligious society rather than in one where one's own faith is shared by a broad majority.

18 Anthony Appiah offers the following argument why the prohibition of an established church in the first amendment to the US Constitution enjoys wide popular support: "Some of us are committed to this because we are religious: we see it as the institutionalization of a Protestant insistence on freedom of conscience. Some of us are committed to it because we are Catholics or Jews or Moslems, who do not want to be pressed into conformity by a Protestant majority. Some of us are atheists who want to be left alone. We can live together with this arrangement provided we all are committed to it, for our different reasons" (Appiah 1996:86). While this is a plausible account for the US context, the first reason does not apply to societies where Catholics, Jews or Moslems form a religious majority. Yet the normative claims liberals make about religious neutrality should also apply in countries like Italy, Israel or Egypt.

19 Quoted in Gutmann (forthcoming).

20 Will Kymlicka acknowledges imperfections of religious neutrality and their impact on minorities but appears to advocate neutralization as the morally required response in most cases (see Kymlicka 1995: 114-5).

21 In Germany courses in ethics have been introduced in the province of Brandenburg, while others have newly admitted Islamic instruction in public schools. In Austria, twelve registered religious denominations enjoy at present the right to give courses in religious instruction, which are paid for, by the state.

22 In contrast with respect for individuals based on their equal dignity as human beings or equal status as citizens, public recognition for group identities is a socially scarce good whose value diminishes as it is more widely distributed. As Fred Hirsch has famously argued, "[i]f everyone stands on tiptoe, no one sees better" (Hirsch 1976: 5).

23 In the US context Michael Walzer (1998) defends a broader principle of separation of voluntary associations from state power that does not merely apply to religion, but equally to political parties or ethnic groups. None of them should be able to wield coercive state power. A partial response to this is to point out that, in contrast with an obligatory school prayer, optional religious instruction is not coercive in this sense (although it involves the general power of the state to raise taxes, which are then used to support these activities). This still leaves unanswered Walzer's question why only religious activities and identities should be supported in this way.

24 Tax exemptions for religious organizations should be properly understood as material support rather than as exemptions from a generally binding law. If taxation of income and wealth is legitimate then granting exemptions amounts to the state paying the organization a part of the public revenue. In order to satisfy the condition of equal respect for all citizens tax privileges have to create some benefit for the wider public rather than merely for the group concerned. No such condition needs to be attached to exemptions for Sikhs from carrying motorcycle helmets or for the Amish to send their children to school until age 16.

25 Distinctions of this kind are made even in the US with its otherwise strict conception of neutrality and separation. On 14 June 1999 the Supreme Court refused to hear a challenge by a Maryland college affiliated to the Seventh-Day Adventist Church against its exclusion from a program of state aid to private colleges. The US Court of Appeals for the Fourth Circuit had deemed the college ineligible for support because of the "pervasively sectarian" character of its educational program (New York Times, 15 June 1999).

26 School voucher schemes, which are currently promoted in some US states, are indirect subsidies for private religious education.

27 Neutrality is certainly no easy formula for resolving all religious conflicts, as the load of US Supreme Court cases dealing with the free exercise and non-establishment clauses of the First Amendment shows.

28 In this section I have extensively borrowed from another essay on religious and linguistic education for immigrant minorities for a forthcoming volume edited by Anthony Messina.

29 The Québec legislation, which originally allowed only for French commercial signs, was overruled by the Canadian Supreme Court as a violation of free speech rights. It was then amended to require merely that French must be the more prominent language on bilingual signs. Even this regulation is apparently not strictly enforced in ethnic minority areas.

30 The 1995 Council of Europe's Framework Convention for the Protection of National Minorities, which otherwise signals substantial progress for minority rights in international law, has the same basic flaw of leaving it to each signatory state to specify whether there are any minorities in its territory who are protected under the convention.

31 The general comment on article 27 issued by the UN High Commissioner for Human Rights in 1994 specifies that "the individuals designed to be protected need not be citizens of the State party" or even permanent residents. "Thus migrant workers or even visitors in a State party constituting such minorities are entitled not to be denied the exercise of those rights" (UNHCHR 1994: 2).

32 "It is quite possible for a state not to have an established church. But the state cannot help but give at least partial establishment to a culture when it decides which language is to be used in public schooling, or in the provision of state services" (Kymlicka 1995:111).

33 This problem is particularly acute within the European Union (Kraus 1998). Currently there are 11 official languages and over the next decade the number might increase with Eastern enlargement of the Union. Different from international organizations like the UN or the Council of Europe, the EU cannot easily agree on a limited number of official languages. A neutral solution would be to re-establish Latin or to introduce Esperanto. But this would be like replacing Sundays with Wednesdays. Such neutrality would leave everybody worse off and disconnect the institutions from the citizens. English may become the European lingua franca, but in the European institutions some official status must be given to all the national languages.

34 See Kymlicka (1995: 111-2).

35 The most obvious reason why liberal states' attitude towards linguistic diversity is fundamentally different from that towards religious toleration is their monopoly in school education.

36 See Honneth (1992: 208).

37 See Dworkin (1977, chap. 9; 1981) on the illegitimacy of a utilitarian calculus that includes external preferences.

38 See Bauböck (1999).

39 Welsh in the UK and Rhaeto-Romanic in Switzerland would probably have become extinct had they not been supported by public policies. This is less obvious for the larger regional languages like Catalan and Basque and altogether wrong for Québec. What is at stake in Québec is of course not the survival of the French language per se, but of a French language community in North America.

40 This is why in Québec children of immigrants must go to schools where French is the language of instruction.

41 For Canada see Carens (forthcoming, chap. 3). In other countries, such as Indonesia, Papua New Guinea and some African states, the number of native languages is so great that only few among them can in a meaningful way serve as official regional languages. In these contexts nation-building requires promoting a common lingua franca throughout the territory. Native languages need not become extinct as long as local cultural traditions remain alive, but the strategy of 'nationalizing' them in order to preserve them cannot be successful for all.

42 An exception to this rule emerges from my argument in the previous section. These are religious groups who enjoy special privileges because they are seen as constituent historical parts of the political community or because they still suffer from the effects of past or present oppression in their society.

43 "...people should be able to live and work in their own culture. But like any other right, this right can be waived, and immigration is one way of waiving one's right. In deciding to uproot themselves, immigrants voluntarily relinquish some of the rights that go along with their original national membership" (Kymlicka 1995: 96).

44 See J.S. Mill's argument against a right to sell one's liberty by becoming voluntarily a slave (Mill 1972: 171-2).

45 See Kymlicka (1995: 98-9).

46 Joseph Carens points out that immigrants' renunciation of language claims may be a case of what Jon Elster has called 'adaptive preference formation': "People don't ask for and even say they don't want what they know they cannot have" (Carens, forthcoming, chap. 3).

47 As we have seen above, Kymlicka's argument that immigrants have implicitly waived their cultural rights does not apply to refugees. However, if we derive cultural rights from state responsibilities rather than from immigrant choices, this distinction is less salient. Refugees have not waived any rights to cultural protection but if the receiving country has not been implicated in depriving them of these rights in their home countries, its obligations to offer substitutive cultural rights are not necessarily different from those towards voluntary immigrants. If a receiving country has been implicated in creating the refugee movement it may indeed incur stronger obligations to enable these refugees, if they so wish, to return to their homeland and to retain their culture and language in preparation for return.

48 In many cases (such as Canada and Spain) these federations are asymmetrical in the sense that only national minorities see them as composed of distinct nations, whereas majorities associate their national identity with the state as a whole and regard the territorial division of power as one among equal provinces.

49 A special case that raises interesting problems for democratic theory is Fiji where the descendants of Indian indentured workers have formed a majority outnumbering the indigenous population. Joseph Carens (1992 and forthcoming) defends the Fiji Indians' right to equal citizenship but also public efforts to preserve the indigenous Fijian culture.

50 See Walzer (1983: 42-8).

51 This does not mean that citizenship is differentiated by the territorial claims of national minorities, but unitary when offered to immigrants. As I have argued elsewhere, liberal citizenship ought to be transnationalized in response to immigration (Bauböck 1994). This involves taking into account migrants' political, social, economic and cultural affiliations to their countries of origins. A trend of disconnecting traditional citizenship rights from the formal status of nationality and a growing toleration of dual nationality signal a still reluctant acknowledgement of these multiple ties by liberal democratic states. Both dual citizenship in multinational federations and dual citizenship between sending and receiving countries of migrants respond to the fact that political communities are not as neatly separated from each other as are the territories of independent states. But the two kinds of multiple membership are also quite different: Whereas transnational citizenship expands the range of membership and rights externally beyond the boundaries of state nationality and territory, multinational federalism creates an internally nested structure that contains several self-governing polities within a larger federation.

52 Western democracies that still restrict such liberties for foreign residents are in this respect illiberal.

References

Anderson, Benedict (1983) *Imagined Communities. Reflections on the Origins and Spread of Nationalism*, Verso Editions and New Left Books, London.

Appiah, Anthony (1996) 'Culture, subculture, multiculturalism: educational options', in: Robert Fullinwider (ed) *Public Education in a Multicultural Society*, Cambridge University Press: 65-89.

Arneson, Richard and Shapiro, Ian (1996) Democratic Autonomy and Religious Freedom: A Critique of Wisconsin v. Yoder, in: Ian Shapiro and Russell Hardin (eds.) *Political Order*, Nomos XXXVIII, New York University Press, New York: 365-411.

Bauböck, Rainer (1994) *Transnational citizenship. Membership and Rights in International Migration*, Edward Elgar, Aldershot, UK.

Bauböck, Rainer (1998) Sharing history and future? Time horizons of democratic membership in an age of migration, Constellations, Vol. 4, No. 3, January: 320-45.

Bauböck, Rainer (1999) Liberal justifications for ethnic group rights, in Christian Joppke and Steven Lukes (eds.) *Multicultural Questions*, Oxford University Press, forthcoming.

Bissoondath, Neil (1994) *Selling Illusions: The Cult of Multiculturalism in Canada*, Penguin, Toronto.

Buchanan, Allen (1998) What's So Special About Nations? *Canadian Journal of Philosophy*, supplementary volume 22: 283-309.

Burtt, Shelley (1996) In Defense of Yoder: Parental Authority and the Public Schools, in: Ian Shapiro and Russell Hardin (eds.) *Political Order*, Nomos XXXVIII, New York University Press, New York: 412-37.

Carens, Joseph H. (1992) *Democracy and Respect for Difference*: The Case of Fiji, University of Michigan Journal of Law Reform, vol. 25, No. 3&4: 547-631.

Carens, Joseph H. (1994) 'Cultural Adaptation and Integration. Is Québec a Model for Europe?' in Rainer Bauböck (ed.) *From Aliens to Citizens. Redefining the Status of Immigrants in Europe*, Avebury: Aldershot.

Carens, Joseph H. (1997) *Liberalism and Culture, Constellations*, vol. 4, No.1: 35-47.

Carens, Joseph H. (forthcoming) *Culture, Citizenship, and Community: A Contextual Exploration of Justice as Evenhandedness*. Oxford University Press, Oxford.

Dworkin, Ronald (1977) *Taking Rights Seriously*, Harvard University Press, Cambridge, Mass.

Dworkin, Ronald (1981) 'What is Equality?' part 1: 'Equality of Welfare' part 2: 'Equality of Resources' *Philosophy and Public Affairs*, Nos. 3, 4.

Gavison, Ruth (1999) 'Can Israel be Jewish and Democratic?' Paper presented at the Politics, Ethics and Public Affairs Seminar, Princeton University Center for Human Values.

Geertz, Clifford (1973) *The interpretation of cultures*, Basic Books, New York.

Gellner, Ernest (1983) *Nations and Nationalism*, Blackwell, Oxford.

Gitlin, Todd (1995) *The Twilight of Common Dreams. Why America Is Wracked by Culture Wars*, Henry Holt, New York.

Gutmann, Amy (forthcoming) 'The importance of not establishing religion', in: Rosenblum, Nancy (ed.) *Religion and the Law*, forthcoming.

Gwyn, Richard (1995) *Nationalism Without Walls: The Unbearable Lightness of Being Canadian*, MacClelland and Stewart, Toronto.

Hirsch, Fred (1976) *Social Limits to Growth*, Harvard University Press, Cambridge, Mass.

Hobsbawm, Eric (1990) *Nations And Nationalism Since 1780: Programme, Myth, Reality*, Cambridge University Press, Cambridge.

Hollinger, David (1995) *Postethnic America. Beyond Multiculturalism*, Basic Books, New York.

Honneth, Axel (1994) *Kampf um Anerkennung. Zur moralischen Grammatik sozialer Konflikte*, Frankfurt am Main: Suhrkamp.

Hughes, Robert (1993) *Culture of Complaint. The Fraying of America*, Oxford University Press, New York.

Kant, Immanuel (1984) *Zum Ewigen Frieden*, Reclam Universal-Bibliothek, Stuttgart.

Kraus, Peter (1998) Kultureller Pluralismus und politische Integration: Die Sprachenfrage in der Europäischen Union, *Österreichische Zeitschrift für Politikwissenschaft*, vol. 27, no.4 : 443-458.

Kukathas, Chandran (1992) 'Are There Any Cultural Rights?', *Political Theory*, vol. 20, no. 1: 105-39.

Kukathas, Chandran (1997) 'Cultural Toleration', in Kymlicka, Will and Shapiro, Ian (eds.) *Ethnicity and Group Rights*, Nomos XXXIX, New York University Press, New York: 69-104).

Kymlicka, Will (1989) *Liberalism, Community, and Culture*, Clarendon Press, Oxford.

Kymlicka, Will (1995) *Multicultural Citizenship. A liberal theory of minority rights*, Oxford University Press: Oxford.

Kymlicka, Will (1998a) *Finding Our Way. Rethinking Ethnocultural Relations in Canada*, Oxford University Press, Toronto.

Kymlicka, Will (1998b) *American Multiculturalism in the International Arena*, Dissent, Fall 1998: 73-79.

Leibowitz Yeshayahu (1992) *Judaism, Human Values, and the Jewish State*, Harvard University Press, Cambridge, MA.

Levy, Jacob T. (1998) Classifying Cultural Rights, in Will Kymlicka and Ian Shapiro (eds.) *Ethnicity and Group Rights*, NOMOS XXXIX, New York University Press, New York: 22-66.

Lind, Michael (1995) The Next American Nation. *The New Nationalism and the Fourth American Revolution*, Simon & Schuster, New York.

Locke, John (1956a) The Second Treatise of Government, In: *The Second Treatise of Government and A Letter Concerning Toleration*, with an Introduction by J.W. Gough (ed.), Macmillan, New York.

Locke, John (1956b) 'A Letter Concerning Toleration', in: *The Second Treatise of Government and A Letter Concerning Toleration*, with an Introduction by J.W. Gough (ed.), Macmillan, New York.

MacCormick, Neil (1996) 'Liberalism, Nationalism and the Post-sovereign State', *Political Studies*, XLIV: 553-567.

Margalit, Avishai and Raz, Joseph (1990) National Self-Determination, in Raz, Joseph (1994) *Ethics in the Public Domain*. Essays in the Morality of Law and Poltics, Clarendon Press, Oxford:125-145.

Marshall, T.H. (1965) 'Citizenship and Social Class' in *Class, Citizenship, and Social Development*, essays by T.H. Marshall, Anchor Books, New York.

Mill, John Stuart (1972) 'On Liberty', in *Utilitarianism, On Liberty and Considerations on Representative Government*, H. B. Acton (ed.), Everyman's Library, London:69-185.

Miller, David (1995) *On Nationality*, Oxford University Press, Oxford.

Modood, Tariq (1998) Multiculturalism, Secularism and the State, *Critical Review of International Social and Political Philosophy*, vol. 1, no. 3.

Moore, Margaret (1997) 'On National Self-Determination', *Political Studies*, vol. 45: 900-913.

Nozick, Robert (1974) *Anarchy, State, and Utopia*, Basil Blackwell, Oxford.
Parekh, Bhikhu (1990) The Rushdie Affair: Research Agenda for Political Philosophy, *Political Studies*, vol. xxxviii: 695-709.
Parekh, Bhikhu (1995) 'Cultural Diversity and Liberal Democracy', in: David Beetham (ed.) *Defining and Measuring Democracy*, Sage, London:199-221.
Parekh, Bhikhu (1996) Minority Practices and Principles of Toleration, *International Migration Review*, vol. xxx, No.1: 251-284.
Parekh, Bhikhu (1997) Dilemmas of a Multicultural Theory of Citizenship, *Constellations*, vol. 4, No.1: 54-62.
Parekh, Bhikhu (forthcoming) A Theory of the Multicultural Society, book manuscript.
Phillipson, Robert, Rannut, Mart and Skutnabb-Kangas, Tove (1995) 'Introduction', in Robert Phillipson and Tove Skutnabb-Kangas (eds.) *Linguistic Human Rights. Overcoming Linguistic Discrimination*, Mouton de Gruyter: Berlin.
Philpott, Daniel (1995) 'In Defense of Self-Determination', *Ethics* 105: 352-385.
Poulter, Sebastian (1998) *Ethnicity, Law and Human Rights. The English Experience*, Clarendon Press, Oxford.
Rawls, John (1971) *A Theory of Justice*, Harvard University Press, Cambridge, Mass.
Rawls, John (1993) *Political Liberalism*, Columbia University Press, New York.
Raz, Joseph (1986) *The Morality of Freedom*. Clarendon Press, Oxford.
Schlesinger, Arthur M. Jr. (1992) *The disuniting of America*, Norton, New York.
Shachar, Ayelet (1998) 'Group Identity and Women's Rights in Family Law', *The Journal of Political Philosophy*, vol. 6, No. 3: 285-305.
Smith, Anthony D. (1987) *The ethnic origins of nations*, Oxford, Blackwell, Oxford.
Spinner, Jeff (1994), *The Boundaries of Citizenship. Race, Ethnicity, and Nationality in the Liberal State*, The Johns Hopkins University Press, Baltimore.
Sunstein, Cass and Holmes, Stephen (1999) *The Cost of Rights: Why Liberty Depends on Taxes*, W.W. Norton.
Tamir, Yael (1993) *Liberal Nationalism*, Princeton University Press, Princeton, NJ.
Taylor, Charles (1992) 'The Politics of Recognition', in Amy Gutmann (ed.) *Multiculturalism and The Politics of Recognition*, Princeton University Press: Princeton.
Tempelman, Sasja (1999) 'Constructions of Cultural Identity: Multiculturalism and Exclusion', *Political Studies*, vol. 47, No. 1: 17-31.
Tomasi, John (1995) 'Kymlicka, Liberalism, and Respect for Cultural Minorities', *Ethics* 105, April 1995: 580-603.
Tully, James (1995) *Strange Multiplicities. Constitutionalism in an age of diversity*, Cambridge University Press, Cambridge, UK.
UNHCHR (1994) General comment 23: The rights of minorities (Article 27) at: www.unhchr.ch/tbs/doc.nsf.html
Waldron, Jeremy (1992) 'Minority Cultures and the Cosmopolitan Alternative', *University of Michigan Law Reform*, vol. 25: 751-93.
Waldron, Jeremy (1996) 'Multiculturalism and Melange', in: Fullinwider, Robert K. (ed.) *Public Education in a Multicultural Society*, Cambridge University Press: 90-118.
Walzer, Michael (1983) *Spheres of Justice: A Defense of Pluralism and Equality*, Basic Books, New York.
Walzer, Michael (1997) On Toleration, Yale University Press, New Haven.
Walzer, Michael (1998) 'Drawing the Line: Religion and Politics', Paper presented at the Program in Ethics and Public Affairs Seminar, Princeton University Center for Human Values, September 17, 1998.

Weinstock, Daniel (1998) 'How Can Collective Rights and Liberalism be Reconciled?' in: Bauböck, Rainer and Rundell, John (eds.) *Blurred Boundaries. Migration, Ethnicity, Citizenship*. Avebury, Aldershot.

Young, Iris Marion (1990) *Justice and the Politics of Difference*, Princeton University Press, Princeton.

Young, Iris Marion (1997) 'A Multicultural Continuum: A Critique of Will Kymlicka's Ethnic-Nation Dichotomy', *Constellations*, vol. 4, No.1: 48-53.

13. Autonomy, Diversity and the Right to Culture

EMILY R. GILL

In this paper I consider the value of cultural membership to the individual, particularly as it contributes to the expression of individual autonomy. Some theorists would accord external protections against the larger society to the cultural *structure* of national minorities through group-differentiated rights. Others eschew external protections, but would protect cultural content by supporting the authority of cultural leaders to enforce traditional practices as a condition of membership. Still others would accord legal protections and exemptions to individuals purely on the basis of minority status, so that members of some groups do not suffer undue disadvantage compared with others.

Each of these viewpoints is implicitly grounded on particular assumptions about the extent to which cultural membership is or is not a matter of choice. I maintain that although membership in some culture is a precondition of human agency, membership in any particular culture is not for mature adults a precondition of autonomy, but should instead be regarded as an expression of autonomy. A liberal polity should ensure the existence of a context of choice that maximizes the probability that cultural membership will proceed from individual critical reflection and will thus indeed function as an expression of autonomy.

As a key human good, cultural membership is or should be a matter of individual choice. This requires a context of choice, I believe, that allows such membership to function as an expression of autonomy. The liberal polity, in my view, is committed both to the background conditions for individual autonomy and self-development and also to a culture of diversity which contains a plurality of options. I agree with Will Kymlicka that in order to fulfill our essential human interest in living a life that is good for us, each of us must develop the capacity to live our lives from the inside, in accordance with our self-endorsed beliefs about value, and each of us must be free to question, examine, and revise our particular projects and goals.[1] That is, we must be able to engage in critical reflection. Cultural membership as a set of particular allegiances and commitments may function either to enhance or to inhibit this capacity. In this paper I shall first outline a case for the value of cultural membership to the individual, particularly as this membership functions as a contribution to or an expression of individual autonomy. Second, I shall examine the case for group-differentiated rights for members of national cultures who are effectively national minorities within a liberal nation state.

Although this contingency is the exception in the United States, my interest is motivated by the way divergent responses to separatist versions of cultural membership illuminate the tension between autonomy and diversity when the range of diversity is great. Some theorists would accord external protections against the larger society to the cultural *structure* of national minorities through group-differentiated rights. Others eschew external protections, but would protect cultural *content* by supporting the authority of cultural leaders to enforce traditional practices as a condition of membership. Still others would accord legal protections and exemptions to individuals purely on the basis of minority status. Each of these viewpoints is implicitly grounded on particular assumptions about the extent to which cultural membership is or is not a matter of choice. I maintain that although membership in some culture is a precondition of human agency, membership in any particular culture is not for mature adults a precondition of autonomy, but should instead be regarded as an expression of autonomy. The liberal polity should ensure the existence of a context of choice, which maximizes the probability that cultural membership will indeed proceed from critical reflection and will thus function as an expression of autonomy.

Cultural Membership

Individuality does not spring into existence independently, but is instead developed within a particular framework or contest. Yael Tamir's concept of the contextual individual, for example, 'portrays an autonomous person who can reflect on, evaluate, and choose his conception of the good, but is capable of such choices because he is situated in a particular social and cultural environment that offers him evaluative criteria.'[2] For Kymlicka, cultural membership is a primary good, and its recognition contributes to and expands individual choice. 'Cultural membership is not a means used in the pursuit of one's ends. It is rather the context within which we choose our ends, and come to see their value, and this is a precondition of self-respect, of the sense that one's ends are worth pursuing.'[3] For Tamir, because the contextual individual is both a situated and a choosing self, 'culture can be a precondition of reflective thinking and the exercise of choice, while in itself remaining the object of choice.'[4] Cultural pluralism carries both the instrumental value of affording us choices among cultures (32), and also the intrinsic value of providing a sense of belonging (68), or a space for the expression of one's communal identity (42-48) with its special ties and obligations.

Kymlicka distinguishes between national minorities who may desire some type of self-government to ensure the cultural survival of their distinct societies, on the one hand, and ethnic groups who have immigrated into and want to become full members of the larger, polyethnic society, on the other.[5] Because cultural membership provides a context of choice, including both 'a range of meaningful options' (83) and 'a secure sense of identity and belonging' (105), access to one's culture is an entitlement that we should expect people to desire (86). Although individuals may integrate themselves into cultures other than their original ones, the difficulty of this enterprise suggests that this undertaking should be a matter of choice, not necessity. However, although Kymlicka endorses external protections for societal cultures that promote their integrity within the larger national community, he rejects internal restrictions 'which limit the right of group members to question and revise traditional authorities and practices' (37). That is, freedom of choice requires cultural preconditions like the right to cultural membership, but we should not structure preconditions in ways that hamper subsequent choices.

Specifically, although we are 'dependent on a cultural community for our self-development and for our context of choice,' we may rightly claim independence, 'as self-directed beings, from any of the specific roles and relationships that exist in the community.'[6] On the other hand, cultural membership should not disadvantage individuals as a result of unchosen constituents of their identities. Thus for some, 'special political rights are needed to remove inequalities in the context of choice which arise before people even make their choices' (190). On the other hand, recognition of a cultural structure should not be used for the preservation of any particular cultural character. In Kymlicka's view, 'the cultural community continues to exist even when its members are free to modify the character of the culture, should they find its traditional ways of life no longer worth while' (16.7). The enforced maintenance of a particular cultural character would limit rather than protect the future choices of the members, and 'Liberals are committed to supporting a rights of individuals to decide for themselves which aspects of their cultural heritage are worth passing on.'[7] The same liberal defense of autonomy that upholds the right to cultural membership against the larger society also justifies the claims of the individual against traditional authorities and practices within a minority culture.[8] In both cases, individuals have rights against the group, or groups have rights against the nation state, that ensure both that they can lead lives from the inside, in accordance with their own beliefs about value, and that they can form those values by questioning, examining, and possibly revising their current beliefs about value. Although outside interference causing the disappearance of a culture *in spite of* its members' choices violates their right to cultural membership, its alteration or disappearance *because of* its members' choices to incorporate aspects of the outside world does not.

Cultural membership is also a central concern for Chandran Kukathas, but for him it is the individual right of association, not the right of an already constituted cultural community, that is fundamental. This right nevertheless 'gives considerable power to the group, denying others the right to intervene in its practices - whether in the name of liberalism or any other moral ideal.'[9] By privileging individual autonomy over cultural integrity, Kymlicka in Kukathas' view undermines the very cultural rights he purports to defend. Because disenchanted members may leave, 'what matters most when assessing whether a way of life is legitimate is whether the individuals taking part in it are prepared to acquiesce in it' (124). 'If the groups that compose a liberal society are to maintain their integrity, they must *to some extent* be impervious to the values of the wider liberal society' (121).[10] Overall, where Kymlicka's liberal society champions the substantive values of equality and individual autonomy, Kukathas defends one in which different ways of life can coexist even if some of those ways of life do not value equality and autonomy.[11] While Kymlicka defends cultural membership through the protection of cultural structure, rather than content or practice, Kukathas defends it by protecting its members' right to adhere to practices without the formal recognition of cultural structure.

A key variable lies in fact that where Kukathas perceives cultural membership as chosen by its adherents, Kyrnlicka does not - or at least not initially. For Kymlicka, 'a liberal needs to know whether a request for special rights or resources is grounded in differential choices or unequal circumstances.' In the case of native cultures, cultural minorities 'have to spend their resources on securing the cultural membership which makes sense of their lives, something which nonaboriginal people get for free.'[12] If cultural membership is a background condition or context of choice that necessarily grounds subsequent choices, individuals whose cultural context is disrupted are disadvantaged in a morally arbitrary way on the basis of unchosen constituents of their identities.[13] This interpretation, however, runs the risk of imputing essentialist qualities to particular groups in determining what support may be needed.

Tamir avoids an essentialist approach, arguing that 'Respect is due to cultural preferences not by virtue of their intrinsic contents, but because they reflect autonomous choices.' Each of us is born with a particular identity, but this does not preclude our moving beyond these identities. 'We can reflect on them critically and exercise choices regarding our future commitments and affiliations. ...Moreover, individuals 'should also have the right to define the meanings attached to this membership, that is, they should be the ones to decide on the cultural practices they wish to adopt, and on the ways of expressing them.'[14] Because affirming one's identity with one's native culture and choosing a different cultural identity are equally matters of choice, both options should be subsidized, as it were, by according special rights of identity with one's chosen culture results in unequal circumstances compared with membership in other cultures. 'Membership in a cultural community is a matter of personal choice, but this does not imply that members have chosen to be a minority' (41-42).[15]

Although Tamir and Kymlicka diverge in their views of the extent to which the affirmation of unchosen constituents of identity is a matter of choice, both believe that members of a cultural community should be free to modify its character or to define for themselves the meaning of their membership. Yet no culture can celebrate or even tolerate all practices, not even the culture of the liberal polity. The larger community decides on the legitimacy of given practices, thus still controlling the content of cultural identity by extending or withdrawing its protection. Thus, the right to a cultural context involves not only a cultural claim but also a political one, a facet of cultural identity not always recognized by its defenders.[16] Another way of putting this point is that the liberal polity itself is the legal expression of a particular cultural structure. On this view, it is 'not merely ...a gathering of individuals striving to improve their lot, but rather ...a community struggling to preserve its distinctive character.'[17] The question is how this distinctive character may be expressed. In my view, particularistic cultural membership has value when it expresses and enhances the critical reflection, which is the hallmark of individual autonomy. It does not have value when it hinders this autonomy.

Minority Cultures

If cultural membership provides a context of choice, as Kymlicka asserts, it implicitly functions as a precondition of the development of the capacity for autonomy, which in turn enables us to question, examine, and revise or reaffirm our current projects and goals. But as a precondition, it is then in some sense a given, and not itself subject to critical reflection and possible revision. As Geoffrey Braham Levey writes, 'Those groups whose cultural rights Kymlicka's theory was originally designed to defend - namely, indigenous groups - tend to be among the nonliberal groups whose self-government rights require some other defense than his autonomy-based theory.'[18] That is, Kymlicka implicitly justifies cultural membership by its contribution to the capacity for autonomy, but simultaneously suggests that the groups for whom a defense of cultural membership is most crucial are those least likely to emphasize the development of this capacity. Because nonliberal groups generally do not value autonomy, for such groups cultural membership cannot be its precondition.

Levey, however, would reverse the relationship to interpret cultural membership as the expression of autonomy rather than as its precondition. I agree. On maturity, we affirm our original cultural membership or affiliate with a different culture as a matter of implicit choice, ideally grounded in critical reflection. Liberals should base the protection of cultures or of particular cultural practices directly on the value of individual autonomy, bypassing the intermediate value of cultural membership as a context of choice. Disparate treatment is unjust not 'because people are being denied some abstract access to a culture as a context of choice. It is that citizens are being denied ...a particular and preferred option that is entirely consonant with liberal values' (237). And the proper justification for self-government rights is not a right to respect for cultural membership as a context of choice, but a right to autonomy (239-240).

If cultural membership is an expression of autonomy, however, this does not mean, Levey argues, that we must equate with autonomy every expression of this membership, accommodating or even supporting 'every personal choice, idiosyncratic whim, or experiment in individuality' (235). That is, even if we interpret cultural membership as an expression of autonomy rather than as its precondition, autonomy itself still has preconditions, even if cultural membership in one's culture of origin is not one of them. Membership in some culture is a precondition of any sort of human agency, but membership in any particular culture on maturity is an expression of autonomy. My focus in this section of the paper, then, will be on the nature of preconditions that maximize the likelihood that cultural membership will represent an expression of autonomy.

The Common Moral Standpoint

For Kukathas, dilemmas concerning cultural accommodation are entirely unnecessary. They arise, however, because liberals assume the centrality of the political community and its common moral standpoint, when the state is in reality merely an association of diverse associations, or 'an area of convergence of different moral practices.'[19] Thus, although it is acceptable for illiberal subgroups themselves to prevent the formation of liberal subgroups within their own midsts, it is morally illegitimate for liberals to prevent the formation of illiberal subgroups within the state (93-99). Even Kymlicka, however, suggests that although liberals should condemn injustice and encourage reform, they must live with illiberality within national minorities as they do with illiberal laws in other countries.[20] Intervention is sometimes justified by systematic violations of human rights (169), but the actual point of intervention is a practical and empirical matter. In practice, then, Kukathas and Kymlicka share a reluctance to allow the national political community to interfere with the practices of cultural minorities, implying that change should emanate from the minority cultural itself. The difference is that whereas Kymlicka would empower individuals to influence cultural character from the bottom up within a secure cultural structure, Kukathas wants cultural traditions or authorities to have primacy and to sanction any change from the top down, so that individual members who want change would leave rather than changing the culture from within. Even Kukathas suggests that 'the acceptability of cultural norms and practices depends in part on the degree to which the cultural community is independent of the larger society.'[21]

As the legal expression of a particular cultural structure, however, the liberal polity cannot and should not, I believe, avoid the instantiation of a common moral standpoint. Michael Walzer reminds us that the nature of a political society is not a finished product of a moment in time, but instead emerges through ongoing negotiation that represents 'the gradual shaping of a common ...political life.'[22] Although the state may be an area of convergence for different moral practices, the nature of this convergence changes over time. Domestic violence, for example, was in western countries once deemed a private matter, while the notion of marital rape was considered an oxymoron. Even a community by Kukathas' definition is open to the possibility and probability, then, of displaying a common moral standpoint.

If all communities then share some understanding, which emerges and is negotiated and renegotiated over time, no external rule exists which dictates what this understanding should look like. Whether the public realm simply represents a convergence of different moral practices, as Kukathas argues, or instead embodies a common moral standpoint, which regulates some of the practices of subcultures, makes no difference. Even an area of convergence that allows the widest possible scope for varied cultural practices still emerges from a common moral standpoint at that time in that polity. Although a polity may reject certain *kinds* of standpoints, those that conflict with the understanding that is currently shared, it cannot reject the notion of a common standpoint altogether. And although the polity may decide to practice *laissez-faire*, it is still affirming a distinct conceptualization of what the public realm should look like, or a metatheory of the public realm which is itself a moral standpoint. Its stance is neither culturally nor morally neutral.

Autonomy and Cultural Structure

Given the ineluctability of nonneutrality, then, how do we maximize the likelihood that cultural membership in a liberal polity will represent an expression of autonomy, resulting from critical reflection rather than unthinking affirmation? John Rawls's political conception of the person describes citizens as capable of taking responsibility for their ends, including their tastes and preferences, and of adjusting them in the light of realistically formed expectations, whether or not these tastes and preferences have arisen from our actual choices.[23] Yet Rawls also distinguishes between citizens' public or institutional identity, which remains the same even when they revise their determinate conceptions of the good, and their moral, noninstitutional, or private identity, which they may view as informed and constituted by religious, philosophical, and moral convictions and attachments characteristic of comprehensive conception of the good (31). As Kymlicka points out, however, Rawls then implicitly assumes that these ethical convictions may constitute our identities to such a degree that we cannot stand back to question, examine, and revise projects and goals informed by these convictions. Although Rawls wants to avoid imposing a robust conception of autonomy on those who do not value this capacity, his description of nonpublic identity, argues Kymlicka, is actually a communitarian one.[24] Those burdened by constitutive commitments may experience difficulty in divesting themselves of these in order to exercise political judgment, while those who are successful may find that this habit permeates their private identities, causing them to value autonomy more comprehensively than their expressed commitments allow.

This contradiction bears on the extent to which we are responsible for our desires and preferences. First, if our constitutive convictions prevent us from questioning, examining and revising these commitments, how then can we take responsibility for them? Rawls states that we are responsible for our tastes and preferences whether or not these emanate from choices we have actually made. If this is true, which I believe it is both ontologically and also as a requirement for successful social cooperation, then we must regard all of our moral commitments as potentially revisable. Second, although Kymlicka faults Rawls for limiting the potential revisability of our nonpublic moral commitments, Kymlicka himself implies that cultural membership is a nonrevisable commitment. As we have seen, he would grant unique protection to those who maintain allegiance to their culture of origin. Culture protection is not problematic in itself for me, because I understand the capacity for autonomy only to require critical reflection on our projects and goals; this capacity is served whether we reaffirm or revise our current commitments. But the degree to which a subculture encourages critical reflection is a necessary if not sufficient indicator of the extent to which its members are acting autonomously.

Other aspects of Kymlicka's account, however, are in fact problematic. First, cultures or groups that do not encourage critical reflection are more likely to be cultures of origin than are cultures that comprise many new adherents, the point made by Levey. The rights that enable a culture of origin to maintain its distinctiveness perhaps render even more difficult its members, efforts to engage in critical reflection. But Kymlicka views cultures of origin as contexts of choice that provide meaningful options and sources of beliefs about value, whereas cultures of choice apparently do not perform these functions or require this protection. Kukathas and Tamir avoid this distinction and its attendant difficulties, Kukathas by eschewing cultural rights altogether, and Tamir by extending them to members of any group with minority status.

Second, I believe that *any* given culture can function as a context of choice for its members, providing both a range of meaningful options and a source of beliefs about value. Although our upbringing is indeed a constitutive part of our identity,[25] any new culture with which we later associate ourselves becomes our new context of choice, providing perhaps a different range of options and a source of different beliefs about value. Together, do these not provide a different, but still essential, sense of identity and belonging? If, as Kymlicka declares, 'nothing is "set for us," nothing is authoritative before our judgment of its value' (51), cultures of origin and cultures of choice should be equally central to our identities. If, as Tamir suggests, the individual is situated in a particular environment offering evaluative criteria, the cultural environment may either be one of origin or one of subsequent choice, either of which offers evaluative criteria. To the extent that cultural membership may be regarded as a precondition of autonomy, everyone is culturally situated, whether by origin or choice, and thus the claim that cultural membership requires protection is generalizable enough to appear trivial.

Third, despite his critique of the communitarianism he perceives in Rawls's account of our moral commitments, Kymlicka's own conception of cultural membership as a precondition of autonomy is open to similar criticism. Although we might hypothetically allow minority cultures to disintegrate and then assist their members' assimilation to other cultures, the unique role of one's culture of origin in identity formation leads Kymlicka to conclude that this solution will not do (173 and 176). But on this argument, notes Don Lenihan, 'then any cultural group which wants to make a claim to special protection (rights) against assimilation by another group must demonstrate that the move will better promote the well-being of its members than assimilation.'[26] But this conclusion is welfare-based rather than autonomy-based, and contradicts Kymlicka's general intuition that we must ourselves endorse the values that ground our lives, whatever others might believe, if we are to lead what are good lives for *us*.

Finally, Kymlicka's privileging of one's culture of origin blurs the distinction he maintains between cultural structure, which he would protect as a context of choice, and cultural character, which members should be free to change. If cultures of origin play a unique role, then in theory they should be maintained in their original character for paternalistic reasons against any impetus to change, even from inside the culture (416).[27] Once again, his claim to special significance for cultures of origin emphasizes their constitutive role in individual identity formation, but without showing how they function as preconditions of autonomy in ways that chosen cultures cannot. As Allen Buchanan suggests, 'An appreciation of the value of cultural membership cannot by itself ...support a right to the continued existence of any particular culture. What is important is that an individual be able to belong to a culture, some culture or other, not that he be able to belong, indefinitely, to any particular culture.'[28] A culture's function as a context of choice, Buchanan maintains, is both to limit the range of alternatives to a manageable set and to offer continuity and structure for otherwise fragmented goals (356). Thus, it provides a framework within which choices are made as a precondition of agency, and certain kinds of choice, those grounded in critical reflection, will constitute an expression of autonomy. But the presence of a range of options and a set of evaluative criteria, although necessary conditions of human agency, appear in all cultures, not only in our cultures of origin.

Moreover, cultures are interdependent. Even when they seem isolated or seemingly closed to outside influences, the very fact that they continue thus reflects the larger society's willingness to leave them alone. Just as the individual is dependent on social and cultural structures for central components of identity, cultures and national communities are also dependent on wider political or international structures that indirectly support them.[29] But if cultures are interdependent, perhaps the larger culture is really our context of choice, containing a range of options and a set of evaluative criteria, including all of the options and criteria of its component subcultures, plus those which are generated by our combining options and criteria from *different* cultures as we attempt to live our lives from the inside, and to examine, question, and possibly revise our current projects and goals. If cultures persist as resources, this is not as self-contained entities, but as components of a larger, more cosmopolitan culture. Individuals only have genuine choice and evaluative capacity, contends Jeremy Waldron, when they are not insulated from different practices from those to which they are accustomed. 'Either people learn about value from the dynamics of their culture and their interactions with others or their culture can operate for them at most as a museum display on which they pride themselves' (109).

Kymlicka responds that although options may be derived from varied sources, this does not obviate the value of separate cultures, who understand their identities as dynamic, not static: they 'demand the right to decide for themselves what aspects of the outside world they will incorporate into their cultures.'[30] But to what extent may we change cultural character or content without also altering cultural structure? Walzer writes, for example, that although many governments provide for their citizens' welfare, they do not necessarily provide the same goods even understand the same goods in the same way. In medieval Europe, the cure of bodies was private, while the cure of souls was public. 'Eternity was a socially recognized need; and every effort was made to see that it was widely and equally distributed. ...Among modern citizens, longevity is a socially recognized need; and increasingly every effort is made to see that it is widely and equally distributed.'[31] Both of these 'cures' have arisen in what we call western culture. But is the shift in emphasis from soul to body merely one of content and character? Or, because the change was preceded by the disestablishment of many state churches and by the secularization of the culture, is the shift also one of structure? In the end, although I sympathize with the effort to distinguish between cultural structure and character, I do not think the distinction can bear the weight that Kymlicka desires. If members of cultures may instantiate change while remaining in their cultures of origin, this is likely to change the cultural structure as well as its character. If, however, its members wish to preserve its structure, they will have to accord weight to cultural tradition or authority, which is likely to prevent not only structural change but also alternations in content and character.

Freedom of Association

The most difficult question concerning the cultural membership of national minorities is that of who within a culture has the authority to determine the meaning of that culture as context of choice. As we saw earlier, this is the major point of disagreement between Kymlicka, for whom the right to determine for oneself the meaning of cultural membership is an individual right, and Kukathas, for whom the culture as a voluntary association determines this meaning without infringing on individual rights as long as individual members acquiesce and are free to leave if they do not. For Kukathas, introducing the guarantee of meaningful individual choice into a culture that does not prize this value undermines the culture itself, even if the guarantee occurs under the rubric of a change in character. Here, 'the change constitutes not a response to the new circumstances confronting it but a change enforced by the wider society interfering in its internal practices.'[32] Some communities into which people are born do not themselves prize freedom, but 'it is the freedom to accept or reject the restriction on one's freedom that is important.'[33] Freedom is therefore grounded on the liberty to leave associations, which also implies freedom to form new associations. This explains why Kukathas does not advocate the group-differentiated rights supported by Kymlicka; members of cultures are free to bear the costs of remaining within them, just as they are free to leave, without special consideration. Freedom need not require the inner freedom of autonomy or self-direction, but only a liberty to follow one's conscience without interference from others (15-16). This requires a wider society, which upholds freedom of association, and probably the other freedoms 'embodying a liberal political culture.'[34]

Kukathas, then, defends cultural membership by protecting members' rights to adhere to particular practices, thereby maintaining cultural character without the formal recognition of cultural structure. Although this formulation avoids some of Kymlicka's problems, it faces difficulties of its own. First, although he believes that the larger political society should be an association of diverse associations without its own common moral standpoint as we have seen Kukathas seemingly allows the larger society to provide the slack to individuals not provided by their particular cultures, by affording them a forum into which to exit. And if the larger political society is, as he suggests, a liberal political culture, it cannot lack a common moral standpoint. It provides equality and the scope for autonomy not afforded by more particularistic cultures, even if this is by default. This logic exemplifies Waldron's point that particular cultures are dependent on and are sustained by the wider community. In Kukathas' case, it is the existence of a wider community that makes meaningful the opportunity to exit.

Second, Kukathas suggests that because intolerable practices will cause members to leave, associations are self-policing, and members who remain have acquiesced and are free. A. John Simmons has suggested, however, that concerning the principle of fair play, 'acceptance of "open" benefits which are not readily avoidable, like regular police patrols of one's neighborhood, cannot generate the same obligation as benefits which are merely "readily available," such as special police protection I might receive with a restraining order.'[35] We should not be required to alter our life styles to avoid *benefits* that generate obligations we do not want to honor. But if we cannot be thought to acquiesce in the receipt of benefits that are avoidable only through extraordinary effort, why must we be assumed to acquiesce in the assumption of burdens that may also be avoidable only with similar difficulty? Leslie Green notes that refusing to extirpate a practice because exit is possible is not the same as endorsing it. 'If a certain social structure is unjust, it cannot become just merely by becoming avoidable.'[36]

Third, although cultural rights may protect minority cultures against the majority, they do not protect internal minorities, who may be as powerless against protected minorities as the latter would be without protection against the majority. This point appears an objection to Kymlicka's formulation of group-differentiated rights, but it also recreates my initial difficulties with Kukathas' assumption that legitimacy is defined by acquiescence. Internal minorities may accept the lives they lead, but they know neither their potential alternatives nor what they might desire with this knowledge. Their context of choice is limited because their range of options is narrow and their set of evaluative criteria is small, even assuming a lack of conscious psychological coercion. Kukathas states that if the liberty to exit is to have meaning, the society into which group members exit must have many of the characteristics of a liberal political culture. I suggest that if liberty to remain in one's culture of origin is to have meaning, it must afford awareness to its members that there are other ways of life, which emphasize other values. Neither Kymlicka nor Kukathas fully appreciate the position of internal minorities or dissenters, Kymlicka because he limits formal protection to certain minorities, and Kukathas because he relies on self-protection through the liberty to exit.

Autonomy-Based Liberalism

In my view, cultural membership as an expression of autonomy implies the presence of critical reflection as we live our lives from the inside and question, examine, and revise or reaffirm our projects and goals. Does this mean that liberals should not permit or facilitate ways of life that do not meet this demanding sort of standard, and that such ways of life are *not* in fact expressions of autonomy? Tamir makes a helpful distinction between *rights-based liberalism*, committed to equal concern and respect for individuals and their interests however these were formed, and *autonomy-based liberalism*, which values cultures only insofar as they may contribute to the development of their members' capacities for autonomy. Rights-based liberalism not only tolerates but respects 'decent illiberal cultures which do not foster the ideal of personal autonomy but which respect their members and allow them some means of participation and social influence.'[37] Tamir's approach is a compromise, which neither respects all cultures equally, nor respects only those, which encourage their members to live autonomous lives. As long as a culture admits 'a measure of liberty of conscience and freedom of thought,' or allows its members 'some means of participation and social influence' (167-168), it is a decent and reasonable community.

But *how much* liberty of conscience, freedom of thought, participation, and social influence is enough for us to conclude that a community is decent or reasonable? A liberal polity has principled reasons based on liberty and toleration to refrain from enforcing its own animating values on its subcultures. Yet whatever meaning we assign, after debate, to 'reasonable' and 'decent' as descriptions of subcultures whose practices we will accept or respect, we are endorsing these practices as part of our common or established moral standpoint as a polity. This does not mean that compromise is never in order. It does mean that we must be clear about what we are doing, which is compromising the value of the development of the capacity for autonomy for the sake of other values.

The crux of the dilemma is that on the one hand, a liberal polity must be tolerant of diversity, without which the larger culture will be homogeneous and without a range of options and evaluative criteria. On the other hand, to make full use of the available options and criteria, individuals must be able to reflect critically on the nature of the life that is good for them if they are to endorse the lives that they live, by imagining themselves with different projects and goals, and by either reaffirming their current lives or revising them so that they can endorse them anew. In other words, autonomy is worth more in a context of choice that offers diversity, but diversity is also worth more than individuals possess the capacity for autonomy. The views that we have considered with respect to cultural membership all in one way or another imply that a life grounded in rational deliberation and critical reflection is indeed superior to one, which is not so grounded. Although Kymlicka, unlike me, views cultural membership as a precondition of autonomy rather than as its expression, his desire to protect cultures of origin is still based on the desire to protect choice. Although this does not guarantee critical reflection, it opens up a space within which this activity may take place. Tamir's formulation makes cultural membership both a precondition and an object of choice. Although her rights-based liberalism ignores preference formation, she accords respect to illiberal cultures only if they meet certain conditions – ones that may foster personal autonomy. Moreover, that she links the ability to lead a satisfying life with the ability to view oneself as an active member 'of a worthy community'[38] implies the possibility of critical reflection in determining this worthiness. As Levey notes, Tamir's 'rights-based liberalism draws on the force of individual autonomy more than she realizes.'[39]

Even Kukathas, as we have seen, relies on the liberal culture of the larger society to influence nonliberal subcultures, especially through its provision of a place into which those exercising freedom of exit may enter (8). Additionally, freedom of exit is itself arguably a liberal norm, which, unlike others, should in his view be forced on groups who do not voluntarily embrace it as the price of toleration. 'But simply, why is the right to choose to leave any less a liberal good (or any more a neutral framework) than is respecting the autonomy of the person?'[40] Moreover, for aboriginal cultures the freedom to dissociate has historically been a function of the law imposed by European settlers, not of spontaneous generation.[41] Finally, freedom of exit itself is an option best appreciated in a context of critical reflection. Individuals who know they may leave may also come to understand their original cultural membership as a matter of choice and personal commitment, whether or not they actually do leave. Freedom of exit is a necessary but insufficient protection for individuals against the tyranny of their cultures. Those for whom leaving is psychologically a viable option may engage in critical reflection as they consider their options, thus embracing characteristics of personal autonomy.

Cultural membership in some culture indeed provides a context of choice by providing a range of options and a set of evaluative criteria. In my opinion, a larger range and a broader set provide a richer and fuller context of choice. But as individuals scrutinize their options and use evaluative criteria to live their lives, their practice of cultural membership can become an expression of autonomy. The liberal polity in my view should attempt to influence these practices so that cultural membership is likely to proceed from critical reflection and will indeed function as an expression of autonomy.

Notes

1 Will Kymlicka, *Liberalism, Community and Culture* (Oxford: Clarendon Press, 1991), 12-13.

2 Yael Tamir, *Liberal Nationalism* (Princeton: Princeton University Press, 1993), 33. Also see Charles Taylor, *Multiculturalism and 'The Politics of Recognition'* (Princeton: Princeton University Press, 1992), 25 and 32.

3 Kymlicka, *Liberalism, Community and Culture*, 192; also see 164-165 and 169-172.

4 Tamir, *Liberal Nationalism*, 7; also see 20-32.

5 Will Kymlicka, *Multicultural Citizenship: A Liberal Theory of Minority Rights* (Oxford: Clarendon Press, 1995), 10-11; see 14-15, 26-33, 45-48, and 58-59. Also see 76 for Kymlicka' s definition of a societal culture.

6 Kymlicka, *Liberalism, Community and Culture*, 127; also see 59-61, 87-89, 165-172, 185-193, and 237-242.

7 Will Kymlicka, 'The Rights of Minority Cultures: Reply to Kukathas,' *Political Theory* 20 (February, 1992), 142. Also see Kymlicka, *Multicultural Citizenship*, 104 and 113.

8 Kymlicka, *Liberalism, Community and Culture*, 197; also see Kymlicka, *Multicultural Citizenship*, 152-155 and 125.

9 Chandran Kukathas, 'Are There Any Cultural Rights?' *Political Theory* 20 (February, 1992), 117-118.

10 Emphasis original.

11 Chandran Kukathas, 'Cultural Rights Again: A Rejoinder to Kymlicka,' *Political Theory* 20 (November, 1992), 680.

12 Kymlicka, *Liberalism, Community and Culture*, 186-187.

13 Kymlicka, *Multicultural Citizenship*, 126.

14 Tamir, *Liberal Nationalism*, 37; also see 7-8.

15 Compare Kymlicka, *Liberalism, Community and Culture*, 189-190 and 237-242.

16 Bernard Yack, 'Reconciling Liberalism and Nationalism,' *Political Theory* 23 (February, 1995), 171-172.

17 Tamir, *Liberal Nationalism*, 127; see 124-130 and 160-162.

18 Geoffrey Braham Levey, 'Equality, Autonomy, and Cultural Rights,' *Political Theory* 25 (April, 1997), 227; also see 232-238, especially 233.

19 Chandran Kukathas, 'Cultural Toleration,' *Ethnicity and Group Rights: Nomos XXXIX*, ed. Ian Shapiro and Will Kymlicka (New York: New York University Press, 1997), 84; see 72-83.

20 Kymlicka, *Multicultural Citizenship*, 168. Also see 163-170 and Kymlicka, 'The Rights of Minority Cultures,' 144-145. But compare with Kymlicka, Multicultural Citizenship: 94.

21 Kukathas, 'Are There Any Cultural Rights?' 133.

22 Michael Walzer, 'Response to Kukathas,' *Ethnicity and Group Rights: Nomo XXXIX*, ed. Ian Shapiro and Will Kymlicka (New York: New York University Press, 1997), 108; see 105-111.

23 John Rawls, *Political Liberalism* (New York: Columbia University Press, 1993), 186; see 185-187, 33-34, and Kymlicka, *Liberalism, Community and Culture*, 36-40.

24 Kymlicka, *Multicultural Citizenship*, 162; see 158-163.

25 Kymlicka, *Liberalism, Community and Culture*, 175.

26 Don Lenihan, 'Liberalism and the Problem of Cultural Membership: A Critical Study of Kymlicka,' *Canadian Journal of Law and Jurisprudence* 4 (July, 1991), 415; see 415- 419 and 402-406.

27 Also see 419 and John Tomasi, 'Kymlicka, Liberalism, and Respect for Cultural Minorities,' *Ethics* 105 (April, 1995), 586-595.

28 Allen Buchanan, 'The Morality of Succession,' *The Rights of Minority Cultures*, ed. Will Kymlicka (New York: Oxford University Press, 1995), 357.

29 Jeremy Waldron, 'Minority Cultures and the Cosmopolitan Alternative,' *The Rights of Minority Cultures*, ed. Will Kymlicka (New York: Oxford University Press, 1995), 103. See 99-105 and Joseph Raz, 'Multiculturalism: A Liberal Perspective,' Dissent (Winter, 1994), 77-79.

30 Kymlicka, *Multicultural Citizenship*, 104.

31 Michael Walzer, *Spheres of Justice: A Defense of Pluralism and Equality* (New York: Basic Books, 1983), 87; also see 8 and 314.

32 Kukathas, 'Are There Any Cultural Rights?' 122; see 118-129. Compare Kymlicka, *Liberalism, Community and Culture*, 195-200; Kymlicka, 'The Rights of Minority Cultures,' 140-146; and Kymlicka, *Multicultural Citizenship*, 152-155.

33 Chandran Kukathas, 'Freedom of Association and Liberty of Conscience,' paper delivered at the 1995 meeting of the American Political Science Association, 10-11.

34 Kukathas, 'Are There Any Cultural Rights?' 134; see 124-134.

35 A. John Simmons, 'The Principle of Fair Play,' *Readings in Social and Political Philosophy*, ed. Robert M. Stewart (New York: Oxford University Press, 1986), 76-77.

36 Leslie Green, 'Internal Minorities and their Rights,' *The Rights of Minority Cultures*, ed. Will Kymlicka (New York: Oxford University Press, 1995), 266; 262-267.

37 Yael Tamir, 'Two Concepts of Multiculturalism,' *Journal of Philosophy of Education (Society of Great Britain)* 29 (1995), 168; see 166-172. Also see Tomasi, 'Kymlicka, Liberalism, and Respect for Cultural Minorities,' 595-603, and Richard Sinopoli, ' Associational Freedom, Equality, and Rights Against the State,' *Political Research Quarterly* 47 (December, 1994), 891-908, especially 902-904.

38 Tamir, *Liberal Nationalism*, 73. On the contextual individual's role as both a situated and a choosing self, see 7.

39 Geoffrey Braham Levey, 'Liberalism and Cultural Toleration,' The Ineluctability of Autonomy,' paper delivered at the 1997 meeting of the American Political Science Association, 12.

40 Adeno Addis, 'On Human Diversity and the Limits of Toleration,' *Ethnicity and Group Rights: Nomos XXXIX*. ed Ian Shapiro and Will Kymlicka (New York: New York University Press, 1997), 149, n. 37.

41 Levey, 'Liberalism and Cultural Toleration,' 9; see 7 and 9-10.

14. Collective Rights: The Case of Indigenous Peoples

ALEXANDRA XANTHAKI

Introduction

Indigenous expectations for a *Declaration on the rights of indigenous peoples* that would include a wide range of collective rights have sparkled lively debates between states, indigenous representatives and experts in the "United Nations working group on indigenous peoples". Indigenous representatives insist that the individualistic view of the world is totally alien to the indigenous ideas of the world, their traditions, their past and their present. An exclusive emphasis on individual rights has not and cannot give effective guarantees for indigenous peoples, who require the simultaneous protection as collectivities in order to survive and flourish as distinct peoples and cultures.

Collective rights emphasize the value of protecting indigenous cultures and existence *per se* and reject assimilation and integration as valid modes of relating to indigenous peoples.[1] Indigenous peoples have stated:

> The concept of indigenous peoples' collective rights is of paramount importance. It is the establishment of rights of peoples as groups, and not merely the recognition of individual rights, which is one of the most important purposes of this Declaration. Without this, the Declaration cannot adequately protect our most basic interests. *This must not be compromised.*[2] (emphasis added)

In contrast, some states use the liberal theory in order to reject the notion of collective rights. The French delegate, for example, stated in the 1996 working group on indigenous peoples that "collective rights did not exist in international human rights law, and therefore his government had reservations with regard to those articles that aimed to establish collective rights".[3] In similar fashion, the USA explains its rejection of indigenous collective rights on the basis that:

> International instruments generally speak of individual not collective rights. (...) Making clear that the rights guaranteed are those of individuals

> prevents governments or groups of violating or interfering with them in the name of the greater good of a group or a state (...) In certain cases, it is entirely appropriate or necessary to refer to indigenous communities or groups, in order to reinforce their individual civil and political rights on the basis of full equality and non-discrimination. But characterizing a right as belonging to a community, or collective, rather than an individual, can be and often is construed to limit the exercise of that right (since only a group can invoke it), and thus may open the door to the denial of the right to the individual. This approach is consistent with the general view of the United States, as developed by its domestic experience, that the rights of all people are best assured when the rights of each person are effectively protected.[4]

The traditional approach of liberal rights theory recognizes only two categories of rights holders: the individual and the society. In their historical evolution, human rights have been perceived as the rights that individuals have against state power. Opponents of collective rights base their arguments on cosmopolitanism, a theory which advocates for autonomous individuals who are free from their cultural tradition and can, therefore, make autonomous decisions, in contrast to the communitarian theory according to which the self has attachments to the culture he/she has grown up in.[5] Liberals argue that the establishment of collective rights will reflect a totalitarian vision of the society and will raise tribalism or nationalistic attitudes.

The extensive philosophizing on the need for cultural membership and collective rights is generally perceived by international lawyers as very engaging and very relevant to legal debates on claims for collective rights; yet, sometimes it appears to be lagging behind new developments in international law. If international law is defined as the system of rules and principles that govern the international relations,[6] its normative direction on the issue cannot be ignored. In this paper, I will focus on three elements which form the direction international law has taken in the debate on cultural membership and collective rights: the perception of groups as concentric circles, the idea of togetherness in difference and the model of critical pluralism.

Groups as Concentric Circles

The liberal emphasis on the dichotomy between the individual and the state ignores the existence of any intermediate groups. The rejection of collective rights derives from a notion of "monotheism of the state", namely unlimited sovereignty of the state and the view that the state should be the only source of authority in each political system. However, this model appears to be inconsistent with the existing norms of international law as well as the international political realities. In the post-national state, although sharing the state's national identity, citizens have in most cases other loyalties as well. These loyalties may lie in groups smaller than the state such as families, local communities, ethnic, religious and cultural groups, as well as groups bigger than the state, such as regional organizations (e.g. the European Union) or even the international society. All these groups represent a series of multiple loyalties that the individual has and consequently incorporate various cultures that influence the individual. For example, a Sami that lives in Finland has been exposed to the specific culture of his family, the culture of his village (which sometimes has a different linguistic dialect), the Sami culture, the Finish culture as well as the European culture.

International law is in the process of recognizing various sub-national groups other than the state. International norms are in the process of expanding the number of entities that enjoy legal personality – if only for some purposes. Currently, non-state entities such as inter-governmental organizations, regional organizations, non-self governing territories, liberation movements and insurgent communities, non-governmental organizations, corporations and autonomous local administrations can act to some extent as agents in the international arena.[7]

International law goes even further and recognizes the importance of groups in the life of the individual. The 1989 UNESCO *Recommendation on the Safeguarding of Traditional Culture and Folklore* protects the culture of sub-national groups. Also, the *Convention on the Rights of the Child* states that education must develop respect for the child's "own cultural identity, language and values" as well as for "the national values of the country in which the child is living".[8] Although the human rights system gives the central role to the individual, protection is also given to the person as a member of groups, such as the family,[9] ethnic, national, religious and linguistic groups[10] and nations (peoples).[11] Even though most of these provisions establish individual rights or individual rights in collective capacity, their spirit recognizes the importance of groups for the individual and prescribes that these groups should be protected.

By protecting the various sub-groups that surround the individual, it appears that international law perceives these groups as forming *concentric circles* around the person. Apart from having his/her own attributes and choices as an independent agent, the person is also influenced by his/her immediate group (such as her family), peer group (such as the local group), ethnic, religious and cultural group, his/her nation (peoples), state, continent/region and finally, loosely by the main culture we all share as citizens of a common world. The closer the circle to the person, the more influence it has on him/her. In order to protect the individual, all the various "circles" – loyalties – around him/her need to be protected.[12] Thus, international law includes a different set of protection for the individual (by establishing individual rights), but also his/her family, ethnic, cultural or religious group, the society he/she lives in, and finally the culture of her continent and the culture of the world itself (by establishing collective rights).[13] As Waldron argues:

> Just as the allegedly self-made individual needs to be brought to a proper awareness of her dependence on social, communal and cultural structures, so too in the modern world particular cultures and national communities have an obligation to recognize their dependence on the wider social, political, international and civilization structures that sustain them.[14]

The illustration of the self and its various cultural memberships as concentric circles seem to represent an accurate and viable perception of the link between the person, non-state groups and society. It follows the communitarian approach on the importance of the cultural frameworks, but it is liberated from the trap of the "one culture". It recognizes that more than one culture can play a valuable role to the individual's choices; it accepts that in the post-national world individuals can have several loyalties without them being opposing or dangerous to the national unity and it indicates the interplay that exists among cultures.

This approach has also been upheld by personalism. Personalists consider the individualistic tradition and the communitarian approach to be complementing rather than contrasting. According to the *Encyclopaedia of Philosophy*, personalism is a "philosophical perspective or system for which person is the ontological ultimate and for which personality is thus the fundamental explanatory principle". Personalists regard the person as an essential part of the community, and distinguish it from the "individual" who is regarded as an isolated entity.[15] The term "person" or "personality" implies relationships with others in the community and a corresponding link on the community and the relations between persons and society.[16] Personalists believe that a person is inseparable from the context of the world and of the others. The person lives in community with others and not as an isolated individual; thus, personalists support the establishment of community rights, particularly for communities smaller than the state. However, personalists do not ignore the negative consequences of group membership; thus, rights exist to counteract the tyranny of the state as well as the tyranny of groups and they can be claimed against the state as well as groups.[17] The personalist perspective of rights offers a western conception of human rights, which is not constrained to individual rights.

The model of personalism appears to be a viable model for indigenous peoples and the recognition of their rights. The Indian Crees, for example, share the culture of their reservation, the culture of the overlapping American Indian community and they also share characteristics of the Canadian culture; they also feel part of the North American culture as well as members of the international community. Their lives and choices represent a mixture of characteristics of these cultures and they want to preserve and protect all of these characteristics. Their collective rights will protect them from the states and the other groups; their individual rights will protect them against all authorities, including the indigenous one. In this spirit, the establishment of collective rights for indigenous seems trouble-free.

Collective rights do not constitute a new area for international law. The existing norms protect various aspects of groups. For example, Articles 1 and 2 of the *Convention on the Prevention and Punishment of the Crime of Genocide* enumerates those acts, which constitute genocide "when intended to destroy, in whole or in part a national, ethnical, racial and religious group". Moreover, article 1(4) of the *Convention on the Elimination of All Forms of Racial Discrimination* rejects the term racial discrimination for special measures that are adopted for the sole purpose of securing adequate advancement of certain ethnic groups.[18] Also, the *UNESCO Declaration on Race and Racial Prejudice* establishes the responsibility of the state to protect human rights and fundamental freedoms on an equal footing for individuals and groups.[19] The various instruments on minorities, such as article 27 of the ICCPR and the United Nations Declaration on Minorities, also protect groups. More recently, various collective rights have been established *per se*, such as the right to self-determination, the right to development, the right to peace, the right to co-ownership of the common heritage of the mankind, the right to a healthy environment and – most relevant to our discussion – the right to preserve one's cultural identity.[20]

Still, even though group rights complement individual rights, there are certain cases where there is a conflict between collective and individual rights. The question is: which one will prevail in cases of conflict? Liberals tried to find a way for the adjudication of all these rights by giving a narrow interpretation of collective rights and by regarding them, as much as possible, as individual rights collectively pursued – and whenever that was not possible to rank them far behind the individual rights. This line of thought is manifested in the establishment of minority rights in international law as individual rights under collective capacity, rather than collective rights.[21]

It seems that establishing a general rule of hierarchy of rights would be counter-productive. Garet argues that any framework of accommodation of individual and collective rights would violate the principle of non-derivation among the three elements of a human being, namely personhood, communality and sociality.[22] William Pertney explicitly rejects any hierarchy between collective and individual rights, although his general interpretative principles to facilitate their co-existence imply a prevalence of individual rights: firstly, "the particular collectivity must not be impaired in its capacity to continue either by the State or by claims on behalf of individuals"; and secondly, "a particular collectivity must respect the maximum individual rights consenant with the preservation of the group".[23] Johnston notes that "in light of the potential diversity of group claims, it might be premature to attempt to construct a generalized framework for their adjudication".[24]

If community is seen as a constituent of individual identity, then enhancing the collective rights needs not diminish the individual rights. By recognizing the importance of sub-national groups, international law seems to emphasize the circumstances of mutual reinforcement between groups. Gutmann adopts an integrationist approach and comments that it may be possible "to find ways in which local communities and democracy can be vitalized without violating individual rights".[25] Johnston argues that "collective and individual interests are not (...) inevitably antagonistic. The supposed antithesis seems to be based on a particular and intolerant conception of the nature of group rights."[26]

International law also seems to oppose a pre-determined hierarchy among rights. Conflicts between rights is a common phenomenon of the legal profession. Any conflicts between rights, principles and norms are generally solved on an *ad hoc* basis, after taking into account various considerations. In possible conflicts between a collective and an individual right, the same process would be used.

Kymlicka opposes this process and accepts interference in the minorities' cultures when the individual rights of the members of the groups are violated. However, this interference is not clear-cut. He suggests many criteria that will determine the prevalence of the individual right, including

> (...) the severity of discrimination within the community, the extend of division within the community, the existence of any treaty obligations, the nature of the proposed interference, and so forth. For example, there is a

large difference between coercively imposing liberalism and offering various incentives for liberal reforms.[27]

Kymlicka favors a search for agreement on fundamental principles. In any case, the two cultures will have to find a *modus vivendi*. Hence, if a minority culture is non-liberal, "liberals inside the culture will seek to promote their liberal principles through reason or example, and liberals outside would lend their support to any efforts the community makes to liberalize their culture".[28]

Togetherness in Difference

The 1966 UNESCO *Declaration of the Principles of International Cultural Co-operation* declares that "in their rich variety and diversity, and in the reciprocal influences they exert on one another, all cultures form part of the common heritage belonging to all mankind".[29] According to the declaration, cultural co-operation is a right and a duty for all peoples and nations. All nations must respect the distinctive character of each culture, while promoting their enrichment in an atmosphere of friendship and peace. Cultural co-operation aims at the mutual benefit of all the nations practicing it and should be exercised in a spirit of broad reciprocity.[30] Both the Framework Convention on National Minorities by the Council of Europe and the OSCE Copenhagen Document re-assert the spirit of tolerance and intercultural dialogue, mutual respect and understanding that should exist among the minorities and the majority.[31] The idea of reciprocity among cultures is emphasized in the comment of the *Committee on Human Rights* in relation to the protection of cultural rights:

> The protection of these rights is directed to ensure the survival and continued development of the cultural, religious and social identity of the minorities concerned, *thus enriching the fabric of society as a whole.* (emphasis added)[32]

International law adopts, in relation to the various groups and their cultures, a multicultural policy, namely a policy that leads to equality among the groups and equal treatment. Through the celebration of difference or diversity, international law has fostered a constructionalist approach to culture, namely a view to culture as a relational concept: there can be no act of identification that does not already entail an act of differentiation.[33] However, differentiation is not viewed as exclusion. All the groups understand themselves as participants in the same society, subject to inter-action, exchange and inter-dependency. The interaction causes, sometimes, friction and conflicts that are resolved following institutions and procedures of discussion that all participants have accepted as legitimately binding. These groups are heterogeneous, and have a differentiated place in public life. Young calls this model "the heterogeneous public".

International law seems to approve the connection between the various groups that Young calls "togetherness in difference". Although Young is primarily interested in social groups, her approach of "togetherness in difference" seems very relevant to cultural groups. Various groups are seen as:

> (...) as overlapping, as constituted in relation to one another and thus, as shifting their attributes and needs in accordance with what relations are salient. In my view, this relational conception of difference as conceptual helps make more apparent both the necessity and possibility of political togetherness in difference.[34]

In her model, Young suggests a conception of difference that better recognizes the heterogeneity and diffusion of groups – a more fluid and explicitly relational conception of difference.

> In this conception, difference does not mean otherness, or exclusive opposition, but rather specificity, variation, heterogeneity. Difference names relations of both similarity and dissimilarity that can be reduced neither to coextensive identity nor overlapping otherness. Different groups potentially share some attributes, experiences or goals. Their differences will be more or less salient depending on the groups compared and the purposes of the comparison. The characteristics that make one group specific and the borders that distinguish it from other groups are always *undecidable*.

Young's approach recognizes that multiculturalism within the state is valuable and that all cultures are important for the development of the individual and the society in general. Cultures are not only permitted, but also even assigned to have an input in the cultural life of the state and, in turn, the state guarantees group related rights and policies.[35] Cultures are not seen as contrasting, but as overlapping; differences are seen as "variations" and are not ignored, but celebrated. Young's model indicates that apart from the cultures that form concentric circles, there are other cultures involved in the forming and development of the individual in a parallel way. It is, thus, viable in a multi-national society to have the same amount of loyalty to two ethnic groups or two cultural groups.

Critical Pluralism

UNESCO, which includes 186 state-members, is dedicated to the development of international intellectual co-operation. The recent UNESCO World Commission Report emphasizes the importance of cultural pluralism and political democracy. The Report states that "the challenge today (...) is to develop a setting that ensures that development is integrative and that there are best practice institutions built on genuine commitment to being inclusive".[36]

Multiculturalism can exist only in a pluralistic society, where an array of choices and opportunities would maintain a marketplace of goods, ideas, cultural and political options. In this context, individuals that are not hopelessly dependent on specific cultural attachments will be able to make their own choices. This framework can be found in a pluralistic society that is advocated by cosmopolitans.[37]

Pluralism is viewed by many states as the main challenge to the state's sovereignty.[38] The two concepts (pluralism and state sovereignty) are perceived as opposing and challenging. In the post-national state, these perceptions are inconsistent with reality. In fact, the recent events in Former Yugoslavia indicate that pluralism may be the only way of maintaining a state's sovereignty. If the state denies its multicultural character, its citizens will inevitably feel dissatisfied and oppressed. As seen in the context of Eastern Europe and the former Soviet Union, oppressed groups are likely to revolt and try to undermine the state's sovereignty. In contrast, if pluralism and sovereignty are viewed as supplementing principles of this new order, collective rights will be recognized in the cultural groups of the state (pluralism) and the state can maintain its role as a decision maker, the manager of the various activities (sovereignty).

Adeno Addis makes the distinction between two forms of pluralism: *paternalistic* pluralism and *critical* pluralism. In paternalistic pluralism, minorities are viewed as the "others" and their rights are protected as a means to "save" them from the majority. In this model, the minorities themselves do not engage in a dialog about their rights, because they are seen as unable to do so. It is the enlightened majority that decides how to "save" them. Evident examples of this policy have been the policies of many governments towards indigenous peoples.[39]

Unlike paternalistic pluralism, *critical* pluralism views minorities as partners in the creation or recreation of the society. The state actively engages in a dialog with minorities in order to find the best way and resources to make minority cultures flourish. Moreover, the state creates institutions that enable the rest of the population to open itself up to all groups, by accepting them all as dialog partners.[40] Critical pluralism also believes in multiplicity: groups are seen as "contingent rather than essential"[41] and their very meaning can be moulded and re-shaped through dialog.

The idea of critical pluralism is realized through the various provisions on participation of minority groups to the decision-making process of the society they live in.[42] The UN Declaration on Minorities proclaims that members of minorities have the right to participate effectively in decisions at the national and, where appropriate, regional level.[43] Especially the *ILO Convention 169 concerning indigenous and tribal peoples in independent countries* adopts a broad concept of participation in relation to indigenous peoples: States should not only consult indigenous peoples on matters which affect them directly; the consultations must be undertaken with the objective of achieving agreement or consent to the proposed measures.[44]

In the dialog process, groups are conceived as equal partners rather than negotiators or imitators of the dominant groups. The critically pluralist society does not transcend group differences; cultures are not surpassed but acknowledged and celebrated. Institutional dialog is very important, because it leads to the revisibly and re-evaluation Kymlicka argues for; groups are involved in mutual corrective engagements. Groups are re-conceptualized and re-cast and their differences are adjusted and reconstituted in a process of constant and genuine dialogue. Through dialog groups are challenged to accommodate in their own world the objective reality of the other. They interact, exchange ideas and benefit from the cultures of all the groups rather than just from their own culture exclusively. As Falk notes:

> One role of the robust society is to overcome both normative and cultural blindness to human suffering. The raising of awareness requires deliberate efforts to counterpart the vulnerability of previously excluded groups; lessening vulnerability in turn depends on developing decentralized participatory democracy. (...) Democratization is both a vital precondition and a crucial ingredient of human rights protection.[45]

Conclusions

The concepts of concentric loyalties, togetherness in difference and critical pluralism appear to be supported by the existing norms of international law. These concepts form the basis for the equal co-existence of collective rights with individual rights and combine the essence of liberalism with collective rights. If indigenous communities are accepted and recognized as bearers of rights and duties, there is a greater chance to develop a coherent set of doctrines to accommodate their real problems and concerns. The inclusion of a wide range of collective rights in the United Nations Declaration on the Rights of Indigenous Peoples will render affirmative action for these communities easier and indigenous nations that have suffered discrimination for so long will eventually be compensated.

Notes

1 See Commission on Human Rights, Consideration of a Draft United Nations Declaration on the Rights of Indigenous Peoples, Information received from non-governmental and indigenous organisations, World Council of Peoples, UN Doc. E/CN.4/1995/WG.15/4, para. 23.

2 United Nations Sub-Commission, Indigenous Peoples Preparatory Meeting: Comments on the First Revised Text of the Draft Declaration on Rights of Indigenous peoples, July 1989, UN Doc. E/CN.4/Sub.2/AC.4/1990/3/Add.2.

3 See Commission on Human Rights, Report of the working group established in accordance with Commission on Human Rights Resolution 1995/32, E/CN.4/1997/102, para. 108.

4 See US Delegation comments on section 1 of the draft declaration in the 1995 working group on indigenous peoples (on file with the author). The same comments are included in Commission on Human Rights, *Consideration of a Draft United Nations Declaration on the Rights of Indigenous peoples, Information received from Governments*, United States of America, UN Doc. E/CN.4/1995/WG.15/2/Add.1, para10-12. Similar views were expressed in the 1998 working group on indigenous peoples, see Commission on Human Rights, *Draft report of the working group established in accordance with Commission on Human Rights Resolution 1995/32*, E/CN.4/1998/WG.15/CPR.1, para. 40. In the same meeting, Japan and Sweden were also very negative concerning the establishment of collective rights.

5 On the issue of communitarianism and cosmopolitanism, see among others W. Kymlicka, *The Rights of Minority Cultures*, Oxford: Oxford University Press, 1995; S. Avineri and A. de-Shalit, *Communitarianism and Individualism*, Oxford: Oxford University Press, 1995; M.J. Sandel, *Liberalism and the Limits of Justice*, Cambridge: Cambridge University Press, 1992; W. Kymlicka, *Liberalism, Community and Culture,* Oxford: Clarendon Press, 1991; 4 (1991) 2 *Canadian Journal of Law and Jurisprudence*; 77 (1989) 3 *California Law Review*, 479-594; C. Kukathas, "Are there any cultural rights?", 20 (1992) *Political Theory*, 105-139; Will Kymlicka, "The Right of Minority Cultures, Reply to Kukathas", 20(1992)1 *Political Theory*, 140-145; Michael McDonald, "Liberalism, Community and Culture" in 42 (1992) *University of Toronto Law Journal*, 113-131; Vernon Van Dyke, "The Individual, the State and Ethnic Communities in Political Theory", 29 (1977) *World Politics*, 343-369; R.E. Howard, "Dignity, Community and Human Rights", A.A. An-Na'im (ed.), *Human Rights in Cross-Cultural Perspectives, A Quest for Consensus*, Philadelphia: University of Pennsylvania Press, 1992, 81-102; R.E. Howard, "Dignity, Community and Human Rights", A.A. An-Na'im (ed.),

Human Rights in Cross-Cultural Perspectives, A Quest for Consensus, Philadelphia: University of Pennsylvania Press, 1992, 81-102.

6 Martin Dixon, *Textbook on International Law*, (3d edition), London: Blackstone Press Ltd, 1996, 2.

7 Martin Dixon, *op.cit.*, 109-110; also see Ian Brownlie, *Principles of Public International Law*, (fourth edition), Oxford: Clarendon Press, 1992, 58-70.

8 Article 29.1.c of the Convention on the Rights of the Child.

9 Article 16.3 of the *Universal Declaration* and article 23 of the *International Covenant on Civil and Political Rights* proclaim that "the family is the natural and fundamental group unit of society and is entitled to protection by Society and the State".

10 Such as article 27 of the International Covenant on Civil and Political Rights and the United Nations Declaration on Ethnic, National, Religious or Linguistic Minorities.

11 Such as the right to self-determination, see Article 1 of the International Covenant on Civil and Political Rights and article 1 of the International Covenant on Economic, Social and Cultural Rights; the right of peoples to peace, see United Nations Declaration on the Right of Peoples to Peace; the right to economic, social, cultural and political development, see United Nations Declaration on the right to development.

12 Garet talks about three equally important components of every human being: a/ personhood, namely the individual good; b/ communality, namely the group good; and c/ sociality, the common good. Communality is for Garet as important as the other two elements:

> Not only is groupness an unfathomable *fact* for all our lives, but it is also an unfathomable *value*. We are born into some groups, others we chose, and still ignoring them means closing the eyes to the existing reality. Others chose us. Life not subject to the call of groupness is as difficult for us to imagine as life not subject to the individuating call of personhood or the sociating call of sociality.

13 See Ronald Garet, "Communality and Existence: The Rights of Groups", 56 (1993) *South California Law Review*, 1001-1050.

14 Jeremy Waldron, "Minority Cultures and the Cosmopolitan Alternative" 25 (1995) *University of Michigan Journal. of Law Reform*, 751-793, as reprinted in Will Kymlicka (ed.), *The Rights of Minority Cultures* (Oxford: Oxford University Press, 1995), 93-119, 103.

15 Virginia A. Leary, "Postliberal strands in Western Human Rights Theory" in Abdullah Ahmed An-Na'im (ed.), *Human Rights in Cross-Cultural Perspectives, A Quest for Consensus*, Philadelphia: University of Pennsylvania Press, 1992, 105-132, 108.

16 Leary, *op.cit.*, 106.

17 Leary, *op.cit.*, 118.

18 Similar references to groups are also found in articles 4(a) and 14 of the Convention.

19 Art. 6 para.1 of the Declaration.

20 Article 1 of the *UNESCO Declaration on Race and Racial Prejudice* proclaims that "all individuals and groups have the right to be different, to consider themselves as different and to be regarded as such"; article 2 states that "all individuals and groups have the right to be different".

21 Thus, minority rights are recognised as individual rights that can be exercised "in community with others". For example, see *United Nations Declaration on Ethnic, National, Religious or Linguistic Minorities* and article 27 of the ICCPR.

22 Ronald Garet, *op.cit.*

23 W.F. Pertney, *The Aboriginal Rights Provisions in the Constitution Act*, (Saskatoon: Native Law Centre, 1987), 52 as quoted in Darlene Johnston, *op.cit.*, 189.

24 Ibid, 189-190.

25 Amy Gutmann, "Communitarian Critics of Liberalism", 14 (1985) *Philosophy and Public Affairs*, 308-330, 322.

26 Darlene Johnston, *op cit*, 179-201, 179.

27 See Will Kymlicka, "The Right of Minority Cultures, Reply to Kukathas", 20(1992)1 *Political Theory*, 140-145, 144.

28 Ibid, 140-145, 144.

29 Article 1.2 of the Declaration.

30 Articles 5-8 of the Declaration.

31 Article 6.1 of the 1994 Council of Europe Framework Convention for the Protection of National Minorities and paragraph 36 of the Copenhagen Meeting of the Conference on the Human Dimension of the OSCE (1990).

32 General Comment no. 23 (50) on Article 27, UN Doc. CCPR/C/21/Rev.1/Add.5, 26 April 1994.

33 M. Schulte-Tenckhoff, *The Right of persons belonging to minorities to enjoy their own culture*, Working paper submitted to the 1997 working group on minorities, UN Doc. E/CN.4/Sub.2/AC.5/1997/WP.7, para. 28-30.

34 Iris Marion Young, "Together in Difference: Transforming the Logic of Group Political Conflict" in Will Kymlicka (ed.), *The Rights of Minority Cultures*, (Oxford: Oxford University Press, 1995), 155-178, 157.

35 Iris Marion Young, *op.cit.*, 155-178, 165.

36 World Commission on Culture and Development, *Report: Our Creative Diversity*, chapter II, page 70. UNESCO organised in January 1999 the colloquium "Towards a constructive pluralism" where the idea of pluralism was discussed in depth. See http://www.unesco.org/culture/culturalpluralism/html_eng/overview.ht.

37 Michael McDonald, "Should Communities Have Rights? Reflections on Liberal Individualism" in 4 (1991) 2 *Canadian Journal of Law and Jurisprudence*, 217-237, 224.

38 Michael Walzer, "Pluralism: A Political Perspective" in Will Kymlicka (ed.), *The Rights of Minority Cultures*, (Oxford: Oxford University Press, 1995), 139-154, 145.

39 Adeno Addis, "Individualism, Communitarianism, and the Rights of Ethnic Minorities", in 67 (1992) *Notre Dame Law Review*, 615- 676, 620.

40 Ibid, 621.

41 Ibid.

42 See for example, article 15 of the 1994 Council of Europe Framework Convention for the Protection of National Minorities; also para. 35 of the Copenhagen Meeting of the Conference on the Human Dimension of the OSCE (1990).

43 Article 2.3 of the UN Declaration on Minorities.

44 Article 6.2 of the ILO 169.

45 Richard Falk, "Cultural Foundations for the International Protection of Human Rights", Abdullahi Ahmend An-Na'im (ed.), *Human Rights in Cross-Cultural Perspectives, A Quest for Consensus*, Philadelphia: University of Pennsylvania Press, 1992, 43-64, 48.

15. Defending Women's Rights Internationally

JAMES P. STERBA

There are a number of approaches currently being used to defend women's rights internationally. One approach, the International Law Approach, defends women's rights by appealing to international agreements.[1] For example, according to the United Nations Universal Declaration of Human Rights adopted in 1948, "All human beings are born free and equal in dignity and rights." And subsequent agreements, the International Covenant on Economic, Social, and Cultural Rights, the International Covenant on Civil and Political Rights, and especially the Convention on the Elimination of All Forms of Discrimination against Women adopted in 1979 have all made it easier to defend women's rights as internationally recognized rights. A serious problem with this approach, however, is that 40 of the 133 ratifying states have only accepted the most important of these agreements with respect to the cause of women's rights, the Convention on the Elimination of All Forms of Discrimination against Women, subject to reservations, mostly on religious or cultural grounds, that have, in effect, undermined the very purpose of the agreement as a whole.[2] A second approach to defending women's rights, the Aristotelian Human Capacities Approach, begins with a refurbished Aristotelian account of human flourishing. Employing this approach, Martha Nussbaum and Amartya Sen seek to characterize a universalist and essentialist conception of what is required for a good human life.[3] They then go on to argue that since men and women have the same capacities for a good human life, they should have the same opportunities and resources for developing those capacities as well.[4] The main difficulties with this approach are the challenges that have been raised to its fairly detailed conception of a good life and to its assumption that this conception gives rise to a political obligation to provide everyone with the opportunities and resources for a good life. A third approach to defending women's rights, the Liberal Feminist Approach, begins with standard liberal ideals of autonomy and fair play and then demands that these ideals be applied to women as well as to men. Susan Okin and others have used this approach, for example, to argue against domestic violence, rape, and unequal opportunity for women in education, employment, housing, credit and health care.[5] This approach, however, is challenged by those who simply reject the liberal ideals on which it is premised. A fourth, the Postmodernist Approach, defends women's rights while attempting to take seriously the differences that there are between individuals and between groups. Using this approach, Jane Flax and others have appealed to the particular features of local normative practices to support women's rights.[6] But this approach runs into difficulty because although certain features of local normative practices support women's rights, other features do not, and this approach has no way to resolve such conflicts, viewing them all as simply conflicts of individual or group interest.

Is there anyway to improve upon these defenses of women's rights? I think there is. It involves constructing a defense of women's rights in three stages. The first stage is to show that rationality requires morality. This enables us to effectively respond to those who reject morality in favor of individual or group interest because then we can show that they are rejecting rationality as well. The second stage is to show that only an accessible, secular conception of morality can support the use of coercion against dissenters. This enables us to respond to those who want to impose their religious ideals on others. The third stage is to show that even the most minimal secular conception of morality supports a robust conception of women's rights. This enables us to respond to those who think that they can be moral without endorsing such a conception of women's rights. In this paper, I will sketch the three stages of this defense of women rights and briefly consider how it applies in practice.

Stage One: From Rationality to Morality

Let us begin by imagining that each of us is capable of entertaining and acting upon both self-interested and moral reasons and that the question we are seeking to answer is what sort of reasons for action it would be rational for us to accept. This question is not about what sort of reasons we should publicly affirm or advocate, since people will sometimes publicly affirm or advocate reasons that are quite different from those they are prepared to act upon. Rather it is a question about what reasons it would be rational for us to accept at the deepest level - in our heart of hearts.

Of course, there are people who are incapable of acting upon moral reasons. For such people, there is no question about their being required to act morally or altruistically. Yet the interesting philosophical question is not about such people but about people, like ourselves, who are capable of acting self-interestedly or morally and are seeking a rational justification for following a particular course of action.

In trying to determine how we should act, we would like to be able to construct a *good* argument favoring morality over egoism, and given that good arguments are non-question-begging, we accordingly would like to construct an argument that does not beg the question against egoism. The question at issue here is what reasons each of us should take as supreme, and this question would be begged against egoism if we propose to answer it simply by assuming from the start that moral reasons are the reasons that each of us should take as supreme. But the question would be begged against morality as well if we proposed to answer the question simply by assuming from the start that self-interested reasons are the reasons that each of us should take as supreme. This means, of course, that we cannot answer the question of what reasons we should take as supreme simply by assuming the general principle of egoism:

> Each person ought to do what best serves his or her overall self-interest.

We can no more argue for egoism simply by denying the relevance of moral reasons to rational choice than we can argue for pure altruism simply by denying the relevance of self-interested reasons to rational choice and assuming the following principle of pure altruism:

> Each person ought to do what best serves the overall interest of others.[7]

Consequently, in order not to beg the question against either egoism or altruism, we have no other alternative but to grant the prima facie relevance of both self-interested and moral reasons to rational choice and then try to determine which reasons we would be rationally required to act upon, all things considered.

Here it might be objected that we *do* have non-question-begging grounds for favoring self-interested reasons over moral reasons, if not egoism over altruism. From observing ourselves and others, don't we find that self-interested reasons are better motivators than are moral reasons, as evidenced by the fact that there seem to be more egoistically inclined people in the world than there are altruistically inclined people? It might be argued that because of this difference in motivational capacity, self-interested and moral reasons should not *both* be regarded as *prima facie* relevant to rational choice.

But is there really this difference in motivational capacity? Do human beings really have a greater capacity for self-interested behavior than for moral or altruistic behavior? If we focus for a change on the behavior of women, I think we are likely to observe considerably more altruism than egoism among women, particularly with respect to the care of their families.[8] Of course, if we look to men, given the prevailing patriarchal social structures, we may tend to find more egoism than altruism.[9] But most likely any differences that exist between men and women in this regard, irrespective of whether we consider them to be good or bad, are primarily due to the dominant patterns of socialization - nurture rather than nature.[10] In any case, it is beyond dispute that we humans are capable of both self-interested and altruistic behavior, and given that we have these capabilities, it seems reasonable to ask which ones should have priority.[11]

In this regard, there are two kinds of cases that must be considered. First, there are cases in which there is a conflict between the relevant self-interested and moral reasons. Second, there are cases in which there is no such conflict.

It seems obvious that where there is no conflict and both reasons are conclusive reasons of their kind, both reasons should be acted upon. In such contexts, we should do what is favored both by morality and by self-interest.

Now when we rationally assess the relevant reasons in conflict cases, it is best to cast the conflict not as a conflict between self-interested reasons and moral reasons but instead as a conflict between self-interested reasons and altruistic reasons.[12] Viewed in this way, three solutions are possible. First, we could say that self-interested reasons always have priority over conflicting altruistic reasons. Second, we could say, just the opposite, that altruistic reasons always have priority over conflicting self-interested reasons. Third, we could say that some kind of compromise is rationally required. In this compromise, sometimes self-interested reasons would have priority over altruistic reasons, and sometimes altruistic reasons would have priority over self-interested reasons.

Once the conflict is described in this manner, the third solution can be seen to be the one that is rationally required. This is because the first and second solutions give exclusive priority to one class of relevant reasons over the other, and only a completely question-begging justification can be given for such an exclusive priority. Only by employing the third solution, and sometimes giving priority to self-interested reasons, and sometimes giving priority to altruistic reasons, can we avoid a completely question-begging resolution.

Notice also that this standard of rationality will not support just any compromise between the relevant self-interested and altruistic reasons. The compromise must be a nonarbitrary one, for otherwise it would beg the question with respect to the opposing egoistic and altruistic views. Such a compromise would have to respect the rankings of self-interested and altruistic reasons imposed by the egoistic and altruistic views, respectively. Since for each individual there is a separate ranking of that individual's relevant self-interested and altruistic reasons, we can represent these rankings from the most important reasons to the least important reasons as follows:

Individual A		Individual B	
Self-Interested Reasons	Altruistic Reasons	Self-Interested Reasons	Altruistic Reasons
1	1	1	1
2	2	2	2
3	3	3	3
.	.	.	.
.	.	.	.
.	.	.	.
N	N	N	N

Accordingly, any nonarbitrary compromise among such reasons in seeking not to beg the question against egoism or altruism will have to give priority to those reasons that rank highest in each category. Failure to give priority to the highest-ranking altruistic or self-interested reasons would, other things being equal, be contrary to reason.

Of course, there will be cases in which the only way to avoid being required to do what is contrary to your highest-ranking reasons is by requiring someone else to do what is contrary to her highest-ranking reasons. Some of these cases will be "lifeboat cases." But although such cases are surely difficult to resolve (maybe only a chance mechanism can offer a reasonable resolution), they surely do not reflect the typical conflict between the relevant self-interested and altruistic reasons that we are or were able to acquire. Typically one or the other of the conflicting reasons will rank significantly higher on its respective scale, thus permitting a clear resolution.

Now it is important to see how morality can be viewed as just such a nonarbitrary compromise between self-interested and altruistic reasons. First, a certain amount of self-regard is morally required or at least morally acceptable. Where this is the case, high-ranking self-interested reasons have priority over low-ranking altruistic reasons. Second, morality obviously places limits on the extent to which people should pursue their own self-interest. Where this is the case, high-ranking altruistic reasons have priority over low-ranking self-interested reasons. In this way, morality can be seen to be a nonarbitrary compromise between self-interested and altruistic reasons, and the "moral reasons" that constitute that compromise can be seen as having an absolute priority over the self-interested or altruistic reasons that conflict with them.[13]

Unfortunately, this approach to defending morality has been generally neglected by previous moral theorists. The reason for this is that such theorists have tended to cast the basic conflict with rational egoism as a conflict between morality and self-interest. For example, according to Kurt Baier,

> The very *raison d'etre* of a morality is to yield reasons, which overrule the reasons of self-interest in those cases when everyone's following self-interest would be harmful to everyone.[14]

Viewed in this light, it did not seem possible for the defender of morality to be supporting a compromise view, for how could such a defender say that when morality and self-interest conflict, morality should sometimes be sacrificed for the sake of self-interest? But while previous theorists understood correctly that moral reasons could not be compromised in favor of self-interested reasons, they failed to recognize that this is because moral reasons are already the result of a nonarbitrary compromise between self-interested and altruistic reasons. Thus, unable to see how morality could be represented as a compromise solution, previous theorists have generally failed to recognize this approach to defending morality.

Stage Two: An Accessible, Secular Morality

Now that we have a response to those who would reject morality, and ultimately women's rights, in favor of individual or group interests, we need to more closely examine the question of what sort of morality is required. It is important to see that the morality we are looking for should be able to provide sufficient reasons accessible to all those to whom it applies for abiding by its basic requirements. So it must be a morality that is capable of justifying the use of power to enforce its basic requirements. To do that it must be possible for us to justifiably morally blame those who are coerced for failing to abide by morality's basic requirements. If that were not the case, people could justifiably resist such uses of power because such uses would lack moral legitimacy.[15] People cannot be morally required to do something if they cannot come to know, and so come to justifiably believe, that they are so required. So if a morality is to be able to justify the use of power to enforce its basic requirements, there must be sufficient reasons accessible to all those to whom it applies for abiding by those requirements. What this means is that the morality we are seeking must be secular rather than religious in character because only secular reasons are accessible to everyone; religious reasons are primarily accessible only to the members of particular religious groups who hold them, and as such they cannot provide the justification that is needed to support the use of power to enforce the basic requirements of morality.

Now it might be objected that at least some religious reasons are accessible to virtually everyone who has been exposed to them. Of course, many people have not been exposed even to the teachings of the four dominant religions today, Christianity, Islam, Buddhism and Hinduism, and even for those who have, mere exposure, by itself, is not enough to guarantee the kind of accessibility that would justify the use of power against those who fail to abide by those teachings. For that to be the case, exposure must necessarily lead to the idea that it would be unreasonable to reject these teachings as such. In the case of Christian moral teachings this would mean that it would be unreasonable to reject these teachings as part of a unique Christian salvation history, which has as key events an Incarnation, a Redemptive Death, and a Resurrection.

Of course, this is not to deny that some religious teachings can be given a justification that is independent of their religious origins (e.g., the story of the Good Samaritan[16]) - a justification that is accessible to virtually everyone exposed to them on the grounds that virtually everyone so exposed would understand that it would be unreasonable to reject those teachings so justified. But the objection we are considering does not address the possibility of justifying religious moral teachings in this way. Rather, it claims that religious moral teachings are justified because *as such* they are accessible to virtually everyone exposed to them with the consequence that it would be unreasonable for virtually anyone so exposed to reject them.

But is this the case? Surely many Christian moral teachings, for example, are understandable to both Christians and non-Christians alike, but the sense of "accessible," we have been using implies more than this. It implies that persons can be morally blamed for failing to abide by accessible requirements because they can come to understand that these requirements apply to them and that it would be unreasonable for them to fail to abide by them. So understood, it would seem that, for example, Christian moral teachings *as such* are not accessible to everyone exposed to them. Too many non-Christians, who seem otherwise moral, do not recognize the authority of Christian moral teachings as such, even though they may grant that some of these teachings have an independent justification.

Accordingly, we are looking for a morality that is secular in character and thus one that can provide sufficient reasons accessible to all those to whom it applies for abiding by its basic requirements. It must be a morality that is capable of justifying the use of power to enforce its basic requirements.

Stage Three: From Minimal Morality to a Robust Conception of Women's Rights

Of course, exactly how morality as compromise, understood now as an accessible, secular morality, is to be worked out is a matter of considerable debate. Libertarians with their ideal of liberty, think that such a morality imposes only minimal requirements on us. Aristotelians, like Nussbaum and Sen, and Liberal Feminists, like Okin, think that it is much more demanding. To resolve this dispute in favor of the views of Nussbaum, Sen, and Okin, I propose to show that the libertarian ideal of liberty is much more demanding than libertarians allow and, that it, in fact, supports a robust conception of women's rights.

To see that this is the case, let us interpret the ideal of liberty as a negative ideal in the manner favored by libertarians.[17] So understood, liberty is the absence of interference by other people from doing what one wants or is able to do.

Interpreting their ideal in this way, libertarians claim to derive a number of more specific requirements, in particular, a right to life, a right to freedom of speech, press, and assembly, and a right to property. Here it is important to observe that the libertarian's right to life is not a right to receive from others the goods and resources necessary for preserving one's life; it is simply a right not to be killed unjustly. Correspondingly, the libertarian's right to property is not a right to receive from others the goods and resources necessary for one's welfare, but rather a right to acquire goods and resources either by initial acquisition or by voluntary agreement.

Of course, libertarians would allow that it would be nice of the rich to share their surplus resources with the poor. Nevertheless, according to libertarians, such acts of charity should not be coercively required. For this reason, libertarians are opposed to coercively supported welfare programs.

Now in order to see why libertarians are mistaken about what their ideal requires, consider a typical conflict situation between the rich and the poor, keep in mind that most of the poor happen to be women and children.

In this conflict situation, the rich, of course, have more than enough resources to satisfy their basic needs. By contrast, the poor lack the resources to meet their most basic needs even though they have tried all the means available to them that libertarians regard as legitimate for acquiring such resources. Under circumstances like these, libertarians usually maintain that the rich should have the liberty to use their resources to satisfy their luxury needs if they so wish. Libertarians recognize that this liberty might well be enjoyed at the expense of the satisfaction of the most basic needs of the poor; they just think that liberty always has priority over other political ideals, and since they assume that the liberty of the poor is not at stake in such conflict situations, it is easy for them to conclude that the rich should not be required to sacrifice their liberty so that the basic needs of the poor may be met.

Of course, libertarians would allow that it would be nice of the rich to share their surplus resources with the poor. Nevertheless, according to libertarians, such acts of charity are not required because the liberty of the poor is not thought to be at stake in such conflict situations.

In fact, however, the liberty of the poor is at stake in such conflict situations. What is at stake is the liberty of the poor not to be interfered with in taking from the surplus possessions of the rich what is necessary to satisfy their basic needs. When libertarians are brought to see that this is the case, they are genuinely surprised, one might even say rudely awakened, for they had not previously seen the conflict between the rich and the poor as a conflict of liberties.[18]

Now when the conflict between the rich and the poor is viewed as a conflict of liberties, we can either say that the rich should have the liberty to use their surplus resources for luxury purposes, or we can say that the poor should have the liberty not to be interfered with in taking from the rich what they require to meet their basic needs. If we choose one liberty, we must reject the other. What needs to be determined, therefore, is which liberty is morally preferable: the liberty of the rich or the liberty of the poor.

I submit that the liberty of the poor, which is the liberty not to be interfered with in taking the surplus resources of the rich what is required to meet one's basic needs, is morally preferable to the liberty of the rich, which is the liberty to use one's surplus resources for luxury purposes. To see that this is the case, we need only appeal to one of the most fundamental principles of morality, one that is common to all political perspectives, namely, the "ought" implies "can" principle. According to this principle, people are not morally required to do what they lack the power to do or what would involve so great a sacrifice that it would be unreasonable to ask, and/or in cases of severe conflict of interest, unreasonable to require them to abide by.

For example, suppose I promised to attend a departmental meeting on Friday, but on Thursday I am involved in a serious car accident, which puts me into a coma. Surely it is no longer the case that I ought to attend the meeting now that I lack the power to do so. Or suppose instead that on Thursday I develop a severe case of pneumonia for which I am hospitalized. Surely I could legitimately claim that I cannot attend the meeting on the grounds that the risk to my health involved in attending is a sacrifice that it would be unreasonable to ask me to bear. Or suppose the risk to my health from having pneumonia is not so serious that it would be unreasonable to ask me to attend the meeting (a supererogatory request), it might still be serious enough to be unreasonable to require my attendance at the meeting (a demand that is backed up by blame or coercion).

What is distinctive about this formulation of the "ought" implies "can" principle is that it claims that the requirements of morality cannot, all things considered, be unreasonable to ask, and/or in cases of severe conflict of interest, unreasonable to require people to abide by. The principle claims that reason and morality must be linked in an appropriate way, especially if we are going to be able to justifiably use blame or coercion to get people to abide by the requirements of morality. It should be noted, however, that although major figures in the history of philosophy, and most philosophers today, including virtually all libertarian philosophers, accept this linkage between reason and morality, this linkage is not usually conceived to be part of the "ought" implies "can" principle. Nevertheless, I claim that there are good reasons for associating this linkage between reason and morality with the "ought" implies "can" principle, namely, our use of the word "can" as in the example just given, and the natural progression from logical, physical, and psychological possibility found in the traditional "ought" implies "can" principle to the notion of moral possibility found in this formulation of the "ought" implies "can" principle. In any case, the acceptability of this formulation of the "ought" implies "can" principle is determined by the virtually universal acceptance of its components and not by the manner in which I have proposed to join those components together.[19]

Now applying the "ought" implies "can" principle to the case at hand, it seems clear that the poor have it within their power willingly to relinquish such an important liberty as the liberty not to be interfered with in taking from the rich what they require to meet their basic needs. Nevertheless, it would be unreasonable to ask or require them to make so great a sacrifice. In the extreme case, it would involve asking or requiring the poor to sit back and starve to death. Of course, the poor may have no real alternative to relinquishing this liberty. To do anything else may involve worse consequences for themselves and their loved ones and may invite a painful death. Accordingly, we may expect that the poor would acquiesce, albeit unwillingly, to a political system that denied them the right to welfare supported by such a liberty, at the same time that we recognize that such a system imposed an unreasonable sacrifice upon the poor - a sacrifice that we could not morally blame the poor for trying to evade.[20] Analogously, we might expect that a woman whose life was threatened would submit to a rapist's demands, at the same time that we recognize the utter unreasonableness of those demands.

By contrast, it would not be unreasonable to ask and require the rich to sacrifice the liberty to meet some of their luxury needs so that the poor can have the liberty to meet their basic needs.[21] Naturally, we might expect that the rich, for reasons of self-interest and past contribution, might be disinclined to make such a sacrifice. We might even suppose that the past contribution of the rich provides a good reason for not sacrificing their liberty to use their surplus for luxury purposes. Yet, unlike the poor, the rich could not claim that relinquishing such a liberty involved so great a sacrifice that it would be unreasonable to ask and require them to make it; unlike the poor, the rich could be morally blameworthy for failing to make such a sacrifice.

Consequently, if we assume that however else we specify the requirements of morality, they cannot violate the "ought" implies "can" principle, it follows that, despite what libertarians claim, the right to liberty endorsed by them actually favors the liberty of the poor over the liberty of the rich.

Yet couldn't libertarians object to this conclusion, claiming that it would be unreasonable to ask the rich to sacrifice the liberty to meet some of their luxury needs so that the poor could have the liberty to meet their basic needs? As I have pointed out, libertarians don't usually see the situation as a conflict of liberties, but suppose they did. How plausible would such an objection be? Not very plausible at all, I think.

For consider: What are libertarians going to say about the poor, most of whom happen to be women and children? Isn't it clearly unreasonable to require the poor to sacrifice the liberty to meet their basic needs so that the rich can have the liberty to meet their luxury needs? Isn't it clearly unreasonable to require the poor to sit back and starve to death? If it is, then, there is no resolution of this conflict that would be reasonable to require both the rich and the poor to accept. But that would mean that libertarians could not be putting forth a moral ideal because a moral ideal resolves severe conflicts of interest in ways that it would be reasonable to ask and require everyone affected to accept. Therefore, as long as libertarians think of themselves as putting forth a moral ideal, they cannot allow that it would be unreasonable in cases of severe conflict of interest *both* to require the rich to sacrifice the liberty to meet some of their luxury needs in order to benefit the poor and to require the poor to sacrifice the liberty to meet their basic needs in order to benefit the rich. But I submit that if one of these requirements is to be judged reasonable, then, by any neutral assessment, it must be the requirement that the rich sacrifice the liberty to meet some of their luxury needs so that the poor can have the liberty to meet their basic needs; there is no other plausible resolution, if libertarians intend to be putting forth a moral ideal.

In brief, I have argued that a libertarian ideal of liberty can be seen to support a right to welfare through an application of the "ought" implies "can" principle to conflicts between the rich and the poor, most of whom happen to be women and children. In the interpretation I have used, the principle supports such rights by favoring the liberty of the poor over the liberty of the rich. In another interpretation (developed elsewhere), the principle supports such rights by favoring a conditional right to property over an unconditional right to property.[22] In either interpretation, what is crucial to the derivation of these rights is the claim that it would be unreasonable to require the poor to deny their basic needs and accept anything less than these rights as the condition for their willing cooperation.

Practical Applications

The right to welfare supported by a libertarian minimal morality can, in turn, be used to support a robust conception of women's rights. It requires that women receive the same basic resources and opportunities as men. Accordingly, it requires action on a whole range of issues, such as genital mutilation, trafficking in women, polygamy, dowry death, forced marriages, domestic violence, marital rape, rape in police custody, lack of reproductive freedom, unequal nutrition and health care, lack of a right to assemble and to walk in public, lack of equality before the law, lack of equal access to education, and sex-selective infanticide and feticide. While it is undeniable that these are areas where women are denied the same basic opportunities and resources that men have, and so denied the same basic rights that men have, today there is still only a dawning recognition that these are clearly issues of women's rights.

Consider the attitude of the chief of pediatrics at a large hospital in Seattle who when interviewed about the U.S. Congress's criminalization of female genital mutilation said: "I think this is an issue that should be decided by a physician, the family and the child. Privacy should prevail and the brouhaha is inappropriate."[23] But would the same be said if we were dealing with a sexual custom in which a man in order to become marriageable and thereby able to survive economically was allowed to ejaculate some sperm to be saved so that he could still reproduce, and then was held down by four or five people in order for his penis to be cut off? This is the closest male equivalent to female genital mutilation in its least invasive, commonly practiced form. The male equivalent of the more invasive infibulation would be the removal of all of the penis, its roots of soft tissue, and part of the scrotal skin.[24]

Or consider the response that a delegation of Amnesty International received from a military commander in Peru when he was asked whether soldiers were known to commit rape. "Yes, of course," he replied, explaining that when you have men away from their homes for a long time under difficult circumstances, they must have their needs met somehow. The commander did not see any reason to deny that his soldiers raped. Only when the question of torture was raised, did he issue a denial. Torture was different.[25]

Likewise, the rape of women in the former Yugoslavia was hardly mentioned in early reports of the UN's Special Rapporteur until women's NGOs demanded that it be taken seriously. Only under the weight of these events, did the resistance to recognizing rape as a war crime begin to dissipate.[26] And now we have the situation in Kosovo where women who have been raped by Serbs are afraid to even admit it fearing rejection by their own people. As one Kosovo man put it if his wife admitted that she was raped by Serbs, "I would ask for a divorce - even if I had 20 children."[27]

Finally, consider the attitude toward polygamy that a French immigrant from Mali expressed in a recent interview. He said: "When my wife is sick and I don't have another, who will care for me?...[O]ne wife on her own is trouble. When there are several, they are forced to be polite and well behaved. If they misbehave, you threaten that you will take another wife."[28] In monogamous cultures, maybe the counterpart to this behavior is a husband's implicitly or explicitly threatening with divorce a wife who is economically dependent on him.

In each of these three cases we have a clear failure to recognize that women have the same rights as men. The failure is at the practical level. The only good arguments we have here support equal rights for women.

The argument that I have sketched in this paper defends women's rights by first, showing that rationality requires morality, an argument that all defenders of women's rights should welcome, second, showing that only an accessible, secular morality can justify the use of coercion against dissenters, an argument that should be particularly helpful to the international law defenders of women's rights, and third, showing that even the most minimal conception of morality supports a robust conception of women's rights, an argument that should help Nussbaurm, Sen and Okin respond to libertarian objections to their more demanding conceptions of women's rights.

Of course, it will not be easy to overcome the bias and prejudice, which accounts for the failure to recognize women's rights. However, those who claim to endorse women's rights should at least do what they can not to aid those who violate those rights, or at least make their aid contingent upon a continually improving record with respect to women's rights. Accordingly, we could make our economic aid abroad, or even doing business abroad, contingent on an improving record with respect to women's rights, and we could do the same at home, for example, by denying tax-exempt status to both secular and religious organizations that discriminate against women, something we have yet to do in my own country, or even at my own religiously affiliated university. Obviously, there is much more that we could do to promote women's rights both at home and abroad, and we have the best of reasons to do it.

Notes

1 See Julie Peters and Andrea Wolper, eds. *Women's Rights Human Rights: International Feminist Perspectives* (New York: Routledge, 1995).

2 Elissavet Stamatopoulou, "Women's Rights and the United Nations," in Peters and Wolper, p.38.

3 See, for example, Martha Nussbaum, *Sex and Social Justice*, (New York: Oxford University Press, 1999) Chapter 1 and Amartya Sen, "Gender Inequality and Theories of Justice," in *Women, Culture and Development*, ed. Martha Nussbaum and Jonathan Glover (New York: Oxford University Press, 1995), pp.259-273.

4 See Nussbaum, pp.42-7.

5 Susan Okin, "Feminism, Women's Human Rights, and Cultural Differences," *Hypatia* (1998) pp.32-52.

6 Jane Flax,"On Encountering Incommensurability," *Controversies in Feminism* ed. James P. Sterba (Lanham: Rowman and Littlefield, 2000), and "Race/Gender and the Ethics of Difference," in *Ethics: The Big Questions*, ed. James P. Sterba (Oxford: Blackwell, 1998) pp.435-441.

7 I understand the pure altruist to be the mirror image of the pure egoist. Whereas the pure egoist thinks that the interests of others count for them but not for herself

except instrumentally, the pure altruist thinks that her own interests count for others but not for herself except instrumentally.

8 Nell Nodding, *Caring: A Feminine Approach to Ethics and Moral Education* (Berkeley: University of California Press, 1984); Joyce Trebilcot, ed. *Mothering* (Totowa: Rowman and Littlefield, 1983); Susan Brownmiller, *Femininity* (New York: Ballantine Books, 1984).

9 James Doyle, *The Male Experience* (Dubuque: W.C. Brown and Co., 1983); Marie Richmond-Abbot, ed. *Masculine and Feminine* Second Edition (New York: Random House, 1991).

10 Victor Seidler, *Rediscovering Masculinity* (New York: Routledge, 1989); Larry May and Robert Strikwerda, *Rethinking Masculinity* (Lanham: Rowman and Littlefield, 1992).

11 This is not to deny that we usually have greater knowledge and certainty about what is in our own self-interest than about what is in the interest of others, and that this difference in our knowledge and certainty can have a practical effect on what good we should do in particular contexts. It is just that the debate between egoism and morality gets started at the theoretical level where no assumption is made about this difference in our knowledge and certainty, since we can, and frequently do, have adequate knowledge and certainty about both what is in our own self-interest and what is in the interest of others.

12 This is because, as I shall argue, morality itself already represents a compromise between egoism and altruism. So to ask that moral reasons be weighed against self-interested reasons is, in effect, to count self-interested reasons twice - once in the compromise between egoism and altruism and then again when moral reasons are weighed against self-interested reasons. But to count self-interested reasons twice is clearly objectionable.

13 For further discussion, see my *Justice for Here and Now* (New York: Cambridge University Press, 1998), Chapter 2.

14 Kurt Baier, *The Moral Point of View* (New York, 1965) p. 150.

15 The will of the majority if it is to be morally legitimate must be backed up with more than power. The minority must have a moral duty to accept the imposition of the majority, but that could only be the case if the minority would be morally blameworthy for failing to accept that imposition. Moreover, I am assuming throughout this discussion that everyone is morally competent, that is, sufficiently capable of understanding and acting upon moral requirements.

16 *Gospel According to St. Luke*, 10:25-37.

17 See John Hospers, *Libertarianism* (Los Angeles: Nash Press, 1971).

18 *Ibid.*, Chapter 7.

19 I am indebted to Alasdair MacIntyre for helping me make this point clearer.

20 See James P. Sterba,"Is There a Rationale for Punishment?" *The American Journal of Jurisprudence* (1984).

21 By the liberty of the rich to meet their luxury needs I continue to mean the liberty of the rich not to be interfered with when using their surplus possessions for luxury purposes. Similarly, by the liberty of the poor to meet their basic needs I continue to mean the liberty of the poor not to be interfered with when taking what they require to meet their basic needs from the surplus possessions of the rich.

22 For this other interpretation, see my *Justice for Here and Now* (New York: Cambridge University Press, 1998), Chapter 2.

23 *New York Times*, October 10, 1996.

24 Okin, pp.38 and 49.

25 Elizabeth Friedman, "Women's Rights: The Emergence of a Movement. " in Peters and Wolper, p.26.

26 Stamatopoulou, p. 42.

27 *New York Times*, June 21, 1999.

28 Susan Okin,"Is Multiculturalism Bad for Women?" *Boston Review*, October 1997, p.26.

Part IV
State Sovereignty and Human Rights

16. Challenges to the Concepts of 'Sovereignty' and 'Intervention'

CHARLES SAMPFORD*

Introduction

The concepts of sovereignty and intervention are closely intertwined. It is the jurisdictional walls erected along the boundaries of nation states that create the barriers to 'international intervention'.[1] If less significance were invested in those boundaries, the legal and political concepts of 'international intervention' would lose their significance and different concepts and principles would be appropriate.

Sovereignty is under challenge on two fronts. The first is the way that the forces of globalisation are weakening the integrity and strength of sovereign states. In so doing they are fundamentally changing the institutional context of 'strong states' based on independent political communities, which has provided the assumptions on which constitutional and international law have been based. The second lies in a fundamental shift in the basis of political legitimacy - from efficacy (or as I prefer to call it: 'the prior successful use of force') to the active consent of the governed.

These challenges will have profound consequences for the way we think about states, citizens and the interactions between them. Those consequences will include arguments about sovereignty and intervention, the primary subject of this paper. But they will extend far beyond that to the entire ideological context in which such debates are conducted. The forces of globalisation provide a fundamental challenge to liberal democratic values[2] - including liberty, rights, democracy, equality, citizenship, community, welfare and the rule of law. Those values were conceived in and for the strong sovereign states that emerged after the Treaty of Westphalia by the 'North Atlantic Enlightenment'[3] and were the means by which those highly authoritarian states were civilized.[4] However, the values were largely conceived for individual states and the institutions designed to realise those values have been almost exclusively state-based. Thus the declining relevance of states and the declining capacity of their institutions has put many liberal democratic values under a cloud. I argue that this is not a reason for abandoning those values, but it is a reason for reconceiving those values for a world without strong states, and for re-institutionalising them in a new set of institutions that are not so dependent on the state. This process of reconceiving liberal democratic values and re-institutionalising them in and for a more global world calls for nothing less than a new enlightenment. Such a global enlightenment should aim to civilise the increasingly brutal world of global economics, just as the eighteenth century enlightenment began the process of civilising the absolutist post-Westphalian states.

Within this context, I will argue that the decline of the state and the shifting basis of political legitimacy justify humanitarian 'intervention', particularly to prevent the oppression of those whose consent has not been sought by those in power. Indeed, as the walls around sovereign states break down, the term 'intervention' seems less and less appropriate and loses most of its normative stigma.

However, the questions of who can intervene and on what basis remain as strong as ever. I will argue that the same arguments that justify intervention forbid intervention by sovereign states, which are not acting at the instigation and behest of bodies genuinely authorised to do so under international law. I will further argue that those who seek to intervene in the name of international law must subject themselves to that law. This is a fundamental Enlightenment principle long recognized domestically and which must now be enforced internationally by the international community, through the ICJ and ICC and through the ethical rules of the professionals involved. I will argue that this is not only legally and ethically imperative but also in the interests of major would be intervenors.

These issues are amply illustrated by the Kosovo crisis and its aftermath, events that have helped to focus my thinking (and which have led to an almost daily rewriting of this paper). The paper is, in a sense, a virtual paper in which much of the most recent material was gleaned from internet sources.

Before I conclude my introduction, I must issue a necessary disclaimer. I write this paper as a jurisprude and a constitutional lawyer. I do not claim professional expertise in international law, though I hope that the other disciplines I bring to bear support the conclusions I draw as to the directions of all three.

The Institutional and Ideological Context of 'Strong States'

Western legal, constitutional and political theory has been built on the assumption that most polities will be 'strong states' - states that largely passed the Austinian test of sovereignty according to which most legal and political issues arise, and can be resolved, within the state. Such states emerged in Western Europe after the Treaty of Westphalia[5] when the horrors of the Thirty Years War convinced many that the greater danger in international affairs was intervention[6] in other states. They were initially highly authoritarian and justified as such because of the fear of internal chaos.[7] Such states were civilised by the North Altantic Enlightenment in the 18th century and by social democrats in the 19th century. Enlightenment Liberals insisted that such states should justify themselves to their citizens by furthering citizens' rights and by becoming accountable to the citizenry. Initially the mechanism for accountability was the right to revolution proposed by Locke and applied on this side of the Atlantic. Accountability mechanisms were refined through democratic legislatures and administrative law.[8] Social democrats sought to extend the range of rights the growing state secured for its citizens.[9] Those who did not adhere to Marxist millenarianism provided an essentially Whig theory of history, of constant improvement towards a common endpoint in which the rights secured by liberal democratic societies were expanded and the number of such societies increased.[10]

What all theories assumed was the existence of a strong state. The debates were about what values should be applied to its governance - liberty, equality, rights, citizenship, democracy, community, welfare and the rule of law.

The Challenge of Globalisation to the Values of Liberal Democracy

A range of recent trends, which are popularly labelled 'globalisation', have rocked the assumption that a world of strong sovereign states was the natural condition of humankind to which we were all evolving. The 350 years since the treaty of Westphalia can be seen in a fundamentally different light. Rather than a process in which distinct geographic areas were politically crystallised as states, this period could now be interpreted as a relatively brief interlude in the development of political communities and political institutions. Sovereign states are not the end point of constitutional development but a mere transitory phase.[11]

The forces collectively referred to as 'globalisation'[12] have undermined the assumption of the strong state as the context for political debate about the balancing and realising of liberal democratic values. Both detractors and supporters of globalisation have queried the continuing relevance of state-based theory and values. These values were formed in and for strong states. Citizenship, democracy, welfare, and community have clear reference to sovereign states but lack apparent application in a larger, more diffuse global world. The institutions, which promote, sustain and realise those values are very much state based. The rights, duties and sense of belonging that go with citizenship are attached to state institutions.

Democracy is realised through citizen participation in the legislatures of states and their federal elements - and has less mileage if the real power and range of choice open to those legislatures is limited.[13] Welfare and welfare rights such as education and health care are only realised through the institutions of strong, sovereign (and wealthy) states - and even the capacity of these institutions to do so is being increasingly questioned.

Some might think that the decline of state institutions is a convenient excuse for limiting or playing down liberal democratic values. Others argue for the protection and bolstering of strong sovereign states on the basis that only they can deliver rights that cost money to provide.

The Key Centre for Law, Ethics, Justice and Governance, of which I am proud to be Director, is founded on the contrary view, that the values of liberal democracy should be rethought rather than abandoned on the excuse of globalisation, or defended by an attempt to recreate the strong states of the recent past.

It is easy to appreciate the way that globalisation undermines some of the institutions that promote and sustain liberal democratic values in particular countries - for example, by narrowing the choices democratic legislatures can make and by restricting their perceived capacity to provide welfare in a more competitive world. We would argue for the protection and preservation of those institutions wherever possible pending the emergence of new institutions.

More importantly, however, the Centre argues that globalisation clears the way for the wider application of the values of equality, democracy, welfare and community. Most Enlightenment values were claims for all human beings.[14] The Declaration by the French Assembly was of the rights of man. The Declaration of Independence held 'these truths to be self-evident, that all men are created equal...' But despite the universality of the claims, the institutions they created were exclusively devoted to providing rights to their own citizens. A more globalised political philosophy may allow more global aspirations that allow these constitutional values to have global application. The concepts of sovereignty and non-intervention provided the context for the development of liberal democratic values. They also provided protection for those fledgling values from outside influence. However, the sovereign walls that protected those values from interference also acted as a barrier to those values spreading to other jurisdictions.

We at the Key Centre intend to contribute to discussions on these issues through a four-stage process:

1. An examination of the challenges that globalisation poses to the values of liberal democracy.
2. A consideration of how those values might be redefined for a world largely without strong states.
3. A consideration of the institutions (local, national and global) that could realise those values.
4. An examination of the means by which those values could be built into those institutions through basic design, management, ethics regimes and integrity systems.[15]

This process will commence with a conference supported by the Australian-American Education Foundation L at the end of September this year,[16] and continue through a series of workshops, edited collections, monographs and policy papers over the next six years.

This is not the time to describe in detail the conceptual and practical work to be done. However, a number of points should be made.

Not World Government

Reconceived liberal democratic values, to be effective, require institutions to support them. These institutions will not be expected to form part of a world government. To think that the solution to the challenges posed by globalisation to existing strong states is to create a new, larger, universal 'strong state' misses the point. Such a view remains stuck in the assumptions held during the period of strong states. What is likely to emerge is a world where institutions cross previous international boundaries and do not claim, unlike sovereign states, to cover all areas of life.

The strong sovereign state was a post-Westphalian solution to the problems that preceded it. The solution to the problems of post-Wesphalian strong states is unlikely to be the creation of a new ever more encompassing version of the same kind of state.[17] That would be to see the problems of post-Westphalian states as soluble by more and larger of the same.

Not Just the Universal Adoption of 'Western' (or American) Values

The end of the Cold War led to some unedifying bouts of normative triumphalism. It was seen as avindication of what were claimed to be western values and the future was assumed to involve the adoption of these values by all countries. I say 'what were claimed to be western values' because the triumphalists tended to be those who pushed the more libertarian versions of capitalism rather than the American liberal and European social democratic elements which had done so much to civilise capitalism and enable it to survive. Triumphalists ignored the longstanding and unanswered criticisms of libertarian values, to which communism had been a totally failed response, and to which liberalism and social democracy had made more successful, though still tentative, contributions.

I am a universalist in the sense that the process envisaged through the work of the Key Centre involves the pursuit of values that can provide answers to the universal problems of human society as it takes on a more global form. I do not believe that the answers will be culturally specific. Nor do I believe that the sources of those answers will come from any single culture. I am absolutely certain that no culture currently provides all the answers. The values of the Enlightenment as challenged, modified and developed by 250 years of legal, political and social philosophy provide an excellent starting point - not least because of the fundamental Enlightenment shift in the relationship between the state and citizen. Rather than concentrating on the obligations of subject to sovereign, it emphasised that public institutions have to be justified on the basis of how they serve the citizens. The North Atlantic Enlightenment did not hold a monopoly on truth but was an important step forward in the universal struggle to improve the human condition.

What is needed now is an international search for new and revised values to which all may contribute and in which all may learn from the ideas, and failures of all. As in so many other areas, the claim to universality must be accompanied by a surrender to it.

The global search for answers will draw on the attempts of different cultures to seek answers to problems of the human condition. Within each culture, the process will begin with their own values, concepts and stories, making it easier to progress. Different cultures have much to learn from each other. For example, Anglo-American ideology tends to concentrate on individuals but is weak on understanding institutions. There are attempts to reduce institutions to matrices of interpersonal contracts rather than seeing institutions as organic wholes. This preference for individuals and lack of understanding of institutions leads to hostility towards them - particularly 'public' ones. European and Japanese cultures seem (to borrow Komesar's phrase) to "take institutions [more] seriously"[18] and to possess a stronger understanding of their nature. For me, the fundamental point of the Enlightenment was that institutions should serve individuals, rather than the other way around. This does not mean that institutions should be abandoned, but that the manner of their justification should be reconceived -as means of protecting, realising and furthering individual human rights.

A Long Intellectual History

The values of liberal democracy were formed in and for strong states. Although these values were based on long-standing ideals found in most, and probably all, cultures, that context affected the ways in which those ideals were expressed, combined and reconceived as liberal democratic values (for example, the citizen-democracy of Athens gave way to the representative democracy in modern states. Constitutional values for a more global world may be variations on the values of citizenship, democracy and welfare. However, they may also be recombined in new values within new concepts that speak more effectively to the problems of globalisation.[19]

Sometimes the values will not be recombined but reinvented in a different form that may expose more general classes of value of which liberal democratic values were merely the contemporary form. I will take one example - citizenship.

Post-Westphalian authoritarian states saw individuals as 'subjects'. The Enlightenment saw them as 'citizens'. What was new was the idea that institutions such as the state existed to serve individuals rather than the individual in service of the state. The concept of citizenship built upon earlier pre-Enlightenment values of family, tribe and ethnic group. At each stage of human development, membership in the most socially and economically powerful groups has been seen as of enormous value. Exclusion from that group has been a very great punishment (e.g. being disowned by family, being expelled from the tribe or being outlawed from the village). The Enlightenment vaunted membership in the state, then the most significant and powerful social group. However, as the sovereign state wanes in social significance, other memberships become more crucial - including those of work. The new value may be the right to participate in the benefits of social life in the most socially significant groupings.

The Ever Present Danger of Regression

The hope behind our project is that the challenges of globalisation will be met with new values that inform new institutions that can civilise a world of weaker states (as the North Atlantic Enlightenment contributed to civilising the absolutist sovereign states of Western Europe). However, this is by no means guaranteed. If the forces of globalisation lead to destabilisation[20] such benign results are unlikely. There are dangers, that in response to the breakdown of Enlightenment ideals, we may return to pre-Enlightenment ones such as tribal exclusivity, ethnic supremacy and religious fanaticism.

When society breaks down, people will not join the IVR and engage in sincere and open debate about the new ideas that may guide and inspire a new global society. They will run with some existing idea that seems to make some sense. It might be some extremist versions of libertarian capitalism (which a number of eastern European nations were briefly attracted to in the belief that the opposite of what they had was the best[21]). It might be a half-baked TV-version of American capitalism gleaned from soaps broadcast by the former regime in the belief that the transmission of patent nonsense cannot affect people's intellect. [22] It is more likely to be the revisitation of another, older and more deeply felt ideal from the past, given ever more destructive power by the forces of modern technology. In the Balkans and some African countries, it has been ethnic supremacy or tribal domination - values uniquely damaging to multi-ethnic communities. In Afghanistan, Sudan, Timor and, to a lesser extent in the Balkans, it has been religious fanaticism and intolerance. In some cases the breakdown of sovereign states has led to a reversion to the worst features of tribalism and inter-tribal violence writ large by modern technology.[23]

This problem is not confined to newly disintegrating states in the developing world. The western response to the end of the Cold War has not been to transcend the competing global ideologies of capitalism and communism. Instead of learning from the miseries generated by these ideologies, there has been a reversion to earlier ideals of global competition - to what Galbraith calls 'primitive capitalism'[24] - rather than the development of new ideas about the way countries may relate to each other such as those expounded in the Brandt report. [25]

If societies in crisis are no place for rational discussion of new ideas and values, the time to have the seminars *is* now.

A Fundamental Shift in the Basis of Constitutional Legitimacy

The constitutional value that is most under threat is, of course, sovereignty itself. Sovereignty is being weakened as the forces of globalisation ensure that forces outside the walls of the state fundamentally affect, and sometimes determine, what goes on within them. Sovereignty and the consequential ban on intervention are also being undermined normatively. As an essentially Westphalian construct, modern ideas of sovereignty predate the Enlightenment by one hundred years. The greatest threat to sovereignty and the associated stigma attached to intervention lie in the full implementation of Enlightenment values.[26]

In domestic law and political theory, there has been a fundamental shift in the basis of political legitimacy - from what I call 'the prior successful use of force' to 'the consent of the governed' (a shift that was, of course, fundamental to the North Atlantic Enlightenment). That shift occurred first in the USA and France and has come to be almost universally acknowledged as a matter of domestic constitutional law and theory.[27] International law, however, has continued to recognize states and governments on the basis of who exercises effective political control over discrete territories. Even when a democratically elected government is overturned by a coup d'etat, the ambassadors of the new regime are accredited by foreign powers and are allowed to take that country's seat at the United Nations and other international forums. This glaring inconsistency has been a constant feature of democratic nations and has caused considerable tension and great soul-searching.

This inconsistency reflects the fact that the Enlightenment was essentially about the internal workings of states, not their external relations. *It was addressed to the domestic aspects of sovereignty, not its international dimensions.* International law is still based on an idea of sovereignty arising out of the century preceding the North Atlantic Enlightenment. In a fundamental sense, Enlightenment values were not directed towards international law and the external elements of sovereignty and there have only been half-hearted attempts to do so since. When Enlightenment values were imposed, this was done either:

a) in defiance of international law or through a refusal to apply it to the supposedly uncivilised world (e.g. the abolition of the slave trade) or
b) as part of a peace imposed on defeated nations (e.g. the provision of self-determination to the peoples of the Austrian and Turkish Empires after the First World War and the imposition of liberal democracy on the German people after the Second World War).

There were many reasons for this limited role of Enlightenment values in international law. Initially, democratic nations sought the *protection* of sovereignty against the reaction of autocratic states to their new democracies. The French revolution and the revolutions of 1848 were defeated by autocrats allied to the regimes, which the new democracies had ousted.[28] It is only recently that the majority of nation states came to enjoy any real measure of democracy. With the notable exception of American interventions in the Americas, virtually all interventions during this century have been by autocratic states.

The glaring inconsistency between the bases of constitutional legitimacy in domestic and international law has been sustained by a number of factors:

1 The understanding/idea that international law is a law for all states, of which not all are democracies.
2 Cultural relativist notions that different cultures involve different approaches to governance.[29]
3 The understanding that it is necessary to 'do business' in both commercial and political terms with a particular territory and that the only way to do this is through the group who exercises effective power in that territory.
4 The idea that there is no alternative to political authority based on the prior successful use of force in a state where there has never been a democratic government who can speak for the people. Even where a democratic government is ousted, it may not be able to retain the integrity of its representative principles for long.
5 The sorry history of interventions. Nations will rarely intervene solely for the benefit of the citizens of another nation state. They will only do so if it is in their interests. The danger is that nations will intervene to further their interests on the pretext of helping the citizens of the target state, but their 'assistance' will actually work to the detriment of those citizens.[30] Intervening nations generally intervene in the name of international law but are rarely willing to subject themselves to it.

The limited but growing recognition of the possibility of intervention on humanitarian grounds[31] is the first crack in the arguments used to support the principle of non-intervention. In addition, as more and more nations formally embrace democratic ideals, the first two factors listed above are losing much of their force. As most countries want to trade with the outside world, the third factor is very much a two-way street so that states which are the targets of intervention may be as keen for trade as the potential intervenors. The problems referred to in the fourth factor are not as insurmountable as they might once have seemed (as evidenced by, for example, the fact that the ANC was seen in many international forums to speak for the black majority of South Africa). The last three factors concern the way in which intervention occurs. An effective overall response to these issues depends on the development of constitutional theory and the development of new institutions, the reform of old institutions and/or the increased utilisation of existing institutions.

My rash prediction is that, within 10-20 years, the prior successful use of force will be as contemptible a claim to recognition in international law as it is within the domestic constitutional law of existing democracies. Within 20 years, it will be impracticable for authoritarian regimes to overthrow democratic regimes because of the consequent denial of recognition and, to a lesser extent, because the intervention of others will be unequivocally sanctioned. During that period, the justification for what we would now call 'intervention' will have been properly worked out as part of the emerging international constitutional jurisprudence.

A Paradigm Shift

The shift within domestic constitutional theory to the consent of the governed reverses the direction of power, authority and accountability. Power is no longer seen as emanating from the sovereign but instead, stems from the people. Domestically, this puts the people at the centre of constitutional jurisprudence. Instead of asking what power the people 'habitually obey', the question becomes 'whom do you represent'. Internationally, this reversal of power does not merely change the direction of authority and accountability, it affects the units that are recognized. Instead of recognizing regimes on the basis of who habitually obeys them, regimes will be recognised on the basis of those to whom they are accountable.

The full acceptance of this principle means that a government only represents internationally those whose consent it has sought and gained. This would involve little change for democratic regimes. For undemocratic regimes it would mean that the government would be seen as representing only those to whom the regime is accountable, be it a party, an ethnic group or a restricted franchise. This allows non-democratic regimes to be recognised as representing one or more groups within the geographical area of the relevant state with a current capacity to dominate other groups. However, a government that has not sought a mandate from a group of people would not be seen as speaking for those so excluded. This leaves obvious lacunae for those whose consent the government has not sought. It opens the way for others to claim to represent those whose consent has not been sought by the government. In some cases, such credentials would be easily established. Where a democratically elected government is ousted in a military coup, members of that government or their accredited representatives still at large would speak for that government.[32] Recent examples include Timoci Bavadra in Fiji (1987), Aung San Suu Kyi in Burma (1990) and Jean-Bertrand Aristide in Haiti (1991). The lack of recognition of the Cedras coup in Haiti and eventual, restoration of Aristide represented an enormous step forward. The fact that SLORC and Sitiveni Rabuka were recognized by the international community for most purposes is an indication that the shift described here is only just commencing. I would like to think that 1991 represented a sea change and that future coups would be resisted in similar fashion but I am sure that Petersen's analysis based on states' interests provides a better explanation.[33]

Of course, in most cases, it is not nearly so clear who will have the right to speak for those whose consent the government has not sought. It is part of the nature of dictatorships and oligarchies that they will use force to prevent and intimidate the processes by which such credentials could be established. There will usually be a number of voices claiming to speak for the unrepresented in a number of overlapping ways. Sometimes, there will be a body that represents the bulk of the people in one sphere of life that comes to speak more broadly - such as the Catholic Church in communist Poland and COSA TU in South Africa. This means that the excluded will not speak with a strong, clear and unified voice.[34] However, that is no reason for not listening to them and those who are trying to suppress their voices have no standing to suggest that the lack of clarity and unity should be held against the voices that can still be heard despite the efforts of their oppressors.

Consequences of This Paradigm Shift

This paradigm shift will have fundamental consequences for the nature, content and practice of international law. It will lead to a whole new jurisprudence and political philosophy. Taking Enlightenment principles to their logical conclusion and applying them to international law may be an important part of a new 'international enlightenment', which may civilize the new global order in the way that the original Enlightenment civilized the strong sovereign states that emerged after the Treaty of Westphalia. This paper is not concerned to explore all the potential consequences of such a shift. It will concentrate on the implications of this shift for 'intervention'.

However, some other consequences should be noted. At the moment, international legal personality involves the right of those in power to contract on behalf of the state and the people who are within its territory. Even when a contract is beyond the legal power of the rulers, even if it is corruptly entered into and the benefits are corruptly appropriated, the successors to those rulers are bound by its provisions. Sovereign debt is incurred by corrupt regimes and the proceeds are spirited away to bank accounts in the first world. When a democratic regime replaces the former rulers, it is forced to pay back the debt to the original lenders - while the corrupt former leaders enjoy the loan funds from the protection of their first world exile.

The paradigm shift would fundamentally change the dynamics of such arrangements. If the government is not accountable to 'all of its citizens', then the people are not accountable for the actions of the government. When the international debt collectors call, they can legitimately say: 'you did not contract with us, you contracted with them. Look to recover your funds from those to whom you lent them.' They could insist on the principle that governments could not commit those whose consent they had not sought and those to whom they were not accountable. This would make international law look more like domestic law. If hoodlums take over a house and hold the lawful owners in terror, they commit serious offences. If they seek to borrow from a bank on the security of the house, the loan is not only unenforceable against the owners, the bank is also guilty of some very serious conspiracy offences, especially if they knew that the money is being used to buy new guns to terrorise the occupants. The bank and relevant employees could expect life terms at least. Far from having their loans repaid by the occupants, they would be facing enormous damages claims, life sentences and almost certain closure. I am not suggesting that international bankers should suffer these kinds of consequences. All I am suggesting is that, as a matter of international law, there should be no obligation on the new government to repay the loan. The inevitable consequence that loan funds would dry up for all but democracies, rendering dictatorial regimes economically non-viable - is fully intended!

Cheating Does not Count

In this and in all other matters, the government's power to claim to represent a group of people and to make commitments in their name would be dependent on having gained the people's consent. By making recognition dependent on such consent, it will be in the interest of governments to gain it. It also has the wonderful side effect of ensuring that cheating does not count. If you rig the election, it is not clever. It means that you have not gained the consent that is the condition precedent of representing a people in the international community.[35] If you fail to gain the support of the people, then you have forfeited the claim to speak for them and others may claim that right. There is a clear parallel in contract law. If you have obtained the consent of the other party by fraud and deception, the contract is void. It is not clever, it is merely dishonest and what is more, totally ineffective.

Delegation of Power

Once governments are seen as representatives of those whose consent they have obtained, an entirely new question arises:

What powers have they consented to delegate to their representatives?

To a constitutional lawyer, this issue is strangely absent from much international law and is famously ignored by some precepts of international law. One of the core elements of constitutionalism (which was imposed by Enlightenment thinkers on formerly autocratic sovereigns[36]) is that you must establish the constitutional authority for every action by a public body. This is reinforced by the closure rule for public law is 'whatever is not permitted is prohibited'.

Domestically, this is sometimes reconciled with sovereignty by seeing the people as sovereign and the only power they have is that which has been specifically authorised by the constitution, which has been agreed (or perhaps accepted) by the sovereign people.

Raising such questions means that the international community would have to take domestic constitutions seriously. Their international representatives would be seen as just that, representatives, with only the power they have been given. In some cases, different constitutionally endorsed bodies might be authorised to exercise different elements of the people's sovereign power.

Towards the Unification of Public Law and Public International Law

Once such issues were taken seriously by International Law, Public Law (i.e. constitutional and administrative law) and Public International Law will begin to fuse methodologically and doctrinally. Methodologically, the question of what powers public bodies exercise will become a matter of international as well as domestic constitutional law. This will automatically introduce critical elements of domestic constitutional content and doctrine into international law.

In the other direction, the actual limitations on state power caused by globalisation and the increasing domestic reach of treaties will mean that international doctrine and methodology will infuse domestic law in all forms. As the walls between states break down so will the walls between domestic public law and public international law.

This will not only mean that domestic and international public lawyers will have to learn each other's business: their business will be fused.

By the same token, the growing reach of international business and the growing recognition of international agencies means that public and private international law will be increasingly fused. Domestic corporate law (which I have elsewhere called the 'constitutional and administrative law of corporations'[37]) will at least linked, and probably fused, with the new emerging global public law.

Elimination of the Conflict between Sovereignty and Human Rights

This reconception of the basis of international constitutional legitimacy largely eliminates most of the conflict between sovereignty and human rights.[38] This kind of conflict is always possible when the international community recognises, as the sovereign power, any group which had gained effective political control through the 'prior successful use of force'. This formula does not deny the possibility that such force will be exercised to deny the human rights of the excluded groups. If anything, it actively encourages human rights abuses by rewarding the successful exercise of force to secure dominion over a particular territory. It rewards those who mount anti-democratic coups. It rewards those who rig elections. It rewards those who intimidate the population or who rule through and for one ethnic or social group against others.[39]

If sovereignty is seen as extending only over those who have provided consent, then this provides members of that group with a right to democratic participation - and accords the right to those who have been excluded to democratic participation in that or another state. Sovereignty is no longer the recognition of a power over a people but the collective right of a people to participate in, and benefit from, an independent political community, participating as an equal in the community of nations. To put it another way, sovereignty *becomes* a human right.[40]

International Legal Personality

The fact that the group in power is only seen as representing those whose consent it has sought and to whom it is accountable has important consequences for international legal personality. Initially only states had international legal personality. The above paradigm shift would limit the nature of the international legal personality of states. The excluded groups whose consent is not sought and to whom the group in power are not accountable have a right to demand full participation in the processes by which consent is sought and accountability delivered. If that right is denied, then the group in power do not have the right to represent them in the international community. This provides a lacuna which the excluded people have a right to fill and give those who represent the excluded a particularly important right to be heard. A form of international legal personality has to be extended to such representatives. If the emergence of such groups is prevented by the group in power, the right to be heard is not extinguished, it is retained by the individual members of the excluded group. The attempt to silence the representatives of excluded groups would only have the effect of giving everyone a voice.

Legitimating Intervention in Some Cases

If governments represent only those whose consent they have sought, action to prevent them from oppressing those whose consent they have not sought ceases to be seen as 'intervention' in the traditional sense. Those who try to protect the oppressed would not be interfering in the internal workings of a sovereign territory or trying to break down the walls around a sovereign state. They would be assisting in a conflict between international legal persons. What would previously have been called 'intervention' will take on a different character, more like action taken to assist the self-defence of a sovereign government. It might still be called 'intervention' as it will still involve 'coming between' other persons - as when another person seeks to come between two bar room brawlers. However, taking such action will lose its normative stigma.

Of course, this does not mean that all such 'interventions' will be justified. If you intervene in a bar room brawl, you may do much good or much harm. If you assist the bully, if you exacerbate the dispute, if you increase the harm, if you just join in the fight with your mates, you will be in the wrong. If you encourage it or precipitate it, you are as guilty of the breach of the peace as they are. If you seek to intervene in place of the lawful authorities you are usurping their authority in a way that generally endangers the peace.

The Ever Present Possibility of Regression

It is easy to see how such interventions protect the oppression of excluded minorities. However, the future is not necessary benign. Just as challenges to liberal democratic values may lead to regression towards old ideologies, the breakdown of weaker states may not herald a progression to a new world order. Instead it may involve regression towards the interference by strong states in the affairs of weaker ones in which the strong enforce their will against the weak claiming moral superiority where only technological superiority is demonstrated. This may lead to modern versions of 'gunboat' diplomacy - or its more frightening modern version, 'cruise missile' diplomacy). This type of interference has led to serious abuses this century by democratic states as well as dictatorships - abuses that continue to take place.[41] Beyond that it may lead to a re-emergence of empire - the principal international organising force before the emergence of sovereign states (perhaps in a more modern hegemonic guise).

The possibility of regression is the key reason why I am not an intervention 'hawk'. Up to this point, you might be forgiven for thinking that I am about as hawkish as one could be, prepared to level the walls around sovereign states to allow intervention by others for the protection of the rights of citizens against those who gain power without consent. But the issue is not just whether intervention is justified; but who is justified in intervening and what processes should be involved in deciding.

Who Intervenes?

Clearly, those who authorise intervention cannot be those who intervene as that would make them judges in their own cause. Intervention may one day be authorised by treaty within a wide range of states. One might envisage a 'Democratic League' formed by an international treaty between democratic nations.[42] It would set standards for its membership and be authorised to intervene in any of its member nations in a coup situation or if any other action, which fundamentally breached the conditions of membership arose.[43] The treaty could not justify intervention in countries that had not signed. This is the sort of club in which voluntary membership is the only kind. Such remedies will take longer but it is more likely to work in the longer term. However, the kinds of nations, which are likely to sign up to such a treaty are, coups apart, unlikely to be justifiable subjects for intervention.

In the absence of such a treaty, a few principles are suggested as a basis for determining who is justified in intervening.

Those who Seek to Enforce International Law Must be Bound by it

This principle seems so obvious that it is almost embarrassing to mention it. One is cautious to argue for something so obvious. This principle is supported by so many arguments, generated by so many different theories that positing an argument based on any one theory might diminish it in the eyes of those who are hostile to the theory used but reach the same result using their own, preferred theory. Some of the eloquent and convincing arguments in favour of this principle were penned by Lon Fuller.[44] The rule of law can appear to be an unfortunate impediment when someone believes that their actions are right. However, no one is immune from error.[45] The whole point of the rule of law is that it is not for us to decide the legality of our own actions. To do so converts the 'rule of law' into the 'rule of men'.[46]

Where our actions involve the use of force against others, we not only deprive those against whom we strike from the protection of the law, we deprive ourselves of the protection of that law. We become, literally, outlaws. Weak outlaws suffer ostracism or punishment. Strong outlaws tend to become tyrants. When the local policeman uses force outside the bounds of law, the tyranny is profound. When the self-appointed policeman is not just carrying a baton but an arsenal of cruise missiles, it is, quite frankly, terrifying.[47] Whilst the policeman is on your side you may feel a false sense of security. At its best it is the kind of security Hobbes promoted. But that best is rarely obtainable because of the corrupting effect of such power and the west turned its back on such regimes ever since Locke and embraced the Enlightenment.

The rule of law is one of the key values of the North Atlantic Enlightenment. On this side of the Atlantic, the principle of the rule of law took firmer root and received greater institutional support and expression than anywhere else. Of all the values of the Enlightenment, it is the one that needs least normative work for application to a global world. It merely needs to be applied beyond the borders of the strong sovereign states for which it was originally conceived. The main problem with its extension has been the doubt that there is such a thing as international law because of the lack of enforcement institutions. Among those who do accept the existence of international law (as must be the case with those who seek to impose it), there is a lack of confidence in international institutions to enforce that law, and, perhaps, a corresponding overconfidence in the ability of domestic institutions to do so. But however good domestic institutions may be, they are not empowered to adjudicate in matters of intervention by their own state in another.

The rule of law cannot be compartmentalised and confined within the boundaries of Enlightenment states.[48] It needs to be globalized and institutionalised in genuinely international bodies.

To argue that universal international norms must override state sovereignty, also involves recognising that the same international norms override your own claims to state sovereignty.

John Kidd emphasises that no country, not even those who claim for themselves the 'right to humanitarian intervention',[49] are ready to relinquish their sovereign rights. My point is that those who seek to change international law to impair sovereign rights must be the first to accept that such a change also applies to them.

In seeking to enforce international law, the intervening state(s) are trying to make another state, and now those who lead them, accountable for their actions. The intervening state insists, rightly, that the walls around sovereign states should not prevent the leaders of the target state being accountable for their actions.[50] But insisting on lowering the barriers around other states requires accepting the lowering of the barriers around the states that are seeking to justify intervention, at least for the purposes of that intervention (and for the matters for which intervention is sought). In seeking to make the subject state accountable to the international community and its norms, or the national community and its norms, intervening states must be accountable for their own actions.

If the would-be intervenor state insists on its sovereign rights, it is appealing to a set of concepts that are inimical to its intervention.[51]

One of the reasons why intervening states are reluctant to subject themselves to international law is that they feel that they are losing some measure of their sovereignty. They feel that the 'guilty' party should lose its sovereignty but that those who are intervening on the side of 'right' should not have to 'suffer' in the same way.

However, being the subject of laws of which you approve, is not to lose sovereignty. I would not go so far as saying that the highest freedom is being subject to a higher law to which you are committed. Binding yourself to the values you hold dearest is not to give up your freedom... It is the breaking of those rules that negates an important part of your personality.

It is the same with states. I would say to any state, and in particular to the United States 'to be bound by international laws that restate your core values stated at your creation (and in particular was used to justify the bloodshed in creating and holding together its union) is to reinforce your very nature. To seek to defy them is not to deny an international law external to your nation. It is to defy the values with which you sought to justify the nation in the first place.

Even if moral superiority is claimed, moral superiority does not justify breaching international norms reflecting your morality. Such morality requires adherence to those norms and a breach of those norms is a self-abnegation of your own morality.

Where an intervening state considers rules so important that they are prepared to kill for them (and in earlier wars to die for them as well), they must, of necessity, consider those values important enough to follow themselves!

The images of sovereignty and intervention are of states doing what they want without resort to international law. If you take exception to what others are doing within their borders, you are denying the principle that the other state can do what it wants within its borders. If you then intervene and act within those borders yourself, you must, as a matter of logic, accept that what you do within those borders is subject to the same international law that you are enforcing within that same territory.

Remember that International Law Belongs to the International Community

Although international norms have to be enforced, for the moment at least, by individual countries, the law remains the law of the international community. Those nations who volunteer to enforce it must appreciate that they are enforcing it on behalf of that community. This involves respect for the law of the international community, as discussed above. It also involves respect for the institutions of the international community. The most elementary form of respect is, of course, seeking the imprimatur of those institutions whose approval is required by international law. Even where such imprimatur is not required, intervening states should ensure, as far as practicable, that they have the support of a genuine cross section of nation states and international NGOs.

However, the respect goes deeper than that. Actions to enforce international law must not only be approved by and through the appropriate international institutions. The concerns must arise from rather than merely be enforced through, the international community. It is natural that those who are prepared to intervene are among those with the greatest concerns for the abuses which the intervention is designed to address. It is natural that they will take a lead in persuading the relevant international bodies to give them the relevant mandate. However, the majority may not be as deeply concerned as the would-be intervenor and may be worried about some of the consequences of the proposed intervention. The judgements of the relevant international bodies must be respected.

There are pragmatic reasons for this. If the mandate given to an intervening state is abused by being extended in ways that were clearly not intended or if the. mandate was gained in the first place through bullying or bribery, mandates are less likely to be given and more strongly circumscribed. Each such episode eats up an enormous amount of goodwill and makes others less likely to cooperate.

But the most important reason is philosophical. *The international community should not be seen as a means to the ends of sovereign states, as determined by their sovereign will.* The international community should be seen as an independent good.[52]

This is going to be easier for weaker states to accept and harder for strongest states. It is going to be hardest for the United States.

'Wrong Way, Go Back'

If those who intervene are to be bound by international law and act on behalf of the international community, we need to make good use of existing institutions and processes. We should seek to improve those institutions and processes and, where reform is insufficient, develop new institutions and processes. The concern is that, in responding to the challenges induced by globalisation, powerful nations will not look to current and improved processes but return to the ways of the past in which great powers intervened as they wished in the affairs of other nations they considered inferior.

Unfortunately, the last thirteen years have seen an increasing reluctance of the United States to be bound by international law and international institutions. I can understand how it happened every step of the way. In most cases, I agree with the goals and can sympathise with the dilemmas faced in trying to achieve them. Even where I believe that the goals were inappropriate - even, occasionally, unworthy - I can understand how the decisions came to be made. In general, those who have power are less concerned with process. They are concerned with ends, not means. If they perceive an evil and have the power to do something about it, there is a temptation to use that power, irrespective of any process questions that arise. In international law, where it is easier for powerful countries to get away with abusing and ignoring process, this temptation is all the greater.

Nicaragua to Panama

When elements of the Reagan administration started supporting the 'contras' in Nicaragua and using direct force against Nicaragua, these actions were challenged as illegal at home and in the International Court of Justice. Up to that point, the United States had accepted the compulsory jurisdiction of the ICJ and was an admirable leader in submitting to its jurisdiction. However, when a case was brought against it in the ICJ, the US repudiated the Court's jurisdiction and accused the Nicaraguan government of carrying on a political stunt in continuing the case. The Court certainly did not consider the case to be a stunt and went on to deliver judgement against the United States. Not surprisingly, the US did not comply with the judgement. There was a remarkably limited outcry against this failure of compliance. The situation with Nicaragua was followed by the action in Grenada whose legality was highly dubious.

This action was not challenged because the new government of Grenada was being established by the Americans and the British were too friendly to make too much of a public fuss. The action itself, which had the effect of defeating a coup d'etat, was one for which intervention should be justifiable. Had the United States offered help to the exiled Governor General and gained his authorisation, the process would have been perfectly acceptable.

The decade was rounded out with an incursion into Panama of even more dubious validity.

The Gulf War - Momentarily Back on Track

This resume did not make the United States a prime candidate for leadership in enforcing international law. Nevertheless, following the invasion of Kuwait, the United States took a new turn. Its diplomatic and military work was magnificent in bringing together a coalition, securing a clear UN mandate and then winning a brilliant military victory. At this stage it seemed that the US was back on track to be a leader in enforcing international law through internationally legal means.

It was a remarkable achievement to turn this magnificent effort into a failure. Yet President Bush managed to do this by lamenting that he had not ousted Saddam Hussein. The problem is that the removal of Saddam Hussein, however desirable, was not one of the war aims taken to the UNSC. No doubt the US was right that such an aim would not have been approved. But rather than accept that the publicly stated aims were all they could achieve within international law and its institutions and be triumphant that they had achieved that goal so brilliantly, the ousting of Saddam remained a key aim, albeit an unstated and unapproved one. When they did not achieve the unstated aim, three results followed:

- they felt themselves to have failed
- the public considered that they had failed
- the public rejected Bush, turning the failure into a self-fulfilling prophesy

The response to the perceived failure to secure this unstated aim was to engaged in a number of highly dubious actions to secure it, including the fomenting of civil war, the encouragement of coups d'etat and the sanction of regimes whose rigour calls forth strong adjectives. It also led to the stretching of the original mandate and its use in ways that were never intended by other members of the Security Council and almost certainly would not have been approved. This led to the most damaging result - many members of the Security Council felt that the mandate had been abused and that the United States could not be trusted with such mandates. The alleged abuse by the US of its UNSC mandate made it much harder to secure international support on the level of that achieved before the Gulf War. This situation was exacerbated by very serious accusations about the misuse of information gathering by the UN Arms Control Mission under Richard Butler.[53]

The US seems to have become disenchanted with the UNSC because it will not agree to what the US wants and UNSC members are becoming warier of giving the US a mandate for fear that it will be abused. The United States seems to be blaming the other permanent members for not agreeing with US policies and has set about seeking more congenial (or merely pliable?) bodies through which it can act. This is not just a matter of forum shopping but, in the case of NATO, whose brief had to be extended before it could be used in a Kosovo style intervention - it is forum *creation*.

There are two kinds of principles compromised by such action. The first is the principle, discussed above, that those who seek to enforce international law must be bound by it. The other is the essential Kantian principle not to use others merely as means to your own ends. The US has sought to use the UNSC as an instrument for its own ends and it is not surprising that the instrument is very unhappy about it.[54]

Kosovo

This brings us to the Kosovo crisis. In dealing with the very real conundrums of the Balkan region, the United States initially showed great good sense. For the first few years, the US was deeply concerned about the potential break up of Yugoslavia and sought other means of dealing with the crisis. Yugoslavia is a multi-ethnic state in which the mingling of ethnic groups had been facilitated by the existence of multi-ethnic empires (Austrian and Turkish) and by Tito's brand of communism (in which the prevailing ideology was based on class rather than ethnic division, and Tito himself was from a minority ethnic group). In seeking to make Yugoslavia a Serb-controlled state, Milosevic reignited old ethnic nationalisms, sentiments which had led to enormous suffering of the Serb people in the past and would do so again.[55] It is for this reason, that I have no problem placing primary and original blame on Milosevic[56] for shamelessly playing the ethnic card. His attempt at ethnic control led to the demand for ethnic division by other ethnic minorities. The problem is that ethnic division is wrong in principle and disastrous in practice. In practice it is disastrous because it is rarely possible to determine when to stop. If Croatia can secede from Yugoslavia because a majority of its people are Croats who want to leave, then the majority Serbs in Krajina will claim the same right to secede from Croatia (or, in what is a stronger claim, to be exempt from the secession[57]) and pockets of Croats within Krajina do not want to be part of the Krajina secession/retention. This is one of the main reasons why the right to self-determination has never been extended to a right to secession. If self-determination were extended to secession, then there would be no end to the arguments over where lines are to be drawn - and no end to the wars that would be fought to draw them!

As a matter of principle, ethnic partition is offensive. The most fundamental point to come out of the Second World War was that race and ethnicity are no way to run a country. It involves assumptions of racial and ethnic superiority that fundamentally contradict the Enlightenment values of the moral equality of all human beings enshrined in the UN Charter, the International Declaration of Human Rights and the various human rights conventions. The answer to ethnic difference is not ethnic partition but the development of mutual respect, to value the contribution that others make to an enriched multicultural society. The answer is to build political structures to enable the participation of all while trying to steer political divisions away from politically and economically irrelevant distinctions such as race, ethnicity and religion and to try to ensure that political divisions run along the fault lines of real economic and philosophical differences.

I can see why some thought that ethnic partition was the best solution. However, I felt it was wrong at the time and I shared the American foreboding. I was deeply saddened that Germany should have had the astonishing insensitivity to insist that a separate Croatian state be established. I have to say that, on that particular issue, Germany is the one country in this world that is under a bounden duty to keep its counsel.[58] have no anti-German sentiments and have many German friends and colleagues whose moral sense is, if anything, over developed and subject to a level of personal guilt for the past deeds of their forbears' leaders that I feel is misplaced. However, their leaders did not share the restraint and sense of history so sensibly displayed by the Americans at that time.

Once the West made it clear that ethnic partition was to be supported by the West, with Germany leading and the United States following, areas of Yugoslavia with Serb majorities sought to apply the same principle and sought to either remain within the rump Yugoslavia or at least to become independent of the newly independent republics. The Serbs clearly considered that these demands were reasonable and followed the same principle that the West had imposed on them. When their demands were blocked and no provision was made for autonomy, special protection or even consultation, the means used by the Serbs to secure their ends escalated in their ferocity and evil. They used their preponderance of military force indiscriminately, with almost total disregard for the humanitarian principles enshrined in international law. To bolster their arguments for ethnic partition (which the West had not only endorsed in the original break up but continued to entertain in the subsequent plans for Bosnia) the Serbs took the terrible step of 'ethnic cleansing', leading to the worst massacres in Europe since 1957 and possibly 1945. The Serbs did not realise that such conduct would ensure that the West, always on the look out for 'white hat/black hat' simplifications, would demonise them and overlook any complaints about the inconsistency of their treatment.[59]

However, as the inconsistencies multiplied, Serb anger at the apparent discrimination increased. When Croatia intervened in Bosnia with US trained and armed forces, they were praised not condemned. When those same forces drove some 400,000 Serbs from the Krajina in the most spectacularly 'successful' exercise in ethnic cleansing in the Balkan wars, the West was silent. In Kosovo, Serbs expected that the same principles by which the West refused to allow the secession of Krajina and Serbska would be applied to refuse demands by Kosovar Albanians to secede from Yugoslavia. This time, the West's insistence that the separate republics of the old Yugoslav federation should be sacrosanct seemed to be in rump Yugoslavia's favour. The West could not simultaneously deny the rights of Serbs in Krajina and Serbska to secede from Croatia and Bosnia while supporting the rights of Kosovar Albanians to secede from Yugoslavia.[60]

As the KLA stepped up their guerilla war, the Serbs responded very strongly. While having no doubt that there were many excesses by the Serbs, I am genuinely uncertain that the severity of the response was in any way atypical of responses to guerrilla war. Most reports seem to agree that about 2,000 people were killed over two years - on both sides, and including policemen and public officials who were murdered in a deliberate KLA policy. The worst pre-bombing atrocity complained of during the war involved a number of people killed in an attack on a village that was an admitted KLA headquarters. The casualty list seemed totally unexceptional in this kind of warfare. There would have been hundreds of such actions in the Vietnam War in which the 'body count' was far higher without any intention to hurt innocent civilians. If the Vietnam War produced massacres like My Lai, I would expect a dirty little war like that between the KLA and the Serbs to produce many more. If the US army had a number of Lt William Calleys, I would expect that the Yugoslav army to have many more - especially as the KLA was trying to provoke Serb atrocities to generate Western sympathy and military support. The number of casualties actually suggests that the Serb government was showing uncharacteristic restraint in killing civilians. This may have been due to the presence of the Organisation for Co-operation and Security in Europe (OCSE) or because the Serbs were made very aware of the consequences of atrocities. The Serb general staff certainly sought and gained some expert advice of how to conduct a counter-insurgency operation without committing war crimes.

The Serbs seemed to be more intent in using a common tactic in anti-guerrilla warfare to achieve another purpose. Ever since General Templar's defeat of the Communist Malay insurgents, it has been common military practice to remove civilians from the area of operations to ensure the removal of potential supporters, the drying up of potential recruits and the reduction in civilian casualties (not least by ensuring that there were no civilians to confuse with the guerrilla enemy).[61] In Kosovo, I have no doubt that the Serbs noted that the same tactics would also have the effect of driving out the Kosovar Albanians in order to counter the latter's ethnic majoritarian arguments.

However the situation is evaluated, in scale and ferocity, it fell well short of the Cambodian massacres of the Khmer Rouge (which Vietnam intervened to stop and for which they were vilified and ostracised by the USA) and the Hutu massacres in Rwanda (where the USA blocked intervention for many months). In fact, the Serbian attempts to shift peoples to create ethnically pure states is more reminiscent of the postwar movements of peoples agreed to and enforced by the Allied Powers (e.g., the millions of Germans moved from what became Poland and the millions of Poles moved from the parts of Poland that were incorporated in the Soviet Union - then called Byelorussia and now the independent state of Belarus). This does not mean that such action, whether in the 1940s or the 1990s, should be condoned. Such actions undoubtedly provided sufficient basis for the UNSC intervention on the ground that the flood of refugees constituted a threat to the peace and security of the region and were an appalling breach of human rights.

However, neither the US nor any of the other NATO members took their proposed Kosovo intervention to the UNSC. Claiming that Russia and/or China would veto reasonable action, the US tried to treat NATO as if it was an alternative body with the authority to authorise action on behalf of the international community. They presented an ultimatum to the Yugoslavs that would be very difficult for any state to accept. The war was launched with claims that it was a war in defence of 'law and human dignity'[62] and the rise of a 'new global moral order'.[63]

Kofi Anan reminded us all that, under the UN Charter, such action by regional bodies required UNSC approval. A flurry of arguments for the legality of the bombing were presented by US lawyers. I must say that I found them underwhelming. The US and other countries were not prepared to defend their arguments before the ICJ, seeking, successfully, to avoid the Court's jurisdiction. The United States avoided jurisdiction for the simple reason that it had repudiated the ICJ's compulsory jurisdiction in the course of the Nicaragua hearings. The only treaty under which the ICJ might have had jurisdiction over the USA was the Genocide Convention.[64] However, even here, the USA had made a reservation that it could only be sued under the Genocide Convention if it consented in a particular case. Even here, it did not give its consent.

The Court clearly did not think that the genocide case was made out. However, the same cannot be said for the argument about the illegality of the use of force. While the majority ruled on jurisdictional grounds, there were some important dissents. The most significant was that of Christie Weeramantry, generally referred to as 'the Sri Lankan' judge but notably the Acting President and formerly a distinguished law professor at Monash University. The rest of the Court accepted that the intervention raised very serious issues of international law and emphasised that all parties must act in conformity with their obligations under the UN Charter and the special responsibilities of the UNSC. No judge actually said that the intervention was legal. The minority of judges who decided that the court did have jurisdiction over some of the belligerents was prepared to exercise that jurisdiction to order them to stop.

With the commencement of the bombing and departure of the observers, the Serbs 'went for broke' to achieve their aims by an all out attack on the KLA and the wholesale expulsion of Kosovar Albanians. The kind of war that NATO launched was deliberately aimed to minimise Serb civilian casualties and eschewed both ground troops and low level attacks that had some chance of seriously damaging the Serb forces. This kind of war is uniquely designed to enrage the enemy without limiting their capacity to express their rage on those opponents within their reach. When NATO appeared to claim the right to act outside of international law, the Serbs also showed contempt for the constraints imposed by international law. There is no way that an alleged breach of international law by NATO justifies a breach by Yugoslavia or Yugoslav soldiers and paramilitaries.[65] Breaches of international law should be punished. Both sides sought to avoid being brought to account. So far, both have succeeded.

Having started the war and finding that the Yugoslavs did not cave in, the sovereign will of the Americans had to prevail. Contrary to western claims that the Russians would veto, Russia was prepared to support a UN sponsored peacekeeping operation. However, NATO made the unprecedented demand that it, one of the belligerents, should command and form the core of the peacekeeping force. The Russians were told that the war would be escalated unless they agreed. They were also told that IMF loans would be held up if they did not agree.[66] China's support was gained through bribes rather than threats, including promised support for most favoured nation status which, Robert Hunter, former US ambassador to NATO, reported as worth 40-50bn a year to them.

NATO was not appointed by the UNSC to run the peacekeeping force (the resolution left it to 'member states' to organise one). NATO insisted on total control, limiting the Russians (cutting them down from the 50% participation widely reported after the UNSC resolution) and giving control of all areas to NATO members. This insistence of control was at the expense of the mission. Within days there were complaints that there were not enough peacekeepers to control the revenge attacks of returning KLA. This was exacerbated by the insistence of NATO that all the Serbian police had to leave the province. When they found the KLA reluctant to disarm, they made an agreement with them that they would allow some of the KLA members to become a new police force with the rest being turned into a 'national guard' based on the US model - a strange way of 'demilitarising' the KLA as required by the UN!

The NATO intervention in Kosovo, though understandably motivated by concern for the Kosovars was not one that followed the suggested principles in the previous section:

1. The intervening states were not prepared to subject themselves to international law. They appeared to be in flagrant disregard or in some important precepts of international law and sought to avoid being accountable to either the UNSC or the ICJ. Unfortunately, it marked a continuation and escalation of a trend in which the United States sought to avoid any form of accountability for its actions in the ICJ.
2. They did not seem prepared to accept any limitation on their sovereign right to decide how they acted within the territory of another state.
3. Even after agreements had been reached, they sought to defeat the parts of the agreements they did not like - including the apparent promises to the Russians that they would have a substantial part of the peacekeeping forces, that the KLA would be disarmed and that Serbia would have no part in the reconstruction scheme unless they changed their head of state (it should be noted that the 0-8 agreement and the UNSC resolution both mandated a reconstruction scheme for the whole region.
4. They sought to use international bodies for their own purposes rather than act on behalf and for them.

I see this as a most unfortunate precedent for intervention. The intervention did not follow elementary principles of negotiation or peacekeeping and even those who were prepared to defend its legality only did so on the basis that it would *not* be a precedent.[67] For me, it is a clear sign, like motorway signs, which warn you not to enter by the exit lane – 'Wrong Way, Go Back'. We need to look at other ways to regulate intervention other than the opinion of the powerful as to the justice and propriety of their own actions.

Regulating Intervention

The United Nations Security Council (UNSC)

The UN Charter seeks to establish the UNSC as the supreme body for the regulation of international peace and security with what seems to appear as the sole right to authorise armed intervention. The argument is a familiar one and will be briefly repeated here.

The Charter bans the use of force except in self-defence or under the authority of the UNSC. Article 2(4) provides that 'all members shall refrain in their international relations from the threat or use of force against the territorial integrity or political independence of any state'.

The self defence exemption is provided in Article 51, stating that: 'nothing in the present Charter shall impair the inherent right of individual or collective self defence if an armed attack occurs against a Member of the United Nations.'

Under Article 39, the UNSC is empowered to 'determine the existence of any threat to the peace, breach of the peace or act of aggression and shall make recommendation, or decide what measures shall be taken'. Although the role of regional collective security arrangements is acknowledged (particularly for the purpose of Article 51), Article 53 explicitly states that 'no enforcement action shall be taken under regional arrangements or by regional agencies without the authorisation of the Security Council'.

There are limitations on the right of the UNSC to sanction intervention. 'Domestic' matters are not subject to its jurisdiction. It only has power if there exists a 'threat to the peace, breach of the peace or act of aggression'. However, the ambiguities in the meaning of these terms have meant that, in practice, the UN Security Council has determined the extent of its power.[68] Each time intervention was mandated, there was a recitation of the alleged fact of a threat to international peace which gave rise to its jurisdiction. This capacity to increase a highly coercive power without external review would normally be highly dangerous. However, the existence of five permanent members who generally have different perspectives means that the Council is more likely to be accused of failing to use its power when it should rather than abusing it. Nevertheless, the issue remains a live legal question and it has tended to dominate discussion of humanitarian intervention.

Until this year, however, the issue was how far the UNSC could go in authorising intervention. It was widely concluded, that this was the only way such intervention without the consent of the host state was either legal or practicable. Such conclusions were issued with the casual certainty of those who did not entertain any doubt as to the obvious. They not only took note of the explicit statements found in the UN Charter[69] but the support provided by other treaties, declarations and Assembly resolutions, not to mention many academic commentators.

When NATO commenced bombing, there were many assertions that the war was legal.[70] The actual arguments did not feature in the publicity for the war and no senior legal figures with a responsibility for giving independent advice were brought forward. I have to say that I found the arguments underwhelming, with some of them worthy of nothing but contempt (see the discussion of 'veto nullification' below).

This is not to say that I do not accept the possibility that some such argument might be made. I have great respect for the arguments of Professor Anthony d'Amato (not just out of professional courtesy towards a fellow jurisprude). He claims that there is a customary norm of humanitarian intervention which would justify the NATO action. My skepticism is aroused by the lack of an obvious precedent of intervention without UNSC approval so that I remain underwhelmed. However, I heartily agree with him that it should have been argued before the court and that 'the failure of the United States to submit to the international rule of law continues to harm its image in the world.'

Veto Nullification in Theory

I find the 'veto nullification' argument as offensive as it is dangerous. The argument seeks to draw an analogy to 'jury nullification' where a jury refuses to convict because they do not like the law. I have no difficulty with the idea that this is a safeguard against iniquitous laws and that there have been a small number of benign examples of its exercise, though I am underwhelmed by the attempts to build it up into an important constitutional practice. The analogy is, frankly, ridiculous. When members of the Security Council decide to go to war, they are not acting like a jury standing up against an unpopular law and protecting the accused from its operation. It is a government refusing to accept the decision of the 'jury' set up to decide - the UNSC. As it is the job of the UNSC to decide and there are rules about what counts as a decision (which are more generous than the unanimous or 10/12 rules), the NATO decision could be likened to half the jury deciding to go out and lynch the accused before the trial because they are sure that they will not get the requisite majority in the jury. Of course, the instant case does not involve the deliberate killing of just one accused. It extends to the deliberate killing of large numbers of 'enemy' (they are not enemy until the war starts) and large numbers of innocent persons whose deaths are not intended but whose deaths will inevitably result from the action taken.

Veto Nullification in Practice: What did NATO Want that Would Have Been Vetoed in the UNSC?

The essence behind veto nullification and most of the other arguments for not using the UNSC in Kosovo was the claim that the Russians and Chinese would unreasonably veto humanitarian action in Kosovo. This is essentially a counterfactual argument as NATO nations have never put a proposal to the UNSC. NATO might claim that they had private discussions, which revealed that they would veto a reasonable resolution. However, there is real evidence of the reasonableness of the positions taken over the Rambouillet accord and the subsequent arguments over the details of the UNSC resolution that was adopted.

Eight major points of disagreement between NATO and the Russians emerged - three before the war, three during it and the final two after the war.

Pre-war disputes

1. The Rambouillet ultimatum was wrong to insist on NATO troops having the right to go anywhere in Yugoslavia they deemed appropriate and incompatible with the concept of sovereignty.[71]
2. The Rambouillet ultimatum was wrong to insist that the Kosovars should have the right to vote on secession in three years. This was inconsistent with the territorial integrity of Yugoslavia and NATO's claim to respect it.
3. Intervention should only occur with a UNSC mandate.

Disputes during the war

4. Any peacekeepers should be from, as far as possible, neutral countries rather than from one of the belligerents in the conflict (i.e. NATO).
5. Similarly, the peacekeeping force should not be under the command of one of the belligerents.
6. The demand by NATO that Serb forces prove that they were leaving before the bombing would stop was illogical and against all precepts of warfare.

Post war disputes

7. The Russians should have their own zone of operation like the other peacekeepers.
8. The Russians should be allowed to bring in the number of peacekeepers nominated in the original proposal.

On all of these points, I have to say that I find the Russian position was not only the more reasonable, but in some cases the NATO position was unreasonable, illogical, unnecessary and so unlikely to achieve a positive response as to cast doubt upon the bona fides of the NATO negotiating position. I will briefly go through these, dealing with the disputes during and after the war and with the pre-war disputes last.

Disputes during the War

More than one month before the cessation of hostilities, Russia agreed to support a peacekeeping force. They signed up to the G-8 accord, which included the 'deployment in Kosovo of effective international civil and security presences endorsed and adopted by the United Nations capable of guaranteeing the achievement of the common objectives'. The sticking point was the composition of the peacekeeping force.[72] NATO insisted on having the lion's share of the force and the overall command. Such a demand, that one of the belligerents in a war should command the peacekeepers was, to my knowledge, completely unprecedented. It is difficult to see that such a demand is reasonable in principle or practice. As a matter of principle, peacekeepers should be seen to be coming between the two sides. The two sides who are involved in the fighting cannot meet this elementary test.[73] Moving from principle to pure pragmatism, for peacekeepers to have the confidence of both sides, they need to be seen to be sufficiently neutral to act independently of the two sides of the conflict. Even more pragmatically, if a belligerent becomes a peacekeeper, they are more likely to be targets of those who had been on the opposing side of the conflict. It is obviously the kind of demand that is likely to be rejected by those who are independent minded, let alone those who are suspicious of NATO motives (such as the Russians). It is bound to be resisted by those on the other side of the conflict, which will naturally see this as an army of occupation. Such a demand was bound to prolong the negotiations, and the failure to reach agreement was used as a convenient reason to intensify the bombing of increasingly civil targets (bridges, oil refineries, even a TV station).

If NATO believed that the situation justified the waging of war and believed that they should become a belligerent, then they should have seen that taking such action ruled them out of role in the peacekeeping force. Under such circumstances, the peacekeeping role would fall to others. The suggestion that there were no others who could perform that role is an insult to many countries with a record of peacekeeping second to none - including Australia, New Zealand, India, Finland, Sweden and Fiji. There are plenty of other countries with sufficient experience to serve under the command of a seasoned peacekeeper from one of the above named neutral countries. Under these circumstances, Russians would be a better bet than actual belligerents. If NATO troops were to be used, they could at least be from those NATO countries, which did not participate in the hostilities.

One of the most curious disputes was generated by NATO insistence that the bombing would not stop until the Serbs had engaged in significant withdrawals from Kosovo. This is a Catch 22 of which Joseph Heller[74] would have been proud. If NATO insist that the Serbs withdraw but also insist that they will keep bombing for a period after the withdrawal has begun then that logically means that they have the right to bomb the troops after they have left their protected positions and started retreating. The Russians described this as contrary to all military logic and commonsense. In the end, NATO did not insist on it and agreed in advance that they would not bomb the withdrawing troops.

Post-war Disputes

The UNSC mandate was remarkably vague about the composition of the peacekeeping force. It authorized 'member states and relevant international organizations to establish the international security presence in KOSOVO'.[75] Annexes referred to 'the international security presence with substantial North Atlantic Treaty Organization participation must be deployed under unified command and control'. Whereas the head of the civilian division was to be appointed by the secretary general, no such power of appointment was given to him with respect to the military mission - as had been the case in Cambodia.[76]

NATO used this as an excuse to take command of K-FOR and control it as they saw fit. NATO gave each of its own members a part of Kosovo to patrol but denied the Russians any area (something which may well have led the Russians to make their preemptive move to Pristina airport[77]). They also cut the size of the Russian force from the 50% which was initially publicized to only a few thousand while boosting their own numbers and sought to effectively sideline the Russians who were a key part of the agreement and were the only neutral peacekeepers. NATO argued that giving the Russians a separate area to cover would lead to a de facto partition of Kosovo. This does not make sense unless NATO intended to breach the agreement itself. The Russians support Yugoslav sovereignty over Kosovo so they are not going to support its becoming part of another state. The only way that Kosovo would be partitioned on this basis is if NATO intended for the parts of Kosovo they controlled to become independent contrary to the UNSC resolution.[78] Later on, it was claimed that separate Russian areas would attract the Serbs and lead to clashes with the KLA. However, such complaints assume that the Serbs would be driven out of areas controlled by NATO and that the KLA would not be disarmed. The latter implies that NATO will not require the KLA to keep to the UNSC resolution. The former implied that NATO would not provide a credible protection for the Serbs who would accordingly be forced to leave those areas controlled by NATO and that NATO occupation would imply effective ethnic cleansing of Kosovo Serbs. These arguments suggest that NATO would make ineffective peacekeepers and enforcers of the UNSC resolution and that Russian troops would be better at both. I am reluctant to come to such conclusions myself, but they seem to be the necessary consequences of NATO views. As indicated above, I would prefer genuinely independent peacekeepers with neither Russian nor NATO presence.

Pre-war Disputes

The two most outrageous aspects of the Rambouillet ultimatum were:

1. the requirements that NATO troops would have free reign to travel through Serbia, to be immune from its laws and have the right to arrest and detain anyone they pleased (and, interestingly enough for those familiar with American revolutionary history, the right to be billeted wherever they wanted) and
2. the right of the Kosovars to decide on whether they would be able to secede in three years. It is important to note that neither of these was a part of the UNSC resolution (which was, in the end, required, thereby vindicating the insistence that one be sought).

It may well be that NATO went to war and achieved no more than they could have achieved by real negotiations rather than an ultimatum. If this were a legal case, they would have to pay the costs of the action.

Sweet Reason?

I do not hold a brief for either Russia or China and I do not seek to portray either as the epitome of sweet reason or paragons of virtue. The current Chinese regime sent tanks to clear Tien An Minh square of demonstrators. President Yeltsin sent tanks to clear the legislature of its legislators.[79] However, if the above disputes are an indication of the kinds of issues on which nullification might be expected, then NATO has managed to appear unreasonable in the most unreasonable of company. These disputes do not constitute justification for 'veto nullification', they constitute unexpected support for the institution of the veto. Worse than that, the moral and legal high ground can be claimed by those to whom nations concerned with human rights have legitimate and pressing concern Worst of all, if these were the kinds of issues that meant that NATO went to war and remained at war, then it would seem that the war was unnecessary, unjustified, gained what could have been conceded and failed to gain for NATO the points it sought.

Flaws in the UNSC

Having argued that the UNSC role is an important one and finding more time for the veto than most western commentators, I will be the first to admit that the UNSC has important weaknesses. I am certain that, as the economic, institutional and ideological forces described in the earlier parts of the paper gather in momentum, the UN and the UNSC will change. However, for the moment, I will be arguing that the prime need is to supplement the role of the UNSC with a more effective jurisdiction for the ICJ than the replacement, abandonment or sidestepping of the UNSC.

The UNSC is more executive than judicial One of the greatest problems with the UNSC role in regulating conflict and in deciding disputes such as those that arose over the Kosovo bombing lies in the nature and origins of the security council. Established at the end of the Second World War, it was an extension and refinement of the meetings of the 'big three' in Teheran, Yalta and Potsdam. Such meetings were essentially executive in nature as the prosecution of the war had called for leaders able to commit to joint and/or immediate action. There was no time for 'judicial review'. In any case, when the great powers could agree, no further safeguards were seen to be required. However, the constitutional principles to which the Western powers were committed, envisage that all executive actions be subject to the rule of law and that their exercise of power be subject to external review by an impartial body sworn to determine whether it is in power. The executive powers of the Security Council are too great to be exercised without the oversight of an essentially judicial body capable of determining whether the action is within relevant international law.

Interpreting previous decisions of the UNSC, especially where a permanent member has a mandate Where UNSC decision has been made and a mandate given, questions may arise as to the extent of the mandate. The natural place to resolve such an issue is the UNSC. However, if a permanent member of the Security Council acts beyond its mandate, they could veto any motion affirming that the action went beyond the mandate. This reverses the basic principle underlying the UNSC, that enforcement action is only taken if the permanent members do not oppose it. It would also mean that the permanent member would be a judge in its own cause. If mandates are abused, the Security Council will no doubt be more careful in the authority they give to member states and will create mechanisms to ensure that authority is not exceeded, prolonged and used for purposes other than those for which the authority was originally delegated. However, it would be much better to give the power to review to an independent judicial authority - presumably the International Court of Justice (with streamlined procedures for the issue of the equivalent of injunctions and advisory opinions) - than leave such arrangements to the ad hoc results of particular negotiations.

Validating action outside the UNSC Given the obvious imperfections of the UNSC, I can see the argument that some other mechanism might be highly desirable in some cases. I am wary of these arguments as it may turn out that the intervention leads to more suffering than the situation it was designed to overcome - either because the views of those who would exercise- the veto are sound or because the failure to generate wider international support is fatal in itself. I am also wary of such arguments because the weakening of the UNSC may lead to far worse consequences in other conflicts. For these reasons, I would argue for a systemic response to a perceived systemic problem rather than an ad hoc response to individual crises or the attempt to use NATO to supplant the role of the UNSC.

Having said that, I am not going to argue that intervention without UNSC approval would never be justified. The question is, again, 'who is to decide and by what process is the justification established?'.

It cannot be left to the intervening states or group of states that would make them judges in their own cause. It cannot be left to 'spin doctored' statements to the media. My response is 'tell it to the ICJ, don't tell it to the media'. If the ICJ is not impressed then neither am I. If the intervening state does not have sufficient faith in its case to go to the ICJ, then no one else should have faith in that case. War is killing on a massive scale. Without legal sanction, it is premeditated serial mass murder. The only way that it is not premeditated serial mass murder is if its legality can be established. The only way to effectively establish legality is through a court. If there were no court available to establish its legality, then it would be a matter of public debate between the legal champions of the protagonists. But there is a court available. The ICJ is ready, available and, even if not particularly willing, certainly prepared to do so. To refuse to argue your case in court does not make you innocent. It does not make you clever. It destroys the only basis for effectively establishing that you are engaged in a just war rather than mass murder and terrorism.

I did not invent the term 'three strikes and you're out'. When it comes to aerial bombardment, it is 'one strike and you're out if you cannot establish your case'. I did not invent the term 'zero tolerance'. I think it was invented a few blocks from here. I am saying that the international community should have zero tolerance for war without the sanction of international law. Those who avoid having their legal arguments being tested in court are not clever, they are merely making themselves international outlaws -international outlaws because they are claiming to be outside international law.

The ICJ and ICC

The international community should consider it intolerable for anyone to claim to enforce international law without being bound by it.

My simple proposition is that no country may intervene unless it submits itself, at least for that particular intervention, to the jurisdiction of the international court of justice and the international criminal court (when established). No country should engage in any intervention without so subjecting itself, no country should support such intervention without this proviso and no international body should endorse or authorise such intervention without it.

Given the strength of the one remaining superpower and its unwillingness to be bound by international law, diplomats might consider this undiplomatic. No head of government would relish saying so - and few would do it for the kind of people who attract such intervention. This is merely a subset of the discomfort most politicians experience in the presence of principles that do not suit their immediate policy objectives.

The answers to such political discomforts are to rely on strength in numbers and strength in position. The logical starting point is the Secretary General and the Security Council. Mr Kofi Anan quietly reminded us of the necessity for regional alliances to have the authority of the Security Council. The Security Council could insist on this proviso to any authorisation of the use of force.[80] Permanent members should make this proviso their constant refrain and their firm condition for endorsing intervention. Other members of the council might be able to join them with less fear of impunity and the Secretary General would have the backing to be more forthright. I regret the fact that the permanent members most likely to insist on this elementary proviso are not the countries with the proudest records in human rights, democracy and the rule of law. I would like to be surprised and find that those who did have a prouder record could take the lead in this. But if the West cedes moral leadership on such matters to others, then that is going to leave it up to the leadership of such countries.

Beyond the Security Council, I would like to suggest that other countries make the same point, politely if they must, before, during and after the intervention. At the very least, I would suggest that they avoid rushing in to support intervention without this proviso. In resisting pressure to issue a statement of support, there are many excuses they might offer. I would suggest the following as samples:

- That they have to refer the matter to their attorney general for comment;
- That if they come out in support and it is subsequently demonstrated to be wrong, it will look difficult;
- That if they support the United States in taking action without being prepared to submit themselves to the jurisdiction, it will be hard to justify to the opposition why we should submit to the WTO next time you get a ruling in your favour.

I would prefer that they were forthright. They could still say it politely: 'Yes, Bill, I understand all your arguments, and I am sure that they are right. If so, why not be prepared to test them. A positive endorsement by the ICJ would do nothing but support your cause. If you are not prepared to put them to the test, it will undermine the strength of your conviction that you are right.'

But a real friend and ally would say: 'Look Bill, it is wrong, it is hypocritical and it is dangerous.'

Arguments Against the Use of the ICJ

Beware putting too much faith in the judicial remedy In putting emphasis on a judicial solution, I am wary of the obvious dangers and criticisms of putting too much faith in judges. All systems of judicial appointment have their limitations. I am sure that this is true of the ICJ (although one of the dangers, the persistent appointment of ideologically amenable judges by a long running administration, is absent).

It is interesting that the revolutions of 1688 to 1789 did not place much emphasis on courts. The Bills of Rights were not intended to be enforced by the courts against legislatures. The grievances to which the revolutions were directed were the excesses of an overweening domestic sovereign power. The democratic legislature was seen as the answer, not the problem. The Bill of Rights involved protection against such sovereigns and a statement of the principles that would guide the legislatures. Unambiguously so in the case of the UK and French Bill/Declaration. It was ambiguous in the United States until Chief Justice John Marshall and the seminal *Marbury v Madison*.

However, this stage occurred when sovereign legislatures had been established or were in the process of being established. Later on, the necessity of judicial review in an effective *rechstaat* subject to the rule of law came to be taken for granted. The international community is not in sight of such a system and arguably will never get there. More interesting and relevant precedents may be found in the role of courts in challenging and partially taming domestic sovereign power. The courts had a particularly proud role during the reign of James I.[81] I venture to suggest that the ICJ might profitably look to some of these institutional precedents.

I do not believe in establishing judicial control without the possibility of creating new rules. Part of the answer lies within the court(s) themselves. Judicial development of the law will inevitably be generated by the irreducible uncertainties of language and its application and in the judicial handling of internal legal contradictions and mixing of the moral commitments of the law and the individual judges who interpret it. The ICJ has had to be particularly cautious in seeming to go beyond existing international law because of its lack of ready enforcement mechanism and the ability of state parties to excuse themselves from future jurisdiction. Such caution would not be necessary if acceptance of jurisdiction by intervening states was a condition of all mandates to intervene. The court may be encouraged where state parties argue that the development of customary international law supports their case (as the United States might have done if they had taken their arguments to court rather than the media and which Professor d'Amato wishes they had done. Institutions tend to mould their behaviour to sustain relevance. Even judges are sub-consciously affected by the greater power they gain when matters are referred to them rather than to others.

One should not discount the possibility that the court might eventually embrace these powers. If there are some germs within international law that allow intervention without UNSC approval (as some such as d'Amato argue) this may mean that the ICJ comes to be an alternative forum in which to justify intervention. If the UN executive, the UNSC, is blocked, this might lead to increasing use of the ICJ if that avenue appears open. There are parallels in the Warren Court[82] which dealt with critical matters of human rights when the US executive and legislature were unable to move on the matter. More generally, courts may be seen to balance not only executive wrong doing, but to other weaknesses. The ICJ may become an alternative forum in which such matters are debated. It might be a particularly appropriate forum in that issues are dealt with relatively independently and dispassionately and there is a voting mechanism to avoid gridlock at the UNSC. If would-be intervenors are seeking other forums, they should look to the ICJ rather than avoid it. I am not predicting a 'Warren Court' for the ICJ - though I would not rule it out at some stage in the future. The court would, inevitably develop the law in response to new situations, the only issue is the pace of change.

Whatever the pace of change and the degree of future judicial activism by the ICJ, the obvious limitations to judicial solutions are rarely without remedy. Judicial powers rarely go unchecked. Judicial development of rules tends to lead to demand for direct 'legislative' changes to the rules. In this case such changes can be made by countries jointly making treaties or ratifying UN General Assembly resolution that will clarify some of the issues that might otherwise be left to judges. In the longer term, it is likely to strengthen the court and the regime of international law.

ICJ jurisdiction is optional so the court must be tentative This is generally the case. However, if the intervening state accepts its jurisdiction, then the onus is on the state in which intervention is occurring to seek a remedy in the court. If intervening states agree to be bound, then there will be jurisdiction. My suggestion is that no state should sanction, tolerate, support - or, indeed, fail to condemn - any intervention in which the intervenor does not accept that jurisdiction.

'Sitting duck' The basic principle behind ICJ jurisdiction is one of reciprocity. If one state is to be subject to litigation, it must either be because it has agreed to be subject to the ICJ in that case or because it has agreed to be subject to the court's compulsory jurisdiction and is sued by another such state. Otherwise, they are seen as being 'sitting ducks' in Professor d'Amato's words.

In general, I am not so worried about sitting ducks. Those who claim to be law-abiding states should not be concerned that their claims of lawful action should be subject to test. If this attracts others to accept the ICJ's compulsory jurisdiction to get a shot at illegal action by another state, then the state concerned should:

1. be acting lawfully in the first place;

2. should not confine its lawful actions merely to those countries which have accepted compulsory jurisdiction;
3. welcome the fact that others are also accepting the universal jurisdiction of the court.

In any case, states that intervene are not merely sitting passively as the sitting duck image suggests. They are not peacefully minding their own business. In intervening in other states, they are dive bombing other, generally smaller, birds.

The most important flaw in the 'sitting duck' argument is that the intervening state is not the only state in legal jeopardy. If the state in which intervention occurs challenges the intervening states in court, it must also accept the ICJ's jurisdiction. This means that the ICJ can make orders against them too. Although the US and other NATO nations successfully sought to avoid jurisdiction, the Acting President of the ICJ, Christie Weeramantry was not only prepared to make orders to stop the NATO action but also to make orders requiring the Yugoslavs to desist from some of their actions. A court case is a two edged sword and those who come to it without a just cause are likely to suffer from it. Those who claim to have a just cause should be prepared to use the court's jurisdiction rather than avoid it.

How to Convince Powerful Nation States to Accept These Strictures

Why should powerful nations agree to abide by international law when it would involve a restriction on its sovereign power to seek to pursue its sovereign view of the right through whatever channels it wishes.

Most of the above argument has been deontological - arguing matters of moral principle that are so widely accepted in domestic law that it would surprise even the cynics and skeptics that they might be breached. Some of the argument is merely one of consistency. The very assertion of such power indicates the flaw in its use as an argument for overcoming the sovereignty of another nation.

This is where we turn to consequential arguments about interests. While I would prefer that such arguments should be unnecessary where the principles are clear, I know very well that most people find it easier to be convinced by arguments of pure principle if they know that they will benefit from doing so!

If the NATO members are not bound, others might not be bound If NATO members are not bound by international law in doing what they believe is right, then what constrains those against whom intervention is sought? As soon as NATO started bombing the Serbs, seemingly indicating that it would not be bound by the constraints of international law in pursuing its own ends, the Serbs threw away any constraints they had felt before.[83] If NATO was not bound by article 2(4) of the UN Charter, then the Serbs seemed to have decided that they would not be bound by conventions concerning the treatment of civilian populations in time of war. They would use the period to do whatever they could to gain the ethnic majority that had been asserted so successfully against them to date. This is just another version of saying that you cannot claim to enforce international law if you are not bound by it. If the US, UK and France will not accept the UN Charter which it was responsible for drafting and which gives it enormous privileges, then why should anyone else accept any international agreements.

I am not suggesting that the Serb action was justified. However, it is, in retrospect at least, unsurprising. According to Professor Roger Hayden,[84] it actually was predicted. If you are concerned about consequences, then you should be concerned about these. 'There were 45,000 refugees outside the borders of Kosovo when the war began. Now there are almost 800,000. If a full 80% go back, the net effect of the war will have been to quadruple the number of Kosovar refugees.'[85]

The US and EU interest in other international law In an increasingly global economy, US and EU firms are increasingly operating in other markets and in other countries. This makes them stronger in most ways. However, it does make them more vulnerable to the action of other countries from appropriation of property to the most subtle forms of discrimination or merely reluctance in defending US and EU intellectual property rights.[86]

The US is seeking an increasing use of international legal and arbitral mechanisms to protect existing interests, and to further an open trading system in which the power of US firms can be more fully projected. If the US is not prepared to be bound by the most fundamental rules of international law, why should other countries feel bound by these new international rules, which protect US property and commercial interests.[87]

The US and EU not only have more to gain from the effectiveness of international law and international institutions. They have less to fear from them - not least because they will have a far greater say in their structure and the values that go into them. They will lose a lesser measure of their current sovereignty than others will. If they insist on no compromises on their own sovereignty, then others will do likewise.

Protection from terrorism The US and EU are concerned about the dangers that terrorism poses to their citizens and their citizens' property. Yet NATO was essentially making a terrorist argument. Do what we want, or we will inflict pain on you irrespective of international law. The pain inflicted by the NATO bombers exceeded that of IRA or Palestinian bombers by a margin of several thousand percent. If others took the security of US and EU property as citizens as lightly as some NATO countries do of other nations, the 1970s would seem tame.

Of course, the cry of the terrorist is normally the last refuge of the powerless rather than the first resort of the powerful.

The culture of violence One does not have to go to those from aggrieved nations to look for bad examples that the NATO approach might give. If the US and its allies use violence to achieve what it wants irrespective of law, then what does it say to the disgruntled youth of the US and EU. I thought it was telling when the Columbine massacre was reported to a grieving nation, the first lady blamed a culture of violence on TV. I am sure that no irony was meant and that she was not having dig at her husband. However, the violence on TV that I had in mind was that in Kosovo.

The resentment of others For most in the west, where the media seemed to largely ignore the issue and argue that the pure evil of Milosevic justified any action, there was little questioning of the legality of the bombing. Other countries were infuriated. Zakaria argues that it has led to an eruption of anti-American fury reminiscent of the cultural revolution, 'set US/Russian relations back by several decades' (quoting Chernomyrdin) and led 15 European countries to establish itself as a military power with command control and troops independent of US.[88]

If you cannot be trusted to keep to your UN treaty obligations, why would anyone else keep to their agreements? There are widespread statements that Milosevic cannot be trusted. Of course Milosevic could not be trusted. However, nobody could be trusted to keep a deal extorted by threats of the most extreme violence. If you get me in a room and threaten to murder my family, I will agree to almost anything to get out of that room. But can you trust me to keep my word? Of course not. If I can, I will go to the police. If the police will not act because you are not subject to their jurisdiction and cannot be touched by normal legal processes, I will think about whether I can kill you. You cannot trust me because I have no moral obligation to keep to what was forced out of me at the point of a gun. I doubt that Milosevic would recognize a moral obligation if it were handed to him by

Moses himself on a tablet of stone. However, there is no moral obligation here. This is not merely a matter of morals. It is a matter of domestic law. And it is a matter of international law.[89] If the war is legal, then a treaty to end the war is also binding even if extorted by force. However, if the war is illegal, then there can be no obligation to keep to the peace treaty extracted at the end of it.

Concluding Remarks

Obviously, strong countries are not yet convinced to conform to international law or international process. I put little faith in the fact that they have not yet heard all the arguments put above - they will have heard some of them. They may gain confidence from the last three months. However, I doubt that the recent action will stand any serious retrospective examination. Other players will be more wary next time and I hope that other countries are persuaded to take a stronger line in insisting that intervenors subject themselves to the law they are supposedly enforcing.

Other Institutional Support

Domestic Supports

Although the thrust of the institutional supports suggested are international and it is illogical to suggest that they could be purely domestic, domestic supports could play a major role. No liberal democracy should go to war without being convinced that it is legal to do so. A statement from a spin-doctor on CNN is not enough. The very least I would expect is that the Attorney General tenders legal advice to the legislature (or perhaps one house or committee designated for that purpose). That advice should be frank and fearless and should canvass the arguments on both sides. He is making the equivalent of an *ex parte* application. He should do this as a legal professional and be subject to ethical censure and disbarment if it is not done honestly. Better still, a body that is independent in fact as well as theory might be appointed to consider such matters. Given the severity of going to war, I do not see why the rest of the business of the court should not be interrupted to allow an advisory opinion to be given. In some countries, such as my own, the ultimate appellate court may not give advisory opinions.[90] However, the fact that the actual decision would be made by the International Court of Justice removes one of the two arguments against the giving of such opinions (i.e. prejudging[91]). This is not the place to consider the arguments for or against using the ultimate appellate court in such cases. It may well be more appropriate in some countries to have a panel of judges or a panel of judges and other officials (e.g. Speaker of the House or President of the Senate), or some other body. The point to be made here is that all countries should have processes in place to ensure as best they can, that the use of force by their armed forces across national borders is, as far as they can reasonably tell, valid under international law. They should do this a matter of honour and to avoid embarrassing mistakes that would follow the entry into war and the subsequent finding by the ICJ that it was illegal. I would also suggest that the ICJ should be more lenient on countries that overstepped the mark if they had shown that they had gone through a genuine process themselves and had brought the matter to the ICJ immediately afterwards.

Professional Ethics - Lawyers

My comments about the duties of an Attorney General to give honest and independent legal advice and that such attorneys should be held accountable as professional lawyers raises an important part of the means by which values may be institutionalised - through codes of ethics, codes of conduct and the means for their enforcement.

I would suggest that we need an international code of ethics for lawyers that would help to properly internationalise the profession. A duty to respect international law would be included in duties. This would, of course, be a radical shift for lawyers - reflecting the decline of sovereignty. I used to say that the legal profession is one of the most localised of all because the nature of its subject matter is determined by the law they practice which is almost universally that of sovereign jurisdictions. That is no longer true. The weaker states become and the more international law grows in significance, the less true it will become. Lawyers need to develop an affinity to international legal norms and a commitment to the international rule of law.

If there ever is another time when a liberal democracy decides to go to war without sanction of UNSC and without being prepared to subject its actions to the ICJ, I would hope that lawyers around the world and in the country concerned would speak out. I would hope that lawyers working for such a government should threaten to resign and carry out that threat if their country persists with such unsanctioned action. The analogy is that of the lawyer who knows from his client's actions, words and documents that the client intends to commit a criminal act. In most jurisdictions, the lawyer is under a duty to advise the client of the illegality, to refuse to represent him and to report him (lawyer-client privilege explicitly excludes the intention to commit a subsequent criminal act). Few criminal acts are more heinous than the illegal taking of large numbers of lives.

I can envisage a day when those who did not so resign would be disbarred from the international bar and would not be able to appear before any international judicial forums - including those covering international contract disputes, international trade disputes and so on. This would reinforce the essential principal that a state which is not prepared to subject itself to the most fundamental of international laws should not expect, or receive, the international protection of the law in economic matters. These are strong suggestions and would have to await further institutional development of an international profession. However, the profession of lawyers should treat the rule of law as one of the most fundamental of their values and should be prepared to provide the strongest institutional support for those values.

Professional Ethics - Soldiers

Raising the professional ethics of lawyers merely draws one's attention to the professionals who are far more intimately involved - the professional soldiers who actually do the fighting. Should they refuse to take part in intervention that is neither sanctioned by the UNSC nor subject to ICJ/ICC jurisdiction?

This will be seen as a totally shocking suggestion by some. It smacks of mutiny and treason - the most serious offences for any soldier to commit in any state. In a democracy, we are particularly insistent, and expectant, that soldiers will be loyal to the state which speaks for the people. However, treason is an offence against a sovereign state. Once state sovereignty ceases to be absolute, then higher laws can apply. If a state concerned is killing people without lawful sanction, it is committing a serious crime and those who are perpetrating it are engaged in a criminal conspiracy that makes almost all other criminal conspiracies pale into insignificance. Loyalty to the conspiracy may be considered the highest duty by members of the conspiracy (as in the Mafia), but the rest of society regards it as evidence of devotion to the criminal endeavour making the intent more serious and severe punishment more justified. The same should be true of soldiers fighting in illegal wars.

Just as the Nazi war criminals were held to have no excuse at Nuremberg, neither should the individual soldiers and generals who fight wars beyond their boundaries for states, which refuse to submit to the jurisdiction of the ICJ. The fact that their state is not prepared to do so should set off alarm bells. The fact that the state has no independent mechanism to provide advice to the Parliament that the war is legal should send off more alarm bells. Indeed, the professional ethics of soldiers should preclude any aggressive acts that are not subject to such an 'international legality' check.

Democracies expect their soldiers to be loyal and follow orders. However, their adherence to the rule of law should make them particularly mindful of the dilemma generated by an order to act contrary to international law and should seek to protect soldiers from that dilemma by following international law and seeking independent confirmation of the legality of those orders.

When Palestinians planted bombs in airports of countries that did not do as they wished, they were terrorists. If someone drops a bomb on the airport of a country that does not do as his President wishes, it is only the lawfulness of the action that protects him from being justifiably branded a terrorist. State sponsored terrorism is still terrorism.[92] Democracies should have more respect for their soldiers than to put them in this position. The soldiers I know certainly deserve better.

Constraints on the use of force are not new to the professional soldier. The traditional term is not 'ethics' but 'honour'. As John Keegan forcefully puts it, a professional soldier would rather sacrifice his life rather than his honour.[93] Honour is at stake. The trouble with honour is that its grandeur and sweep make it too imprecise in its application. Clear ethical rules are needed to deal with some of these issues. However, the honour of the 21st Century soldier will be determined by their willingness to live by a professional ethic that accepts the primacy of international law in the international use of force.

Other Professional Bodies

If lawyers and the military were to see themselves as international professional associations whose core values include new global values of liberal democracy they could become two of the most important international institutions to promote those values. Such institutions relate individuals to liberal democratic values by interpreting what those values mean for professionals of a particular kind and how that profession may advance global values. But they may not be the only ones. Doctors have a professional interest in alleviating and preventing suffering - and a universal right to health care.

New professional associations might prove important contributors. I have been involved in the establishment of the International Institute for Public Ethics which is intended to build a new profession of 'public ethicists' from those who are charged with implementing ethics regimes in public agencies and educating public officials to make them work.

Business could also play an important role, especially if a number of nations insisted on the linkage I have described above. If their ability to protect their intellectual property and penetrate markets were made dependent on their home countries subjecting their military activities to international law, they might provide a powerful influence on those home countries. I would hope that they would have the good sense to realise that their long term interests are supported by their home countries complying with this most reasonable of requests rather than getting their home countries to bully those who are making the request.

Conclusion

When I told some of my friends about what I was going to say today, they joked that that is the one thing you might say in New York that will have you on a plane out of here by sundown. While dismissing those suggestions with reminders of the North American love of robust debate about values, I appreciate that it may be hurtful for those who see the USA as a moral leader in the world.

One of the reasons why I say it is that in many ways it has been and sometimes still is a moral leader. The words of the North Atlantic Enlightenment ring out over the centuries as some of the finest statements of human aspiration in any language. There have been many echoes and restatements by Abraham Lincoln, Woodrow Wilson, Franklin Roosevelt, Earl Warren, John Kennedy, Martin Luther King - not to forget Bill Clinton's Normandy speech on June 6th 1994).

Much of the moral leadership was gained as part of the North Atlantic Enlightenment that articulated values, which civilized the authoritarian sovereign states that had emerged in the seventeenth century.

However, the moral achievement was not confined to articulating fine values. Americans in particular were aware of the temptations of power. They did not rely on finding or training public officials to be saints who would not succumb to its temptations. Saints are in short supply and no training program can ever deliver enough saints to fulfil all the important public positions of a modern liberal democracy. They realised, better than most, that the point is to design institutions that do not need saints to run them. The founders sought to establish checks to prevent the abuse of power rather than to ensure its saintly exercise. In this they were entirely correct.

We are now witnessing a sea change as fundamental as that heralded by the Treaty of Westphalia. The strong sovereign states that were civilized by the North Atlantic Enlightenment are being fundamentally weakened by the forces of globalisation. We need a new Enlightenment to civilize the global world to avoid its dangers and crystallize its opportunities. That new Enlightenment will involve the reconceiving of those values for a more global world and developing institutions that will support them.

In this essay I have considered the decline of the sovereignty-based objections to intervention to protect human rights and other values. However, such interventions need to be subjected to international versions of Enlightenment values, most notably the rule of law. This requires the enhancement of existing institutions such as the ICJ and ICC or the development of new ones.

Like the original transatlantic Enlightenment, the new global Enlightenment must aim at identifying a set of values and institutions that bind the strong and the weak alike.

Notes

* The author wishes to thank Ms Suzanne Condlln and Dr Yeong-Han Cheong, Research Officers in the Key Centre for their many contributions to the development of this paper including digging out sources, highlighting some of the most important elements, editing and providing footnotes.

1 Lyons defines intervention in terms of crossing boundaries. See, for example, G.M. Lyons and M. Mastanduno, 'International Intervention, State Sovereignty and the Future of International Society', *International Social Science Journal*, 45,4 (1993), pp 517-32.

2 I do not seek to define liberal democratic values here and am particularly conscious that any listing, let alone definition of liberal democratic values will be subject to serious challenge. However, the forces of globalisation affect virtually all such listings and definitions of such liberal democratic values - or certainly any listing that would have received general acknowledgement from 1945 to 1980.

3 I have added the 'North Atlantic' prefix to indicate the importance of the ideological and, especially, institutional contributions made on this side of the Atlantic. I also do so in the hope that the heirs to the American part of the North Atlantic Enlightenment may be reminded of the values they then so gloriously trumpeted.

4 I am conscious of using such a loaded term in an area already overloaded with ideological rhetoric and cultural angst. However, the term is apt in that it emphasises the importance of the control and marginalisation of brute force, the importance of the citizen and the generation of civil society. I am open to other terms but it will do for the moment.

5 See G.M. Lyons and M. Mastanduno, 'International Intervention, State Sovereignty and the Future of International Society' (1993) 45 (4) *International Social Science Journal* 519. Such states saw themselves as part of an international community of states.

6 See A.M. Slaughter Burley and C. Kaysen, 'Introductory Note: Emerging Norms of Justified Intervention' in L.W. Reed and C. Kaysen, eds, *Emerging Norms of Justified Intervention: A Collection of Essays From A Project of the American Academy of Arts and Sciences* (Cambridge, MA: American Academy of Arts and Sciences, 1993), p 8.

7 See, in particular, T. Hobbes, *Leviathan* (London: Dent, 1973).

8 Including judicial review, freedom of information legislation, merits review tribunals, ombudsmen, investigative media and public interest litigation.

9 Political philosophy did not end its development with the US Bill of Rights and I have argued elsewhere that the thinking of the last 200 years is inadequately reflected in the kinds of rights instruments drafted by today's constitutionalists – see 'The Four Dimensions of Rights' in B. Galligan and C. Sampford, eds, *Rethinking Human Rights* (Leichhardt: Federation Press, 1997).

10 While sovereign states were conceived in, and initially seen as limited to, Western Europe, such statehood was extended to other states that could defend themselves and, after decolonisation, to all new states. See G.M. Lyons and M. Mastanduno, 'International Intervention, State Sovereignty and the Future of International Society', *International Social Science Journal*, 45,4 (1993), p 521. The traditional view was that, when states reached a certain point of development they were catapulted into statehood. See J. Chopra and T.G. Weiss, 'Sovereignty Is No Longer Sacrosanct: Codifying Humanitarian Intervention', *Ethics and International Affairs*, 6 (1992), p 107.

11 S.D. Krasner, 'Sovereignty and Intervention', in G.M. Lyons and M. Mastanduno, eds, *Beyond Westphalia? State Sovereignty and International Intervention* (Baltimore, MD: The Johns Hopkins University Press, 1995), p 233.

12 This is not the place to commence a dissertation on the various meanings (let alone interpretations, nuances, slants and ideological hectoring) of 'globalisation'.

13 P.G. Cerny, 'Globalisation and Other Stories: The Search for a New Paradigm for International Relations', *International Journal*, 4,51 (1996), p 620.

14 In their limited vision, it was 'mankind', 'man' etc. However, while the origin and causes of this limited vision are suitable causes for censure, the reinterpretation to a vision including women as well as men seems easy and uncontroversial enough.

15 This would involve examining seriatim and collectively the various techniques available for public governance (including contract, reward, punishment, direct control, budgetary or substantive approval, merits or process review) at a theoretical and practical level.

16 'Beyond the Republic: Meeting the Global Challenges to Constitutionalism' Wednesday 29th September to Friday 1st October, Heritage Hotel, Brisbane, Australia.

17 As in all things, one could be wrong. I am very aware that the EU was seen by some of its founders as a future European federation while others saw it as having more narrow goals (and a few Englishmen still think of it in narrower terms). It is possible that the idealism of global governance will prove successful and I will ruefully look back on my comments as the early musings of a global skeptic, rivaling the pronouncements of the euroskeptics. However, it is my profound impression that the world is moving beyond Westphalian strong states that suggests to me that the future does not lie in an enlarged version of the past. See also S.D. Krasner, 'Sovereignty and Intervention', in G.M. Lyons and M. Mastanduno, eds, *Beyond Westphalia? State Sovereignty and International Intervention* (Baltimore, MD: The Johns Hopkins University Press, 1995), p 235.

18 N.K. Komesar (1984), 'Taking Institutions Seriously: Introduction to a Strategy for Constitutional Analysis.' 51 *University of Chicago Law Review* 366-446.

19 Cf R. Holton, *Globalisation and the Nation State* (London: Macmillan, 1998), p 43 who believes that the values can be combined but does not advocate it.

20 I sometimes wonder if globalisation is actually shorthand for 'global destabilisation'!

21 See Sampford, 'Dworkin's Claim to a Socialist Inheritance' *Bulletin of the Australian Society of Legal Philosophy* (1991) in which I predicted that this infatuation would be very short lived.

22 Ceaucescu's regime reportedly screened old episodes of Dallas and Dynasty in the hope that they would be either harmless or would teach Rumanians the evils of capitalism. It is reported that they were the most popular shows on television and led many to fall in love with western capitalism.

23 Not only through the use of modern weapons but also modern communications (even though many of the killings in Rwanda were through the use of machetes, the genocide of the Tutsis was orchestrated by the Hutu government run radio stations).

24 And what I have called 'vulgar capitalism' - see Sampford, C. 'Dworkin's Claim to a Socialist Inheritance' *Bulletin of the Australian Society of Legal Philosophy* (1991)

25 Note that the last two sets of revolutionary ideals have been global. Global capitalism and global socialism. The failure of the latter has come to a 'revolution' in the sixteenth century sense. We need a third set of revolutionary ideals. We need to transcend socialism not retreat from it to the ideals that preceded global socialism with the faults that spawned it.

26 S.D. Krasner, 'Sovereignty and Intervention', in G.M. Lyons and M. Mastanduno, eds, *Beyond Westphalia? State Sovereignty and International Intervention* (Baltimore, MD: The Johns Hopkins University Press, 1995), p 247.

27 Though not, of course, always honoured in practice.

28 One of the most remarkable of these reactions was the successful attempt of the young Emperor Franz Josef to use non-Germans to drive out the liberal constitutionalists who had sought to offer him the crown of a constitutional pan-German monarchy.

29 Such notions are often infused with concepts of self-determination and political preference that are dependent on democratic ideals. Yet those ideals are denied by the form of government supposedly chosen or preferred.

30 For more on these points, see A.P. Rubin, *Ethics and Authority in International Law* (Cambridge: Cambridge University Press, 1997).

31 Perez de Cuella, quoted in J. Chopra and T.G. Weiss, 'Sovereignty Is No Longer Sacrosanct: Codifying Humanitarian Intervention', *Ethics and International Affairs*, 6 (1992), p 96 and G.M. Lyons and M. Mastanduno, 'International Intervention, State Sovereignty and the Future of International Society', *International Social Science Journal*, 45,4 (1993), p 522. See also United Nations Doc. A/46/1, September 6,1991, pp 10-11.

32 In my earlier work on coups, I suggested that democratic governments have clearly stated lines of authority in the case of coups to ensure that it is clear who speaks for them, even if the key leaders have been killed or imprisoned.

33 See F.J. Petersen, 'The Façade of Humanitarian Intervention for Human Rights in a Community of Sovereign Nations' 12 *Arizona Journal of International and Comparative Law* 871, (1998).

34 It would be flippant to say that the same is true of most governments anyway - so I will keep such comments to the footnotes!

35 This assumes minimum standards for fair elections. These are being formulated for UN supervised elections. These minimum standards could be developed in a number of ways:

- by developing practice in UN supervised elections,
- by international NGOs such as the Stockholm based IDEA (the International Institute for Democracy and Electoral Assistance),
- by the formation of a 'Democratic League' with rules for admission, and,

ultimately, when this principle is established in international law by international law making bodies like the UN General Assembly and by the International Court of Justice.

36 One of the first demands made of nineteenth century monarchs was that the sovereign should 'give' the people a constitution which established who had what powers.

37 See Sampford, C., 'Law, Institutions and the Public Private Divide' 20 *Federal Law Review* 185 (1992).

38 This does not deal with problems of human rights abuses by democratic states.

39 This overcomes the problem that Stephen David highlights. Although some elites in third world countries may represent little more than themselves, use state power for their own ends and interests, and have come to power by illegitimate means (including support from abroad), they have all the benefits of sovereignty, including non intervention without consent.

40 S.D. Krasner, 'Sovereignty and Intervention', in G.M. Lyons and M. Mastanduno, eds, *Beyond Westphalia? State Sovereignty and International Intervention* (Baltimore, MD: The Johns Hopkins University Press, p 231. Some would leave this as a collective right of the people. Others might like to conceive it in terms of individual rights - as a right of all persons to take part in a sovereign government, to be a part of the group to whom a government is accountable (See C. Sampford, 'The Four Dimensions of Rights and their Means of Protection', in B. Galligan and C. Sampford, eds, *Rethinking Human Rights* (Leichhardt: Federation Press, 1997). Either way the point is made that every human being on the planet has the right to participate in such a community and denying them that right is an abuse of their human rights.

41 Kidd is concerned that wider concepts of 'humanitarian intervention' would invite abuse and that would be very difficult to establish a mechanism that would not be influenced by ideological and cultural positions. Similarly, Petersen argues that all 'humanitarian' interventions have been done for other, non-humanitarian reasons. The problem is that countries generally intervene for their own purposes and that it is only by chance that those purposes will only coincide with those of the subject people (see his 'The Façade of Humanitarian Intervention for Human Rights in a Community of Sovereign Nations' 12 *Arizona Journal of International and Comparative Law* 871, (1998).

42 See my arguments to this effect ten years ago at the IVR in Scotland and published in 'Coups d'etats and Law' 13 *Bulletin of the Australian Society of Legal Philosophy* 253 (1989) as well as 'Coups d'etat and Law' in Attwooll, E. (ed.), *Shaping Revolution*, Aberdeen University Press, Aberdeen, 1991, 161.

43 Some might find similarities to the principle that the USSR used to try to run with the Warsaw Pact - once you had joined that bloc you could not get out of it. However, once you have defined the country as the people's chosen government, it is easy to see that no one other than the chosen government can get out of it.

44 L.L. Fuller, *The Morality of Law* (New Haven, CT: Yale University Press, 1977). King Rex found seven ways not to make law by forgetting seven of laws virtues. It

makes one wonder if, with respect to international law, we have a new King Rex in the White House.

45 It may be argued that it worked out OK in the end. But the question is, for whose ends? You can never overcome sovereign boundaries by discussions within your own frame of reference. If the frame of reference in which you claim to speak has universality, then there can be no harm in surrendering the conclusion to a body that is beyond your borders which is imbued with that supposedly universal truth. If not, it indicates that it is not universal or that your own judgment is clouded by issues of national self-interest.

46 I will not translate this traditional phrase into 'rule of persons' as no disrespect is done to women by failing to include them in this derided alternative to the rule of law.

47 Even if we have confidence that the policeman will not strike us, we should be terrified for those who might be - and rationally concerned that one day it *might* be us.

48 In some ways, I would have thought that the United States should be as aware of this as any nation. One of the grievances which led to its revolutionary establishment was the wider power of the British sovereign outside the realm. He was less subjected to the limitation by parliaments and courts than he was in England. It would be a pity if the United States ended up a source of one of the great problems against which their own being was a justified protest.

49 University of Queensland Department of Law Staff Seminar, 29 April 1999.

50 Hobbes and most other prominent 17th century legal and political philosophers were not very strong on accountability, indeed, he did not see it as compatible with sovereignty. However, the most important developments of enlightenment theorists were to insist on domestic accountability, first by revolution (Locke) and then by democracy.

51 R.M. Cassidy, Sovereignty Versus the Chimera of Armed Humanitarian Intervention, *The Fletcher Forum of World Affairs*, 21, 2 (1997), p 50.

52 I was tempted to say that it should be treated as an end in itself. I think I would want to say that only sentient beings could be 'ends in themselves'. The international community is an increasingly important means for supporting and enhancing human flourishing and protecting other species and should be respected for that reason alone.

53 I am not going to buy into this argument but what does not seem to be denied is that bugs were planted by Butler's men which fed raw intelligence to American agencies which passed on the information to the UN Mission. This is indefensible. The US was threatening, and did, bomb Iraq. The kind of information that might be picked up could be of enormous use. Richard Butler might believe that western intelligence agencies would not succumb to the temptation to look at it. I would have thought that most intelligence agencies felt the duty to acquire information by whatever means they could, especially where it involves no risk of detection and no risk for the personnel. If I took a straw poll in this room, I think that Richard Butler would be strongly outvoted with most considering his faith to be so ludicrous as to doubt the truthfulness of its assertion. However, the point is that this should not be left to trust. Institutions should be so arranged to minimise such temptations so that those who have less trust of intelligence agencies can have trust in the process. I have argued elsewhere that we should not try to teach people to be saints but design institutions that don't need saints to run them. When it comes to intelligence agencies, saint-training (or rather re-training) is not an option.

54 F.L. Kirgis, 'The Kosovo Situation and NATO Military Action', *American Society of International Law* (website).

55 It was foolish because the Serbs were not the only ethnic group within the former Turkish Empire that held long suppressed aspirations to recreate their own best memories of historical power- viz Greater Bulgaria, Greater Albania, not to mention Greece's desires to recreate parts of the Byzantine Empire from the fighting in Eastern Turkey to the attempt to deny Macedonia its rights to its own choice of name. This is a problem in the eastern parts of the former Turkish Empire including the Kurds, pan-Arabism, Iraq-Kuwait - not to mention the Jews hope to go back even further in history.

56 I note the claims by Kozyrus that Milosevic's original revocation of Kosovar autonomy was a response to discriminatory treatment of ethnic Serbs by the Kosovar administration which was itself a continuation of discriminatory treatment by Albanians over many years - especially those years when Kosovo was controlled by regimes hostile to the Serbs (Turks before 1911 and Italians during the war). I am in no position to evaluate these claims and the extent to which they justified this or other measures taken by Milosevic in the political maneuvering that preceded the secession of Slovenia and Croatia. We should all be wary of assuming that all guilt lay on the side of the Serbs when others had some very murky backgrounds. Of these, the most disturbing are the clear and acknowledged Ustasha influences on the Croatian secessionists. However, there are many stories about the KLA, for example claims of at least a dozen KLA officials that the then current leader, Hashim Thaci, murdered potential rival leaders (report by Chris Hedges, New York Times, June 2Sth 1999, page 1).

57 It should be noted that the Krajina Serbs moved before Croatia became independent of Yugoslavia. Given the wartime history of Croatia and the treatment of Serbs by the Nazi backed Ustasha, no one should be surprised that the local Serbs were worried about being ruled by a new Croation government that embraced the symbols of the Ustasha and was established at the insistence of the German government against opposition by the Americans.

58 When I put this point of view to a senior British diplomat, he heartily agreed and added that this would only have happened in the two years between the fall of the Berlin Wall and the realisation that taking on the East was a major task even for the rejuvenated Germany.

59 D.G. Haglund and O. Mager, 'Bound to Leave? The Future of the NATO Stationing Regime in Germany', in D. Dewitt, D. Haglund and J. Kirton, eds, *Building A New Global Order* (Oxford: Oxford University Press, 1993), p 315.

60 Source to Kissinger.

61 This was a common feature of American military practice in Vietnam where civilian populations were forcibly removed to new areas and the areas vacated treated as a free-fire zone.

62 Jacques Chirac, quoted by D. Rieff, *Newsweek*, June 14th 1999, p 39.

63 D. Rieff, *Newsweek*, June 14th 1999, p 39.

64 This was the reason why Yugoslavia attempted to argue that the use of force against it amounted to genocide: as a matter of international law it is unnecessary to argue that external aggression without UNSC authority is genocide but they hoped to attract jurisdiction by so arguing.

65 F.L. Kirgis, 'The Kosovo Situation and NATO Military Action', *American Society of International Law* (website).

66 This was reported by Martin Walker on Lateline (ABC TV) on June 8th 1999 and also repeated on June 17th on CNN.

67 For example, Professor Bruno Simma in the European Journal of International Law, May 1999.

68 See F.J. Petersen, 'The Façade of Humanitarian Intervention for Human Rights in a Community of Sovereign Nations', 12 *Arizona Journal of International and Comparative Law* 871, (1998) at p 877.

69 Unlike article 39; article 51 is far more specific. It refers to 'an armed attack ...against a Member of the United Nations'.

70 See 'Lawyer Sam's War' The Economist, April 24th 1999, p 38 and 'Legal Scholars Support Case for Using Force', *New York Times* on 27th March 1999.

71 Given the concerns about the misuse of mandates by the US, this concern would be even more appropriate.

72 As Vyacheslav Nikonov argued on CNN, the best solution would be to have neutral countries that were not part of the conflict to be the peacekeepers.

73 Although Dag Hammerskold had initially demanded complete independence by peacekeepers, Bhoutros Bhoutros-Ghali abandoned the requirement as difficult to achieve in practice (everyone has a history and most societies have cultural sympathies, so no one is really completely neutral) and there are arguments that some cultural understanding may actually improve the work of peacekeepers.

74 The Author of *Catch* 22.

75 The functions were set out in paragraph 9.

76 Given that the UK and USA had shown complete contempt for the lawful role of the UNSC, they may have had good reason to fear that the Secretary General might have more confidence in a military commander who was not from a belligerent nation.

77 The move by the Russians to rush into Pristina airport was criticized in the West as an act of hostility and the Russians acting on their own. However, from the point of view of the Russians, NATO had been acting on its own without reference to the UNSC for three months. Now that there was a UNSC resolution, which clearly included a Russian role, NATO seemed to be trying to cut the Russians out of it by stalling on an agreement on where the Russians would be. It is not as if there had not been enough time to consider this matter. The mixed force had been agreed for more than a month.

78 Given some of the statements of NATO leaders during the conflict, it would be easy to assume that they might be tempted to breach this element of the agreement.

79 President Clinton persists in supporting Yeltsin despite the fact that the parliamentarians who were opposed to Yeltsin were not merely the appointed communist rump but also a majority of the democratically elected representatives.

80 Where the country concerned does not accept the jurisdiction of the ICJ, the authorisation is invalid and of no effect. with regard to the ICC, the Security Council can submit a matter directly to the court.

81 In the case of Proclamations, it was held that the King could not legislate by himself, and it was held that the king could not sit as a judge.

82 The US Supreme Court under Chief Justice Earl Warren.

83 As already argued these constraints may well have been considerable considering the relatively low number of total deaths in the two years preceding the bombing.

84 Professor Roger Hayden is Director of the Centre for Russian and East European Studies at the University of Pittsburgh.

85 See F. Zakaria, *Newsweek,* June 14th 1999, p 25.

86 See also A.P. Rubin, *Ethics and Authority in International Law* (Cambridge: Cambridge University Press, 1997.

87 I am attracted to the slogan: 'no more trade agreements until US is prepared to be bound by the ICJ'.

88 See F. Zakaria, *Newsweek*, June 14th 1999, p 25.

89 See M. Whiteman, *Digest of International Law*, Vol. 12, pp 204-15 (1971); O. Schachter (1984) 82 *Michigan Law Review*, p 1629; *British Year Book of International Law*, Volume 57 (1986), p 614; Y. Dinstein (1988) War, *Aggression and Self-Defence* CUP, p 89; Randelzhofer (1994), *The Charter of the United Nations, A Commentary*, OUP, pp 123-4; B. Simma (1999), 10, *European Journal of International Law.*

90 *Advisory Opinions Case* (1920), CLR.

91 The other argument, that the giving of legal advice is essentially an executive, rather than a judicial, function needs far more argument than can be properly adduced here. One must beware of overly simplistic three way separation of powers which are almost always belied by the uncertainties of definition and the fact that all judiciaries play some executive roles (e.g., the swearing in of presidents or the management of court buildings). The constitutional arguments will vary from country to country as do the natures of the courts.

92 The Geneva Convention on the treatment of prisoners of war may well protect them from prosecution as such, but it does not dignify the action.

93 War and Our World, The Reith Lectures, Hutchinson, London, 1998.

17. State Sovereignty, the Common Good and International Intervention

R.A. AKANMIDU

The general outlook of events in the world shows instances of tumult within nations, which the world cannot ignore. This tumult emanates from different sources but the cases of linguistic and cultural polyglots are the more susceptible to situations of tumult. The deeply entrenched components of human social behavior orchestrate the feelings of showing concern one for another in spite of the constraints of differing nationalities.

From a strictly theoretical perspective, the fact of our differing nationalities also gave way to world's political civilization within which the international community grants recognition of sovereignty to all member nations. This recognition requires that "nations do not intervene in the domestic activity of established governments and that they do not attempt to undermine them or otherwise work for their abolition".[1] While tracing the development of this concept in the terrains of history and international relations, this recognition has influenced among nations the belief in absolute self-dependence invulnerable to external interventions.

The practical difficulty of accepting the doctrine of sovereignty in its absolute terms takes source from the polarization of world's problems, practical interests of nations and the sharing tendencies among them. These represent the impressions inherent in the concept of globalization: that humanity is transiting to a global society. Sovereignty provides an ordering principle for what is internal to States and what is 'external' to them. As Giddens puts it, "a State cannot become sovereign except within a system of other sovereign States, its sovereignty being acknowledged by them, in this there is a strong pressure towards mutual recognition as equals whatever the factual situation in respect of differential power".[2] The concept of sovereignty is unyielding to other meaning when particularly understood from relational profile between nations. The views of Morgenthau, Aron, Maritain, Benn to name but a few, only help to give conceptual strength to Giddens' view.[3]

The objective of this work is to show how the challenges of globalization sustain the integrity of State sovereignty and justify the imperative of intervention on grounds of common good. The relevance of this objective cannot be over-emphasized at a time when some national leaders are caught in a tide of using the instrument of sovereignty to create internal trauma to destabilize global common good. The adopted approach is to begin from the critical to the analytical assessment to establish the integrity of sovereignty through its nature, the inviolability of State sovereignty, globalization and common good and the status of State sovereignty on occasions of intervention.

The Nature of State Sovereignty

The drift to globalization has given new thinking to the concept of sovereignty without having to jettison any aspect of the integrity of the concept. The integrity of the concept is the ultimate legal authority of government, dominion, over a territory and the recognition of these privileges and rights by other nation-states. As Elfstrom puts it "[state] sovereignty entails being recognized as the international representative of the people of a given area, authorized to articulate and press their interests, to speak for them".[4]

The understanding of the integrity of State's sovereignty entails what a people represents in terms of what they are and as they are in themselves to what they are not only as they understand themselves but also the way others know them and understand them. To this extent, sovereignty of States encompasses the *noumenon* (what they are in themselves) and the *phenomenon* (what they are in appearance). The *noumenon* and the *phenomenon* combine to precipitate the understanding of "other's recognition". Therefore, in practice, State sovereignty by nature, is not self-conferred but rather from "other's recognition". Hence, the legitimacy of State sovereignty is inherent in "other's recognition".

The rhetoric of diplomacy notwithstanding, "other's recognition" translates into legality which in turn provides the basis for rights claim by the sovereign nation-state. The legality factor in which claim of rights is embedded forms the basis for equality between nation-states their size, military strength and level of affluence or poverty notwithstanding. This element draws attention to the general principle that nation-states do not intervene in the domestic activity of established sovereign States. Apparently, the concept of sovereignty among nations, by nature, precipitates the basis for equality between world nations both in concept and practice.

Rules of "other's recognition" from the analytic perspective, clearly denies self-conferment of sovereignty by States but it does not represent the mechanism of nurturing. The State has the responsibility of nurturing the status of its sovereignty en route internal mechanism. The way any State can nurture its status of sovereignty by means of internal mechanism is by maintaining peace within its borders politically, economically and socially. When a sovereign State is enmeshed in disputes and conflicts, the factor of "other's recognition" is depressed. Although this form of *status quo* does not undermine State's sovereignty because depressed sovereignty is not sovereignty dissolved. Nevertheless, a depressed sovereignty is both a local and foreign concern.

This aspect of sovereignty as it relates to nation-states has given it novel identity. It is part of the new understanding of the concept of sovereignty which confirms the dimension in which globalization has affected the nature of State sovereignty. It is to this extent that globalization current understanding has reduced state sovereignty to mere State identity. This point will appear in a more definitive way as we proceed in this work.

The Inviolability of State Sovereignty

As the above points intimate, the internalist's concept of sovereignty include reference to the broad perception that it does not point beyond the nation-state. This broad perception undoubtedly spells a misunderstanding because the authority of the State is not insulated without effects on the long-term well-being of the citizens and also that the rule of "other's recognition" is incompatible with the internalist's concept. This rule of "other's recognition" suggests that the complexity of power relations stretches beyond the State.

Edmund's political foresight has interpretation in this complexity when he says that, "the question was posed whether the international community as a whole is not the true holder of sovereignty rather than the individual States".[5]

It is noted that there is a conscious effort to adhere to the postulates of the principle of sovereignty; that each nation-state has autonomy built into political will that has understanding in supreme authority. The adherence to this thinking aggravates the general principle of the inviolability of State sovereignty. Much of what influences the idea of inviolability of State sovereignty relate to the theory of "state solipsism" in which only self can be shown to exist. The external world, in this regard, is merely an idea based on constructions devised by self.

It is plain that the coherence of economic, political and social ties has steadily changed the world that nation-states have personality and integrity so much that sovereign prerogatives in matters of state policies have cross-border implications. As Elfstrom correctly pointed out, "the world has been faced with instances of tumult within nations which it is unable to ignore, either because their scale demands international attention or because the larger community has willy-nilly, become caught up in essentially domestic conflicts".[6] It is to this extent that the world has moved beyond "State solipsism" to "State personalism" in which value is placed on the policies of nation-states with full recognition of the texture of leadership.

From the background such as we have given so far, the inviolability of State sovereignty hinges heavily on the internalist's perception. This perception has significant illustrations in equality and autonomy factors. The equality factor is estimated from the perspective of status that has no reference to size and wealth of the State. Apparently, the equality factor is a package in "other's recognition" and essentially assumed in the recognition. The autonomy factor speaks to State responsibility, freedom to be self-influenced free from external dictates and the wherewithal to act as deem fit. The factors of equality and autonomy do not doubt the sovereignty status of States rather they confirm formal recognition and give strength to the expectations that internal policies of each State should defend this status.

Therefore, State sovereignty carries the prospects of responsibility and deliverance from any form of humiliation such that can discredit the status. To this extent, sovereignty as it relates to States is finding meaning in internal policies, devoid of isolationism that have place in international solidarity. We shall proceed to illustrate the relationship of the internalist perception of sovereignty within the framework of common good and globalization.

Common Good and Globalization

As the above on the internalist perception of sovereignty intimates, the workings of politics within the nation offer little beyond national boundaries. The usual target in this form of political model is the effort to define certain political policies formalized in the context of foreign policies. Foreign policies are defined political positions that promote national interests inherent in the discourse of nationalism and statism. Indeed, global modeling is not a hall-mark of foreign policies.

What seems to matter is that there is no intention to disregard the concept of common good in foreign policy issues. This intention rests principally on the perception that common good is assumed in the life of a nation or State in the sense that it is seen as the object of rationality and so it is the real good of each individual. As Raphael sees it;

> The common good is taken to be the aim of moral volition and the general will is the will that each man has as a citizen or moral agent, not the sum of particular wants each has as a non-moral individual thinking of his own interests in isolation from the interests of others.[7]

The idea of common good, as can be seen in Raphael's view, begins as a set of values that collectively pursue general interest that further public order of the community. Apparently, common good from Nardin's analysis "can be specified as having to do above all with peace, justice, protected liberty and guaranteed rights...for the education of the members of the community and for certain minimum standards of well-being".[8]

As the concept of "common good" shows above, it transcends individual interests but still protects it in a broader form since all individual interests are integrated into it. Common good has understanding in domestic jurisdiction as it docs in international jurisdiction. The restrictive domestic understanding of common good is equally tenable in the broader global terrain. It follows that common good has the same understanding both in the restrictive and global forms. Apparently, the widening terrain beyond the restrictive pursues the same values of justice, peace, security and coexistence, which are also plausible in the restrictive form.

With all of the above, it is worth noting that the tendency of national development to global community only goes by shifting and not by alteration of meaning as the contemporary understanding attempts to suggest "globalization" rather than "common good". Globalization processes, in Waterman's words, "imply that hegemony no longer rests in a single territorial site (national, regional, block) any more than it rests with a single subject (international capitalist class) on a primary determinant (economic, military) or level (the state-national)".[9]

It is especially noteworthy that the conceptual compatibilities as shown above in Waterman's view, that exist between "common good" and "globalization" lend credence to the view that the term "common good" is an approximate meaning of globalization. The upsurge to modernity transforms "common good" to globalization to enhance an understanding that moves with contemporary thinking. Apparently, the concept of globalization is extrapolating from existing idea of common good building in a new dimension of thinking, a new consciousness that humanity belong together, that we are citizens of this world regardless of which country we may belong to, which religion and which sex.

Hence, the evolving global society is seen to be responding to the same exigencies and vulnerabilities that all humanity must live with, sharing together the success of technological breakthroughs and also sharing the consequences of political misadventure, violence and their aftermath. This experience is unavoidable since the increasing sustenance of "common good" in the global society creates a real universal world allowing for universalism that goes beyond mere imagined community but real solidarity that compels sharing together necessities for mutual development pointing beyond extra-territorial identities.

Since we live in a world in which humanity is threatened by all sorts of cultural political, economic, and religious conflicts in a structure of interconnected interests, common good illustrates the promotion, and sharing of values of justice, peace, security and mutual coexistence. Thus, where there are political responsibilities that create a basis for insecurity in one nation, the general "principle of sharing" that is a hall-mark of common good will make isolationism impracticable. Apparently, common good bolsters international interdependence among nations and renders the division of mankind into States increasingly irrelevant with respect to judgments on matters about justice, peace, security and mutual coexistence in world affairs.

This linkage notwithstanding, the relevance of nations and nation-states can be seen both theoretically and practically and to that extent the claim to sovereignty. Elstrom pointed out that nation-states "are important theoretically because they are the basic structures of human political order (and practically) because their existence serves to define the issues of the ethics of international relations".[10] Interestingly, there is no reason why the values of common good that transcend national boundaries cannot be discussed within the framework of national sovereignty. In other words, nation-states still hold to their sovereignty to claim their identity and simultaneously take note that modernization confirms international interdependence.

As this context suggests, the system that promotes common good does not have to dispense with national sovereignty. The sensitivity of this context has increasingly shown itself in the relations between nation-states of the twentieth century. Sometimes nation-states show glaring failure in their moral responsibilities in the upholding of the values of common good and even refuse to show respect to such values and as well seem to disregard the implications of such failure on global interests. This is illustrative of the core issue inherent in this work. The inevitable decline in the values of justice, peace, security and mutual coexistence are too glaring to ignore when under the protection of sovereignty nation-states destabilize the values of common good affecting the global terrain.

This issue points to some constraints on whether intervention, with the aim of restoring the values of common good, is justified. It is in the light of this point that the status of State sovereignty is assessed against the backdrop of international intervention.

Status of State Sovereignty and Intervention

In a case in which international society is identified as an association of nation-states with respect to the general authoritative consensus of common practices and the sharing of experience, the factor of sovereignty is of some relevance. This relevance is in the purview of international morality and in the context of mutual respect, liberty and freedom of each nation-state, and independence as political units. It is in this sense that Nardin explains that the role of international law "seeks to protect the liberty of a people to govern itself according to its own laws and traditions".[11]

The ethics of international relations is characterized with universalism on grounds of mutual interests capable of upholding and recognizing individual differences associated with disparate backgrounds but forming political understanding that promotes common will, good or interest. This characterization is coherent with "other's recognition" as shown in the concept of sovereignty and there is no international law that exist in negation to this position. Sovereignty, as it relates to States, depicts autonomy not transferable analogous to independence, a political shield for identity and an emblem of political entitlements for States.

On this view, sovereignty and individual rights is vulnerable to threats and threats can lead to violation and not to seizure because the strength of state sovereignty is acknowledged in "other's recognition" (i.e. in the recognition of other States). The "rule of recognition" in this context is beyond acknowledgement and identity, it stretches to the protection of convergent interests that have explanation both politically and economically. These interests are of variant forms that speak to the reality that no nation can claim self-sufficiency in these divergences.

It is therefore widely recognized that for big and or small reasons nations need each other to sustain their sovereignty. The task of this work is to lay the foundation of the credibility of the need for one another to sustain the concept of common good in our understanding of global or international society. As Elfstrom correctly pointed out in these words:

> The forces that bring the world closer also magnify the potential for doing well and doing ill. In the past it was easy to remain ignorant of distant suffering and even easier to remain indifferent to it. Yet, though the earth now touches more closely, old ideas of moral responsibility and moral accountability remain.[12]

Surely, scholars who are prone to insist that closeness on earth is a reality are also prone to accept the view that pressures, which sustain the closeness, are facilitated by common good. Apparently, common good as we have repeatedly pointed out above represents a convergence of interests, which imposes on humanity the unavoidable sharing from necessities of and expediencies of existence. The reality of the present world situation is that the nation where one lives determines the political process that sharpens the living profile of the individual but the living profiles of others in the nations do have rippling effects on this living profile. This tendency becomes increasingly apparent as the society of States shares unavoidably from experiences of other States. It has been pointed out by Nardin that;

> The rights of political sovereignty and territorial integrity are not absolute either. The limits of sovereignty on the one hand and of intervention on the other are determined by the standard of international law and morality, and these include an international relation between a government and its own subjects may be judged.[13]

The limitation of State's right of political sovereignty and territorial integrity depend on two major points; namely, cases in which "a government sets out to massacre a number of its own subjects" and the "international minimum standard" regarding the treatment of aliens. These two reasons have, from all indications, come to congeal clearer in human rights matters. Again, these points derive from political accounts, which do not have explanations in the interests that common good promotes in the global society.

It is apparent that all these considerations merit further attention. To this end, this paper is an attempt to broaden on the justification of the limits of State's rights of political sovereignty. Our line of argument follows the construction of a theoretical foundation upon which the justifications are established. This theory is drawn from the distinctive and complex character that governs the sharing principle among States. The complexity of this character is in the context of having a share from other's troubles and successes devoid of alternative option. To be consistent with our discourse above, this theory is rippling and from the mere fact that this is the case, we shall build our justification arguments on the "rippling theory" framework. Let us define the "rippling theory more precisely as follows;

> The consequences of tensions (political, economic, etc) in nation-states are encumbered with intra and international characterizations, which are not agent-specific but agent-general.

At various points above, we have alluded to the view that the strength of the pursuance of common good has introduced a strong tendency for humanity to share from extra-territorial activities whatever forms these take. This reveals in important way humanity's vulnerability to some real and disturbing cases resulting from the behavior of others. It is on account of the weight of other's actions on others, that action of international intervention remains impartial to State sovereignty not only as a political value but as a virtue which is still respected in spite of intervention. Perhaps, it is this sense that Elfstrom contends that "sovereignty overridden is not sovereignty dissolved".[14]

This idea needs some refinement on the basic notion that sovereignty violated is not sovereignty denied. All too often, the significance of the principle of sharing that may not be acceptable but unavoidable by nations justifies the triumph of intervention under the aegis of common good. This justification is three-dimensional; namely, the restorative, reductive and rectification dimensions.

The first justification argument builds on the larger moral framework on which State's political sovereignty is established. This moral framework has interpretation or understanding in what a sovereign State presupposes; the responsibility to determine the course of justice and the defense of fairness in this regard and act in pursuance of the well-being of the citizenry. The whole point on State sovereignty hinges on the detraction of hostilities, avoidance of absurdities within the internal political framework of a nation-state. Thus, the sustenance of justice, peace and well-being of the citizenry is a necessary method of acknowledging the political sovereignty of nation-states. As this view shows, the contemplation of intervention in whatever form is most inappropriate.

Instances in which these goals are not achieved and the realities are that of violent assault by brutal political leaders in a situation of global interest (common good) coupled with the inevitability of rippling theoretical position, state sovereignty becomes an epitome of absurdity and of pain. By this view, the focal point or principle defended in the restorative thesis is that the authenticity and identification of the sovereignty of a nation-state are in "other's recognition" and when this recognition is in disarray or disordered, external intervention measures to restore orderliness is justified. Hence, a sovereign nation-state that is carrying and perpetuating pain is plainly threatening international peace. It is the meeting point between the carriage and perpetuation of pain and rippling theoretical position that restorative thesis is built as our first argument on the justification of international intervention.

From the consideration highlighted above, intervention is justified on grounds of restoration of sanity and for the integration of peaceful arrangement correcting political derailment. To this extent, the restoration of sanity through intervention is not a distortion of state sovereignty; rather, it is a confirmation of it.

A great deal of attention has been given to the general characteristic of emergent problems in the 20th century that always first have national outlook and gradually cumulate and subsequently assume international outlook. Events in different parts of the world with unintended consequences are known to be extra-territorial. These consequences loom much larger when national autonomy that is a hall-mark of State sovereignty is given credit in "other's recognition" under this kind of situation.

When legitimacy is understood in this way, it is often known that consequences of political violence always undermine or disrupt the ways of life of distant peoples. This point becomes much more pertinent in a global society of intertwined interests. The violent political activities of sovereign states are extra-territorial in characterization and consequently mortgaging the peace of the common good. It is from this consideration that the focal principle of reductive thesis states that the control of consequences of violence is more in peace talks than in practice and sharing of consequences of violence is inevitable between nations therefore international intervention is prevention of widespread pains among nations.

In this thesis, there is a contingent connection between the legitimacy and sustenance of State sovereignty, since there is no denial of sovereignty in this mode of intervention. International intervention, in this regard, enforces the entitlement to retain sovereignty for the protection of global common *good* that *ab initio* serves the general interests of the global society.

The key inherent principle in state sovereignty advocates for non-interference in the internal affairs of any sovereign State, though its leaders, should engage in political obligations that are unproblematic to the mutual existence of the collectivities of all sovereign nations.

The whole idea of internal affairs has explanation in autonomy in decision making of nations; the non-imposition of policies by external powers the freedom to determine interests that favor State propagation in pursuit of self-confirmation and sustenance. Apparently, a sovereign nation is expected to confirm its sovereignty on the cohesiveness and sustainable internal policies. Internal policies are representative of internal affairs and internal affairs are defenders of State sovereignty.

To this extent, sovereignty is in itself unstable when internal affairs policies obstruct the peace, justice and security of a sovereign State. When the idea of internal affairs that are so much in the heart of State sovereignty are unstable, violence sets in and the political values of sovereignty itself suffer right in the heart of the nation. In this way, a sovereign nation that has no control over its sustainability cannot have full respect in "other's recognition". Where it is apparent that this *status quo* has become a political standard of conduct, there cannot be any cohesiveness in such a nation. The sovereignty of a nation is pertinently a flexible attribute under constant surveillance of internal policies of nations. It follows from all these points that the claim of sovereignty by States or nations should be a condition of stable internal policies. Further to this, it is always reasonable to concede to the view that sovereign nations that have stable internal policies are naturally immune to external aggression.

In the light of all these, the justification of international intervention from the "rectification thesis" standpoint speaks of the betrayal of good governance *en route* the implementation of bad internal policies of sovereign States. This point is well expressed in "rectification thesis" as follows; the principles of State sovereignty presume good governance unyielding to violence and when the reverse obtains international intervention is rectification of threatened sovereignty of the State.

On account of these theses, international intervention is not a political action that is partial to the claim of sovereignty by States, rather, it is a political action that seeks for normalcy in States that their autonomy is under threat or pressure of derailment. Therefore the sovereignty of States whose internal policies elicit violence are nevertheless entitled to the claim of sovereignty but not to the sustenance of it. Hence, international intervention, political intimidation apart, is no denial of sovereignty of States, it is to strengthen the rights of sovereign States as members of global political community.

Conclusion

The larger part of the political experience in the 20th century witnessed a situation of consistent disloyalty to the values of justice, peace and security by sovereign nation-states. This disloyalty has survived under the claim of sovereignty by world's nations. Much of what had influenced the choice of using sovereignty as a shield to perpetuate vices by some nation-states derived from internal policies that disrespect values that are common among humanity coupled with the persuasion that there are no existing argumentative parameters on which intervention can be justified.

At the tail end of the millennium, there is a strong drive towards a world system that is characterized with a convergence of interests among nations. This convergence of interests is bound to increase the level of intimacy among them while showing in clear terms that the problems of one nation has threatening influence on global common good.

For the 21st century, sovereignty as a political virtue will not be inviolable and its inviolability is for its sake and a protest against tyrannical States that seek only to respect jurisdictions and not values. The arguments in this work hinge on the unavoidability of the sharing principle among nation-states in a world that promotes global common good. The restorative, reductive and rectification theses rest on this fact of global common good for the justification of international intervention among sovereign nation-states.

Notes

1 Gerard Elfstrom. *Ethics for a Shrinking World*. London: The Macmillan Press Ltd.1990, p.86.

2 Anthony Giddens. *The Nation-States and Violence*. Cambridge: Polity Press, 1985. p.282.

3 See H.J. Morgenthau *Politics Among Nations*. New York: Knopf 1960, p.328; Raymaond Aron, *Peace and War*. Malabur: Krieger 1981, p.738; Jacques Maritain, 'The Concept of Sovereignty' in W.J. Stankiewicz (ed.) *In Defense of Sovereignty*. New York: Oxford University Press, p.51; Stanley I. Benn, 'The Uses of 'Sovereignty' in W.J. Stankiewicz (ed.) *In Defense of Sovereignty*, p.77.

4 Gerard Elfstrom. *Ethics for a Shrinking World*, p.90.

5 Sterling E. Edmunds. *The Lawless Law of Nations*. Washington, DC: Byrne & Com. 1925, p.80.

6 Gerard Elfstrom. *Ethics for a Shrinking World*, pp.87-88.

7 D.D. Raphael. *Problems of Political Philosophy*. London: The Macmillan Press Ltd., 1981, p.99.

8 Terry Nardin. *Law, Morality, and the Relations of States*. Princeton: University Press, 1983, p.17.

9 Peter Waterman. *Globalization, Civil society, Solidarity*. The Hague: Institute of Social Studies Working Paper series No 147. 1993, pp. 1, and 4.
10 Gerard Elfstrom. *Ethics for a Shrinking World*, p.273.
11 Terry Nardin. *Law, Morality, and the Relations of States*, p.237.
12 Gerard Elfstrom. *Ethics for a Shrinking World*, p.3.
13 Terry Nardin. *Law, Morality, and the Relations of States*, p.287.
14 Gerard Elfstrom. *Ethics for a Shrinking World*, p.120.

Part V
Global Justice

18. Nation-Building and Global Justice

KOK-CHOR TAN

Some liberals have argued that as part of its nation-building goals, the liberal state may rightly regulate immigration. For example, Will Kymlicka writes: "the existing use of boundaries to define and protect distinct national languages, cultures and identities is not inherently in conflict with liberal egalitarian values" (Kymlicka 1999a ms 33). But given the grossly unequal distribution of wealth and resources between states, Kymlicka emphasizes that this right of a state to restrict admissions is conditional on its fulfilling its obligations of global justice. "If countries are unwilling to share their wealth in this way, then I think they forfeit the right to restrict admission into their borders" (ibid. ms 34). Similarly, Yael Tamir notes that "[l]iberal nationalism ...implies that it is justified for a nation to seek homogeneity by restricting immigration only if it has fulfilled its global obligation to assure equality among all nations" (Tamir, p. 161). To force this thesis into a maxim: states may use their borders to keep people out, but not to keep resources in.

But can one consistently hold that the liberal state may engage in nation-building, including restricting immigration for this purpose, while holding simultaneously that it may not hoard more than its fair share of resources and wealth within its borders? After all, there have been various objections to global distributive justice on account of nationality. For example, some have argued that national self-determination implies that nation-states have a sovereign right over resources in their borders, and hence any "outward" redistribution of such resources is at their discretion (e.g., Miller pp. 103-108); others have argued that justice depends on shared meanings and understandings of common goods which are not available outside the context of a national community (Walzer 1983); and yet others have said that justice presupposes existing shared institutional schemes and these are nonexistent beyond the borders of a nation-state (e.g., Walzer 1983, Sandel 1996). These objections, however, have received much attention in the literature, and I will not pursue them here.[1]

What I wish to focus on, instead, is a particular nationalist objection to global justice that has come to receive some attention in the recent literature. This is the claim that among the central features of nationality is the belief that the interests of co-nationals have greater priority over those of strangers, that co-nationals have specials claims on each other that outsiders do not. As David Miller puts it, "In acknowledging a national identity, I am also acknowledging that I owe a special obligation to fellow members which I do not owe to other human beings" (p. 49). On this view, "there is no general obligation to help poorer states"; a Rawlsian second principle, for instance, would be ruled out as a global principle (ibid. p. 108).

If this claim about nationality is correct, then liberal nationalism and the cosmopolitan aspiration of global justice are fundamentally at odds. Members of rich countries not only may use their borders to restrict the entry of needy foreigners in the name of nation-building, but they may also restrict the transfer of resources to poorer countries in the name of conational priority. The hope then that liberal nationalism in our world could be legitimate would be baseless, and liberals would find themselves in a real bind: either they concede the illegitimacy of nation-building; or they renounce the universalism of liberal equality. It is for this reason that Bhikhu Parekh thinks that "[t]o assert that 'healthy' nationalism need not be anti-internationalist is to be naive in the extreme" (Parekh p. 317).

Must liberal nationalism entail the thesis that co-nationals take priority? Or, can the liberal nationalist have it both ways: be a nationalist while remaining an egalitarian internationalist? I wish to explore this question.

Liberal Cosmopolitanism

Liberalism is commonly regarded as an individualist political morality in that it takes the individual to be the ultimate unit of moral worth and concern, and that she is entitled to equal respect and concern. It is in this sense that liberalism can be said to be fundamentally a cosmopolitan political morality.[2] But it is important to get clear on what liberal cosmopolitanism entails, and what it need not entail. Following Charles Beitz, I think it will be useful to draw a distinction between institutional cosmopolitanism and moral cosmopolitanism. Institutional cosmopolitanism pertains "to the way the world's political institutions should be set up"; it holds that an ideal global political order is one in which state boundaries and membership do not carry the same moral or political weight as they currently do (Beitz 1999b p. 287). A democratic world government or global state would be the exemplary manifestation of institutional cosmopolitanism. Moral cosmopolitanism, on the other hand, is the idea that the individual is the ultimate unit of moral worth and concern, and how we ought to act or what kinds of institutions we ought to establish "should be based on an impartial consideration of the claims of each person who would be affected" by our choices, irrespective of her citizenship, nationality and other socially contingent factors about her (ibid). Put simply, moral cosmopolitanism is concerned, not with *institutions* as such, but with the *justificatory* basis of institutions (ibid).

It should be clear that there is no necessary connection between moral cosmopolitanism and institutional cosmopolitanism. A moral cosmopolitan could argue, for example, that a world order structured around nation-states is one in which cosmopolitan moral ideals are most effectively realized (e.g., Goodin). So, while institutional cosmopolitanism would be quite straightforwardly at odds with the notion of nation-building, nothing about moral cosmopolitanism itself is inconsistent with this idea.[3]

So, liberalism, commonly understood, is cosmopolitan in at least the *moral* sense. Whether liberalism entails institutional cosmopolitan is not an issue I will get into here. I shall start from the premise of liberal nation-building, and ask whether this is compatible with the moral cosmopolitan ideals of global justice.[4]

Liberal Nation-Building

In his defense of nationality, David Miller argues that democratic politics "are likely to function most effectively when they embrace just a single national community" (p. 90). This is because the virtues of mutual trust and respect, moderation and self-restraint, to which one may add the ideal of public reason (Rawls 1993), are crucial for a functioning democratic political community; and common nationality provides the catalyst for engendering and nurturing these virtues. As well, the ideals of distributive justice presuppose a community in which "members recognize such obligations of justice to one another" (Miller p. 93). In other words, "[w]here citizens of a state are also compatriots [i.e., co-nationals], the mutual trust that this engenders makes it more likely that they will be able to solve collective action problems, to support redistributive principles of justice, and to practice deliberative forms of democracy" (Miller p. 98).

Traditionally, it has been thought that liberalism and nationalism are antithetical ideals; and to the extent that liberal democracy and liberal egalitarianism must presuppose an underlying national community, liberalism is doomed to failure in the eyes of its critics (e.g., MacIntyre, Sandel 1992).

However, an increasing number of liberal theorists are coming to accept that some sense of shared identity is required to sustain liberal democratic institutions, and that this may call for more than (pace Habermas) an allegiance to shared political values and principles (Kymlicka 1995, McMahan, Yack). They acknowledge that the liberal democratic state must be undergirded by a common national community; and to inculcate and foster this common nationality, the liberal state has to engage in some form of nation-building (Kymlicka 1999a, Tamir). The state may thus adopt certain policies to integrate all citizens into what Kymlicka has called a societal culture - i.e., a set of public and social institutions operating with a common language (Kymlicka 1999a, 1995).

Moreover, liberal nationalists claim that nationality provides the moral precondition for individual autonomy, by providing the cultural context of choice within which individuals form, pursue and revise their conceptions of the good life; and within which they also acquire their sense of identity and belonging (Kymlicka 1989, 1995; Margalit and Raz; Tamir).

Briefly put then, liberal nation-building, it is argued, serves the three core liberal ideals of autonomy, democracy, and social justice (Kymlicka 1999a). It is in the context of a national community that these liberal values can be best and most fully realized.

The above sketch of liberal nationalism is, of course, not endorsed by all liberals. But let us assume for the purpose of this discussion that liberal nation-building is an important and essential liberal good for the reasons offered above, and that it is to this end of cultivating a common nationality that liberal states may regulate immigration, along side other nation-building policies. The question I want to ask is whether this project of nation-building is consistent with the cosmopolitan ideals of global justice.[5]

Nationality and Individual Autonomy

As mentioned, it is commonly held that part of what it means to belong to a nation, a "morality of community" (Tamir), is the recognition that fellow members have special claims on us, that we may (or are even required to) privilege their needs over those of strangers. As Parekh writes, "The nationalist privileges the moral claims of one's fellow nationals and assigns only a limited moral weight to those of outsiders" (p. 316). This doctrine of conational priority is one commonly cited reason for doubting the compatibility of nationalism and global justice.

But does nationality entail giving priority to the interests of co-nationals? In particular, is *liberal* nationalism tied to this priority doctrine? To answer this question, perhaps it will be helpful to proceed by recalling the different goals of liberal nation-building, and examine whether the successful pursuit of these goals depends on conational partiality.

Consider first, then, the goal of securing the cultural context of choice for individual autonomy and the basis of individual identity. If it is right that a person's national institutions, practices and traditions serve as the cultural framework within which she meaningfully forms, pursues and revises her conceptions of the good, then it follows quite plainly that liberal nationalism has to promote and foster a *particular* national or societal culture. Liberal nationalism is openly premised on the basic idea that individuals have certain predispositions or inclinations towards their own national culture: their own national culture, and not another, gives their choices meaning; their nationality, but not another, provides the basis of their identity.

Thus liberal nation-building is unavoidably biased in a sense: it aims to engender and promote a given national culture for the benefit of its adherents. It helps secure for members of a nation access to that nation's cultural resources, without doing the same for non-nationals outside its borders.

But nothing about privileging co-nationals' access to their nation's cultural resources entails prejudicial attitudes or hostility towards other nations. The liberal nationalist can accept that the cultural institutions of other nations are as valuable to their respective members, as her own institutions are to her; and that other states are as entitled to promote their own national cultures as her own state is.[6] But more to the point, such partiality is not antithetical to the aspirations of global justice: nothing in the privileging of co-nationals' access to a cultural context is incompatible with the demands for global equality. These are two very different and independent goals.

A more problematic form of co-national partiality is that which wants to privilege co-nationals' access to material resources as well. It is conational partiality in this sense - that of privileging their access to the primary goods (if we like) of income and wealth - that poses a serious obstacle to global equality; and it is co-national partiality in this sense that is specifically at issue in debates about national partiality and global justice.

But must liberal nationalism require or rest on this form of conational partiality? More precisely, does the promoting of the national cultural context of choice require the liberal state to privilege co-nationals' access to material resources, over that of non-nationals? It seems far from clear that it does. While the liberal nationalist's argument for autonomy necessarily entails favoring the claim of co-nationals to their national culture, it says nothing, one way or the other, about privileging their claim to material resources.

Thus, liberal nationalism clearly privileges, if we like, the *cultural* well-being of co-nationals - this is precisely its aim; but it does not follow from this that it has to privilege their *material* well-being as well. Once the different ways in which liberal nationalism privileges co-nationals are sorted out, we can see that the sort of co-national partiality that is inimical to global justice does not come into play at all in the promotion and protection of a nation's cultural context. (From now on, co-national partiality, and its cognate terms, refer specifically to partiality in this relevant sense).

Partiality and Liberal Democracy

Consider, next, the second objective of liberal nationalism - that of facilitating deliberative democracy. As mentioned, the virtues of democratic citizenship - e.g., civility, mutual respect and trust, self-restraint and public reasonableness - presuppose a shared identity or solidarity amongst citizens. Moreover, "democratic politics is politics in the vernacular": a common national language allows citizens to engage in political deliberation, to understand the symbols and customs of political deliberation, and is moreover itself an expression of democratic self-determination (Kymlicka 1999a ms 32).

But we have seen that there is no tension between promoting and participating in a particular societal culture while remaining a committed liberal universalist. That is, liberal nationalists can be actively partial towards co-national's access to their national language (or languages) without also having to be partial towards their living standards (i.e., we may privilege the language, but not the material interests of the users of that language). To repeat an earlier point, these are very distinct and separable categories of partiality. A "politics in the vernacular" can be secured without hindering liberal egalitarian commitments globally.

But what about the other ideals, in particular those of mutual trust and respect? Does the realisation of these depend on some form of compatriot favoritism? To get a grip on this question, perhaps a more basic question to ask is: why should deliberative democracy depend on mutual respect and trust? When this is clarified, we can perhaps better see whether the idea of conational partiality needs to be invoked at all.

The reason why deliberative democracy depends on mutual trust and respect is that, for successful democratic deliberation, individuals are required to respect each other as autonomous agents capable of advancing and accepting reasonable and rational arguments in defense of each other's positions, and to respect the outcome of the democratic procedure even if it is not in their favor. And citizens are able to respect a losing outcome because they trust that should the democratic process rule in their favor next time, the opposing side would also honor that result.

If this is the exact function of mutual respect and trust with respect to democracy, it is not clear to me if conational partiality is a relevant factor here. How does conational partiality motivate the respecting of co-nationals as autonomy rational agents, and the trust that they will also honor democratic outcomes regardless of how their interests are affected? More arguments are needed here. Just assuming that solidarity, trust and respect, loyalty, fellow feelings and co-national partiality (the commonly cited list of national sentiments) must simply go together as a package begs the question. While some forms of nationalism may insist on as inseparable from all these other national sentiments, liberal nationalism need not. There is nothing in the liberal nationalist goal of promoting deliberative democracy that depends on it.

In any event, if there is a problem here - if the fostering of trust and respect necessary for deliberative democracy is dependent on conational partiality - then this is a problem for deliberative democracy in general, rather than a problem peculiar to liberal nationalism.[7]

So it remains to be shown that the fostering of mutual respect and trust, for the purpose of democratic deliberation, must rest on the practice of conational partiality. And if it must, this is a problem not specific to nationalism as such, but to democratic theory. Moreover, on the contrary, one could as well speculate that rather than fostering mutual respect and trust within a nation, if co-national partiality in turn means that other nations are treated unjustly, this could as well undermine trust and respect, breeding, instead, mutual suspicion and contempt. Engel's observation that "a nation cannot become free and at the same time continue to oppress other nations" is quite apt here (cited in Cunningham p. 104). So, instead of enabling deliberative democracy, co-national partiality at the expense of treating non-nationals unjustly may in fact disenable it.

Nationality and Social Justice

So the first two goals of liberal nation-building, the promotion of autonomy and democracy, are realizable independently of co-national partiality. Let us turn to the third goal of liberal nation-building, that of producing social justice within the state. As mentioned, the liberal welfare state assumes citizens to be "mutually indebted and morally engaged to begin with" (Sandel 1992 p. 23), that they share a common moral world. Thus liberal citizens are expected to look beyond kin and neighbors, and to include fellow citizens, who are virtually strangers, within their scope of moral concern. One way the moral horizons of individuals can be broadened beyond their parochial and traditional ties is through the establishment of a common nationality. Common nationality thus provides the bond that transcends the physical and personal gulf between citizens of a modern state by drawing them into a common "morality of community" (Tamir).

But this creation of a moral community inevitably leaves some out, namely, non-citizens outside the country's borders. Hence the immediate worry here is that in as far as liberal nationalism succeeds in expanding our moral world beyond our parochial ties, it succeeds only by limiting that world to the nation-state. Liberal nationalism risks championing a kind of moral isolationism, wherein an abiding sense of moral identity is enhanced nationally through excluding or weakening that identity globally.

If this is right, the project of liberal nation-building is in trouble: the right of a state to maintain its culture by means of regulating its immigration policy, which is dependent on its fulfilling its obligations of global justice, has to be forfeited because the project of creating a national identity undercuts that very commitment. Of the three goals of nation-building, the goal of promoting social justice within the state seems to pose the most serious obstacle to the liberal commitment to global justice.

But this worry may be too quickly voiced. If liberal nation-building aims to extend the moral boundaries of individuals to include fellow citizens who are practically strangers, and *succeeds* in doing so, then why should we think that such efforts cannot be sustained beyond the national boundary? As Charles Jones asks, why not capitalize on this "expansionary momentum" to expand the scope of our moral concern beyond co-nationals to include also foreigners (Jones p. 160)? To assume that the construction of our moral world has to suddenly cease at our national borders seems arbitrary at best. To be sure, more arguments must be provided here to suggest this possibility (though there are evidence that this can be done; e.g., the European Union); but neither should one foreclose the discussion by assuming national boundaries to be morally impermeable, or that they fix the outermost limit of our moral sphere.

Parekh worries that "[I]f people are constantly told that they should care for each other because they belong together and if their educational, cultural, and other institutions are designed, as they must be, to reinforce this message, their moral imagination gets so emasculated and moral resources so depleted that outsiders will come to mean little to them" (p. 316). But this worry is exaggerated. That people are taught that they should "care for each other [i.e., co-nationals]" does not mean that they must be taught to care exclusively for each other; that our institutions must be designed to "reinforce this message" of national affinity, does not mean that these institutions cannot also be designed to reinforce our cosmopolitan commitments.

Thus Amy Gutmann (responding to similar worries raised by Nussbaum) argues that education for democratic citizenship, and educating people to be moral *cosmopolitans* (in the sense that they are taught their duties to humanity at large), are not mutually exclusive projects (Nussbaum p. 16, Gutmann p. 71). In fact, Gutmann goes on to argue that global justice might be best realized through democratic citizenship participation and education. She notes: "Democratic citizens have institutional means at their disposals that solitary individuals, or citizens, of the world, do not. Some of those institutional means are international in scope... but even those tend to depend on the cooperation of sovereign societies for effective action" (Gutmann p. 71).

If this is right, liberal nationalism, rather than thwarting cosmopolitan aspirations, in fact provides one realistic vehicle for pursuing these aspirations. Take away national solidarity, and we take away democratic citizenship, and in doing that, we surrender the arena within which liberal citizens can fight for a better world. Moreover, it might be said that the weakening of national ties will have the opposite effect of driving people back into their sub-national and parochial moral communities, instead of turning them into enlightened cosmopolitans. So, rather than expanding our moral horizons, disbanding national solidarity - without a viable alternative basis of solidarity - may in fact deflate them (Kymlicka 1999c).

But it might be objected that if the aim of nation-building is to create a moral community, attempts to expand this moral community outwards thwarts that very aim. "Justice presupposes a bounded world" as Walzer has put it; yet aspirations to global justice threatens that very world. Either we give preferences to co-nationals (i.e., maintain a limited but viable moral world), or we treat everyone equally, but incapacitate ourselves morally. In other words, caring equally for all is incompatible with caring for our own - the demands of domestic justice and the demands of global justice pull us in opposite directions.[8]

Now if the above is a comment about our moral attitudes, it is rather implausible. It assumes that individuals can consistently inhabit a morally split mental-world; that one's intolerance of injustice at home is indirectly proportionate to one's intolerance of injustices abroad. I would think, on the contrary, that there is more of a unity and consistency in moral attitudes, such that one who is indifferent about injustices abroad would tend also to be indifferent about injustices domestically, and vice versa. The sorts of attitudes that would lead one to ignore foreign injustices are similar in kind to the sorts that would lead one to ignore domestic injustices (barring those directly affecting one and one's immediate circle). After all, we cannot say of co-nationals that they have a stronger pull on us because they are more familiar or intimate. Co-nationals are for the most part also strangers; thus to the morally indifferent, there is no significant difference between a local or foreign stranger. If we can't succeed in making people care for strangers outside their borders, we would not too, I think, have succeeded in making them care for strangers *within* their borders; and that we do succeed in making people care for strangers within, gives us hope that they too can be made to care for strangers without.[9] The belief that the demands of global justice and nationalism involve conflicting moral sentiments is ill-founded.

But the objection, that the demands of national justice and global justice are in conflict, could be read as a comment about the *absolute* scarcity of resources. Given that we have only so much, *all things being equal*, we should (or are at least permitted to) give priority to our own (e.g., Miller p. 75). That is, nationalists (liberal or not) will insist on redistributing scarce resources first to their co-nationals before the needs of strangers can be countenanced. Limited resource prevents us from meeting both demands of justice.

This is potentially a serious objection. If we can only do so much as a matter of justice, then surely we have to decide where and how to limit our commitment. The main problem here, though, is that the both the objection's premises - that of absolute scarcity and the "all things being equal" clause - are quite indefensible.[10]

But grant for a moment the truth of these premises: can liberal nationalism still be reconciled with global justice? At this point liberal nationalists are faced, I will concede, with a serious moral dilemma. But this is not because liberal nationalism cannot be reconciled with global justice, but because, quite simply, the notion of global justice no longer applies in such a world.[11] Under such a condition (a condition outside the realm of justice), principles of justice between nations do not apply, and conational priority cannot be said to be just or unjust. So this hypothetical case tells us nothing about the merits or demerits of liberal nationalism vis-à-vis global justice. Desert Island scenarios cannot tell us what justice requires; their sole purpose is to show us its limitations.

But to return to the real world: I have argued that liberal nation-building and global justice are not contradictory aspirations. And if, from the liberal point of view, the legitimacy of the former is dependent on the realization of the latter, then liberal nationalists should take an active interest in combating global inequality. One thing they have to work hard to ensure, in particular, is that the attainment of a morality of community does not come at the cost of some sort of moral isolationism. Crucially, this means that in educating citizens to be liberal *nationalists*, we do not turn them into *illiberal* internationalists only then can nation-building be undertaken consistently with liberal principles; and there is no reason, I hope to have shown, to think why this can't be done.

Conclusion

I have tried to show that there is no inherent conflict between liberal nation-building and the liberal commitment to global justice. The goals of securing and protecting a cultural context of choice, and of enabling democracy through common language and mutual trust and respect are achievable without yielding to conational partiality. And while the fostering of a common moral community via common nationality may be thought, on first glance, to be antithetical to a cosmopolitan moral point of view, it need not be so.

If this is right, then the requirement that liberal states may restrict immigration in the name of nation-building, only if they do not neglect their duties of justice to poorer countries, is not self-contradictory. Liberal nationalists can accept Lichtenberg's exhortation that "first you equalize resources [globally], then you can have your cultural belonging" (p. 183). Or if this puts it too ordinately, we could say that liberals can have their cultural belonging only if they also work towards equalizing resources globally *at the same time*.

Nothing in the above claims that co-national partiality is never justified. Once a just allocation of resources is obtained, individuals and states may do as they wish with their fair share of resources, including apportioning more of these to co-nationals and other national projects, than to non-nationals. What is objectionable, from the point of global justice, is the claim that co-national partiality may determine what that baseline just allocation is. And liberal nationalism does not endorse this claim.

The liberal half of the "liberal nationalist" equation, if we like, sets constraints on the nationalist - half-nationalist projects and undertakings, including those that aim to privilege the material well-being of co-nationals, can be undertaken only within the perimeters of justice. And where these perimeters lie is to be set independently of the idea that co-nationals take priority.

Notes

1 See, e.g., Beitz 1979, 1999b and Pogge 1989.

2 Of course, there are some liberals e.g., the "communitarian-liberals" if we may so label them, who reject this cosmopolitan ideal; but our focus here will be on cosmopolitan liberals. Non-cosmopolitan liberals will sense no tension between nation-building and global justice - they simply reject the latter. See e.g., David Miller, Chap. 3; Walzer.

3 Kymlicka makes a similar liberal distinction in terms of cosmopolitan in "ideology" and cosmopolitan in "practice" (Kymlicka 1999a); Pogge makes this distinction in terms of "legal cosmopolitanism" and "moral cosmopolitanism" (Pogge 1992a), 1.

4 Cosmopolitanism is understood from now to mean specifically moral cosmopolitanism.

5 In fact, given that one common reason for rejecting liberal *nationalism* is the belief that. nationalism is at odds with duties of global justice (e.g., Lichtenberg, Parekh), showing that liberal nationalism and global justice are not mutually incompatible ideals will serve to remove one common liberal objection to liberal nationalism.

6 This is one crucial condition, which sets liberal nationalism apart from *illiberal* forms of nationalism. Also, in this regard, liberal nationalists should accord minority nations within the state special rights to mitigate the effects of state nation-building. Sée Kymlicka 1999a; 1995. But I will leave this important point aside here, and focus more on the implications of nation-building, if any, for global justice.

7 Richard Miller in a recent paper seems to suggest this. Miller's central claim is that equal respect for all requires greater concern for some, namely, compatriots who share common democratic social schemes. I would argue that Miller's distinction between equal respect and unequal concern is mistaken, but I will not pursue this point here.

8 See Rawls's "strains of commitment" (Rawls 1971 p. 145).

9 Consider the dismal foreign aid contributions (and isolationist policies) of Western governments who are also hostile to domestic welfare programs.

10 I will not pursue this point here, but see Nathan and Pogge, 1992b, 1998, respectively.

11 See Hume and Rawls on the circumstances of justice.

References

Beiner, R. (ed) (1998). *Theorizing Nationalism.* SUNY, Albany.

Beitz, C. (1999a). 'Social and Cosmopolitan Liberalism.' *International Affairs* 75/3: 515-529.

Beitz, C. (1999b). 'International Liberalism and Distributive Justice: A Survey of Recent Thought.' *World Politics* 51.

Beitz, C. (1983). 'Cosmopolitan Ideal and National Sentiment.' *The Journal of Philosophy.*

Beitz, C. (1979). *Political Theory and International Relations.* Princeton University Press, Princeton.

Cohen, J. (ed.) *(1996).For Love of Country* . Beacon Press, Boston.

Cunningham, F. (1995). *The Real World of Democracy Revisited.* Humanities Press, Atlantic Highlands.

Goodin, R. (1988). 'What So Special About Our Fellow Countryman?' *Ethics* 98/4.

Gutmann, A. (1996). 'Democratic Citizenship.' In J. Cohen.

Habermas, J. (1992). 'Citizenship and National Identity: Some Reflections On the Future of Europe.' *Praxis International* 12/1: 1-19.

Jone, C. (1999). 'Patriotism, Morality, and Global Justice.' In *Global Justice.* Shapiro and Brilmayer (ed). NYU Press, New York.

Kymlicka, W. (1999a). 'Territorial Boundaries: A Liberal Egalitarian Perspective.' In David Miller and Sohail Hashmi (eds.). *Boundaries, Ownership and Autonomy.* Princeton University Press, Princeton.

Kymlicka, W. (1999b), 'From Enlightenment Cosmopolitanism to Liberal Nationalism.' In Steven Lukes (ed.). *The Enlightenment: Then and Now.* Polity Press.

Kymlicka, W. (1999c). 'Citizenship in an era of Globalization: Commentary on Held.' In Shapiro and Hacker-Cordon (eds.).

Kymlicka, W. (1995). *Multicultural Citizenship.* Oxford UP, Oxford.

Kymlicka, W. (1989). *Liberalism, Community and Culture.* Oxford UP, Oxford.

Lichtenberg, J. (1998). 'How Liberal Can Nationalism Be?' In Beiner.

Margalit, A. and J. Raz (1990). 'National Self-Determination.' *Journal of Philosophy* LXXXVII.

MacIntyre, A. (1984). 'Is Patriotism a Virtue?'. The Lindley Lectures. University of Kansas.

McKim, R. and McMahan, J. (eds.) (1997). *The Morality of Nationalism.* Oxford UP.

Miller, D. (1995). *On Nationality.* Oxford University Press, Oxford.

Miller, R. (1998). *Philosophy and Public Affairs* 27/3.

Nussbaum, M. (1996). 'Patriotism and Cosmopolitanism.' In J. Cohen.

Parekh, B. (1998). 'The Incoherence of Nationalism.' In Beiner.

Pogge, T. (1998). 'The Bounds of Nationalism.' In *Rethinking Nationalism.* Couture, Nielsen, and Seymour (ed). University of Calgary Press, Calgary.

Pogge, T. (1992a). 'Cosmopolitanism and Sovereignty.' *Ethics* 103/1.

Pogge, T. (1992b). 'An Institutional Approach to Humanitarian Intervention.' *Public Affairs Quarterly,* 6/1.

Pogge, T. (1989). *Realizing Rawls.* Cornell UP, Ithaca.

Sandel, M. (1996). *Democracy's Discontent.* Harvard UP.

Sandel, M. (1992), 'The Procedural Republic and the Unencumbered Self.' In Avineri and De-Shalit (eds.). *Communitarianism and Individualism.* Oxford: Oxford UP.

Shue, H. (1988). 'Mediating Duties'. *Ethics.*

Tamir, Y. (1993). *Liberal Nationalism.* Princeton UP, Princeton.

Walzer, M. (1983). *Spheres of Justice.* Basic Books, New York.

Yack, B. (1999). 'Myth of the Civic Nation.' In Beiner.

19. Retroactive Justice: Trials for Human Rights Violations under a Prior Regime

MAKOTO USAMI*

The Problem

The twentieth century has witnessed grave human rights violations conducted by a considerable number of governments around the world. Surprisingly, human rights have been more frequently infringed upon by repressive governments during peacetime than during international or civil war.[1] A typical example of abuses under a tyrannical regime is the killing and torture of citizens through massacres, summary or extrajudicial execution, death squads, and "disappearances."

This situation is being reversed as suppressive governments are replaced by democratic governments committed to human rights protection in Mediterranean countries, Latin America, Eastern Europe, the former Soviet Union, and Africa. Democratization has also occurred in some countries in Asia. Successor civilian governments in these countries face the problem of how to deal with killings and torture committed under their predecessors. The legal remedies available for the new governments, which are not necessarily exclusive, include the criminal prosecution and punishment of those found responsible, the purgation of chargeable officials and officers, the establishment of truth commissions, the provision of compensation for victims, the official restoration of victims' deprived rights and interests, and the grant of amnesty or pardon.

If one looks at the fact of governmental inhumanity against citizens on a massive scale, one tends to say that those involved in such inhumanity deserve prosecution and punishment. Namely, one will prefer the across-the-board prosecution to purgation and truth commissions and will reject amnesty. Moreover, criminal trials for human rights violations may be able to prevent such violations in the future, to facilitate the consolidation of democracy, and to enhance respect for the rule of law.

In certain circumstances trials for past abuses, however, entail the problem of retroactive justice or punishment through application of ex post facto laws. Situations can arise in which there were no legal rules definitively prohibiting killings and torture committed by military or police officers. These acts may have been considered as legitimate policy at the time they were conducted. In other situations, these atrocities were made explicitly legal by self-amnesty laws. Ex post facto laws breach the established principle of *nullum crimen, nulla poena sine lege* in the criminal process, and more generally violate the rule of law. The *nulla poena* principle requires that preexisting laws define the acts of crime and determine the kinds and limits of possible punishments for the crimes. Retroactive laws in criminal justice do not merely constitute a lapse in legal predictability but treat individuals unfairly.

International law on human rights is often said to resolve the retroactive justice problem in the prosecution of perpetrators. Indeed, numerous states signed and ratified treaties forbidding killings and torture, and a growing number of international law scholars have argued that these abuses violate customary international law. Moreover, some human rights experts have urged that international law, both conventional and customary, imposes on a successor government an affirmative obligation to prosecute and punish human rights violations conducted under its predecessor. As I will argue, however, the scope of international law is much more limited than these commentators assume. Initially it will be noted that treaties and alleged customary law fall short of resolving the retroactive justice problem. Next, the concept of obligation to prosecute will be examined both from the theoretical perspective of legal sources and from the practical perspective of the political consequences which may follow from this obligation. These considerations will show, I hope, that international law provides an unsatisfactory approach to the problem.

Ex post facto laws invoked in trials for past human rights abuses create a persistent problem unresolved by the proof of preexisting laws. This is the problem of how to reconcile the need for prosecution and punishment with the *nulla poena* principle. I will characterize this problem as "dirty hands," the idea of which has been developed in political ethics. Dirty hands is a circumstance in which one needs to use the wrong means to achieve the best ends most effectively. Such characterization has normative implications for three aspects of these trials: the process of retroactive law enactment and the process of the trials themselves; other possible legal remedies provided concurrently with the trials or as an alternative to them; and the principles and strategies related to creating reactions in the international community. In considering these implications, I will try to bring a new perspective to the concept of retroactive justice.

Before my inquiring into the subject, I will briefly make two methodological remarks. First, this article is somewhat multidisciplinary in the sense that it deals with concepts conventionally within the philosophy of law, while simultaneously exploring ideas more closely connected to international law and political ethics. I am not insensitive to the risk such an approach involves—that of manipulating concepts and ideas without deeply understanding their backgrounds in unfamiliar disciplines. Nevertheless, the possible fruits of the multidisciplinary approach seem to outweigh this risk in discussing retroactive justice. It is indispensable before analyzing a normative problem in prosecution to examine the claims that international law resolves the problem or that prosecution is justified as a fulfillment of international obligation. Also, applying the idea of dirty hands to this problem will be helpful in exploring the persistence of conflicting values in public life.

The second methodological remark concerns how to treat practical facets of interpretative theory. When one evaluates an interpretative theory, one needs to take into account the strands of an interpreted social practice which support this theory as well as the possible consequences the theory may produce. No interpretation of a practice can be convincing without demonstrating facts backing it up. Also, an interpreter is required to suggest what consequence would follow if her theory was commonly accepted. Based on these considerations, in my assessment of alleged customary international law on human rights, I will emphasize the significance of state practice and of the allegation's effects upon a transitional society.

Ex Post Facto Laws

In the literature of contemporary legal philosophy, there seems to be a loose consensus on how to deal with ex post facto laws. Authors substantially agree that a retroactive law is permissible or even advisable when the normative deficit it creates is outweighed by its objective necessity. Ex post facto laws are discussed by H. L. A. Hart (1958: 618-620) and by Lon L. Fuller (1958: 652-657) in the context of a case involving the informer who legally betrayed her husband to the Nazi police. Hart suggests that the choice of whether to punish this informer should have been made as a choice between the evil of leaving her unpunished and the sacrifice of a moral principle endorsed by most legal systems. Although Fuller is critical of Hart's suggestion in the context considered, he does not totally reject retroactive laws. Fuller (1969: 53) instead observes that in a system of generally prospective legal rules, retrospective rules can be not only tolerable but essential to advance the cause of legality. In her critical examination of legalism, Judith N. Shklar (1964: 147, 209-210, 220) argues that political trials, whose most notable example is the International Military Tribunal at Nuremberg, can be justified only by the political values these trials implement. Martin P. Golding (1993: 181-182, 190-191) notes that a retroactive law may be the best way for a successor government to clean up a mess left by the predecessor government when a society's need to express its moral judgment on its past outweighs the concern of upsetting reasonable legal expectations.

Hart's basic approach seems applicable to the context of a case involving an abusive regime's sanctioned attacks upon citizens, as Golding implies. There is a difference, of course, between a case of idiosyncratic betrayals conducted by private citizens and that of systematic killings and torture committed by public officials and officers who are conventionally expected to serve citizens. The latter acts appear to deserve punishment much more than the former. Because of this difference, one might be inclined to assert that prosecution and punishment of official killings and torture, unlike those of personal betrayals, do not entail any normative loss at all. But the normative loss caused by ex post facto laws is a persistent characteristic of trials for official perpetrators. Consequently, where there is a choice of whether to punish the perpetrators by invoking a retroactive law, it is always of importance to weigh the normative loss against the law's necessity.

The first thing to do to develop such a weighing approach is to identify both the necessity for, and the loss incurred by prosecution and punishment. Let me begin with identifying the necessity. Trials for human rights abuses are said to have several varieties of social function (e.g. Zalaquett 1989: 37; Malamud-Goti 1990: 2-3, 11-12; Nino 1996: 129-134, 142-147). The following two can be unequivocally assigned to the public interest. First, these trials are one of the most effectual measures to prevent human rights violations in the future. The preventive function of trials falls into three categories. The trials can prevent those who were punished from committing the same atrocities over again. Punishment also has a deterrent effect over the whole society, by discouraging the commission of future violations. Further, the trials may contribute to the hindrance of human rights abuses in some other countries where tyrannical regimes remain.

The second unequivocal source of the social interest of criminal trials is that they facilitate instituting or restoring democracy. Prosecution and punishment highlight the democratic character of a new regime, by making a clear distinction between its previous suppressive regime and itself.

Moreover, the trials can foster democratic culture, since they provide the public with the opportunity of public discussion and collective deliberation on the social tragedy of killings and torture.

It is noteworthy, however, that these outcomes are not exclusively produced by trials. Possible human rights violations in the future can be prevented to a lesser degree by purgation or truth commissions. Public discussion and collective deliberation on the tragedy may also result to some degree through the process of truth commission.

Other functions attributed to trials for perpetrators are more controversial. Some analysts (e.g. Orentlicher 1991: 2542-2543) contend that these trials enhance respect for the rule of law. There can be three arguments for this contention. First, as democracy is gradually formed with help from the trials, the high level of appreciation for the rule of law grows in society. This could be said to stem from the idea that the rule of law is connected with the ideal of collective self-government stating that citizens have a duty to obey the laws enacted by democratically elected representatives. The second argument concerns how the trials are carried out. The merit of the rule of law is showcased when the trials take place before impartial courts, with ample opportunity for the accused to be heard and with strict adherence to the procedures governing evidence (Nino 1996: 146 cf. Shklar 1964: 168-170). The third argument is more realistic. The trials effectively eliminate or disgrace the former officials and officers who oppose the principles a successor government commits to (Shklar 1964: 149). Since the rule-of-law ideal is among these principles, the trials strengthen the ideal.

In evaluating the three arguments, a distinction between thin theories and thick theories of the rule of law may be useful. Thin theories only demand governance through preexisting laws which satisfy several formal conditions. Thick theories additionally demand that preexisting laws be enacted democratically or that these laws secure rights of the accused. The former two arguments mentioned above presuppose thick views, but thin views may be more desirable. Robert S. Summers (1988: 161) gives three justifications for thin theories.[2] First, thin conceptions of the rule of law have more discrete clusters of values than thick conceptions, and so arguments relying on the thin conceptions can have more unified focus and force. Second, because thin theories are politically more neutral than thick theories, the thin-theory-based arguments are more likely to call the attention of various political regimes. Third, thin views, unlike thick views, do not obscure the possibility that the real sacrifice of the rule of law may be called for to resolve conflicts with other values within a legal system. The ideal of democracy is a value which is distinct from the rule of law.

When the former ideal is promoted by vitiating the latter, a sacrifice is made. That sacrifice cannot be overlooked. Also, the preservation of rights of the accused does not contribute to the rule of law, although the preservation itself is another value and is expected to enhance general respect for the law. In contrast with the former two arguments relying on thick theories of the rule of law, one cannot deny the third argument if one takes a direct view of the actualities of a transitional society. In sum, prosecution and punishment may help a successor government to establish the rule of law only by eliminating the government's political opponents.

Let us turn to the identification of the loss that might result from criminal trials. I distinguish legal loss and political loss. Legal loss means that ex post facto laws break the *nulla poena* principle and more generally the rule of law. Such a breach is critical for two reasons: First, ex post facto laws applied in criminal law can create more monstrous results than in other areas, since criminal law can deprive individuals of their liberty and even of their lives in some legal systems. If the rule of law should be maintained at all, criminal law is the first area in which retroactive laws ought to be excluded.

The second reason concerns the nature of legal loss. The significance of the rule of law is commonly thought to be to secure legal predictability, enabling citizens to make an informed choice of courses of action. Admittedly, this predictability is of great importance, particularly in criminal law, for the reason mentioned above. But it is not realistic to assume that citizens choose their actions in everyday life recognizing the contents of all provisions in the applicable criminal code. Nor is such an assumption coherent with the principle of *ignorantia legis neminem excusat*. The idea that what the *nulla poena* principle protects is not actual expectation but counterfactual—"reasonable"—expectation suggests that legal predictability is a somewhat fictional idea. Rather, the quintessence of the rule of law in the context of criminal law is to hold individuals responsible only for acts which they could reasonably have expected were banned and punishable under the law when they acted. In doing so, the law treats individuals fairly. Ex post facto laws disregarding the limits of individual responsibility thus are not merely instrumentally detrimental to individuals but intrinsically unfair. The unfairness of retroactive laws also stems from the general commitment of a successor government to the rule of law. If the government enacts retrospective laws only in a case involving grave human rights violations under its predecessor, while refraining from doing so in other criminal cases, then this discriminative treatment of violators is unfair.

The existence and degree of political loss depends upon circumstances surrounding a new government. In the common case that the government is fragile and unstable, it may be overthrown by the *coup d'etat* criminal trials may provoke (Zalaquett 1989: 27-28). If some of the officials involved in past abuses retain their office in the subsequent government, the government's attempts to prosecute will face strong objections from these officials. If those who supported or collaborated with the prior government amount to a substantive portion of the population, trials may make it difficult to bring about national unification (Zalaquett 1989: 37-38). Additionally, a virtual certainty of prosecution will hinder some repressive governments from voluntarily relinquishing power; however, this concern may be outweighed by the international preventive function of punishment (Orentlicher 1991: 2549).

To sum up, what makes it necessary to prosecute and punish perpetrators is the prevention of human rights violations in the future, the consolidation of democracy, and the establishment of the rule of law through eliminating political opponents. On the other side, the legal loss caused by criminal trials is the unfair treatment of individuals and the breach of legal predictability; the resulting political loss consists of destabilizing effects on the transitional government and obstructive effects on national union.

The Scope of International Law

The development of international law on human rights appears to have resolved the retroactive justice problem in trials for torturing and killing citizens. Indeed, during the last half century, a multitude of states signed and ratified treaties forbidding various categories of human rights violations including killings and torture. The right to life is secured by article 6(1) of the International Covenant on Civil and Political Rights (International Covenant),[3] article 2 of the European Convention for the Protection of Human Rights and Fundamental Freedoms (European Convention),[4] and article 4(1) of the American Convention on Human Rights (American Convention),[5] among others. Torture is prohibited by article 7 of the International Covenant, article 3 of the European Convention, article 5(2) of the American Convention, and so forth. The purpose of the Convention on the Prevention and Punishment of the Crime of Genocide (Genocide Convention)[6] is to prevent and punish acts relating to genocide; that of the Convention Against Torture and Other Cruel,

Inhuman or Degrading Treatment or Punishment (Torture Convention)[7] is to make the deterrence of torture more effective.

Furthermore, a growing number of international law scholars, particularly in the United States, notably Oscar Schachter (1985: 333-338), have argued that the obligations to protect human rights which are incumbent upon all states derive from customary law. Customary human rights law has been formed, it is argued, through treaties like the ones mentioned above, references in resolutions of the United Nations to the Universal Declaration of Human Rights, national constitutions and laws in major legal systems, and statements by national officials condemning other states for human rights abuses. Along the same line, the *Restatement* (American Law Institute 1987: 161-165) enumerates human rights accepted as customary norms. Since the idea of customary human rights law concerns substantive law opposed to procedural law, I will call proponents of this idea substantive internationalists.

The substantive internationalist claim is controversial for the three reasons supplied by Bruno Simma and Philip Alston (1992: 88-100). First and foremost, the fact that official killings and torture have been conducted all over the world, while many states have signed human rights treaties arouses doubt that the state practice supporting customary law exists in this matter. What has been traditionally recognized, with *opinio juris*, as indispensable to customary international law is a general, uniform, consistent, and settled practice. Recent attempts to conceal facts of outrages through "disappearances" may represent an emerging *opinio juris* on human rights, but do disprove the assertion of state practice of respect for these rights. Next, it is noteworthy that there is a remarkable correlation between the rights listed as customary norms and the rights incorporated into the U.S. Bill of Rights. The correlation might be an instance of what can be called legal chauvinism. Why is freedom from hunger or the right to basic health care, for example, excluded from the list of customary norms? This is in part because the infringements on these social rights have not been condemned as human rights violations. This answer leads us to the third reason: the official statements cited as the evidence of customary law are almost exclusively Western in origin. In referring to these points, I do not intend to say that human rights do not have universalistic values beyond the borders of Western culture and society. Nor do I deny that human rights norms have evolved among a growing number of states during the last several decades. I only suggest that it is difficult at the present to demonstrate the existence of customary human rights law and to identify the rights as accepted in the international community as a whole.

The problem peculiar to the context of retroactive justice is that neither conventional law nor alleged customary law constitutes preexisting law in trials for past abuses. International law on human rights obliges states to take proper actions such as enacting laws and establishing institutions regarding the rights. But this law does not definitively prohibit officials and officers from infringing on these rights. Enacted laws must be prospective not retrospective, according to the *nulla poena* principle established in conventional law by provisions like article 15(1) of the International Covenant, article 7(1) of the European Convention, and article 9 of the American Convention. The need for ex post facto laws remains, however.

One possible way to consider international human rights norms in conventional or customary law as legitimate preexisting laws in domestic criminal trials is for a national court to acknowledge the norms as self-executing. This means that the court applies these norms directly to a human rights violations case. However, that is not a promising approach. First, in a considerable number of states courts have no constitutional authority to apply international law to domestic cases. The second reason concerns a distinction between civil case and criminal case. True, several provisions of some treaties such as the International Covenant and the European Convention may be recognized as self-executing in civil cases. But even these provisions cannot be so in criminal cases, since they do not provide the kinds and limits of punishment required by the *nulla poena* principle. The lack of punishment provisions is also the case in customary law. Third, courts in most states have not acknowledged customary norms as self-executing in any kind of human rights case, with a few exceptions including the well-known decision in *Filartiga v. Pena-Irala.*[8]

Some of the literature on international law and human rights urges that both conventional law and customary law impose upon a successor government an obligation to prosecute and punish those found responsible for past human rights abuses. Naomi Roht-Arriaza (1990), focusing on examples of Latin American countries, argues that criminal law treaties, "ensure and respect" provisions, and guarantees the right to a remedy to constitute the conventional law basis for an obligation to investigate and prosecute (462-483) and that the customary law basis exists for such an obligation (489-504). Similarly, Diane F. Orentlicher (1991: 2551-2595) maintains that an obligation to prosecute and punish atrocities is imposed both by several human rights treaties and by customary norms. I will call these analysts procedural internationalists. If their argument is correct, it will justify prosecution and punishment as a fulfillment of obligation in international law. This argument about a procedural aspect of criminal trials does not demonstrate preexisting substantive law, of course. Rather, the argument implies that an international obligation to prosecute overrides a national one to respect the rule of law. In the rest of this section, I will examine to what extent the procedural internationalist argument is correct.

There are international criminal treaties which explicitly provide an obligation to prosecute certain human rights violations. The treaties frequently cited as the grounds of an obligation to prosecute include the Genocide Convention and the Torture Convention. Article 4 of the Genocide Convention provides that persons committing genocide shall be punished. The Convention applies to only a specific category of human rights abuses, however, as article 2 clearly states. For one thing, the victims of genocide must be members of a national, ethnical, racial, or religious group. On the other hand, those who are tortured and killed under a repressive regime are typically actual, perceived, or alleged political opponents. But acts directed against such political groups were deliberately excluded from the Convention's definition of genocide. This was the outcome of pressure from suppressive governments wishing to avoid international interference in their domestic affairs (Kuper 1981: 24-30). Moreover, genocide means killings and other acts committed with intent to destroy a substantial portion of a target group. Many acts which are clearly atrocities but lacking in this intent are excluded from the definition of genocide. It follows from these limitations that the Convention covers only a specific type of abuses.

The Torture Convention covers a whole range of torture irrespective of what kind of group the victim belonged to or what intent the torturer had. Article 7 provides that if a state party does not extradite the alleged offender, the state party should submit the case to its competent authorities for the purpose of prosecution. Nevertheless, the Convention is far from establishing an obligation to prosecute all actual torturers. First, the Convention is the relatively new treaty which was opened for signature on February 4, 1985 and which entered into force on June 26, 1987. For instance, in Argentina, where harsh torture had been committed before the military government had given way to its civilian successor in 1983, the new government ratified the Torture Convention in 1986, and a sort of amnesty law, the "due obedience" law, was passed on June 4, 1987, 22 days before the Convention entered into force. The second reason for the Torture Convention's ineffectiveness is that a rather small number of state parties are presently bound by it. The Convention had only 82 parties as of July 1995.

General human rights treaties do not explicitly impose on state parties an obligation to prosecute, but do oblige the state parties to ensure rights set forth therein. These treaties include the International Covenant, the European Convention, and the American Convention. Procedural internationalists assert that "ensure" provisions in these treaties selectively imply an obligation to prosecute. However, a state party has a wide range of alternative measures to ensure human rights. Backward remedial measures encompass the purgation of those chargeable for past abuses, the establishment of investigative commission on the abuses, the provision of compensation for victims, and the restoration of victims' deprived rights. Forward constructive measures include the signing and ratification of human rights treaties, the recognition of the jurisdiction of international human rights courts, the revision of the constitution and relevant laws, the drastic reformation of the military, the establishment of human rights bureaus in ministries, and the introduction of a human rights component into the training of law enforcement personnel (cf. Zalaquett 1989: 38). There is no doubt a large gap between "ensure" provisions and the idea of an international obligation to prosecute.[9]

Faced with the fact that conventional law provides a patchwork quilt of obligations to prosecute, procedural internationalists assert that customary law obliges all states to prosecute crimes against humanity. The crimes were originally presumed to be, with war crimes, committed in connection with the war, but were later reinterpreted to extend to abuses committed during peacetime. Crimes against humanity mean killing, torture, and other kinds of inhumane acts when these acts are committed as a part of a widespread or systematic attack against a civilian population on national, political, ethnic, racial, or religious grounds. This category of crime covers, unlike that of genocide, acts of attack against political groups. If an obligation to prosecute those who committed crimes against humanity is drawn from customary human rights law, then the customary law will provide states with a seamless web of obligations. It is still more difficult, however, to verify the state practice necessary for customary law on obligation to prosecute than for customary law on human rights (cf. Scharf 1996: 57-59). Since 1945 prosecution has not been instituted at all in a majority of cases involving the official killing of citizens during peacetime, and amnesty has been granted instead of or after prosecution (Balint 1996: 244-247).

Another consideration in opposition to the procedural internationalist argument stems from the practical consequences this argument might produce when an obligation to prosecute past abuses is interpreted as virtually absolute. Such an interpretation seems appropriate in the light of the procedural internationalist position that the obligation in conventional law cannot be overridden by domestic law (Roht-Arriaza 1990: 483-488) and that it is hardly permissible for a successor government to invoke necessity to overcome the obligation in customary law (505). The obligation interpreted as virtually absolute will force a new government to institute criminal trials even when the government's existence is at stake. The subsequent collapse of democratic government would cause the reoccurrence of grave human rights violations. Orentlicher (1991: 2549) suggests that pressure from the international community for compliance with such a mandatory obligation will provide a counterweight to organized opposition to prosecution. But this suggestion is too optimistic. International pressure may expose the fragility of the government to the public, and may confirm the military officer's belief that the military needs to protect the state's sovereignty from outside powers (cf. Nino 1991: 2631-2637). When the pressure intensified by foreign democratic governments brings about a political crisis in a transitional society, it is not these demanding governments who will pay the huge political cost. It is the new government and ultimately the public in that society.

The examination of international law on human rights suggests several precepts. That the substantive internationalist argument does not hold exemplifies the formidability of retroactive justice. Under circumstances in which no domestic laws explicitly prohibited official killings and torture at the time of committing these acts, the legal loss caused by criminal trials pertinaciously remains even when the necessity for the trials outweighs the resulting political loss. The problem of legal loss must be managed in ways that do not embrace striving to prove preexisting laws. The procedural internationalist argument can be one approach to this task, but it fails to justify prosecution unless the involved repressive state ratified a criminal treaty in advance. The procedural internationalists' failure also highlights the undesirable consequences which mandatory prosecution might bring about. A more promising approach therefore will acknowledge the persistency of retroactive justice on one hand, while also leaving a successor government room for discretion on the other.

Dirty Hands

There are some attempts to resolve the retroactive justice problem from perspectives outside of international law. The most notable is Carlos Santiago Nino's (1996: 158-163) argument which invokes the idea that decision in the practice of law should be justified by moral norms and by the epistemic superiority of democracy over undemocratic regimes. Nino distinguishes between a case in which democracy had existed before human rights abuses were conducted under a suppressive regime and a case in which democracy had not. In the former case, he argues that these abuses should be judged according to substantive and procedural laws enacted in the former democracy. He reasons that the laws authorizing the abuses are null and void because of the epistemic inferiority of the undemocratic regime under which the authorizing laws were enacted. In the latter case, past atrocities should be punished according to the laws enacted under the present democracy, which coincide with ideal moral norms.

These arguments seem to be open to objection for three reasons. First, applying the laws coincident with moral norms to a human rights violations case does not resolve the retroactive justice problem, because the *nulla poena* principle requires preexisting laws, not preexisting moral norms. Instead of demonstrating the viability of preexisting laws, Nino essentially tries to justify ex post facto laws through their coincidence with morals. Second, this attempt to justify retroactive laws is not itself successful. I agree with his claim that decision in the practice of law should be justified by moral arguments (cf. Usami 1993: 77-82). These moral arguments, however, do not belong to common morality governing all individuals but to legal morality permeating only among legal professionals. Obligations and responsibilities in legal morality derive from the role of jurists. The two kinds of morality are generally convergent; otherwise legal morality could not draw its persuasive power from common morality. Nonetheless, the two can diverge. Suppose that for some reason the "cold-blooded" murderer who had killed ten people received a mild punishment. People of moral sense may believe that he be given another trial. But for lawyers and judges, who accept legal morality, the resulting double jeopardy should be not merely unconstitutional but monstrous, even though they may feel resentment at the mild punishment. The same should be true for retroactive laws. Thus it does not follow from invoking morality in the justification of legal decision that ex post facto laws are justifiable. Third, if the law which had been expressively nullified under a prior regime was suddenly applied to a criminal case after political transition, it would be reasonable to say that such an application is unfair to the accused.

The pertinacious unfairness of retrospective laws places those who were involved directly or indirectly in prosecution of perpetrators in a moral predicament. This predicament seems to be properly characterized as dirty hands. The idea of dirty hands, which dates back to Machiavelli (1995: 30-31, 49, 54-55), was rearticulated by Michael Walzer (1973) and has been developed by many authors in contemporary political ethics. This idea has been often interpreted as the moral dilemma in which one cannot help but use the wrong means to achieve the best ends. In this dilemma, the only way to avoid doing morally wrong is to abandon one's primary purpose completely. But such a conception of dirty hands seems too restrictive, because the conception fails to cover a wide variety of the non-dilemma situations which may deserve ethical scrutiny. More desirable may be a broad conception stating that dirty hands refers to all circumstances in which one needs to employ the morally wrong means if one seeks to obtain the best ends in the most effective way. Dirty hands is more perplexing to public officials than to private citizens. For the former individuals, whose role is to serve the latter, face the choice of whether to impair moral values not only in a case of their own private interests involved but in a case of the public interest at stake.

A considerable body of literature on dirty hands has devoted little attention to acts in the legal process, instead focusing mainly on acts in the political realm. For many authors assume that dirty hands is a characteristic of politics in part because politicians are in cutthroat competition for power and because victorious politicians can resort to violence. Among exceptions in the literature are the discussion of client control made by public interest lawyers (Luban 1988: 319-341) and the examination of the Solicitor General's acts influencing the decisions in *Brown v. Board of Education* (Winston 1998).

The idea of dirty hands will be also applicable to the context of trials for past human rights violations. The leaders of a successor government have an obligation, in role morality, to promote the public interest, and this interest in a transitional society includes the prevention of human rights abuses and the consolidation of democratic institutions and culture. Also, it is at the discretion of the leaders to institute trials for past atrocities unless the state signed and ratified an international criminal treaty before political transition. These leaders thus have good reason to arrange criminal trials when the leaders believe that the trials are the most effectual measure to prevent human rights abuses and to consolidate democracy. And yet the necessity for prosecution and punishment does not sweep away another obligation of the leaders: to show respect for principles in the practice of law including the *nulla poena* principle. The result is that in terms of the distinction J. L. Austin (1979: 176-177) makes, these leaders are able to excuse the trials but are unable to justify them. Although justification and excuse can be close in the actual vindication of action, they are conceptually distinct. A justification is at least an assertion of innocence and at most a claim of praise. An excuse is the defense against wholesale condemnation which entails an admission of fault. Trials for past abuses are excusable when their necessity outweighs the political loss they may cause; however, the trials are not justifiable because of the residual legal loss.

Those who face dirty hands are not just the leaders of a new regime. Judges in trials for human rights violations make their hands still more dirty than those of the leaders by declaring the accused guilty. For these judges, as legal professionals, have a stronger obligation to adhere to legal principles than legislators or executives, and the judges are not expected to promote the public interest in any other way than through adherence to the law. Some people might say that a difference between politicians' role and that of judges is a matter of what Thomas Nagel (1978: 85) calls ethical division of labor. Judges should do what they are required and authorized to do, it would be argued, within their official positions instead of what they believe should be done, all things considered. This line of argument leads to the conclusion that while the political leaders should arrange the trials, the judges should pronounce all the accused not guilty in recognition of the principle that criminal retroactive laws are null and void. I disagree with this conclusion. It is excusable for the judges to declare those found involved in past atrocities guilty by applying ex post facto laws, since a portion of the public interest at stake here is to deter grave human rights violations which are fatal to the decent practice of law. Others might go further, claiming that these judges should pronounce some individuals guilty even when the judges believe they were not involved. This would eliminate, the argument goes, opponents against the new government's principles including the rule-of-law ideal. But if judges pretend to find people guilty while believing that they are innocent, the law collapses. The end does not always excuse the means.

The other group who encounters dirty hands is the public. Citizens place themselves in such a quandary when democracy begins to be instituted or restored. They indirectly do wrong by electing the leaders who made a campaign pledge to prosecute past abuses or by generally supporting prosecution.[10]

To interpret trials for past violations as dirty hands has several normative implications. The first concerns the process of enacting retroactive laws, the contents of these laws, and the process of conducting the trials. The trials should be held in such a way that both publicity and what I call excusableness maximization are maintained. As Dennis F. Thompson (1987: 22-23, 32) argues, when public officials secretly or deceptively commit wrong deeds, these officials make their hands doubly dirty by adding secrecy or deception to the wrong of their acts *per se*. To avoid doubly dirty hands, the leaders of a new government should not allege that international law is preexisting laws necessary to punishment or that the state has an obligation to prosecute according to general human rights treaties or customary international law. Nor should they hold secret trials. Rather, when these leaders conclude that the trials are the best policy, the leaders are to enact an ex post facto law, to sincerely persuade the public of the law's necessity, and to make open trials take place.

The principle of excusableness maximization demands that criminal trials be invulnerable to any other legal objection than that of retroactive laws. Namely, ex post facto laws invoked are required to clearly define crimes punishable in the trials and to exclude the death penalty from possible punishments, at least in the countries where this penalty was abolished. Also, the accused should be given ample opportunity to be heard, and fair procedural rules governing evidence and testimony should be strictly followed. When these conditions all are met, excusableness is maximized, although the trials are still unjustified.

An example of flagrant breach of both publicity and excusableness maximization is the military trial of Nicolae and Elena Ceausescu conducted in Romania in December 1989. After the two-hour summary trial was held secretly, they both were executed. Such a trial cannot be excusable.

The second implication relates to how to choose legal measures to deal with past human rights violations. If political leaders expect that criminal trials may provoke *coups d'etat* or strenuous objections within the government or that the trials will hinder national unity, they need to exclude the trials from the policies carried out. Let us take an overview of the merits and liabilities of remedial measures other than trials. Purgation administered according to ex post facto laws is incompatible with the rule of law, although it does not violate the *nulla poena* principle. This measure belongs to the realm of dirty hands, since the legal loss incurred by the measure remains even when its necessity outweighs the resulting political loss in given political circumstances. The purgation is thus covered by demands of publicity and of excusableness maximization. This policy will make a smaller contribution to human rights protection and democratization than trials, and will encounter weaker political opposition. A truth commission, which is consistent with the rule of law, is expected to enable citizens to share the facts of social tragedy and to hopefully advance democratic discussion and deliberation. In doing so, the truth commission also seems to contribute to the prevention of human rights abuses. Political objections to this policy may be more easily contrived than those directed against purgation. Compensation for victims and the restoration of their deprived rights are demanded by the ideal of corrective justice pervading the practice of law. A common problem in implementing the compensation is not political opposition but financial scarcity. Amnesty and pardon, despite their strong provocativeness from the perspective of common morality, are not contrary to any principle in legal morality. These two policies may facilitate human rights protection and democratization in certain circumstances in which they are effective in bringing about national unification.

These considerations supply guidelines for the choice of legal measures. Because victims deserve compensation regardless of what political circumstances surround the government, compensation should be always included in any set of policies carried out. A choice of any other policy depends upon the political situation. In a case of expected political reaction severely destabilizing a fragile government or of social cleavage hindering national unity, a list of possible policies needs to include amnesty or pardon. Truth commissions can be combined with amnesty or purgation, depending on the political environment. Purgation can supplement remedies produced by criminal trials when the number of those indicted is considerably small. The flexible approach these guidelines suggest will be able to more successfully manage political issues in a transitional society than the absolutist one applied by procedural internationalists.

Finally, the dirty hands conception of trials has a broad implication for the question of how the international community deals with a successor government. It would be not only unwise but cruel for other states and international bodies to single-mindedly demand prosecution and punishment while neglecting the reality of a transitional society. An alternative is that the international community takes a supportive attitude toward helping the successor government implement what it chose, instead of demanding that the new government do what foreign states decided. International assistance for the government's backward measures could properly include the dispatch of legal advisors for fair trials, the provision of information on experiences of truth commissions in other states, and financial aid intended to compensate the victims of past abuses. Assistance for forward policies, such as sending legal advisors for the revision of relevant laws and providing temporary financial aid to revitalize the economy, will enhance the reliability of the new government among citizens. In providing both forms of support, the international community may indirectly make it easier for the government to hold criminal trials.

Conclusion

One can ask two normative questions as to criminal trials for human rights violations conducted under a previous regime. Does the retroactive justice problem arise when these trials take place for the acts which were not punishable according to the domestic law at the time of doing them? Is the prosecution of violators obligatory or discretionary in the eyes of the law? To the former question, legal philosophers give an affirmative answer, while substantive internationalists imply a negative one. The negative answer is objectionable, since international law on human rights cannot stand in the place of preexisting laws in national criminal trials. Because these trials breach the *nulla poena* principle, they have intrinsic unfairness and produce instrumental detriment. To the latter question, procedural internationalists answer that the prosecution is obligatory according to international human rights law. But the obligatory conception of prosecution has a considerably limited scope: only a few criminal treaties oblige state parties to prosecute. The mandatory conception also has an undesirable practical consequence that a successor government is obliged to prosecute even though the prosecution may cause a political crisis.

Some people might summarize my conclusion in the following way: a retroactive law in trials for human rights abuses, which are discretionary, is unfair and detrimental. So summarized, my position may look disappointing to those who share resentment against grave human rights violations. But such an interpretation is misguided. My point is that whenever an ex post facto law is invoked in the trials, one should not shut her eyes to the fact that the practice of law suffers from the legal loss caused by this law, even when the law's necessity overweighs its political loss. The political leaders, the judges involved, and the public in a transitional society surely make their hands dirty. And I cannot keep my own hands clean when I argue that retroactive laws are to be invoked where they are the most effective measure to promote the public interest.

Notes

* I wish to thank Ko Hasegawa, Dennis Thompson, and Kenneth Winston for their valuable comments on an earlier version of this article. My thanks are also due to Steven Rich for his editorial advice.

1 According to an estimation (Rummel 1994: 15), the nearly 169.2 million dead were caused mostly by repressive regimes during peacetime in comparison with the approximately 34 million dead from international or civil wars between 1900 and 1987.

2 My reference to justifications Summers gives does not demonstrate my complete agreement with his arguments on the rule of law. One divergence between Summers's position and mine is that while he seems to regard the rule of law as an external constraint to the practice of law, I consider the rule of law as an internal principle that functions in the practice once it is established.

3 G.A. Res. 2200, 21 U.N. GAOR Supp. (No. 16) at 52, 999 U.N.T.S. 171.

4 213 U.N.T.S. 221, Europ. T.S. No. 5.

5 O.A.S. Official Records, OEA/ser. K./XVI/1.1, doc. 65 rev. 1, corr. 1 (1970).

6 G.A. Res. 260A(III), 78 U.N.T.S. 277.

7 G.A. Res. 39/46, 39 U.N. GAOR Supp. (No. 51) at 197, U.N. Doc. A/39/51 (1984).

8 630 F. 2d 876 (2d Cir. 1980).

9 To fill this gap, procedural internationalists invoke the authoritative interpretations rendered by the Human Rights Committee and the Inter-American Court of Human Rights. But looking closely at the interpretations should make it clear that these institutions do not read "ensure" provisions as obliging state parties selectively to prosecute (Scharf 1996: 49-51).

10 If a secret agreement to punish a limited number of perpetrators was made as part of the regime transition, would not the public have their hands dirty because of their lack of information on the agreement? Or, would they do still since the agreement was implemented in the name of the public? I leave this question open, which it would take another article to investigate.

References

American Law Institute. 1987. *Restatement of the Law Third: The Foreign Relations Law of the United States*. Vol. 2. St. Paul: American Law Institute Pub.

Austin, J. L. 1979. A Plea for Excuses. *Philosophical Papers*. 3rd ed. Ed. J. O. Urmson and G. J. Warnock. Oxford: Oxford University Press. 175-204. (Originally published 1957.)

Balint, Jennifer L. 1996. Conflict, Conflict Victimization, and Legal Redress, 1945-1996. *Law and Contemporary Problems* 59: 231-247.

Fuller, Lon L. 1958. Positivism and Fidelity to Law—A Reply to Professor Hart. *Harvard Law Review* 71: 630-672.

Fuller, Lon L. 1969. *The Morality of Law*. Rev. ed. New Haven: Yale University Press. (1st ed. 1964.)

Golding, Martin P. 1993. Retroactive Legislation and Restoration of the Rule of Law. *Jahrbuch fur Recht und Ethik* 1: 169-192.

Hart, H.L.A. 1958. Positivism and the Separation of Law and Morals. *Harvard Law Review* 71: 593-629.

Kuper, Leo. 1981. *Genocide*. Harmondsworth: Penguin Books.

Luban, David. 1988. *Lawyers and Justice: An Ethical Study*. Princeton: Princeton University Press.

Machiavelli, Niccolo. 1995. *The Prince*. Ed. and Trans. David Wootton. Indianapolis: Hackett Pub. (Originally Published 1532.)

Malamud-Goti, Jaime. 1990. Transitional Governments in the Breach: Why Punish State Criminals? *Human Rights Quarterly* 12: 1-16.

Nagel, Thomas. 1978. Ruthlessness in Public Life. *Public and Private Morality*. Ed. Stuart Hampshire. Cambridge: Cambridge University Press. 75-91.

Nino, Carlos Santiago. 1991. The Duty to Punish Past Abuses of Human Rights Put into Context: The Case of Argentina. *Yale Law Journal* 100: 2619-2640.

Nino, Carlos Santiago. 1996. *Radical Evil on Trial*. New Haven: Yale University Press.

Orentlicher, Diane F. 1991. Settling Accounts: The Duty to Prosecute Human Rights Violations of a Prior Regime. *Yale Law Journal* 100: 2537-2615.

Roht-Arriaza, Naomi. 1990. State Responsibility to Investigate and Prosecute Grave Human Rights Violations in International Law. *California Law Review* 78: 449-513.

Rummel, R.J. 1994. *Death by Government*. New Brunswick: Transaction Pub.

Schachter, Oscar. 1985. *International Law in Theory and Practice: General Course in Public International Law*. Recueil des cours: Collected Courses of the Hague Academy of International Law 1982-V. Dordrecht: Martinus Nijhoff Pub.

Scharf, Michael. 1996. The Letter of the Law: The Scope of the International Legal Obligation to Prosecute Human Rights Crimes. *Law and Contemporary Problems* 59: 41-61.

Shklar, Judith N. 1964. *Legalism*. Cambridge, Mass.: Harvard University Press.

Simma, Bruno and Philip Alston. 1992. The Sources of Human Rights Law: Custom, Jus Cogens, and General Principles. *Australian Year Book of International Law* 12: 82-108.

Summers, Robert S. 1988. The Ideal Socio-Legal Order. Its "Rule of Law" Dimension. *Ratio Juris* 1: 154-161.

Thompson, Dennis F. 1987. *Political Ethics and Public Office*. Cambridge, Mass.: Harvard University Press.

Usami, Makoto. 1993. *Kokyoteki Kettei to shite no Ho: Ho-Jissen no Kaishaku no Kokoromi [Law as Public Decision: Interpreting the Practice of Law]*. Tokyo: Bokutaku-sha Pub.

Walzer, Michael. 1973. Political Action: The Problem of Dirty Hands. *Philosophy and Public Affairs* 2: 160-180.

Winston, Kenneth I. 1998. Moral Opportunism: A Case Study. *Integrity and Conscience*. Nomos XL. Ed. Ian Shapiro and Robert Adams. New York: New York University Press. 154-184.

Zalaquett, Jose. 1989. Confronting Human Rights Violations Committed by Former Governments: Principles Applicable and Political Constraints. *State Crimes: Punishment or Pardon*. Ed. The Justice and Society Program of Aspen Institute. Queenstown: Aspen Institute. 23-69.

20. Left-Libertarianism and Global Justice

NICOLAUS TIDEMAN
PETER VALLENTYNE

1. Introduction

We address the question of what obligations of economic justice citizens of one country have to citizens of other countries. We hold that there are some such obligations, and although we hold that these obligations are obligations of individual citizens, we speak loosely of obligations of one country to another - understood as the composite obligations of the citizens of one country to citizens of another.

We are concerned here with *duties of justice*, which we understand as *enforceable* duties of morality. They are the moral duties that agents have that other agents are morally *permitted to coerce* them to fulfill. On most views, not all moral duties are duties of justice, since there are some duties (such as helping one's elderly mother, perhaps) that are not legitimately enforceable by others. We believe that there are duties of justice between (citizens of different) countries.

We address the issue of global economic justice by addressing the question of who owns what in the world. There are three categories of things that must be considered: *beings with moral standing* (beings that matter morally for their own sake), *natural resources* (unproduced resources with no standing, such as land, air, water, etc.), and *artifacts* (produced resources with no standing). For simplicity, we assume that all beings with moral standing are agents (rational choosers), and we thus ignore the important and difficult problem of the status of children, fetuses, and animals (which we believe have some sort of non-full moral standing). We also assume that there is just one generation of agents, and we thus also ignore the important problems concerning future generations. These gross simplifications permit us to focus on the core issues of global economic justice that arise in a context of a single generation of agents.

2. A Brief Statement of the Problem

What does economic justice require in the way of wealth distribution among countries? We focus on two kinds of wealth (1) human wealth, which are the personal characteristics of the citizens that are conducive to a good life (e.g., what capacities they have); (2) non-agent resource wealth, which are the non-agent resources of the country that are conducive to a good life (e.g., land, machines, etc.). Furthermore for each of these two types of wealth, we can distinguish between: (a) the initial wealth (i.e., the initial personal characteristics of the citizens, and the initial natural resources), (b) the created part of the wealth (e.g., the personal characteristics that the citizens choose to develop and the artifacts that they choose to produce). Making the distinction between the initial and the created parts is of course almost always difficult in practice, and even in theory there are many murky issues. We believe, however, that sense can be made of this distinction, and simply assume it here.

We both agree that inequalities in wealth that are appropriately attributable to the choices of the agents involved (e.g., the extent to which they develop their capacities or produce artifacts) are not issues of justice. (Recall that we are here assuming a single generation of agents. Where there are multiple generations, this view may need to be modified.) Although this is a controversial issue, we simply assume it in what follows. Hence in what follows we are only concerned with inequalities in unchosen (initial) personal characteristics and natural resources.

Our question then is: To what extent do agents of one country owe agents of another country payments if their unchosen (initial) natural resources or personal characteristics are more valuable?

3. Left-Libertarianism: A First Gloss

We defend a *left-libertarian* theory of justice, and discuss its implications for global justice. In our simplified world there are agents, natural resources, and artifacts. *Libertarian* theories of justice hold that *agents*, at least initially, own themselves, and thus owe no service to others, except through voluntary action. The most familiar libertarian theories (e.g., Nozick [1974]) are *right-libertarian* in that they hold that *natural resources* are initially unowned and, under a broad range of realistic circumstances, can be privately appropriated without the consent of, or any significant payment to, the other members of society. *Left-libertarian* theories, by contrast, hold that natural resources are owned by the members of society in some egalitarian manner, and may be appropriated only in ways that are compatible with the rights of all to natural resources. Left-libertarian theories have been propounded for over two centuries,[1] but in recent years there has been a revival of interest in them. Theories roughly of this sort (but with some important qualifications noted below) have been explored (but not defended) by Gibbard [1976] and Kolm [1985, 1986], advocated by Grunebaum [1987], Steiner [1994], Van Parijs [1995], and Tideman [1991, 1994, 1997, 1998], and criticized by Cohen [1995].

Left-libertarianism has two central ideas: (1) Agents own themselves. (2) The value of natural resources is owned in some egalitarian sense. Different left-libertarian theories have different conceptions either of self-ownership or of the relevant form of egalitarian ownership of natural resources (and indirectly of the ownership of artifacts). We start by explaining and motivating the thesis of self-ownership for agents. Then we discuss some different conceptions of egalitarian ownership of natural resources.

The core idea of self-ownership is that agents own themselves in much the same way that they can own inanimate objects. This ownership is typically taken to include, at a minimum (1) full *control rights* over (power to grant and deny permission for) the *use* of their persons (e.g., what things are done to them) and (2) full *immunity from payment* for the possession and exercise of these rights (ensuring, for example, that the rights are not merely rented). One of us (Vallentyne) holds that self-ownership also includes (3) full *rights to transfer* the rights they have to others (by sale, rental, gift, or loan), so that individuals are able to sell themselves into slavery. The other of us (Tideman) denies (3), and holds that no one can rightly be compelled, on pain of physical punishment or loss of liberty, to fulfill a personal service commitment. On the other hand, this view does permit a person to pledge his/her accumulated physical wealth as security for a personal service commitment.

Another way of expressing this difference in views is to say that Vallentyne regards the agents who own themselves as people in the normal intuitive sense (e.g., that can live for fifty years or more), while Tideman holds that the agents that own themselves can cut themselves off from their histories if they are prepared to forego the assets to which their histories would otherwise entitle them. Vallentyne's view gives an agent who does not change his/her mind a more valuable ownership of him/herself, while Tideman's view ensures that any person that one encounters owns him/herself to the greatest extent that a person can.

Self-ownership, on either view, is plausible because it imposes appropriate constraints on how individuals may be treated by others without their consent. Killing, torturing, or enslaving innocent individuals without their consent is unjust no matter how effective it may be as a means to some moral goal. Some form of self-ownership is necessary to recognize adequately that agents have the *formal right to control the use of their person*. There are some things (such as physical contact of various sorts) that others may not do to an agent without his/her consent, and those very things are permissible if the agent gives his/her consent and the owners of other resources involved give their consent. The view that agents have the right to control the use of their persons is, of course, highly controversial. A constraint against killing an agent need not be accompanied by the right of the agent to waive the constraint, as self-ownership holds. (One might hold, for example, that killing is always wrong—even with the consent of the agent.) A full argument would need to address many important relevant issues that we here ignore.

The assumption that some form of self-ownership imposes constraints on the promotion of equality need not be the assumption that self-ownership as we define it imposes such constraints. Our concept of self-ownership gives agents both *control rights* over the *use* of their persons and various *tax immunities*. One can endorse a partial form of self-ownership (e.g., control rights) without endorsing full self-ownership (e.g. with full tax immunities). So, much more argument is needed for a full defense of self-ownership. We hope that we have said enough to give it at least some plausibility.

Self-ownership is one central ideal of left-libertarianism. The other is egalitarian ownership of the value of natural resources. There are many forms that this egalitarian ownership can take, and we defend one form.

One basic issue concerns the level of jurisdiction at which egalitarian ownership applies. One view is that the land occupied by each country is owned in some egalitarian manner by its citizens, but that non-citizens have no claim to the value of that land. This would be egalitarian internally, but viewed globally, this might involve an extremely inegalitarian distribution of rights over natural resources. Those who live in countries that control less valuable natural resources would thereby have less valuable ownership rights. Natural resources were not created by any (non-divine) agent, and no agent has any special entitlement to a greater share merely because he/she happened to be there first. Hence, any plausible view treats the egalitarian ownership of natural resources as holding at the global level (the entire world). This crucial claim is assumed in what follows.

1 According to one version of left-libertarianism, natural resources are *jointly owned* in the sense that authorization to use, or to appropriate,

is given through some specified collective decision-making process (e.g., by majority or unanimous decision). One form of this approach—advocated (seemingly, at least) by Grunebaum [1987]—holds that collective approval is needed for any *use*, as well as appropriation, of natural resources. But as Fressola [1981] and Cohen [1986, 1995] have argued, this is implausible, since it holds that, for agents like us, no one has the right to *do anything* (e.g., stand in a given spot, eat an apple, or even breathe) without authorization from other members of society. For every action requires the use of some natural resources (e.g., occupying a spatial location), and thus no one is permitted to do anything without approval from others.

2 A more plausible form of joint ownership of natural resources—held perhaps by Grotius [1625] and Pufendorf [1672], and explored by Gibbard [1976]—holds that prior to any agreement agents are permitted to *use* natural resources in conformance with specified terms of *common use,* but they have no *exclusive* rights of use (no private ownership). Roughly, this means that they are permitted to use natural resources in various ways (occupy locations, breathe air, eat apples) as long as those resources are not then in use by others (and perhaps subject to certain conditions of sustainability), but they have no rights over any natural resources that they are not currently using. On this view, the initial rights over natural resources are like rights over public park benches. One has a right to use a resource (e.g., sit in one), but once one stops using it, one has no right to prevent others from using it.

3 Even this form of joint ownership of natural resources, however, is implausible. For it has the implication that no *appropriation* (i.e. acquisition of exclusive rights of use) could be just in the absence of actual collective agreement. It is most implausible to hold that the consent of others is required for just appropriation when communication with all relevant others is impossible, extremely difficult, or expensive (as it almost always is). And even when communication is relatively easy and costless, it is unclear why one needs the consent of others as long as one makes an appropriate compensatory payment for the natural resources appropriated.

A different sort of approach holds that agents may use, or appropriate, inappropriate natural resources without the permission of others, but if they do so, they acquire certain obligations. Below we suggest that some form of this approach is plausible. But first we must see that some forms clearly are not. An extreme form of this approach holds that anyone who *uses* natural resources (which is of course everyone) *forfeits all rights* of self-ownership (e.g., acquires an enforceable duty to do whatever maximally promotes equality). A slightly less extreme form allows agents to use natural resources subject to the rules of common use without any loss of self-ownership, but holds that anyone who *appropriates* (claims rights of exclusive use over) natural resources forfeits all rights of self-ownership. Both these views hold that agents are "initially" self-owners, and are thus "formally" versions of libertarianism. Neither is plausible because they allow self-ownership to be lost too easily.

A plausible conception of the ownership of natural resources must be compatible with reasonably *secure* (not easily lost) self-ownership. At a minimum it should allow inappropriate resources to be *used* by agents *without the permission of others* and *without any loss of the rights of self-ownership*—as long as it does not violate the property rights of others. Without some such condition of permissible use of natural resources, self-ownership has no real force, since it could be lost through the unavoidable use of natural resources. In addition, a plausible conception of the ownership of natural resources should be *unilateralist* in the sense of allowing agents to *appropriate* inappropriate natural resources without the consent of others—and with no loss of self-ownership—as long as they make an appropriate payment (to be discussed below).[2]

In what follows, then, we consider some unilateralist conceptions of natural resource ownership (in conjunction with self-ownership). *Radical right libertarians*—such as Rothbard [1978, 1982] and Kirzner [1978]—hold that that there are no payment requirements for the appropriation of inappropriate resources. Agents are free to take ownership of whatever inappropriate natural resources they find (or mix their labor with). Obviously, this is a non-starter from a viewpoint that requires egalitarian ownership of resources. *Nozickean right libertarians*—such as Nozick [1974]—hold that the only payment requirements are those of a Nozickean proviso, which requires roughly that (taking account of the general benefits of a system of exclusive rights to natural resources), no individual be made worse off (in some appropriate sense) by the appropriation (compared with the situation before appropriation).[3] It seems quite plausible that satisfaction of some form of a Nozickean proviso is a *necessary* condition for just unilateral appropriation. But Nozickean libertarians are mistaken in holding that it is *sufficient* for just appropriation. For a world without the possibility of appropriating exclusive rights to natural resources would leave people very poor. Little if any compensation is required by a Nozickean proviso. There is no excuse for those who first appropriate natural resources to insist that the whole gain in efficiency from institutions for exclusive appropriation of natural resources must be assigned to them, when there are alternative protocols for assigning the gain that would preserve most if not all of the efficiency gain. Those who wish to impose an institution and justify it on grounds of efficiency have, at most, a claim to the gain as compared to the next most efficient institution, not a claim to the gain as compared to no institution.

Georgist libertarians—such as eponymous George [1879, 1892], Steiner [1977, 1980, 1981, 1992, 1994], and Tideman [1991, 1994, 1997, 1998]—hold that agents may appropriate inappropriate natural resources as long as they pay the competitive value of the rights they claim.[4] Because of potential problems with future generations (which we are here ignoring), the rights involved are usually understood as temporary in nature, and thus the competitive value is understood as the competitive *rent* owed for the rights claimed. For simplicity, we also make this assumption.

We believe that Georgist libertarianism is plausible. It allows agents to use and appropriate unowned natural resources as long as they pay the competitive value of the rights they claim. Furthermore, it holds that agents fully own the artifacts that they produce with their labor, as long as they pay the rent on the underlying natural resources they own and the owners of any other labor, natural resources, or artifacts involved in the production have consented (e.g., in return for a payment) to the use of these resources and have renounced any claim to the product. Thus, for example, if I produce some apples on some land that I have claimed, then I own the apples as long as I have paid any required rent for the land. If I hire someone to work for me, and rent some machinery from someone, then I own the apples as long as I have paid any required rent for the land, the wages to the hired hand, and the rent for the machinery.

We address below the question of how the rent payments are to be divided up. One of us suggests that they should be divided up equally, and one of us argues that they should be used to promote equality of effective opportunities for a good life (and thus divided up unequally). The point to note here is that, however they are divided up, the duty to make payments is limited to the competitive value of the rights over natural resources that one claims. There are no duties to contribute simply because someone is in need. Nor does the amount that agents are required to contribute depend on how fortunate they are with respect to their personal endowments (capacities, etc.) or their situational endowments (wealth, opportunities, etc.). The duty to make payments to others is based solely on the value of the natural resources one appropriates. If one appropriates none, one owes nothing.

Purist egalitarians reject this limited egalitarian duty. They hold that equality must be promoted whenever possible. No constraints are imposed in principle on how this may be done. We believe, however, that the egalitarian duty is indeed limited in two ways. First, violations of self-ownership are not permitted no matter how effective they may be in promoting equality. Agents may not be killed, tortured, or assaulted without their consent. Nor may they be coerced into providing involuntary services for others (e.g., mandatory labor for the state). Nor do agents owe any taxes merely because they exist or because they use natural resources in ways that do not reduce the value of the opportunities of others. Second, although agents do owe taxes (rent) if they appropriate natural resources, these taxes are based solely on the competitive value of the rights over the resources that they claim. No taxes are owed for simply having or exercising one's talents. For example, setting taxes for each agent at some fraction of the value of his/her actual or maximally valuable annual product is inadmissible.

So, the Georgist conception of egalitarian ownership of natural resources is plausible because it recognizes that agents must pay the full competitive value of any rights of over natural resources they claim, but it denies that agents have an unlimited duty to promote equality.

If Georgist left-libertarianism is accepted, then we can draw one implication for global justice. Each country is required by justice to make a payment for distribution among all countries equal to the value of the rights they have claimed over unimproved natural resources. Countries that have appropriated more valuable natural resources owe more than those who have appropriated less valuable natural resources.

So far, so good. We now consider how these rent payments are to be allocated among countries.

4. Distributing the Rent Payments

So far we have addressed the obligations to make payments for natural resources appropriated. We now turn to how these payments are to be distributed. For simplicity we ignore the important question of how administrative expenses are factored in and simply discuss how the payments should be distributed if it could be done without any administrative cost.

There is, of course, a very wide range of possible answers to the question of how the rent payments should be distributed. One might hold, for example, that a utilitarian principle should be applied. We simply assume here that some sort of egalitarian principle should be applied. After all, natural resources are in some sense the common property of all.

One of us (Tideman) holds that the rent payments should be *divided equally* among all agents in the world. The net effect of this idea, in conjunction with the idea that competitive rent is owed for rights claimed over natural resources, is that agents and countries effectively owe rent payments only to the extent that they appropriate more than an equal per capita share of the value of natural resources. For if they appropriate just a per capita share, their share of the rent payments equals the rent they owe, and hence no net rent is due.

The other of us (Vallentyne) holds that the rent payments should be divided *so as to promote effective equality of opportunity for a good life.* There are, of course, many issues here that a full theory of equality promotion would have to address. What makes for a good life? How exactly are effective opportunities understood? On what basis are effective opportunities assessed? Are the requisite interpersonal comparisons possible? How is equality measured? These important issues are not addressed here, except to stipulate that the relevant equality promotion is to be done by making people's lives better, and not by leveling-down.[5] For present purposes it suffices to contrast this view with the previous one. On Vallentyne's view, the rent payments are not normally divided up equally but rather divided up unequally so as to equalize effective opportunities for a good life (whatever exactly that requires). Someone who has advantageous unchosen personal capacities (e.g., a strong, beautiful, intelligent person with a happy disposition) gets less (and perhaps nothing) from the rent payments than a person with disadvantageous personal capacities (e.g., a weak, ugly, stupid person with a depressive disposition). (If our model had more than one generation, we might ask whether those who bring weak, ugly, stupid people with depressive dispositions into the world have an obligation to compensate those who thereby receive less rent.) The same point applies to those who have advantageous unchosen situations (e.g., those who come to start life in an especially desirable physical or social location). The most basic point on this view is simply that the division of the rent payments should compensate for unchosen inequalities in opportunities for a good life.

Because we both agree that the demands of equality are limited to how the rent payments should be spent, we both agree that agents and countries do not have a duty of justice to do whatever is necessary to promote equality. The economic duties of agents and countries are determined by the value of the natural resources that they appropriate, and do not depend on the needs or relative deprivations of others (except of course to the extent that this affects the competitive value of the rights claimed).

At issue is how the independently generated rent payments are to be divided. Tideman endorses the view that each agent has a right to an equal share of the value of natural resources. Vallentyne endorses the view that justice requires that the value of natural resources be used to promote effectively equality of opportunity for a good life. At issue between the two views is the question of whether disadvantages in unchosen characteristics entitles one to a greater share of the value of natural resources (the rent payments). This is a deep and controversial issue that we cannot develop here. Suffice it to say that the equal share view is a form of external resourcism—the view that justice is concerned only with the distribution of external (non-personal resources), and that the effectively equality of opportunity view is a form of welfarism—the view that justice is concerned with the distribution of all resources (personal and external) and with how they affect the opportunity for a good life.

In terms of global justice, this issue is relevant only if there are differences among countries in the average value of the effective opportunities for a good life. One way that there can be such differences is by there being differences in the distribution of innate personal capacities of the citizens (initial immunity to disease and depression, disposition to intelligence, strength, etc.). In the world as it is, for reasonably large countries the differences on average in such characteristics are likely to be quite small. Furthermore, even where there are significant differences, our knowledge of the differences is likely to be very limited. Hence, in practice in typical cases it is unlikely that there will be a difference between the two approaches with respect to the impact of differences of innate personal capacities. As we now indicate however, there are other sources where the two approaches to the division of the rent payments are likely to yield significant differences in practice.

First, even if countries differ little on average in the distribution of innate personal capacities, the (e.g. socially inherited) *initial (unchosen) beliefs, values, and practical knowledge* of adults may have a significant impact on their effective opportunity for a good life. If individuals in one country start adult life with many more false beliefs (e.g., false superstitions about how to avoid disease and depression, about how to develop intelligence and strength, etc.), that reduces the value of their effective opportunity for a good life. Likewise, if the individuals start life with *values* that are very difficult to satisfy, and very difficult to change, this too may have a significant impact on the value of their effective opportunities for a good life. To the extent these factors have such an effect, the equality promotion model of the division of the rent payments, but not the equal division model, gives countries with a greater proportion of such disadvantaged individuals a greater share of the rent payments.

So far we have considered ways in which individuals might be disadvantaged in their effective opportunity for a good life by their own personal characteristics. Individuals can also be disadvantaged by the personal characteristics of their neighbors, and by the general social climate in their country and in neighboring countries. The extent to which others in one's country are disposed to trust and cooperate with others (whether this is innate or socially conditioned), for example, very much affects one's effective life opportunities. The two models of division of the rent payments are likely to differ because of such differences.[6]

Yet another factor in the determination of effective opportunities for a good life is the vicinity to desirable natural resources. Although those who appropriate natural resources owe competitive rent for the rights claimed, the starting geographical positions of agents affect their effective opportunities for a good life. First, citizens may have unchosen psychological attachments to their geographical region of origin, even if it is otherwise less desirable. More generally, the costs of moving to take advantage of desirable natural resources depend very much on where one starts. So this is yet another factor that affects the effective opportunities for a good life.

Finally, the artifacts (roads, machines, etc.) with which the citizens of a country start their adult life are another source of inequality in effective opportunity for a good life. Strictly speaking, in our simplified model in which there is only one generation of agents, there are no such artifacts, but it is worth mentioning here because in real life they are likely to be a major source of inequality of effective opportunity for a good life. We have not here addressed the status of such artifacts, but for the record one of us (Tideman) holds that those who own artifacts have a right to transfer them to others by gift without any taxation, and one of us (Vallentyne) denies that individuals have such a right. The point here is simply to note that to the extent that there is transmission of artifactual wealth from one generation to a later generation, this too is a factor in generating inequality of effective opportunity for a good life among countries.

In sum, there are likely to be significant differences in practice between the two models of rent payment division. It ultimately boils down to whether one views the value of natural resources as a fund to be divided equally or as a fund for the promotion of effective equality of opportunity for a good life.

5. Conclusion

We have given the outline of a left-libertarian theory of justice according to which each agent, initially at least, owns him/herself, and natural resources are owned in some egalitarian sense. Self-ownership, we have suggested, is needed to provide agents with adequate protection against interference from others. Egalitarian ownership of natural resources is plausible because none of the agents created these resources. Furthermore, this egalitarian ownership is most plausible when understood as *global* (and not merely national) egalitarian ownership of the value of natural resources. We have defended a version of Georgist left-libertarianism according to which those who appropriate natural resources are required to pay competitive rent for the value of the rights they claim. This generates a fund of rent payments that is to be divided among the citizens of the world.

There are many important unresolved issues in this approach. In particular, we, the authors, disagree about how the rent payments are to be divided. Tideman holds that the rent payments should be divided equally among all agents, whereas Vallentyne holds that the rent payments should be spent so as to promote effectively equality of opportunity for a good life among agents. In addition to these, there are many other important issues that need to be addressed. We identify some of the main ones in the appendix.

On any plausible view of left-libertarianism, however, national boundaries are arbitrary in principle (although not in practice), and those countries that have appropriated more than their per capita share of the value of natural resources, and for which the average unchosen advantage is greater than the global average, owe payments to those countries that that have appropriated less than their per capita share of the value of natural resources, and for which the average unchosen advantage is no greater than the global average.

Notes

1 Early exponents of some form of self-ownership combined with some form of egalitarian ownership of natural resources include: Ogilvie [1781], Spencer [1793], Paine [1795], Colins [1835], Huet [1853], Dove [1850, 1854], Spencer [1851],George [1879, 1892], and Walras [1896]. For insightful discussion of some of these early views, see Cunliffe [1987, 1988, 1990a, 1990b, 1998].

2 We leave open here what agents must do in addition to making an appropriate payment. The most plausible view, we believe, simply requires that they stake a claim (assert certain rights). The payment owed would thus depend on what rights are claimed. Other possible views are that agents must discover the natural resource,

or that they must mix their labor with it. Although we believe neither of these views to be plausible, for generality we leave open this issue.

3 Locke [1690] was not a Nozickean libertarian. For he disallowed appropriation that would lead to spoilage, he rejected the right of voluntary self-enslavement, and he held that one had a duty to provide the means of subsistence to those unable to provide for themselves. He arguably also rejected the Nozickean proviso, since he may have meant "enough and as good" to mean "an equally valuable share".

4 For discussion of the views of Henry George, and of contemporary Georgist economists, see: Andelson [1991], Harrison, Hudson, Miller and Feder [1994], Tideman [1994], and Wenzer [1997]. Van Parijs [1995] also defends charging competitive rent for the appropriation of natural resources. He is not, however, a Georgist libertarian because he endorses charging rent on (or taxes equal to up to 100% of the value of) all non-personal assets that were "given" to an agent (as opposed to produced by him/her).

5 Vallentyne would defend the view that equality should be promoted among the Pareto optimal arrangements (i.e., arrangements for which no one's opportunity set can be improved except by making someone else's opportunity set worse).

6 Another factor that can affect life opportunities is the material wealth inherited from previous generations of one's country. Given, however, that we are assuming only a single generation, this factor won't arise.

References

Ackerman, B., [1980], Social Justice in the Liberal State, New Haven, Yale University Press.

Andelson, R.V., ed., [1979], Critics of Henry George, London, Associated University Presses.

Andelson, R.V., ed. [1991], Commons Without Tragedy, London, Shepheard-Walwyn.

Brody, B., [1983], "Redistribution Without Egalitarianism", Social Philosophy and Policy, 1, p.71-87.

Christman, J., [1994], The Myth of Property, New York, Oxford University Press.

Cohen, G.A., [1986], "Self-Ownership, World Ownership, and Equality: Part II," Social Philosophy and Policy 3, p.77-96.

Cohen, G.A., [1989], "On the Currency of Egalitarian Justice", Ethics 99, p.906-44.

Cohen, G.A., [1995], Self-Ownership, Freedom, and Equality, Cambridge, Cambridge University Press.

Colins, H., [1835], Du Pacte Sociale, et de la Liberté Politique considerée comme complément moral de l'Homme, vol. 2, Paris, Moutardier.

Cunliffe, J., [1987], "A Mutualist Theory of Exploitation?", in Modern Theories of Exploitation, ed. A. Reeve, London, Sage.

Cunliffe, J., [1988], "The Liberal Rationale of 'Rational Socialism'", Political Studies, 36, p.653-662.

Cunliffe, J., [1990a], "The Neglected Background of Radical Liberalism; P.E. Dove's Theory of Property", History of Political Thought, 11, p.467-490.

Cunliffe, J., [1990b], "Intergenerational Justice and Productive Resources; A Nineteenth Century Socialist Debate", History of European Ideas, 12, p.227-238.

Cunliffe, J., [1998], "The Liberal Case for a Socialist Property Regime; The Contribution of Francois Huet", History of Political Thought, forthcoming.

Dove, P.E., [1850], The Theory of Human Progression and Natural Probability of a Reign of Justice, The Science of Politics, Part 1, Edinburgh, Johnstone and Hunten.
Dove, P.E., [1854], The Elements of Political Science, The Science of Politics, Part 2, Edinburgh, Johnstone and Hunten.
Fressola, A., [1981], "Liberty and Property", American Philosophical Quarterly, 18, p.315-322.
Gauthier, D., [1986], Morals by Agreement, London, Oxford University Press.
George, H., [1879], Progress and Poverty, New York, Robert Schalkenbach Foundation.
George, H., [1892], A Perplexed Philosopher, New York, Robert Schalkenbach Foundation.
Gibbard, A., [1976], "Natural Property Rights", Nous, 10, p.77-86.
Grotius, H. [1625], The Rights of War and Peace, ed. A.C. Campbell, London, M. Walter Dunne, 1901, Hyperion Reprint Edition, 1979.
Grunebaum, J., [1987], Private Ownership, New York, Routledge & Kegan Paul.
Harrison, F., Hudson, M., Miller, G.J., and Feder, K., [1994], A Philosophy for a Fair Society, London, Shepheard-Walwyn.
Huet, F., [1853], Le Régne Social du Christianisme, Paris, Firmin Didot Frères.
Kirzner, I., [1978], "Entrepreneurship, Entitlement, and Economic Justice", Eastern Economic Journal 4, p.9-25. Reprinted in Reading Nozick, ed. J. Paul, Oxford, Basil Blackwell, 1981, p.383-401.
Kolm, S.C., [1985], Le Contrat Social Libéral (Théorie et Pratique du Libéralisme), Paris, Presses Universitaires de France.
Kolm, S.C., [1986], "L'Allocation des Ressources Naturelles et le Libéralisme." Revue Economique, 37, p.207-241.
Kolm, S.C., [1987b], "The Freedom and Consensus Normative Theory of the State: The Liberal Social Contract", dans Individual Liberty and Democratic Decision-Making: The Ethics, Economics, and Politics of Democracy, edited by P. Koslowski, Tübingen, J.C.B. Mohr.
Kolm, S.C., [1996a], Modern Theories of Justice, Cambridge (Massachusetts), MIT Press.
Lindholm R.W. and Lynn, A.D. Jr., eds., [1982], Land Value Taxation, Madison, University of Wisconsin Press.
Locke J., [1690], Two Treatises of Government, ed. by P. Laslett, New York, Cambridge University Press, 1960.
Mavrodes, G., [1974], "Property", The Personalist, 53, p.245-262.
Nozick, R., [1974], Anarchy, State, and Utopia, New York, Basic Books.
Ogilvie, W., [1781], "The Right of Property in Land", in The Pioneers of Land Reform, ed. M. Beer, New York, Alfred Knopf, 1920.
Otsuka, M., [1998], "Self-Ownership and Equality, A Lockean Reconciliation", Philosophy and Public Affairs 27, p.65-92.
Paine, T., [1795], "Agrarian Justice", in The Thomas Paine Reader, ed. M. Foot and I. Kramnick. Harmondsworth, Penguin Books, 1987.
Rothbard, M., [1978], For a New Liberty, The Libertarian Manifesto, revised edition, New York, Libertarian Review Foundation.
Rothbard, M., [1982], The Ethics of Liberty. Atlantic Highlands, Humanities Press.
Spence, T., [1793], "The Real Rights of Man", in The Pioneers of Land Reform, ed. M. Beer. New York, Alfred Knopf, 1920.
Spencer, H., [1851], Social Statics, New York, Augustus M. Kelley.
Steiner, H., [1977], "The Natural Right to the Means of Production", Philosophical Quarterly, 27, p.41-49.
Steiner, H., [1980], "Slavery, Socialism, and Private Property", Nomos, 22, p.244-65.

Steiner, H., [1981], "Liberty and Equality", Political Studies, 29, p.555-69.
Steiner, H., [1987], "Capitalism, Justice, and Equal Starts", in Equal Opportunity, ed. E. Frankel Paul, F.D. Miller, J. Paul, and J. Ahrens, Cambridge (Massachusetts), Basil Blackwell, p.49-71.
Steiner, H., [1992], "Three Just Taxes", in Arguing for Basic Income, ed. P. Van Parijs, New York, Verso, p.81-98.
Steiner, H., [1994], An Essay on Rights, Cambridge (Massachusetts), Blackwell Publishers.
Tideman, N., [1991], "Commons and Commonwealths: A New Framework for the Justification of Territorial Claims", in ed. R.V. Andelson, Commons Without Tragedy, Savage, Maryland, Barnes and Noble, p.109-129.
Tideman, N., ed., [1994], Land and Taxation, London, Shepheard-Walwyn.
Tideman, N., [1997], "The Shape of a World Inspired by Henry George", unpublished manuscript, Department of Economics, Virginia Polytechnic and State University.
Tideman, N., [1998], "Applications of Land Value Taxation to Problems of Environmental Protection, Congestion, Efficient Resource Use, Population, and Economic Growth", in ed. D. Netzer, Land Value Taxation: Can It and Will It Work Today? Cambridge (Massachusetts), Lincoln Institute of Land Policy, p.263-276.
Vallentyne, P. [1998], "Critical Notice of G.A. Cohen's Self-Ownership, Freedom, and Equality", Canadian Journal of Philosophy 28, p.609-626.
Van Parijs, P., [1990], "Equal Endowments as Undominated Diversity", Recherches Economiques de Louvain, 56, p.327-355.
Van Parijs, P., [1991], Qu'est-ce qu'une société juste?, Paris, Le Seuil.
Van Parijs, P., [1992], "Competing Justifications of Basic Income", in Arguing for Basic Income, ed. P. Van Parijs, New York, Verso, p.3-43.
Van Parijs, P., [1995], Real Freedom for All, New York, Oxford University Press.

Appendix

Important issues that a full left-libertarian theory would need to address

1 The notion of competitive rent: Exactly how is competitive rent determined? What are the initial allocations of rights relative to which demand and supply operate (e.g., common use of natural resources as modified by past just appropriations)? What is the relevant process for determining the competitive value (market-clearing price? second price auction?)? Do problems of multiple equilibria (multiple possible competitive prices) arise, and if so, how are they handled?

2 Dealing with existing beings with partial moral standing (i.e., that are not full agents): How is the theory extended to deal with sentient beings with no potential for agency (low level animals, defective humans), sentient beings with no agency but with the potential for agency (normal fetuses, infants), sentient beings with partial agency (children, great apes)?

3 Dealing with future beings with moral standing: How are the following issues to be dealt with in light of the definite or possible existence of future beings with moral standing: the of use non-renewable resources, gifts to later generations, procreation?

4 Implementation: To whom is rent to be paid where there is no government or no government that distributes the rent appropriately (e.g., if the government is grossly inefficient or corrupt)?

21. Global Ecological Citizenship and Human Rights

PETER D. SWAN

Introduction

The contours of citizenship in the welfare state were laid out by T.H. Marshall in his famous essay, "Citizenship and Social Class".[1] While for Marshall, modern citizenship is concerned with the promotion of equality of membership in the nation state; his analysis provides a point of departure for understanding the possibilities for the further development or expansion of citizenship and environmental governance in what Ulrich Beck has referred to as the "risk society".[2]

Marshall's emphasis on the dynamic or evolutionary character of citizenship is particularly significant because it allows us to recognize that the development of citizenship has been open-ended. It also illustrates the expansionary character of rights discourse as the assertion of some rights claims require the articulation of further rights in order to provide the conditions that are necessary for the exercise of existing rights. This at least suggests the possibility for the reconceptualization of citizenship and its extension to cover more and more areas of social life.[3] In addition Marshall's emphasis on full participation in the national community makes an important connection between citizenship and democracy. This has specific implications for the development of new forms of citizenship that seek to "socialize" environmental decision-making by opening it up to non-expert cultures at both the national and global levels.

For the last three decades, environmental groups in North America and elsewhere have been demanding rights to environmental protection and rights for participation in environmental decision-making. Such demands have taken on a new impetus during the last decade with the increasing perception that we are now entering a period of unprecedented danger by living in a "risk society" marked by the possibility of technological and ecological catastrophe on a grand scale.[4] The reconceptualization of environmental or ecological rights[5] as part of a new generation of citizenship rights will form the focus for this paper.

While recognizing that it is at the level of the nation-state that the institutionalization of ecological rights must take place, in this paper, I will explore the possibility that ecological citizenship and its associated form of rights must also increasingly operate at the international or global level. The context of citizenship has been changed by the phenomenon of globalization since Marshall first presented his analysis of modern citizenship in 1949. After successive waves of immigration, the populations of Western societies are no longer as homogeneous as Marshall's postwar Britain. Most of the North-Atlantic liberal democracies grant rights to non-members living within their borders as immigrants or as refugees.[6] In addition many of the most important decisions affecting the lives of individuals are no longer made at the level of the nation-state but rather at the international or transnational level. Not only do many of the most serious problems facing humanity such as environmental degradation and risks exist on a global scale, but also the moral and political responses to these problems must take place at the global or planetary level.

In the first section of this paper, I will refer to the recent work of Ulrich Beck to show the global character of the environmental crisis. Without disparaging the importance of addressing environmental issues at the local and national levels, I will argue that appropriate responses to this crisis must also be directed at issues of the globalization of risks. I will contend that effective responses should not only focus on the management of the crisis by scientific and technical experts but also should emphasize the need to democratize decisions about risk at the global level. It is this need for the democratization of environmental decision-making that raises the issue of extending the boundaries of citizenship to the global or planetary level. Just as Marshall associated earlier forms of modern citizenship with civil, political and social rights, I will try to show that demands for ecological citizenship also require the development of forms of environmental or ecological rights that are compatible with furthering the claims of citizens at the global level.

In the final section of the paper, I will briefly discuss the relationship between environmental rights and human rights. I will then suggest an outline for an approach to environmental rights as human rights that is more explicitly political in character. Drawing on the concept of the "right to have rights" from Hannah Arendt and Claude Lefort, I will suggest a framework for interpreting environmental human rights as equal rights of public access to deliberation and decision-making about environmental risks.

The Democratic Response to the Globalization of Risks

Citizenship, whether in the form articulated by T.H. Marshall or in relationship to its expansion through new generation of rights, has almost always been associated with membership in the modern nation-state. However, the centrality of national sovereignty can no longer be taken for granted. Many of the rights and obligations that have traditionally been associated with the nation-state are now legitimized at the international and transnational level and thus transcend the traditional boundaries of nations.[7] These developments can best be explained in terms of the process of globalization or more specifically of "Western globalization". According to David Held, this process can be defined in terms of two distinct but related phenomena: a world-wide linkage of political, economic and social activity; and an intensification of world-level interactions and interconnections both within and between states and societies.[8] In addition to these new connections that are usually associated with economic globalization,[9] there has been the growth of a number of transnational political and legal structures that restrict the state monopoly of control over populations within their borders. As an example, citizens within states that are part of a regional federation of states such as the European Union may appeal to supranational courts for infringements of their rights by their own countries.[10] These developments have been accompanied by the emergence of universalistic norms relating to the rights of individuals that are formalized within international conventions and charters rather than in state law.[11]

Increasingly membership in national communities is no longer the sole criterion for the assertion of rights claims. On one hand individuals who have exhausted all domestic avenues increasingly turn to international and transnational institutions for redress. On the other, a developing concept of substantive citizenship implies that many of the rights that are normally associated with citizenship are exercised by immigrants and guest workers in states in which they are not citizens.[12]

However, just as the intensification of interaction at the global level forces us to reconceptualize the relationship between citizenship and cultural rights, so does the universalization of ecological and technological risks force us to rethink the character of environmental rights and citizenship. Environmentalists have long argued that the effects of pollution or other forms of degradation often cannot be confined within the boundaries of a single nation. Chemical pollution in a river flowing through more than one country is likely to affect residents of all the countries along the river; acid rain as a product of industry in one country potentially will affect the water quality of other countries. Nor can such effects be confined temporally for they also represent dangers to future generations of humans and other species.

The extent of the dangers of ecological destruction has been given a particularly articulate formulation in Ulrich Beck's concept of the risk society. According to Beck, developments in the nuclear and chemical industries have greatly increased our susceptibility to large-scale disasters and to chronic illnesses. More recently, Beck has clarified the global character of risk society and its implications for the democratic restructuring of decision-making processes around ecological and technological risks. Accordingly,"[r]isk society, fully thought through, means world risk society. For its axial principle, it challenges, are dangers produced by civilization which cannot be delimited in space or time."[13]

The recognition of the global character of risks suggests that we can no longer rely exclusively on sovereign nations or traditional concepts of national citizenship to respond to the global dimensions of risks. However, proposed institutional responses to perceptions of the globalization of risk may be quite different. The dominant response encourages a more centralized form of risk management based on increasing the power of international or transnational institutions that continue to rely upon and to promote the authority of technical and bureaucratic expert responses to the perception of crisis.

Beck contests this approach by arguing that the recognition of the need to address environmental risks at both the local and global levels results as much from the ability of environmental actors to articulate environmental dangers as matters of common concern through public dialogue as it does from scientific diagnosis.[14] He does not deny that environmental risks do exist. However, he insists that we should not simply accept the definitions of risks as provided by experts. It also is important to grant recognition to the validity of local or lay ecological knowledge as important sources of public knowledge about risks.[15]

Accordingly Beck argues that in order to facilitate the recognition of the validity of lay knowledge and to further the democratization of decision-making about "what sort of nature and society we want",[16] it is necessary to place more emphasis on democratic forms of deliberation in the ecological public sphere. This is more compatible with the promotion of what he refers to as the emerging realm of subpolitics in "global civil society". As such, the politics of a global risk society represents a dual challenge to traditional ideas of state sovereignty for not only does it emphasize the significance of interactions at the international and transnational levels but it also focuses on an increasingly important role for non-state actors such as NGO's and social movements in an arena where, until recently, only states have been recognized as valid actors.

Global Ecological Citizenship

In opposition to earlier writers such as Ophuls and Heilbroner[17] who argued that the ecological crisis required a strong government, Beck proposes a "reinvention of politics" through the democratization of decision-making about environmental risks. His conception of a democratic resolution of the crisis within areas of life that are outside the realm of "official politics" supplies a model that is an alternative to both authoritarian state responses to the ecological crisis and a postmodernism suspicious of all projects of emancipation. This focus on "socializing" decision-making about risks suggests that the determination of acceptable levels of ecological hazards can never be regarded simply as a matter of expert decisions about investment, economic efficiency or political efficacy. These are decisions that all citizens must confront because they are crucial to the survival of both local and planetary ecosystems.[18]

There is evidence that the recognition of the need for this democratic confrontation of risk has led to the appearance of new and powerful actors on the international scene. As demonstrated by the successful organization of a multinational boycott in Europe in 1995 that succeeded in getting Shell Oil to dispose of one of its obsolete oil rigs on land rather than at sea, increasingly Non-Governmental Organizations (NGO's) such as Greenpeace are emerging as forces that promote "globalization *from below*".[19] According to Beck this is evidence of a "subpoliticization of world society" where politics takes place "outside the representative institutions of the political systems of nation-states".[20] Increasingly individuals and groups are bypassing the official institutions of political will-formation and participating directly in political decisions affecting the environment.

It is in this form of participation at the international level that we see the first anticipations of a "global citizenship" in which the rights and obligations that are normally attached to membership in national communities are articulated at a transnational and planetary level.[21] Global citizenship as a normative undertaking in relation to environmental politics has recently been explored by Richard Falk[22] and by Bart van Steenbergen.[23] From these works we see that there is a multiplicity of images associated with the concept of global citizenship.

While Falk suggests at least five partly overlapping ideas that are applicable to citizenship at the global level,[24] from the perspective of ecological politics, the most relevant parts of Falk's typology are the world managers and the transnational activists. Focusing on key terms such as sustainable development, world manager focus on solving issues of global risk through an extensive technical/managerial approach that is to be coordinated through the "concerted action of states and international institutions" and is the antithesis of the democratization of risk decisions.[25]

As opposed to the expertise based managerial model of environmental governance, Falk's "transnational activists" try to address the democratic deficit of current approaches to environmental decision-making. According to Falk, these activists are either parts of transnational social movements or members of NGO's such as Greenpeace or Amnesty International that operate to promote political consciousness across international boundaries. Such activists tend to operate in what has come to be known as global civil society. More recently some of these organizations have been accepted as actors within international organizations. Although this recognition of a growing role for global activists is important, Falk's contribution to the discussion of global citizenship remains somewhat sketchy. The exact character of their roles to date remains unclear, and he does not acknowledge the danger that activist groups also may have to water down their demands as the price for their recognition as participants in international bodies. In part because he remains unreflective about existing power relations and about the potential role of these new actors, Falk does not succeed in clarifying the relationship between transnational activists and a process of democratizing environmental decision-making at the global level.

Bart van Steenbergen elaborates on Falk's model by conceptualizing a framework for global ecological citizenship that is a specific response to the ecological crisis and which relies on a more radical ecocentric approach to environmental decision-making. His ideal for global citizenship is found in the concept of the "earth citizen" who has a sense of his or her own organic attachment to nature.[26] Thus conceived, the concept of "earth citizenship" shows a desire to extend citizenship in such a way that it reflects recognition of our increasing responsibility for nonhuman nature.

Following Marshall, van Steenbergen acknowledges that the centrality of the concept of participation to the redefinition of citizenship. However, rather than referring to the active involvement in a polity, his conception of participation emphasizes that individuals must take an active role in a "natural community" that is seen as necessary to the constitution of meaning and identity for individuals.[27]

Although this is an interesting elaboration of ecological citizenship, van Steenbergen's focus on an "organic" connection of humans to the earth is a retreat not only from the global political emphasis of Falk's "transnational activists" but also from the Marshall's social democratic interpretation of the role of citizens. By his own admission, a serious concern for ecology may impose limits on the action/activist orientation of modern citizenship because ecology emphasizes contemplation and the restraint on action.[28] Although citizenship must necessarily refer to the obligations that citizens have to both present and future human members of the world community and to nonhuman nature as part of a planetary ecological community, a viable concept of ecological citizenship cannot sacrifice individual and collective autonomy to duties and obligations towards an already constituted social or natural community.[29]

Although they represent important attempts to sketch the contours of ecological citizenship, a closer evaluation of the above formulations suggests that they may replicate problems revealed in the liberalism/ communitarian debate. While Falk's transnational activists represents the extension of a liberal individualistic conception of politics to transnational activists at the global level, van Steenbergen merely substitutes the idea of an already constituted natural community of human and non humans for an existing political community. A more democratic concept of ecological citizenship must be accompanied by a theorization of the articulation of new rights claims in and their institutionalization in appropriate forms.[30] In the rest of this paper, I will discuss some of the environmental rights that may be associated with ecological citizenship and the character of their relationship to human rights.

Environments Rights and Human Rights

Just as previous stages of modern citizenship required the civil, political and social, the concept of global ecological citizenship implies the need to formulate new ecological or environmental rights at both national and international levels. However, there has been "a shift in the major organizing principle of membership in contemporary polities".[31] Unlike earlier forms of modern citizenship, global citizenship can no longer be based on membership in national communities. Accordingly, individuals as global citizens may make rights claims based on the more abstract concept of universal personhood rather than on nationality. As asserted by global citizens, individual rights claims thus can be reconceptualized as universal human rights claims that are often legitimated at the international or transnational levels.[32]

Like the newly emerging social and cultural rights of non-citizens, global ecological citizenship can be grounded in human rights discourse. Recently some writers have suggested that in struggles in developing countries, human rights and environmental rights are separate but mutually reinforcing rights.[33] This bolsters the view by other theorists that although environmental protection and human rights have different societal values, these values are overlapping and that the two processes may be brought together to achieve a number of common objectives.[34]

Within this latter conception, the relationship between environmental rights and human rights has taken two dominant forms: as included within an expanded interpretation of existing human rights or as a new generation of human rights.[35] Environmental rights as "pure human rights" can be subsumed under existing civil, political or social rights such as the right to life or to security of the person. According to this interpretation the meaning of the above rights can be widened so that they can encompass environmental rights. A second interpretation would attempt to duplicate the logic of Marshall's argument with regard to the significance of social rights as establishing a basis for the equal exercise of first generation rights. According to this interpretation, environmental rights would be needed to provide the preconditions for the exercise of the other rights.

Environmental rights, interpreted as a right to environment, can also be seen as separate from previous forms of human rights and thus could be formulated as an addition to these rights. Conceived of as a new form of human rights, environmental rights would focus on the provision of certain levels of environmental quality such as rights to clean air and clean water as substantive rights and also on rights of access to wilderness. To the extent that such rights would require action by both states and international bodies to provide environmental protection for people, they would most resemble social rights in their logical structure.

Most of the existing discussion on ecological or environmental rights as human rights focuses on whether or not the two forms of rights are mutually compatible. While this is an important question, for the sake of argument I am going to assume that they are compatible. In my opinion, the more important issue is the relationship of environmental rights to the democratization of decisions on environmental risks that I believe is central to global ecological citizenship. For that reason, I will now turn my attention to a specific formulation of human rights that I believe is capable of addressing the relationship between environmental protection and struggles to democratize social and political decisions in emerging environmental public spheres of global civil society.

Environmental Rights and the "Right to Have Rights"

To refer to a definitive form that environmental or ecological rights must take would be both premature and undesirable. Instead I would like to explore a more explicitly political interpretation of the role of human rights discourse that I believe can provide a conceptual framework for analyzing ecological rights as arising either from the reinterpretation of existing rights or from the formulation of new rights.

An important starting point for exploring the political character of environmental rights as human rights is provided by the concept of "the right to have rights" as formulated initially by Hannah Arendt and later elaborated upon by the French political philosopher, Claude Lefort. As I am interpreting it, the right to have rights is a basic human right from which further more specific rights claims can be made.

Within the context of analyzing the growth of totalitarian governments, Hannah Arendt contends that:

> We became aware of the existence of a right to have rights (and that means to live within a framework where one is judged by one's actions and opinions) and a right to belong to some kind of organized community only when millions of people emerged who had lost and could not regain these rights because of the new global situation.[36]

Although this formulation has been interpreted as saying that basic human rights are meaningless in the absence of the concrete protection of inclusion in a national polity through the granting of citizenship rights, recent commentaries have tried to provide a more "democratic" reading of the right to have rights by interpreting it as referring to more than existing rights of citizenship.[37] A more fruitful line of inquiry for our purposes can be found in attempts to give the "right to have rights" a more intersubjective explanation that emphasizes the importance of political communication. According to a recent interpretation by James Bohman, this basic right makes sense primarily as a right of equal access to the public world.[38] Accordingly, we need to be able to participate on an equal basis in public affairs in order to articulate our opinions and have them listened to and to ensure that our actions may have some effect.[39] However, the right to have rights entails more than mere access to the public sphere. It also refers to a broad concept of political equality that means that humans not only have access to the public space but that they also can initiate action with others and initiate acts of deliberation with others about matters of common concern.[40] Without rights of access that can also address the social inequalities that act as obstacles to the initiation of deliberation, people have little opportunity to define issues of common concern. As a result, public deliberation is reduced to the one-way discourse of expertise that allows the powerful to continue to marginalize other voices and to set the public agenda as they see fit.[41] Without the right to have right, there is no deliberative equality and the public space is diminished.

The relationship of the politics of rights to the preservation and enhancement of the public space also is central to understanding Claude Lefort's more explicitly democratic interpretation of the right to have rights. According to Lefort, the key to the universality of rights lies in their articulation within a public space in civil society that is separate from the state. Accordingly any diminishing or elimination of the public space is interpreted as a degradation of human rights.[42] However, like Hannah Arendt, who recognizes that institutional guarantees remain effective only so long as they reflect "the living power of the people",[43] Lefort acknowledges that no institution, including the state can guarantee either rights themselves or the continued existence of the public space. Rights are gained and secured only in their declaration and practice by individuals in the presence of others who recognize the validity of their claims. According to Lefort, this recognition of human rights is based on the right to have rights. Consequently, the recognition of this basic right leads to the generation of other rights and the opening up of the possibility of a potentially endless democratic adventure, the outcome of which is indeterminate.[44]

This conception of the appropriate relationship between human rights and democratic politics relates justice to the existence of a public space that encourages individuals and groups to both speak and to listen to others. The size of that space is dependent on the extent of the mutual recognition of participating speakers and actors within its shifting boundaries.[45] Lefort's politics of rights thus depends on an intersubjective construction of rights in the public spaces of civil society.

The failure of norms and institutions to satisfy the requirements of the basic right to have rights leads to claims that question these norms and institutions.[46] Interpreted in this manner, the right to have rights can provide the basis for critique of the partiality of existing rights and their failure to promote political equality defined in terms of access to the public world. In this way, the discourse of human rights can provide a fundamental critique of the inadequacy of existing institutions and also provide the impetus to generate new interpretations of existing legal rights and the political articulation of new rights. This discourse should be central to the articulation of a new regime of rights to support the emergence of democratic ecological citizenship at both the national and global levels.

Within the context of global ecological citizenship/politics, rights to equal access to the public world and to the equal capacity to initiate deliberation and action within it are central. However, the exact form, that such environmental rights as part of the development of environmental citizenship should take, remains up for discussion. As suggested above, proposals for environmental human rights as a "fundamental right to environmental quality or to environmental protection" would require states or international organizations to guarantee acceptable levels of protection from technological and ecological risks. Although this kind of right has already been adopted in certain state constitutions in a number of international covenants, critics have questioned the adequacy of a right that closely resembles existing social rights. According to the more progressive critics, not only does this type of right raise the specter of citizens remaining as the passive clients of the state welfare regulations but also it may not be suitable for dealing with the complexities of contemporary society.[47] According to Karl-Heinz Ladeur and Ida Koppen, because of the "ever-provisional knowledge basis of decisions", environmental rights must be structured in such a way as to allow for flexibility and the reversibility of decisions.[48] Accordingly, only a procedural form of rights that provides for the participation of all affected persons in the defining and creation of changing forms of "common interests" is adequate to the conditions of uncertainty in a risk society.[49]

This conception of procedural environmental rights is intended to be sufficiently reflexive to deal with the uncertainties of the environmental risks produced by economic, technological and political decisions. Yet it may not be sufficiently open to address either the actual exigencies of struggles around environmental rights or the complex indeterminacy of the social struggles that are envisioned in the concept of the right to have rights. As James Bohman suggests, in order for meaningful participation to take place, the reasons given in deliberation must receive consideration by other participants and acquire public significance.[50] Even with the availability of genuine procedural opportunities for participation, persistent forms of social inequalities can become political inequalities that undermine the democratic character of deliberation in environmental matters. As illustrated by the recent struggles by the environmental justice movement in North America, racism and the lack of economic resources have made it very difficult for marginalized groups to have an effective voice in the decisions that affect their lives. In risk decisions such as those involving the siting of hazardous wastes facilities, this marginalization is further reinforced by the prioritization of expert knowledge.[51] These forms of social and cognitive inequality thus become variants of political and deliberative inequality. Not only are groups and individuals systematically prevented from initiating politically significant deliberations on environmental matters but also they often are implicated in the decisions of the dominant actors. The very silence that is produced by inequality is turned into its opposite by more powerful deliberators who present this as a form of tacit consent to decisions whose more immediate consequences are more likely to be felt by members of the excluded groups.[52]

I therefore would argue that a more adequate conceptual framework for environmental rights at either the domestic or international level can be located within the recursivity that is implicit in the idea of the right to have rights. Despite their intended flexibility, procedural environmental rights on their own may be insufficiently open to struggles for recognition and inclusion around environmental issues to promote the degree of political equality necessary for the democratic "subpolitics" envisaged in the more radical images of ecological citizenship.

Within the context of rights discourse as a questioning of the adequacy of existing rights and especially of those rights that are "granted" by the state, a more reflexive conceptualization of ecological rights must also present a view of rights as open to reinterpretation and revision. While I can agree with the prioritization of the role of procedural rights in promoting democratic decision-making on environmental matters, I do not believe that purely procedural participatory rights are sufficient on their own. Drawing on Nancy Fraser's analysis of needs talk, I would argue that rights also are embedded in chains of "in order to" relationships. Once we open up environmental rights as either human rights or institutionalized rights for interpretation, we also have to consider what other deliberative skills or opportunities have to be provided in order for those who have been excluded to reflexively participate in decision-making. In other words, the successful establishment of participatory rights claims will lead to the need for groups to publicly articulate further claims that are necessary to either provide substance to the initial claims or to reveal the partiality of justice involved in the initial claims. It is only by conceptualizing environmental rights as involving a more general right to criticize the justice of existing institutions, including existing rights, that environmental groups and individuals will be able to contest their current subordinate role in risk decision-making and also to challenge the established boundaries of the political at both the domestic and global levels.

Conclusion

The above discussion of global ecological citizenship represents a challenge to the continued authority of the nation-state for two separate but related reasons: the impetus for new rights and citizenship emerge from civil society or global civil society; and the development of ecological citizenship emphasizes the discourse of human rights rather than legal rights of membership. Neither challenge, however, is intended to deny the continuing relevance of the state itself or of citizenship within its boundaries. Although the activities and deliberation of civil society are increasingly being recognized as significant in this era of globalization, this development is by no means unique in history. To some extent, civil society is being rediscovered rather than being invented. The earlier forms of citizenship rights, discussed by Marshall, also emerged first from struggles in civil society and only later were given state recognition.

In addition, we must consider the limited character of struggles for rights by groups in civil society. Such struggles over rights are fragmented and disparate by nature. They emerge from different groups in society with no conception of a unified struggle to overthrow all existing power relations. For the most part, movements struggling for recognition and inclusion are self-limiting in character.[53] Their struggles for rights are intended not as a means to the conquest of state power but rather as attempts to nourish and expand individual and collective autonomy through the expansion of a public space separate from the power of both the economy and state.[54]

The "foundation" of global ecological citizenship in universal personhood and human rights can be considered as a challenge to both the state and to the ideal of national citizenship. However, again it is necessary to qualify the extent of this challenge. As interpreted within the context of the right to have rights, an absolute separation of a person's roles as person and as citizen is difficult to maintain in practice. Thus the rights, which an individual claims as a moral person, may also be claimed by that person as a citizen. *That, which can be justified intersubjectively in a universal moral context, must also be justifiable in the more particular discourses used by citizens to make claims*. Human rights claims thus arise out of the context of violations within states as concrete political communities and are directed against those states. Even when the focus is on violations of human rights in the international arena, states remain as the primary addressees of human rights claims.[55]

Although the state must continue to play a major role in human rights discourses directed at global ecological politics, it is important to reiterate that such emerging rights are not simply "granted" to moral persons by that state or by any international associations of states. As was the case with first and second generations of citizenship rights, the rights attached to ecological citizenship arise from struggles for rights and recognition in civil society within specific nations and within global civil society. The rights and responsibilities of global ecological citizenship are those that humans give each other as "global citizens" and as inhabitants of particular communities. Such rights and responsibilities must be articulated in public spaces that are constituted by democratic deliberation: a deliberation in which people, speaking from the perspective of specific experiences of environmental injustice, have genuine opportunities to initiate.

Notes

1 T. Marshall and Tom Bottomore, *Citizenship and Social Class* (1992).

2 Ulrich Beck, *Risk Society: Towards a New Modernity* (1992), somewhat guardedly and I use the term "risk society" and without accepting all the implications of Beck's usage. However, for the purposes of this paper, the term is useful for revealing the contours of our contemporary environmental crisis.

3 However, there also are important conceptual limits to Marshall's model. One of the potential problems lies with the functionalism at the root of this analysis that is associated with his evolutionary approach. While his analysis is essentially accurate from an historical point of view, the legal institutions of citizenship are not simply created as a response either to the perception of broader social needs or to satisfy the demands of capitalism as many readings of Marshall have suggested.

4 See generally U. Beck, supra note 2.

5 Although some theorists attribute different meanings to the use of the terms "environmental" and "ecological", in this paper, when discussing citizenship and rights, I will use the terms synonymously.

6 See Yasemin N. Soysal, *Limits of Citizenship: Migrants and Postnational Membership in Europe* (1994); and W. Rogers Brubaker, *Citizenship and Nationhood in France and Germany* (1992).

7 Y.M. Soysal, *ibid.*, at p. 164.

8 D. Held, 'Democracy and the New International Order' in D. Archibugi and D. Held, eds., *Cosmopolitan Democracy: An Agenda for a New World Order* (1995), at p. 100.

9 *Ibid.*, at p. 101.

10 See Jean L. Cohen, 'Rights, Citizenship, and the Modern Form of the Social: Dilemas of Arendtian Republicanism' (1996), 3 *Constellations* at p.164

11 Y.M. Soysal, *supra* note 8, at p. 144.

12 See W. Rogers Brubaker, *supra* note 6 at pp. 36-38 for the distinction between formal and substantive citizenship.

13 U. Beck, 'World Risk Society as Cosmopolitan Society' (1996), 13, *Theory, Culture & Society* 1 at p.1. This characterization of "world risk society" is not new in Beck's work. The formulation of "Risk society" from the beginning represented a critique of modernity as a whole and hence both implicitly and explicitly had a global application.

14 For an analysis of the role of "discourse coalitions" of environmentalists and other concerned groups in defining the environmental agenda see Maarten A. Hajer, "Ecological Modernization as Cultural Politics" in Scott Lash et al., eds., *Risk, Environment & Modernity: Towards a New Ecology* (1996); and Maarten A. Hajer, *The Politics of Environmental Discourse: Ecological Modernization and the Policy Process* (1995).

15 For a more extensive discussion of the role local knowledge in defining environmental risks see B. Wynne, 'May the Sheep Safely Graze? A Reflexive view of the Expert-Lay Divide' in Scott Lash et al., eds., *Risk, Environment & Modernity: Towards a New Ecology* (1996).

16 M. Hajer (1996) *supra* note 14 at p. 259.

17 See William Ophuls, *Ecology and the Politics of Scarcity*, (1977); and Robert Heilbroner, *An Inquiry into the Human Prospect* (1974).

18 See U. Beck, "From Industrial to Risk Society", (1992) 9 *Theory, Culture & Society*

19 U. Beck, *supra* note 13, at p. 17 (emphasis in original) See also Ronnie D. Lipshutz, 'Reconstructing World Politics: The Emergence of Global Civil Society', in (1992) 21, *Millennium: Journal of International Studies* 389, Beck's interpretation of the role of NGO's may be overly optimistic. His interpretation tends to equate these organizations with new social movements in civil society. Other critics have argued that such an equation may be overly simplistic. See Alex Demirovic, 'NGO's: Social Movement in Global Order' paper presented at the Annual Meetings of the APSA, New York, September 1996.

20 Ulrich Beck, *supra* note 13 at p. 18.

21 For the purposes of the present paper, I will continue to use the term citizenship as if it were not problematic at the global level. To the extent that citizenship is associated with democratic participation, with the possession and assertion of rights and with embracing responsibilities for one's co-residents in a community it remains relevant to politics beyond the nation-state. As long we are concerned about the democratization of decisions about risk, about human rights and about the embracing of responsibility for present and future generations of humans and for other species inhabiting the planet as an ecological community, citizenship remains applicable to politics in a "risk society". I therefore believe that we can continue to use the term to describe a basis for a "globalization from below".

22 Richard Falk, 'The making of Global Citizenship', in Bart van Steenbergen, ed., *The Condition of Citizenship* (1994), 126.

23 Bart van Steenbergen, "Towards a Global Ecological Citizenship", in Bart van Steenbergen, ed., *The Condition of Citizenship* (1994), 141.

24 Supra note 22 at pp. 132-38. Falk's five aspects of global citizenship are the global reformer, the global businessperson, the world manager focusing on economic and environmental problems, the politically conscious regionalist, and the transnational activist.

25 *Ibid.* at pp. 135-36.

26 B. van Steenbergen, *supra* note 23 at pp. 149-51.

27 *Ibid.* at pp. 146-47.

28 *Ibid* at pp. 142-43.

29 Too often ideas about the duties citizenship have been used as part of the discourse of deregulation by neo conservatives to justify the transfer of collective state obligations for environmental protection to the individual. For a recent example of this phenomenon, see Canadian Ministry of the Environment, *A Primer on Environmental Citizenship* (1994). Despite the way that the discourse on environmental responsibility has been opportunistically used to further a conservative political agenda, it should not be dismissed as irrelevant to ecological democracy. Although in this paper, I attribute greater significance to the role of environmental rights, a more comprehensive theoretical framework for ecological citizenship will require an elaboration of a critical concept of ecological responsibility/care. For the start of a discussion of a such a critical concept of responsibility that emphasizes the importance of democratic deliberation as a means of structuring our ideas about duties, see Richard J. Bernstein, "Rethinking Responsibility" in (1994) 61 *Social Research* 833.

30 Although his concept of "global citizen activists" may be more compatible with a democratic theory of environmental decision-making, Falk also fails to connect global citizenship to an appropriate form of rights discourse.

31 Y.N. Soysal, *supra* note 6 at p. 164.

32 Y.N. Soysal, *supra* note 6 at p. 164. For a similar connection between personhood and human rights see Stanley I. Benn, 'Rights' in P. Edwards, ed. *The Encyclopedia of Philosophy* (1969), at pp. 195-99.

33 See James W. Nickel and Eduardo Viola, 'Integrating Environmentalism and Human Rights' in (1994) 16 *Environmental Ethics*, 265.

34 See Dinah Shelton, 'Human Rights, Environmental Rights, and the Right to Environment' (1991), 28 *Stanford Journal of International Law*, 103 at 105; and Leonard J. Waks, 'Environmental Claims and Citizen Rights' in (1996) 18 *Environmental Ethics*, 133.

35 D. Shelton, *ibid.*, at pp. 104-05; and 117-25.

36 Hannah Arendt, *The Origins of Totalitarianism* (1973), at p. 298.

37 Jeffrey C. Isaac, 'A New Guarantee on Earth: Hannah Arendt on Human Dignity and the Politics of Human Rights', in (1996), 90 *American Political Science Review* 61 at p. 67 Isaac's interpretation of the politics of human rights generally is very similar to the position that I am presenting here. However, in order to find this interpretation in Arendt, he has to overlook aspects of her work in which she is explicitly critical of the discourse of rights. For a more negative assessment of Arendt's views on human rights and their relevance to international politics, see Jean L. Cohen, *supra* note 10.

38 James Bohman, 'The Moral Costs of Political Pluralism: The Dilemmas of Difference and Equality in Arendt's "Reflections on Little Rock"' in Jerome Kohn and Larry May, eds., *Hannah Arendt: Twenty Years Later* (1996).

39 *Ibid.*, at p. 63.

40 *Ibid.*, at pp. 63-4.

41 *Ibid.*, at p. 64. This association of the right to have rights with the need to link economic poverty with the "political poverty" that results in the inability to initiate deliberation is particularly important with respect to political participation in environmental decision-making as I will discuss briefly below.

42 Claude Lefort, 'The Politics of Human Rights' in Claude Lefort, *The Political Forms of Modern Society* (1986); and Claude Lefort, 'Human Rights and the Welfare State' in Claude Lefort, *Democracy and Political Theory* (1989), at p. 41.

43 Hannah Arendt, *On Violence* (1970), at p. 7.

44 Claude Lefort (1989), *supra* note 50 at p. 37.

45 Claude Lefort (1989), *supra* note 50 at p. 41.

46 This interpretation of the critical functions of rights means that the assertion of rights must constitute an active questioning of existing forms of right, especially those granted by the state.

47 Ida Koppen and Karl-Heinz Ladeur, 'Environmental Rights' in Antonio Cassese et al., eds. *Human Rights and the European Community: The Substantive Law*, (1991) at p. 4.

48 *Ibid.*, at pp. 12 and 43.

49 *Ibid.*, at p. 14.

50 J. Bohman, *supra* note 46 at p. 64.

51 See Peter D. Swan, 'Environmental Justice and Minority Ecological Rights' in Juha Räikka, (ed.) *Minority Rights: Some Conceptual Issues* (1996).

52 J. Bohman, *supra* note 46 at p. 64.

53 Claude Lefort (1986), *supra* note 50 at p. 262.

54 See Peter D. Swan, 'Rights and Democratic Politics: The Contributions of Jürgen Habermas and Claude Lefort' in (1990) *Archiv für Rechts Und Sozialphilosophie* 215, at p. 223.

55 For a similar argument with respect to human rights as moral rights see Rainer Forst 'The Basic Right to Justification: Toward a Constructivist Conception of Human Rights' (1999), 6 *Constellations*, 35 at p. 52.

Part VI
Self-Determination

22. Therapeutic Jurisprudence and the Rights of Self-Determination

JAMES M. COOPER*

It is time for therapeutic jurisprudence to go international. As a budding jurisprudential movement, therapeutic jurisprudence has continually gained credibility in legal circles. First undertaken as a scholarly approach to mental health,[1] the movement has expanded its scope of analysis to become a mental health approach to law generally. Scholars have applied this mental health approach to criminal law,[2] civil actions,[3] disability law,[4] evidence law, labor arbitration law,[5] commercial law,[6] and mediation debates.[7] For Professor Bruce Winick, "[d]efining therapeutic jurisprudence broadly thus cedes to therapeutic jurisprudence scholars wide latitude in selecting their scholarly agendas."[8]

It is clear that this legal movement which studies the role of the law as a therapeutic agent,[9] is being used more frequently to analyze the goals and purposes of law. Therapeutic jurisprudence focuses on the law's impact on emotional life and psychological well-being.[10] Therapeutic jurisprudence considers the law's therapeutic or anti-therapeutic effects, seeks to enlarge the therapeutic functions, and delimits the non-therapeutic functions. Moreover, "[t]herapeutic jurisprudence proposes the exploration of ways in which, consistent with principles of justice and other constitutional values, the knowledge, theories, and insights of the mental health and related disciplines can help shape the development of the law."[11]

In essence, therapeutic jurisprudence focuses on various forms of self-determination. Each of the above contexts in which therapeutic jurisprudence has been applied has at its core an issue of self-determination. The defendant is provided with rights to participate in the procedure, be it criminal, medical, or otherwise. Procedural justice studies have focused on ways in which a process is deemed fair – when the participant in the legal process is accorded respect, dignity and a voice in the matter at hand.[12] Professor Winick's work "has praised the law's commitment to the principle of individual autonomy on the basis that *self-determination is therapeutically advantageous*" (emphasis added).[13]

However, it is not just the individual that deserves autonomy and all the therapeutic benefits that attend that set of rights. It is all people. The American and French revolutions moved the notion of self-determination from the individual to the nation.[14] Article 1 of both International Covenants on Human Rights further enshrined this collective right: "All people have the right of self-determination. By virtue of that right they freely determine their economic, social and cultural development."[15] For Professor James Crawford, "self-determination is plainly a collective rather than an individual right, although obviously enough individuals are to be involved in the exercise of the right, and a majority of them at least will benefit directly from it in the sense of retaining or achieving a measure of self-government in accordance with their wishes or preferences."[16] Hence, therapeutic jurisprudence must recognize other forms of self-determination, including those traditionally considered in the international realm. Domestic lawyers' efforts to empower their clients should be mirrored by international lawyers who deal in *trans-statal* and *international* matters.[17]

The proponents of therapeutic jurisprudence have alluded to the strength that an international perspective can bring to the endeavor. "[T]herapeutic jurisprudence can be more international and comparative in scope, allowing for greater opportunities for interchange between scholars of different nations."[18] Although therapeutic jurisprudence has been applied to a number of mental health and criminal law issues in countries outside the United States,[19] it has yet to be used as an analytical tool concerning international legal concepts.

It is now time to look at international law in terms of its therapeutic nature. The definition of what constitutes *therapeutic* in therapeutic jurisprudence has been given wide latitude. Professor David Wexler contends that "as a mere heuristic, therapeutic jurisprudence has eschewed a tight definition of 'therapeutic', and has similarly left open the nature of the party or person on whom the therapeutic or antitherapeutic consequences might be visited."[20] With such license,[21] we can find a number of therapeutic experiences in international law.

If *therapeutic* effects are defined as emotionally beneficial, nothing rivals the arrival of a people, nation, province, trust territory, or colony to formal and recognized statehood.[22] Take for example the newly independent state of Eritrea. As a province of Ethiopia, Eritrean liberation movements fought against rule from Addis Ababa for 30 years until Tigrean and Eritrean rebels toppled the Ethiopian dictator Mengistu Haile Mariam and his Communist regime in 1991. The Eritrean People's

Liberation Front (EPLF) took power soon after and prepared for a three-day referendum in the area concerning independence from Ethiopia in April 1993.[23] On May 14, 1993, following Eritrea's declaration of independence on April 27, the United Kingdom recognized the new East African state.[24] The U.N. Security Council recommended to the General Assembly on May 26, 1993 that it grant Eritrea membership in the United Nations.[25] On May 28, 1993 the General Assembly passed a resolution granting Eritrea membership in the United Nations. At midnight on Sunday, May 30, 1993, Eritrea formally became a state as Isayas Afewerki, leader of the EPLF was elected president by the front's ruling council before the proclamation of independence.[26] The festivities that came with the recognition by the international community was evidence of the therapeutic nature of independence. After three decades of struggle, self-determination had fully been realized.

While other substantive and procedural aspects of international law have therapeutic properties, it is the recognition of statehood by other sovereign states in the international system that has come to symbolize self-determination.[27] There are many forms of political and social organization, but the sovereign state is the primordial corporate form.[28] It is no surprise that this is the ultimate goal for national liberation groups and other peoples seeking self-determination:

> Every state, by the very fact that it is a state, is endowed with certain fundamental or inherent, or natural, right. Writers differ in enumerating what these rights are, but generally five rights are claimed, namely self-preservation, independence, equality, respect, and intercourse.[29]

To date international law has been about the law of states. They are the only subjects of international law. They can legitimately raise armies, impose taxes, sign treaties, and have a seat in the United Nations among other equal sovereign states.[30]

In the global village, however, each of us is a potential villager with a desire for a meaningful voice. All other actors who have some capacity for international relations themselves – non-governmental organizations ("NGOs"), multinational corporations, regional governments, national liberation movements, indigenous peoples, the global biosphere and individuals – have little standing in international law and are, more often than not, objects rather than subjects of the international legal regime.[31] To gain this standing is to become an integral part of the discourse that *juridically* constitutes international law. This is fundamentally what the right of self-determination has been about – the pursuit of internationally recognized statehood.

It is now time to expand the *level* of therapeutic jurisprudence just as it is time to understand traditional doctrinal international law as a stultifying and regressive set of rules.[32] At its heart is the right of self-determination – a normative value that very often conflicts with the fundamental right of statehood – territory integrity and political independence. There are endless cases of minorities, indigenous peoples, and other groups within a sovereign state that are seeking the right of self-determination. This leads to instability, oppression, and, increasingly, armed conflict. The inability to reconcile these two divergent visions of the international system has led to much instability and the failure of international law to dictate a direction for the future. In order to reduce this tension, statehood should not be the only exercise of self-determination.

This Article seeks to blaze a new path for the right of self-determination – one that unfolds its therapeutic properties and expands those agents who can exercise it. Self-determination, an internationally recognized,[33] yet completely misunderstood human right, has as many antecedents as it does abuses. Part I of this Article traces both the positive and negative therapeutic nature of right of self-determination. Originally formulated as a collective human right to lead peoples to their destiny,[34] self-determination has tremendous therapeutic properties that can bring salvation and autonomy to a nation, territory, or people once recognized by the rest of the international community.[35] As a sovereign state, new rights are conferred upon this juridical body to which it had previously been denied. But, there are also negative aspects to this exercise, for there are few countries in the world that do not have an ethnic minority or special interest group seeking to exercise some form of alternative self-determination within the same territory. Herein lies the tension in international law: the territorial integrity and political independence of many current states are at risk if internal bodies that also pursue self-determination form into secessionist movements.

Part II examines how this devolution and disintegration of sovereign states have been precluded by international law, thereby limiting in practice the rights of some groups to self-determination. The right of self-determination has become closely aligned with the recognition of statehood in the international community and this has been the focus of international law.[36] In the era of decolonization, self-determination meant the independence of former colonial states, with their respective borders already intact. The further division of states into smaller states was not permitted. State sovereignty brought with it, the inviolability of borders and political independence.[37] Self-determination was a once and once only right of territories under colonial and alien rule.[38]

Part III of this Article examines the decline of the statist view of self-determination and the corresponding changes that have come with new forms of non-state-based self-determination. Today, sovereign borders are increasingly losing their meaning. With the advent of international telecommunications and the globalization of national economies, state borders are fast disappearing. It is now time to redefine self-determination and change our international system from one based on states as principal actors to one where peoples exercise self-determination in any number of vehicles - the Internet, transnational corporations, religious affiliations, and professional associations. It may be only a matter of time before Microsoft Windows users recognize their own potential for self-determination, for they already constitute a powerful global force.[39] Perhaps billionaire entrepreneur Bill Gates, chairman of Microsoft, already has more of a right to a seat at the United Nations General Assembly than, for example, Burkina Faso. Part III ends with a look at ways to change the notion of self-determination and expand its meaningful exercise by non-state actors. The first agents to adapt to these changes, must be the practitioners of international law. States have, for too long, held a grip on membership in the international community. That monopoly is due for an end, an event unto itself that will have incredible therapeutic qualities.

I. Therapeutic and Anti-Therapeutic Notions of Self-Determination

A. Therapeutic Notions of Self-Determination

Self-determination is by no means a new concept in the history of political thought. Based on the Enlightenment, it is a natural extension of the fundamental liberties that philosophers such as John Locke, Jean-Jacques Rousseau and John Stuart Mill espoused. And while its historical antecedents are European, it was in the United States of America that self-determination got its legs.[40] In 1776, the breakaway American republic embraced the principle of self-determination and turned it into a collective right with therapeutic properties. The thirteen Colonies had long been denied their rights as British subjects.[41] They were being taxed, yet had no right of representation in the British Parliament in London. The American rebels proclaimed the birth of a new nation, fully independent from the mother country – the ultimate therapeutic event.

For psychiatrist Franz Fanon,

> "[d]ecolonization never takes place unnoticed, for it influences individuals and modifies them fundamentally. It transforms spectators crushed with their inessentiality into privileged actors, with the grandiose glare of history's floodlights upon them. It brings a natural rhythm into existence, introduced by new men, and with it a new language and a new humanity. Decolonization is the veritable creation of new men."[42]

In essence, self-determination was about independence. In theory, it provides the "territorial integrity" in the form of recognized borders and "political independence" in the form of recognized state functions. The ultimate event of therapeutic international law is an independence day. This is a celebration of the day the state got independence from some other political unit. There are those states which have celebrated the first day of independence in recent memory. The political changes in South Africa, the Czech Republic and Republic of Slovakia, and Eritrea are all examples. There is nothing more therapeutic than singing a national anthem and seeing the flag of one's nation flying in the United Nations Plaza with all the sovereign states of the world.

But self-determination is not always about division and dissolution. Sometimes self-determination has been in the form of reunification. The uniting of West and East Germany after four a half decades was such an example. These examples where the right of self-determination has been exercised are all state-related. Clearly self-determination has been strictly limited to sovereign states and those national liberation movements the international community deem worthy of joining its ranks as an equal member.

B. Anti-Therapeutic Notions of Self-Determination

In traditional therapeutic jurisprudence: "sometimes, of course, therapeutic considerations arguably will conflict. Legal rules may affect an individual both positively and negatively."[43] So too it is with the right of self-determination in an international context. Like all psychological phenomena, the effect of self-determination is not always positive. "The nation, as Self, with its self-conceived subjects, and the nation as Other, in relation to those individuals and collectivities which are not conceived as part of its Self, are treated as an actual modification of human reality, a natural source of actual effects, in relation to which all, self and other, must accommodate their self-conceived reality and their willed action."[44] As it is now practiced the exercise of self-determination brings with it an isolation of *other*. Depending on how the group defines *self* the self-determination can be exclusionary based on religion, language, color, gender, ethnicity, and nation. The same feeling that attracts members of some nation to seek self-determination by obtaining sovereign statehood, repels others who do not belong to this nation. It is hardly surprising that self-determination has been the primary cause of all major conflicts in this century.[45] The shot that killed Archduke Ferdinand of the Austro-Hungarian Empire during his visit to Sarajevo in 1914 came from the gun of a Serb nationalist, intent on self-determination for Serbia. The First World War followed suit.[46]

The most overtly anti-therapeutic aspect of the pursuit of self-determination is demonstrated by National Socialism in Germany.[47] German aggression leading up to the Second World War was based on visions of self-determination. Adolf Hitler's quest for *lebensraum*, or living space, led to his conquest of Europe. In 1938, the German peoples in Austria were co-opted into the Reich. Hitler then set his sights on ethnic Germans imprisoned, as he saw it, under alien Czech rule. The Sudetenland's German-speaking citizens joined the Third Reich and soon thereafter the rest of Czechoslovakia fell. The next area where German-speakers lived was the Free City of Danzig (today's Gdansk). Hitler demanded that this city become part of the Reich. On September 1, 1939, Hitler's self-determination on behalf of the German people resulted in the invasion of Poland and the beginning of the Second World War. The *other* to Hitler's Aryan master race were the Jews, six million of whom he systemically exterminated using instruments of the state.[48] Out of the ashes of the conflict and the Holocaust, another new international order was founded from which a new right of self-determination was born.

In the decolonization process, the natural avenue for self-determination following the end of the Second World War, the anti-therapeutic nature of self-determination reared its ugly head. According to Fanon decolonization, "which sets out to change the order of the world, is, obviously, a program of complete disorder."[49] The motherland, a European power, had trouble decoupling itself from its department, territory or colony. Seeds of dissent are sown early and manifest themselves in later political processes, often in the form of alternative notions of self-determination and attempts at secession. This would be the struggle with which international law would struggle as the developing world became independent.

II. Self-Determination in Current International Practice and Law

A. Self-Determination in International Practice

According to the United Nations Charter, a fundamental principle of this new organization would be "to develop friendly relations among nations based on respect for the principles of equal rights and self-determination of peoples..." According to the International Court of Justice, the right of self-determination became *ius cogens,* a peremptory norm of international law from which no derogation would be permitted. Soon, self-determination became somewhat of an international mantra, especially for states seeking independence from European colonial rule.

But in a Cold War environment in which decolonization was on the rise, self-determination had to be controlled. As the globe split down the middle along the ideological spectrum, proxy wars had to be contained so as to avoid superpower, and thus nuclear conflicts. Too volatile in nature, the right of self-determination in the United Nations Charter era had to be restricted.[50] Newly independent states retained old, often haphazard colonial boundaries that had never taken account of the conflicting nations within them. Stability, it was naively thought, could be preserved in this process.

Left as an unfulfilled right for many people stuck in artificial boundaries, the principle of self-determination was open to the perversion of Cold War politics. When Soviet tanks rolled into Prague in 1968, the Kremlin announced that its forces were merely assisting the socialist people of Czechoslovakia with the right to self-determination. The so-called Brezhnev Doctrine would be exercised again in 1979 in Afghanistan when the regime in Kabul needed similar assistance in guiding its people in its pursuit of self-determination. These are examples of the negative or anti-therapeutic aspects of this ill-defined international legal right.

But the geopolitical perversion of the right of self-determination was not restricted to the Soviets. American foreign policy manipulated the principle of self-determination to root out the threat of communism by claiming that the *Contra* rebels in Nicaragua and the *mujahedeen* fighters in Afghanistan were national liberation movements and, therefore, worthy of U.S. support. Similarly, the U.S. invasions of the Dominican Republic,[51] Grenada,[52] Panama,[53] and Haiti[54] were also explained away by some U.S. policy hacks as instrumental to bringing about self-determination in those countries.

The Gulf Conflict of 1991, showed the limitations of the right of self-determination and the vacuum that this supposed peremptory norm of international law had created.[55] By invading the Emirate of Kuwait in 1990, the Iraqis had denied the Kuwaitis the right to self-determination. Then U.S. president George Bush justified an attack on Iraq by telling the world that the conflict was about democracy and self-determination. According to President Bush, the military build-up and subsequent multilateral invasion of Kuwait and Iraq were merely collective responses to Kuwait's plea for assistance in restoring their self-determination. After all, surmised the U.S. President, weren't the Kuwaitis entitled to this fundamental right?

But as important as self-determination for the Kuwaitis may have been, there was a distinct lack of effort in the Bush administration to address perhaps a more pressing issue of self-determination in the region. In the closing days of the Gulf Conflict, Iraqi troops turned their attention away from Kuwait, and attacked Kurdish villages in response to their repeated demands for an independent Kurdistan. Although the U.S. helped with relief efforts to feed the starving Kurdish masses in Iraq as they escaped the brutal oppression of Saddam Hussein's regime,[56] it made no attempt to help them realize their dreams of a Kurdish state.

This selective and highly politicized approach to self-determination created an international double-standard.[57] Although the international community upheld the right of self-determination, it severely restricted its application in the aftermath of the Gulf Conflict. So, the Kuwaiti people should be able to exercise self-determination in the form of statehood, but the Kurds had to do so under the jurisdiction of Iraq. In a scene reminiscent of Wilsonian sophistry at the end of the First World War, legal *philosophes* and political pundits at the end of the Gulf Conflict made all sorts of convoluted arguments to explain why some nations could exercise self-determination in the form of statehood while other nations were merely minorities in someone else's state.

What emerged was a shaky New World Order and a recipe for disaster. A few months after the Gulf Conflict, the world, quite literally, fell apart in a helter-skelter frenzy characterized by conflicting notions of self-determination. New international actors appeared on the global scene and challenged the primacy of states, those actors whose territorial integrity and political independence had been deemed sacrosanct.

First, came the break-up of the Socialist Federal Republic of Yugoslavia in June 1991.[58] Then came the dissolution of the Soviet Union in August 1991, which also sparked demands for self-determination amongst the former Soviet republics. Membership in the international community was not closed.[59] Germany and Austria unilaterally recognized Croatia and Slovenia as states, in flagrant violation of existing international law,[60] and helping to fuel further ethnic rivalries in Bosnia-Hercegovina, and that is now manifesting itself in Kosovo, Albania, and Macedonia. This recognition that sparked the disintegration of the Former Socialist Federal Republic of Yugoslavia was clearly an indication that the right of self-determination had been balkanized. Some peoples or nations that aspired to statehood were granted inclusion in the international community and received the therapeutic experience of recognition and sovereignty. Others did, and still do, not. Dr. Boutros Boutros Ghali, U.N. Secretary-General, wrote that:

> The United Nations has not closed its door. Yet if every ethnic, religious or linguistic group claimed statehood, there would be no limit to fragmentation, and peace, security and economic well-being for all would become even more difficult to achieve.[61]

We must then examine the weak foundations laid down by international law concerning self-determination.[62] For Professor Winick: "In cases in which a rule of law may impose conflicting therapeutic effects on different groups, there also may be disagreement about which group's interests should be considered more important."[63] That has been the nub of the argument concerning who has the right to exercise self-determination. To date, it is states that make those rules and states which control the barriers to entry into the international community.

B. Self-Determination in International Law

Winick has admitted that "[A]s postrealists, we understand that there often is a wide gulf between the law of the books and law in action."[64] The confusion in life reflecting the confusion in book is not the case with respect to international law and the right of self-determination. In addition to treaties, a major source of international law is custom which itself is composed of state practice and *opinio juris*. The inconsistent and contradictory state practice concerning the recognition of states – the result of a highly selective exercise of self-determination – is merely reflected in the international law concerning this troubling area. While the exercise of self-determination does not feature prominently in the Charter of the United Nations, there are specific references to it in Articles 1(2) and 55.[65] Since that time, however, there has been a plethora of United Nations resolutions and conventions that have directly and indirectly dealt with this emerging international right.[66] The majority of the states making up the United Nations achieved their respective independence during the era of decolonization that began in the late 1950s as this newly emergent right began to take its current and unbending form. The right was even found to be a principle of *ius cogens*, a principle of international law from which no derogation was permitted.[67] Yet all the while, there has been no reigning and jurisprudentially recognized definition of *people*.[68] To make matters more difficult, some international instruments refer to the beneficiary of the right of self-determination as "peoples". As international lawyers committed to therapeutic jurisprudence, we must therefore explode the definition beyond traditional notions of statehood.

Like the practice of past eras, this right was applied in an uneven fashion. Initially, state sovereignty was supreme and the right of self-determination could only be applied in a patriarchical manner: for the national liberation of colonies to full statehood in the community of states. The context was, as Judge Dillard states in his separate concurring opinion in the International Court of Justice's decision in the *Western Sahara* case confined:

> The pronouncements of the Court thus indicate, in my view, that a norm of international law has emerged applicable to the decolonisation of those non-self-governing territories which are under the aegis of the United Nations.[69]

Such a restriction manifested itself in the first fifty years of the United Nations.[70] All secessionist attempts – save one (Bangladesh[71]) – failed. Statehood was not granted to the province of Katanga when it attempted to separate from the Belgian Congo following the independence of the latter.[72] Not only did the international community fail to recognize the secessionist movement, but it sent troops under United Nations control to put an end to the civil war that the Katangan action brought about.[73] A few years later, moreover, when Biafra attempted to leave the Nigerian state, only a handful of African states recognized its independence. The United Nations virtually ignored the large-scale human rights abuses committed against the Biafran people in the ensuing civil war, seeing the conflict as an internal matter.[74] U.N. General-Secretary U Thant went so far as to state:

> So far as the question of secession of a particular secession of a member state is concerned, the United Nations' attitude is unequivocable. As an international organization, the United Nations has never accepted and does not accept *and I do not think it will ever accept the principle of secession* of a part of its member state.[75]

Thus, the international law of self-determination was such that it was a once and once only right: a colonial territory could declare itself independent from its colonial master, but that was the final exercise of its right of self-determination. No further subdivision, secession or separation was to be permitted. The international community was quite clear in its practice and the practice of its Member States. International law, for a change, was a little more ambiguous. Indeed, the United Nations declarations concerning self-determination carried with it an obligatory clause regarding the preservation of territorial integrity of states. State sovereignty was to continue unabated. Yet despite the consistent state practice of not recognizing a secessionist movement's attempt at statehood, there was some contradictory soft law out of the United Nations. The 1970 General Assembly Declaration on Principles of International Law Concerning Friendly Relations and Co-operation among States in Accordance with the Charter of the United Nations,[76] described as "the cornerstone of the United Nations approach to the concept"[77] of self-determination, demonstrates the fundamental contradiction between the right of self-determination and the preservation of territorial integrity. The Declaration states in part:

> By virtue of the principle of equal rights and self-determination of peoples enshrined in the Charter, all peoples have the right freely to determine, without external interference, their political status and to pursue their economic, social and cultural development, and every State has the duty to respect this right in accordance with the provisions of the Charter.

Nothing in the foregoing paragraphs shall be construed as authorizing or encouraging any action which would dismember or impair, totally or in part, the territorial or political unity of sovereign and independent States conducting themselves in compliance with the principle of equal rights and self-determination and thus possessed of a government representing the whole people belonging to the territory without distinction as to race, creed or color.

Every state shall refrain from any action aimed at the partial or total disruption of the national unity and territorial integrity of any other State or country.

While it can be argued that this declaration does not provide for the right to secession, the second paragraph listed above has been viewed as an affirmation of the applicability of the principle to peoples within existing States and the necessity for governments to represent the governed.[78] Yet in the third paragraph listed above the inviolability of the territorial integrity of a state is enshrined. It is no surprise then, that this area of law is one that many scholars find slippery and frustrating. It is even less shocking to discover that international law is full of these contradictions –

all of which leads to anti-therapeutic experiences. National liberation groups, like that in East Timor,[79] go without international recognition for their goal of statehood.

III. The Decline of State Centricity: Toward a More Therapeutic Form of Self-Determination

For Winick, "a proper concern of therapeutic jurisprudence is consideration of alternative legal arrangements that might produce more functional behavior."[80] In the international legal context of self-determination, this means changing the primordial role that the state enjoys. It cannot be too difficult, for the state is withering on its own. Harsh economic realities were forcing the abdication of certain state functions, and in many Western industrialized democracies, the modern state was rapidly losing its *raison d'etre*. It could no longer keep pace with the escalating costs of social welfare. With the erosion of such essential services as public health care and education, private medicine and schools increased exponentially, offering top-rate services for those who could afford them. Similarly, social upheavals were challenging the state's monopoly of force. An increase in urban crime created a demand for private toll roads, gated communities, and private security firms, as fewer and fewer citizens relied on the state to protect them.

Since the end of the Cold War, the nation-state, if such a thing ever really existed, is quickly disappearing.[81] Just as the Socialist Federal Republic of Yugoslavia was about to fall apart in 1991, while he was in Europe to tow the state sovereignty line, U.S. Secretary of State James Baker III commented:

> Perhaps the most striking phenomenon across all of Europe today is the combined and simulanteous devolution and evolution of the nation-state. While the nation-state remains by far the most significant political unit, its political role is being increasingly supplemented by both supranational and subnational units. In other words, some of the nation-state's functions are being delegated "upward" and others "downward".[82]

States are no longer constituted by one nation. Indeed, the French state, the first nation-state, was a rough collage of Bretons, Provencales, and Normans. In the late eighteenth century, a French identity was foisted upon these peoples and, somehow it managed to stick. But this too is changing. With immigration, France and other European states have become less like nation-states and more like multinational states, comprised of competing nationalities. Contemporary France is no longer just a state of Frenchmen. Today it includes Algerians, West Africans and other immigrants from La Francophonie.

As the nation-state erodes around the world, policy makers are scrambling for a whole new set of criteria to define what is a "people" or a nation. Great Britain, which is itself originally made up of Northern Irish, Scots, Welsh and English, is today quickly becoming an even more multi-racial, multi-ethnic state as a result of an influx of immigrants from around the world. Contemporary Germany is increasingly made up of Turks and Eastern European populations. This is the therapeutic opportunity – the moment to move to alternative forms of self-determination. To do this, we must recognize the *international* of other international actors and give them standing, a voice in the international community.

A natural place to start is with non-governmental organizations, for they continue to proliferate. Even the United Nations – the exclusive club whose membership is limited exclusively to states – has recognized their importance and expertise in certain disciplines, including accurate reporting and documentation of facts. ECOSOC Resolution 1503, for example, provides for the involvement of NGOs in the reporting of human rights abuses. The work that the International Committee of the Red Cross and other NGOs in promoting an international treaty banning the deployment of landmines is a case in point. Likewise, the pioneering work that Amnesty International has undertaken in bringing to justice dictators like Chilean General Augusto Pinochet demonstrates the power of such non-state actors.

The globalization of culture has also challenged traditional definitions of *self* and *determination*. We have begun to define what we are (our *self*) in new manners and categories over the last few decades. Today, there are a plethora of new vehicles by which we can define and *determine* ourselves. We are no longer just American, French, British, Russian, Spanish or Argentine. We are bankers, students, jurists, Microsoft Windows-users, senior citizens, and supporters of Greenpeace.[83] There are many sides to our *selves*, just as there are many ways in which we choose to *determine* those *selves*.

The rise of transnational corporations offers yet another challenge to the sovereignty and primacy of states. Of the world's 100 largest economies, 47 are multinational corporations. In 1997, Wal-Mart Stores Inc. did over $119.3 billion in business. In the same year, the gross domestic product of Greece was $119.1 billion.[84] Which one has more power in the international realm? Which one deserves a seat at the United Nations?

Youth culture is another transborder movement that has enormous potential to challenge traditional international order. With rising unemployment, few future prospects, increased educational costs, anti-social attitudes, common socialization through popular culture, and collective anger, the youth of today have more in common with each other internationally than they do as citizens of their respective states. Similarly, other transborder movements, such as Africanism and Arabism, are not confined within state borders. The unifying power of Islam is one particular form of a self-determination movement that goes beyond state boundaries and has enormous potential influence on the future of international relations.

New forms of economic and military re-organization are also threatening the traditional role of the state. On the military front, NATO now requires that new member states cede their military command and supplies to the Alliance as well as work towards joint ventures in peacekeeping. Throughout the world, there is a move towards economic regionalization. The dictates of the World Trade Organization and the move towards open markets and freer global trade have translated into a decline in state power over tariffs, import substitution, subsidies and trade policy. In the case of Europe, the phenomenon of *subsidiarity* on the demise of the state is even more pronounced. As the European Community morphed into the European Union in 1995, the fifteen members began to work towards a common monetary union and foreign policy, ceding much of the decision-making functions once exclusively held by states to the European Parliament in Brussels.

In short, there are a number of competing forms of political and social organization that vie with the sovereign state for international membership in the international community – with all its attendant decision-making functions.[85] This then is a call to action. If international law is truly the official discourse of international society,[86] the *nomos*, or prevailing values, must be defined by its actors. For Professor Thomas Franck, "The postmodern tribal-secessionist crisis which defines the new era compels international lawyers to rethink their most fundamental norms, in particular those concerning title to territory, and its relation to human personality and group identity."[87] If lawyers do not understand the changes that are occurring and the need for these changes, they will not be effective in managing the conflicts that come from competing self-determination movements.[88]

But international law is indeed about people and liberating the notion of self-determination from its confines of statehood will go a long way in ensuring that the rules and practice of international law can be more therapeutic. Indeed, this goes beyond a perceived crisis for state sovereignty; the internationalization of events can be deemed a therapeutic process. States, which to a certain point in history could do to their internal subjects whatever it wished, must now open its internal matters. More issues are internationalized now. We have real-time global media coverage to thank. Now we can watch the issue unfold before us courtesy of satellite television. More things are accessible now and there are more avenues where actions are internationalized. When we connect on the Internet and have information relayed to us on computer resting in other jurisdictions is an international event. Long distance telephone calls are an international event. Each one of these mechanisms is a therapeutic means.

IV. Conclusion

While traditional international law, has looked to states as the primary constituent actors on the international stage, we are facing a world where every person is a people, for the purpose of the right of self-determination. International law must recognize the world as it is today.[89] It is the ultimate recognition that we are facing a world where every person is a *people* for the purposes of Article 1 of the International Covenants on Human Rights.

Self determination has been a sacred tenet of international law, yet it has been largely founded on legal inadequacies and fictions. For too long, international law and the international system have been dominated by states and their apologists. As states lose their meaning, it is little wonder that international law – the law between states – has also become largely ineffective and a lesson in anti-therapeutic behavior. It is time for international law to achieve its true purpose – to be a necessary part of a "process of communication."[90] Indeed, international law seems primed for some analysis through the lens of therapeutic jurisprudence. For Dino Kritisiotis, "International law offers a much more constructive communicative medium (with all the prospects and risks that this entails) than naked power could ever hope to do. Its very rules promise peace; they preach pacifism."[91]

With the decline of sovereign states, the emerging international system is not unlike early forms of biological life. In the same way that a single cell joins other cells to form larger organisms, the individual will move from among various international bodies. This emerging *social mitosis-osmosis* transcends borders, and will eventually destroy the modern state.[92] In a few years, the international system as we know it, will be unrecognizable. Strangely, George Bush may have got it right when he stated before the United Nations General Assembly:

> "I see a world of open borders, open trade, and, most importantly, open minds. A world that celebrates the common heritage that belongs to all the world's people taking pride not just in hometown or homeland but in humanity itself."[93]

As the state becomes increasingly marginalized by the developments in international life – legislative, technological, and financial – international law must solve the tension between territorial integrity of states and the right of self-determination. International law must decouple the right of self-determination from the fundamental notion of the state. This decoupling will assist in reducing the tension in international law, widen the groups who wish to exercise this new vision of self-determination, and bring more peace and justice to our world. In enhancing the numbers of groups and variety of actors benefiting from the empowering effects of self-determination, this movement in international law will fulfill the vision of therapeutic jurisprudence.

Notes

* B.A., LL.B. (University of Toronto), LL.M. (Cantab.), Barrister and Solicitor (Ontario, Canada), Fellow, Cambridge Commonwealth Society. Mr. Cooper is the Executive Director of the McGill Center for Creative Problem Solving at California Western School of Law, San Diego, California. The author wishes to thank William Aceves, Toni Christiani, Rhona Smith, Aaron Schwabach, and Ellen Waldman for their comments on earlier drafts of this Article.

1 Tom R. Tyler, The Psychological Consequences of Judicial Procedures: Implications for Civil Commitment Hearings 3, in Law in a Therapeutic Key (David B. Wexler and Bruce J. Winick, eds. 1996) (hereinafter "Therapeutic Key").

2 David B. Wexler, Therapeutic Jurisprudence and the Criminal Courts 157 in Therapeutic Key, *supra* note 1.

3 Bruce Feldthusen, The Civil Action for Sexual Battery: Therapeutic Jurisprudence?, 845 in *Therapeutic Key, supra* note 1.

4 Rose A. Daly-Rooney, Designing Reasonable Accommodations through Co-Worker Participation: Therapeutic Jurisprudence and the Confidentiality Provision of the Americans with Disabilities Act 365, in *Therapeutic Key, supra* note 1.

5 Roger I. Abrams, Frances E. Abrams, and Dennis R. Nolan, *Arbitral Therapy* 499, in *Therapeutic Key, supra* note 1.

6 Jeffrey L. Harrison, Class, Personality, Contract and Unconscionability 525, in Therapeutic Key, *supra* note 1.

7 Ellen A. Waldman, The Evaluative-Facilitative Debate in Mediation: Applying the Lens of Therapeutic Jurisprudence, 82 Maro. L. REV. 155 (1998).

8 Bruce J. Winick, *The Jurisprudence of Therapeutic Jurisprudence*, 3 Psychol. Pub. Pol'y & L. 184, 195 (1997).

9 *Ibid.*, 185.

10 David B. Wexler, Practising Therapeutic Jurisprudence: Psycholegal Soft Spots and Strategies, *Revista Juridica* U.P.R. 317 (1998).

11 Winick, *supra* note 9, 185.

12 See e.g., E. Allan Lind et al., Voice, Control and Procedural Justice: Instrumental and Noninstrumental Concerns in Fairness Judgments, 59 *Personality & Soc. Psychol.* 952, 952-59 (1990).

13 *Ibid.*, 184. Winick has written on the development of substantive due process protection for self-determination as well as protection of self-determination in the areas of marriage, family, and procreation. *See* Bruce J. Winick, *On Autonomy: Legal and Psychological Perspectives*, 37 Vill. L.R. 1705.

14 Ozi Umozurike, Self-Determination in International Law 6 (1972).

15 International Covenant on Civil and Political Rights 1966, 999 U.N.T.S. 171, and International Covenant on Economic, Social and Cultural Rights 1966, 993 U.N.T.S. 3, Article 1(1).

16 James Crawford, *The Rights of Peoples: 'Peoples' or 'Governments'*, The Rights of Peoples 59 (James Crawford, editor, 1988).

17 Indeed, today the very definition of *international* affairs must be queried. Colloquially, *international* has come to mean relations between sovereign states, but a more precise understanding of the word leads us to understand it to possible signify relations between nations that exist within a single state, or relations among those nations in many states. In truth, as we live in a world beyond that of the states, the word *international* no longer makes sense. It is a leftover of the days of the sovereign nation-state.

18 Winick, *supra* note 9, 204.

19 Indeed, scholars outside the United States have embraced therapeutic jurisprudence. See David Carson, Therapeutic Jurisprudence for the United Kingdom?, 6 J. Forensic Psychiatry 433 (195); Bruce Feldthusen, The Civil Action for Sexual Battery: Therapeutic Jurisprudence?, 25 Ottawa L.Rev. 205 (1993); Eilis S. Magner, Therapeutic Jurisprudence: Its Potential in Australia, 67 Revista Juridica U.P.R. 121 (1998).

20 David B. Wexler, New Directions in Therapeutic Jurisprudence: Breaking the Bounds of Conventional Mental Health Law Scholarship, 10 N.Y.L. Sch. J. Human Rts. 750, 765 (1993).

21 "Therapeutic jurisprudence has left the concept of 'therapeutic' intentionally vague." Winick, *supra* note 9, 192.

22 "Any consequence that is arguably therapeutic and in at least some sense related to psychological functioning would seem to be within the broad contours of therapeutic jurisprudence." Winick, *supra* note 9, 194. "The history of the revolt and the fact of its victory will guide us in the unknown future. They will teach us never to despair even in conditions of enslavement. For a nation, enslaved, dispersed, beaten, decimated, on the brink of utter destruction, can yet arise to rebel against the fate, and so come to life again." Menachem Begin, *the Revolt* 487 (1951).

23 Song and dance over referendum, Independent, April 24, 1993, at 15, col 1.

24 Foreign and Commonwealth Office (UK) Press Release No. 78, May 18, 1993.

25 United Nations Information Office (UK), Doc. NS/20/93, May 27, 1993.

26 Eritrea gains statehood, *Times* (UK), May 25, 1993, at 12, col 8.

27 There is a reason that literature of therapeutic jurisprudence is filled with words like "empowerment", "self-esteem".

28 According to Professor Brierly, "for the practical purposes of the international lawyer sovereignty is not a metaphysical concept, nor is it part of the essence of statehood; it is merely a term which designates an aggregate of particular and very extensive claims that states habitually make for themselves in their relations with other states." J.L. Brierly, the Law of Nations. An Introduction to the International Law of Peace 47 (1963) (6th ed., Sir Humphrey Waldock, ed.).

29 *Ibid.*, 49. For Dino Kritsiotis, however, international law already provides tools to a number of international actors, for "it provides a voice and a language for a greater range of participants in the international system, including those who have traditionally been excluded from the great power rivalries of yesteryear: minorities, indigenous peoples, non-governmental organizations, and individuals." Dino Kritiotis, *The Power of International Law as Language*, 34 Cal. Western L. Rev. 397, 405 (1998), citing Robert Y. Jennings, *Universal International Law in a Multicultural World*, in Liber Amicorum for the Rt. Hon. Lord Wilberforce 39, 40-41 (Maarten Bos & Ian Brownlie, eds., 1987).

30 "The unexamined premise in world order thinking has been that *only* governmental solutions can organize planetary life, that only existing governmental structures and their leaders can command the authority required for this essential undertaking, and that only argument and persuasion can release the political energy needed to overcome the inertia that sustains the state system in the face of the most unmistakable writing on the wall." Richard Falk, *The End of World Order*, in International Law (1995) (Barry E. Carter and Phillip R. Trimble, (eds.) 80.

31 See Christopher D. Stone, Should Trees Have Standing? Toward Legal Rights for Natural Objects, 45 S. Cal. L. Rev. 450 (1972).

32 See generally, Philip Allott, Eunomia. New Order for a New World (1990).

33 See generally, Antonio Cassese, Self-Determination of Peoples (1995); Hurst Hannum, *Rethinking Self-Determination*, 34 Va. J. Int'l L. 1 (1993); W.M. Reisman, *Coercion and Self-Determination: Construing Charter Article 2(4)*, 78 A.J.I.L. 642 (1984); Antonio Cassese, *Political Self-Determination – Old Concepts and New Developments*, in UN Law/Fundamental Rights: Two Topics in International Law (1979) (Antonio Cassesse, editor).

34 "All people have the right of self-determination. By virtue of that right they freely determine their political status and freely pursue their economic, social and cultural development." Article 1 of the International Covenant on Civil and Political Rights 1966, 999 U.N.T.S. 171, and Article I, International Covenant on Economic, Social and Cultural Rights 1966, 993 U.N.T.S. 3, article 1(1).

35 "Today, in their immense majority these peoples have become sovereign states through the legitimate exercise of their self-determination. The final hour of colonialism has struck, and millions of inhabitants of Africa, Asia and Latin America rise to meet a new life and demand their unrestricted right of self-determination and to the independent development of their nations." Che Guevara, Speech before the United Nations General Assembly, December 11, 1964, reprinted in Che Guevara and the Cuban Revolution 321 (1987).

36 "The principles of international law, or the primary principles upon which the others rest, can be deduced from the essential nature of the state." Brierly, *supra* note 29, 49.

37 "Externally, a state is sovereign if the exercise of power internally to the state is not subject to external superior power or to other constraints or restrictions legal in

nature." Neil MacCormick, Beyond the Sovereign State, 56 Modern L. Rev. 14 (1993).

38 James M. Cooper, 'The Challenge to the State in International Law', 170, 172 in *Law, Justice and the State* II (1995) (edited by Michel Troper and Mikael M. Karlsson).

39 "Now that computing is astoundingly inexpensive and computers inhabit every part of our lives, we stand at the brink of another revolution." Bill Gates, *the Road Ahead* (1995).

40 In discussing the republican form of government that the United States of America would take, John Madison wrote: "It is evident that no other form would be reconcilable with the genius of the people of America; with the fundamental principles of the Revolution; or with that honorable determination which animates every votary of freedom to rest all our political experiments on the capacity of mankind for self-government." John Madison, The Federalist Papers 240 (1961).

41 "A nation, without a national government, is, in my view, an awful spectacle. The establishment of a Constitution, time of profound peace, by the voluntary consent of a whole people, is a prodigy, to the completion of which I look forward with trembling anxiety." Alexander Hamilton, The Federalist Papers 527 (1961).

42 Frantz Fanon, The Wretched of the Earth 36 (1963).

43 Winick, *supra* note 9, 194.

44 Philip Allott, 'Nation as Mind Politic', 24 *Int'l L. and Politics* 1361, 1373 (1992).

45 See MacCormick, *supra* note 38, 17: ("One of the main upshots of universal sovereign statehood was two disasters – world wars.")

46 See generally, Jay Winter, The Experience of World War I (1989); Marc Ferro, The Great War (1973).

47 The Treaty of Versailles – the peace that was concluded from the ashes of the First World War – has been blamed for much conflict in its wake. Centered around the principle of self-determination, the treaty brought to an end the multinational empires and created new states. "This was the belief that Europe should be organized on the principle of nationality, and that violations of this principle had had a large part in bringing on the war." Gerhard L. Weinberg, *A World at World Arms. A Global History of World War II* 9 (1994). The Nazi regime in Germany was focused on righting the perceived wrongs of Versailles. Moreover, for Professor Habsbawm, "the national conflicts tearing the continent [of Europe] apart in the 1990s were the old chickens of Versailles once again coming home to roost." Eric Hobsbawm, Age of Extremes. The Short Twentieth Century 1914-1991 31 (1994). Versailles is alive and well unfortunately.

48 "The Jews were seen as the most immediate threat to racial purity inside Germany, and as the main motor of resistance outside the country. A policy of extreme anti-Semitism would accordingly be a central concern of the government in peace first and in war later." Gerhard L. Weinberg, A World At World Arms. A Global History of World War II, 21 (1994).

49 Fanon, *supra* note 43, 36.

50 "International law thus became not law of a human society but a regulator of the external interactions of sovereigns." Martti Koskenniemi, 'Book Review of *Eunomia. New Order for a New World* (by Philip Allott)', 87 A.J.I.L. 160, 162-163 (1993).

51 See generally, Ved P. Nanda, *The United States Action in the 1965 Dominican Crisis: Impact on Wolrd Order – Part I*, 43 Denver L. J. 439 (1966); A.J. Thomas Jr. and Ann Van Wynen Thomas, The Dominican Republic Crisis 1965 (1967).

52 See generally, John Moore, Grenada and the International Double Standard, 78 A.J.I.L. 145 (1984).

53 See generally, Abraham D. Sofaer, The Legality of the United States Action in Panama, 29 Col. J. Transnat'l L. 281 (1991); Ved P. Nanda, The Validity of United States Intervention in Panama Under International Law, Agora: U.S. Forces in Panama, 84 A.J.I.L. 494 (1990).

54 See generally, Julie Ann Waterman, The United States' Involvement in Haiti's Tragedy and the Resolve to Restore Democracy, 15 N.Y.L. Sch. J. Int'l & Comp. L 187 (1994).

55 See generally, Robert E. Frankel, Recognizing Self-Determination in International Law: Kuwait's Conflict with Iraq, 14 Loy. L.A. Int'l & Comp. L.J. 359 (1992).

56 See generally, Ved P. Nanda, Tragedies in Northern Iraq, Liberia, Yugoslavia and Haiti – Revisiting the Validity of Humanitarian Intervention Under International Law – Part I, 20 Denv. J. Int'l L & Pol'y 305 (1992).

57 "Almost all states support the 'right' to self-determination by some groups but oppose such claims by others." Malvina Halberstam, *Self-Determination in the Arab-Israeli Conflict: Meaning, Myth, and Politics*, 21 N.Y.U Int'l L. & Pol. 465, 468 (1989).

58 See generally Marc Weller, The International Response to the Dissolution of the Socialist Federal Republic of Yugoslavia, 86 A.J.I.L. 569 (1992).

59 See European Community, Declaration on the Guidelines on the Recognition of New States in Eastern Europe and the Soviet Union, EPC Press Release 129/91 (December 16, 1991); 31 I.L.M. 1485 (1992).

60 See EPC Declaration of August 27, 1991 (Brussels), EPC Press Release 82/91.

61 United Nations, Report of the Secretary-General on an Agenda for Peace – Preventive Diplomacy, Peacemaking and Peace-Keeping, (June 17, 1992) paragraph 17, 31 I.L.M. 953 (1992).

62 "[I]n Europe the basic principle of re-ordering the map was to create ethnic-linguistic nation states, according to the belief that nations had the 'right to self-determination'. President Wilson of the USA, whose opinions were seen as expressing those of the power without whom the war would have been lost, was passionately committed to this belief, which was (and is) more easily held by those far from the ethnic and linguistic realities of the regions which were to be divided into neat nation-states. The attempt was a disaster, as can be seen in the Europe of the 1990s." Hobsbawm, *supra* note 43, 31.

63 Winick, *supra* note 9, 195.

64 Winick, *supra* note 9,186.

65 According to Article 1(2) of the Charter, one of the purposes of the United Nations is "To develop friendly relations among nations based on respect for the principle of equal rights and self-determination of peoples, and to take other appropriate measures to strengthen universal peace;" Chapter IX of the Charter begins with Article 55 which provides: "With a view to the creation of conditions of stability and well-being which are necessary for peaceful and friendly relations among nations based on respect for the principle of equal rights and self-determination of peoples, the United Nations shall promote: higher standards of living, full employment, and conditions of economic and social progress and development; solutions of international economic, social, health, and related problems; and international cultural and educational cooperation; and universal respect for, and observance of human rights and fundamental freedoms for all without distinction as to race, sex, language, or religion." Charter of the United Nations, Articles 1(2) and 55.

66 ("After World War II, self-determination entered its normative zenith.") Thomas M. Franck, Fairness in International Law and Institutions 144 (1995).

67 Hector Gros-Espiell, Special Rapporteur, Implementation of United Nations Resolutions relating to the Right of Peoples under Colonial and Alien Domination to Self-Determination, U.N. Doc E/CN.4/Sub.2/40, June 5, 1978.

68 "Although the principle of self-determination grants a right to *peoples*, one should co-ordinate that principle with all the other rules of international law, in order to grasp the scope of people's international personality. International rules cannot have as their addressees loose aggregates of individuals." Antonio Cassese, International Law in a Divided World 93 (1986).

69 Advisory Opinion on the Western Sahara, [1975] I.C.J. Reports 12, at 121.

70 Winick has noted that "paternalism is often antitherapeutic." Winick, *supra* note 9, 192.

71 See generally, Thomas M. Franck and Nigel S. Rodley, After Bangladesh: The Law of Humanitarian Intervention by Military Force, 67 A.J.I.L. 275 (1973); Ved P. Nanda, Self-Determination in International Law: The Tragic Tale of Two Cities – Islamabad (West Pakistan) and Dacca (East Pakistan), 66 A.J.I.L. 321 (1972); The Secretariat of the International Commission of Jurists, The Events in East Pakistan, 1971 (1972).

72 See generally, Howard Weisberg, 'The Congo Crisis 1964: A Case Study in Humanitarian Intervention', 12 *Virg. J. Int'l L.* 261 (1972).

73 See generally, Georges Abi-Saab, The United Nations Operation in the Congo 1960-1964 (1978).

74 During the Biafra crisis that tore apart Nigeria, Professor Arthur Leff wrote: "Forget all the blather about international law, sovereignty and self-determination, all that abstract garbage: babies are starving to death." Arthur Leff, N.Y. Times, October 4, 1968, at 46, col. 3, quoted in T. Farer, Humanitarian Intervention: The View from Charlottesville, in Richard B. Lillich, ed., Humanitarian Intervention and the United Nations 151 (1973) at 151.

75 7 U.N. Monthly Chronicle (Feb. 1970) at 36.

76 General Assembly Resolution 2625 (XXV), October 24, 1970.

77 Robin C.A. White, Self-Determination: Time for a Re-assessment, 28 Netherlands Int'l L. Rev. 147, 147 (1981).

78 Rosenstock, The Declaration of Principles of International Law Concerning Friendly Relations: A Survey, 65 A.J.I.L., 713 (1971) at 732.

79 See Laura Silber, Portugal restarts talks on E Timor, Fin. Times, April 23, 1999, 6; Sander Thoenes, E Timor officials critical of vote, Fin. Times, April 29, 1999, 6; Brandi J. Pummell, The Timor Gap: Who Decides Who is in Control?, 26 Denv. J. Int'l L & Pol'y 655 (1998).

80 Winick, *supra* note 9, 194.

81 "[I]t seems obvious that no state in Western Europe any longer is a sovereign state." MacCormick, *supra* note 38, 16. "[T]he state is simultaneously *too large* to satisfy human needs and *too small* to cope with the requirements of guidance needed by an increasingly interdependent planet." Falk, *supra* note 31, 82.

82 James A. Baker III, "The Euro-Atlantic Architecture", Address to the Aspen Institute, Berlin, June 18, 1991, Transcript from the U.S. Department of State Bureau of Public Affairs, Washington, D.C., at 2.

83 "[T]he state system is now being superseded. In this context, one set of plausible possibilities is the globalization of social life in a way that allows cooperative organizational forms to flourish." Falk, *supra* note 31, 81.

84 John Stopford, *Multinational Corporations*, 113 Foreign Policy, 12, 16 (1998).

85 "To escape from the idea that all law must originate in a single power source, like a sovereign, is thus to discover the possibility of taking a broader, more diffuse, view of law." MacCormick, *supra* note 38, 8.

86 "As international society is ultimately the society of all (subordinate) human societies, so international law has ultimately to do with the organization of all aspects of social life." Martti Koskenniemi, "Book Review of *Eunomia. New Order for a New World* (by Philip Allott)", 87 A.J.I.L. 160, 161 (1993).

87 Thomas M. Franck, Fairness in International Law and Institutions 144 (1995).

88 Professor Anthony D'Amato has long lamented that international lawyers "revert to the Oppenheimian notion that international law is all about states and not at all about people." Anthony D'Amato, *The Invasion of Panama Was a Lawful Response to Tyranny*, 84 A.J.I.L. 516, 516 (1990).

89 "One thing which is necessary for jurisprudence or the philosophy of law to do in the present state of affairs is to guard against taking a narrow one-state or Community-only perspective, a monocular view of these things." MacCormick, *supra* note 38, 5. "We seem caught in a historical movement where the burdens of the old order are too great to bear, and yet the new alternative order that hopefully lies beyond the presently perceived horizon of attainability casts no shadow backwards from the future that can be reliably and persuasively discerned." Falk, *supra* note 31, 80.

90 W. Michael Reisman, International Lawmaking: A Process of Communication, 75 ASIL Proc. 101 (1981).

91 Kritsiotis, *supra* note 30, 405.

92 For Professor Falk, the imminent disintegration of the state system is akin to the collapse of the church-based feudal system several centuries ago in Europe. "Compared to the ferment of the seventeenth century with the new logic of the state system taking over the feudal logic, our transitional challenge is more dangerous and bewildering. The statist logic has not yet been seriously challenged by an alternative logic..." Falk, *supra* note 80.

93 U.S. President George Bush, "The UN: World Parliament of Peace", Address before the United Nations General Assembly, New York, October 1, 1990. U.S. Department of State, Bureau of Public Affairs, Current Policy No. 1303 at 3. The words of Professor Brierly come to mind: "We have begun to realize that a world society will not come into existence without conscious human effort." Brierly, *supra* note 29, 44.

23. The Ethics of Self-Determination: Democratic, National and Regional

OMAR DAHBOUR

Introduction

In the last fifty years, the principle of self-determination has been incorporated into international law, despite continuing disagreements about its definition, meaning, and justification. In this paper, I distinguish three different versions of the principle (which I will call the democratic, national, and regional principles of self-determination). Each of these versions gives emphasis to a different aspect of the general concept of self-determination: the democratic principle emphasizes the political aspects, the national principle highlights cultural issues, and the regional principle focuses on the social dimensions. My argument here is that, first, the democratic principle is adequately recognized in international law; second, the national principle - despite its philosophical advocates - should not be legally recognized; and, third, the regional principle, though relatively ignored, best characterizes the core issue underlying many struggles over sovereignty, nationality, and territory today.

While, as I hope will become clear, the democratic and national principles of self-determination are a familiar part of current discussions in international law, the regional principle is less so - and requires some reflection on the definition and meaning of the concept of a "region." In this paper, I do not try to define what a region is, nor resolve jurisdictional disputes over the extent of regions. What I advocate here is a particular principle of regionalism that relies on an ecological definition of regions as the basis for claims to autonomy and self-determination. Regions are to be seen, not as based on language, culture, or history, but on similar economies, ecologies, and ways of life. It is the uniqueness of regions in this respect, I argue, that warrants claims to their self-determination. The extent of regions - which will often be substate localities, but may in certain instances be suprastate entities - is not the issue; it is the principle of regions as distinctive foci for material life that I think is worthy of consideration.

Finally, I think it vitally important, in the present climate of military and imperial triumphalism resulting from the NATO attack on Yugoslavia, to insist that advocacy of self-determination not be taken to mean the undermining of the idea of state sovereignty that is an important principle in international law. As will become clearer below, it is the compatibility of regional self-determination with state sovereignty that is one of its most important features, especially in contradistinction to the national principle's contribution to subverting the sovereignty of existing states.

It is essential to begin my argument by noting the precise differences between the three principles referred to above. When self-determination is regarded as a democratic principle, it is equivalent to the idea that peoples in already existing political communities ought to participate in their own governance. But when self-determination is understood to apply to national groups, it is not self-rule as such that is at issue. This is because the national principle could be (and is) the basis for demands made against avowedly democratic states. It is the boundaries of the unit, entity, or territory within which self-rule is to be exercised that is the focus of claims to national self-determination, rather than the type of regime within these boundaries.[1] Finally, when self-determination is thought of in regional terms, it indicates an interest in the autonomy necessary to protect and enhance the self-sufficiency and distinctiveness of peoples in particular geographical regions or localities.

Limitations of the Democratic Principle

The democratic principle of self-determination has come to be accepted as an integral part of international law, at least since the promulgation of the Universal Declaration of Human Rights and the United Nations Charter at the end of the 1940s.[2] This is not to say that there have not been some persistent critics of the adoption of any idea of self-determination. Such critics have generally been suspicious either of the philosophical underpinnings of self-determination per se or of the elasticity of the term, which seems to allow for a variety of misapplications.[3]

Nevertheless, most international jurists have come to view self-determination as justified on the basis of considerations of consistency, in the following sense. The democratic principle constitutes the assertion that, when there exists a political entity of some kind, its people ought to be self-governing. This would seem to be a simple extension of the act of recognizing *any* political entities as self-governing - for instance, through treaties or membership in international organizations such as the U.N.[4] If Britain or France, for instance, are recognized as being legitimate international actors (that is, independent states), then why not also recognize British Guiana or French West Africa as such, since they are already accorded separate status even by their imperial rulers? Obviously, such an idea was most effectively used to justify the independence of colonies from their colonizers. But are there any entities to which it is now applicable in the postcolonial era?

One view of how the democratic principle might be extended from a colonial to a postcolonial context is to ensure that, within existing states, no groups or categories of persons are systematically excluded from the same degree of political participation as others. Something like this idea was used to criticize the apartheid regime in South Africa.[5] An even more contemporary case might be that of Palestine.[6] The Palestinian problem raises the issue of whether, when a group lacks political participation within an existing state, it may legitimately claim statehood for itself. This would require some specification of when a group has a kind of *neo*colonial status, about which there is no consensus in international law. But such an idea does not seem to be, prima facie, an illegitimate extension of the democratic principle.

It is also crucial to distinguish the democratic principle from the contemporary advocacy of a right to democracy, in the sense of a democratic regime. This is obviously a very different type of idea, since it goes some way toward undermining the principle of political sovereignty by establishing a right of peoples, not only to independence from other states, but also to a specific form of governance.

So, while the democratic principle does not mandate establishment of particular forms of regime, it is generally recognized today in the sense of justifying political independence for all peoples. Regardless of the scope of this principle, however, it is likely to be insufficient either to mollify nationalists who seek new states or to address the concerns of those who seek to preserve regionally distinct ways of life.

This is because, in the first case, the aim of democratic self-determination is not to ensure that particular cultural nations have states of their own, but to ensure that peoples generally have the right to participate politically in some state. While undoubtedly this will not satisfy nationalists, I think that it should.

A second problem, however, is truly unaddressed by the democratic principle - that of the self-determination of indigenous peoples or exploited regions which seek to protect or maintain a distinctive society or way of life within a state. This is, of course, a variant of the classic problem of the domination of minorities within a majoritarian political system - but as applied to minorities constituted not by opinion, interest, or nationality, but by particular places, needs, or material cultures. This problem, I believe, is best addressed through the regional principle outlined below.

The National Principle and the Right to Culture Argument

The national principle of self-determination can be defined as the idea that nationalities may rightfully determine the boundaries, membership, and political status of their own communities, including asserting a right to statehood. When this principle is understood as aimed at enabling individuals to express their cultural identities, it becomes equivalent to a "right to culture" - namely, the idea that the right of individuals to express, participate in, and propagate a distinctive culture requires that the cultural groups of which they are members be able to establish independent states within which these activities can be pursued.

This right to culture argument is based on the claim that there is an important connection between individual well-being and the welfare of what Avishai Margalit and Joseph Raz have called "encompassing groups" (of which nationalities are the primary example).[7] It also depends on the idea that self-determination means the "right to decide" about the conditions of well-being for a group. So, even if one might contend that a national group's well-being is not served by a separate state, the decision of the group to seek a state is regarded as *sufficient* reason for their claim to be honored.

The connection between encompassing groups and individual well-being supposedly generates a "right to culture" - a right to be able freely to participate in a group's cultural life. But this doesn't seem to entail a corresponding right to a state. Those philosophers who argue that it does, however, ultimately rely on a belief that possession of a state is essential in order for cultures to flourish.[8] Why do they think this?

First, without the state, cultural survival cannot be assured. In certain circumstances, cultural groups may be thought to require an independent state in order to receive adequate recognition from others.[9] This is especially so today, according to Will Kymlicka, since the only cultures that can escape marginalization are increasingly "societal cultures" - those that can use state institutions to ensure their dominance within a given territory.[10]

A second connection between a right to culture and a right to a state has to do not with cultural survival, but with cultural enjoyment.[11] Yael Tamir emphasizes this in arguing that cultures, in order to be fully enjoyed, must be experienced on a large (national) scale; and this requires the action and cooperation of a state that can organize the distinctive traits of a culture - for example, national holidays, official languages, cultural symbols such as flags or costumes, sports teams able to compete internationally, and so forth.[12]

The basic defect of the right to culture argument is that there is no necessary connection between the well-being of individuals and their membership in nation-states. The creation of such states would either be irrelevant to the survival of group cultures or harmful to the free self-development of individuals. The concept of encompassing groups upon which the ethical justification of the national principle rests assumes the equivalence of personal identities with national identities. Yet, this is surely false.

It is based on the notion that there is such a thing as "national character," and that, even if it does not subsume all of what we know to be culture, it is nevertheless a very important part of it.[13] But asserting that persons have one (and only one) national identity, and that this identity is readily recognizable, distorts the very processes by which cultures are constituted by presupposing the static and necessary character of cultural differences.[14] While national identities are undoubtedly a part of the cultural experiences of many individuals, they are not equivalent to cultures in general.[15]

Furthermore, there are ways in which giving nations the right to states may actually restrict and undermine individual self-determination. This is because any particular cultural identity that individuals embody or adopt may only further their own life-plans temporarily or in limited ways. It cannot be assumed that particular national identities will necessarily always serve as the basis for people's self-identification or mutual recognition, especially if such national identities are regarded as excluding cultural syncretism or personal transformation.[16]

The ability of persons to lead fulfilling lives seems to be best served when individuals have the maximum opportunity to change their group affiliations and cultural identities in relation to changing needs and interests. It is not only group membership, but also individuals' ability to change membership, that is important.[17] This is the reason why, in the principal documents of international law, cultural rights have always been stipulated as the rights of individuals to cultural expression.

However, it may be that it is the enjoyment of cultures rather than their survival that is really at issue. Perhaps it is not enough for persons to see themselves as members of a cultural nationality, and as embodying particular practices, customs, languages, and so on, as they choose. A more "heroic" form of cultural identification in which individuals live vicariously through the state may be the true culmination of cultural development.[18] But this also seems false, inasmuch as nation-states actually enhance just those aspects of culture (and only those aspects) that ratify their own power. The "unreal universality" of states, as Marx put it, is, on this account, of more importance than the variety of real human cultures.[19]

If an instance of a claim of national self-determination, such as that of the secessionist movement in Québec, is examined, it should be clear that a general right to culture - that is, a right that is asserted absent any particular injustice or oppression - is insufficient to justify the principle. On the one hand, if the existence of Québeçois culture were threatened by the increasing globalization of a commodity culture, for instance, it is undemonstrable that such an eventuality could be prevented by statehood, since many cultures with sovereign states are still subject to such a threat. Furthermore, the survival of Québecois culture would not be sufficient warrant for an independent state, since the continued existence of such a culture cannot simply be assumed to benefit or interest many people living there. On the other hand, the enjoyment of state symbols and ceremonies is clearly not a significant enough benefit to justify political independence, given the probable costs of creating such a new state. Absent specific state policies of cultural suppression, there is no good reason, on cultural grounds, to advocate self-determination for national groups.

Self-Determination, Regional not National

To consider whether the principle of self-determination requires any further specification than the political or democratic one currently given to it in international law, we need to consider some aspects of the general idea of self-determination, as it was first formulated by Immanuel Kant, among others. Lewis Hinchman, in an article on Kant's concept of self-determination, has specified three basic elements of the principle: [1] a particular meaning given to the concept of autonomy that is the core of the idea of self-determination, [2] a definition of the agent or "self" who seeks self-determination, and [3] a principle that provides limitations on when a claim of self-determination is warranted.[20] All these elements are designed to set limits on self-determination, so that it does not become an indeterminate expression of the will. It is precisely this indeterminacy - that is, the lack of these elements - that Elie Kedourie and others have pointed to in the national principle as justifying violent and protracted conflicts between national groups.

I think that, properly understood, a regional principle of self-determination could supply these elements, while still specifying conditions for the autonomy of communities that have not been identified within the current framework of international law. First of all, the concept of autonomy would involve prevention of the exploitation or oppression of regions and localities either by states, corporations, or other neighboring regions within the same country. Second, the selves seeking self-determination would be regions defined not by ethnonational characteristics, but by ecological criteria that specify distinctive ways of life. And third, the principles of limitation on claims of self-determination would be those of the territorial integrity and political sovereignty of states that are basic to existing international law.

To further specify the nature of autonomy in the regional principle, it should be remembered that it is a principle of "communal" (not individual) autonomy. In regional terms, communal autonomy is best understood as what Allen Buchanan has called the elimination of "discriminatory redistribution." This latter term means the forcible reallocation of goods, resources, and benefits (including property rights and tax monies) from one region to another (or to extraregional corporations, governments, or persons) by a central state.[21] Two cases in which the regional principle would apply are those of indigenous peoples who are trying to preserve a distinctive way of life and those of localities that are attempting to maintain economic self-sufficiency in terms of an ecologically sustainable form of development. In both cases, it is the redistribution of natural resources or material wealth (through expropriation or taxation, for example) from one population or area to another that is unjust or discriminatory and that would therefore provide grounds for a claim of self-determination.

Thus, the regional principle should be invoked under the following condition - when a group of persons living within a well-defined region of a country and pursuing a distinctive way of life is systematically disadvantaged by an entrenched and continuing pattern of discrimination in the allocation of goods and resources that prejudicially affects their ability to pursue their own way of life. The warrant for this principle is that neither the concepts of human rights nor democratic self-government adequately address the problems of what have been called "internal colonialism" or "regional exploitation." The regional principle is designed to do this.

Two kinds of cases may help to clarify what is meant by discriminatory redistribution. First, there is the case of indigenous peoples such as American Indians (e.g., the Mayan people in Mexico). The attempted destruction of American Indian peoples' ways of life by European immigrants, and the states that they have established in the Americas, provides a prima facie reason for claiming self-determination within autonomous regions. This has, in fact, been the basis of attempts to redress the extreme disenfranchisement of American Indians in Mexico, the U.S., Canada, and other countries.

The regional principle is a way of giving reasons for such a claim not in terms of the specific cultural identities of indigenous peoples, but in terms of the preservation of distinct regional ways of life. The difference between these two approaches is that policies that result in suppression of indigenous ways of life may coexist with the right of individuals to engage in cultural practices. Without communal autonomy to maintain territorially specific regional cultures, however, such cultural practices - while allowable - become meaningless. This is not, of course, true of all cultures; and this is why the issue is fundamentally distinct from that of a general right to cultural expression. Indigenous peoples' rights seem to be applicable largely to those cultures that maintain economic and ecological relationships noticeably different from industrial capitalism and its variants.

A second kind of case is that of regions of a country subject to economic exploitation that disrupts the ability of such regions to sustain a way of life distinctive from the rest of the country. Usually such discriminatory redistribution occurs through excessive taxation; but it may also occur through tariffs that affect production of goods in particular regions, changes in land tenure that grant property rights to outside peoples or corporations, or the imposition of restrictions on forms of economic production such as farming or fishing. Such measures have threatened the livelihood and way of life of peoples in many regions of the world; examples could be drawn from the Maritime provinces of Canada, the Amazon River basin in Brazil, and the Siberian region of Russia, among others. In all such cases, self-determination is at issue because a redistribution of resources has unfairly reallocated material wealth and opportunities - unfairly in the sense that they adversely affect the ability of peoples to live independent, self-sustaining lives based on particular regional environments.

What both cases of internal colonialism and regional exploitation thus present us with are examples of the lack of regional self-determination for peoples with ways of life that diverge from those politically dominant within larger countries. This is not a problem that can be grasped within a nationalistic framework, since the idea of national culture is not adequately descriptive of differences between local and regional ecologies. It is also not one that a democratic principle can address, since it may actually be the decisions of democratic majorities within particular countries that lead to the problem in the first place.

Conclusion

The analysis of these cases should lead us to conclude, I would argue, that a regional principle of self-determination can specify a dimension of injustice - that of the discriminatory redistribution of resources by region or locale - that is currently unaddressed in international law. It is important to note, however, that invoking this principle ought to be restricted to cases in which regionally distinctive ways of life become unsustainable as a result of forced redistributions (rather than merely more costly). In addition, while identifying a concept of the type of region that is entitled to make a claim of self-determination cannot be done definitively, a principle by which such regions could be defined can be given - namely, that of those locales that possess human ecologies distinct from other regions of a country. Finally, the regional principle should be understood as a principle of autonomy (rather than statehood) in order that self-determination remains an idea compatible with international legal principles of territoriality and sovereignty.

While my approach has emphasized the social dimension of self-determination, this is not to say that there are never problems of political or cultural self-determination - only that those advocating self-determination for national groups have not shown that this principle is required in order to deal with such problems. Furthermore, I would argue that it is injustices resulting from economic exploitation and ecological destruction of traditional societies and environments that most urgently needs redress in the current period. When aimed at redressing these injustices, the principle of self-determination may come to mean not attainment of the illusory community of the nation-state but a new type of autonomy that can protect ecologically distinct, but equally sustainable, forms of economic life within larger political communities.

Notes

1 Jürgen Habermas, 'Citizenship and National Identity: Some Reflections on the Future of Europe', *Praxis International*, vol. 12, no. 1 (Apr. 1992): 1-18.

2 Wentworth Ofuatey-Kodjoe, *The Principle of Self-Determination in International Law* (New York: Nellen, 1977), 150.

3 See Elie Kedourie, *Nationalism*, 4th ed. (Oxford: Blackwell, 1993), and e.g., Gebre Hiwet Tesfagiorgis, 'Self-Determination: Its Evolution and Practice by the United Nations and Its Application to the Case of Eritrea', *Wisconsin International Law Journal* 6 (1987).

4 Antonio Cassese, 'The Self-Determination of Peoples', in *The International Bill of Rights: The Covenant on Civil and Political Rights*, ed. Louis Henkin (New York: Columbia University Press, 1981).

5 However, to some extent, the apartheid regime was regarded as a special case in international law; see Rupert Emerson, 'Self-Determination', *American Journal of International Law* 65 (1971), 468.

6 On the Palestinian case in international law, see W. Thomas Mallison and Sally V. Mallison, *An International Law Analysis of the Major United Nations Resolutions Concerning the Palestine Question* (New York: United Nations, 1979), and Heather Wilson, *International Law and the Use of Force by National Liberation Movements* (Oxford: Clarendon Press, 1988).

7 Margalit and Raz, 'National Self-Determination', 454.

8 Robert Musil, 'Nation as Ideal and Reality', in *Precision and Soul: Essays and Addresses*, tr. Burton Pike and David S. Luft (Chicago: University of Chicago Press, 1990).

9 Taylor, 'Politics of Recognition', 60-61.

10 Kymlicka, *Multicultural Citizenship*, 80.

11 On nationalist uses of the concept of cultural enjoyment, see Slavoj Zizek, 'Eastern Europe's Republics of Gilead', *New Left Review*, no. 183 (Sept.-Oct. 1990): 50-62, and *Tarrying with the Negative: Kant, Hegel, and the Critique of Ideology* (Durham, N.C.: Duke University Press, 1993).

12 Tamir, *Liberal Nationalism*, 85.

13 Yael Tamir, 'The Right to National Self-Determination', *Social Research*, vol. 58, no. 3 (Fall 1991), 577.

14 Iris Young, *Justice and the Politics of Difference* (Princeton, N.J.: Princeton University Press, 1990), 157.

15 And, as Ross Poole has pointed out in his book, *Morality and Modernity* (London: Routledge, 1991, 98-99), they are only one form that cultures have taken, often by obliterating other local or transnational forms.

16 Ronen, *Quest for Self-Determination*, 52.

17 Ronen, *Quest for Self-Determination*, 61.

18 Tamir, 'Right to National Self-Determination', 585.

19 Karl Marx, 'On the Jewish Question', in Robert Tucker (ed.), *The Marx-Engels Reader*, 2nd ed. (New York: Norton, 1978), 34.

20 Lewis Hinchman, 'Autonomy, Individuality, and Self-Determination', in James Schmidt (ed.), *What Is Enlightenment? Eighteenth-Century Answers and Twentieth-Century Questions* (Berkeley: University of California Press, 1996).

21 On the concept of 'discriminatory redistribution', see Allen E. Buchanan, *Secession: The Morality of Political Divorce from Fort Sumter to Lithuania and Quebec* (Boulder, Colo.: Westview Press, 1991).

Part VII
Diverse Experiences of Human Rights

24. Human Rights and Human Responsibilities: An East Asian Perspective

CHONGKO CHOI

Foreword

Frankly speaking, as an East Asian legal philosopher, I feel some uneasiness about the "Western" theories of rights and human rights. Rudolf von Jhering's assertion that the struggle for rights (Kampf ums Recht) is a moral duty sounds to me extreme and exaggerated, judged by the standard of East Asian social consciousness. Especially with R. Dworkin's famous book Taking Rights Seriously (1977), the rights-based theory seems to enjoy the dominant role in the contemporary jurisprudence.

On the other hand, we see current debates between liberalism (or libertarianism) and communitarianism. On the issue of human rights also, there seems to be different views from these two positions.[1]

Methodologically, two ways are possible for the discussion of human rights and responsibilities. One is the logical analysis of the concepts of rights and responsibilities and of the relationship of each other. The other is the ideological explanations of rights and responsibilities in the historical contexts.

Following, I will review the concepts of rights and responsibilities from the comparative perspectives of East and West.[2] Then I will discuss briefly the East Asian jurisprudence on rights and responsibilities. The Universal Declaration of Human Responsibilities (1997) is servered as an example of global ethics based on "responsibility". I want to assert that East Asian jurisprudence is keenly concerned with the harmony between rights and responsibilities.

I. Reconsidering of Rights and Duties

The coherence of rights and responsibilities is commonplace in everyday thought and conversation, such as "Consumer Rights and Responsibilities" and "Rights and Responsibilities of Mass Media". Yet despite its occurrence at various levels of discourse, the connection between rights and responsibilities in the abstract has received little attention from philosophers.[3] Philosophers ask whether rights and duties are logically correlative, that is, whether one's possession of a right logically assumes one is owed some duty by others and conversely, whether one's bearing a duty logically implies that another or others possess a right against one.

Since the 17th century, problems connected with rights have steadily engaged the attention of political and legal philosophers. John Locke is a key figure in the rise of "rights" to a place of preeminence in western liberal culture. Natural law, traditionally the doctrine of people's duties and obligations, has become the doctrine of the natural rights of people. Until the 17th century, the problems of political ethics were problems not of rights but, rather of the duties a man owed to his lord, his king, his church, or his God. Oliver W. Holmes explains his *The Common Law* (1881) as the history of people's duties and their evolution. Nevertheless, "rights" have come into prominence as a notion crucial to an understanding of relationship between people and their government. Of course, the concept of right had its ups and downs. Neither Utilitarians nor Marxists found it particularly useful in formatting their political ideals.[4] It is not essay to judge whether human being is essentially right-based or duty-based. Therefore, there is constant discussions on human rights and human duties.

Joseph Raz points out inherent limitations of rights-oriented doctrines and the need to regard rights as subduable and devised from a more fundamental doctrine of well-being on the one hand, and a complementary need to give duties a central role in our understanding of moral and political life, independent of their role in protecting and promoting right, on the other hand. He argues that the commonly distorted perception of duties, which is supposed to make plain their subordination to rights, in fact leads to belittling of the role of rights. He emphasizes that the role of rights is subordinate and thus is to be understood from a wider and a more fundamental perspective, in which they are no more than the equal of duties.[5]

The role of duties in practical reasoning is seen to be to subject the action of one person to the will or the interests of another. But this picture is fundamentally mistaken: there are self-regarding duties, duties, which arise out of their subjects' own well-being. Furthermore, duties may be intrinsically good, and their existence may be essential to the existence of valuable activities and relationships.

Jack Donnelly says:

> Rights do have a correlative duties. Many (but no all) duties have correlative rights, but particular rights and duties may stand in a great variety of relations to one another, and many rights are held independently of the discharge of duties. One has human rights simply because one is a human being.[6]

Like this, the logical analysis of the relationship between rights and duties is going further in the contemporary jurisprudence.

II. Universal Decreation of Human Responsibilities

As a good example of the correlation of rights and duties, I would like to compare the Universal Declaration of Human Rights (1948) and UniversalDeclaration of Human Responsibilities (1997).[7] A group named Interaction Council including 24 former heads of states formulated this Declaration.[8] The group aimed to have this Declaration engrossed by the UN. When I read this document composed in 19 articles, I find progress toward a deeper understanding on human rights. I have the impression that this Declaration of Human Responsibilities reaches maturity of the Declaration of Human Rights of 50 years ago. The preamble of the Declaration manifests that the exclusive insistence on rights can result in conflict, decision, and endless dispute, and the neglect of human responsibilities with a possibly outcome of lawlessness and chaos. Art. 1 of the Declaration of Human Rights declares; "All human beings are born free and equal in dignity and rights. They are endowed with reason and conscience and should act towards one another in a spirit of brotherhood". Art. 4 of the Declaration of Human Responsibilities declares; "All people, endowed with reason and conscience, must accept a responsibility to each and all, to families and communities, to races, nations, and religions in a spirit of solidarity: what you do not wish to be done to yourself, do not do to others". What is I find impressive here is the fact that the Golden Rule is cited here manifestly as global ethics.[9]

Art. 7 of the Declaration of Human Rights says: "All are equal before the law and are entitled without any discrimination to equal protection of the law". Art. 3 of the Declaration of Human Responsibilities says, "No person, no group or organization, no state, notary or police stands above good and evil; all are subject to ethical standards. Everyone has a responsibility to promote good and to avoid evil in all things". The Declaration of Human Responsibilities adopts new provision of human responsibilities on environment: "Every person is infinitely precious and must be protected unconditionally. The amenable and the natural environment also demand protection. All people have a responsibility to protect the air, wether, and soil of the earth for the sake of present inhabitants and future generations (Art. 7)". Art. 3 of Declaration of Human Rights says, "Everyone has the right to life, liberty and security of the person". Art. 5 of the Declaration of Human Responsibilities says, "Every person has a responsibility to respect life. No one has the right to injure, to torture, or to kill another human person".

Art. 12 of the Declaration of Human Rights says: "No one shall be subjected to arbitrary interference with his privacy, family, home or correspondence, nor to attacks upon his honor and reputation. Everyone has the right to the protection of the law against such interference or attackers". Art, 12 of the Declaration of Human Responsibilities says: "Every person has a responsibility to speak and act truthfully. No one, however high or mighty, should speak lies. The rights to privacy and to personal and professional confidentiality is to the respected. No one is obliged to tell all the truth to everyone all the time".

Art. 10 of the Declaration of Human Rights says; "Marriage shall be entered into only with the free and full consent of the intending spouses. The family is the natural and fundamental group unit of society and is entitled to protection by society and the state". Art. 18 of the Declaration of Human Responsibilities says: "Sensible family planning is the responsibility of every couple. The relationship between parents and the children should reflect mutual love, respect, appreciation, and concern. No parents or other adults should exploit, abuse, or maltreat children".

Art. 17 of the Declaration of Human Rights says: "Everyone has the right to own property alone as well as in association with others. No one shall be arbitrarily deprived of his property". Art. 11 of the Declaration of Human Responsibilities says: "All property and wealth must be used responsibly in accordance with justice and for the advancement of the human race. Economic and political power must not be handled as an instrument of domination, but in the service of economic justice and of the social order".

Art. 18 of the Declaration of Human Rights says, "Everyone has the right to freedom of thought, conscience and religion; this right includes freedom to change his religion or belief, and freedom, either alone or in community with others and in public or private, to manifest his religion or belief in teaching, practice, worship and observance". Art. 15 of the Declaration of Human Responsibilities says, "While religious freedom must be guaranteed, the representatives of religion have a special responsibility to avoid expressions of prejudice and acts of discrimination toward those of different beliefs. They should not incite or legitimize hatred, fanaticism, and religious wars, but should foster tolerance and mutual respect between all people".

Art. 19 of the Declaration of Human Rights says, "Everyone has the right to freedom of opinion and expression: this right includes freedom to hold opinions without interference to seek, receive and impart information and ideas through any media and regardless of frontiers". Art. 14 of the Declaration of Human Responsibilities says; "The freedom of the media to inform the public and to criticize institutions of society and governmental actions, which is essential for a just society, must be used with responsibility and discretion. Freedom of the media carries a special responsibility for accurate and truthful reporting. Sensational reporting that degrades the human person or dignity must at all times be avoided". Additionally, the Declaration of Human Responsibilities declares: "All people, given the necessary tools, have a responsibility to make serious efforts to overcome poverty, manipulation, ignorance, and inequality. They should promote sustainable development all over the world in order to assure dignity, freedom, security, and justice for all people (Art. 9)". "No politicians, public servants, business leaders, scientists, writers, or artists are exempt from general ethical standards, nor are physicians, lawyers, and other professionals who have special duties to clients. Professional and other coders of ethics should reflect the priority of general standards such as these of truthfulness and fairness". Finally, the Declaration of Human Responsibilities concludes: "Nothing in this Declaration may be interpreted as implying for any state, group or person any right to engage in any activity or to perform any aimed at the destruction of any of the responsibility, rights, and freedom set forth in this Declaration and in the Universal Declaration of Human Rights of 1948".[10]

In the expressions of the Universal Declaration of Human Responsibilities, we see a deep and rich progression of legal thought finding rights and responsibilities as two sides of the same coin, I want to point that such development of world legal thought matches the East Asian legal philosophy of right and duty.[11] The East Asian jurisprudence is based on the "practical reasons" which constitute the articulated principles and rules about human conduct and customs.[12]

III. Confucian Theories of Rights and Responsibilities

I think the biggest task of human rights theory is to harmonize the "universality" and culture-boundedness of human rights.[13] In this context, I would like to point to some recent intellectual efforts of the East Asian scholars to build up relevant theories of human rights.

A symposium was held in 1995 at the East-West Center, Honolulu, and the result was published as a book *Confucianism and Human Rights* (1998).[14] This book confirms that Confucianism is not incompatible with human rights even though it has no matching term for the Western word "human rights". It held that Asian values of Confucianism need not reject any of the prescriptions of the Universal Declaration of Human Rights as stated in 1948. There is no intrinsic tension between Confucianism and human rights.[15] I appreciate Wejen Chang's efforts to build up the Confucian theory of norms and human rights. He concludes that Western and Confucian ideas are conceptually compatible but practically different.[16] He suggests a two-step approach for a good human life that people first learn the Confucian norms and become compassionate and respectful towards one another and then be assured that they have certain "rights".

Chungying Cheng also tries to transform theoretic Confucian virtues into human rights in five ways. According to him, the modern West, in developing the notion of rights and duties, comes out of the Aristotelian tradition of virtue ethics, which A. MacIntyre hopes to reclaim. The point would be how to preserve the Confucian virtues while at the same time extrapolating from them an ethics of rights for modern society. Cheng argues the possible transformation of Confucian virtues into rights in the cultivation of virtue by individuals in a community with a view to awaking an individual sense of consciousness of duty to the community, which in turn should call forth an awareness of the individual's legitimate potential to participate in public affairs.[17]

It is worth while to observe how the Chinese legal scholars are trying to build up human rights theories based on traditional Confucian philosophy and ethics. In a book named *Human Rights and Chinese Values* (1995), the Chinese scholar Du Gangjian attempts to relate human rights to Chinese culture, naming the four paths of the Confucian Analects and the four principles of a New Theory of Benevolence.[18] According to Du, the four principles derived from the Analects for the human rights are 1) human rights, 2) tolerance, 3) resistance, 4) new-constitutionalism. All together these comprise what he calls a "new benevolence theory", to compare with the classical Confucian theory. The classical components of the benevolence theory in the Analects include the paths of benevolence, tolerance, justice and government. Du argues the compatibility of Classical Chinese Confucian philosophy and modem principles of human rights. He emphasizes that the modem concept of human rights is not alien to Chinese soil. What struck me is his earnest intellectual efforts to combine his thesis with G. Radbruch's legal philosophy. He maintains, "G. Radbruch's juristic theory has had a significant effect upon the development of legal culture and socio-economic reforms in modem East Asia".[19] It is very interesting that Radbruch's relativistic jurisprudence is introduced as a progressive liberal theory supporting human rights in the Socialistic People's Republic of China.

Korean legal scholars also are engaging actively in the discussion of human rights and practices. South Korea established a Constitutional Court in 1988 according to the German and Austrian model of *Verfassungsgericht* and is preparing a Governmental Committee on Human Rights. As a divided nation, North Korea is still suffering severe damages in the area of human rights. Nevertheless, human rights and dignity is considered to be the most important concept of Korean jurisprudence.[20]

We see here that East Asian legal philosophers are eager to reevaluate their cultural tradition positively, combining the rights and duties on the new level. They feel proud that they have a rich tradition out of which to propose theories of human rights and human duties. They try to suggest a new virtue-ethics and right-responsibilities jurisprudence in their own tongue. Politically, it is understandable that Chinese and Korean jurisprudents are trying to build up the human right theories rather than theories of human responsibilities. The intellectuals are inclined by nature to resist the "dictatorial" political powers, which ignore the human rights. Notwithstanding the current attention on human rights, I believe, they are acknowledging a basic primacy of human responsibility.

There is a correspondence between responsibilities and virtues, the latter being derived from the former, as the following suggests:

Virtues	**Responsibilities**
Truthfulness	Duty to tell the truth
Nonmalfeasance	Duty not to harm
Fairness	Duty to be just
Benevolence	Duty to be beneficent
Conscientiousness	Duty to be sensitive to one's duty
Faithfulness	Duty to be loyal as well as faithful
Love	Duty to do what promotes another's good

Although derived from the right kind of actions, the virtues are nonetheless very important for the moral life: They provide the dispositions that generate right action.[21]

Conclusion

We see Western jurisprudence also renewing discussion of rights and responsibilities. The one-sided rights-based theory is criticized by the Communitarian responsibility-based ethics. Apart from that discussion, East Asian jurisprudents are concerned with building up their own philosophies of rights and responsibilities. It is not easy, because theory-building must use "Western" concepts, to make itself understandable in the context of western thought. This presents both a dilemma and opportunity for East Asian jurisprudence. Nevertheless, at least in regard to the problem of human rights and responsibilities, we observe a corresponding resonance in the Western jurisprudence also especially in the Universal Declaration of Human Responsibilities. Globalization is matched by global problems, and global problems demand global solutions based on ideas, values and norms respected by all cultures and societies. A better social order, both national and international, cannot be achieved by laws, prescriptions and conventions alone, but needs the help of a global ethic. If one person or government seeks to maximize freedom but does it at the expense of others, a large number of people will suffer. If human beings maximize their freedom by plundering the natural resources of the earth, then future generations will suffer. Of course, to create a true philosophy of human rights and responsibilities dialogue between Western and East Asian scholars is constantly needed.

Notes

1 Stephen Mulhall and Adam Swift, *Liberals and Communitarians*, 2n ed. 1996. esp. pp. 272-81; Jack Donnelly, *Universal Human Rights in Theory and Practice*, Comell Univ. Press, 1989.

2 In this paper, I use the terms duties and responsibilities in a interchangeable way. I know, there are many sophisticated distinctions between both concepts. But I don't want to be restrained by these theories.

3 John Neigh, On Rights and Responsibilities, *Law and Philosophy*, vol. 7, 1988, p. 149.

4 Joseph Raz, Liberating Duties, *Law and Philosophy*, vol. 8, No.3, 1989, p. 4.

5 J. Raz, ibid. pp. 4-5.

6 Jack Donnelly, Human Rights and Asian Values: A Defense of "Western" Universalism, Joanne R. Bauer/Daniel A. Bell (ed.), *The East Asian Challenge for Human Rights*, Cambridge Univ. Press, 1999, pp. 78-79.

7 In Germany, this declaration is translated as *Allgemeine Erklilärung des M enschenpflichte,* See, Helmut Schmidt (hrg.), *Allgemeine Erklilärung der Menschenpflichte*, Piper Verlag/ München, 1997.

8 The proposed Declaration has the endorsement of the following individuals: Helmut Schmidt (Former Chancellor of Germany), Malcolm Fraser (Former Prime Minister

of Australia), Jimmy Carter (Former President of USA), V. Giscard d'Estaing (Former President of France), Lee Kuan Yew (Former Prime Minister of Singapore), Kiichi Miyzawa (Former Prime Minister of Japan), Shin Hyon Hwak (Former Prime Minister of the Republic of Korea), etc. China has not endorsed yet.

9 About the Golden Rule for the contemporary relevance, Amitai Etzioni, *New Golden Rule: Community and Morality in a Democratic Society*. N. Y. 1997; and *The Spirit of Community: Rights, Responsibilities and Communitarian Agenda*, N. Y. 1993.

10 The text of the UDHRe is printed in: *The Responsible Community*, vol. 8, No.21, 1998; Mary Maxwell, Toward a Moral System for World Society: A Reflection on Human Responsibilities, *Ethics and International Affairs*, vol. 12, 1998, pp. 179-193.

11 Chongko Choi, Asian Concept of Rights and Duty, *Asian Jurisprudence in the World*, Seoul, 1997.

12 Chongko Choi, Law and Practical Reason from the Asian Viewpoint, paper presented at IVR Congress in Göttingen (Oct. 18-22, 1991).

13 Many books and reports has been published, including Federico Mayer(ed.), *Taking Action for Human Rights in the Twenty-First Century*, UNESCO Publishing, 1998; Morigiwa Yasutomo(ed.), *Law in a Changing World: Asian Alternatives*, ARSP Beiheft Nr. 72, 1998; Nicholas Wheeler(ed.), *Human Rights in Global Politics*, Cambridge Univ. Press, 1998.

14 Book review, Chongko Choi, in: *Philosophy East and West*, vol. 49, No.3, 1999 (forthcoming).

15 De Bary/Tu Weiming (ed.), *Confucianism and Human Rights*, Columbia Univ. Press, 1988, p. 313.

16 Wejen Chang, 'The Confucian Theory of Norms and Human Rights', in: *Confucianism and Human Rights*, 1998, p. 134.

17 Chungying Cheng, 'Transforming Confucian Virtues into Human Rights', *Confucianism and Human Rights*, p. 151.

18 Du Gangjian/Song Gang, Relating Human Rights to Chinese Culture: The four paths of the Confucian Analects and the Four Principles of a New Theory of Benevolence, in; Michael C. Davis (ed.), *Human Rights and Chinese Values: Legal, Philosophical and Political Perspectives*, Oxford Univ. Press 1995, pp. 35-55.

19 Du Gangjian, op. cit, p. 39; For discussion, Keifu Suzuki, *Human Rights and Relativism in China* (Japanese), Tokyo, 1997; Joanne R. Bauer/Daniel A. Bell(ed.), *The East Asian Challenge for Human Rights*, Cambridge Univ. Press, 1999.

20 William Shaw (ed), *Human Rights in Korea*, Harvard Univ. Press, 1991.

21 Louis P. Pojman, *Ethics: Discovering Right and Wrong*, Belmont/CA, 1995, p. 174.

25. Legal Moralism and the European Court of Human Rights

RICHARD NUNAN

> Moral people, as they are termed, are simply beasts. I would sooner have fifty unnatural vices than one unnatural virtue. It is unnatural virtue that makes the world, for those who suffer, such a premature Hell.
>
> Oscar Wilde, 1897[1]

On April 1, 1894, the Marquess of Queensbury, infuriated with what he regarded as a scandalous dalliance between his son, Lord Alfred Douglas, and the Anglo-Irish playwright Oscar Wilde, fired off the following letter to Douglas:

> Your intimacy with this man Wilde...It must either cease or I will disown you and stop all money supplies. I am not going to try and analyze this intimacy, and I make no charge; but to my mind to pose as a thing is as bad as to be it.
> Your disgusted, so-called father, Queensbury[2]

To this Douglas telegrammed a less-than-diplomatic response the following day: "What a funny little man you are."

Things went from bad to worse between father and son until the following February, when Queensbury left a calling card at Wilde's club, addressed: "For Oscar Wilde, posing as a Somdomite" [sic]. Following this rather public accusation, Wilde decided, with Douglas's urging, to sue Queensbury for libel. Unfortunately for Wilde, the available evidence, including correspondence between him and Douglas, supported rather than refuted the charge, and Wilde lost the lawsuit. Subsequently, Wilde himself was had up on criminal charges under Section 11 of the *Criminal Law Amendment Act* of 1885, which provided that:

> Any male person who, in public or private, commits, or is a party to the commission of, or procures or attempts to procure the commission by any

> male person of, any act of gross indecency with another male person, shall be guilty of a misdemeanor, and being convicted thereof shall be liable at the discretion of the court to be imprisoned for any term not exceeding two years, with or without hard labor.

Wilde's initial trial, conducted in April of 1895, resulted in a hung jury. But he was successfully convicted the following month in a retrial. Upon sentencing, the presiding judge in the case issued a sample of judicial vitriol that has rarely been surpassed:

> It is no use for me to address you. People who can do these things must be dead to all sense of shame, and one cannot hope to produce any affect upon them. It is the worst that I have ever tried...that you, Wilde, have been the center of a circle of extensive corruption of the most hideous kind among young men, it is equally impossible to doubt. I shall, under such circumstances, be expected to pass the severest sentence that the law allows. In my judgment it is totally inadequate for such a case as this. The sentence of the Court is that you shall be imprisoned and kept to hard labor for two years.

The Parliamentary Act which led to this sad tragedy, together with Section 61 of the earlier *Offenses Against the Person Act* of 1861 (prescribing penal servitude for life[3] for "the abominable crime of buggery, committed either with mankind or with any animal") remained on the books in England until the Sexual Offenses Act of 1967, which finally implemented some of the recommendations issued in the Wolfenden Report a decade earlier. (This was the report, familiar to philosophers thanks to the subsequent debate between Patrick Devlin and H.L.A. Hart,[4] which advocated legalization of prostitution and homosexuality on the ground that certain consensual privately conducted activities were "not the law's business"). This reform measure did not apply in Northern Ireland, however. For at that time, just prior to resumption of hostilities between Catholic and Protestant extremists, the Six Counties were still governed by a separate, and quite conservative, Northern Ireland Parliament. Nor, of course, did it apply in the Irish Republic, where acts issued from Westminster have had no authority since the creation of the Irish Free State in 1922. Nonetheless, British law, including its Victorian relics, was adopted wholesale into the Irish legal system in the 1922 Free State Constitution, and reaffirmed in the Irish Republic's 1937 *Constitution of Ireland*.[5]

So after 1967, both Northern and Southern Ireland found themselves in the ironic position of sustaining laws, which had once been used by England to destroy one of Ireland's literary progeny, laws that were now repudiated by England. Moreover, both Irish governments vigorously defended these laws against subsequent attacks. And yet today, thirty years later, the Irish Republic has one of the more liberal legal systems in the world with respect to issues of sexual orientation. This development, and others like it in the area of morals legislation, cannot be credited primarily to some remarkable epiphany of the Irish government. The real credit belongs to a few courageous Irish citizens, and to the concept of international judicial review, as exhibited through a series of European Court of Human Rights (ECHR) decisions implementing the right of privacy provision in Article 8 of the *European Convention on Human Rights*. In this paper, I propose to examine these cases, and other related ones, with an eye to determining the extent to which the Court, and its advisory arm, the European Commission of Human Rights, have felt entitled to rewrite, and have actually rewritten, the brief for legal moralism in the domestic law of member states of the Council of Europe.

I

Legal moralism, of course, is the principle propounded by Patrick Devlin in "The Enforcement of Morals"[6] (and, with a rather different justification, a century earlier by James Fitzjames Stephen,[7] in his response to John Stuart Mill's defense of the harm principle[8]). On Devlin's view, the State may intervene in the lives of individual citizens not only to protect a sphere of individual autonomy (Mill's harm principle), but also to sustain and promote certain shared values which imbue a community with its unique identity, on the theory that such shared values are essential to the very survival of that community as a distinct society. Legal moralism has its place in European human rights law through references, in various articles of the *European Convention on Human Rights*, to the latitude which signatory States have in honoring enumerated rights when "the protection of health or morals" is at issue, and through the practice, in both the Commission and the European Court of Human Rights, of affording member States of the Council of Europe a "wide margin of appreciation" where matters of moral weight are concerned.[9]

The original cases in question, one for each jurisdiction, were Irish equivalents of *Bowers v. Hardwick* (478 U.S. 186), the 1986 U.S. case in which the United States Supreme Court upheld a Georgia sodomy law. The Northern Ireland case, *Dudgeon v. United Kingdom* (7525/76, ECHR Series A, No. 45, 1981), was very similar to *Bowers*, in that a police investigation into the private affairs of Jeffrey Dudgeon, a citizen of Northern Ireland, served as the catalyst, which instigated the case. In the Irish Republic, *Norris v. Attorney General* (1984 I.R. 36; 10581/83, ECHR

Series A, No. 142, 1988) differed from *Bowers* insofar as David Norris, a lecturer in English at Trinity College Dublin, and a member of the Irish Senate, instituted his legal proceeding in the absence of any direct provocation by the State. He simply contended that the statutes in question violated several provisions of Article 40 of the Irish Constitution (the first of four lengthy articles enumerating constitutional protections for various "Fundamental Rights"), and should therefore be struck down on the authority of Section 1 of Article 50 (*supra*, note 5). Both cases were like *Bowers* in their outcomes, however: the plaintiffs each lost in their respective local courts of last appeal. But unlike Michael Hardwick, both Jeffrey Dudgeon and David Norris had one further card to play: they could take their respective cases to the European Court of Human Rights, under the right of privacy articulated in Article 8 of the *European Convention on Human Rights*.

The *Convention* is a post-war declaration akin to (and inspired in part by) the slightly older United Nations *Universal Declaration of Human Rights* (which contains a similar privacy provision). Both documents were motivated in turn by a fervent wish to avoid any repetition of the human rights abuses witnessed during the Nazi occupation of Europe. The *Convention* was also fueled by the conviction, shared among most of the original members of the Council of Europe (and partially motivating the Council's creation as well), that, for the present at least, the *Universal Declaration* could not reasonably be regarded as more than a hortatory aspirational document. Given the enormous diversity of nations sharing U.N. membership, any real consensus on human rights issues was still a long way off. But given the shared history and political ideals of Western European nations, a binding declaration of human rights could realistically be drafted among that subset of U.N. members:

> Although the question of human rights had been discussed at length by the United Nations, it had not yet been possible to draft a text, which held well in International Law. The universal declaration lacked precision. It could not be otherwise in view of the differences in civilization and forms of Government existing in different member States of the United Nations. It would be a very different matter if the question was reconsidered on a purely Western European basis, in which case a text might be elaborated which would be binding in the legal sense.[10]

The prediction that a regional international court could be effective in Europe has been borne out, and the cases contesting the criminalization of homosexual acts number among the more dramatic illustrations of this thesis. *Dudgeon* came first, in 1981. *Convention* Article 8, the basis for Dudgeon's appeal, holds that:

1. Everyone has the right to respect for his private and family life, his home and his correspondence.
2. There shall be no interference by a public authority with the exercise of this right except such as is in accordance with the law and is necessary in a democratic society in the interests of national security, public safety, or the economic well-being of the country, for the prevention of disorder or crime, for the protection of health or morals, or for the protection of the rights and freedoms of others.

The Court quickly decided that the N.I. statutes at issue violated Provision 1: "the offenses are committed whether the act takes place in public or in private, whatever the age or relationship of the participants involved, and whether or not the participants are consenting. It is evident from Mr. Dudgeon's submissions, however, that his complaint was in essence directed against the fact that homosexual acts which he might commit *in private* with other males capable of valid consent are criminal offenses under the law of Northern Ireland" (*Dudgeon*, §39; italics added). The Court was equally prompt in ascertaining that the opening test in Article 8(2)—the presence of an actual state interference—was satisfied: "The maintenance in force of the impugned legislation constitutes a continuing interference with the applicant's right to respect for his private life" (*Dudgeon*, §41).

Unlike U.S. courts, which often set the bar very high for finding violations of the right of privacy in the first place, the ECHR has always been fairly liberal about the breadth of the scope of privacy rights. In the *Bowers* majority opinion, by contrast, Byron White chose to caste the issue in terms of a putative right to engage in consensual homosexual sodomy, and went on to contend that we should not recognize such specific rights as "fundamental". White offered this reasoning in the face of Harry Blackmun's unusually blunt dissent, suggesting that the court majority was deliberately pursuing its own ideological agenda by framing the issue in a way that completely ignored the facts of the case. Blackmun argued that there certainly was a fundamental right at issue here: Louis Brandeis's "right to be let alone"—the previously recognized right of privacy.

One reason for this difference in judicial temperament undoubtedly has to do with the fact that, unlike the explicit reference in Article 8 of the *Convention*, privacy in the U.S. Constitution is an innumerated, judicially-recognized, constitutional right. White clearly was concerned that the Court might be in danger of discovering historically novel personal rights not embedded in the intent or language of the Constitution, and therefore sought to impose narrow limits on the scope of unenumerated rights which the Court has been wrestling with ever since it explicitly ratified the right of privacy in *Griswold v. Connecticut* [381 U.S. 479 (1965)].

Robert Wintemute has pointed out a different (but not incompatible) possible explanation for this contrast between the U.S. and European courts of last resort.[11] Where the U.S. Supreme Court, and the lower federal courts, have a long history (going back, at least in principle, as far as *Palko v. Connecticut* [302 U.S. 319 (1937)] and *Korematsu v. United States* [323 U.S. 214 (1944)]) of invoking the due process clauses of the Fifth and Fourteenth Amendments, and the equal protection clause of the Fourteenth, to set fairly high justificatory standards for permissible governmental interference with the lives, liberty, or property of individual citizens, the European Court of Human Rights has tolerated a much broader standard of permissible justifications for contested domestic laws of the various member States of the Council of Europe. Given the innate conservatism of courts everywhere, it is not surprising that the U.S. Court makes up for a previously established weak screening system at the level of justificatory rationales for restrictions on individual rights, by imposing a higher threshold for falling within the scope of the right in the first place. In the same vein, the European Court makes up for the exclusionary scope of the right by shifting the burden of proof concerning the rationality of the contested law. Unlike the U.S. Courts, the European Court frequently assigns that burden to the protesting individual rather than to the member State.

Indeed, the European Court's disposition to be deferential to legislative rationales for disputed legal practices was written into many of the substantive provisions of the *European Convention on Human Rights*. The language, which limits the right of privacy by carving out exceptions for what, is "necessary in a democratic society" for the sake of various state interests (including especially "the protection of health and morals" and "the rights and freedoms of others") is not idiosyncratic to Provision 2 of Article 8. Similar language appears in Articles 9, 10, 11, and Protocol 4. These constraints have led the Court, as well as respondent member States, to invoke a "margin of appreciation," both out of respect for local democratic autonomy, and in recognition of the likelihood that local authorities are generally better placed to recognize and provide for local needs, and to sustain a nation's distinctive moral ethos.

Consequently, the serious question which confronted the Court in *Dudgeon* was not whether there was any violation of Jeffrey Dudgeon's privacy right, but whether the 'moral exception' clause in Provision 2 justified the interference with that recognized privacy right, whether the Parliamentary Acts under dispute were "necessary in a democratic society" to protect "the rights and freedoms of [particularly vulnerable] others" and, more generally, "the moral ethos or moral standards of a society as a whole." While the European Court certainly acknowledges the legitimacy of such claims in the abstract, and in many specific cases, which it has adjudicated, it didn't buy that argument in this instance:

> As compared with the era when that legislation was enacted, there is now a better understanding, and in consequence an increased tolerance, of homosexual behavior to the extent that in the great majority of the member States of the Council of Europe it is no longer considered to be necessary or appropriate to treat homosexual practices of the kind now in question as in themselves a matter to which the sanctions of the criminal law should be applied; the Court cannot overlook the marked changes which have occurred in this regard in the domestic law of member States....No evidence has been adduced to show that this [new tolerance] has been injurious to moral standards in Northern Ireland or that there has been any public demand for stricter enforcement of the law. (*Dudgeon*, §60)

As a direct result of the Court's ruling, the Homosexual Offenses Order was passed in 1982, in order to limit the scope of the 1861 and 1885 Acts to special cases such as military personnel, bringing Northern Irish law into line with England's 1967 Sexual Offenses Act.

One reason, of course, why the European Court of Human Rights might have been more disposed to dismiss Northern Ireland's moral exception case for its anti-sodomy laws could have been the fact that the legal institutions in force there were essentially indistinguishable from those operating in England, where such laws had been abandoned nearly 15 years earlier. The same argument might not be so readily applicable in the Irish Republic, which was governed by a written constitution, modeled in large part on the U.S. Constitution, and which was predominantly Catholic. Neither of these traits is shared by Northern Ireland. Indeed, in the 1984 sodomy decision of the Irish Supreme Court, ruling against David Norris's plea for legalization, Chief Justice O'Higgins reasoned that while England, and even Northern Ireland, might be governed by the Wolfenden Committee's conviction "that homosexuality was concerned only with private morality and that the law had no business entering into that field," he would not assume that the same principle applies under the Irish Constitution unless there were "very clear and express provisions in the Constitution" to suggest that (*Norris* (I.R.), 63-64).

There is some reason to acknowledge that O'Higgins' argument is not without merit. For the 1937 Irish Constitution does indeed embody some features hostile to the concept of homosexual rights, having to do with the presence in that document of two potentially incompatible visions of national self-identity. There is now a widely shared view among Irish scholars of constitutional law and legal history that Eamon de Valera, the Irish Constitution's James Madison, was trying "to reconcile the [Lockean] notion of inalienable popular sovereignty with the older medieval conception of a theocratic state."[12] More specifically, de Valera was an admirer of the ideals of Enlightenment liberalism, as expressed in the U.S. Constitution, from whose text and amendments he borrowed freely, and also of Thomistic natural law theory and the contemporary social teachings of the Catholic Church, as represented by papal encyclicals published this century in the years prior to de Valera's drafting of the Constitution. The end result is a singularly peculiar mix of two very different legal traditions which have frequently worked at cross purposes during subsequent acts of constitutional interpretation in the Irish courts, and in popular referenda on constitutional issues.

On the liberal side, Article 1 asserts an inalienable right of self-governance; in Article 40 we find recognition of citizen equality before the law, due process rights, freedom of speech and assembly; in Article 43 a right to private property; and Article 44 asserts freedom of conscience. On the theocratic side, the Constitution's Preamble reads, in part:

> In the name of the Most Holy Trinity, from Whom is all authority and to Whom, as our final end, all actions both of men and States must be referred, we, the people of Éire, humbly acknowledging all our obligations to our Divine Lord, Jesus Christ...and seeking to promote the common good...do hereby adopt, enact, and give ourselves this Constitution.

More specific theocratically motivated provisions include a recognition of the family as the "natural" primary unit of society, a state obligation to "endeavor to ensure that mothers shall not be obliged by economic necessity to engage in labor to the neglect of their duties in the home," and a provision prohibiting divorce (Article 41). The State reserves the right to constrain the exercise of the right to private property (Article 43) to whatever extent it deems necessary to achieve satisfaction of "The Principles of Social Justice" set forth in Article 45 (which include, among others, a right to an adequate means of livelihood, and the principle "that the ownership and control of the material resources of the community may be so distributed amongst private individuals and the various classes as best to subserve the common good"). And finally, many of the individual rights covered in Article 40 are "subject to public order and morality."

The history of constitutional adjudication in Ireland, especially since the 1970s, has been a history of failed efforts to reconcile the conflicting elements in these two traditions. O'Higgins' reaction to Norris's argument is a case in point. He simply opted for the theocratic interpretation, specifically invoking the Preamble as evidence of a natural law justification for ruling against David Norris's claim that the anti-sodomy laws of 1861 and 1885 violated an unenumerated right of privacy under Article 40 (*Norris* (I.R.), 64-65).

Despite the Irish government's plea that local autonomy ought to apply in matters of protection of morals, as an essential component of Ireland's right to define its own identity through democratic self governance, and despite O'Higgins' argument that the Irish Republic's legal system and its moral ethos were *sui generis*, the European Court of Human Rights ruled that *Norris* was in essence no different than *Dudgeon*, and quoted extensively from its decision in the earlier case:

> Yet the [Irish] Government has adduced no evidence which would point to the existence of factors justifying the retention of the impugned laws which are additional to or are of greater weight than those present in the aforementioned *Dudgeon* case. (*Norris* (ECHR), §46.)

In short, the Court found that, with respect to private consensual sexual relationships at least, the margin of appreciation which the Court often invokes to defer to the considered judgment of local authorities (even in favor of limited interference with human rights recognized by the *Convention*), was insufficient to justify reaffirmation of a putative local moral ethos through the criminalization of homosexual acts. Moreover, the Court concluded that the margin of appreciation was insufficient not only in Northern Ireland, where that claim might arguably be compromised by the fact that Northern Ireland was part of a larger polity which clearly did not embrace criminalization, but also in the Republic, which was not subject to that objection, and which was overwhelmingly Catholic (an argument for the potential strength of local moral antipathy to homosexual acts).[13]

II

From the perspective of political ideals informed by the philosophy of Enlightenment liberalism, the European Court's intervention in Irish judicial review, the decisions in *Dudgeon* and *Norris* are to be applauded. They represent the implementation of progressive social forces emerging from a more ecumenical European community. Individual countries—and Ireland is surely not alone in this regard—could do with an awakening from their various parochial dogmatic slumbers. And even then the arousal can be rather slow. It took Ireland five years, two changes of government, and threats of renewed litigation from Senator Norris, before it finally came out with a decriminalization act in May of 1993, including a common age of consent at 17. Interestingly, this act included none of the special exemptions incorporated in English laws legalizing homosexuality: the Irish military, for example, cannot discriminate on grounds of sexual orientation. The decriminalization law was followed in quick succession by an employment anti-discrimination law covering sexual orientation (in October, 1993), and legislation prohibiting medical insurers from discriminating against lesbians and gay men, effective July of 1994. Going far beyond the requirements of the European Court, this body of legislation represents a remarkable reversal for a country where, until recently, an Irish homosexual was characterized as an Irishman who prefers women to a pint. (Lesbianism was apparently so far removed from the Irish public consciousness that it didn't even rate a punch line.)

Is there a downside to the European practice of subjecting local judicial decisions or legislative measures to the threat of international review? Well, I suppose there is. Irish conservatives and communitarians, as well as traditionalists in other European countries, have complained not only about the application of the *European Convention of Human Rights* via the European Court of Human Rights in Strasbourg, but also about the application of EC treaties to domestic laws via the European Court of Justice in Luxembourg. On their view, both courts have sporadically interfered with the democratic implementation of local social mores, to the point of threatening the right of self-government and legitimate cultural differences.

In Ireland, the major sore spots on this score have not been gay rights, to which the Irish electorate seems to have no fervent opposition (Catholicism and the theocratic elements of the Irish constitution notwithstanding), but divorce, contraception, and abortion, all of which cut much closer to the bone with respect to the theocratic dimension of the Irish polity. Divorce has now been legalized in Ireland, thanks to a recent (1995) constitutional referendum amending (by a bare majority) a provision, which prohibited divorce. But a decade earlier, back in 1986, another such divorce referendum lost by nearly two-thirds of the vote. Interestingly enough, the European Court of Human Rights rejected an appeal at that time to compel the Dáil, the lower house of the Irish Parliament, to introduce divorce legislation in order to conform with Articles 8 and 12 of the *European Convention on Human Rights*.[14] At least on some occasions, the European Court on Human Rights is inclined to take the "moral exception" clause seriously, an issue to which I will return in the final section of this paper.

A similar problem arose more recently, initially in the context of EC law, with respect to Ireland's constitutional amendment prohibiting abortions. The amendment itself was motivated by two earlier judicial decisions based on some of the liberal ideals expressed in the Irish Constitution. In a case concerning compulsory fluoridation of municipal water (*Ryan v Attorney General* [1965 I.R. 294]) the Irish courts first came to recognize an unenumerated right to privacy as an implication of Article 1940s assurance that: "The State guarantees in its laws to respect, and, as far as practicable, by its laws to defend and vindicate the personal rights of the citizen." This unenumerated right was subsequently applied to justify reversal of a law preventing married couples from access to contraceptives (*McGee v Attorney General* [1974 I.R. 284]). Watching contemporaneous events in the U.S. Courts, and thus fearing an Irish equivalent of *Roe v Wade* [410 U.S. 113 (1973)] following hard upon the heels of this Irish *Griswold v Connecticut*, the government then undertook to back the abortion amendment, which won voter approval in 1983.

Just as the fugitive slave law became necessary for effective enforcement of the property rights of U.S. slave owners at the end of the eighteenth century (the basis for Roger Taney's infamous decision in *Scott v Sanford* [60 U.S. 393 (1857)]), the Irish abortion amendment could not be effectively enforced unless Irish citizens were denied access to information about English abortion clinics, and denied the right to travel to them. While access to information and the right to travel between EC/EU countries is protected under EC/EU law, the EC Commission on Legal Services, an advisory body on EC law, concluded in 1991 that the Maastricht protocol on the Irish abortion question created an exception to the exercise of these rights in the context of abortion counseling or travel, as part of the public policy exemption granted to Ireland on the abortion question. The EC at least professed to operate on the principle that EC treaties should not force any EC country to import the ethics of its EC neighbors.

Nonetheless, in 1992 the issue came to a head. First, the Irish Supreme Court reversed a government decision to enforce these policies by denying permission for a fourteen year-old girl to travel to England for an abortion after being raped by the father of a friend (*Attorney General v X*). The Court's action was basically a mercy judgment, made in the midst of a public furor over the government's callous response to the situation. The Court did however use the judgment as an occasion to reaffirm the general principle that the mother of an unborn child did not have an unqualified right to travel. Later that same year, Ireland ran afoul of the European Court of Human Rights on the issue of freedom of information with respect to abortion, after a Dublin pregnancy counseling organization successfully appealed an unfavorable Irish Supreme Court ruling against its activities.[15] And finally, at the end of November, yet another Irish abortion referendum designed to modify the constitutional amendment was offered to address these conflicts with EC practice and with human rights law. Two of the three components of the amendment, those affirming freedom of information and the right to travel, were approved, but a third, making abortion permissible (in Ireland) to save the life of the mother, was not.

Using Ireland as a specific illustration of the larger issue of conflict between local autonomy and respect for human rights as understood in international tribunals, what are we to make of what has happened with the evolution of gay rights, Irish abortion law, and Irish divorce law with respect to the unfolding of the Irish national political identity? As I explained earlier, the Irish Republic's constitutional discourse is subject to two competing internal conceptions of the political ideals to be pursued (theocratic and liberal). Even if it might be argued that the Irish people were not fully cognizant of what they were voting on during the constitutional referendum back in 1937, there is something to be said for the view that de Valera may have "gotten it right" with respect to the historical antecedents of the political sensibilities of the Irish citizenry of that era. It is quite reasonable to suppose that the Irish people, and not just de Valera himself, were deeply influenced by both theocratic and liberal considerations. While it is also legitimate to question whether this combination makes any coherent sense, that is not to say that one strain (the liberal one?) is within the pale of acceptable conceptions of constitutionalist ideals, and the other (the theocratic one?) is not. However distasteful classical liberals might find some Catholic theocratic values, those values cannot readily be dismissed on grounds of moral bankruptcy (unlike, e.g., the slave economy of the antebellum South).

On the other hand, we also need to take into account the two kinds of external judicial influences on that debate (EC/EU law, and the *European Convention on Human Rights*). By voting to ratify the *European Convention on Human Rights* back in 1953 (via their representatives in the Dáil), or to approve the 1972 referendum which created the third Amendment to the Constitution, making EC law part of domestic Irish law, did the Irish people effectively reconstitute their political self-identity as a nation, or were they simply voting without recognizing the potential consequences, or perhaps voting under economic duress? The latter characterization is especially relevant where pressure to conform to EC and EU practices is at issue, given the dire economic consequences (for Ireland, at least), of going it alone.

Indeed, the significant increase in Irish prosperity, which came with EC membership, suggests that the Irish people have quite willingly embraced those economic advantages, even at the expense of turning their backs on traditional Irish moral attitudes. This may be part of the message delivered in the Irish ratifications of the 1992 referendum on the Maastricht Treaty, and again of the 1998 referendum on the Treaty of Amsterdam. As *Irish Times* correspondent Gerard Brady wryly observed during the public debate about Maastricht: "It is ironic that scarcely more than a single generation of material affluence has done more to weaken the religious faith and the moral fibre of the Irish people than two centuries of persecution." Or as Conor Cruise O'Brien put it in May of that year: "If the Irish people are offered a choice between God and Mammon, the outcome will be: Number One: Mammon. Number Two: God."[16] Motives are not always pure in electoral deliberations. I suspect that, as often as not, the evolution of national self-identities, even when configured through democratic constitutional referenda, simply "happen". Such identities are, inevitably, and to at least a considerable extent, visited upon us rather than chosen, via our contingent responses to largely intractable social forces. Nonetheless, when those forces are themselves products of a broader democratic vision informed by widely shared intuitions about human rights, they can be forces for political growth rather than for externally imposed tyranny. What has happened to the evolution of gay rights in Ireland, especially in the Republic, bears out this conclusion.

Arguably, the case of domestic legitimating is somewhat clearer with respect to Ireland's submission to the judgments of the European Court of Human Rights than it is in the area of EC/EU law. In August of 1950, when the ratification of the *European Convention on Human Rights* was still in doubt, the Council of Europe's Committee of Ministers decided to make Articles 25 and 46 of the *Convention* optional for the signatory States. Article 25 gives individuals (as well as member States) the right to petition the European Commission of Human Rights, which fulfills a screening role as the sole authority permitted to bring *individual* petitions it judges meritorious before the Court (member States can appeal directly to the Court). Article 46 gives the Court jurisdiction to actually hear and try cases reported to it by the Commission. In February of 1953, Ireland was the first nation in the Council of Europe to voluntarily submit its domestic judicial decisions to Articles 25 and 46.[17] Moreover, all Council members retain the drastic option of withdrawing from the Council and repudiating the *Convention*, an option which Greece exercised temporarily, from 1969 until 1974.

No other nation in the Council has exercised the devolution option. There are of course considerable political pressures against doing so, and thus appearing to repudiate not only the *Convention*, but also the human rights to which it gives expression. Nonetheless, given the essentially voluntary nature of this participation, it is reasonable to contend that the Court does not really subvert the domestic democratic processes of member States like Ireland.

III

Even if we concede that member States of the Council of Europe are willing participants in the subjection of their own laws to international oversight in Strasbourg, we can still ask: what safeguards are in place to insure that the European Court retains moral legitimacy when its exercise of judicial review results in the repudiation of domestic law? Basically, the answer to this question is reflected in the history of the Court's behavior. Despite its occasional liberalizing influence on domestic legal practices, both the Court and the Commission are, like the U.S. Supreme Court, fundamentally conservative institutions. The rights enumerated in the *Convention* are often honored in the breach in both bodies, for the sake of preserving local autonomy in the face of *prima facie* conflicts between domestic judicial decisions and the Articles of the *Convention*. Thus, while the Court did not receive any cases from the Commission prior to 1960,[18] and ruled on only seven cases during the 1960s, and 24 in the seventies, the Commission was assailed during its first two full decades of activity with far more cases, especially from individuals. But most of these never reached the Court, for the Commission would routinely dismiss them as "manifestly unfounded," and only the Commission could present petitions from individuals to the Court.

By way of example, it took over twenty years from the date of its initial activity before the Commission even ruled a homosexual rights application admissible. In *X v.U.K.* (7215/75, 1977), a challenge to England's higher age of consent for male-male sexual relations (21) than for male-female or female-female relations (16), the Commission ruled, for the first time, that the case was at least admissible (worth considering) under the *Convention*'s antidiscrimination Article 14, as applied to the right of privacy enumerated in Article 8. But even that case never made it to the Court, as the Commission found no violation a year later (19 D.R. 66, at 79-80).

Prior to this case, the Commission simply ruled all homosexual rights applications inadmissible, including a similar case just two years earlier. In *X v. Germany* (5935/72, 1975), a challenge to Germany's inequality between male-male and female-female ages of consent (21 and 14, respectively), the Commission did acknowledge that a "person's sexual life is undoubtedly part of his private life of which it constitutes an important aspect." But it didn't regard that fact as sufficient to rule the case admissible, choosing instead to cite German sociological studies alleged to reveal "a specific social danger in the case of masculine homosexual[s]...result[ing] from the fact that [they] often constitute a distinct socio-cultural group with a clear tendency to proselytize adolescents and that the social isolation in which it involves the latter is particularly marked" (3 D.R. 46, at 56).

Much earlier, and repeatedly, when confronted with petitions against unconditional criminalization of homosexual acts (the issue identical to the domestic policies eventually overturned in *Dudgeon* and *Norris*) the Commission ruled them inadmissable.[19] Thus, in *X v. Germany* (1960, 530/59), the Commission simply concluded that: "the Convention allows a High Contracting Party [signatory State] to punish homosexuality since the right to respect for private life may, in a democratic society, be subject to interference as provided for by the law of that Party for the protection of health or morals" (3 Y.B. 184, at 194).

To justify its (partial) change of heart in *X v. U.K.*, the Commission explained that it was "taking into account the development of moral opinion in recent years concerning State interference with the private, consensual sexual lives of adults" (11 D.R. 36 at 43). Two more decades elapsed, however (despite the fact that both the Commission's and the Court's case loads mushroomed dramatically in the eighties and nineties), before the Commission saw fit to draft a final report accepting the argument that such a disparity in the age of consent actually violated Article 8, taken together with Article 14. In *Sutherland v. U.K.* (25186/94, 1997), the Commission concluded that the continuing disparity between the age of consent for male-male sexual relations (reduced to 18 under the Criminal Justice and Public Order Act of 1994) and for male-female or female-female relations (still 16), constituted a discriminatory limitation (Article 14) on the exercise of the right of privacy (Article 8) for young male homosexuals.

To explain this further reversal of its original position, the Commission first offered the following summary of its previous position:

> In its Report in...*X. v. the United Kingdom* the Commission...observed that the age limit of 21 might be regarded as high in the present era, especially when contrasted with the current position in other Member States of the Council of Europe.... However, the Commission held that it could not disregard the fact that the question had been examined by the Wolfenden Committee, whose recommendations had been adopted by Parliament and incorporated in the 1967 legislation; nor could it ignore the fact that the issue had been before Parliament again and was being then currently re-examined by the Criminal Law Revision Committee and the Policy Advisory Committee on Sexual Offence. In addition, the Commission took the view that there was a realistic basis for the respondent Government's opinion that, given the controversial and sensitive nature of the question involved, young men in the 18-21 age bracket who were involved in homosexual relationships would be subject to substantial social pressures which could be harmful to their psychological development. (*Sutherland*, § 40)

Underlying this explanation is the tacit acknowledgment that, the Commission is always prepared to alter its views in light of changing perceptions of present conditions, at least one important element of which may be the collective practice or views of the other signatories to the *Convention*. But against those views have to be weighed any countervailing domestic deliberations conducted in a democratically constituted forum, as occurred in Britain via the Wolfenden Committee and subsequent Parliamentary deliberations, which, in the Commission's 1977 case, at least, resulted in reaffirmation of the concern expressed earlier in *X v. Germany*: young men confused about their sexual identity might be subject to manipulation and abuse by predatory older homosexual males.

Despite the deference, which the Commission avowed it owed to local sentiment, such considerations are not absolute. The Commission reversed its *X v. U.K.* decision in *Sutherland* simply because it no longer found the special vulnerability argument persuasive, once the local medical establishment had reversed course:

> The Commission, however, observes that its Report in *X. v. the United Kingdom* is now nearly 20 years old....[M]ajor changes have in the meantime occurred in professional opinions - particularly those of the medical profession - on the subject of the need for the protection of young male homosexuals and on the desirability of introducing an equal age of consent....In particular,...the Council of the British Medical Association (BMA), which in 1981 gave evidence to the Policy Advisory Committee that boys and girls of the same age did not possess the same degree of emotional and psychological maturity, observed in 1994 that most researchers now believed that sexual orientation was usually established

> before the age of puberty in both boys and girls and referred to evidence that reducing the age of consent would be unlikely to affect the majority of men engaging in homosexual activity, either in general or within specific age groups. The BMA Council concluded in its Report that the age of consent for homosexual men should be set at 16 since the then existing law might inhibit efforts to improve the sexual health of young homosexual and bisexual men... It is further noted that equality of treatment in respect of the age of consent is now recognized by the great majority of Member States of the Council of Europe.[20]

"In the light of these modern developments" (§60) the Commission concluded, even while acknowledging that British authorities had reviewed and debated this issue once again just three years earlier (during the 1994 Parliamentary debate which led to the explicit rejection, in both houses, of a proposal that 16 become a universal age of consent, and acceptance of 18 as the appropriate minimum for male-male relationships), that the revised medical opinion and general trend among member States now exercised the greater weight.[21]

The Commission's approach in *Sutherland* suggests once again that the Commission and the Court exert a liberalizing influence on local law by taking the side of contemporary scientific research and the relatively cosmopolitan perspective of the larger European Community, when confronted with ill-defended traditionalist policies of individual member States. But appearances can be quite deceiving. The ultimate disposition of *Sutherland* has since been passed on to the European Court of Human Rights, and there is no assurance that the Court will simply reaffirm the Commission's finding of a violation (even though it often does).[22] Two of the Commission dissents in *Sutherland*, and the Court's repudiation of the Commission's report in yet another privacy case, *X, Y and Z v. U.K.* (21830/93, 1997), illustrate how easy it is for the Court to choose an unpredictable path in its disposition of privacy cases.

The problem is that it's easy to question judicial perceptions about the collective "received view" of member States on any issue before the Commission or the Court, and even if such skepticism is itself occasionally implausible, protesting member States, European Court justices, or commissioners, can always question the Court's (or the Commission's) authority to subvert the results of democratic deliberations in those member States. Thus, on the first point, we find *Sutherland* Commission dissenters Herndl and Békés arguing that:

> While, as we believe, all States parties to the Convention share the view expressed by the Court that the Convention is a living instrument which

> must be interpreted in the light of present-day conditions, ...it is also true that when interpreting its provisions, the developments and commonly accepted standards in the policy of the Member States of the Council of Europe in the relevant field will have to be taken into account. In the field of the minimum age of consent for sexual relationships there does, however, not seem to exist a common standard. A number of States parties to the Convention still maintain different minimum ages for homosexual and heterosexual relations, sometimes as far as four years apart.

On the second point, we find Commissioner Martinez objecting, in his dissent, that since the British Parliament had carefully weighed the issues recently on its own, the Commission was overstepping the legitimate bounds of its judicial authority by taking up the cause of the losing side in Parliament.[23]

The Court itself took a similar view that same year, in the case of *X, Y and Z v. U.K.* There the issue turned on an unmarried couple's request to have X registered as the father of *Z*, who was *Y*'s child by means of government-sponsored artificial insemination from an anonymous sperm donor. *X* and *Y* had been together in a stable union for more than a decade prior to a hospital ethics committee's approval of the artificial insemination procedure. They were unmarried because British law prohibited *X*, a female-to-male transsexual, from marrying a female partner. In accordance with Britain's Human Fertility and Embryology Act of 1990, however, *X* had willingly consented to acknowledge himself as the father of any resulting child.[24] The applicants' complaint centered on the fact that the British government declined to act on *X*'s request because of *X*'s transsexual status: only applicants who were biologically male could be registered as fathers.

In its 1995 report, the European Commission concluded that the British government's refusal to recognize *X* as *Z*'s father had indeed violated the applicants' right to respect for their family and private life under Article 8 of the *Convention*. In reaching this conclusion, the Commission was heavily influenced by the Court's 1986 *Johnston v. Ireland* decision (see note 14, *supra*). In that case the issue of parental recognition grew out of Ireland's prohibition against divorce. Some years after Roy Johnston and his first wife had arranged an amicable separation, Johnston came to be involved in a long-term stable union with Janice Williams-Johnston. But the couple could not marry, because such a marriage would have been bigamous under Irish law. Consequently, Nessa Williams-Johnston, their child by this union, was effectively illegitimate, as the Irish State refused to grant Roy Johnston legal recognition as Nessa's father. The European Court ruled that, whatever might be said about the parents' rights of privacy and respect for family life (no interference, in the majority's view), at least Nessa's Article 8 rights, in particular her right to respect for family life, had been violated. Irish divorce laws notwithstanding, the Irish government needed to take steps (undefined) to insure that Nessa enjoyed precisely the same rights as legitimate children in Ireland.

Despite the obvious parallels between *X, Y and Z* and *Johnston*, the Court did not see fit to concur with the Commission's findings in *X, Y and Z*, and for much the same reasons that the dissenters objected in *Sutherland*. On the one hand, in *X, Y and Z* (§44), the Court questioned the Commission's assertion "that there is a clear trend in Contracting States towards the legal acknowledgement of gender re-assignment (see e.g. the domestic law of Germany, Italy, the Netherlands, Sweden and Turkey, and also the Recommendation 1117 (1989) of the Parliamentary Assembly of the Council of Europe on the condition of transsexuals, which recommends the introduction of legislation by member States, *inter alia*, to allow the rectification of birth registers)." (Commission Report, §67.) This skepticism licensed the Court's next move (also §44), to insist that, in the absence of any general consensus among Council States, Britain "must be afforded a wide margin of appreciation" in its democratic policy-making deliberations concerning the legal status of transsexual families.

One glaringly inconsistent feature of the Court's decision in *X, Y and Z*, when contrasted with the *Johnston* case, was its willingness to dismiss (in §48 ff.) a series of concerns raised by the applicants about the limited scope of *Z*'s legal rights, owing to the State's refusal to recognize *X* as her father. In *Johnston*, when Ireland contended that the legal problems associated with Nessa Williams-Johnston's illegitimate status could be dealt with piecemeal, by a variety of ad hoc legal maneuvers of which her parents could avail themselves, the Court did not regard this response as adequate to the task of insuring sufficient respect for Nessa's family rights under Article 80:

> Examination of the third applicant's present legal situation, seen as a whole, reveals, however, that it differs considerably from that of a legitimate child. In addition, it has not been shown that there are any means available to her or her parents to eliminate or reduce the differences. (*Johnston*, §75)

Earlier, in §71-72, the Court acknowledged that Nessa's parents were able to take some steps to integrate their daughter into the family, such as circumventing problems of interstate succession by drafting a will for Roy Johnston which explicitly included Nessa, arranging for Johnston's health insurance to cover Nessa, and drafting a formal separation agreement with

Johnston's first wife under which both parties renounced succession rights over each other's estates (§12, referenced in §71). Nonetheless, the Court went on to declare that: "As envisaged by Article 8, respect for family life implies in particular, in the Court's view, the existence in domestic law of legal safeguards that render possible *as from the moment of birth* the child's integration into his family" (*Johnston*, §72; italics added). In *Johnston*, the Court subsequently concluded that Ireland failed to satisfy this standard.

In *X, Y and Z*, by contrast, even though *Z* was confronted with diminished legal protections in England similar to those afflicting Nessa Williams-Johnston in Ireland, the Court concluded that, in *Z*'s case, the family integration standard invoked in *Johnston* cut no ice with the Court. It wasn't even mentioned. Instead, the comparable ad hoc solutions available to *X and Y* were considered to be sufficient unto the day:

> The applicants identify a number of legal consequences flowing from this lack of recognition. For example, they point to the fact that if *X* were to die intestate, *Z* would have no automatic right of inheritance. The Court notes, however, that the problem could be solved in practice if *X* were to make a will....The Court considers, therefore, that these legal consequences would be unlikely to cause undue hardship given the facts of the present case. (*X, Y and Z*, §48)

Returning now to the original question that motivated this section, concerning the nature of the safeguards available to sustain the Commission's and Court's moral authority when either holds a member State's policy to be in defiance of rights enumerated in the *Convention*, the answer seems to depend heavily on both the nature of the policy and the orthodoxy of the petitioners. Despite the strong parallels between the *Johnston* and *X, Y and Z* cases, the Court behaved very differently in each. First of all, even though Ireland's position on the divorce issue was clearly out of step with the views of other member States in the Council of Europe, a phenomenon which the Court professes to take seriously in its deliberations, and even though that prohibition arguably undermined the right to marry enumerated in *Convention* Article 12,[25] the Court was nonetheless prepared to afford Ireland "a wide margin of appreciation" in determining how to insure the adequate "'respect' for family life" called for in Article 8 of the *Convention*. (*Johnston*, §55) Nonetheless, the Court was unwilling to allow that margin to encompass legal differentiation between Nessa Williams-Johnston and the legitimated offspring of recognized marriages. Why then couldn't it do the same for *Z*?

In my opinion, the Court's higher level of empathy with Nessa's plight suggests that the Court regarded her family situation as somehow more legitimate than that of a family union involving a transsexual partner. At one point in *Johnston*, the Court appeared to assert that the margin of appreciation encompassed Ireland's social experiment with the prohibition of divorce because it was being conducted "in a society adhering to the principle of monogamy" (*Johnston*, §52). The idea seems to be: (heterosexual) monogamy is a goal worthy of pursuit, therefore we on the Court are willing to tolerate some restrictions on the human rights of *adult* citizens of a member State for the sake of this goal. The obverse side of this analysis, applied to the case of *X, Y, and Z*, can be used equally well to explain why the Court was unprepared to extend the same rights to *Z* that it insisted Nessa Williams-Johnston must enjoy: the Court was unconvinced that the "social experiment" undertaken by *X* and *Y* encompassed any goal especially worthy of pursuit, and was therefore more willing to tolerate a member State's restrictions not only on the legal rights of adults, but even those of children, as a way to discourage socially unorthodox behavior.

As a footnote to this analysis, it is also worth noting that the European Commission of Human Rights does not have a more exemplary track record than the European Court of Human Rights on the issue of protecting privacy and family rights in Article 8. Just three years prior to its report on *X, Y and Z*, in a relatively perfunctory dismissal under both Articles 8 and 14, the Commission ruled inadmissible ("manifestly unfounded") a lesbian couple's request for legal recognition of parental authority of the biologically unrelated partner over the other partner's child (by donor insemination), despite the fact that such recognition would have been unproblematic for an unmarried opposite-sex couple under Dutch law (*Kerkhoven v. Netherlands*, 15666/89, 1992). In response to the applicants' discrimination charge under Article 14, the Commission simply noted, without argument, that "as regards parental authority over a child, a homosexual couple cannot be equated to a man and woman living together" (*Kerkhoven*, §2).

Conclusion

What is the message we are to take away here? Apparently, it is the following: that the Commission regards homosexual unions as too unorthodox to be worthy of full coverage under the rights enumerated in the *Convention*, but transsexual unions are sufficiently close to the norm to warrant greater, albeit still incomplete, coverage. The Court simply endorses a higher standard of orthodoxy, lumping transsexual partnerships together with homosexual ones, and affording heterosexual couples with a multiple partnership history the kind of status, which the Commission would extend to transsexual couples.

This record of shifting standards and arbitrary dividing lines in the Commission and the Court does not entail that the *European Convention on Human Rights* fails to function as a progressive social force in member States. It does. In the particular area we've been examining in detail, the privacy rights of the sexually unorthodox, Council of Europe members, collectively at least, have a significantly better track record than U.S. federal and state jurisdictions. I believe this development is a direct consequence of the *Convention*'s influence. The ECHR ban on outright criminalization of sexually unorthodox activities between consenting adults represents one such advance over U.S. legal practices, but this gesture alone has encouraged some member States to institute other voluntary measures designed to reduce legislatively or judicially imposed discrimination against homosexuals, bisexuals, and transsexuals. Nonetheless, if the issues examined in this paper illustrate anything, they indicate that making privacy an enumerated right is no guarantee of greater coherence in judicial adjudication. European privacy law is, unfortunately, almost as big a mess as the corresponding mess the U.S. courts have produced over an unenumerated right of privacy during the past three decades.

Notes

1 As quoted in Jeffrey Weeks, Coming Out: Homosexual Politics in Britain, from the Nineteenth Century to the Present (1977), 33.

2 The passages quoted subsequently in conjunction with Wilde's three trials can be found on the Internet site, Oscariana.

3 This was the language of the act as amended by the Statute Law Revision Act of 1892, instituted in response to a generic provision of the 1891 Penal Servitude Act (Subsection 1.2), limiting terms of penal servitude to a maximum of two years, in the absence of explicit provisions to the contrary. In a similar vein, the 1892 amendment set the sentence for attempted buggery (Section 62 of the 1861 Act) to a period of not more than ten years.

4 See Patrick Devlin, The Enforcement of Morals (Oxford: Oxford University Press, 1965), and H.L.A. Hart, Law, Liberty, and Morality (Stanford, CA: Stanford University Press, 1963).

5 Article 50, § 1 of the 1937 Constitution provided that: "Subject to this Constitution and to the extent to which they are not inconsistent therewith, the laws in force in Saorstát Éireann [the Irish Free State] immediately prior to the date of the coming into operation of this Constitution shall continue to be of full force and effect until the same or any of them shall have been repealed or amended by enactment of the Oireachtas [the two houses of the Irish Parliament]."

6 Proceedings of the British Academy 45 (1959), 129-51. Revised and reprinted as "Morals and the Criminal Law," in The Enforcement of Morals (supra, note 4), 1-25.

7 Liberty, Equality, Fraternity, ed. by R. J. White (Cambridge: Cambridge University Press, 1967). (Reprint of 2d edition, 1874; 1st edition published in 1873.)

8 On Liberty, ed. by Elizabeth Rapaport (Indianapolis: Hackett Publishing, 1978). (Originally published in 1859.) Mill's harm principle reads: "The only purpose for which power can rightfully be exercised over any member of a civilized community against his will is to prevent harm to others. His own good, either physical or moral, is not a sufficient warrant. He cannot rightfully be compelled to do or forbear because it will be better for him to do so, because it will make him happier, because in the opinion of others, to do so would be wise or even right" (Mill, 9).

9 Both of these elements are discussed at length subsequently.

10 1 Council of Europe, Collected Edition of the Travaux Préparatoires (1975), 24, as quoted in Mark W. Janis amd Richard S. Kay, European Human Rights Law (University of Connecticut Law School Foundation Press, 1990), 23. These remarks were expressed by Representative Rasmussen, of Denmark. For a good discussion of the influences out of which the Convention evolved, see Janis & Kay, 1-38.

11 Sexual Orientation and Human Rights (Oxford: Clarendon Press, 1995), 99-100.

12 N.S. Mansergh, Survey of British Commonwealth Affairs: Problems of Imperial Policy, 1931-39 (1952), 297 [as quoted in F.S.L. Lyon, Ireland Since the Famine (London: Fontana Press, 1973), 538]. See, more generally, Lyon, 538-50.

13 The Court makes no direct reference to the theocratic arguments in O'Higgins' majority opinion in Norris (1984). Instead, it simply reaffirms (at ¶42) the European Commission's earlier conclusion that Ireland presented no argument, let alone a compelling one, to distinguish the Republic from Northern Ireland's situation in Dudgeon. See especially §63 of the Commission's report on Norris [44 D.R. 132 (1987)].

14 Case of Johnston and Others v. Ireland, 9697/82, ECHR Series A, No. 112 (1986). Article 12 establishes a right to marry.

15 Society for the Protection of Unborn Children (SPUC) v Open Door Counselling, 1988 I.R. 593; Case of Open Door and Dublin Well Woman v. Ireland 14234/88, ECHR Series A, No. 246 (1992).

16 Both remarks as quoted in Mary Kenny, "The Real Irish Question: Europe or Church?" The Sunday Telegraph (London), June 7, 1992.

17 Sweden accepted the principle of individual petitions in February of the previous year, but did not accept the jurisdiction of the Court until 1966. Denmark was the only other nation to accept both Articles prior to 1955.

18 Although the Commission was authorized to hear interstate petitions in 1953, and individual petitions in 1955, there was relatively little activity in the fifties (only two government-initiated and three individual cases ruled admissible). The Court itself was not constituted until 1958, and did not hear its first case until 1960 (Lawless v. Ireland, ECHR Series A, No. 1 (1960); Re Ó Laighléis 1960 I.R. 93).

19 The Commission rejected a string of such cases from Germany and Austria in 1955, 1956, 1957, 1960, 1963, and 1967.

20 Sutherland, §59. It is also worth noting, although the Commission merely records this observation without comment, that in the 1994 Parliamentary debate Tony Blair argued, in defence of a uniform age of consent, that what was true for 16-year-old male homosexuals would be at least equally true for 16-year-old heterosexual or

lesbian females: they too could be subject to exploitation by predatory older partners (Sutherland, §28).

21 "In contending that there remains a reasonable and objective justification for maintaining different ages of consent for homosexual males and for heterosexuals, the Government place considerable reliance on the fact that the issue was recently and fully debated by a democratically elected Parliament which, on a free vote, decided to reduce the minimum age of consent to homosexual acts to 18 but rejected a proposal to assimilate the age of consent to that for heterosexuals."

22 The Commission agrees with the Government that some weight should be attached to the fact that the issue has been recently considered by the legislature and that the reduction of the minimum age to 16 was rejected. Nevertheless, this factor cannot of itself be decisive. Of more importance is the sufficiency of the reasons advanced to justify maintaining a different age of consent" (Sutherland, §61-62).

23 The case may be rendered moot before the Court completes its evaluation because, subsequent to the Commission's report, there has been overwhelming support in the House of Commons for bills, which would institute 16 as a universal age of consent. Approval has been blocked twice thus far (July, 1998 and April, 1999) by the House of Lords. But the Labour government, with considerable opposition support, may now invoke the Parliament Act to override the House of Lords after another year's delay. (See, e.g., "Rebel peers say no to lower age of gay consent," Manchester Guardian, 4/14/99, and "Lords overturn vote on consent age for gays," Irish Times 7/23/98.) "Je signale que le Parlement britannique a pesé les arguments pour l'un et l'autre âge et que, par la voie démocratique de la majorité des voix, il s'est décidé pour l'âge de 18 ans. Pourtant, on dirait, d'après les paragraphes 59 et 60 du rapport, que les 15 membres représentant la majorité de la Commission européenne des Droits de l'Homme, dans cette affaire prennent fait et cause pour la minorité parlementaire. Ceci, selon mon avis très personnel, s'apparente à une sorte d'excès de pouvoir."

24 The Act provides, in §28(3), "where an unmarried woman gives birth as a result of AID with the involvement of her male partner, the latter, rather than the donor of the sperm, shall be treated for legal purposes as the father of the child" (X, Y, and Z v. U.K. §21).

25 The Court denied this, on the somewhat specious ground that Article 12 does not contain a right to dissolution of a marriage (§52-54). Judge de Meyer took the contrary view in his dissent (§5), and it is undeniable that for those of its citizens who have married once, and do not reside abroad, Ireland's policy has the practical effect of making a second marriage impossible.

26. The Paradox of Remedies

LOUIS E. WOLCHER*

I

"An unjust law", wrote St. Thomas Aquinas, "has the nature, not of law, but of violence."[1] Although Aquinas believed that the category of law includes only just human ordinances - only those conforming to the law of nature[2] - his remark echoes an attitude that goes well beyond the perspective of natural law. That attitude can be summarized as one which holds to the syllogism that if a thing properly counts as law according to whatever criteria the thinker happens to employ, then it follows that the thing does not have the nature of violence. For example, a natural lawyer might imagine that if a law passes Aquinas's test of "right reason," then it becomes akin to a beneficent datum of nature - just part of the right and natural order of things. Alternatively, a positivist might think that the law's legitimate political pedigree assures its status as a mere "social technique" for controlling violence; law would not be violence, but would be opposed to violence, according to this opinion. And adherence to either of these points of view would tend to assure that law is always kept outside the sphere of those practices that are noticeable (and hence subject to criticism) as violence. In the stark antithesis between law and violence that is brought out by this expansive and rather naive reading of Aquinas's remark, we can see in the clearest possible terms the possibility of an attitude that always conceals from itself the element of brutality that is manifested or that lies coiled within the law whenever and wherever law appears. It was just this kind of thinking that Rousseau objected to in his famous remark on the origins of the state: "All ran headlong to their chains, in hopes of securing their liberty; for they had just wit enough to perceive the advantages of political institutions, without experience enough to enable them to foresee the dangers."[3]

Standing opposed to the Pollyannaish attitude about law's methods that I have just described is the point of view of those thinkers who like the law, but who do not let their fondness for it delude them into imagining that it is a non-violent means. Hobbes is a good example. To be sure, Hobbes thought that law's violence is the lesser of two evils - the state of nature wherein there is a "warre ...of every man, against every man" is much worse.[4] But in his statement that "Soveraigne Power [is] not so hurtful as the want of it"[5] we find evidence of the kind of person who is willing to admit that law is something that hurts, even if he also claims, in the very next breath, that law's benefits do outweigh its burdens. Perhaps the apotheosis of this way of thinking is Kant's notion that no matter how peaceful in fact a person may be, if he does not submit to the law's authority - if he stubbornly persists in living in a lawless state of nature - his proximity alone is enough to justify law-loving people to "use violent means to compel [him] to enter into a juridical state of society."[6] Kant's idea that human beings have an innate right to liberty (defined as negative freedom - freedom from violence) comes down to saying that the individual's right to liberty underwrites the power of the state to use painful coercion against those who, by refusing to kiss the lash of law, are *ipso facto* guilty of "lawless violence." Law, on this view, is merely a washed-out and remote kind of coercion that stands opposed to another kind of coercion that is more vivid and immediate; and the latter, which is characterized by its lawlessness, is the only kind of coercion that deserves the epithet "violence." But whatever *word* one may use to name law's methods, it is still possible to find out something disquieting about their nature, at least if one does not take too distant a view of them. It is possible to notice, for example, that the blood on the hands of the state's executioner has exactly the same hue and texture as the blood on the hands of the outlaw. In short, law may call itself the kind of coercion that is legitimate, but in admitting or showing the violent nature of its methods it reveals something deeply troubling about itself.

Nowhere is this admission more obvious than in the field of legal remedies. Here law's violent methods are laid bare by the mere existence of remedial *law*: legal texts that purport to restrain law's methods in advance by announcing a calculus - an economy, really - of legitimate force. The announcement of such an economy of force would never have been thought necessary or appropriate if those who made and those who have perpetuated remedial law had the kind of attitude that I have attributed to Aquinas: namely, if they conceived of the realm of law in general as standing altogether outside the realm of violence. The mere existence of remedial law is a concession that there can be such a thing as too much (or too little) of the good thing that we call law - too much or too little *violence*, in other words, from the one source that usually gets away with calling the things that it accomplishes, if not completely good, then at least routine, ordinary, and perfectly proper.

The theme of this essay is the relation between legal remedies and legal rights, and what that relation has to tell us about the relation between law and violence. But these remarks are not about what a metaphysically inclined philosopher of law might call the real relationship that subsists between rights and remedies. Nor do I propose to don the frock of a preacher or moral philosopher and speak about the right relationship - the relationship that should exist - between these two. Instead, I will describe a certain enigma that emerges if one thinks of the relation between rights and remedies in terms of the question of priority. On the one hand, rights precede remedies in the same way that chickens precede the eggs they sometimes lay: only if there first exist rights that are *then* violated can sanctions be imposed. On the other hand, remedies precede rights in the same way that eggs precede the chickens that cannot come into being without them: only if remedial force is credibly promised in advance can there exist such a thing as a legal right in the first place. Thus the paradox of rights in relation to remedies is like the paradox of chickens in relation to eggs: in both cases the question that leads to the paradox is "Which comes first?" And in both cases it seems that the answer that can be validly derived takes the paradoxical form "A comes first *and* B comes first".

The question of priority between rights and remedies presupposes a framework for answering that not only produces the paradox, but hinders us from seeing any way out. But this paradox is not just an inconsequential word-puzzle, fit only for the quiet musings of a logician. The right-remedy distinction yields a paradox that is interesting and productive because it says something profound about the ambivalence that we feel in contemplating the use of violence as a means. I will show that the paradox can be dissolved only by discarding the frame of reference that gives rise to it. My claim is that rights and remedies cease to be distinguishable from one another when the question that we ask is not which comes first, but rather how it is that the official acts of violence that we call "enforcing rights by means of remedies" come to acquire legitimacy. At this level, the right question to ask is one that transcends the distinction between rights and remedies. And the right question is: What role does official violence play in the ceaseless cycle of violence that we call history?

If one's attention stays focused completely within the orbit of national law, the question just asked naturally seems to limit itself to the relation between the state and the people on whom the state's official violence and threats of violence are brought to bear. From this rather narrow perspective, which is Hobbesian, law seems to be about the violent mediation of relations between individuals and groups who otherwise might fall into an even more violent state of anarchy. But it turns out that the point of view of the supra-national set of institutions that calls itself "international human rights law" yields far more perspicuity on the problem. International human rights law seeks to limit the proper sphere of state violence, and it seeks to do this most especially in cases where national law calls that violence legitimate. Moreover, the means, by which international human rights law accomplishes this task in a given case also can be called violent, in the sense of non-consensual, even if it is true that the origin of its enforcement authority always lies in a prior act of general consent by the state. For once it has given its general consent, the state's subsequent political, strategic, and diplomatic necessities often turn its submission to a particular judgment rendered by a supra-national body charged with the enforcement of human rights law into something that the state feels it *must* do. In this essay, I will use as my primary example of this kind of supra-national law the enforcement of the European Convention on Human Rights by the new European Court of Human Rights.[7] Forty states have bound themselves to honor the provisions of the Convention, and to submit to the jurisdiction of the Court, which now can be invoked unilaterally at the instance of individual complainants. And it will be seen that the Court's case law exhibits its own version of the paradox of remedies.

The paradox of remedies at the supra-national level reveals a dimension of the problem of official violence that Hobbes did not and could not envision. I will trace the symbolic relationships that are created by the Convention among the triad that is formed by the terms "state," "individual," and "European Court of Human Rights." I will also draw attention to the real relationships of power that these symbolic relationships help to nurture and sustain. By way of foreshadowing what is to come, permit me to utter a rather blunt truism: People have no right under the Convention to be free of violence as *such* when it is committed against them by the state. In other words, legal violence as a means is not abolished by the Convention. I think that this truism betrays something troubling - something ambivalent and even a bit *conspiratorial* - about what the Court does when it enforces the Convention by giving or withholding a remedy. Law is "legitimate" violence that always seeks to deny its origin in the "illegitimate" violence that makes up the contingent meandering of history. The right-remedy distinction reenacts law's founding moment, when there is no legal right without the prior use of a force - a completely unauthorized force - that makes the idea of legal rights imaginable in the first place. Furthermore, the two systems of official violence - national and supra-national - are linked together in a cycle of mutual dependence. The supra-national system of human rights law needs official state violence in order to maintain its authority to use violent means to limit it; whereas the system of national law needs the threat of supra-national official violence in order to insure that the vast majority of its acts go undetected as violence.[8] But in order to arrive at the place where these perhaps shocking claims can be seen clearly and evaluated properly, it will first be necessary to take an excursion into traditional legal theory.

II

As it is traditionally conceived, the main philosophical problem about the relationship between legal rights and legal remedies is to decide which of these two comes first. To begin with, we often say that rights precede their enforcement by way of sanctions for violations, because we think that punishment is illegitimate unless there first existed a rights-creating rule with which the alleged wrongdoer could have complied. John Austin's command theory of law is a notable example of this way of thinking. As Austin put it, "unless the party knew he was violating his duty, or unless he might have known that he was violating his duty, the sanction could not operate, at the moment of the wrong, to the end of impelling him [to obey the command]."[9] H.L.A. Hart's notion of the "internal aspect of rules" is another good illustration of the point of view that wants to put rights before remedies. Unlike Austin, Hart's concept adopts the perspective of those who apply the law rather than the perspective of the primary actors to whom the law's statements of duty are addressed:

> [T]he judge, in punishing, takes the rule as his guide and the breach of the rule as his reason and justification for punishing the offender. He does not look upon the rule as a statement that he and others are likely to punish deviations, though a spectator might look upon the rule in just this way. The predictive aspect of the rule (though real enough) is irrelevant to his purposes, whereas its status as a guide and justification is essential.[10]

This passage reminds us of the undeniable logical distinction between the grounds of a decision and its causes, as well as of the more debatable psychological fact that judges employ substantive rules as the reason or justification for sanctions, and not as grounds for a prediction that they will impose sanctions if the rules are violated.[11] And Hart's description undoubtedly fits the way most judicial opinions are written - for in that medium discussions of entitlement almost always precede discussions of remedy. But there is a hint of something more strident in this passage. Hart almost seems to be asking us to believe that, from the standpoint of the judge at least, questions about rights *always* come before questions about remedial force, whether this occurs in the rhetorical context of writing an opinion for a decision that has already been reached, or in the altogether different pragmatic context of a judge who is trying to discover how he should decide.[12]

So on the one hand, we have a picture that puts rights before remedies. But on the other hand, we also know that remedies *realize* rights, and that they do this in at least two different senses. First, they give justice to the one whose rights are violated - if not the equivalent of her loss, then at least *something* to compensate her for what was due her under the law of rights - while at the same time they punish the wrongdoer for his transgression. This result is more or less Aristotle's doctrine of corrective justice, which calls for the law both to rectify the victim's unjust loss by restoring him to the *status quo ante*, and to deprive the wrongdoer of the unjust gain that is represented by his having disturbed the state of equilibrium that was in existence just before he violated the victim's rights.[13] As Professor Dinah Shelton notes in her comprehensive new study of remedies in international law for human rights violations, corrective justice is the traditional philosophy of remedial justice within the international legal system.[14] But quite apart from all considerations of justice on account of what has happened between the parties in the past (the so-called "*ex post* perspective"), we also know that remedies have an ex ante instrumental dimension: they are means to secure future compliance. They transform the substantive legal text's lofty pronouncements about the rights that people have into warnings that others cannot safely ignore, lest they be visited with unpleasant consequences. Remedies are the unpleasant consequences. When we are thinking in this mode, we imagine that remedies enter into the body of rights and animate them - make them "effective," as we so often put it. But (and here is the source of the paradox within traditional legal theory) remedies seem to animate legal rights just as much as, and no more than, the remedial law not just determines, but *pre*-determines. Remedies, broadly conceived, represent what the pragmatist William James might have called the "cash value" of the idea of rights.[15] That is to say, without remedies (or with substantially weaker remedies than happen to exist now) the idea of rights would occupy a much-degraded practical position in people's lives.

However much we may want to animate legal rights, we also know that this animation comes at a cost whenever it is accomplished by means of the texts that we call "remedial law." For remedial law helps to make it possible for Oliver Wendell Holmes's "bad man" to calculate in advance both the expected costs and the expected benefits of violating rights. The "bad man," Holmes wrote, "does not care two straws for the axioms and deductions" of substantive law, but only about "what the courts will do in fact."[16] Anyone who has the bad man's disposition can rest secure in the knowledge that when the time comes for him to answer for the consequences of his misdeeds the remedial law will protect him from "too much" punishment. By thus giving rights to the class of future wrongdoers, remedial law seems to transform legal duties into practical options. It seems to say: "Either do X, or accept penalty y for not doing it - it is entirely up to you." Indeed, there are some philosophers who read this conditional statement as expressing the essence of law itself. Hans Kelsen's "Pure Theory of Law," for example, completely rejects the notion that a legal duty - and with it a legal right - are independent of the notions of submission or non-submission to the threat of a sanction.[17] The concept of a "legal right," for Kelsen (at least during his neo-Kantian phase) means simply that the legal subject *qua* "violated party" participates in the creation of a sanction (and hence of law) as the consequence of a specific unlawful act that was directed against him.[18]

If we thought that remedial law existed only for the benefit of nasty people like Holmes's bad man, we might imagine ourselves able to do without it. Something like Kelsen's notion of legal sanctions would remain, of course, but there would be no general statement of any content that would fill in the form "penalty Y" in advance of sanctions being imposed in concrete cases. We might then trust judges and juries to "do the right thing" by way of sanctions, without giving them any guidance whatsoever about what the right thing is. We might even keep the results secret, to prevent the bad man from making any inductive generalizations about the probable size of sanctions in future cases. But although this imagined solution resembles in some respects the actual state of English and American common law in pre-modern times, it is doubtful that it would appeal to very many people today. The procedure just described not only would make rights-holders understandably nervous about the practical value of their rights,[19] it turns out that we have another, equally fundamental, reason for mistrusting it. For even the bad man's opposite - someone I will call the "good woman" - wants to know the details of remedial law in advance, and her reason for wanting to know this goes beyond her desire to compute the expected legal value of her entitlements in case they are violated. If remedial law and practice[20] give Holmes's bad man the wherewithal to predict the material or social gain that could be his if he violated someone else's rights, they also give the good woman the basis for predicting the risk of acting in accordance with her best judgment about the right course of action to take in pursuing her goals. The good woman genuinely wants to fulfill all of her legal duties - she may even view obedience to the law as a moral obligation - but at the same time she knows that the legal system is less than perfect in its ability to determine whether her behavior is in accordance with her legal obligations. She knows that defendants in legal proceedings do not in fact receive what Ronald Dworkin has called "the most accurate trials possible, hang the cost."[21] They get considerably less than this under procedural rules that strike a balance between fairness to litigants and the public's interest in the cost-efficiency of the legal system. Thus remedial law and practice give the good woman the wherewithal to predict the *expected* value of any action that she proposes to take. For even if she contemplates acting in a way that she rightly feels will violate no one's legal rights, there is still some possibility that legal sanctions will be applied against her in the context of a procedural system that is less than perfect. Remedial law helps her to calculate the expected value of this chance. If, as a matter of ethics, the right (conceived as doing one's duty) is always before the good (conceived as living a good life), then the possibility of the right being erroneously held to be wrong is also before the good as a matter of the rational decision-making apparatus of anyone who has the kind of disposition that I have attributed to the good woman.

It follows that we cannot blithely relegate the predictability of sanctions and their amounts to the category of that which is of interest only to those who are contemplating the "violation of rights." Indeed, the predictability of sanctions seems no less entailed than the predictability of duties within any theory of law that makes fair notice of legal rules and their consequences the criterion of a lawful state, or a state in which the rule of law obtains.[22] The problem is: the more predictable the quantum of sanctions becomes, the deeper the paradox of remedies grows. For the more explicit the consequences of violation become in the interest of fair notice, for planning purposes, to the good woman, the more explicit they also become to the bad man who thinks of his legal duties merely as practical options. Remedial specificity as a means of fair notice comes down to remedial specificity as a means of facilitating the calculations of interest by everyone. This conclusion is implied by the first two sentences of the following quotation from John Rawls's discussion of the "Rule of Law," although it is completely missed by the third:

> While a coercive mechanism is necessary [for the Rule of Law], it is obviously essential to define precisely the tendency of its operations. Knowing what things are within their power to do or not to do, citizens can draw up their plans accordingly. One who complies with the announced rules need never fear an infringement of his liberty.[23]

The last sentence of this passage is consistent with the first two only if mistakes never happen in the legal system. But since mistakes do happen in the real world where our rational calculations take place, Rawls's commitment to legal clarity as a condition of the possibility of the Rule of Law seems to entail a precise antecedent definition of the "tendency of operations" of remedies no less than of primary duties.

Many legal theorists are simultaneously repelled by and attracted to the picture of remedial law that I have been describing. In The Metaphysical Elements of Justice, for example, Kant finds himself troubled by the case of a slander that is committed by someone from the "higher classes."[24] He concedes that the law's normal penalty of a fine may be inadequate to achieve equality of retribution (his criterion of remedial justice), for he notes that "someone who has a good deal of money can easily afford to make insults whenever he wishes." Hence Kant sees the existence of predetermined remedies as a problem. His solution, however, is to predetermine a new rule in the very realm of remedial law that presented him with the problem in the first place: He argues that the law should require the wrongdoer who is privileged not only to make a public apology to his victim, "but also at the same time to kiss his hand, even though he be socially inferior."[25] Professor Shelton, addressing an analogous problem in the case of remedies for international human rights violations, expresses the same kind of love-hate relationship with the concept of predetermined remedies. Hear what she says about the size of damage awards against states:

> The level of award that would serve to deter an individual is likely to be inadequate when the state is the defendant because any compensation awarded will be paid from the public treasury, which has resources far beyond those of individual wrongdoers. The level of the award or the nature of the remedy must be such that the state is deterred and not permitted to purchase an option to continue violating human rights.[26]

Shelton thinks that the prospect of small damage awards is bad because it allows the state to purchase an option to violate human rights; but her solution (the pre-determination of large damage awards) occurs in the same realm - the realm of remedial means - that gave rise to the problem in the first place. In other words, she, like Kant, argues for raising the *price* of the option, not for eliminating the option altogether. Moreover, neither Shelton nor Kant notices that the problem of remedial explicitness is connected to the problem of marginal deterrence *in general*: that is, the bigger the remedy is known to be in the context of any legal system that is capable of making errors (which is to say, any legal system), the larger is the predicted set of marginal behaviors that will be deterred, without regard for their value. This means that we can expect marginally good (or neutral) behaviors to be deterred along with marginally bad ones. For the good woman, just like the bad man, has her counterparts in any area that the law touches, including the behaviors of those state officials that are touched by international human rights law. If one works through the implications of taking an instrumental point of view on the law, it turns out that sanctions play the role of an "equal opportunity deterrer," bullying down behaviors that we might call good (or at least not bad) just as well as those that we are inclined to call bad.

An example or two drawn from instances of enforcement of the European Convention on Human Rights will help to make this all a bit more concrete. Suppose, for example, that the substantive law of international human rights guarantees to *all* individuals the right not to have their lives taken by the state except under certain circumstances, but the remedial law withholds an award of damages to the families of some of those whose lives are wrongfully taken - namely, those who are judged morally unworthy by a court. In that case would-be executioners would seem to have one less reason not to end the lives of those whom they, or those who organize their operations, think will be judged morally unworthy by a court. I have in mind here the example of the decision by the European Court of Human Rights in *McCann and Others v. U.K.*[27] There the Court found, on the one hand, that the killing of three suspected I.R.A. terrorists in Gibraltar by forces of the United Kingdom deprived these men of the right to life that was guaranteed them by Article 2 of the Convention; and yet, on the other hand, it refused their survivors all pecuniary or non-pecuniary damages for the violation. The brief explanation that the Court gave for this denial of a monetary remedy was as follows: "[H]aving regard to the fact that the three terrorist suspects who were killed had been intending to plant a bomb in Gibraltar, the Court does not consider it appropriate to make an award under this head."[28] Remarks and results such as this can make it appear that the Court's law of remedies corresponds to what Max Weber called "khadi-justice": namely, the kind of legal system in which there is a "failure to distinguish in a principled fashion between legal and extra-legal (ethical or political) grounds for decision."[29] Indeed, some scholars of the old Court's remedial practices have come to just this conclusion.[30] But be that as it may, the appearance that the *McCann* decision's remedial aspect creates of ceding something like an option to agents of the state to kill those who they judge to be morally unworthy seems unavoidable. And had the decision gone the other way, the equally unavoidable appearance would have been created that the Convention's liberal remedial scheme threatened to make the state timid and indecisive - and thus potentially ineffective - whenever it considered adopting life-threatening methods to deal with the scourge of terrorism. Naturally, one's particular value-position will probably influence the relative weight that one gives to these opposing appearances in deciding whether *McCann* was "rightly decided." But this is only because their status as apparent tendencies of a possible remedial rule has already been assured.

Consider another example: Perhaps the apotheosis of the feeling that remedial law creates rights for wrongdoers is the remedial protection that texts like the Convention give against excessive sanctions imposed by national courts in certain contexts. Now those who would violate the rights of others under national codes can know in advance that if they take - or are unable to avoid[31] - the fateful step towards violation they will be able to wear the mantle of "human rights" if the sanctions that are imposed on them exceed what the Convention is interpreted to allow. A good example of this kind of thing is the decision of Britain's Court of Appeal in *Rantzen v. Mirror Group Newspapers*,[32] which reduced a jury's damage award in a libel action, and announced that there would be a heightened level of appellate scrutiny for such awards in the future, based in large part on the protection that Article 10 gives against excessive penalties in the context of freedom of expression. Article 10 authorizes penalties under national law for the protection of the "reputation or rights of others," but only if they are "necessary in a democratic society." The *Rantzen* decision announces an interpretation of this limitation with which the shabbiest of the tabloids (and other would-be libelers) cannot be unhappy. Yet a decision to the contrary would have been read in some quarters as a dangerous threat to freedom of expression: Some would have noticed with alarm the chilling effect that unreviewable damage awards could be expected to have on people like the good woman, who want to speak their mind and contribute to public debate in a truly non-libelous way, but who now are inclined to keep silent from fear of the possibility of jury error.

By means of these and countless other examples it can be made to appear that the substantive law, which at one time seemed to create and command respect for legal rights, does not precede the remedial law after all. On the contrary, substance seems to be utterly penetrated and determined by remedies from the very outset. The legal philosopher Lon Fuller dramatized this position in the following passage, which he wrote not to express a conviction of his own but rather as a way of sharpening the traditional conception of the paradox:

> Now there is a very simple way of escaping the imbroglio that surrounds the word "right." This consists in recognizing that the word "right" can be given only one meaning that is intelligible and defensible. Startling as it may seem to those steeped in traditional thinking, this meaning is that which defines a right, not as the "cause" of a remedy, but as a way of expressing the existence of a remedy.[33]

Fuller's way of putting the relationship between rights and remedies brings out a feature of the problem that is very important for my purposes. The legal manifestation of power that occurs whenever courts adjudicate cases always has a tendency to crave and seek legitimacy in an authority that is prior to its exercise. However, that power would show itself to be an emperor with no clothes, as it were, if it *explicitly* put might before right - if the written decision that explains and justifies that power put legal remedies before legal rights, in other words. For Fuller's text, which does just that, comes down to saying that the coercion that is entailed by a remedy rests on no ground other than itself. The word "right" is merely the name for the court's inclination to use remedial force, and, conversely, the phrase "no right" is merely the name for the court's inclination to withhold it.[34]

On the other hand, if the law seeks to escape the troubling implications of this state of affairs by restoring the "official" relationship of priority between remedies and rights - if it insists that the texts which create rights are the preexisting *basis* on which remedies are awarded - then the emperor will have reacquired his clothes at the cost of his power to do anything. For why should anyone care about either having or honoring a mere legal right that is scribbled on a piece of paper unless it is already *law* - unless, in short, it is already backed up by a credible promise of enforcement? Even those philosophers who think that there exists a general moral obligation to obey the law, at least in the context of a just state, generally recognize that what morality provides a sufficient reason to obey is an already *coercive* law, and not some other thing. John Finnis, for example, argues that there is a moral duty to obey the law because it is not fair to take the benefits that law's already coercive order provides (such as the benefit that comes when law "enforces against [one's] neighbors the obligation not to burn down [one's] buildings") without also accepting its burdens in those cases where short-run self-interest counsels disobedience.[35] Thus, even deontological moral theories like Finnis's concede the premise that coercion lies at the heart of the law that we have an alleged moral duty to obey. This is the same problem of violence that lies at the heart of the traditional paradox of remedial law - a paradox that Wittgenstein's criticism of the seemingly unholy relationship between formal ethical laws and the sanctions that attend their violation brings sharply into view: "When an ethical law of the form, 'Thou shalt...' is laid down, one's first thought is, 'And what if I do not do it?"[36]

III

By way of summary, and as a foundation for what is to come: So long as the only law in existence is the so-called "substantive" law (including the laws that give people legal rights) the problem of legal violence is merely the problem of the legitimacy of the official act of enforcement seen in *general* terms. In other words, the question is merely whether the officers of the state are authorized to enforce, in a vague and rather loose sense of the word "enforce," this or that law in this or that particular context. But let there also exist an economy of force that rises to the level of law-in short, let there be *remedial law* (either statutes, or precedent, or both) - and a brand new problem emerges. Now it can be asked: What authorizes this amount of enforcement, as opposed to some other amount? The naive answer - that the nature of the right always determines the amount of force that is authorized to vindicate it - no longer suffices in an environment where there is remedial law. For wherever remedial law predetermines the nature, measure, and amount of force that can be used to vindicate a right, and does so in general terms (which is, after all, what the rule - form always does), then that very same law makes force at variance with the remedial law *pro tanto* "illegitimate." In other words, if remedial law authorizes a penalty or remedy in the amount of X, then this means that a judge's act of enforcing the substantive law by giving an award to the plaintiff of X + y is illegitimate. His act is naked force - force shorn of the legitimacy that the law is supposed to give to the act of enforcement. But of course, whenever remedial law enters into the calculus of legitimacy in this way - whenever it admits the possibility of the argument that "too much" or "too little" enforcement was given - then the distinction between rights and remedies is completely erased. No longer is it possible to argue that the remedy "ought" to restore what the law of rights gave the victim of a violation the right to expect, for remedial law also enters into the world of "ought" to condemn *in advance* violence in the name of law that deviates from what it authorizes the judge to inflict.

Thus, it is primarily in the realm of determining the legitimacy or illegitimacy of the official violence that is undertaken in the name of law that the distinction between rights and remedies no longer holds. In this realm a law is a law, regardless of the adjective ("substantive" or "remedial") that precedes it. In this realm the judge "ought" to enforce rights, but he also "ought" to enforce them in conformity with the law's economy of force: too much force is illegitimate violence by the state; too little force is the state's illegitimate retroactive authorization of the violent overthrow of rights that public remedies are supposed to rectify. The point is not that the tail of remedies occasionally or even always wags the dog of rights.[37] The point is that in this realm it no longer makes any sense to draw a distinction between the dog and its tail. "What opposes unites," said Heraclitus in one of his most famous fragments.[38] What oppose within the category of law are paired concepts like command vs. sanction, primary duty vs. secondary duty, and right vs. remedy. What unites these opposing sub-concepts is precisely their claim to the status of being what we call "law." But this is a status that, if it is to be seen clearly and evaluated in a thoroughly undogmatic way, must enter into a radical new opposition that is capable of transcending the old one. The criterion of efficiency that is offered by many market-based theories of political economy fails in this task, for it requires that people possess stable and enforceable entitlements that they can then use as bargaining chips in negotiating a contract that itself would be enforceable (non-consensually) in some manner or other. The realm of exchange, in other words, already presupposes the distinction between rights and remedies, and hence is incapable in principle of dissolving it.[39] And while natural law may at first blush seem to offer the hope of affording a productive opposition that could dissolve the distinction (natural law vs. all of what we call positive law), this hope is dashed by natural law's refusal to recognize that the use of just but violent means to achieve just ends is itself a problem. In other words, natural law does not make a problem out of legal violence in general, but only the legal violence that it calls unjust by this or that criterion. In shutting its eyes to the problem of the use of violent means *in general*, natural law thus winds up reproducing the paradox of remedies within the realm of just law and its methods.

But I am not interested in attempting to *solve* the traditional version of the paradox of remedial law here. In the manner of Wittgenstein, I think that all this philosophical fuss about which comes first, the right or the remedy, is the product of an enormous grammatical confusion. People have taken their eyes off the ball, as it were, and the only cure for this is to begin looking at the ball - to begin looking at the way human beings really use legal words when they do things like sentencing people to prison and ordering states to pay damages on account of their human rights violations. Thus, I have developed the paradox in its traditional form up to this point only because it has the value of bringing into view a much deeper phenomenon. This is the phenomenon that Walter Benjamin characterized, in a rather uncharitable way, as "something rotten in law."[40] For the problem that traditional philosophers of law have had in working through the relationship between rights and remedies owes its existence to certain disquietude that we all feel, at some level, about law's use of violence as a means. This disquietude that owes its existence to the uneasy relationship between law and violence was first uncovered in Benjamin's 1921 essay "Critique of Violence", and his treatment of it remains to this day one of the most radically original discussions of the problem in Western legal thought.

Benjamin noticed that while existing law purports to authorize the violence that *conserves* the legal order (the violence that we commonly call "enforcement of the law"), another kind of violence is always responsible for having founded the legal order in the first place. This violence at the origin of law takes the form, for example, of wars, conquests, revolutions, and compromises induced by explicit or implicit threats, and it founds a law that is only *thereafter* capable of being conserved. If, as some say, law is the ground of legitimate violence,[41] then law itself has no ground - it only has a cause. Founding violence is no more than "violence crowned by fate,"[42] as Benjamin so aptly puts it, for it can rely for its own authority on nothing but the brute historical fact that it succeeded. In Jacques Derrida's version of this same point, the origins, foundations, and grounds of law's authority - which includes its origin in our customs and their dominant interpretation - "can't by definition rest on anything but themselves, [for] they are themselves a violence without ground."[43] Any attempt to trace law to its origins always gets us down to the bedrock of what is received. And it would get us nowhere to say that what is received, in turn, must have a ground for its own reception. For anything that we could call the ground-of-this-ground would also have to be groundlessly *received* in just the way it is, and not some other way, in order for it to be comprehensible to us at all.[44]

Law is thus founded in a spasm of violence that is neither legitimate nor illegitimate, but rather a kind of violence that transcends the distinction. And now that it has been founded in blood or the threat of it, law seeks above all else to preserve *itself* - and this means to preserve its status as the only grammatically correct noun to which the descriptive phrase "legitimate violence" may be applied. Law's interest in maintaining its monopoly of force vis-à-vis individuals cannot be explained by its desire to ensure the attainment of legally valid ends. For if that were all there were to it, then there would exist no need for the legal prohibition against individuals taking the law into their own hands in order to achieve the very same ends.[45] Law "wishes to have a formal existence," as Stanley Fish puts it,[46] in order to preserve itself as the only legitimate means to the ends that it calls legitimate. And law most of all preserves its grammatical monopoly over the word "legitimate" by seeking to deny or obscure its origins. Law purports to authorize in advance - to make legitimate and hence unproblematic - the enforcing violence that conserves it as the font of all future legitimacy. But here the law comes up against a perplexing grammatical problem. Expressed in set theoretical terms, one might say that the problem is that legal rules and the particular cases to which they can be made to apply do not have the same "multiplicity." There does not exist a one-to-one correspondence between the words of a legal rule and the words that express the facts of a particular case. The first falls into the grammatical category of "rule," in other words, and the second falls into the grammatical category of "cases of application." How then is an already-founded law supposed to be able to perform the task of making legitimate the subsequent enforcing violence that is supposed to conserve just precisely *it* (the already-founded law)? In order to get this job done at all, it would seem that the law must already somehow dictate or underwrite in advance the acts that are undertaken in its name, for otherwise enforcement in the name of the law would not be an act that conserved anything that could rightly be said to have preceded it.

How could the law dictate or underwrite in advance the multitude of acts that are taken in its name? Traditional legal theory imagines that there are two standpoints on the problem of legal duties: the predictive, which equates legal duty with the chance of suffering in the event of disobedience, and the normative, which makes the existence of law into the ground of legal duty whether or not punishment follows disobedience. Yet the terms in which these different standpoints are usually discussed very often reconciles them by hypostatizing a mysterious content to go along with those inky words written on a page that we are wont to call legal statements. H.L.A. Hart, for instance, has this to say about how the two standpoints might be "illuminatingly combined":

> Thus, the normative account might be said to give correctly the meaning of such statements as that a person has a legal duty to do a certain action, while the predictive account emphasizes that very frequently the point or purpose of making such statements is to warn that suffering is likely to follow disobedience. Such a distinction between the meaning of a statement and what is implied or intended by its assertion in different contexts is of considerable importance in many areas of legal philosophy.[47]

In this passage we are able to glimpse a powerful sort of enchantment with the possibility of a law-governed will - that old Kantian dream. In this dream, the possibility of such a will brings the normative and predictive standpoints together on a common ground: namely, the power of language to *ground* the projects of the will, whatever form they may take. Hart's version of the nonnative standpoint pictures a will that is governed by what the meaning of the legal expression "says" the will ought to do, while in the predictive standpoint he pictures a will that decides what it would like to do by hearing what the same legal expression "tells" it about the likelihood of sanctions. Hart, of course, had the old-fashioned idea that words have "core meanings" as well as "penumbras."[48] But the most important thing to notice is his latent presumption that language is capable of speaking to us at all.

Let us slow down our thinking to a snail's pace. It we do that, and also go to the immense trouble of discarding all of our prejudices about what the "meaning" of a law is or has to be, we ought to be able to admit to ourselves that a legal rule always takes the form of a linguistic sign: the material manifestation of speech or writing. Let us depict this form as "a." By the same token, the form of all statements and explanations of what we think a legal rule "means" (or alternatively, what it "plausibly means" to a community of like-minded persons) is "b" - yet another linguistic sign. And finally, the form of all descriptions of the conditions under which we might think that the application of a legal rule is "legitimately assertable"[49] is "c" - once again, a linguistic sign. But the signs "a", "b", and "c" are merely special instances of the form of the linguistic sign in general - let us depict it as "x." And the linguistic sign "x" - which is to say, any linguistic sign - always stands inert before its application. Which is to say, it always just lies there on the page unless and until we pick it up. The gap between a sign and its application is nowhere closed except by the *deed* of applying the sign: the deed of using the legal rule-sign, for example, to subsume what is called "facts" under what is called the "general rule."[50] This deed which imagines itself as taking the particular case under the wing of the rule is always a human act. By this I mean that it is not the act of an official of the state, for example, but rather the act of the human being who is called an "official of the state." In the case of law, this is a deed the end-point of which is always violence or the withholding of violence. It is a deed that looks yearningly to the rule-sign ("a"), or the sign that expresses the meaning of the rule-sign ("b"), or the sign that describes the warranted conditions of the rule's assertability ("c"), for the permission, the authority, the grounds, in a word, for the *legitimacy*, of itself. Yearn as it may, however, it is the deed itself which always closes the gap between the sign and its application. It is the deed itself, which legitimates the violence that it is, or that it precedes in the manner that the violent pull of a gun's trigger precedes the bullet that emerges from its barrel.

Heidegger's concept of the hermeneutic circle,[51] Wittgenstein's concept of the language-game,[52] and Derrida's concept of *différance*:[53] each of these concepts bears witness, in its own special way, to an irreducible minimum for the program of any philosophy of language (or law) that aspires to call itself undogmatic. That minimum is: We use signs, and they do not use us, except in the sense that we let them use us in countless acts of hearing, speaking, reading, and writing, that are like surrendering, but that are themselves also a kind of use. To compare this last kind of use to a "surrender" is by no means to reproach it - for we could not get along without uses of this sort; rather, it is to put human beings back into the foreground of the philosophy of language and of law. But here there is a great danger of going astray, for the tangible expressions of these thinkers' concepts also take the form of linguistic signs ("hermeneutic circle," "language-game," and "*différance*"). And these signs too, no less than more mundane words like "buggy whip" and "toggle bolt," are destined to just lie there on the musty pages of forgotten books unless and until they are appropriated in deeds by those who are alive - by those whose deeds are their lives. (Why is it so very difficult to get across this profoundly simple, and simply profound, point?)

It follows that the ever-present and never-closed gap between a legal rule and its application is not merely the entailment of what might be called a *theory* of language. For a theory explains facts that could be otherwise, whereas the impossibility of closing the gap of which I speak is not the kind of impossibility that has an imaginable antithesis. This impossibility is not like the kind of impossibility that we have in mind when we say things like this: "As far as we know, it is impossible for a human being to run the mile in less than a minute." As the visually spectacular achievements of the science fiction industry demonstrate, this latter kind of impossibility is characterized by our ability to depict or describe the state of affairs that we are excluding as impossible. What it asserts not to be the case could (logically) be the case, even if this excluded antithesis is inconsistent with all that we know about the laws that govern empirical reality.[54] But the kind of gap between a legal rule and its application that I am speaking about in this essay is present even when the language of the rule is at its clearest - even when the plain meaning of the rule leaves us no room to escape. For even the clearest case requires us to *act* to resolve it. Indeed, the clear or easy case, far from being a refutation of the existence of a gap between a rule and its application, actually raises the problem of violence in the clearest possible terms. For why should we act in this way to violently enforce the habitual way of doing things, if the foundation of that way is the accidental success of the historical violence that brought it into being? The point is not that there are no good answers to this question (or at least what counts as "good answers" from this or that point of view). The point is that if we rarely ask this question in the first place, we almost never ask it in the context of the so-called easy case. We usually do not see law's enforcement of the rights that are involved in an easy case *as* violence, and this allows us to avoid having to worry about the problem of its moral worth. For as Benjamin put it, "a cause, however effective, becomes violent, in the precise sense of the word, only when it bears on moral issues."[55] The easy case is one of those particularly deep ruts into which history happened to have thrown us at birth. While we are in this rut, the moral plain that should be visible to us whenever and wherever one man lifts his hand against another is obscured from our view. And we oblige the past by continuing to plod along the rut in the present like a blindered mule in harness, cutting it deeper still for those who will follow behind us.

The gap between rule and application that looms in the midst of every case before it is decided is not to be "explained" by a theory of language according to which even the clearest rule only *seems* to be clear from the point of view of a reader whose own historical context accounts for that seeming.[56] For what do we gain by thus obliterating the grammatical distinction between the words "appearance" and "reality"? This way of thinking comes down to merely crossing out some of the words in our dictionary. For one cannot sensibly deny the existence of "real" (non-contingent) clarity in legal rules unless one knows and can say what it would be like for that clarity to be real. Nothing whatsoever about the gap of which I speak can be explained by such a theory's stipulation that all cases of absolute clarity are to be spoken of as cases of "absolute clarity as seen from a particular point of view." For without an antithesis, the words "particular point of view" completely lose any foothold in the world. What I mean here is that if we cannot use these words to draw distinctions between cases to which they apply and cases to which they do not, then they *explain* nothing whatsoever, at least in the normal sense of the word "explain." No, the gap between a legal rule and its application is present even when the language of the rule *really* is clear. For legal rules do not use us to close the gap between them and the cases they control. The relation is always the other way around, even in those cases where we feel most acutely that the rule leaves us no choice. The gap exists because a legal rule does nothing until we use it. We close the gap by acting to extinguish all other possibilities of acting. A course of action, in other words, can be *merely* clearly and plainly determined by a rule. My use of the word "merely" signifies that a course of action can really be clearly and plainly determined, but only so far as we ourselves let the words "clearly and plainly determined" go in the act of evaluating what we do either before or after we have done it. For it is also the case that we are the ones who close the gap between the words that we use to evaluate a course of action and their application. We do this in another course of action - the one that we call an "act of evaluation."

It should be plain by now that the word "violence," as I use it here, does not stand for a category of behaviors that are metaphysically secure owing to an explicit and true definition of the word "violence." It does not even stand for a shadowy and undefined category of force the concrete examples of which verge on a description of the causes and conditions of all the things that human beings do when they live in a state of law, in the manner that is suggested by the following passage written by Jacques Derrida:

> There are, to be sure, laws that are not enforced, but there is no law without enforceability, and no applicability or enforceability of the law without force, whether this force be direct or indirect, physical or symbolic, exterior or interior, brutal or subtly discursive and hermeneutic, coercive or regulative, and so forth.[57]

Rather, the word "violence" as I use it here stands opposed to its antithesis - the word "non-violence" - in an opposition that is purely formal and grammatical. This opposition is brought to life, as all words are, by the human act of applying it. Nor is it necessary for me to define or even adumbrate the "true nature" of the conceptual distinction between violence and non-violence, for nothing of significance turns on how I might define or adumbrate the distinction. Rather, the word "violence" names anything that we notice as violence. Which is to say, it names anything that we notice under the aspect of a word that has connotations which disquiet us - a word that connects what law does, for example, to certain pictures and images of the violent that haunt us in our waking hours or in our dreams. In short, to apply the word "violence" to the law is to be troubled by the law's methods. The minimum program of such an application involves dwelling within the tragedy that is inherent in law - inherent in even the best of laws. It is, if not to criticize in a noisy and public way, at least to experience *concern* in the face of what we do and are capable of doing when we take up and use the language of the law.[58]

The perspective that I am describing stands radically opposed to any ethical system that would separate words and deeds, or norms and actions according to norms. Take Kant, for example, who famously stipulated that "a good will is good not because of what it performs or effects, nor by its aptness for attaining some proposed end, but simply by virtue of the volition."[59] For Kant, the contingent relation between the will and its effects makes what we do (the consequence of our willing) an unsuitable site for morality. He thought that goodness had to rest on something other than itself. So he discovered the categorical imperative ("Act only on a maxim by which you can will that it, at the same time, should become a general law"),[60] and offered this form of words as a suitable building site for any will that would aspire to do the right thing in life. In a word, Kant's ethical system is based on the allegedly *non-contingent* relation between the general laws that the will lays down, by means of the categorical imperative, and the subsequent act of willing that proceeds on the basis of those laws. He failed to see that the relation between the expression of a general law for willing and a particular act of will that is founded on such a law is no less contingent than the relation between any linguistic sign and what we do with it. Kant's impulse was to provide good willing with a foundation. But the foundation he laid is made of paper and ink. It consists in words that the will seizes upon to cover up the violence of the deed that it is about to commit. Having let these words perform their allotted role, the good will then lets them encourage it never to grieve over what it has done in the name of "duty."

Recall the condition mentioned earlier: that the law must already dictate or underwrite in advance the acts that are undertaken in its name if it is to make legitimate and hence unproblematic the enforcing violence that conserves it as the font of all future legitimacy. It follows from what I have said that this condition is satisfied only to the extent that we *let* it be satisfied.[61] The problem of prior authorization by something that is outside of us thus haunts the law in the manner of a ghost - a ghostly non-presence of anything demonstrably solid that would distinguish legal violence from the "illegitimate" historical violence that we like to imagine legal violence rising up to oppose. If, as some of the more radical American Legal Realists thought, law is the official decision to give or withhold a sanction,[62] then it no longer makes sense to speak of law as the reason or justification for legal violence, except as a part of the rhetorical flourishes that accompany the brute act of sanctioning. Rather, by the law of identity, law is that violent decision, which is always just itself and not some other thing. But if that is so, where has the spirit of law gone, and what is to distinguish the violence done in its name from the "illegal" violence that it is supposed to suppress? Contrariwise, the claim that legally right answers can precede the act of sanctioning as their possible ground requires that we believe that the linguistic signs which express a general rule or system of rules (including any imaginable theory of rules) are capable of "saying" something in advance about their application. But if this is so, where are we to find the sanctioner who can be trusted to hear this message in its pure form, completely unsullied by any act of hearing? Where is this hearer who has not first fallen into the act of hearing it just the way he does, and not some other way?

The thesis of law's radical indeterminacy that I am advancing here is not, as some might think, the tepid and shopworn claim that no absolutely definitive and correct legal arguments can be found to justify any official act. Of course such arguments can be found - but only as far as our deeds let those words "absolutely definitive and correct legal arguments" extend. The thesis of radical indeterminacy is simply the claim that human beings are the ones who do the violence of the deed in all cases that we call the enforcement of law. Anyone who would deny this kind of indeterminacy is, at bottom, denying the existence of human agency. His implicit picture is one in which the people who enforce the law are reduced to being merely the objects of the objects that they have created - legal rule-signs - instead of being elevated into the tragic status of responsible subjects: people who use their own hands to commit violent deeds against other people. Whereas, from the point of view of the kind of radical indeterminacy that I am describing, the more plausible is the interpretation of a legal rule's scope and application as authority for a particular act of enforcement, the *greater* is the violence of this deed - in just the same way that blows from many hands usually hurt more than a blow received from a single hand.

To the extent, therefore, that we let the law be indeterminate - to the extent that we let ourselves see those who enforce it as choosing one among many competing interpretations of it - then to that extent we can also see that the violence that purports to conserve an already existing law actually founds new law each time it bursts forth. In such cases, since the violence of the act of enforcement no longer stands on unambiguous and solid ground, the violence that purports to conserve the law passes over into a violence that founds it. The paradox that Walter Benjamin first uncovered in "Critique of Violence" can thus be put this way: Law pretends to legitimate the violence that conserves it (we would call this "remedies"), but in reality the enforcement action that is taken in its name founds new law each and every time *this exact result* was not unambiguously predetermined by the law. Such an enforcing violence thus fails to ground itself in any authority beyond its own performance. It is a naked and literally law-less violence.

IV

Having brought into view the general problem of law's use of violence as a means, it is now time for me to begin addressing the particular relationship that exists between violence and what the European Court of Human Rights does when it enforces the Convention by means of its remedial powers. Now Kant, in the course of discussing his doctrine of right as it affects public law, has this to say about the right to punish:

> The *right to punish* is the right a ruler has against a subject to inflict pain upon him because of his having committed a crime. The head of a state can therefore not be punished; one can only withdraw from his dominion.[63]

Of course, Kant's reference to the relation between law and the infliction of pain has the advantage of putting the general subject of my remarks in a context that makes explicit what I have been trying to show all along: that when all is said and done the enforcement of law, any law, is a matter of coercion.[64] But in addition to this, Kant's statement about punishment also betrays a certain attitude towards the distinction between legitimate and illegitimate force that is productive for my theme. This attitude may be summarized in the form of three propositions. First, it holds that there is a category of violence that is illegitimate because it is contrary to the law. Here the English phrase "to violate the law" evokes a telling connection between legally impermissible behavior and the illegitimate use of force, for it connotes an identification of such behavior (however passive it may be in fact) with violence against the law. Second, the attitude of which I speak nods with approval at the violence that the state commits when it punishes someone who has done violence to the law. In other words, the state has a right, and perhaps even a duty, as Kant himself says elsewhere,[65] to use force against the offender. The third proposition is that the state, which enjoys a monopoly over the exercise of legitimate violence, is not itself rightfully subject to the infliction of punishment. In other words, the existence of such a category as *legitimate* violence against the state is a logical if not a moral impossibility.

It has been forty-six years since the European Convention on Human Rights went into effect, five years since Protocol 9 gave individuals the right of direct access to the old Court, and less than a year since Protocol 11 brought into being the new European Court of Human Rights. Forty states have now bound themselves both to the law that is expressed in the Convention's specification of human rights and fundamental freedoms, and to the Court's powers over them. Under Article 34 it is now unequivocally the case that "[t]he Court may receive applications from any person, non-governmental organisation or group of individuals claiming to be the victim of a violation by one of the High Contracting Parties of the rights set forth in the Convention or the protocols thereto." The individual applicant thus sets in motion a legal process that can result not only in a finding that the respondent state has violated the Convention, but also a judgment awarding the applicant money to be paid by the state as "just satisfaction" under Article 41. It would appear that the form of the new Court puts its human actors in a position to realize, as never before in history, the founding aspirations of the 1948 Congress of Europe, which adopted a resolution stating its conviction that,

> in the interest of human values and human liberty, the [proposed] Assembly should make proposals for the establishment of a Court of Justice *with adequate sanctions* for the implementation of this Charter [of Human Rights], and to this end any citizen of the associated countries shall have redress before the Court, at any time and with the least possible delay, of any violation of his rights as formulated in the Charter.[66]

Of course, it is also true that the Court does not enjoy the other remedial powers that were favored by the 1948 Congress, such as the power to order states to change their internal laws and practices. It is also true that the Court can summon no army or police force to physically coerce states into complying with its judgments. Indeed, the Committee of Ministers - which is the closest approximation under the Convention to an executive arm for the Court - pointedly does not "enforce" compliance with the Court's judgments. Instead, as Article 46(2) so delicately and diplomatically puts it, it merely "supervises" their execution by the state. Moreover, the inability of applicants to enforce the Court's judgments directly in the national courts of the Convention's signatories represents another significant limitation on the Court's power.[67] But on the other hand, it should never be forgotten that what is always left over after the smallness of a power is taken into account is still a kind of power. As the first paragraph of Article 46 stipulates, the High Contracting Parties do "undertake to abide by any final judgment of the Court in any case to which they are parties." And, as scholars of the old Court's work have noted, the level of compliance in fact by states with the Court's judgments has been quite high.[68]

States do not comply with the Court's judgments because they enjoy complying. There is an important sense in which the Convention overthrows Kant's doctrine that there is no such thing as legitimate violence against the sovereign. For make no mistake about it: the applicant who succeeds in winning a judgment before the European Court of Human

Rights has brought coercion to bear upon the responding state even if the Court cannot enforce its judgment directly. Here I do not refer merely to Hans Kelsen's doctrine that international law is a coercive system because "the specific consequences of an unlawful act are reprisal and war."[69] I mean to invoke a wider notion of the relation between law and coercion, namely, the one that is associated with Max Weber's sociology of law. Weber defined law as an order that is "externally guaranteed by the probability that physical or psychological coercion will be applied by a staff of people in order to bring about compliance or avenge violation."[70] He also stipulated that "the means of coercion are irrelevant," giving as examples the statutes of a voluntary association and the administration of an order by a staff of people who can only exercise various forms of merely psychological coercion.[71] And while I do not wish to claim that anything of importance for my theme turns on how the words "law" and "coercion" are defined, Weber' s definition does have the advantage of demonstrating why states take the trouble of resisting, sometimes fiercely, the claims that are made against them in the European Court of Human Rights. They resist applications to this "staff of people," as Weber would have put it, because the prospect of an unfavorable result is painful to them. It is painful either for the shame and the depletion of public funds that it visits upon them, or for the dishonor that will be theirs if they break the promise that they made to abide by the Court's judgments. In short, thc act that the European Court of Human Rights performs when it hands down a remedy to enforce the Convention is an act of punishment. It is violence against the state: a deed that enters the category of the *legitimate* on account of the state's own previous consent to the possibility of its infliction in general terms, but that also enters the category of the *violent* on account of the trouble that the state takes to avoid its actual infliction in particular cases.

V

There is something enabling about this violence. I am not speaking merely of the improved position that vigorous enforcement of the Convention gives to victims and potential victims of human rights violations. It is of course a matter of the highest importance that the Court's work in enforcing the convention is often an instrument for correcting manifest injustice, and, from a certain point of view, that its work makes it possible for people to enjoy, or at least dream of enjoying, privileges and opportunities that would never have been theirs were it not for the existence of the Convention. But it is also true that the enabling aspect of the violence to which I refer has its dark side - a side that is rarely mentioned. From the standpoint of the state, there is something sweet that goes along with the bitter of the possibility represented by the Court's jurisdiction. It was Michel Foucault who drew attention, in the clearest sort of way, to the danger of thinking that power is a one-way street - that it always comes down to a simple relation between those who have it and those who do not have it and submit to it. "Power," he said, "must be analysed as something which circulates, or rather as something which only functions in the form of a chain. It is never localised here or there, never in anybody's hands, never appropriated as a commodity or piece of wealth."[72] In Foucault's theory of power, the individual is never to be seen merely as an isolated atom, the vis-à-vis of a power that is brought to bear upon him from the outside. Rather, Foucault says, "[t]he individual is an effect of power, and at the same time, or precisely to the extent to which it is that effect, it is an element of its articulation. *The individual which power has constituted is at the same time its vehicle.*"[73]

I would like to make use of Foucault's concept of a power that circulates to bring out something important about the enabling aspect of the violence that is implicit in the Court's jurisdiction to enter judgments against states at the instance of individual applicants. For despite appearances to the contrary, the position that the Convention occupies on the relation between the individual and the state is far from unambiguous. And this means that the position that it occupies in competing conceptions of European liberalism is also far from unambiguous.

There are two main historical traditions of liberalism in the West, and the European Convention on Human Rights plays a significant role in the continuation of both. In the first place, there is the liberalism of Locke, Voltaire, Montesquieu, and von Humboldt: the liberalism that sets the state in opposition to the individual, and that defines liberty as independence from constraints that are imposed by the state. This is the liberalism of the minimal state, of radical individualism, and of laissez-faire. But there is a second liberalism, grounded in Rousseau's conception of human perfectibility, and Kant's notion that freedom is obedience to the moral law. In its right-wing Hegelian version, this liberalism identifies freedom with the organic development of society into ever higher and more spiritual forms, with the result that an individual's obedience to the morally perfected state becomes the highest expression of his liberty. In the left-wing egalitarian version of the second liberalism, freedom means ruling oneself through the medium of a state that one has made one's own by means of democratic participation. In both versions of the second liberalism, unlike the first, the state does not stand in opposition to the individual as a threat to his liberty. Instead, the state is either the end towards which liberty, conceived as self-realization, tends (the right-wing version), or else it is the means for achieving a liberty conceived as self-rule (the left-wing version).[74] In the democratic, egalitarian version of the second liberalism, the state is seen as a progressive instrument that can be used to free humanity from misery, ignorance, and oppression - including the oppression that comes whenever laissez-faire policies lead, as they inevitably do, to those inequalities and asymmetries in private power that the liberalism of the first type rules off-limits to the exercise of public power.

To the extent that the Convention announces and gives certain enforceable rights to individuals vis-à-vis the state conceived as a potential wrongdoer - as a potential violator of "human rights" - then the Convention may be seen as a document that is written in the spirit of the first liberalism. For despite the requirement in Article 35 that applicants exhaust all domestic remedies, the very existence of the jurisdiction and powers of the new European Court of Human Rights exhibits a Lockean spirit of mistrust towards the state. The Court is quite literally a counter-force to the force of the state. It occupies a place outside the sphere of state power where individuals can come to claim redress against the state, while standing in the role of a "victim" (as Article 34 puts it) of official violence. But on the other hand, it cannot be overlooked that the Convention merely sets limits on what its signatories are permitted to do to individuals. The state is left alone by the Convention and the Court when it coerces the individual within a context that is seen as lying within its proper domain. And moreover, there is something far from indifferent in this act of leaving the state alone. For the Convention and the Court do not just tolerate the state that stays within its limits, they also give legitimacy to the force that the state employs within its proper sphere. The lawful state is like the lawful individual: both are entitled to claim the sobriquet "good citizens" within their respective communities. And a good citizen of the community of nations is also one that tends to look good to its own citizens. The lawful state is the state that can avoid being tarred with the brush of contempt for the Convention, just as the lawful individual is one that can avoid being sanctioned by the law. And whether the lawful state's tendencies are Lockean, statist, or both at the same time, it can now claim the mantle of legitimacy in the first sense of liberalism to validate all of its policies, including those that may be progressive in the second sense of liberalism. The message is that the activist state that abides by the Convention is no longer to be feared, because all legitimate cause for fear has been eliminated by the fact that it has not been shown to have violated the rights that are specified in the text of the Convention.

The violence that always lies at least just beneath the surface of legitimate state law - law washed clean of reproachability by its compliance with the Convention - may thus be seen as part of a chain of power that "circulates," as Foucault might have put it. The links in the chain are the individual, the state, and the Court. State power, which now stands in the shadow of the possibility of being monitored by the Court's counter-power, triggered at the instance of the individual, is thereby rendered unproblematic *as* violence, *as* force, *as* coercion within its proper sphere. This is the sweet that comes with the bitter of the Court's jurisdiction, if one looks at it from the standpoint of the state. And the sweetness is rendered all the sweeter by the fact that the Court very frequently does not award damages to successful applicants, and that when it does award them, as one leading text recently put it, they "tend not to be very high."[75]

VI

The remedies that the European Court of Human Rights gives to enforce the Convention - for all of their paucity in most cases and their apparent randomness[76] in many - can now be seen as playing an altogether different role on the stage of European political theory than they are conventionally assumed to play. In a world that no longer believes in the divine right of kings to rule and to punish, perhaps it is not too much to say that the European Convention on Human Rights plays the role of the Divine, and the human beings who are the judges of the Court the role of the angels, in distributing legitimacy to the states that submit to the Convention's authority.

And where, pray tell, has the traditional conception of international human rights gone - the one that sees texts like the Convention and the existence of institutions like the Court as being essential and valuable bulwarks against at least some of the forms of oppression and injustice in this world - namely a certain subset of those that are inflicted by the state? At the risk of being accused of ducking the question, permit me to call upon Goethe's *Faust* for assistance. By way of preparation for the end of my remarks, I will briefly paraphrase both the struggle that Faust went through when he set out to translate the gospel, and the solution that finally gave him peace.

"*Im Anfang war das Wort*": "In the beginning was the Word." So reads the standard German and English translations of the Gospel

According to St. John.[77] Sitting in his study, Faust puzzles over this text, seeking to translate it afresh, and in accordance with its true spirit. He rejects "*das Wort*" as an unsuitable name for what was there in the beginning, reasoning thus: "To set so high a value on a "word" is impossible: I must translate it some other way, if the spirit is giving me real enlightenment."[78] Nor will "*Sinn*" do, for Faust cannot bring himself to agree that it is merely by Sinn (which I will let hover in translation somewhere between "thought" and "meaning")[79] that all things are done and made.[80] The word *Kraft* (which means "power" or "energy") is closer to the mark, but still does not seem quite right.[81] And then, finally, the right word hits him with the force of a revelation:

> *Mir hilft der Geist! auf einmal seh ich Rat*
> *Und schreibe getrost: Im Anfang war die* Tat*!*
>
> ("The spirit helps me! Now I see the answer
> And boldly write: 'In the beginning was the *Deed*!'")

I believe that good-hearted people want so desperately to achieve a world in which human beings are treated *in fact and at all times* with dignity and respect that they project mythical creatures into the language of their legal documents - "rights" and "duties" - that they hope will subdue the baser instincts of people and governments. But we forget or have failed to learn that the essence of law, like everything else human, lies in the doing of it. We suppress our awareness of the tragedy that comes on the heels of *all* violence - the legitimate as well as the illegitimate. We draw back from the radical and apparently anarchistic implications of Walter Benjamin's contention that the categorical imperative does not go far enough. Kant had merely laid it down that we should act in such a way that at all times we use humanity both in our persons and in the persons of all others "always as an end, and never *merely* as a means."[82] Whereas Benjamin drew attention to the extremely uncomfortable fact that positive law, if it is at all conscious of its roots, will certainly always claim "to acknowledge and promote the interest of mankind in the person of each individual."[83] And who can seriously deny Benjamin's thesis that whenever and wherever in history the state has made this claim, it has also linked this alleged interest of mankind to the preservation of something quite particular and contingent: namely, "the representation and preservation of an order imposed by fate"?[84] So Benjamin tried to go Kant's categorical imperative one better by writing down this shocking sentence: "One might, rather, doubt whether this famous demand does not contain too little, that is, whether it is permissible to use, or allow to be used, oneself or another *in any respect* as a means."[85]

What would the world look like if Benjamin's implied version of the categorical imperative were taken seriously? We cannot or will not answer this question, for our fear of the violence that would come our way in a world where others are not restrained and coerced for our benefit gets in our way of imagining humanity constituted as a kingdom of absolute ends, where no one is ever used as a means. We may all want to be coequal citizen-sovereigns of what Kant called the kingdom of ends; but deep down we know that law's violent methods make us all into potential subjects in a kingdom of means whose ruler is a sovereign other than ourselves. Unlike Benjamin, most of us have a love-hate relationship with the law's use of violence as a means. Our relationship with it causes us to look the other way when the unpleasantness that we call "legitimate" violence is visited on others.

Now a widespread belief in the existence of the mythical creatures ("rights" and "duties") that we have made mayor may not help bring about the world we desire. Here I am tempted to agree with Nietzsche's remark that the only correct answer to the Kantian question, "How are synthetic judgments a *priori* possible?," is that "such judgments must be *believed* to be true, for the sake of the preservation of creatures like ourselves."[86] But if we put our superstitious belief in them aside for a moment, it ought to be clear to us that our mythical creatures *themselves* will never rise up and accomplish anything for humanity. Only you - or rather, only *we* - can do that, for good or for ill. What this says about the probable existence and size of the next remedy from the European Court of Human Rights, or from any other court, I cannot say. But I can say that the violence that will be done in that deed, whatever shape it may take, is bound to play its fated role in constituting and perpetuating the world's ceaseless cycle of violence. And judging from history, the one characteristic of those who do law's deeds that seems to remain constant is their impulse to conceal the violent nature of the acts that they are committing, not just from others, but from themselves. For as Wittgenstein said, "What the eye doesn't see the heart doesn't grieve over."[87]

Notes

* Professor of Law, University of Washington School of Law, 1100N.E. Campus Parkway, Seattle, Washington 98105- 6617, U.S.A. Email address: wolcher@u. washington.edu. This paper is based on the text of a lecture that the author gave to

the judges and staff of the European Court of Human Rights in Strasbourg, France, on March 19, 1999.

1 'The Summa Theologica', in *Introduction to Saint Thomas Aquinas*, Anton Pegised. (New York: Modern Library, 1948), p. 633 (Q. 93, Art. 3).

2 *Id.* at 649 (Q. 95, Art. 2)("As Augustine says, *that which is not just seems to be no law at all*... [I]f in any point it departs from the law of nature, it is no longer a law but a perversion of law.").

3 'A Discourse on the Origin of Inequality', in Jean-Jacques Rousseau, *The Social Contract and the Discourses*, trans. G.D.H. Cole (New York: Alfred A. Knopf, 1993), pp. 32-125, at 98.

4 Thomas Hobbes, *Leviathan* (New York: Penguin Books, 1968), p. 185.

5 *Id.* at 238.

6 Immanuel Kant, *The Metaphysical Elements of Justice*, trans. John Ladd (Indianapolis: Bobbs-Merrill, 1965), p. 77.

7 'Convention for the Protection of Human Rights and Fundamental Freedoms', in *Human Rights Today: European Legal Texts* (Strasbourg: Council of Europe Publishing. 1999). pp. 9-38.

8 In the United States the role of the "supra-national system of human rights law" is played primarily by the United States Constitution and the jurisdiction of federal courts to enforce it against the states and the other branches of the federal government. The widespread internal acceptance (if not celebration) of this institutional arrangement creates the impression in the minds of many Americans that since the state and federal governments are already bound to respect "human rights" (as codified in the Constitution and enforced by the federal courts), therefore the United States qua state in the international sense has no need to accept the enforcement authority of international human rights organizations. Although this essay concerns itself primarily with the relation between national and supra-national law, its frame of reference easily could be extended by analogy to the situation created within the United States by the existence of our federal system, as we have historically received and interpreted it.

9 John Austin, *Lectures on Jurisprudence* (4th ed. 1879), at 485.

10 H.L.A. Hart, *The Concept of Law* (Oxford: Clarendon Press, 1961), p. 10.

11 For an interesting attempt to prove that it is psychologically possible for a judge to employ something that could plausibly be called a "prediction theory of law", see Anthony D'Amato, 'The Limits of Legal Realism', 87 *Yale Law Journal* 468 (1978).

12 The distinction between these two contexts is Dewey's. John Dewey, 'Logical Method and Law', 10 *Cornell Law Quarterly* 17,23-27 (1924). For the case against the kind of empirical claim that is mentioned in text, see Paul Gewirtz, 'Remedies and Resistance', 92 *Yale Law Journal* 585, 678- 79 (1983)(asserting the existence of a 'permeable wall between rights and remedies: The prospect of actualizing rights through a remedy... makes it inevitable that thoughts of remedy will affect thoughts of right, that judges' minds will shuttle back and forth between right and remedy.").

13 'The Nicomachean Ethics', in *The Complete Works of Aristotle*, Jonathan Barnes ed. (Princeton: Princeton University Press, 1984), pp. 1728-1867, at 1786-87. The concepts of "unjust gain" and "unjust loss" in Aristotle's theory of corrective justice are notoriously ambiguous. For the argument that they should be understood normatively (relative to the parties "due") rather than materially (relative to their pre-existing resources), see Ernest Weinrib, 'The Gains and Losses of Corrective Justice', 44 *Duke Law Journal* 277-97 (1994).

14 Dinah Shelton, Unpublished Manuscript on Remedies for International Human Rights Violations, ch. II, p. 32 (copy in the possession of this essay's author).

15 See William Earle, 'William James', in 4 *The Encyclopedia of Philosophy*, Paul Edwards ed. (New York: MacMillan, 1967), p. 247.

16 Oliver Wendell Holmes, 'The Path of Law', 10 *Harvard Law Review* 457, 460 (1897).

17 For Kelsen, while the "ought" of legal duty seems to be addressed to the citizen, the more important "ought" of law's conditional statement is addressed to the official who is responsible for imposing a sanction in case the first norm is violated. But, he reasons, "[i]fit is assumed that the first norm ...is valid only if the second norm attaches a sanction. .., then the first norm is certainly superfluous in an exact exposition of the law." Thus, he concludes: "If at all existent, the first norm is contained in the second, *which is the only genuine legal norm*." Hans Kelsen, *The Pure Theory of Law* (Berkeley: University of California Press, 1924, Max Knight trans., 1967)(emphasis added). Some have read Kelsen's theory as "a strong endorsement of libertarianism," on the premise that it endorses the view that law does not command the observation of duties, but always leaves it up to the citizen to choose between being obedient to the law and being sanctioned by the law, in accordance with the form of the conditional statement. Anthony D'Amato, *Analytic Jurisprudence Anthology* (Cincinnati: Anderson, 1996), p. 55.

18 Hans Kelsen, *Introduction to the Problems of Legal Theory*, trans. Bonnie Litschewski Paulson and Stanley Paulson (Oxford: Oxford University Press, 1992), pp. 44-45.

19 See David Schoenbrod, Angus Macbeth, David Levine, and David Jung, *Remedies: Public and Private* (St. Paul: West, 1996), p. 2 ("A judge with unfettered discretion over remedy can effectively nullify the prohibitions in constitutions, statutes, and cases.").

20 I mean to include here all of the materials that the bad man needs to make an accurate prediction: not just the texts that make up remedial law, but also the attitude towards those texts and the bad man's anticipated course of action that those who will enforce the law can be expected to take. Lon Fuller was right when he said that the bad man, if he is to become a good predictor of consequences, must "learn to look at the law through the eyes of the good man," to the extent that the good man is the one who will decide his case. Lon Fuller, *The Law in Quest of Itself* (Evanston: Northwestern University Press, 1940), p. 95. This does not imply, of course, that the bad man has *to become* a good man: he need only become skilled in predicting the probable moral judgments that others will in fact make - skilled, in other words, in the craft of descriptive ethics.

21 Ronald Dworkin, *A Matter of Principle* (Cambridge: Harvard University Press, 1985), pp. 72-73. Dworkin spends all of chapter 3 arguing that people do not have a right to a "perfect" legal system that excludes all possibility of error. But the point in text is that whether or not they have a right to it, they do not get it in fact, and probably never have gotten it in all of human history. And this is a circumstance of which even the good woman is entitled to take notice.

22 Lon Fuller's concept of the 'internal morality of the law' is a good example of this kind of theory. See Lon Fuller, *The Morality of Law* (New Haven: Yale University Press, 1969), p. 39, where Fuller makes both the failure to publicize the rules that people are "expected to observe," and the 'failure of congruence between the rules as announced and their actual administration,' as two of the criteria he employs to decide that something that calls itself law is 'not properly called a legal system at

all.' Since Fuller believes that law is the "enterprise of subjecting human conduct to the governance of rules," *id.* at 122, there seems to be no reason in principle to distinguish, within his system, between substantive rules and remedial rules.

23 John Rawls, *A Theory of Justice* (Cambridge: Harvard University Press, 1971), p. 241.

24 *Supra* n.6, at 101.

25 *Id.*

26 *Supra* n.14, at 48.

27 21 E.H.R.R. 97 (1995).

28 *Id.* at ¶ 219.

29 Anthony Kronman, *Max Weber* (Stanford: Stanford University Press, 1983), pp. 76-77.

30 *See* e.g. Shelton, *supra* n.14, at 54 ("The European Court ...seems to give unjustified weight to the character and reputation of the victim. All too frequently the Court's decision to award compensation, and the amount awarded, are explicitly linked to its assessment of the worthiness of the victim."); Alastair Mowbray, 'The European Court of Human Rights' Approach to Just Satisfaction', (1997) *Public Law* (Winter) 647-59, at 658-59 ("the Court makes moral judgments about the nature of different types of applicants, such as convicted criminals and terrorists, when evaluating their claims for just satisfaction.").

31 Sometimes rights violations are unavoidable, as when Shakespeare's Antonio found himself unable to repay Shylock due to the unexpected failure of his ships to arrive in time. On such occasions, even those who did not plan to violate another's rights may be comforted to know that the remedy for violation will be rigorously limited to the taking of a pound of flesh, without the right to shed a single drop of blood. William Shakespeare, The Merchant of Venice Act IV, Scene I, in *The Complete Works of William Shakespeare* (Roslyn, NY: Walter J. Black, 1937), pp. 241-46.

32 (1994) Q.B. 670.

33 Lon Fuller, *The Problems of Jurisprudence* (Brooklyn: Foundation Press, 1949), p. 632.

34 The linkage between rights and remedies in the realm of the legitimacy of official violence in the name of law was a favorite theme of the American Legal Realists. Consider the analysis of the relation that is contained in Jerome Frank's 1930 book *Law and the Modern Mind* (Gloucester: Peter Smith, 1970). Frank took Leon Tulin's famous analysis of the role of penalties in criminal law as evidence that judges "work back from conclusions to principles," rather than the other way around. *Id.* at 111. Tulin made a study of the kind of case where a drunk driver recklessly (but not purposefully) runs over another person. Leon Tulin, 'The Role of Penalties in Criminal Law', 37 *Yale Law Journal* 1048 (1928). He found that the courts of some states held that such drivers can be indicted for the statutory offence of "assault with intent to kill," whereas courts of other states rejected this conclusion, holding such drivers indictable for the lesser statutory crime of "reckless driving." This looks like an important disagreement about substantive law. But on closer inspection, Tulin found that drunk drivers in the two different types of jurisdictions actually received roughly the same punishment for the same type of act. It turns out that the penalty for assault with intent to kill in the first group of states was the same as the penalty for reckless driving in the second group of states, whereas the penalty for reckless driving in the first group was "too lenient," and the penalty for assault with intent to kill in the second group was "too severe." Frank's conclusion from Tulin's findings was as follows: "In other words, the courts in these cases began with the results they

desired to accomplish: they wanted to give what they considered to be adequate punishment to drunken drivers; their conclusions determined their reasoning." Frank, *supra* at 110. For Frank, then, substantive law did not determine the choice of remedy in these cases - rather, the remedy determined the choice of substantive law. And if, as Frank thinks, choice of remedy ("adequate punishment") was determined on the basis of the judge's innate sense of rightness, *id.* at 111-12, citing Joseph Hutcheson, 'The Judgment Intuitive: The Function of the "Hunch" in Judicial Decisions', 14, *Cornell Law Review*, 274 (1929), then this can only mean that it was not determined in accordance with any kind of law that underwrote in advance the infliction of the penalty.

35 John Finnis, 'The Authority of Law in the Predicament of Contemporary Social Theory', 1 *Notre Dame Journal of Law, Ethics, and Public Policy*, 113, 116-20, 136-37 (1984).

36 Ludwig Wittgenstein, *Tractatus Logico-Philosophicus*, trld. D.F. Pears and B.F. McGuinness (Atlantic Highlands, NJ: Humanities Press, 1961), pp, 71-72 (¶ 6.422).

37 *Cf.* Dan Dobbs, *Law of Remedies* (St. Paul: West, 2d ed., 1993), pp. 23-24 ("sometimes the remedial tail wags the substantive dog," as in those situations where "rights will not be established unless a remedy can be administered.").

38 Heraclitus, Fragments, trans. T.M. Robinson (Toronto: University of Toronto Press, 1987), p. 15 (Fragment 8).

39 I have discussed this problem elsewhere in terms that usefully elaborate on the point made in text:

> [A]n irreducible remedial entitlement must exist at the core of the bargaining process in order to make the [Coase] theorem coherent. ...[T]he Coase Theorem presuppose[s] a bargain. A bargain, however, may be perceived as worthless, or at least worth less, if it is not meaningfully enforced. This observation leads naturally to the question: what rule will enforce the parties' hypothetically costless bargain to employ remedy X rather than standard remedy in case of breach? It is no answer to posit as controlling whatever remedy the parties negotiate, because this answer forces us to ask anew what remedy will enforce the bargain that enforces the bargain, and so on in an endless regression.

Louis Wolcher, 'The Accommodation of Regret in Contract Remedies', 73, *Iowa Law Review*, 797-892, at 837 (1988).

40 'Critique of Violence', in Walter Benjamin, *Reflections: Essays, Aphorisms, Autobiographical Writings*, trans. Edmund Jephcott (New York: Schocken Books, 1986), pp. 277-300, at 286.

41 Here I have in mind the kind of elaborate argument that people have legal rights that precede the public act of enforcing them that is put forward by Ronald Dworkin in the form of his 'right answers' thesis. See, e.g., Ronald Dworkin, Law's Empire {Cambridge: Harvard University Press, 1986), pp. 225- 75; Ronald Dworkin, *A Matter of Principle* (Cambridge: Harvard University Press, 1985), pp. 119-45; Ronald Dworkin, *Taking Rights Seriously* (1977), pp. 279-90.

42 *Id.*

43 Jacques Derrida, 'Force of Law: The Mystical Foundation of Authority', trans. Mary Quaintance, 11 *Cardozo Law Review* 920-1045 (1990), p. 943.

44 See *id.* at 939, quoting Pascal: 'Custom is the sole basis for equity, for the simple reason that it is received; it is the mystical foundation of its authority. Whoever traces it to its source annihilates it.'

45 See *supra* n.40, at 281.

46 Stanley Fish, 'The Law Wishes to Have a Formal Existence', in Austin Sarat and Thomas Keams eds., *The Fate of Law* (1991), pp. 159-62.

47 H.L.A. Hart, 'Problems of Philosophy of Law', in 6 *The Encyclopedia of Philosophy*, Paul Edwards ed. (New York: Macmillan, 1967), pp. 264-76, at 266.

48 H.L.A. Hart, 'Positivism and the Separation of Law and Morals', 71 *Harvard Law Review*, 90 (1958).

49 The phrase is Kripke's. Saul Kripke, *Wittgenstein on Rules and Private Language* (Cambridge: Harvard University Press, 1982), p. 78. It comes in the course of his description of what he takes to be Wittgenstein's theory of meaning: "All that is needed to legitimize assertions that someone means something is that there be roughly specifiable circumstances under which they are legitimately assertable, and the game of asserting them under such conditions has a role in our lives. No supposition that 'facts correspond' to these assertions is needed." *Id.* at 77-78.

50 For an interesting discussion of this point, see Marijan Pavcnik, 'Legal Decisionmaking as a Responsible Intellectual Activity: A Continental Point of View', 72 *Washington Law Review* 481 (1997).

51 I have summarized this concept elsewhere as follows:

> The concept of the "hermeneutic circle" can be illustrated by paying close attention to the question "What is the meaning of the words 'is' and 'meaning'?". The meaning of the words in italics must already be understood by the reader (if only vaguely and unthematically) in order for the enquoted words to be interrogated as to *their* meaning. Yet the words that do the questioning, and the words that are questioned, are also the *same* words. One way to express this connection is to say that there is a "circle" running between that which is doing the questioning and that which is questioned. The circle is called "hermeneutic" to draw attention to the fact that what is going on here is an interpretation. (The word "hermeneutic" comes from the Greek hermēneutikē, meaning 'interpretive', and before Heidegger it was primarily used as the name for the science or art of biblical interpretation.)

Louis Wolcher, 'The Man in a Room: Remarks on Derrida's Force of Law', 7 *Law and Critique* 35-64, at 37 n.9 (1996).

52 See Ludwig Wittgenstein, *Philosophical Investigations*, trans. G.E.M. Anscombe (New York: Macmillan, 3d ed., 1968), p. 5e ("I shall... call the whole, consisting of language and the actions into which it is woven, the 'language-game'.").

53 See Jacques Derrida, *Edmund Husserl's* Origin of Geometry: *An Introduction*, trans. John Leavey (Lincoln: University of Nebraska Press, 1989), p. 156:

> The impossibility of resting in the simple maintenance [nowness] of a Living Present, the sole and absolutely absolute origin of the De Facto *and* the De Jure, of Being and Sense, but always other in its self-identity: the inability to live enclosed in the innocent undividedness [indivision] of the primordial Absolute, because the Absolute is present only in being deferred-delayed [différant] without respite, this impotence and this impossibility are given in a primordial and pure consciousness of Differance. Such a *consciousness*,

with its strange style of unity, must be able to be restored to its own light. Without such a consciousness, without its own proper dehiscence, nothing would appear.

54 See Louis Wolcher, 'Ronald Dworkin's Right Answers Thesis Through the Lens of Wittgenstein', 29 *Rutgers Law Journal* 43-65, at 57-60 (1997), where Wittgenstein's concept of "bipolarity," which informs the discussion in text, is further elucidated.

55 *Supra* n.40, at 277.

56 See. e.g., Anthony D'Amato, 'Pragmatic Indeterminacy', 85 *Northwestern Law Review*, 148 (1990).

57 *Supra* n.43, at 925-27.

58 Derrida's remarks about the relation between law and justice in the "easy" case make a similar point: "Every time that something comes to pass or turns out well, every time we placidly apply a good rule to a particular case, to a correctly subsumed example, according to a determinant judgment, we can be sure that law (*droit*) may find itself accounted for, but certainly not justice." *Supra* n.43, at 947. On the other hand, Derrida's willingness in that same essay to let justice be identified with deconstruction ("Deconstruction is justice," *id.* at 945) seems a bit too strong, a bit too much like a metaphysical *justification* in advance for the "practice" of deconstruction, to capture the point I want to make. See supra n.51, at 60 ("Can one fail to hear in this 'Deconstruction is justice', if not authority for a particular deconstruction, at least a kind of authority - a kind of permission - for deconstruction in general?").

59 Immanuel Kant, *Metaphysical Foundations of Morals, in The Philosophy of Kant*, Carl Friedrich ed, (New York: Modern Library, 1993), pp. 154-229, at 155.

60 *Id.*, at 187.

61 Least of all is this condition satisfied in the body of remedial jurisprudence that the old Court has handed down to the new one in the context of enforcing the Convention. The Court itself has declared that "as is borne out by the adjective 'just' and the phrase "if necessary", the Court enjoys a certain discretion in the exercise of the power conferred by Article 50 [now 41]," Judgment of 6 November 1980, *Guzzardi*, A.39 (1981), at 42. And students of the Court's remedial decisions have often confessed an inability to find much of a rational relationship between, on the one hand, the texts of Article 41 and the Court's prior interpretations of it and, on the other hand, its decisions in concrete cases. See, e.g., Frank Newman and David Weissbrodt, *International Human Rights: Law, Policy, and Process* (Cincinnati: Anderson Publishing, 1996), at 485 ("Possibly the Court is now examining the facts of cases and dispensing justice on a case-by-case basis. The equities governing particular awards are not always readily apparent."); Mowbray, *supra* n.30, at 649 ("An unsatisfactory aspect of the Court's provision of this type of non-pecuniary damage [for distress and anxiety caused by officials' noncompliance with the Convention] has been its failure to justify or explain the different levels of awards."). In short, the Court's remedial law is indeterminate even by the more conventional measure of indeterminacy that distinguishes between rule-signs that have "clear meanings" and those that do not.

62 See Frank, *supra* n.34, at 138 ("The law, therefore, consists of decisions, not of rules. If so, then *whenever a judge decides a case he is making law*').

63 'The Metaphysics of Morals', in Immanuel Kant, *Practical Philosophy*, trans. Mary Gregor (Cambridge: Cambridge University Press, 1996), 353-603, at 424.

64 The English word "enforce," which is what remedies are supposed to do *vis-à-vis* the law, visibly carries this connotation of coercion - one that is often lost in other languages. As Jacques Derrida put it not too long ago:

> When one translates 'to enforce the law' into French, by 'appliquer la loi', for example, one loses this direct, literal allusion to the force that comes from within to remind us that law is always an authorized force, a force that justifies itself or is justified in applying itself, even if this justification may be judged from elsewhere to be unjust or unjustifiable.

Supra n.43, at 925.

65 "The law of punishment is a categorical imperative, and woe to him who crawls through the windings of eudaimonism in order to discover something that releases the criminal from punishment or even reduces its amount by the advantage it promises, in accordance with the Pharisaical saying, 'It is better for one man to die than for an entire people to perish.' For if justice goes, there is no longer any value in human being's living on the earth." *Supra* n.63, at 473.

66 Council of Europe, *Report of the Control System of the European Convention on Human Rights* (H(92) 14), December 1992, at 4 (¶ 6)(emphasis added).

67 Jacobs and White say that "[t]he procedure for executing the Court's judgments cannot be regarded as satisfactory," and draw attention in particular to the fact that the Court's judgments, unlike those of the Court of Justice of the European Communities, are not enforceable directly in national courts. Francis Jacobs and Robin White, *The European Convention on Human Rights* (Oxford: Clarendon Press, 1996), p. 392.

68 See, e.g., Neville Hunnings, *The European Courts* (London: Cartermill International, 1996), p. 337. Another recent assessment of the old Court's decisions concludes that "[o]n the whole... the Court's judgments have had a significant impact, in that the respondent State has often been prepared to take not only individual but also general measures of corrective action, including legislative reform." R. Macdonald, F. Matscher, and H. Petzold, *The European System for the Protection of Human Rights* (Dordrecht: Martinus Nijhoff, 1993), p. 636.

69 *Supra* n.18, at 108.

70 Max Weber, *Economy and Society* (Berkeley: University of California Press, 1978), vol. I, p. 34.

71 *Id.* at 35.

72 Michel Foucault, *Power/Knowledge: Selected Interviews and Other Writings 1972-1977* (New York: Pantheon Books, 1980), at 98.

73 *Id.* (emphasis added).

74 I owe this insight to the analysis of liberalism contained in J.G. Merquior, *Liberalism Old and New* (Boston: Twayne Publishers, 1991), p. 13.

75 Macdonald, Matscher and Petzold, *supra* n.68, at 635.

76 See Mowbray, *supra* n.30, at 650 (complaining of the 'worrying lack of transparency in reasoning' in the Court's remedial jurisprudence).

77 The German is from 'Faust Übersetzt Das Evangelium', in Goethe: *Selected Verse*, David Luke ed. (London: Penguin Books, 1964), p. 185. The English is from John 1:1 (King James).

78 'Ich kann das *Wort* so hoch unmoglich schiitzen,
Ich muss es anders iibersetzen,
Wenn ich vom Geiste recht erleuchtet bin.'

Goethe: *Selected Verse, supra* n.77, at 185.

79 Here I prefer to follow the direction of Philip Wayne, who translates *Sinn* as "thought" in *Faust: Part One* (London: Penguin Books, 1949), p. 71, rather than as the more insipid word "Mind" that is employed by most modem translators of Goethe.

80 *Ist es der* Sinn, *der alles wirkt und schafft?* Goethe: *Selected Verse*, supra n.77, at 185.

81 "*Schon warnt mich was, dass ich dabei nicht bleibe*": "Something warns me not to leave it at that." *Id.* at 185.

82 *Supra* n.59, at 195.

83 Benjamin, *supra* n.40, at 285.

84 *Id.*

85 *Id.* at 285 n* (emphasis added).

86 Friedrich Nietzsche, 'Beyond Good and Evil', in *The Philosophy of Nietzsche* (New York: Modem Library, 1954),392-93.

87 Ludwig Wittgenstein, *Remarks on the Foundations of Mathematics*, G.H. von Wright, R. Rhees, and G.E.M. Anscombe eds. Cambridge: MIT Press, 1983), p. 205.

27. The Success of Feminist Jurisprudence in India

NIDHI GUPTA*

Introduction

"*A woman is never fit for independence. In her childhood her father protects her, in youth her husband and in old age her sons.*" This statement was made by Manu, the first codifier of law in ancient India. Tulsidas, author of great Indian epic "*Ramcharitmanas*", which forms the basis of philosophy for vast sections of Hindu society in the country classified women in the group of "idiots", "illiterates", "low castes" and "animals". Such utterances are ironical, for women occupied a very important position; in fact superior to man in ancient India. A plethora of goddesses were created who enjoyed equal status with their husbands. Kali, the most significant goddess of Hindu pantheon epitomizes powers of women - in fact the absolute power of any kind. The concept of "*Ardhnareshwara*" depicts God as half man and half woman, which is a physical representation of the idea that God is beyond gender.

It is not strange that such a dichotomy of thought apparent in contemporary context manifests in the form of paradoxical status of women in India. On one hand joint participation of husband and wife is mandatory to perform any religious ritual for Hindus, on the other hand some wives are burnt by their husbands and family members for they could not bring a purse large enough for the groom's family (system named as dowry). A woman heading one of the national political parties – is expected to become the prime minister and that too a very powerful one just like the one and only woman prime minister - Mrs. Indira Gandhi, at the same time we have witnessed woman being shot dead at point blank range in an elitist party in Delhi by a rich young man from an influential political background for saying "no". A female child is "put to sleep" as soon as she is born by her mother or father or even grandmother by feeding poison or slipping a buck of paddy into her milk so that her slender throat would be split. And all this is done out of "love" to save her from poverty and misery she may have been inflicted with at grown up stage.[1] Such cases may not really be the norm uniformly applicable to the country but it is horrifying to see that they happen. In contemporary India, which is almost an antithesis to ancient India the society continues to discriminate against women under the guise of protecting religiosity and plurality of ethnicity.

The above account offers a peculiar complexity prevalent in Indian situation for feminist jurisprudence. Fortunately many things are being done to address the problems of gender bias and the rights of women through legal pronouncements. This paper attempts to bring forth some of the issues concerning women as they have been meticulously shaped by law, thanks to the proactive role of the feminist movement in the backdrop of religious and customary hurdles.

It is rather interesting to note that the women's movement in India dates back to a period of subservient status of the people under colonial rule. The movement began mainly with securing social rights for women. It had in fact laid the foundation stone of the citadel that feminist movement in India has shaped, which has place for all women irrespective of religion, caste, economic or social status.

Since the last two decades, in addition to various societal, economic and political causes, various laws have attracted the wrath of the women's movement for perpetuating patriarchy and gender bias. Legal feminism or feminist jurisprudence in India can be said to have emerged as a distinct category of the feminist movement in the late 1970s as a reaction towards some of the overtly biased judicial decisions. It now enjoys a formidable presence in the feminist movement by unveiling the insidious nature of various laws ostensibly meant for ameliorating the status of women. It has also been successful in influencing reforms in legislation dealing with issues relating to violence against women, dowry, marriage, divorce, alimony, adoption, inheritance and sensitizing judiciary in the direction of innovative and progressive law making through conception of new legal categories like sexual harassment, cruelty against women etc.

The success of legal feminism is praiseworthy for unlike the west, discipline is not institutionalized in India. None of the universities and law schools offers specific courses on women and law. There is no systematic exploring of techniques and methods revealing gender bias and invidious social meaning accorded to women. No sophisticated distinction exists between feminist legal theory and feminist jurisprudence enabling abstraction of issues for better insight to further relate them to the reality. Stray and sporadic writings of a few spirited academicians and lawyers deserve the credit of making our legal system gender sensitive and compatible with international norms and regulations.

Given its cultural and social peculiarities the feminist concerns in India though same in some areas are much different in others from that of the western part of the world. Prioritization of concerns is a tough task but keeping in view the scope of this paper the attempt is to discuss the role of feminist jurisprudence relating to only two major issues. First, sexual harassment and violence against women, which gives the cause of common concern to women world wide, second a problem having its roots in age old traditions and rituals and very specific to Indian women i.e. of dowry deaths. An effort has been made to highlight a few important judicial pronouncements, which reflect a definite change in the perceptions of the society and increasing clarity amongst women groups on the subject of legal feminism.

Not trying to disparage these gradual but significant achievements along with desired changes it is necessary to make explicit the prevailing gender bias in law and society. Continuation of such bias is a warning against any kind of complacency and has neutralizing effect on special and unique mandate of equality in Indian constitution. The myopic vision and sinister ideology of some sections of the society and undeniably at times some of the economic and political causes result in watering down the noble edict of our constitution makers for empowerment and emancipation of women. Before starting with the critical appraisal of the issues involved it is vital to include a brief account of mandate of equality as laid out in the Indian Constitution.

Equality and Indian Constitution

The Indian Constitution adopting the rule of law mandate provides for the equality before law and equal protection of laws for every individual. Feminist groups often criticize this kind of mandate for its patriarchal roots and for perpetuating male dominance.[2]

Inclusion of Article 15, clause 3[3] in the constitution as a part of fundamental rights imparts a unique strength to Indian constitution to withstand this stream of criticism. This Article authorizes positive discrimination for women without attracting the restrictions of the other provisions of equality under Article 14[4] and 15(1)[5] of the constitution, which includes sex as one of the grounds to prohibit discrimination. Indian legislature has promulgated various laws aiming exclusively at protection and empowerment of women with a shield of art. 15(3) to withstand the test of constitutional validity. Given below are some examples from different codes on special provisions meant for women:

- Section 354 of Indian Penal Code which protects the modesty of only a woman;
- Section 125 of Criminal Procedure Code obliges husband to maintain his wife;
- Section 437(1) of Cr. P.C. authorizes special treatment of women accused of a non-bailable offence in matter of bail;
- Section 13 of Hindu Marriage Act differentiates between husband and wife as to grounds of divorce;
- 73rd and 74th amendment in constitution provide for reservation of one third of seats for women in local councils for governance;
- Reservation of women in government jobs and educational institutions through administrative measures.

It is interesting to note that most of these laws have been challenged for their constitutional validity on grounds of equality, but under rising influence of feminist movement have successfully withstood these challenges.

With this brief background of the Indian Constitution, the core areas of concern are now discussed in the following paragraphs to examine the reasons for the failure to achieve the true spirit of the constitution.

Sexual Harassment

The menace of sexual harassment of women by male bosses and colleagues is not a new one. It has always worked in the direction of neutralizing the equality mandate as well as the special provisions made under Art. 15(3). Hostile sexual behavior of men towards women in public sphere especially at work places has always been a major impediment for emancipation of women. After a protracted struggle of feminist activists for abating this danger the Supreme Court recognized sexual harassment as a form of sexual discrimination in a recent judgment of *Vishaka v. State of Rajasthan.*[6] The court accepted that the present civil and penal laws in India do not adequately provide for specific protection of women from sexual harassment at the work place. The three-judge bench of the Supreme Court, which also included a woman judge, acknowledged the arduous efforts of women activists and non-governmental organizations for focusing attention towards this aberration and assisting in finding suitable methods for realization of the true concept of "Gender Equality".

Accepting the general recommendations of CEDAW[7] (Convention for Elimination of Discrimination against Women) in respect of its Art. 11

the Supreme Court defined sexual harassment and laid down guidelines to be respected as enacted legislation, till the same is replaced by a formal legislation enacted for the purpose.[8]

Definition of Sexual Harassment

As per the judgment sexual harassment includes such unwelcome sexually determined behavior (whether directly or by implication) as:

a) Physical contact and advances.
b) A demand or request for sexual favors.
c) Sexually colored remarks.
d) Showing pornography.
e) Any other unwelcome physical, verbal or non-verbal conduct of sexual nature.

It is considered discriminatory when the woman has "reasonable grounds" to believe that her objection would disadvantage her in connection with her employment or work environment or when it creates a hostile work environment.

Duty of Employer

It shall be the duty of the employer or other responsible persons in work place or other institutions to prevent or deter the commission of acts of sexual harassment and to provide the procedures for resolution, settlement or prosecution of acts of sexual harassment by taking all steps required.

Preventive Steps

The judgment provides that all employers or persons in charge of the workplace whether in public or private sector should take the following steps to prevent sexual harassment:

a) Express prohibition of sexual harassment as defined above at work place should be notified, published and circulated in appropriate ways.
b) The Rules/Regulations of Government and public sector bodies relating to conduct and discipline should include rules/regulations prohibiting sexual harassment and provide for appropriate penalties in such rules against the offender.

c) As regards private employers steps should be taken to include the aforesaid prohibitions in the standing orders under industrial employment (Standing Orders) Act, 1946.

d) Appropriate work conditions should be provided in respect of work, leisure, health and hygiene to further ensure that there is no hostile environment towards women at work places and no employee woman should have reasonable ground to believe that she is disadvantaged in connection with her employment.

Other Measures

The judgment provides for criminal proceedings to be initiated by the employers, when such conduct amounts to a specific offence under Indian Penal Code or under any other law. It further states that when such conduct amounts to misconduct in employment as defined by the relevant service rules, appropriate disciplinary action should be initiated by the employer in accordance with those rules.

Employers are instructed to ensure that witnesses are not victimized or discriminated against while dealing with complaints of sexual harassment. Further, the victims of sexual harassment should have option to seek transfer of the perpetrator or their own transfer.

An employer would be required to create an appropriate complaint mechanism for redress of the complaint made by the victim. This complaint mechanism would provide, where necessary, a complaints' committee that would be headed by a woman and not less than half of its members would be women. Further, to prevent the possibility of any undue pressure or influence from senior levels, such complaints' committee should involve a third party, either a non-governmental organization or other body who is familiar with the issue of sexual harassment.

This judgement has a silver lining in an otherwise grim scenario of insecurity for women given the prevailing feudalistic tendencies of judiciary as well as dominant groups in society. This encouraging decision is the result of intensified demands of feminist groups and National Commission for Women in the wake of the brutal gang rape of the social worker Bhanwari Devi in State of Rajasthan while trying to perform her duty of preventing a child marriage. Though this case is still pending in the Rajasthan High Court the greatest cause of concern is the acquittal of the accused by session's court due to lack of sufficient evidence. This incident revealed the hazards to which a working woman may be exposed and the depravity to which sexual harassment can degenerate.

Even this judgment of the Supreme Court could have been interpreted as another hollow declaration and as an occasional display of sensitivity but for another very recent judgment of the Supreme Court in March 1999 in the case of *Apparel Export Promotion Council v. A.K. Chopra.*[9] Relying on the decision in Vishaka's case the Supreme Court recognized the demoralizing effect of such incidents upon women and once again emphasized that present civil and penal laws in the country are not well equipped to deal with the cases of sexual harassment at the work place.

Being aware of the utmost necessity of checking rapidly growing menace of sexual harassment especially for working women, the Supreme Court said: "In a case involving charge of sexual harassment or attempt to sexually molest the courts are required to examine the broad possibilities of a case and not get swayed by insignificant discrepancies or narrow technicalities or dictionary meanings of the expression molestation. They must examine the entire material to determine the genuineness of the complaint. The statement of the victim must be appreciated in the background of the entire case."

A three-judge bench of the Supreme Court delivered this landmark and progressive judgment while reversing the order of Delhi High Court. The High Court had quashed the punishment order given by a disciplinary committee for accused on the charges of molesting a subordinate lady employee. High Court opined that punishment was not justified and adequate since the accused had only tried to molest and he had not in fact molested the complainant. Interpreting the word molestation this court had observed "The entire disposition relates that accused A.K. Chopra tried to touch her but he did not manage to make even slightest physical contact with the lady. There being no physical contact between accused and the lady there cannot be any attempt to "tried to molest" on the part of the accused".[10] To everybody's surprise even after proven misconduct of the accused which did not withstand the test of decency and modesty and which projected unwelcome sexual advances the learned bench of High Court did not find the matter serious enough and decided to reduce the punishment of the accused.

Under the rising pressure of feminists groups against such decisions the Supreme Court could not avoid undoing the great harm purported to be done to working women. Accepting prevention of sexual harassment and abuse as a part of constitutional mandate in India, the court declared "The contents of fundamental rights guaranteed in our constitution are of sufficient amplitude to encompass all facets of gender equality including prevention of sexual harassment and abuse. The courts are under a constitutional obligation to protect and preserve those fundamental rights. That sexual harassment of a female at place of work is incompatible with the dignity and honor of a female and needs to be eliminated and that there can be no compromise with such violations, admits of no debate".[11]

The refusal of the bench to accept even an unqualified apology by the accused is exemplary of its determination to leave no stone unturned to eradicate this evil. Court rightly asserted that any lenient action in such a case is bound to have demoralizing effect on working women. Sympathy in such cases is uncalled for and mercy is misplaced.

Another judgment important from the point of view of success of feminist jurisprudence but at the same time reflecting the biased attitude of some sections of society about role of women is that of *Rupan Deol Bajaj v. Kanwar Pal Singh Gill.*[12] Besides other things this case is significant because of involvement of senior officers of Indian Civil Services, which is the premier service for governance in the country. In this case once again the Supreme Court reversed the judgment of a High Court, wherein the court had quashed the complaint of the victim, Mrs. Bajaj, a senior officer of the Indian Administrative Services on some procedural grounds. She had complained of being slapped on her posterior by Mr. Gill, then Director General of Police, in full public view. The allegations involved outraging the modesty of woman under section 354 of Indian Penal Code or insulting the modesty of woman under section 509 of Indian Penal Code. High Court quashed the complaint finding the complained offence too trivial[13] to be cognizable and for the reason of unreasonable and unexplained delay of eleven days in lodging the first information report.

Expressing its gender sensitive attitude the Supreme Court held that the offence of outraging the modesty of a woman is made out. In the absence of any definition of modesty in the Penal Code the court applied its dictionary meaning "in the present context" which is given as "womanly propriety of behavior, scrupulous chastity of thought, speech and conduct (in man or woman), reserve or sense of shame proceeding from instinctive aversion to impure or coarse suggestions." Court concluded that "keeping in view the total fact situation it could not but be held that alleged act of the accused in slapping the appellant on her posterior amounted to outraging her modesty for it was not only an affront to the normal sense of feminine decency but an affront to the dignity of the lady – sexual overtones or not, notwithstanding".[14] While rejecting the defense contention of absence of intention[15] and of the triviality of offence the Supreme Court attempted to view the whole thing from a woman's perspective. Court held that intention was immaterial if offence was likely to outrage the modesty of appellant, as the alleged act was committed in the presence of a gathering comprising the elite of society.

The gender sensitivity and sagacity of the court was reflected in not accepting the defense of triviality with the recognition that keeping in view Indian society Mrs. Bajaj or any woman of ordinary sense and temper would never buy even bigger ignominy and trauma by bringing in such a complaint if the ignominy and trauma to which she was subjected to was so slight. Once again the Supreme Court attempted to check the unwelcome biased trend in some sections of judiciary while expressing the need for gender sensitivity of our legal system. Again, not with the intention of disparaging the success it is pertinent to mention that the complainant had to fight this battle for seven years in spite of being a high profile Government officer.

Legal feminism bagged itself another major success in 1991 with the Supreme Court's pronouncement that the right to privacy is a part of right to life under article 21[16] of the Constitution and a woman even of easy virtue is entitled to privacy.[17] This observation was made by the court while reversing the order of the High Court where the latter had set aside the dismissal order of a police inspector on proven charges of perverse conduct against a woman. The main defense argument of the accused was the unchastity of that woman. The High Court found it dangerous to believe upon the uncorroborated version of such a woman who herself had admitted of being a woman of easy virtue for the reason of having illicit, extra-marital relations with another man. Evidence was also led to show that she was known as a "vagrant" in locality. Considering all the facts and circumstances the Supreme Court concluded that an evidence of a woman could not be thrown overboard merely because she is a woman of easy virtue. Court further said "Even a woman of easy virtue is entitled to privacy and no one can invade her privacy as and when he likes. So also it is not open to any and every person to violate her person as and when he wishes. She is entitled to protect her person if there is an attempt to violate it against her wish. She is equally entitled to protection of law."[18]

This decision is indeed commendable specially considering norms of Indian society where chastity is the biggest virtue expected of a woman and where a single deviation is sufficient to diminish her credibility.[19] Reversal of departmental dismissal order by High Court reveals the same mind set of the judges, but fortunately the open mindedness of some of the judges is facilitating the process of emancipation of women.

For the purpose of realizing true equality, this kind of open mindedness is desired not only from judiciary but also from all departmental authorities. Very often cases of sexual harassment are not taken seriously specially at the work place. Objectionable behavior tends to be ignored considering it part of the game as a very natural, obvious side effect to be borne by women for the audacity of crossing the barrier of public and domestic sphere. In the wake of these judgments it is expected of all concerned departmental authorities or other responsible persons to follow the norms and guidelines in right earnest to realize the dream of true equality.

Violence Against Women

Various surveys and the reports on crime statistics released from time to time by the police department reveal that the cases of violence against women in public as well as in domestic sphere are on the rise. This certainly makes them more and more vulnerable resulting in their oppression. Present laws concerning rape and assault are not sufficient to cover the various kinds of sexual assault women have to face. Necessity to create new categories to deal with such incidence and reforms in existing laws can not be denied. The belief that domestic sphere does not need any kind of legal regulation or intervention has resulted in the absence of laws to deal with cases of domestic violence which present an equally grave threat to women. Now with increasing awareness many countries have legislated directly or indirectly to deter and punish the cases of domestic violence. In India such cases are dealt with as penal offence in categories like dowry death and cruelty. Discussed below are some of the reforms in existing laws and new categories for the purpose of dealing with violence against women in both the spheres. An analysis has also been made of the other reasons which hamper effective implementation of these laws.

Rape

The first stepping stone for legal feminism in law concerning sexual violence against women was laid in 1980. This victory came in the wake of a rape case popularly known as *Mathura rape case*[20] where the Supreme Court by reversing the conviction order of the High Court acquitted the accused on ground of non-resistance and for not raising any alarm by the victim. The fact of being used to sexual intercourse in the past also weighed against her in proving a case of rape.

The decision had sent shock waves amongst all women's organizations and groups especially due to the obvious insensitivity of judges towards prevailing social reality. Given the vulnerable position of many sections of society due to existing social and economic disparity, acquittal of the accused keeping in mind their presumed authority as police personnel had great demoralizing effect. Pressurized by tremendous activities of feminist groups certain amendments were introduced in Indian Penal Code 1860 through Criminal Law (Amendment) Act, 1983. All demands of feminists were not acceded but many important changes were made through this act which are listed as follows:

- Changing the element of consent it was made explicit that consent was invalid if it was obtained by putting in fear not only her own self but also by putting any person in whom she is interested in fear of death or of hurt.[21]
- New sections 376-A, 376-B, 376-C, 376-D were incorporated to introduce the notion of "Custodial Rape"[22] and in limited sense "Marital Rape".
- Minimum mandatory punishments of seven years in ordinary rape and ten years in custodial rape were introduced.
- A new section 114-A was introduced in the Evidence Act, which provides for the presumption of absence of consent in case of custodial rape, rape of pregnant woman and gang rape.
- With the aim of saving a victim from social victimization or ostracism section 228-A was added in the Indian Penal Code. This section made disclosure of identity of a victim of sexual offences a punishable offence.
- Section 327 of Criminal Procedure Code was amended to provide in camera proceedings, i.e. allowing the presence of no one but the person immediately connected with the case. This section also prohibited the publication of any such proceedings.

These changes, especially the inclusion of the category of custodial rape and enhanced mandatory punishment, was indeed a welcome and progressive step. Another success in matters relating to sexual violence was through the judgment of the Supreme Court in 1995 in case of *Delhi Domestic Working Women's Forum v. Union of India.*[23] In this judgment while drawing attention to drawbacks in the existing system, specially in respect to provisions relating to compensation to victims, the bench has recommended special consideration for rape victims. The Union of India was directed by the court to set up a Criminal Injuries Compensation Board and to furnish victims with compensation.

Speaking of the psychological and physical trauma a victim of rape has to bear, judges directed the National Commission of Women to draft a scheme for trial of rape victims. Court acknowledged that in the name of trial, victims are subjected to another verbal rape in court through indecent cross examination and vulgar innuendoes which victims regard worse than the rape itself.

Changing perceptions and gender sensitivity of judiciary is evident from the views of a judge in another recent case. Criticizing this common trend of judiciary to discharge many cases of rape on the basis of lack of sufficient corroboration of evidence Dr. Anand J. observed: "The inherent bashfulness of the females and tendency to conceal outrage of sexual aggression are factors which court should not overlook. Seeking corroboration of her statement before relying upon the same as a rule in such cases amount to adding insult to injury. Why should evidence of a girl or a woman who complains of rape or sexual molestation be viewed with doubt, disbelief or suspicion?"[24]

Without belittling these welcome and much desired changes, it is pertinent to point out that the ray of hope in the form of these progressive judgments is often eclipsed by biased and feudalistic attitudes of many judges. Even a very quick and cursory analysis of most of the cases involving rape and sexual assault draws attention to the facts of quashing of complaints and discharge of accused on technical and procedural grounds. In maximum cases victims are at the mercy of judges as they are allowed to reduce the minimum mandatory punishment at their discretion and which is often done on frivolous grounds. Cases of attempted rape are frequently dealt under the offence of outraging the modesty of women, which prescribes the maximum punishment of only two years. With their callous attitude, judges express more sympathy towards violators, resulting in light sentences.[25]

The whole situation demands complete metamorphosis in attitudes of society, police as well as judiciary. Moreover, the whole criminal justice system is still crying hoarse for more changes in law. Keeping in view social conditions there is utmost necessity for recognition of marital rape, inclusion in custodial rape of categories like rape by men in position of social and economic authority as rape is very often used as a weapon of revenge against various disadvantaged groups or to subdue workers and other weaker sections. Amendments are also sought for in section 155(4) of Indian Evidence Act, which provides that during a rape trial evidence can be laid about the past sexual history of the victim.[26] In a study titled "Gender and judges: A judicial point of view", most of the judges agreed that the moral character of a woman is relevant in sexual abuse cases.[27]

Apathetical attitude of judiciary and police and negative reaction of society towards victims is working against the deterrent effect of these apparently strict laws. A large number of cases are either unreported or are reported after long delay, resulting in diminished evidence. Every case of sexual assault or rape brings more disrepute and public humiliation to the victim as compared to the culprit. The decision to report a case and seek legal remedy is often suicidal, since being a part of a rape trial as a victim is nothing short of playing the lead role in a pornographic serial show.

Implicitly it is conveyed that rape or sexual assault is basically due to women's own fault for being in company of men who by virtue of their patriarchal superior status are authorized to act as they wish. Seemingly such assaults are some sort of punishment which few unfortunate women have to bear for being a part of this "(Hu)Mankind". Correctly said, woman is not yet the considered fully human.[28]

Dowry Deaths

Dowry is the name for a large purse which a woman's parents are expected to pay to the groom or to his parents. It is one of the most horrendous social evils, which has infected almost all sections of Indian Societies. This age old and now illegal social practice epitomizes the patriarchal and male dominant nature of Indian society. It is a kind of fine to be paid by a family of every girl for the crime of having a female child and a reward which every groom's family is entitled to receive for being blessed with a male child. This evil is also the cause of other evils affecting women, like high female illiteracy rate and rising rate of girl infanticide.

Perceiving dowry as a kind of social evil which needs legal eradication, the Dowry Prohibition Act was passed in 1961. In spite of this enactment during the 1970s and 1980s dowry related crimes proportioned very high amongst crimes related to women. Feminist groups attribute the reason for the same to social practices and to this act as well. As a result of widespread activity for overhauling the law related to dowry this act was amended twice in 1984 and 1986 to incorporate certain important changes like

- Making it cognizable and a non-bailable offence.
- Increased punishment for giving and taking dowry to a period not less than five years.
- No limitation for a period within which a dowry complaint could be filed.
- Burden of proof being shifted from complainant to the person being prosecuted for dowry.

Besides the changes in this Act two other major achievements for feminists were the addition of section 304-B and a new chapter XX-A with only one section 498-A through Criminal Law Amendment Act 1983 in Indian Penal Code. Section 304-B provides for punishment in case of death of a married woman within seven years of marriage, of burns or bodily injury under suspicious circumstances. Section 498-A was a watershed for dealing with violence against women in domestic spheres. This section aimed at curbing the menace of dowry covered many areas of domestic violence. It punishes a husband of a woman or any relative of the husband for subjecting her to cruelty. Cruelty is defined as:

- any willful conduct, which is of such a nature as is likely to drive the woman either to commit suicide or to cause grave injury or danger to life, limb or physical or mental health of the woman.
- harassment of the woman with a view to coerce either her or any person related to her to meet unlawful demand for any property or valuable security or is on account of failure by her or any person related to her to meet such demand.

Along with this a new Section 113-A was added in the Indian Evidence Act to reverse the presumption of innocence against the accused.

Sensitivity of judiciary towards this issue is well expressed through the Supreme Court judgment in G. Renuka v. M. Papa Rao.[29] Court held that dowry being deep rooted in our system needs to be tackled in a phased manner. Consequently court concluded that in spite of the fact that giving and taking of dowry is an offence, nonetheless when same is given the receiver holds it as trust for benefit of the woman for whom it is given.[30] Thus beneficiary can file a suit for recovery of the same as trust property. In this case despite the defense argument being technically correct decision was made keeping in view the interest of women. This case is an excellent example of primacy of social justice for women to legal justice.

In spite of these seemingly effective laws and favorable judicial trends, feminists have to accept their limited success in this particular area. Though in a number of cases petitions led by women's organizations have resulted in conviction of the accused but this legislation and favorable judgments do not have the required deterrent effect. This illegal practice is reigning unabated in society. This sad state of affairs can be attributed to widespread corruption and the cavalier attitude of police as well as the judiciary along with the deeply entrenched patriarchal system. Many cases go unreported, are badly investigated or are discharged on frivolous grounds. In large numbers of cases, the accused are not booked under section 304-B even in the case of a woman's death, either on technical grounds or lack of evidence. Criminals very often manage to go free upon the benefit of doubt or get light sentences, as the deciding judge does not find the crime of killing or burning of a wife grave enough for rigorous punishment. It has been pointed out that it is cheaper for an Indian man to kill his spouse and obtain a new one with another dowry than to divorce his wife and pay her maintenance.[31]

Accepting the legal system's shortcomings in this regard it is to be noted that social causes arising from patriarchal society bears the responsibility for this evil practice. In an economically strangled hyper populated society non-supportive of unmarried women almost every woman internalizes her inferior status as compared to man. She is made to feel obliged for being accepted by a superior "man". Religious sanctions for marriage as a sacrament induces the woman to bear silently all kinds of injustice and exploitation. Dowry harassment cases are brought to light only in the extreme situation of death or burning.

Since the dowry system has a direct relation to other evils affecting women, a solution to this problem cannot be found in isolation. Reforms are required in all spheres, public as well as private, and not only in the legal system but in the way of "thinking the whole system – legal as well as social".

Conclusion

After a long struggle feminist jurisprudence now stands on a distinct platform having carved out its own niche in the feminist movement in India. It has been assisted in this endeavor by many women groups, non-governmental organizations, National Commission for Women and individuals.

The various judicial pronouncements are a silver lining to an otherwise grim scenario for women in Indian society, a society which is struggling hard to escape from the clutches of obsolete religious traditions and customs. Such progressive judgments are setting a healthy trend in direction of checking objectification, stigmatization and victimization of women. Notwithstanding all the constraints courts are following international obligations arising from different conventions in an attempt to make status of women in India comparable to world standards. Gender sensitization of the judiciary is manifested in the form of high conviction rates of the accused. It may not have sufficient deterrent effect, but with increasing awareness comparatively higher number of incidents are made public and violations are condemned.

Surely, it is too early to be proud of any success since these attitudinal changes, tendency to see things from women's perspective, attempt to incorporate women's experiences while interpreting and implementing laws can only be considered as a beginning to face many more challenges. Creation of sexual harassment or cruelty as distinct categories is indeed welcome change but that is not enough. The whole criminal justice system is in need of drastic changes and gender sensitization. Many specific reforms are required to curb the rising rate of crimes against women. Laws as well as implementation procedure has to be strict enough to achieve the objective of deterrence.

The challenges for legal feminist are not restricted to revealing and reversing gender bias in the legal system. There is imminent need to strike at the roots of issues. It is an uphill task with feminist groups to make sure that this innovative and proactive judicial law making does not end up being a mere contributor to the list of legislation. This demands considerable courage and endurance from women, keeping in view prevalent stereotypical ideas about role of women in society.

The success of legal feminism in seeking desired changes in laws reflects the potential of feminist jurisprudence in India. With support of many international organizations efforts can be made to institutionalize feminist jurisprudence. There are all the reasons for optimism that with the combined efforts from all sections of society and also through well-organized, formal and streamlined contributions from academicians, women can be emancipated from their paradoxical status. The concept of equality as propounded in the Indian Constitution can thus be realized ushering the country to a new era.

Notes

* Associate Professor of Law, Indian Institute of Comparative Law, 6/146 Malviya Nagar, Jaipur, India

1 Gita Aravamudan, 'Whose Baby is She Anyway', *The Hindu*, October 16, 1994. Reference is to the village of Alligundam in Vsilampathi Taluk of Madurai District in South India. Statistics collected by the Indian Council for Child Welfare (ICCW), which is doing woman work in that area show that out of the 1,194 females born during the second half of 1993, 156 were suspected to have been killed. They managed to prevent another 243 infanticides.

2 Ann Scales, The Emergence of Feminist Jurisprudence: An Essay, 95 *Yale Law Journal*, 1373 (1986).

3 Article 15(3) says: "Nothing shall prevent the state from making special provisions for women and children."

4 Article 14 provides: The state shall not deny to any person equality before law or the equal protection of laws within the territory of India.

5 Article 15(1) says: The state shall not discriminate against any person on grounds only of religion, race, caste, sex, place of birth or any of them.

6 A.I.R. 1997 S.C. 3011.

7 India became a party to this convention in 1993.

8 This was done in exercise of power available under Article 32 of the Indian Constitution for enforcement of fundamental rights and was to be treated as law as declared by the Supreme Court under Article 141 of the constitution.

9 A.I.R. 1999 S.C. 625.

10 ibid., para 10.

11 ibid., para 27.

12 1995(6) S.C.C. 194.

13 Section 95 of I.P.C. provides a defence in the form of triviality of offence. The section says, "Nothing is an offence by reason that it causes, or that it is intended to cause, or that it is known to be likely to cause any harm, if the harm is so slight that no person of ordinary sense and temper would complain of such harm".

14 1995(6) S.C.C. para 14 and 15.

15 Intention is one of the essential elements for constituting offence under section 354 I.P.C.

16 Art.21 of the Indian Constitution provides "no person shall be deprived of his life and personal liberty accept according to procedure established by Law". The Supreme Court has given very broad interpretation to "Right to Life" through various judicial pronouncements.

17 *State of Maharashtra v. Madhukar Narayan Mandikar*, A.I.R. 1991 S.C. 207.

18 ibid., para 8.

19 Analysis of number of rape cases substantiates this fact where past sexual history of victim has important bearing on the conviction.

20 *Tuka Ram v. State of Maharashtra*, A.I.R. 1979 S.C. 185.

21 Section 375 (3) I.P.C.

22 Under this category rape by men in a position of authority over a woman was considered more serious than ordinary rape.

23 1996 (1) S.C.C. 14.

24 A.I.R. 1996 S.C. 1393 at 1400.

25 Serious doubts are raised about sentencing policy of courts in cases *Raju v. State of Karnataka, Krishna v. State of Karnataka*. The sentence was reduced in these cases on the ground of long delay. Ironically the court recognized rape as a crime of passion and used the same argument in favour of accused to reduce the sentence.

26 Gender bias is overt in this provision since not a word about the accused's past sexual history is relevant.

27 Nivedita M. C. Monga, Gender bias in law, in a compendium on Gender Inequalities, eds. Anil Kalia and Deepa Bajaj, Child Survival India, Delhi.

28 Catherine A. Mackinnon, Reflections on Sex Equality under Law, 100 *Yale Law Journal*, 1281, (1991).

29 A.I.R. 1995 A.P. 130.

30 Section 6 of Dowry Prohibition Act, 1961 legislates the same.

31 Partha Banerjee, A matter of extreme cruelty: "Bride burning and dowry deaths in India", 1.1 Injustice Studies, (Nov.1997).

Name Index

For Product Safety Concerns and Information please contact our EU
representative GPSR@taylorandfrancis.com
Taylor & Francis Verlag GmbH, Kaufingerstraße 24, 80331 München, Germany

www.ingramcontent.com/pod-product-compliance
Ingram Content Group UK Ltd.
Pitfield, Milton Keynes, MK11 3LW, UK
UKHW020025200926
475702UK00014B/2066

* 9 7 8 1 1 3 8 7 2 1 6 8 5 *